# Discovering
# Advanced
# Algebra
### An Investigative Approach

## Solutions Manual

DISCOVERING

MATHEMATICS™

**Key Curriculum Press**
Innovators in Mathematics Education

**Teacher's Materials Project Editor:** Joan Lewis

**Project Editors:** Christian Aviles-Scott, Heather Dever

**Project Administrator:** Erin Gray

**Editorial Assistant:** Eric Martin

**Writers:** Ellen Bracken, Kendra Eyer

**Accuracy Checker:** Dudley Brooks

**Production Editor:** Angela Chen

**Copyeditor:** Margaret Moore

**Editorial Production Manager:** Deborah Cogan

**Production Director:** Diana Jean Ray

**Production Coordinator:** Ann Rothenbuhler

**Text Designer:** Jenny Somerville

**Art Editor:** Jason Luz

**Composition, Technical Art:** Interactive Composition Corporation

**Art and Design Coordinator:** Marilyn Perry

**Cover Designer:** Jill Kongabel

**Printer:** Alonzo Printing

**Executive Editor:** Casey FitzSimons

**Publisher:** Steven Rasmussen

Key Curriculum Press
1150 65th Street
Emeryville, CA 94608
(510) 595-7000
editorial@keypress.com
www.keypress.com

Printed in the United States of America
10 9 8 7 6 5 4 3     09 08 07 06

ISBN-13: 978-1-55953-608-0
ISBN-10: 1-55953-608-X

# Contents

# Chapter 12

# Chapter 13

# Introduction

The *Solutions Manual* for *Discovering Advanced Algebra: An Investigative Approach* contains solutions to the exercises at the end of each lesson, to the questions in each Exploration, and to the Extensions, Improving Your Reasoning Skills, Improving Your Visual Thinking Skills, Improving Your Geometry Skills, and Take Another Look activities. You can find solutions for the Investigations and Exploration activities from the student book in the *Teacher's Edition*.

The solutions in this *Solutions Manual* are more complete than those offered as annotations in the *Teacher's Edition* or in the selected answers in the back of the student book. Although complete solutions for the problems are provided here, keep in mind that often there is more than one method students might use to solve a particular problem. Also, the answers will vary for some problems, depending on assumptions that students make or how they round values. For problems that could have many different answers, a sample solution is given.

Refer to these solutions when your students have difficulty solving a problem and need some assistance in determining a possible approach toward solving it. You might also want to provide a copy of certain solutions for students who have been absent for an extended period of time.

# CHAPTER 0

## LESSON 0.1

### EXERCISES

**1. a.** Begin with a 10-liter bucket and a 7-liter bucket. Find a way to get exactly 4 liters in the 10-liter bucket.

**b.** Begin with a 10-liter bucket and a 7-liter bucket. Find a way to get exactly 2 liters in the 10-liter bucket.

**2. a.** Choose two points on the line, such as $(0, 4)$ and $(5, 2)$, and substitute them in the formula for slope: $\frac{change\ in\ y}{change\ in\ x} = \frac{2-4}{5-0} = -\frac{2}{5}$.

**b.** Using the points $(0, 1)$ and $(2, 4)$, $slope = \frac{change\ in\ y}{change\ in\ x} = \frac{4-1}{2-0} = \frac{3}{2}$.

**3.** Possible answer: $(14, 13)$ and $(-1, 4)$. Because $slope = \frac{change\ in\ y}{change\ in\ x} = \frac{3}{5}$, you can find other points on the line by starting with the known point, $(4, 7)$, and repeatedly adding or subtracting 5 (*change in x*) from the *x*-coordinate and correspondingly adding or subtracting 3 (*change in y*) from the *y*-coordinate. Other possible points are $(19, 16)$ and $(-6, 1)$.

**4.** The line has slope $\frac{12}{16}$ and goes through $(0, 0)$, so the slope from $(0, 0)$ to any point $(x, y)$ on the line will be $\frac{y}{x} = \frac{12}{16}$.

**a.** $a = 12$. Find 9 on the *y*-axis and trace to the line. This matches 12 on the *x*-axis.

**b.** $b = 7.5$. The point on the line with *x*-coordinate 10 has *y*-coordinate 7.5.

**5.** Sample answer: Use three objects such as coins to represent the wolf, the goat, and the cabbage. Draw both banks of the river on paper and use an index card as a boat. Act out the problem trying to never leave the wolf and the goat together or the goat and the cabbage together.

**6.** Use the slope formula: $\frac{change\ in\ y}{change\ in\ x} = \frac{(y_2 - y_1)}{(x_2 - x_1)}$.

**a.** $\frac{10 - 5}{7 - 2} = \frac{5}{5} = 1$

**b.** $\frac{7 - (-1)}{8 - 3} = \frac{8}{5} = 1.6$

**c.** $\frac{-6 - 3}{2 - (-2)} = -\frac{9}{4} = -2.25$

**d.** $\frac{-2 - 3}{-5 - 3} = \frac{-5}{-8} = \frac{5}{8} = 0.625$

**7. a.**

25 ft, $x$, 10 ft

**b.**

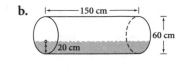

150 cm, 60 cm, 20 cm

**c.**

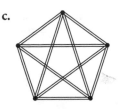

**8. a.** 312 g. Find 11 oz on the horizontal axis and trace to the line, then trace from the line to the vertical axis; this is about 312 g.

**b.** 12.5 oz. Find 350 g on the vertical axis and trace to the line, then trace from the line to the horizontal axis; this is about 12.5 oz.

**c.** 437 g. Find 15.5 oz on the horizontal axis and trace to the line, then trace from the line to the vertical axis; this is about 437 g.

**d.** 6.2 oz. Find 180 g on the vertical axis and trace to the line, then trace from the line to the horizontal axis; this is about 6.2 oz.

**e.** Using the approximate point $(15, 425)$ and the definite point $(0, 0)$, the slope is $\frac{425}{15} = \frac{85}{3} \approx 28.3$. There are about 28.3 grams in an ounce.

**9. a.** Sample answer: Fill the 7-liter bucket and pour the contents into the 10-liter bucket. Fill the 7-liter bucket again and pour 3 liters from the 7-liter bucket into the 10-liter bucket, completely filling the 10-liter bucket and leaving 4 liters in the 7-liter bucket. Empty the 10-liter bucket and pour the 4 liters from the 7-liter bucket into the 10-liter bucket.

**b.** Sample answer: Fill the 10-liter bucket and pour the contents into the 7-liter bucket, completely filling the 7-liter bucket and leaving 3 liters in the 10-liter bucket. Empty the 7-liter bucket and pour the 3 liters from the 10-liter bucket into the 7-liter bucket. Fill the 10-liter bucket and pour 4 liters into the 7-liter bucket, completely filling the 7-liter bucket and leaving 6 liters in the 10-liter bucket. Empty the 7-liter bucket. Pour the 6 liters from the 10-liter bucket into the 7-liter bucket. Fill the 10-liter bucket and pour 1 liter into the 7-liter bucket, completely filling the 7-liter bucket and leaving 9 liters in the 10-liter bucket. Empty the 7-liter bucket and pour 7 liters from the 10-liter bucket into the 7-liter bucket, completely filling the 7-liter bucket and leaving 2 liters in the 10-liter bucket.

**10.**

$$x \cdot \boxed{x} + x \cdot \boxed{2} + 3 \cdot \boxed{x} + 3 \cdot \boxed{2}$$

The outer rectangle has length $(x + 2)$ and width $(x + 3)$, so the area is length times width, or $(x + 2)(x + 3)$. The areas of the inner rectangles are $x^2$, $2x$, $3x$, and 6. The sum of the areas of the inner rectangles is equal to the area of the whole outer rectangle, so $(x + 2)(x + 3) = x^2 + 2x + 3x + 6$.

**11. a.** $(x + 4)(x + 7) = x^2 + 4x + 7x + 28$

**b.** $(x + 5)^2 = x^2 + 5x + 5x + 25$

|     | $x$   | 5    |
| --- | ----- | ---- |
| $x$ | $x^2$ | $5x$ |
| 5   | $5x$  | 25   |

**c.** $(x + 2)(y + 6) = xy + 2y + 6x + 12$

|     | $x$  | 2    |
| --- | ---- | ---- |
| $y$ | $xy$ | $2y$ |
| 6   | $6x$ | 12   |

**d.** $(x + 3)(x - 1) = x^2 + 3x - x - 3$

|     | $x$   | $-1$   |
| --- | ----- | ------ |
| $x$ | $x^2$ | $-1x$  |
| 3   | $3x$  | $-3$   |

**12.** Take the goat across and come back. Next take the wolf across and bring the goat back. Next take the cabbage across and come back. Last, take the goat across.

**13. a.** $n + 3$, where $n$ represents the number

**b.** $v = m + 24.3$, where $v$ represents Venus's distance from the Sun in millions of miles and $m$ represents Mercury's distance from the Sun in millions of miles.

**c.** $s = 2e$, where $s$ represents the number of CDs owned by Seth and $e$ represents the number of CDs owned by Erin.

**14. a.** 0.375   **b.** $1.\overline{4}$   **c.** 0.64   **d.** $0.3\overline{571428}$

**15. a.** $\frac{375}{1000} = \frac{3}{8}$   **b.** $\frac{142}{100} = \frac{71}{50} = 1\frac{21}{50}$

**c.** $\frac{2}{9}$   **d.** $\frac{35}{99}$

**16. a.** $c = 5$ m. Substitute 3 and 4 for the lengths of the legs in the Pythagorean formula and solve for the hypotenuse. $c^2 = a^2 + b^2 = 3^2 + 4^2 = 9 + 16 = 25$, so $c = \sqrt{25} = 5$ m.

**b.** $a = \sqrt{7} \approx 2.6$ cm. Substitute 3 for the length of one leg and 4 for the length of the hypotenuse, and solve for the length of the other leg. $a^2 + b^2 = c^2$, so $a^2 = c^2 - b^2 = 4^2 - 3^2 = 16 - 9 = 7$, and $a = \sqrt{7}$ cm $\approx 2.6$ cm.

**c.** $x = 13$ in. Solve for the length of the hypotenuse of the smaller right triangle, following the steps in 16a. The length of the hypotenuse is 5 in. Use this length to find the length of the hypotenuse, $x$, of the larger right triangle: $x^2 = 5^2 + 12^2 = 25 + 144 = 169$, so $x = \sqrt{169} = 13$ in.

**EXTENSIONS**

**A.** All segments are horizontal, or vertical, or have a slope of 1 or $-1$. If more segments were added, you would be able to tell from the graph how to get any amount into either bucket.

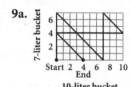 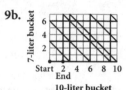

**B.** See the solutions to Take Another Look activities 1 and 3 on page 12.

## LESSON 0.2

**EXERCISES**

**1. a.** Subtract 12 from both sides.

**b.** Divide both sides by 5.

**c.** Add 18 to both sides.

**d.** Multiply both sides by $-15$.

**2.** C. 5 letters $+ \left(\frac{3\text{ letters}}{\text{member}}\right)(c$ members$) = 32$ letters, or $5 + 3c = 32$

**3. a.** $c = 32 - 5 = 27$

**b.** $5c = 32 - 3 = 29$, so $c = \frac{29}{5} = 5.8$

**c.** $3c = 32 - 5$, so $c = \frac{27}{3} = 9$

**4.** B. $x$ represents the number of dozens of calls made on the first day. The expression $2x + 3$ represents doubling the number of dozens of calls on the second day in addition to three dozen calls. The total number of calls made in two days is 75 dozen.

**5. a.** $x = 75 - 3 = 72$

**b.** $3x + 3 = 75$, so $3x = 72$, and $x = 24$

**c.** $2x = 75 - 3 = 72$, so $x = 36$

**6. a.** $L$ represents the cost of a single large bead. $S$ represents the cost of a single small bead. $J$ represents the amount that Jill will pay for her purchase.

**b.** Cents

**c.** Anita's purchase of 6 large beads and 20 small beads for $2.70

**7. a.** $-12L - 40S = -540$

**b.** $12L + 75S = 855$

**c.** Add the equations from 7a and b.

$$\begin{array}{r} -12L - 40S = -540 \\ +12L + 75S = \phantom{0}855 \\ \hline 35S = \phantom{00}315 \end{array}$$

**d.** $S = \frac{315}{35} = 9$. The small beads cost 9¢ each.

**e.** $L = 15$. Substitute $S = 9$ in Equation 1 or 2 and solve for $L$. $6L + 20(9) = 270$, so $6L = 270 - 180 = 90$, and $L = 15$. The large beads cost 15¢ each.

**f.** $J = 264$. Substitute $L = 15$ and $S = 9$ in Equation 3 and solve for $J$. $8(15) + 16(9) = J$, $J = 264$. Jill will pay $2.64 for her beads.

**8. a.** $a$ represents the number of denarii that $A$ has.

**b.** $b$ represents the number of denarii that $B$ has.

**c.** If you take 7 denarii from $B$ and give them to $A$, then $A$'s sum equals five times $B$'s new amount.

**d.** If you take 5 denarii from $A$ and give them to $B$, then $B$'s sum equals seven times $A$'s new amount.

**9. a.** Solve Equation 1 for $a$. Substitute the result, $5b - 42$, for $a$ in Equation 2 to get $b + 5 = 7((5b - 42) - 5)$.

**b.**

| | |
|---|---|
| $b + 5 = 7((5b - 42) - 5)$ | Original equation. |
| $b + 5 = 7(5b - 47)$ | Subtract the 5. |
| $b + 5 = 35b - 329$ | Distribute the 7. |
| $b - 35b = -329 - 5$ | Subtract $35b$ and 5 from both sides. |
| $-34b = -334$ | Combine terms. |
| $b = \dfrac{-334}{-34} = \dfrac{167}{17}$ | Divide both sides by $-34$ and reduce. |

**c.** Substitute $\frac{167}{17}$ for $b$ in the equation $a + 7 = 5(b - 7)$ and evaluate.

$$a + 7 = 5\left(\frac{167}{17} - 7\right)$$

$$a = \frac{835}{17} - 42$$

$$= \frac{835}{17} - \frac{714}{17} = \frac{121}{17}$$

**d.** $A$ has $\frac{121}{17}$, or about 7, denarii, and $B$ has $\frac{167}{17}$, or about 10, denarii.

**10. a.** Let $g$ represent the number of Georgian great-grandchildren, let $f$ represent the number of Floridian great-grandchildren, let $h$ represent the amount that each Georgian got from the will, let $c$ represent the amount that each Floridian got from the will, and let $d$ represent the amount that each great-grandchild eventually ended up with.

**b.** $g + f = 36$, $h = c + 700$, $gh + fc = 206100$, $d = h - 175$, $36d = 206100$

**c.** $g = 27$, $f = 9$, $h = 5900$, $c = 5200$, $d = 5725$. Here is one way to solve the system. First solve the fifth equation for $d$ and then find $c$ and $h$ by substitution:

| | |
|---|---|
| $36d = 206100$ | The fifth equation. |
| $d = \dfrac{206100}{36} = 5725$ | Divide both sides by 36 and evaluate. |
| $d = h - 175$ | The fourth equation. |
| $5725 = h - 175$ | Substitute 5725 for $d$. |
| $h = 5725 + 175 = 5900$ | Add 175 to both sides and evaluate. |
| $h = c + 700$ | The second equation. |
| $5900 = c + 700$ | Substitute 5900 for $h$. |
| $c = 5900 - 700 = 5200$ | Subtract 700 from both sides and evaluate. |

Next solve for $f$ in terms of $g$: $g + f = 36$, so $f = 36 - g$. Substitute this expression for $f$ in the third equation and solve for $g$.

| | |
|---|---|
| $gh + fc = 206100$ | The third equation. |
| $5900g + 5200(36 - g) = 206100$ | Substitute 5900 for $h$, 5200 for $c$, and $36 - g$ for $f$. |
| $5900g + 187200 - 5200g = 206100$ | Distribute 5200. |
| $700g + 187200 = 206100$ | Combine terms. |
| $700g = 206100 - 187200$ | Subtract 187,200 from both sides. |
| $700g = 18900$ | Subtract. |
| $g = \dfrac{18900}{700} = 27$ | Divide both sides by 700 and evaluate. |

Then substitute 27 for $g$ and solve for $f$: $f = 36 - 27 = 9$. So $g = 27$, $f = 9$, $h = 5900$, $c = 5200$, and $d = 5725$.

**d.** There are 27 Georgian great-grandchildren and 9 Floridian great-grandchildren. According to the will, each great-grandchild living in Georgia received $5,900 and each great-grandchild living in Florida received $5,200. After the great-grandchildren evened it out, each received $5,725.

**11.** Sample answers:

   **a.** Draw a 45° angle, then subtract a 30° angle; 45° − 30° = 15°. Or draw a 60° angle and subtract a 45° angle; 60° − 45° = 15°.

   **b.** Draw a 45° angle, then add a 30° angle; 45° + 30° = 75°.

   **c.** Draw a 45° angle, then add a 60° angle; 45° + 60° = 105°. Or draw a 90° angle, add a 45° angle, then subtract a 30° angle; 90° + 45° − 30° = 105°.

**12. a.** $3x + 21$     **b.** $-12 + 2n$     **c.** $4x - x^2$

**13. a.** $47 + 3(17) = 98$

   **b.** $29 - 34(-1) + 14(-24) = -273$

**14. a.** $slope = \dfrac{7 - 7}{8 - 4} = \dfrac{0}{4} = 0$

   **b.** $slope = \dfrac{5 - 3}{2 - (-6)} = \dfrac{2}{8} = \dfrac{1}{4} = 0.25$

**15.** Fill the 4-cup pan with milk and pour from the pan to the soda can, completely filling the 12-ounce $\left(1\frac{1}{2}\text{ cup}\right)$ can and leaving $2\frac{1}{2}$ cups in the pan. Empty the soda can and pour from the pan to the soda can again, this time leaving 1 cup in the pan.

**16.** A horizontal line has slope 0. A vertical line has undefined slope. (In The Geometer's Sketchpad® a vertical line is given the slope ∞.) A line that increases from left to right has positive slope. A line that decreases from left to right has negative slope.

## EXTENSION

See the solution to Take Another Look activity 4 on page 12.

## LESSON 0.3

### EXERCISES

**1. a.** $(15 \text{ ft})\left(\dfrac{1 \text{ s}}{3.5 \text{ ft}}\right) \approx 4.3 \text{ s}$

   **b.** $(25 \text{ ft})\left(\dfrac{12 \text{ in.}}{1 \text{ ft}}\right)\left(\dfrac{2.54 \text{ cm}}{1 \text{ in.}}\right) = 762 \text{ cm}$

   **c.** $\left(\dfrac{32 \text{ mi}}{1 \text{ gal}}\right)(15 \text{ gal}) = 480 \text{ mi}$

**2. a.** Let $e$ represent the average problem-solving rate in problems per hour for Emily, and let $a$ represent the average rate in problems per hour for Alejandro.

   **b.** This is the equation for Monday. 3 hours times $e$ problems per hour plus 1 hour times $a$ problems per hour is equal to 139 problems.

   **c.** $2e + 2a = 130$

   **d.** ii. Substitute the values in both equations to see if they satisfy the equations. Points i and ii satisfy the first equation. Points ii and iii satisfy the second equation. The last point doesn't work in either equation. $(e, a) = (37, 28)$.

   **e.** Emily averages 37 problems per hour and Alejandro averages 28 problems per hour.

**3.** 150 mi/h

### Method 1

Write down the things you know and the things you might need to know.

| Know | Need to know |
|---|---|
| Speed of first lap: 75 mi/h | Speed of second lap (mi/h): $s$ |
| Average speed for both laps: 100 mi/h | Length of one lap (mi): $l$ |
|  | Time for first lap (h): $t_1$ |
|  | Time for second lap (h): $t_2$ |

Next look at units to help you write equations connecting the pieces of information.

$$\begin{cases} t_1 = \dfrac{l}{75 \text{ mi/h}} & \text{The speed, time, and distance for the first lap.} \\[2mm] t_2 = \dfrac{l}{s} & \text{The second lap.} \\[2mm] t_1 + t_2 = \dfrac{2l}{100 \text{ mi/h}} & \text{The average speed needed for both laps to qualify.} \end{cases}$$

Solve the equations for $s$.

$t_1 + t_2 = \dfrac{2l}{100}$    The equation for the average speed.

$\dfrac{l}{75} + \dfrac{l}{s} = \dfrac{2l}{100}$    Substitute expressions for $t_1$ and $t_2$.

$\dfrac{1}{75} + \dfrac{1}{s} = \dfrac{1}{50}$    Divide both sides by $l$ and reduce $\frac{2}{100}$.

$75s\left(\dfrac{1}{75} + \dfrac{1}{s}\right) = 75s\left(\dfrac{1}{50}\right)$    Multiply both sides by $75s$.

$s + 75 = \dfrac{3}{2}s$    Evaluate.

$75 = \dfrac{1}{2}s$    Subtract $s$ from both sides.

$150 = s$    Multiply both sides by 2.

Benjamin must go at least 150 mi/h on the second lap to qualify for the race.

### Method 2

The length of the lap may seem important, but you don't have enough information to find it. Maybe this value is arbitrary. Start by picking a number for the length, then check to see if it does matter. So choose the length of a lap to be 5 miles.

Next look at the units. The rate (speed) is used to change one unit into another. In this case, $\frac{miles}{hour} \cdot hours = miles$. Use this formula to write three equations:

First lap $\quad 75t_1 = 5 \qquad\qquad t_1 = \frac{1}{15}$ hour

Second lap $\quad st_2 = 5 \qquad\qquad t_2 = \frac{5}{s}$ hour

Both laps $\quad 100(t_1 + t_2) = 10 \quad t_1 + t_2 = \frac{1}{10}$ hour

Combine this information to write one equation for time: $\frac{1}{15} + \frac{5}{s} = \frac{1}{10}$ hour. Solve this equation for $s$.

$$\frac{1}{15} + \frac{1}{s} = \frac{1}{10} \qquad \text{The original equation.}$$

$$15s\left(\frac{1}{15} + \frac{5}{s}\right) = 15s\left(\frac{1}{10}\right) \qquad \text{Multiply both sides by } 15s.$$

$$s + 75 = \frac{3}{2}s \qquad \text{Evaluate.}$$

$$75 = \frac{1}{2}s \qquad \text{Subtract } s \text{ from both sides.}$$

$$150 = s \qquad \text{Multiply both sides by 2.}$$

Benjamin must go at least 150 mi/h to qualify for the race. If you go back and try a different value for the length of a lap, you will find the same result.

**4. a.** $7.5a - 22.5$

   **b.** $12 + 4.7b + 28.2 = 40.2 + 4.7b$

   **c.** $5c - 2c + 24 = 3c + 24$

   **d.** $294 - 8.4d + 12.6d = 294 + 4.2d$

**5. a.** $4.5a - 31.5 = 26.1$, so $4.5a = 57.6$, and $a = \frac{57.6}{4.5} = 12.8$

   **b.** $9 + 2.7b + 8.1 = 20.7$, so $2.7b = 3.6$, and $b = \frac{3.6}{2.7} = \frac{4}{3} = 1.\overline{3}$

   **c.** $8c - 2c + 10 = 70$, so $6c + 10 = 70$, $6c = 60$, and $c = \frac{60}{6} = 10$

   **d.** $294 - 8.4d + 12.6d = 327.6$, so $294 + 4.2d = 327.6$, $4.2d = 33.6$, and $d = \frac{33.6}{4.2} = 8$

**6.** 8 h. Let $d$ represent the number of hours Alyse worked past 8:00 P.M. Alyse earns $15.40(1.5) = \$23.10$ for each hour past 8:00 P.M. Set up an equation using the information given and solve it for $d$.

$$15.4(35 - d) + 23.1d = 600.6 \qquad \text{The equation for Alyse's total pay.}$$

$$539 - 15.4d + 23.1d = 600.6 \qquad \text{Distribute 15.4.}$$

$$539 + 7.7d = 600.6 \qquad \text{Collect like terms.}$$

$$7.7d = 61.6 \qquad \text{Subtract 539 from both sides.}$$

$$d = \frac{61.6}{7.7} = 8 \qquad \text{Divide both sides by 7.7.}$$

Alyse worked 8 hours past 8:00 P.M.

**7. a.** $volume = (area \ of \ base)(height)$, or $V = Bh$, so $486 \ in.^3 = B \cdot 9 \ in.$, and $B = \frac{486 \ in.^3}{9 \ in.} = 54 \ in.^2$

   **b.** $V = Bh = \left(3.60 \ m^2\right)(0.40 \ m) = 1.44 \ m^3$

   **c.** $V = Bh$, so $h = \frac{V}{B} = \frac{2.88 \ ft^3}{2.40 \ ft^2} = 1.20 \ ft$

   **d.** $V = lwh = 12960 \ cm^3 = (30 \ cm) \cdot w \cdot (18 \ cm)$, so $w = \frac{12960 \ cm^3}{(18 \ cm)(30 \ cm)} = 24 \ cm$

**8.**

| Container | Bottle | Erlenmeyer flask | Round flask |
|---|---|---|---|
| **Source** | Well | Lake | Spring |
| **Element** | Calcium | Iron | Sulfur |
| **Position** | Left | Center | Right |

**Method 1**

List all the information in groups and organize your information in a large table like the one below. (*See table at bottom of page.*) Number the facts so that you can record where each piece of information comes from. The first fact says that sulfur is not in the center and maybe is on the left or right.

**Lesson 0.3, Exercise 8**

| | Erlenmeyer flask | Round flask | Bottle | Calcium | Sulfur | Iron | Lake | Well | Spring |
|---|---|---|---|---|---|---|---|---|---|
| **Left** | | | | | | | N4 | | |
| **Center** | | | N3 | | N1 | | | | N3 |
| **Right** | | | | N4 | | | | | |
| **Lake** | | | | N4 | | | | | |
| **Well** | N5 | | | | N5 | | | | |
| **Spring** | | | N3 | | | | | | |
| **Calcium** | | N6 | | | | | | | |
| **Sulfur** | N5 | | | | | | | | |
| **Iron** | Y2 | | | | | | | | |

You don't record "maybes" with this method, so put an N in the Sulfur-Center cell. Take each fact and convert it to a yes or no in the table.

Next, in each small block it takes two noes to make a yes in the same column or row. But one yes will make four noes, two in the column and two in the row. Fill in the lower-left block to get two noes and one yes in each row and column.

|         | E.F. | R.F. | Bottle |
|---------|------|------|--------|
| Calcium | N    | N6   | Y      |
| Sulfur  | N5   | Y    | N      |
| Iron    | Y2   | N    | N      |

Now look back at the facts and use these yeses and noes to fill in more blanks. The calcium is in the bottle and the lake water is not high in calcium, so the lake water is not in the bottle. (See first table at bottom of page.)

Repeat these steps to complete the table. (See second table at bottom of page.)

## Method 2

Create a table to hold the information. Make a second table to record the decisions you make as you solve the problem. In many cases you will need to make a choice. Note the occasions when you choose and when you don't. If you find a contradiction, go back to the last choice you made and choose differently. The numbers in these tables indicate the numbers of the facts.

| Fact | Choice                        |
|------|-------------------------------|
| 1    | Sulfur on left                |
| 2    | E.F., iron in center          |
| 3    | Bottle on left, spring on right |
| 4    | Contradiction                 |

|           | Left     | Center  | Right     |
|-----------|----------|---------|-----------|
| Container | 3 Bottle | 2 E.F.  |           |
| Element   | 1 Sulfur | 2 Iron  |           |
| Source    |          |         | 3 Spring  |

Here, choices were made for each of the first three facts. By the fourth fact, calcium should be to the left of the lake water, but the only slot open for calcium is the position on the right. Something is wrong, so you need to back up and try new choices. Remember to keep track of all the choices you have tried. When you can complete the table without a contradiction, you have the solution.

| Fact | Choice                          |
|------|---------------------------------|
| 1    | Sulfur on right                 |
| 2    | E.F., iron in center            |
| 3    | Bottle on left, spring on right |
| 4    | Calcium on left, lake in center |
| 5    | Well on left                    |
| 6    | R.F. on right                   |

---

**Lesson 0.3, Exercise 8**

|        | Erlenmeyer flask | Round flask | Bottle | Calcium | Sulfur | Iron | Lake | Well | Spring |
|--------|------------------|-------------|--------|---------|--------|------|------|------|--------|
| Left   |                  |             |        |         |        |      | N4   |      |        |
| Center |                  | N           | N3     | N       | N1     |      |      |      | N3     |
| Right  | N                |             |        | N4      |        |      |      |      |        |
| Lake   |                  |             | N      | N4      |        |      |      |      |        |
| Well   | N5               | N           |        |         | N5     | N    |      |      |        |
| Spring |                  |             | N3     | N       |        |      |      |      |        |

|        | Erlenmeyer flask | Round flask | Bottle | Calcium | Sulfur | Iron | Lake | Well | Spring |
|--------|------------------|-------------|--------|---------|--------|------|------|------|--------|
| Left   | N                | N           | Y      | Y       | N      | N    | N4   | N    | Y      |
| Center | Y                | N           | N3     | N       | N1     | Y    | N    | Y    | N3     |
| Right  | N                | Y           | N      | N4      | Y      | N    | Y    | N    | N      |
| Lake   | Y                | N           | N      | N4      | N      | Y    |      |      |        |
| Well   | N5               | N           | Y      | Y       | N5     | N    |      |      |        |
| Spring | N                | Y           | N3     | N       | Y      | N    |      |      |        |

|  | Left | Center | Right |
|---|---|---|---|
| Container | 3 Bottle | 2 E.F. | 6 R.F. |
| Element | 4 Calcium | 2 Iron | 1 Sulfur |
| Source | 5 Well | 4 Lake | 3 Spring |

**9. a.** Equation iii. The area painted is calculated by multiplying painting rate by time. Equation iii represents the sum of Paul's area and China's area equaling the whole area, or

$$\left(\frac{96 \text{ ft}^2}{15 \text{ min}}\right)t + \left(\frac{96 \text{ ft}^2}{20 \text{ min}}\right)t = 96 \text{ ft}^2$$

**b. i.** $15t + 20t = 1$

$$35t = 1$$

$$t = \frac{1}{35} \approx 0.03$$

**ii.** $1440t + 1920t = 96$

$$3360t = 96$$

$$t = \frac{96}{3660} \approx 0.03$$

**iii.** $\frac{(60)96t}{15} + \frac{(60)96t}{20} = 96$

$$384t + 288t = 5760$$

$$672t = 5760$$

$$t = \frac{5760}{672} = \frac{60}{7} \approx 8.57$$

**c.** The solution to the correct equation, $\frac{96t}{15} + \frac{96t}{20} = 96$, is $t \approx 8.57$. Therefore it would take ~9 minutes for Paul and China to paint the wall.

**10.** Sadie plays with the catnip-filled ball.

| Position | 1 (left) | 2 | 3 | 4 (right) |
|---|---|---|---|---|
| Name | Rocky | Sadie | Winks | Pascal |
| Age | 8 | 5 | 13 | 10 |
| Sleeps | Floor | Box | Chair | Sofa |
| Toy | Stuffed toy | Catnip ball | Silk rose | Rubber mouse |

List all the information in groups and organize your information in a large table. (*See table at bottom of page.*) Then take each fact and convert it to a yes or no in the table. Number the facts so that you know where each piece of information comes from. The first fact says that Rocky and the 10-year-old cat are not next to each other in the photo. Place an N1 in the Rocky-10 cell. Continue with this method as you read once through the nine statements.

Next, in each small block it takes three noes to make a yes in the same column or row. But one yes will make six noes, three in the column and three in the row. For example, fill in the center box to get three noes and one yes in each row and column.

**Lesson 0.3, Exercise 10**

|  | Rocky | Sadie | Pascal | Winks | 5 | 8 | 10 | 13 | Rubber mouse | Silk rose | Stuffed toy | Catnip ball |
|---|---|---|---|---|---|---|---|---|---|---|---|---|
| P1 (left) |  | N4 |  |  |  |  |  |  |  |  |  |  |
| P2 |  |  |  |  |  |  |  |  |  |  |  |  |
| P3 |  |  |  |  |  |  |  |  |  | Y3 |  |  |
| P4 (right) |  |  |  |  |  |  |  |  |  |  |  |  |
| Chair |  | N4 |  |  | N2 | N2 |  |  | N2 |  |  | N9 |
| Sofa |  | N4 |  |  |  |  | Y6 |  |  |  |  |  |
| Box |  |  |  | N8 |  | N8 | N8 |  |  |  |  |  |
| Floor |  |  |  |  |  | Y5 |  |  |  |  |  |  |
| 5 |  |  | N7 |  |  |  |  |  | N2 |  |  |  |
| 8 |  |  |  |  |  |  |  |  | N2 |  |  |  |
| 10 | N1 |  |  |  |  |  |  |  |  |  | N8 |  |
| 13 |  |  |  | Y8 |  |  |  |  |  |  | N8 |  |
| Rubber mouse |  |  |  |  |  |  |  |  |  |  |  |  |
| Silk rose |  |  |  |  |  |  |  |  |  |  |  |  |
| Stuffed toy |  |  |  | N8 |  |  |  |  |  |  |  |  |
| Catnip ball |  |  |  |  |  |  |  |  |  |  |  |  |

| | 5 | 8 | 10 | 13 |
|---|---|---|---|---|
| Chair | N2 | N2 | N | Y |
| Sofa | N | N | Y6 | N |
| Box | Y | N | N8 | N8 |
| Floor | N | Y5 | N | N |

Now look back at the facts and use these yeses and noes to fill in more blanks. Because Winks is 13 and sleeps in the blue chair, the cat that plays with the rubber mouse is age 10. The 5-year-old cat lives in a box, so Pascal does not live in a box, and the 8-year-old cat plays with a stuffed toy. The oldest cats sleep on the furniture, so Sadie is not age 10 or 13. *(See first table at bottom of page.)*

Pascal is the 10-year-old cat, so he plays with the rubber mouse and is not in the third position.

Reading through facts 2, 8, and 9, you can deduce that Winks plays with the silk rose, so he is in the third position and Sadie can only be in the second position. Pascal sleeps on the furniture, leaving Rocky on the left of Sadie in the first position and Pascal in the fourth position. Winks is next to Pascal and Sadie in the photo, so the catnip belongs to Sadie. The 8-year-old cat plays with the stuffed toy, so Sadie must be age 5 and sleep in a box. Therefore, Rocky is age 8 and sleeps on the floor. Continue following the same method of deduction and the three noes lead to a yes, one yes leads to six noes. *(See second table at bottom of page.)*

Now the table is complete, and you can see that Sadie plays with the catnip-filled ball.

**Lesson 0.3, Exercise 10**

| | Rocky | Sadie | Pascal | Winks | 5 | 8 | 10 | 13 | Rubber mouse | Silk rose | Stuffed toy | Catnip ball |
|---|---|---|---|---|---|---|---|---|---|---|---|---|
| 5 | | | N7 | N | | | | | N2 | | N | |
| 8 | | | N | N | | | | | N2 | N | Y | N |
| 10 | N1 | N | Y | N | | | | | Y | N | N8 | N |
| 13 | N | N | N | Y8 | | | | | N | | N8 | |

| | Rocky | Sadie | Pascal | Winks | 5 | 8 | 10 | 13 | Rubber mouse | Silk rose | Stuffed toy | Catnip ball |
|---|---|---|---|---|---|---|---|---|---|---|---|---|
| P1 (left) | Y | N4 | N | N | | | | | N | N | Y | N |
| P2 | N | Y | N | N | | | | | N | N | N | Y |
| P3 | N | N | N | Y | | | | | N | Y3 | N | N |
| P4 (right) | N | N | Y | N | | | | | Y | N | N | N |
| Chair | N | N4 | N | Y | N2 | N2 | N | Y | N2 | Y | N | N9 |
| Sofa | N | N4 | Y | N | N | N | Y6 | N | Y | N | N | N |
| Box | N | Y | N | N8 | Y | N | N8 | N8 | N | N | N | Y |
| Floor | Y | N | N | N | N | Y5 | N | N | N | N | Y | N |
| 5 | N | Y | N7 | N | | | | | N2 | N | N | Y |
| 8 | Y | N | N | N | | | | | N2 | N | Y | N |
| 10 | N1 | N | Y | N | | | | | Y | N | N8 | N |
| 13 | N | N | N | Y8 | | | | | N | Y | N8 | N |
| Rubber mouse | N | N | Y | N | | | | | | | | |
| Silk rose | N | N | N | Y | | | | | | | | |
| Stuffed toy | Y | N | N | N8 | | | | | | | | |
| Catnip ball | N | Y | N | N | | | | | | | | |

*Discovering Advanced Algebra Solutions Manual*
©2004 Key Curriculum Press

**11.** **a.** $r^{5+7} = r^{12}$  **b.** $\frac{1}{3}s^{6-2} = \frac{s^4}{3}$

**c.** $\frac{t^{1+3}}{t^8} = \frac{t^4}{t^8} = t^{4-8} = t^{-4} = \frac{1}{t^4}$

**d.** $3\left(2^4 u^{2 \cdot 4}\right) = 3 \cdot 16u^8 = 48u^8$

**12.** **a.** 4 years  **b.** $\frac{16}{12} = \frac{4}{3} = 1.\overline{3}$

**c.** 4 years  **d.** $\frac{24}{20} = \frac{6}{5} = 1.2$

**13.** **a.** $x^2 + 1x + 5x + 5$  **b.** $x^2 + 3x + 3x + 9$

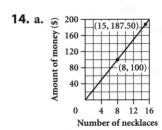

**c.** $x^2 + 3x - 3x - 9$

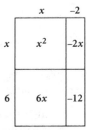

**14.** **a.**

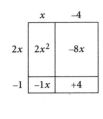

**b.** $75. Move up to the line from 6 on the horizontal axis. The corresponding value on the vertical axis is approximately 75, so she will get $75 for 6 necklaces.

**c.** $\frac{\$100}{8} = \$12.50$ per necklace

**IMPROVING YOUR REASONING SKILLS**

1000 hours in 45 days would require someone to be online for more than 22 hours per day. The advertisement is probably unreasonable because the average human being needs to sleep more than 2 hours per day.

**EXTENSION**

See the solution to Take Another Look activity 2 on page 12.

## CHAPTER 0 REVIEW

**1.** Sample answer: Fill the 5-liter bucket and pour 3 liters into the 3-liter bucket, leaving 2 liters in the 5-liter bucket. Empty the 3-liter bucket and pour the remaining 2 liters from the 5-liter bucket into the 3-liter bucket. Fill the 5-liter bucket and pour 1 liter into the 3-liter bucket, completely filling the 3-liter bucket and leaving 4 liters in the 5-liter bucket.

**2.** **a.** $x^2 + 3x + 4x + 12$  **b.** $2x^2 + 6x$

**c.** $x^2 + 6x - 2x - 12$  **d.** $2x^2 - 8x - 1x + 4$

**3.** Substitute the given values in the Pythagorean Theorem and solve.

**a.** $3^2 + 3^2 = x^2$

$$x^2 = 18$$

$$x = \sqrt{18} \text{ cm} = 3\sqrt{2} \text{ cm} \approx 4.2 \text{ cm}$$

**b.** $y^2 + 12^2 = 13^2$

$$y^2 = 169 - 144 = 25$$

$$y = \sqrt{25} \text{ in.} = 5 \text{ in.}$$

**4.** Approximate answers from the graph will vary slightly.

**a.** 168 mi. Choose a point on the line for Car A, then set up and solve a proportion.

$$\frac{120 \text{ mi}}{5 \text{ gal}} = \frac{m}{7 \text{ gal}}$$

$$(5 \text{ gal}) \cdot m = (7 \text{ gal})(120 \text{ mi})$$

$$m = \frac{(7 \text{ gal})(120 \text{ mi})}{5 \text{ gal}} = 168 \text{ mi}$$

Car A can drive 168 miles.

**b.** 9.5 gal. Choose a point on the line for Car B, then set up and solve a proportion.

$$\frac{180 \text{ mi}}{5 \text{ gal}} = \frac{342 \text{ mi}}{g}$$

$$(180 \text{ mi}) \cdot g = (5 \text{ gal})(342 \text{ mi})$$

$$g = \frac{(5 \text{ gal})(342 \text{ mi})}{180 \text{ mi}} = 9.5 \text{ gal}$$

Car B needs 9.5 gallons of gasoline.

**c.** Set up and solve a proportion for each car.

Car A: $\dfrac{120 \text{ mi}}{5 \text{ gal}} = \dfrac{m}{8.5 \text{ gal}}$

$$(5 \text{ gal}) \cdot m = (8.5 \text{ gal})(120 \text{ mi})$$

$$m = \frac{(8.5 \text{ gal})(120 \text{ mi})}{5 \text{ gal}} = 204 \text{ mi}$$

Car B: $\dfrac{180 \text{ mi}}{5 \text{ gal}} = \dfrac{m}{8.5 \text{ gal}}$

$$(5 \text{ gal}) \cdot m = (8.5 \text{ gal})(180 \text{ mi})$$

$$m = \frac{(8.5 \text{ gal})(180 \text{ mi})}{5 \text{ gal}} = 306 \text{ mi}$$

Subtract to find the difference: $306 - 204 = 102$. Car B can go 102 miles farther than Car A.

**d.** For Car A the slope is $\frac{120}{5} = 24$, which means the car can drive 24 miles per gallon of gasoline. For Car B the slope is $\frac{180}{5} = 36$, which means the car can drive 36 miles per gallon.

**5. a.** 

| | |
|---|---|
| $3(x - 5) + 2 = 26$ | The original equation. |
| $3x - 15 + 2 = 26$ | Distribute 3. |
| $3x - 13 = 26$ | Add. |
| $3x = 39$ | Add 13 to both sides. |
| $x = 13$ | Divide both sides by 3. |

To check your answer, substitute 13 for $x$ and evaluate both sides: $3(13 - 5) + 2 = 3(8) + 2 = 26$.

**b.**

| | |
|---|---|
| $3.75 - 1.5(y + 4.5) = 0.75$ | The original equation. |
| $3.75 - 1.5y - 6.75 = 0.75$ | Distribute $-1.5$. |
| $-1.5y - 3 = 0.75$ | Add. |
| $-1.5y = 3.75$ | Add 3 to both sides. |
| $y = -2.5$ | Divide both sides by $-1.5$. |

To check your answer, substitute $-2.5$ for $y$ and evaluate both sides: $3.75 - 1.5(-2.5 + 4.5) = 3.75 - 1.5(2) = 0.75$.

**6.** Let $n$ represent the unknown number.

**a.** $2n + 6$

**b.** $5(n - 3)$

**c.** $2n + 6 = 5(n - 3)$. Solve for $n$:

$$2n + 6 = 5n - 15$$
$$2n = 5n - 21$$
$$-3n = -21$$
$$n = 7$$

**7.** Let $m$ represent the number of miles driven, and let $c$ represent the total cost in dollars of renting the truck.

**a.** $c = 19.95 + 0.35m$

**b.** Possible answer: $61.25. Assuming that Keisha makes five trips, she will drive the 12-mile distance nine times (not ten times) because she doesn't need to return to the old apartment after the fifth time. Then $m = 9(12) + 10 = 118$, and $c = 19.95 + 0.35(118) = \$61.25$. If she goes back to her apartment to clean or return the keys, $c = 19.95 + 0.35(130) = \$65.45$.

**c.** $(24 \text{ mi})\left(\dfrac{\$0.35}{1 \text{ mi}}\right) = \$8.40$

**8. a.** Let $w$ represent the mass in grams of a white block, and let $r$ represent the mass in grams of a red block.

**b.** $4w + r = 2w + 2r + 40$; $5w + 2r = w + 5r$

**c.** $w = 60$; $r = 80$. Solve the first equation to get an expression for $r$ in terms of $w$.

$$4w + r = 2w + 2r + 40$$
$$-r = -2w + 40$$
$$r = 2w - 40$$

Substitute $2w - 40$ for $r$ in the second equation and solve for $w$.

$$5w + 2(2w - 40) = w + 5(2w - 40)$$
$$5w + 4w - 80 = w + 10w - 200$$
$$9w - 80 = 11w - 200$$
$$-2w = -120$$
$$w = 60$$

To find $r$, substitute 60 for $w$ in either equation and solve.

$$4(60) + r = 2(60) + 2r + 40$$
$$-r = 120 + 40 - 240 = -80$$
$$r = 80$$

**d.** The mass of a white block is 60 grams and the mass of a red block is 80 grams.

*Discovering Advanced Algebra Solutions Manual*
©2004 Key Curriculum Press

**9.** 17 years old. Let $a$ represent Amy's age in years.

$$6(a - 5) = 2(2(a + 1))$$

$$6a - 30 = 2(2a + 2) = 4a + 4$$

$$2a = 34$$

$$a = 17$$

Amy is 17 years old.

**10.** 12 pennies, 8 nickels, 15 dimes, 12 quarters. Let $p$ represent the number of pennies, $n$ represent the number of nickels, $d$ represent the number of dimes, and $q$ represent the number of quarters. Translate the information into equations.

$$\begin{cases} p + n + d + q = 47 \\ p + 5n + 10d + 25q = 502 \\ p = q \\ p + q = n + d + 1 \end{cases}$$

| | |
|---|---|
| $p + n + d + q = 47$ | Scott has 47 coins. |
| $p + 5n + 10d + 25q = 502$ | The value of all the coins equals $5.02. |
| $p = q$ | The number of pennies equals the number of quarters. |
| $p + q = n + d + 1$ | The sum of the number of pennies and quarters is one more than the sum of the number of nickels and dimes. |

Substitute $(n + d + 1)$ for $(p + q)$ in the first equation and solve for $n + d$.

$$p + n + d + q = 47$$

$$(p + q) + n + d = 47$$

$$n + d + 1 + n + d = 47$$

$$2n + 2d = 46$$

$$n + d = 23$$

Substitute 23 for $n + d$ and $q$ for $p$ in the fourth equation and solve for $p$ and $q$.

$$p + q = (n + d) + 1$$

$$q + q = 23 + 1$$

$$2q = 24$$

$$q = 12, \ p = 12$$

Substitute 12 for $p$ and $q$ in the second equation to get another equation involving only $n$ and $d$.

$$p + 5n + 10d + 25q = 502$$

$$12 + 5n + 10d + 25(12) = 502$$

$$5n + 10d + 312 = 502$$

$$5(n + 2d) = 190$$

$$n + 2d = 38$$

Combine the two equations with $n$ and $d$ and solve for $d$ by elimination.

$$\begin{array}{r} n + 2d = 38 \\ -n + (-d) = -23 \\ \hline d = 15 \end{array}$$

Substitute 15 for $d$ and solve for $n$.

$$n + (15) = 23$$

$$n = 8$$

Scott has 12 pennies, 8 nickels, 15 dimes, and 12 quarters.

**11. a.** $h = -16(0)^2 + 48(0) = 0$. Before the ball is hit, it is on the ground.

**b.** $h = -16(2)^2 + 48(2) = 32$. Two seconds after being hit, the ball is 32 feet above the ground.

**c.** $h = -16(3)^2 + 48(3) = 0$. After three seconds, the ball lands on the ground.

**12. a.** $4x^{-2+1} = 4x^{-1} = \dfrac{4}{x}$

**b.** $\dfrac{1}{2}x^{2-3} = \dfrac{1}{2}x^{-1} = \dfrac{1}{2x}$

**c.** $x^{3 \cdot 5} = x^{15}$

**13. a.** $y = 2^0 = 1$

**b.** $y = 2^3 = 8$

**c.** $y = 2^{-2} = \dfrac{1}{2^2} = \dfrac{1}{4}$

**d.** $32 = 2^x$, so $x = 5$

**14. a.** $(5 \text{ gal})\left(\dfrac{4 \text{ qt}}{1 \text{ gal}}\right)\left(\dfrac{4 \text{ c}}{1 \text{ qt}}\right)\left(\dfrac{8 \text{ oz}}{1 \text{ c}}\right) = 640$ oz

**b.** $(1 \text{ mi})\left(\dfrac{5280 \text{ ft}}{1 \text{ mi}}\right)\left(\dfrac{12 \text{ in.}}{1 \text{ ft}}\right)\left(\dfrac{2.54 \text{ cm}}{1 \text{ in.}}\right)\left(\dfrac{1 \text{ m}}{100 \text{ cm}}\right) =$ 1609.344 m

**15.**

| Sales Rep | Mr. Mendoza | Mr. Bell | Mrs. Plum |
|---|---|---|---|
| **Client** | Mr. Green | Ms. Phoung | Ms. Hunt |
| **Location** | Conference room | Convention hall | Lunch room |
| **Time** | 9:00 A.M. | 12:00 noon | 3:00 P.M. |

List information in groups and organize it in a table. The answers in the chart are marked with capital letters when the relationship comes directly from the clues and lowercase letters when they are deduced from other relationships. Once you determine which sales representative is meeting with which client, where, and when, you can stop filling in cells. *(See first table at bottom of page.)*

## TAKE ANOTHER LOOK

1. Use a volume model, in which the length, width, and height each represent a factor, and the volume represents the product. The volume model has eight different sections. This volume model represents $x^3 + 4x^2 + 3x^2 + 2x^2 + 8x + 6x + 12x + 24$.

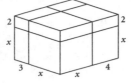

2. The sample answers in the chart are marked with capital letters when the relationship comes directly from the clues and lowercase letters when they are deduced from other relationships. Once all bottles are determined, no more cells are filled in.

*(See second table at bottom of page.)* See the solution to Lesson 0.3, Exercise 8 for a table of answers.

3. Distribute the first factor over the second by multiplying each term in the second factor by the entire first factor. Then use the distributive property again to eliminate the parentheses.

$$(x + 2)(x + 3) = (x + 2)(x) + (x + 2)(3)$$
$$= (x \cdot x + 2 \cdot x) + (x \cdot 3 + 2 \cdot 3)$$
$$= x^2 + 2x + 3x + 6$$

4. Lines with slopes less than $-1$ are steep and decreasing, lines with slopes between $-1$ and $0$ are less steep and decreasing, lines with slope $0$ are horizontal, lines with slopes between $0$ and $+1$ are increasing, and lines with slopes greater than $+1$ are steeper and increasing. A slope of $1$ or $-1$ creates a line at a 45° angle on a square coordinate grid.

**Chapter 0 Review, Exercise 15**

| | Mr. Green | Ms. Hunt | Ms. Phoung | Lunch room | Conference room | Convention hall | 9:00 A.M. | 12:00 noon | 3:00 P.M. |
|---|---|---|---|---|---|---|---|---|---|
| Mr. Bell | N | | | | n | | n | y | n |
| Mr. Mendoza | | | | n | Y | n | y | n | n |
| Mrs. Plum | | | | | n | | n | N | y |
| Lunch room | n | Y | n | | | | | | |
| Conference room | y | n | n | | | | | | |
| Convention hall | N | n | y | | | | | | |
| 9:00 A.M. | Y | n | n | | | | | | |
| 12:00 noon | n | n | y | | | | | | |
| 3:00 P.M. | n | y | N | | | | | | |

**Chapter 0 Review, Take Another Look activity 2**

| | Erlenmeyer flask | Round flask | Bottle | Calcium | Sulfur | Iron | Lake | Well | Spring |
|---|---|---|---|---|---|---|---|---|---|
| Left | n | n | y | | | | N | y | n |
| Center | y | n | N | | N | | y | | N |
| Right | | y | n | N | | | | | y |
| Lake | | | | | | | | | |
| Well | N | | | | N | | | | |
| Spring | | | | | | | | | |
| Calcium | n | N | y | | | | | | |
| Sulfur | N | y | n | | | | | | |
| Iron | Y | n | n | | | | | | |

# CHAPTER 1

## LESSON 1.1

### EXERCISES

**1. a.** 20, 26, 32, 48. Find the four terms using recursion:

$u_1 = 20$      The starting term is 20.

$u_2 = u_1 + 6 = 20 + 6 = 26$    Substitute 20 for $u_1$.

$u_3 = u_2 + 6 = 26 + 6 = 32$    Substitute 26 for $u_2$.

$u_4 = u_3 + 6 = 32 + 6 = 48$    Substitute 32 for $u_3$.

**b.** 47, 44, 41, 38

$u_1 = 47$

$u_2 = 47 - 3 = 44$

$u_3 = 44 - 3 = 41$

$u_4 = 41 - 3 = 38$

**c.** 32, 48, 72, 108

$u_1 = 32$

$u_2 = 1.5(32) = 48$

$u_3 = 1.5(48) = 72$

$u_4 = 1.5(72) = 108$

**d.** $-18, -13.7, -9.4, -5.1$

$u_1 = -18$

$u_2 = -18 + 4.3 = -13.7$

$u_3 = -13.7 + 4.3 = -9.4$

$u_4 = -9.4 + 4.3 = -5.1$

**2. a.** Arithmetic; $d = 6$     **b.** Arithmetic; $d = -3$

    **c.** Geometric; $r = 1.5$    **d.** Arithmetic; $d = 4.3$

**3.** $u_1 = 40$ and $u_n = u_{n-1} - 3.45$ where $n \geq 2$

| $n$ | 1 | 2 | 3 | 4 | 5 | 9 |
|-----|----|------|------|------|------|------|
| $u_n$ | 40 | 36.55 | 33.1 | 29.65 | 26.2 | 12.4 |

**4.** $u_1 = 6$ and $u_n = u_{n-1} + 3.2$ where $n \geq 2$; $u_{10} = 34.8$

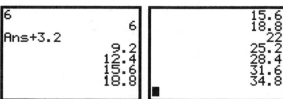

**5. a.** $u_1 = 2$ and $u_n = u_{n-1} + 4$ where $n \geq 2$; $u_{15} = 58$

   **b.** $u_1 = 10$ and $u_n = u_{n-1} - 5$ where $n \geq 2$; $u_{12} = -45$

   **c.** $u_1 = 0.4$ and $u_n = 0.1u_{n-1}$ where $n \geq 2$; $u_{10} = 0.0000000004$

   **d.** $u_1 = -2$ and $u_n = u_{n-1} - 6$ where $n \geq 2$; $u_{30} = -176$

   **e.** $u_1 = 1.56$ and $u_n = u_{n-1} + 3.29$ where $n \geq 2$; $u_{14} = 44.33$

   **f.** $u_1 = -6.24$ and $u_n = u_{n-1} + 2.21$ where $n \geq 2$; $u_{20} = 35.75$

**6.** $u_1 = 4$ and $u_n = u_{n-1} + 5$ where $n \geq 2$; $u_{46} = 229$. Organize the information from the graph in a table:

| $n$ | 1 | 2 | 3 | 4 |
|-----|---|---|----|----|
| $u_n$ | 4 | 9 | 14 | 19 |

The starting term is 4 and the common difference between successive terms is 5. Therefore the following recursive formula generates the sequence on the graph: $u_1 = 4$ and $u_n = u_{n-1} + 5$ where $n \geq 2$.

Use either the recursive sequence or Home screen recursion on the calculator to find the 46th term: $u_{46} = 229$.

**7.** $u_1 = 4$ and $u_n = u_{n-1} + 6$ where $n \geq 2$

| Figure | 1 | 2 | 3 | 4 | 5 | 12 | 32 |
|--------|---|----|----|----|----|----|-----|
| Segments | 4 | 10 | 16 | 22 | 28 | 70 | 190 |

**8. a.** 13 minutes. Organize the information in a table:

| Minute | 0 | 1 | 2 | 3 | 10 | 13 |
|--------|----|------|------|------|----|------|
| Gallons | 20 | 22.4 | 24.8 | 27.2 | 44 | 51.2 |

The water is flowing over the top of the bathtub when you check at 13 minutes.

   **b.** 29 minutes. Add two more rows to the table in 8a and extend the columns:

| Minute | 0 | 1 | 2 | 3 | 10 | 13 | 20 | 29 |
|--------|----|------|------|------|----|------|----|------|
| Gallons with added water | 20 | 22.4 | 24.8 | 27.2 | 44 | 51.2 | 68 | 89.6 |
| Gallons drained | 0 | 3.1 | 6.2 | 9.3 | 31 | 40.3 | 62 | 89.9 |
| Gallons remaining | 20 | 19.3 | 18.6 | 17.9 | 13 | 10.9 | 6 | -0.3 |

The tub is empty when you check at 29 minutes.

   **c.** $u_0 = 20$ and $u_n = u_{n-1} + 2.4 - 3.1$ where $n \geq 1$, or $u_0 = 20$ and $u_n = u_{n-1} - 0.7$ where $n \geq 1$

**9. a.** $\left(\dfrac{57 \text{ km}}{1 \text{ h}}\right)(7 \text{ h}) = 399 \text{ km}$

**b.** 10 hours after the first car starts, or 8 hours after the second car starts. Let $t$ be the number of hours after the first car starts, $d_1$ be distance traveled in kilometers by the first car, and $d_2$ be distance traveled in kilometers by the second car.

**Method 1**

Organize the information in a table:

| Time (h) $t$ | 2 | 3 | 4 | 5 | 10 |
|---|---|---|---|---|---|
| Distance of first car $d_1$ | 114 | 171 | 228 | 285 | 570 |
| Distance of second car $d_2$ | 0 | 72 | 144 | 216 | 576 |

From the table, you see that after a total of 10 hours, the second car will have passed the first car.

**Method 2**

Set up equations and evaluate. From the information given, you know that $d = r \cdot t$, $d_1 = 57t$, and $d_2 = 72(t - 2)$. Set $d_1 = d_2$ and solve for $t$.

$$57t = 72(t - 2) = 72t - 144$$

$$-15t = -144$$

$$t = \frac{-144}{-15} = 9.6 \approx 10 \text{ h}$$

**10. a.** The differences are 245, 273, 225, 229, 283, 211, and 289. The average is about 250, so a recursive formula is $u_1 = 250$ and $u_n = u_{n-1} + 250$ where $n \geq 2$.

**b.** $u_9 = 2250$, $u_{10} = 2500$, $u_{11} = 2750$, $u_{12} = 3000$, $u_{13} = 3250$

**c.** $\dfrac{100000}{250} = 400$, so $u_{400} = 100000$. There will be approximately 400 defective batteries in 100,000.

**11. a.** $80 - 0.25(80) = \$60$, or $80(1 - 0.25) = 80(0.75) = \$60$

**b.** Write a sequence. $u_1 = 80$ and $u_n = 0.75u_{n-1}$ where $n \geq 2$. $u_4 = 33.75$, so the price during the fourth week is $33.75.

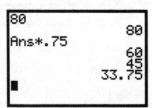

**c.** Continue evaluating the sequence until the term is less than 10. The ninth term is about 8.01, so the vacuum will sell for less than \$10 during the ninth week.

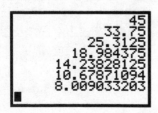

**12. a.** $3.2$; $\dfrac{51 - 35}{5} = 3.2$

**b.** $25.4, 28.6, 31.8, \ldots, 38.2, 41.4, 44.6, 47.8, \ldots, 54.2$

**c.** $172.6$. Use either recursive sequences or Home screen recursion on your calculator.

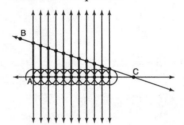

**13.** Sample answer: Construct two lines that intersect, $\overleftrightarrow{AB}$ and $\overleftrightarrow{BC}$. On one line, $\overleftrightarrow{AB}$, use congruent circles to mark off ten equally spaced points. Construct lines perpendicular to $\overleftrightarrow{AB}$ through each point. The segments between $\overleftrightarrow{AB}$ and $\overleftrightarrow{BC}$ represent an arithmetic sequence.

**14. a.**

| Elapsed time (s) | Distance from motion sensor (m) |
|---|---|
| 0.0 | 2.0 |
| 1.0 | 3.0 |
| 2.0 | 4.0 |
| 3.0 | 5.0 |
| 4.0 | 4.5 |
| 5.0 | 4.0 |
| 6.0 | 3.5 |
| 7.0 | 3.0 |

**b.**

**15. a.** $\dfrac{70}{100} = \dfrac{a}{65}$. Multiply by the product of the denominators, $100 \cdot 65$: $6500 \cdot \dfrac{70}{100} = 6500 \cdot \dfrac{a}{65}$, or $70(65) = \dfrac{a}{100}$, $a = \dfrac{70(65)}{100} = 45.5$.

**b.** $\dfrac{115}{100} = \dfrac{b}{37}$; $3700 \cdot \dfrac{115}{100} = 3700 \cdot \dfrac{b}{37}$, $115(37) = 100b$, $b = \dfrac{115(37)}{100} = 42.55$

*Discovering Advanced Algebra Solutions Manual*
©2004 Key Curriculum Press

**c.** $\frac{c}{100} = \frac{110}{90}$; $900 \cdot \frac{c}{100} = 900 \cdot \frac{110}{90}$, 

$90c = 100(110)$, $c = \frac{100(110)}{90} \approx 122.2\%$

**d.** $\frac{d}{100} = \frac{0.5}{18}$; $1800 \cdot \frac{d}{100} = 1800 \cdot \frac{0.5}{18}$, 

$18d = 100(0.5)$, $d = \frac{100(0.5)}{18} \approx 2.78\%$

**16.** 17 square units. Sample answer:

**Method 1**

Enclose the triangle in a rectangle and subtract the areas of the right triangles on the outside.

Area of rectangle $= 4 \cdot 9 = 36$ square units

Area of $\triangle CFB = \frac{1}{2}(4)(1) = 2$ square units

Area of $\triangle ADC = \frac{1}{2}(2)(9) = 9$ square units

Area of $\triangle AEB = \frac{1}{2}(2)(8) = 8$ square units

Area of $\triangle ABC = 36 - 2 - 9 - 8 = 17$ square units

**Method 2**

The slopes of $\overline{AB}$ and $\overline{BC}$ are negative reciprocals of each other, so $\overline{AB} \perp \overline{BC}$. Find their lengths using the distance formula, and use the formula $A = \frac{1}{2}(AB)(BC)$. Call point $D$ the origin.

$AB = \sqrt{(0-8)^2 + (2-4)^2} = \sqrt{68}$ square units

$BC = \sqrt{(8-9)^2 + (0-4)^2} = \sqrt{17}$ square units

Area of $\triangle ABC = \frac{1}{2}\sqrt{68} \cdot \sqrt{17} = 17$ square units

**17.** Evaluate both offers.

7% increase per week: $390 + 390(.07) = \$417.30$, or $390(1.07) = \$417.30$

Additional $25 per week: $390 + 25 = \$415.00$

Sherez should accept the 7% increase, which is an additional $27.30 per week.

**IMPROVING YOUR REASONING SKILLS**

1, 1, 2, 3, 5, 8, 13, 21, 34, 55, 89, 144, . . . ; $u_1 = 1$, $u_2 = 1$, and $u_n = u_{n-1} + u_{n-2}$ where $n \geq 3$. The recursive rule for the Fibonacci sequence is defined by two preceding terms, which is different from the other sequences you have studied.

**EXTENSION**

See the answers to Take Another Look activities 1 and 3 on pages 23 and 24.

## LESSON 1.2

**EXERCISES**

**1. a.** $r = 1.5$; $\frac{150}{100} = 1.5$, $\frac{225}{150} = 1.5$, $\frac{337.5}{225} = 1.5$, 

$\frac{506.25}{337.5} = 1.5$

**b.** $r = 0.4$; $\frac{29.375}{73.4375} = 0.4$, $\frac{11.75}{29.375} = 0.4$, 

$\frac{4.7}{11.75} = 0.4$, $\frac{1.88}{4.7} = 0.4$

**c.** $r = 1.03$; $\frac{82.4}{80} = 1.03$, $\frac{84.87}{82.4} = 1.02997$, 

$\frac{87.42}{81.87} = 1.03005$, $\frac{90.04}{87.42} = 1.03$

**d.** $r = 0.92$; $\frac{191.36}{208.00} = 0.92$, $\frac{176.05}{191.36} = 0.91999$, 

$\frac{161.97}{176.05} = 0.92002$

**2. a.** Growth; $1.5 - 1 = 0.5$, 50% increase

**b.** Decay; $0.4 - 1 = -0.6$, 60% decrease

**c.** Growth; $1.03 - 1 = 0.03$, 3% increase

**d.** Decay; $0.92 - 1 = -0.08$, 8% decrease

**3. a.** $u_1 = 100$ and $u_n = 1.5u_{n-1}$ where $n \geq 2$; $u_{10} \approx 3844.3$

**b.** $u_1 = 73.4375$ and $u_n = 0.4u_{n-1}$ where $n \geq 2$; $u_{10} \approx 0.020$

**c.** $u_1 = 80$ and $u_n = 1.03u_{n-1}$ where $n \geq 2$; $u_{10} \approx 104.38$

**d.** $u_1 = 208$ and $u_n = 0.92u_{n-1}$ where $n \geq 2$; $u_{10} \approx 98.21$

**4.** A, ii. decay; B, i. growth; C, iii. constant

**5. a.** $(1 + 0.07)u_{n-1}$, or $1.07u_{n-1}$

**b.** $(1 - 0.18)A$, or $0.82A$

**c.** $(1 + 0.08125)x$, or $1.08125x$

**d.** $(2 - 0.85)u_{n-1}$, or $1.15u_{n-1}$

**6. a.** $0.8$; $\frac{64}{80} = 0.8$, $\frac{51}{64} \approx 0.8$, $\frac{41}{51} \approx 0.8$

**b.** 11 in.; $u_0 = 100$ and $u_n = 0.8u_{n-1}$ where $n \geq 1$; $u_{10} \approx 11$

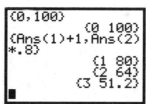
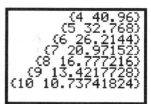

**c.** 21 bounces; 31 bounces

**7.** 100 is the initial height, but the units are unknown. 0.20 is the percent loss, so the ball loses 20% of its height with each rebound.

**8.** Possible answer: The sum of $250,000 was invested at 2.5% annual interest in 2003.

**9. a.** Write a recursive formula that generates the total number of workers and evaluate it for each of the next five years:

$u_0 = 12$ and $u_n = 1.2u_{n-1}$ where $n \geq 1$

$u_1 = 14.4$, $u_2 = 17.28$, $u_3 = 20.736$, $u_4 \approx 24.883$, and $u_5 \approx 29.860$

The number of new hires for each year is the number of workers for that year minus the number of workers for the previous year.

Year 1: $u_1 - u_0 = 14.4 - 12 = 2.4$

Year 2: $u_2 - u_1 = 17.28 - 14.4 = 2.88$

Year 3: $u_3 - u_2 = 20.736 - 17.28 = 3.456$

Year 4: $u_4 - u_3 \approx 24.883 - 20.736 = 4.147$

Year 5: $u_5 - u_4 \approx 29.860 - 24.883 = 4.977$

Rounding, the number of new hires for the next five years is 2, 3, 3 (or 4), 4, and 5.

**b.** About 30 employees. Add the 17 or 18 new hires to the initial 12 employees.

**10. a.** $u_0 = 2000$ and $u_n = (1 + 0.085)u_{n-1}$ where $n \geq 1$

**b.** 8.5%. $\frac{2170}{2000} = 1.085$, so $1 - 1.085 = 0.085$, or 8.5%.

**c.** 14 years ($6266.81). Use the recursive formula or add values to the table until the balance passes 3(2000), or $6000.

**11.** $u_0 = 1$ and $u_n = 0.8855u_{n-1}$ where $n \geq 1$; $u_{25} = 0.048$ or 4.8%. It would take about 25,000 years to reduce to 5%.

**12. a.**

| Generations back $n$ | 1 | 2 | 3 | 4 | 5 |
|---|---|---|---|---|---|
| Ancestors in the generation $u_n$ | 2 | 4 | 8 | 16 | 32 |

**b.** Start with 1 and recursively multiply by 2. $u_0 = 1$ and $u_n = 2u_{n-1}$ where $n \geq 1$.

**c.** $u_{30}$; 30 generations ago, Jill had 1 billion living ancestors.

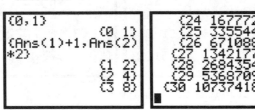

**d.** 750 years ago; 30(25) = 750

**e.** The population of the planet at that time was less than 1 billion. Jill must have some common ancestors.

**13. a.** $\frac{6.5}{12} \approx 0.542\%$

**b.** 500(1.00542) = $502.71

**c.** $u_0 = 500$ and $u_n = \left(1 + \frac{0.065}{12}\right)u_{n-1}$ where $n \geq 1$; $u_{12} = \$533.49$

**d.** $u_{29} = \$584.80$

**14. a.** $\frac{77654 - 39175}{39175} = \frac{38479}{39175} = 0.9822 = 98.22\%$

**b.** You might guess $\frac{0.9822}{30} = 0.0327 = 3.27\%$, or if you think that growth is not linear, you might guess 3% or less.

**c.** Using $u_{1970} = 39175$ and $u_n = (1 + 0.0327)u_{n-1}$ where $n \geq 1971$ yields $u_{2000} = 102857$. Sample explanation: The percentage used in the recursive formula is an average and does not account for population surges during later years.

**d.** 2.3%  *(See table at bottom of page.)*

**e.** Using $u_{1970} = 39175$ and $u_n = (1 + 0.023)u_{n-1}$ where $n \geq 1971$ yields $u_{1985} = 55099$. The average is 58,414.5. The mean works only if the growth is arithmetic.

**15. a.** 3; $\frac{162}{18} = 9$, $3^2 = 9$

**b.** 2, 6, . . . , 54, . . . , 486, 1458, . . . , 13122

**c.** $u_{11} = 118{,}098$

**16.** 248.6 million; $(1 + 0.132)x = 281.4$, so $x = \frac{281.4}{1.132} \approx 248.6$

**17. a.** $\frac{160 \text{ m}}{40 \text{ s}} = 4$ m/s  **b.** $\frac{40 \text{ m}}{4 \text{ m/s}} = 10$ s

**c.** 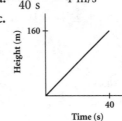  **d.**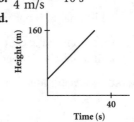

---

**Lesson 1.2, Exercise 14d**

| Guess (p) | Find $u_{2000}$ ($u_{1970} = 39175(1 + p)u_{n-1}$ where $n \geq 1971$) | Check: 77,654? |
|---|---|---|
| 3% (or 0.030) | 95,088 | too high |
| 2% (or 0.020) | 70,960 | too low |
| 2.5% (or 0.025) | 82,172 | too high |
| 2.2% (or 0.022) | 75,255 | too low |
| 2.4% (or 0.024) | 79,801 | too high |
| 2.3% (or 0.023) | 77,495 | closest |

*Discovering Advanced Algebra Solutions Manual*
©2004 Key Curriculum Press

**e.**

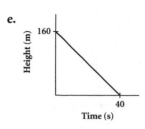

**18. a.** $u_1 = 180$ and $u_n = u_{n-1} - 7$ where $n \geq 2$

    **b.** $u_{10} = 117$     **c.** $u_{27} = -2$

**19. a.** $3.5x = 151.7$, so $x = \frac{151.7}{3.5} \approx 43.34$

    **b.** $0.88x = -599.72$, so $x = \frac{-599.72}{0.88} = -681.5$

    **c.** $18.75x = 16$, so $x = \frac{16}{18.75} \approx 0.853$

    **d.** $x = 16 - 0.5(16) = 16 - 8 = 8$

**20. a.** $y = 47 + 8(0) = 47 + 0 = 47$

    **b.** $y = 47 + 8(1) = 47 + 8 = 55$

    **c.** $y = 47 + 8(5) = 47 + 40 = 87$

    **d.** $y = 47 + 8(-8) = 47 - 64 = -17$

### EXTENSION

By guess-and-check, perhaps coupled with the "rule of 70" (divide 70 by the interest rate to get the approximate number of years required for doubling), $\left(1 + \frac{0.07}{12}\right)^n$ first exceeds 2 when $n = 120$ months, or 10 years. $\left(1 + \frac{0.07}{360}\right)^n$ first exceeds 2 when $n = 3566$, about a month less than 10 years.

## LESSON 1.3

### EXERCISES

**1. a.** 31.2, 45.64, 59.358; shifted geometric, increasing

    **b.** 776, 753.2, 731.54; shifted geometric, decreasing

    **c.** 45, 40.5, 36.45; geometric, decreasing

    **d.** 40, 40, 40; arithmetic or shifted geometric, neither increasing nor decreasing

**2. a.**     $a = 210 + 0.75a$

    $0.25a = 210$

        $a = \frac{210}{0.25} = 840$

    **b.**     $b = 0.75b + 300$

    $0.25b = 300$

        $b = \frac{300}{0.25} = 1200$

    **c.**     $c = 210 + c$

    $0 \neq 210$; no solution

    **d.**     $d = 0.75d$

    $0.25d = 0$

        $d = \frac{0}{0.25} = 0$

**3. a.**     $a = 0.95a + 16$

    $0.05a = 16$

        $a = \frac{16}{0.05} = 320$

    **b.**     $b = 0.95b + 16$

    $0.05b = 16$

        $b = \frac{16}{0.05} = 320$

    **c.**     $c = 0.9c$

    $0.1c = 0$

        $c = \frac{0}{0.1} = 0$

    **d.**     $d = 0.5d + 20$

    $0.5d = 20$

        $d = \frac{20}{0.5} = 40$

**4. a.** $u_0 = 200$ and $u_n = 1.08u_{n-1}$ where $n \geq 1$

    **b.** $u_0 = 0$ and $u_n = 0.5u_{n-1} + 10$ where $n \geq 1$

**5. a.** The first day, 300 grams of chlorine were added. Each day, 15% disappears, and 30 more grams are added.

    **b.** Assume that terms stop changing, set the value of the next term equal to the value of the previous term, and solve the equation.

| | |
|---|---|
| $u_n = 0.85u_{n-1} + 30$ | Recursive formula. |
| $c = 0.85c + 30$ | Assign the same variable to $u_n$ and $u_{n-1}$. |
| $0.15c = 30$ | Subtract $0.85c$ from both sides. |
| $c = 200$ | Divide both sides by 0.15. |

The amount of chlorine levels off at 200 g.

**6. a.** $u_0 = 24000$ and $u_n = \left(1 + \frac{0.034}{12}\right)u_{n-1} - 100$ where $n \geq 1$

    **b.** 24,000; 23,968; 23,935.91; 23,903.73; 23,871.45

    **c.** After four months the account balance is $23,871.45.

    **d.** $u_{12} = \$23,609.96$, $u_{36} = \$22,789.00$

**7. a.** The account balance will continue to decrease (slowly at first, but faster after a while). It does not level off, but it eventually reaches 0 and stops decreasing.

    **b.** \$68. The interest earned the first month is $24000\left(\frac{0.034}{12}\right) = \$68$. Withdrawing \$68 each month maintains a balance of \$24,000.

**8. a.** $u_0 = 7000$ and $u_n = (1 - 0.12)u_{n-1} + 600$ or $0.88u_{n-1} + 600$ where $n \geq 1$; $u_{10} = 5557$ trees

    **b.** 5000 trees. The number of trees sold will be exactly equal to the number planted.

**c.** $c = 0.88c + 600$

**d.** Initial values greater than 5000 decrease, and initial values less than 5000 increase. Regardless of the initial value, all stop changing at 5000.

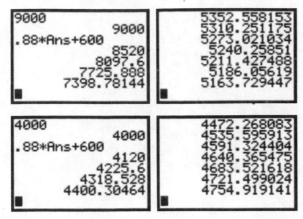

**e.** The long-run value will be the same as long as the nursery continues to sell and plant at the same rate.

**9.** $u_0 = 20$ and $u_n = (1 - 0.25)u_{n-1}$ where $n \geq 1$; 11 days ($u_{11} \approx 0.84$ mg)

**10.** Yes, the long-run value was $\frac{16}{0.25}$, or 64 mL, and it is now $\frac{32}{0.25}$, or 128 mL.

**11. a.** Sample answer: After 9 h there are only 8 mg, after 18 h there are 4 mg, after 27 h there are still 2 mg left.

**b.**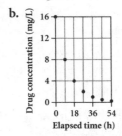

**c.** 8 mg. Write a recursive formula. $u_0 = 16$ and $u_n = \frac{1}{2}u_{n-1} + c$ where $n \geq 1$. Substitute the long-run value, 16, and solve for $c$.

$u_n = \frac{1}{2}u_{n-1} + c$  Recursive formula.

$16 = \frac{1}{2}(16) + c$  Substitute 16 for $u_n$ and $u_{n-1}$.

$8 = c$  Subtract 8 from both sides.

The person should take 8 mg every 9 h to maintain a balance of 16 mg/L.

**12. a.** $p_1 = 32$, $p_2 = 16\sqrt{2}$, $p_3 = 16$, $p_4 = 8\sqrt{2}$, ..., $p_9 = 2$ in.

**b.** $a_1 = 64$, $a_2 = 32$, $a_3 = 16$, ..., $a_9 = 0.25$ in.². You can also use the perimeter found in 12a: $\frac{2}{4} = 0.5$, so $(0.5 \text{ in.})^2 = 0.25$ in.².

**c.** $r_1 = \frac{p_1}{a_1} = 0.5$, $r_2 = \frac{\sqrt{2}}{2}$, $r_3 = 1$, $r_4 = \sqrt{2}$, ..., $r_9 = \frac{2}{0.25} = 8$. The ratio gets larger and larger without limit.

**13. a.** $u_2 = -96$; $u_5 = 240$. $d = 128 - 16 = 112$; $u_2 = u_3 - 112 = 16 - 112 = -96$, $u_5 = u_4 + 112 = 128 + 112 = 240$

**b.** $u_2 = 2$; $u_5 = 1024$. $r = \frac{128}{16} = 8$; $8u_2 = u_3$, $u_2 = \frac{16}{8} = 2$, $u_5 = 8u_4$, $u_5 = 8(128) = 1024$

**14. a.** $u_{1998} = 760$ and $u_n = (1 + 0.1)u_{n-1}$ where $n \geq 1999$

**b.** The range of the moose population is between 859 and 909. $1010(1 - 0.15) = 1010(0.85) = 858.5$ and $1010(1 - 0.1) = 1010(0.9) = 909$.

**15.** Let $u_0$ be the original height of the ball and $n$ be the number of bounces. The recursive formula $u_0 = 1$ and $u_n = 0.97u_{n-1}$ where $n \geq 1$ yields $u_{23} \approx 0.5$. The ball will bounce 23 times before it rebounds to half its original height.

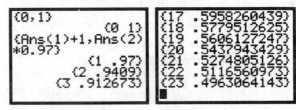

**IMPROVING YOUR VISUAL THINKING SKILLS**

At each step, the same amount of red paint is in the white as there is white paint in the red. For example, after the first mixing, the "white" can contains 3.25 qt of white paint and 0.75 qt of red paint; the "red" can contains 0.75 qt of white paint and 2.25 qt of red paint. With numerous repetitions, the two cans will get closer and closer to the same shade of pink, but theoretically they will never be exactly the same.

**EXTENSIONS**

**A.** Research results will vary.

**B.** See the answers to Take Another Look activity 2 on page 23.

**LESSON 1.4**

**EXERCISES**

**1. a.** 0 to 9 for $n$ and 0 to 16 for $u_n$

**b.** 0 to 19 for $n$ and 0 to 400 for $u_n$

**c.** 0 to 29 for $n$ and $-178$ to 25 for $u_n$

**d.** 0 to 69 for $n$ and 0 to 3037 for $u_n$

*Discovering Advanced Algebra Solutions Manual*
©2004 Key Curriculum Press

**2. a.** Geometric; $u_0 = 20$ and $u_n = 1.2u_{n-1}$ where $n \geq 1$

   **b.** Arithmetic; $u_0 = 80$ and $u_n = u_{n-1} - 5$ where $n \geq 1$

   **c.** Arithmetic; $u_0 = 0$ and $u_n = u_{n-1} + 8$ where $n \geq 1$

   **d.** Geometric; $u_0 = 90$ and $u_n = 0.7u_{n-1}$ where $n \geq 1$

**3. a.** Geometric, nonlinear, decreasing

   **b.** Arithmetic, linear, decreasing

   **c.** Geometric, nonlinear, increasing

   **d.** Arithmetic, linear, increasing

**4. a.** 840. $c = 0.75c + 210$, so $0.25c = 210$, and $c = \frac{210}{0.25} = 840$

   **b.  i.** Possible answer: $u_0 = 200$

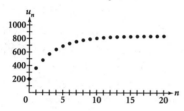

   **ii.** Possible answer: $u_0 = 1000$

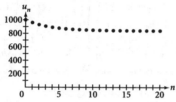

   **iii.** $u_0 = 840$

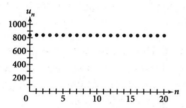

   **c.** When the starting value is below the long-run value, the graph increases toward the long-run value. When the starting value is above the long-run value, the graph decreases toward the long-run value. When the starting value is the long-run value, the graph is a constant, horizontal, linear pattern at the long-run value.

**5. A. iii.** The graph of an arithmetic sequence is linear.

   **B. ii.** The graph of a nonshifted geometric sequence will increase indefinitely or have a limit of zero.

   **C. i.** The graph has a nonzero limit, so it must represent a shifted geometric sequence.

**6. a.** $u_0 = 18$ and $u_n = -0.75_{n-1}$ where $n \geq 1$

**b.** Because each term alternates signs, the graph is unique; each point alternates above or below the $n$-axis. The points above the $n$-axis create, however, a familiar geometric pattern, as do the points below the $n$-axis. If the points below the $n$-axis were reflected across the $n$-axis, you would have the graph of $u_0 = 18$ and $u_n = +0.75u_{n-1}$ where $n \geq 1$.

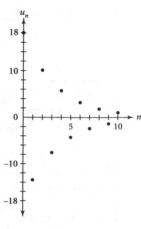

**c.** 0. $c = -0.75c$, so $1.75c = 0$, and $c = 0$

**7.** The graph of an arithmetic sequence is always linear. The graph increases when the common difference is positive and decreases when the common difference is negative. The steepness of the graph relates to the common difference.

**8.** The graph of a geometric sequence is usually nonlinear and usually approaches the $n$-axis or recedes more and more quickly from it. The graph increases when the common ratio is greater than 1 and decreases when the ratio is between 0 and 1. The change in steepness of the curve is related to the common ratio.

**9. a.**

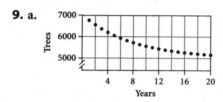

   **b.** The graph appears to have a long-run value of 5000 trees, which agrees with the long-run value found in Exercise 8b in Lesson 1.3.

**10. a.** After approximately seven days. Write a recursive formula and/or make a graph that represents the concentration of fluoride in drinking water over the next several days.

$u_0 = 3.00$ and $u_n = (1 - 0.15)u_{n-1}$ (or $u_n = 0.85u_{n-1}$) where $n \geq 1$

$u_7 \approx 0.96$, which is less than 1 mg/L, the minimum concentration.

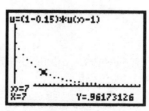

$[-1, 31, 1, -1, 5, 1]$

**b.** Add 0.50 to the recursive formula and regraph.

$u_n = 0.85u_{n-1} + 0.50$   where $n \geq 1$

The concentration
of fluoride is
increasing toward
a long-run value
of approximately
3.3 mg/L.

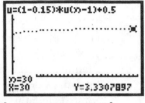

$[-1, 31, 1, -1, 5, 1]$

**c.** Add 0.10 to the original formula and regraph.

$u_n = 0.85u_{n-1} + 0.10$   where $n \geq 1$

The concentration
of fluoride is
decreasing toward a
long-run value of
approximately
0.67 mg/L.

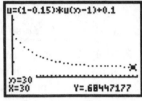

$[-1, 31, 1, -1, 5, 1]$

**d.** 0.225 mg. Let $f$ be
the amount of
fluoride added
daily and $c$ be the
long-run value
where $c = 0.85c + f$.
Substitute 1.50 for
$c$ and solve for $f$:

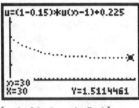

$[-1, 31, 1, -1, 5, 1]$

$1.50 = (0.85)1.50 + f$, so $f = 1.50 - 1.275 = 0.225$. Approximately 0.225 ppm of fluoride
needs to be added daily.

You could also note that each day, the amount
lost must be exactly replaced and on any day, the
amount lost is 15% of 1.50 mg, or 0.225 mg.

**11.** Possible answer: The common difference is $d = \frac{60 - 40}{55 - 50} = \frac{20}{5} = 4$, so $u_{50} = 40$ and $u_n = u_{n-1} + 4$ where $n \geq 51$.

**12.** Possible answer: $u_{1950} = 7.6$ and $u_n = (1 + 0.026)u_{n-1}$ where $n \geq 1951$

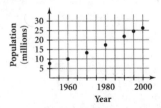

**13. a.** $u_1 = 547.5$, $u_2 = 620.6$, $u_3 = 675.5$, $u_4 = 716.6$, $u_5 = 747.5$

**b.** $\frac{547.5 - 210}{0.75} = 450$. Subtract 210 and divide the
difference by 0.75.

**c.** $u_0 = 747.5$ and $u_n = \frac{u_{n-1} - 210}{0.75}$ where $n \geq 1$

**14. a.** $10^a = \frac{47,500,000}{4.75} = 10,000,000 = 10^7$, so $a = 7$

**b.** $a = \frac{0.0461}{10^{-2}} = 4.61$

**c.** $a = 0.348$

**15. a.** $33\frac{1}{3}$. $c = 0.70c + 10$, so $0.3c = 10$, and
$c = \frac{10}{0.3} = 33\frac{1}{3}$.

**b.** $66\frac{2}{3}$. $c = 0.70c + 20$, so $0.3c = 20$, and
$c = \frac{20}{0.3} = 66\frac{2}{3}$.

**c.** 100. $c = 0.70c + 30$, so $0.3c = 30$, and
$c = \frac{30}{0.3} = 100$.

**d.** The long-run value grows in proportion to the
added constant. $7 \cdot 33\frac{1}{3} = 233\frac{1}{3}$

**EXTENSION**

Sequences explored will vary. When the common ratio
of a sequence is greater than 1, the sequence does not
approach a limit.

**EXPLORATION · RECURSION IN GEOMETRY**

**QUESTIONS**

**1.** They are very nearly the same, except near the
center and at the edge of the spiral. The center
of the Fibonacci spiral breaks down into two
congruent squares, but the golden rectangle spiral
continues inward indefinitely. Both spirals poten-
tially continue outward indefinitely. The construction of the golden rectangle spiral starts with a
finite outside edge (though the reverse process of
adding a square to the longer side could always be
carried out to continue expanding it outward).

**2.** Golden-rectangle spiral ratios: 1.618, 1.618, 1.618,
1.618, 1.618, 1.618, . . .

Fibonacci spiral ratios: 1, 2, 1.5, 1.667, 1.6, 1.625,
1.615, 1.619, 1.618, . . .

The sequence of ratios for the Fibonacci spiral
approaches the golden ratio in the long run.

**3.** Possible answer: A recursive rule in geometry
usually produces a geometric design. The measurements of the shapes at each stage of the recursion
process produce sequences that can be expressed
with an algebraic recursive rule.

**LESSON 1.5**

**EXERCISES**

**1. a.** Investment, because a deposit is added

**b.** $450

**c.** $50

**d.** 3.9%

**e.** Annually (once a year)

**2. a.** Loan, because a payment is subtracted

**b.** $500

**c.** $25

**d.** 4%

**e.** Quarterly (four times a year)

**3. a.** $32000 \cdot \dfrac{0.049}{12} = \$130.67$

**b.** $32000 \cdot \dfrac{0.059}{12} = \$157.33$

**c.** $32000 \cdot \dfrac{0.069}{12} = \$184.00$

**d.** $32000 \cdot \dfrac{0.079}{12} = \$210.67$

**4. a.** $u_0 = 10000$ and $u_n = u_{n-1}\left(1 + \dfrac{0.10}{12}\right) - 300$ where $n \geq 1$

**b.** $u_0 = 7000$ and $u_n = u_{n-1}\left(1 + \dfrac{0.1875}{12}\right) - 250$ where $n \geq 1$

**c.** $u_0 = 8000$ and $u_n = u_{n-1}\left(1 + \dfrac{0.06}{4}\right) + 500$ where $n \geq 1$

**d.** $u_0 = 0$ and $u_n = u_{n-1}\left(1 + \dfrac{0.070}{12}\right) + 100$ where $n \geq 1$

**5.** $u_0 = 500$ and $u_n = u_{n-1}\left(1 + \dfrac{0.0325}{12}\right)$ where $n \geq 1$; $u_{60} = \$588.09$

**6. a.** $u_0 = 1000$ and $u_n = u_{n-1}\left(1 + \dfrac{0.065}{4}\right)$ where $n \geq 1$; $u_{40} = \$1905.56$

**b.** $u_{80} = \$3631.15$     **c.** $u_{120} = \$6919.38$

**7. a.** $u_0 = 1000$ and $u_n = (1 + 0.065)u_{n-1}$ where $n \geq 1$; $u_{10} = \$1877.14$

**b.** $u_0 = 1000$ and $u_n = \left(1 + \dfrac{0.065}{12}\right)u_{n-1}$ where $n \geq 1$; $u_{120} = \$1912.18$

**c.** $u_0 = 1000$ and $u_n = \left(1 + \dfrac{0.065}{360}\right)u_{n-1}$ where $n \geq 1$; $u_{3600} = \$1915.43$

**d.** The more frequently the interest is compounded, the more quickly the balance will grow. That is, after 10 years, an investment compounded daily will be greater than an investment compounded monthly, which will be greater than an investment compounded annually.

**8. a.** Both deposit $1000 to start and $1200 each year. There is no difference.

**b.**

| Year | 0 | 1 | 2 | 3 |
|---|---|---|---|---|
| Beau | $1000.00 | $2265.00 | $3612.23 | $5047.02 |
| Shaleah | $1000.00 | $2303.38 | $3694.04 | $5177.84 |

Shaleah's account always has a higher balance. The difference between Beau's and Shaleah's balances gets greater over time.

**9. a.** $1000000 = 5000\left(1 + \dfrac{0.085}{12}\right)u_{45} + d;\ d = \$123.98$

**b.** For $u_0 = 5000$ and $u_n = \left(1 + \dfrac{0.085}{12}\right)u_{n-1} + 123.98$ where $n \geq 1$

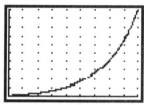

[0, 540, 60, 0, 900000, 100000]

**10. a.** $1990; $1979.85; $1969.55; $1959.09; $1948.48; $1937.70

**b.** 94 months, or 7 years 10 months

**c.** $93(40) + \left(40 + u_{94}\right) = 3720 + (40 - 35.53) = \$3724.47$

**11. a.** $0 = 60000\left(1 + \dfrac{0.096}{12}\right)u_{24} - p;\ p = \$528.39$

**b.** For $u_0 = 60000$ and $u_n = \left(1 + \dfrac{0.096}{12}\right)u_{n-1} - 528.39$ where $n \geq 1$

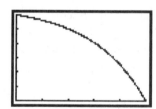

[0, 300, 60, 0, 60000, 10000]

**12. a.** $20(0.10) = 2$ mL

**b.** $220(0.05) = 11$ mL

**c.** $20 - 2 + 11 = 29$ mL

**d.** $240 - 29 = 211$ mL, or $220 - 11 + 2 = 211$ mL

**e.** After 3 seconds: 43.2 mL of NO and 196.8 mL of $N_2O_2$. After 10 seconds: 68.2 mL of NO and 171.8 mL of $N_2O_2$. In the long run: 80 mL of NO and 160 mL of $N_2O_2$.

**13.** Something else. The differences are not the same $\left(\frac{1}{2}, \frac{1}{6}, \frac{1}{12}, \ldots\right)$, the ratios are not the same $\left(\frac{1}{2}, \frac{2}{3}, \frac{3}{4}, \ldots\right)$, and the limit is zero. So the sequence is not arithmetic, not geometric, and not shifted geometric.

**14. a.** $c = 0.7c$, so $0.3c = 0$, and $c = 0$

 **b.** There is no long-run value. The sequence increases faster and faster.

 **c.** 4

**15. a.** $\left(12 \text{ in.}^2\right)\left(\dfrac{2.54 \text{ cm}}{1 \text{ in.}}\right) = \left(12 \text{ in.}^2\right)\left(\dfrac{n \text{ cm}}{12 \text{ in.}}\right)$,

 $(2.54 \text{ cm})(12 \text{ in.}) = (1 \text{ in.})n$,

 $n = \dfrac{(2.54 \text{ cm})(12 \text{ in.})}{1 \text{ in.}} = 30.48 \text{ cm}$

 **b.** $\left(125 \text{ mi}^2\right)\left(\dfrac{1 \text{ km}}{0.625 \text{ mi}}\right) = \left(125 \text{ mi}^2\right)\left(\dfrac{n \text{ km}}{200 \text{ mi}}\right)$,

 $(1 \text{ km})(200 \text{ mi}) = (0.625 \text{ mi})n$,

 $n = \dfrac{(1 \text{ km})(200 \text{ mi})}{0.625 \text{ mi}} = 320 \text{ km}$

 **c.** $\left(0.926n \text{ m}^2\right)\left(\dfrac{1 \text{ yd}}{0.926 \text{ m}}\right) = \left(0.926n \text{ m}^2\right)\left(\dfrac{140 \text{ yd}}{n \text{ m}}\right)$,

 $(0.926 \text{ m})(140 \text{ yd}) = (1 \text{ yd})n$,

 $n = \dfrac{(0.926 \text{ m})(140 \text{ yd})}{1 \text{ yd}} = 129.64 \text{ m}$

**EXTENSIONS**

 **A.** Sample answer: Interest for investments such as CDs or money markets are generally compounded monthly or daily. Interests rates for loans are always higher than those for investments so that the banks can earn a profit. Investments have compounding interest (interest is earned on principal and the interest), whereas loans generally have simple interest (interest is only paid on the principal).

 **B.** See the solution to Take Another Look activity 4 on page 24.

 **C.** Sample answer: In both states, the salary is about a quarter of the house price, so you need to look at things more closely. Assuming that interest rates are the same in both states (7%) and that you have $20,000 to use as a down payment, you end up having monthly payments that are about $300 more in California. If you add your parents' interest-free loan to your down payment, you pay only about $200 dollars more per month. You probably make about $500 more a month in California (after taxes), so with your parents' help you could afford to live in either state. However, you should take into account that the cost of living also is more in California.

**EXPLORATION · REFINING THE GROWTH MODEL**

**QUESTIONS**

 **1.** $u_n = u_{n-1}\left(1 + 1.25\left(1 - \frac{u_{n-1}}{5000}\right)\right)$. Net growth rates: 124%, 122%, 119%, 111%, 96%, 69%, 30%. Population: 112, 249, 544, 1150, 2260, 3800, 4940.

 **2. a.** Greater than 0   **b.** Less than 0

 **c.** Close to 0.20   **d.** 0

 **3.** Sample answer: The population begins at 100 and grows to 750. The growth rate starts near 35% and shrinks to 0%. It takes about 6 years to get halfway to the maximum and about 13 years to pass 700 daisies.

**CHAPTER 1 REVIEW**

**EXERCISES**

 **1. a.** Geometric; $r = \dfrac{192}{256} = 0.75$

 **b.** $u_1 = 256$ and $u_n = 0.75u_{n-1}$ where $n \geq 2$

 **c.** $u_8 \approx 34.2$

 **d.** $u_{10} \approx 19.2$

 **e.** $u_{17} \approx 2.57$

 **2. a.** Arithmetic; $d = 7 - 3 = 4$

 **b.** $u_1 = 3$ and $u_n = u_{n-1} + 4$ where $n \geq 2$

 **c.** $u_{128} = 511$

 **d.** $u_{40} = 159$

 **e.** $u_{20} = 79$

 **3. a.** $-3, -1.5, 0, 1.5, 3$; 0 to 6 for $n$ and $-4$ to 4 for $u_n$

 **b.** 2, 4, 10, 28, 82; 0 to 6 for $n$ and 0 to 100 for $u_n$

 **4. a.** $u_0 = 14.7$ and $u_n = (1 - 0.20)u_{n-1}$ where $n \geq 1$

 **b.**

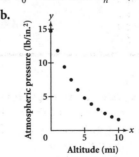

 **c.** $u_7 = (1 - 0.20)u_6 = 0.80(3.85) \approx 3.1 \text{ lb/in.}^2$

 **d.** 11 mi; $u_{10} \approx 1.58 \text{ lb/in.}^2$ and $u_{11} \approx 1.26 \text{ lb/in.}^2$

 **5. A. iv.** The recursive formula is that of an increasing arithmetic sequence, so the graph must be increasing and linear.

**B. iii.** The recursive formula is that of a growing geometric sequence, so the graph must be increasing and curved.

**C. i.** The recursive formula is that of a decaying geometric sequence, so the graph must be decreasing and curved.

**D. ii.** The recursive formula is that of a decreasing arithmetic sequence, so the graph must be decreasing and linear.

**6.** $12.4 \text{ gal} + \dfrac{4.2 \text{ gal}}{1 \text{ min}} \cdot 18 \text{ min} = 12.4 \text{ gal} + 75.6 \text{ gal} = 88 \text{ gal}$

**7.** $u_6 \approx 5300$; $c = (1 - 0.24)c + 1250$, $0.24c = 1250$, $c \approx 5200$; $u_0 = 5678$ and $u_n = (1 - 0.24)u_{n-1} + 1250$ where $n \geq 1$

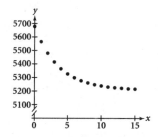

**8. a.** $u_0 = 500$ and $u_n = \left(1 + \dfrac{0.055}{4}\right)u_{n-1}$ where $n \geq 1$; $u_{20} = \$657.03$

**b.** $u_0 = 500$ and $u_n = \left(1 + \dfrac{0.055}{4}\right)u_{n-1} + 150$ where $n \geq 1$; $u_{20} = \$4,083.21$

**9.** Possible answer: $u_{1970} = 34$ and $u_n = (1 + 0.075)u_{n-1}$ where $n \geq 1971$

**10.** $\$637.95$. $u_0 = 80000$ and $u_n = \left(1 + \dfrac{0.089}{12}\right)u_{n-1} + p$ where $n \geq 1$ gives $u_{30} = 0$ if $p = 637.95$

 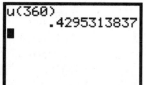

**TAKE ANOTHER LOOK**

**1.** The area of the tables generates a sequence proportional to 1, 2, 3, . . . . The perimeters of the nested squares generate the sequence 4, 8, 12, 16, . . . . The growth is arithmetic; $u_1 = 4$ and $u_n = u_{n-1} + 4$ where $n \geq 2$. The areas of the nested squares generate the sequence 1, 4, 9, 16, . . . . The growth is neither arithmetic nor geometric; you can write the recursive rule $u_n = u_{n-1} + 2n - 1$, or $u_n = n^2$ where $n \geq 1$. The heights of the nested squares generate the sequence 1, 2, 3, 4, . . . . The growth is arithmetic; $u_1 = 1$ and $u_n = u_{n-1} + 1$ where $n \geq 2$.

The perimeters of the other nested polygons generate the sequence 3, 4, 5, 6, . . . . The growth is arithmetic; $u_1 = 3$ and $u_n = u_{n-1} + 1$ where $n \geq 2$.

Using $s = 1$ and $A = \dfrac{ns^2}{4 \tan\left(\frac{360°}{n}\right)}$, their areas generate the sequence $\dfrac{\sqrt{3}}{4}$, 1, $\dfrac{5}{4 \tan 72°}$, $\dfrac{3}{2 \tan 60°}$, . . . , which generalizes to $u_n = \dfrac{n}{4 \tan\left(\frac{360°}{n}\right)}$ where $n \geq 3$. The growth is neither arithmetic nor geometric.

Invented geometric patterns will vary.

**2.** Sample answer: Consider a loan of $\$32,000$ to be paid off in 60 months at 7.9% annual interest, compounded monthly $\left(u_0 = 32000\right)$.

| Monthly payment | Final balance | Difference |
|---|---|---|
| $0 | $47,438.84 | |
| $1 | $47,365.56 | $73.28 |
| $2 | $47,292.27 | $73.29 |
| $3 | $47,218.99 | $73.28 |

Each difference is approximately $\$73.28$, so the final balances form an arithmetic sequence with a common difference of about $\$73.28$. Divide $\$47,438.84$ by $\$73.28$ to determine how many times you must repeat the sequence for the final balance to be 0: $\dfrac{47438.84}{73.28} \approx 647.36$. The monthly payment should be about $\$647.36$. (Actually, because the differences are not exactly $\$73.28$, the closest you can get to 0 after 60 months is with a monthly payment of $\$647.31$.)

**3.** Sample arithmetic probability sequence:

| Radius | Circle area | Annulus area | Probability |
|---|---|---|---|
| 1 | $\pi$ | $\pi$ | $\frac{1}{16}$ |
| 2 | $4\pi$ | $3\pi$ | $\frac{3}{16}$ |
| 3 | $9\pi$ | $5\pi$ | $\frac{5}{16}$ |
| 4 | $16\pi$ | $7\pi$ | $\frac{7}{16}$ |
| | Totals | $16\pi$ | 1 |

Sample geometric probability sequence (begin with areas of bull's-eyes and annuluses as a geometric sequence and work backward through the area formula):

| Radius | Circle area | Annulus area | Probability |
|--------|-------------|--------------|-------------|
| 1 | $\pi$ | $\pi$ | $\frac{1}{15}$ |
| $\sqrt{3}$ | $3\pi$ | $2\pi$ | $\frac{2}{15}$ |
| $\sqrt{7}$ | $7\pi$ | $4\pi$ | $\frac{4}{15}$ |
| $\sqrt{15}$ | $15\pi$ | $8\pi$ | $\frac{8}{15}$ |
| | Totals | $15\pi$ | 1 |

**4.** Result will vary.

## CHAPTER 2

### LESSON 2.1

#### EXERCISES

**1. a.** Mean: $\frac{28 + 31 + 26 + 35 + 26}{5} = \frac{146}{5} = 29.2$ min. Median: arrange the data in numerical order and find the middle value: {26, 26, **28**, 31, 35}; 28 min. Mode: 26 min.

**b.** Mean: $\frac{11.5 + 17.4 + \cdots + 17.4 + 19.0}{6} = \frac{104.1}{6} =$ 17.35 cm. Median: arrange the data in numerical order and find the mean of the two middle values: {11.5, 17.4, **17.4, 18.5**, 19.0, 20.3}; $\frac{17.4 + 18.5}{2} = 17.95$ cm. Mode: 17.4 cm.

**c.** Mean: $\frac{19}{8} = 2.375 \approx \$2.38$. Median: $\frac{2.25 + 2.50}{2} =$ 2.375 $\approx \$2.38$. Mode: none.

**d.** Mean: $\frac{14}{7} = 2$. Median: 2. Modes: 1 and 3.

**2. a.** $12 \cdot 3 = 36$ days

**b.** The middle value (median) is 14 days.

**c.** Possible answer: {7, 14, 15}. There are several data sets with the same statistics. The first value must be less than or equal to 8, the last value must be greater than or equal to 14. The first and last values must sum to $36 - 14 = 22$.

**3.** Minimum: 1.25 days; first quartile: 2.5 days; median: 3.25 days; third quartile: 4 days; maximum: 4.75 days

**4. B.** The five-number summary is 470, 510, 558, 574, 593. All plots have the right minimum and maximum; A, B, and D have the right $Q_1$; B and C have the right median; and A and B have the right $Q_3$. Plot B is the only one that matches the data set.

**5. D.** The five-number summary is 37, 40, 42, 50, 51. Data sets B and D have the right minimum and maximum; C and D have the right $Q_1$ and $Q_3$; and A, C, and D have the right median. Data set D is the only one that matches the box plot.

**6.** The means and the medians for each student are the same, 84. Neither the mean nor the median reveals the larger variation of Oscar's scores.

**7.** The bottom box plot is longer because it reflects the longer range of Oscar's scores. There is no left whisker for the top box plot because the first quarter of Connie's scores is made up of a single repeated score. The median isn't in the center of the top box because the second quarter of Connie's scores is spread over a longer interval than the third quarter of her scores. There is a bigger range for the first quarter of Oscar's scores than for the fourth quarter, so the left whisker is longer than the right one in the bottom box plot.

**8. a.**

20  30  40  50  60  70
**Home runs**

**b.** 25, 51, 58, 65, 72. Minimum: 25; first quartile: 51; median: 58; second quartile: 65; maximum: 72.

**c.** Find the sum of Homer's home runs and divide by 11 to obtain the mean. $\bar{x} = \frac{622}{11} \approx 57$ home runs.

**d.** 98 home runs. Let $x$ equal the number of home runs Homer needs to hit next season to have a 12-year mean of 60. The sum of all home runs in the first 11 years is 622. Set up an equation and solve for $x$.

$$\frac{622 + x}{12} = 60$$
$$622 + x = 60 \cdot 12 = 720$$
$$x = 720 - 622 = 98$$

**9. a.** Connie: $range = 86 - 82 = 4$; $IQR = 85 - 82 = 3$. Oscar: $range = 96 - 72 = 24$; $IQR = 94 - 76 = 18$.

**b.** $range = 72 - 25 = 47$; $IQR = 65 - 51 = 14$

**10.** Possible answer: {9, 10, 11, 12, 13, 14, 15}. Because $7 \cdot 12 = 84$, the seven values must sum to 84; $9 + 10 + 11 + 12 + 13 + 14 + 15 = 84$.

**11.** Possible answer: {62, 63, 64, 65, 70, 70, 70}. The middle value must be 65, and there must be more 70's than any other value.

**12.** Possible answer: {33, 50, 60, 70, 80, 83, 91}. Five of the values are fixed and two are missing: 33, 50, ?, 70, ?, 83, 91. The first missing value is between 50 and 70, and the second is between 70 and 83.

**13. a.** Juniors: $\bar{x} \approx 12.3$ lb; seniors: $\bar{x} \approx 8.6$ lb

**b.** Juniors: $median = 10$ lb; seniors: $median = 8$ lb

**c.** Each mean is greater than the corresponding median.

**14. a.**

**Backpack Weights**

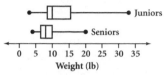

Five-number summaries: juniors: 3, 8.5, 10, 15.5, 33; seniors: 4, 6.5, 8, 10, 20

**b.** Sample answer: The juniors box plot has a higher maximum and $Q_3$ than the seniors box plot, so the juniors carry more weight in general. The juniors also have a greater spread of weights. Both data sets are skewed right.

**c.** The means are greater because both data sets are skewed right.

**15. a.** Chemical: 2.29816, 2.29869, 2.29915, 2.30074, 2.30182; atmospheric: 2.30956, 2.309935, 2.31010, 2.31026, 2.31163

**b.**

Chemical

Atmospheric

2.297    2.302    2.307    2.312

Mass (g)

**c.** Sample answer: Both graphs are skewed right. There is a significant difference in the range and *IQR* for the two sets of data. The mass of the nitrogen produced from the atmosphere is heavier than the mass of the nitrogen produced from chemical compounds, so the box plots support Rayleigh's conjecture.

**16. a.** 51, 54, 57; $u_1 = 42$ and $u_n = u_{n-1} + 3$ where $n \geq 2$

**b.** 250, 625, 1562.5; $u_1 = 16$ and $u_n = u_{n-1} \cdot 2.5$ where $n \geq 2$

**17. a.** $\sqrt{\dfrac{436}{6}} = \sqrt{72} = \sqrt{36 \cdot 2} = 6\sqrt{2} \approx 8.5$

**b.** $\sqrt{\dfrac{782 + 1354}{24}} = \sqrt{\dfrac{2136}{24}} = \sqrt{89} \approx 9.4$

**c.** $\sqrt{\dfrac{49 + 121 + 16 + 81 + 100}{4}} = \sqrt{\dfrac{367}{4}}$
$= \sqrt{91.75} \approx 9.6$

**18.** On credit, she will have paid for the drum set after 11 months. Her total cost will be \$430.01. Use the recursive formula $u_0 = 400$ and

$u_n = \left(1 + \dfrac{0.15}{12}\right)u_{n-1} - 40$ where $n \geq 1$, and find when her balance would be 0.

With savings, she could buy the drum set after 10 months.

Sample advice: If it is worth it to Rebecca to pay \$30 extra to have the drum set now, she should buy it on credit; otherwise, she should wait.

**19. a.** $x = 15 - 8 = 7$

**b.** $x = \dfrac{15}{3} = 5$

**c.** $3x = 7$, so $x = \dfrac{7}{3} = 2.\overline{3}$

**IMPROVING YOUR GEOMETRY SKILLS**

This problem does not specify what is meant by *compare*, so you can answer in several ways. First you can compare the relative areas of the regions: area I < area II < area III < area IV. You can also look at the ratios of the areas. The ratio of area I to area II to area III to area IV is 1 : 2 : 4 : 5.

**EXTENSIONS**

**A.** Results will vary.

**B.** See the solutions to Take Another Look activities 1 and 2 on pages 31 to 32.

**C.** Results will vary.

**D.** Answers will vary. You can use geometry software to investigate this problem.

**LESSON 2.2**

**EXERCISES**

**1. a.** $41 + 55 + 48 + 44 = 188$, so $\bar{x} = \dfrac{188}{4} = 47.0$

**b.** $-6, 8, 1, -3$. Subtract 47 from each data value.

**c.** $s = \sqrt{\dfrac{(-6)^2 + (8)^2 + (1)^2 + (-3)^2}{4 - 1}} = \sqrt{\dfrac{110}{3}}$
$\approx 6.1$

**2. a.** $\bar{x} = \dfrac{571}{9} \approx 63.4$

**b.** $-18.4, -0.4, 10.6, 5.6, 8.6, -10.4, 8.6, 9.6, -13.4$. Subtract 63.4 from each data value.

**c.** 11.2. The sum of the squares of the deviations from 2b is 1010.24.

$$s = \sqrt{\dfrac{1010.24}{9-1}} \approx 11.2$$

**d.** Minutes

**3. a.** 9, 10, 14, 17, 21

**b.** *range* $= 21 - 9 = 12$; $IQR = 17 - 10 = 7$

**c.** Centimeters

**4. a.** 18, 22, 28, 30, 35

**b.** *range* $= 35 - 18 = 17$; $IQR = 30 - 22 = 8$

**c.** Grams

**5.** Possible answer: {71, 79, 80, 84, 89, 91, 94}. The median is 84. Because the mean is also 84, and $7 \cdot 84 = 588$, the values must sum to 588. The minimum and maximum must have a difference of 23, and $Q_1$ and $Q_3$ must have a difference of 12.

**6.** She would not let CDs be shipped that measure more than 12.012 cm or less than 11.988 cm.

**7.** 20.8 and 22.1. $15.60 + 2(2.20) = 20$ and $15.60 - 2(2.20) = 11.2$, so outliers are less than 11.2 or greater than 20. These two outliers are the same ones found by the interquartile range.

**8.** $IQR = 10 - 7 = 3.0$ lb.

$$s = \sqrt{\dfrac{(-0.2)^2 + (9.8)^2 + \cdots + (-3.2)^2 + (6.2)^2}{30-1}}$$

$$= \sqrt{\dfrac{1004}{29}} \approx 5.9 \text{ lb}$$

The standard deviation is larger here but not always. The data set given in the possible answer for Exercise 5 is a counterexample.

**9. a.** Possible answer:

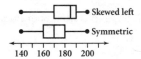

**b.** The skewed data set will have a greater standard deviation because the data to the left (below the median) will be spread farther from the mean.

**c.** Possible answer: symmetric: {140, 160, 165, 170, 175, 180, 200}; skewed left: {140, 170, 180, 185, 187, 190, 200}. When the values are in order the difference between the first and last values is the same in each data set, so both data sets have the same range; the difference between the second and sixth values is the same in each data set, so both data sets have the same interquartile

range; and the quartile values for the second data set are higher than the corresponding ones of the first data set, so the second data set is skewed left.

**d.** In the example in 9c, the standard deviation for the symmetric data set is 18.5 cm and the standard deviation for the skewed data set is 19.4 cm. These support the answer to 9b.

**10. a.** Add each deviation to 46.3: 47.1, 45.9, 47.9, 47.4, 45.1, 46.0, 45.7, and 45.3 cm.

**b.** $s = \sqrt{\dfrac{7.46}{7}} \approx 1.03$ cm

**c.** Below the mean: 45.1 cm; above the mean: 47.9 cm and 47.4 cm. Add to and subtract from the mean one standard deviation: $46.3 + 1.03 = 47.33$ cm and $46.3 - 1.03 = 45.27$ cm.

**11. a.** First period appears to have pulse rates most alike because that class had the smallest standard deviation. It is possible, however, that one of the other classes had one extreme outlier that greatly increased the standard deviation.

**b.** Sixth period appears to have the fastest pulse rates because that class has both the highest mean and the largest standard deviation. However, if sixth period were skewed left and some other period were skewed right, then it could be the other class.

**12. a.** Juneau: $\bar{x} = \dfrac{486}{12} = 40.5°\text{F}$; $s = \sqrt{\dfrac{1463}{11}} \approx 11.5°\text{F}$. New York: $\bar{x} = \dfrac{645}{12} \approx 53.8°\text{F}$; $s = \sqrt{\dfrac{2876.28}{11}} \approx 16.2°\text{F}$.

**b.** **Mean Temperatures**

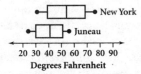

Five-number summaries: New York: 31, 39, 54, 68.5, 76; Juneau: 24, 30, 41, 51, 56

Juneau: *median* $= \dfrac{40 + 42}{2} = 41°\text{F}$; $IQR = 51 - 30 = 21°\text{F}$. New York: *median* $= \dfrac{51 + 57}{2} = 54°\text{F}$; $IQR = 68.5 - 39 = 29.5°\text{F}$.

**c.** Juneau has a smaller spread of temperatures because it has a lower standard deviation and a lower interquartile range.

**d.** Because both data sets are symmetric, the standard deviation and the interquartile range do an equally good job of describing the spread.

**13. a.** *median* $= 75$ packages; $IQR = 86.5 - 67.5 = 19$ packages

**b.** $\bar{x} = \dfrac{2022}{25} \approx 80.9$ packages; $s = \sqrt{\dfrac{14576.65}{24}} \approx 24.6$ packages

*Discovering Advanced Algebra Solutions Manual*
©2004 Key Curriculum Press

**c.** $86.5 + 1.5(19) = 115.0$ and $67.5 - 1.5(19) = 39.0$. Outliers are less than 39.0 or greater than 115.0. There are two outliers: 147 and 158.

Five-number summary: 44, 67.5, 75, 86.5, 158.

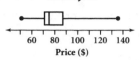
Hot Chocolate Mix

Packages

**d.**
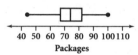
Hot Chocolate Mix

Packages

Five-number summary: 44, 67, 74, 82, 100

**e.** *median* = 74 packages; *IQR* = $82 - 67 = 15$ packages; $\bar{x} = \frac{1717}{23} \approx 74.7$ packages; $s = \sqrt{\frac{3365.27}{22}} \approx 12.4$ packages

**f.** The mean and standard deviation are calculated from all data values, so outliers affect these statistics significantly. The median and *IQR*, in contrast, are defined by position and not greatly affected by outliers. While the median and *IQR* shifted down by 1 and 4, respectively, the mean and standard deviation shifted down by 6.2 and 12.3, respectively.

**14. a.** Multiply each data value by 0.28. The five-number summary is 12.32, 18.9, 21, 24.22, 44.24.

Hot Chocolate Mix

Income ($)

*median* = $21.00; *IQR* = $24.22 - 18.9 = \$5.32$; $\bar{x} = \frac{566.16}{25} \approx \$22.65$; $s = \sqrt{\frac{1142.8089}{24}} \approx \$6.90$.

If you divide each of these statistics by the same statistic in Exercise 13, you see that each of the original statistics has been multiplied by about 0.28. The shapes of two graphs are exactly the same; only the scale is different.

**b.** *median* = $75(0.35) = \$26.25$; *IQR* = $86.5(0.35) - 67.5(0.35) = 30.275 - 23.625 = \$6.65$; $\bar{x} = 80.9(0.35) \approx \$28.32$; $s = 24.6(0.35) \approx \$8.61$

**c.** The revised five-number summary is 24, 47.5, 55, 66.5, 138. *median* = $74 - 20 = 55$; *IQR* = $66.5 - 47.5 = 19$; $\bar{x} = \frac{1522}{25} \approx 60.9$; $s = \sqrt{\frac{14576.64}{24}} \approx 24.6$. You can subtract 20 from the original median and mean. The statistics that measure spread (*IQR* and standard deviation) remain the same.

**d.** *median* = $75 - 10 = 65$ packages; *IQR* = 19 packages; $\bar{x} \approx 80.9 - 10 = 70.9$ packages; $s \approx 24.6$ packages

**15. a.** Mean: $\frac{1610.46}{20} = \$80.52$; median: $\frac{74 + 76}{2} = \$75.00$; modes: \$71.00, \$74.00, \$76.00, \$102.50

**b.**
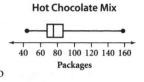
CD Players

Price ($)

The five-number summary is 51, 71, 75, 87, 135.5. The box plot is skewed right.

**c.** *IQR* = $87 - 71 = \$16$. Outliers: \$112.50 and \$135.50. Outliers are $1.5(IQR) = 1.5(16) = 24$ from an end of the box. Outliers are less than 47 or greater than 111.

**d.** The median will be less affected because the relative positions of the middle numbers will be changed less than the sum of the numbers.

**e.** Revised five-number summary: 51, 71, 74, 82.87, 102.5
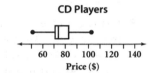
CD Players

Price ($)

The median of the new data set is $74.00 and is relatively unchanged.

**f.** Sample answer: Based on the box plot without outliers, Matt could start with a first bid of $51.00 (the minimum for the CD player), but set his maximum bid at $82.87. That way, he may exceed the median price, but he still will pay less than 25% of the previous selling prices he researched.

**16.** Sample answer: $u_0 = 2400$ and $u_n = u_{n-1} - 1.3 \cdot 60$ where $n \geq 1$. After 20 minutes, she is still 840 meters from school ($u_{20} = 840$).

**17. a.** $x = 59$

$\dfrac{x + 5}{4} + 3 = 19$    The original equation.

$\dfrac{x + 5}{4} = 16$    Subtract 3 from both sides.

$x + 5 = 64$    Multiply both sides by 4.

$x = 59$    Subtract 5 from both sides.

**b.** $y = 20$

$\dfrac{3(y - 4) + 6}{6} - 2 = 7$    The original equation.

$\dfrac{3(y - 4) + 6}{6} = 9$    Add 2 to both sides.

$3(y - 4) + 6 = 54$    Multiply both sides by 6.

$3y - 12 + 6 = 54$    Distribute.

$3y - 6 = 54$    Combine terms.

$3y = 60$    Add 6 to both sides.

$y = 20$    Divide both sides by 3.

**18. a.** Offensive team: $\bar{x} = \frac{2902}{11} \approx 263.8$ lb; *median* $\approx$ 255 lb. Defensive team: $\bar{x} = \frac{2703}{11} \approx 245.7$ lb; *median* = 250 lb.

**b.**

**Players' Weights**

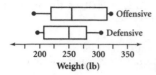

Five-number summaries: offensive: 190, 220, 255, 315, 322; defensive: 196, 207, 250, 280, 305

Sample observations: The lightest and heaviest players are on the offensive team. The offensive team has greater mean and median weights. The spread of the weights of the offensive team is greater than that of the defensive team. Over a quarter of the offensive players weigh more than any of the defensive players.

## EXTENSIONS

**A.** See the solution to Take Another Look activity 4 on page 32.

**B.** Results will vary.

## LESSON 2.3

### EXERCISES

**1. a.** 2

**b.** $2 + 1 + 0 + 1 + 4 + 1 = 9$

**c.** Possible answer: {2.3, 2.7, 3.5, 5.7, 6.2, 6.2, 6.6, 6.8, 7.4}. The data set must have two values between 2 and 3, one value between 3 and 4, one between 5 and 6, four between 6 and 7, and one between 7 and 8.

**2. a.** i. 10; ii. 15; iii. 20; iv. 25

**b.** Histograms i, ii, and iv show one value at about 240. Histogram iii is missing the value around 240 cm.

**3. a.** 5 values

**b.** 25th percentile

**c.** 95th percentile

**4. a.**

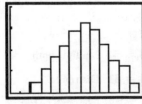

[0, 13, 1, 0, 200, 50]

**b.** It is mound-shaped because 7 is the most likely sum when rolling a pair of dice, then 6 and 8, then 5 and 9, then 4 and 10, then 3 and 11, and then 2 and 12.

**c.** You can find the mean by summing the products of *sum* · *frequency* and dividing by 1000.

$$\frac{2(26) + 3(56) + \cdots + 12(21)}{1000} \approx 7.0$$

You can find the median by identifying the bin containing the 500th and 501st values. Both values are in the 7 bin, so the median is 7.

**5. a.** The numbers of acres planted by farmers who plant more than the median number of acres vary more than the numbers of acres planted by farmers who plant fewer than the median number of acres.

**b.**

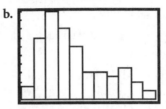

[0, 11, 1, 0, 20, 2]

**c.** There are 95 acres in this distribution. The median number of acres planted in corn is probably about 3. The part of the box to the left of the median would be smaller than the part to the right because there are more values close to 3 on the left than on the right. The whiskers would range from 0 to 11.

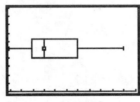

[0, 11, 1, 0, 20, 2]

**6.** Possible answers:

**a.** SAT scores for all students in one year

**SAT Scores**

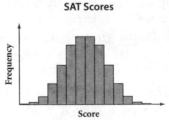

**b.** Number of good photos developed from a roll of 24 exposures

**Number of Good Photos**

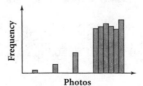

*Discovering Advanced Algebra Solutions Manual*
©2004 Key Curriculum Press

**c.** Number of pets owned by students in the class

**Number of Pets**

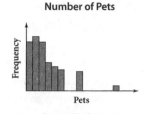

**d.** Number rolled on a standard die

**Number Rolled on a Die**

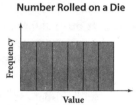

**7. a.**

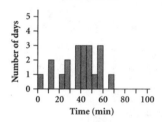

The five-number summary for homework is 4, 27.5, 40.5, 49, 65 and for television is 5, 26, 36.5, 58, 95. The range for homework is $65 - 4 = 61$ and the range for television is $95 - 5 = 90$, so television has the greater spread.

**b.** Television will be skewed right. Neither will be mound-shaped.

**Homework**

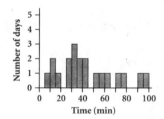

**Television**

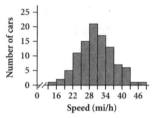

**c.** Homework: $median = \frac{40 + 41}{2} = 40.5$ min; $IQR = 49 - 27.5 = 21.5$ min; $\bar{x} = \frac{767}{20} = 38.4$ min; $s = \sqrt{\frac{5314.6}{19}} \approx 16.7$ min. Television: $median = \frac{35 + 38}{2} = 36.5$ min; $IQR = 58 - 26 = 32$ min; $\bar{x} = \frac{844}{20} = 42.2$ min; $s = \sqrt{\frac{12309.36}{19}} \approx 26.0$ min.

You can argue that either $IQR$ or the standard deviation is the better measure of spread. Both show that television has greater spread than homework.

**8. a.** About 88% of the students, or $0.88(1500) = 1320$ students, scored lower; about 12% of the students, or $0.12(1500) = 180$ students, scored higher.

**b.** Mary scored higher than 95% of the students in the class.

**c.** 99th percentile

**d.** About 10% of the students, or $0.10(1500) = 150$ students, earned an A.

**e.** A percent score expresses number correct (presumably indicating percentage of content mastered), whereas a percentile rank compares one score relative to others. Opinions will vary.

**9. a.**

**Speed Limit Study**

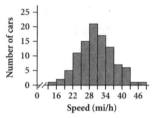

**b.** Between 37 mi/h and 39 mi/h. Because 100 cars were surveyed, the 85th percentile speed occurs with the 86th entry. By summing the frequencies until the total reaches 86, you can see that it is in the 37–39 bin.

**c.** Possible answers: 35 mi/h, 40 mi/h. 40 mi/h would ensure that at least 85% of drivers comply with the limit.

**d.** Sample answers: road type and surface (such as curve or hill), location and type of access points (such as intersections or entrances), existing traffic control devices (such as signs or signals), accident history, traffic volume, limitation of setting speed limits in 5 mi/h intervals

**10. a.** $2 + 11 + 22 + 26 + 27 + 20 + 8 + 2 = 118$ cars

**b.** Between 57 mi/h and 59 mi/h. Because $0.85(118) = 100.3$, the 85th percentile speed occurs with the 101st car. This will occur in the 57–59 bin.

**c.** Possible answer: 60 mi/h. This will ensure that at least 85% of the drivers will be in compliance with the speed limit.

**11. a.** The sum of the deviations is 13, not 0.

**b.** $33 - 13 = 20$

**c. i.** Add each deviation to 747: {747, 707, 669, 676, 767, 783, 789, 838}; $s = \sqrt{\frac{24466}{7}} \approx 59.1$; $median = \frac{747 + 767}{2} = 757$; $IQR = 786 - 691.5 = 94.5$.

**ii.** Add each deviation to 850: {850, 810, 772, 779, 870, 886, 892, 941}; $s = \sqrt{\frac{24466}{7}} \approx 59.1$; $median = \frac{850 + 870}{2} = 860$; $IQR = 889 - 794.5 = 94.5$.

**d.** Translating the data doesn't change the standard deviation or the interquartile range. The measures of spread are not dependent on the mean or median, only on the way the data are distributed.

**12. a.** A recursive routine to model this is $u_0 = 8.99$ and $u_n = u_{n-1} + 0.50$ where $n \geq 1$. Using this formula, a four-topping pizza will cost $10.99 ($u_4 = 10.99$).

**b.** Using the formula from 12a, an eight-topping pizza should cost $12.99. Buying the special saves you $12.99 - 12.47 = \$0.52$.

**13.** Find both runners' speeds in meters per second. Courtney's speed is $\frac{100 \text{ m}}{12.3 \text{ s}} \approx 8.13$ m/s. For Marissa, first convert yards to meters.

$$100 \text{ yd}\left(\frac{3 \text{ ft}}{1 \text{ yd}}\right) = 300 \text{ ft}$$

$$300 \text{ ft}\left(\frac{12 \text{ in.}}{1 \text{ ft}}\right) = 3600 \text{ in.}$$

$$3600 \text{ in.}\left(\frac{2.54 \text{ cm}}{1 \text{ in.}}\right) = 9144.00 \text{ cm} = 9.144 \text{ m}$$

Marissa's speed is $\frac{9.144 \text{ m}}{11.2 \text{ s}} \approx 8.16$ m/s. Marissa runs faster.

## EXTENSIONS

**A.** See the solution to Take Another Look activity 3 on page 32.

**B.** Results will vary.

## EXPLORATION · CENSUS MICRODATA

### QUESTIONS

**1.** Sample conjecture: Asian Indian residents of Berkeley make more money than white residents. A summary table indicates that this is true, as the mean and median are both significantly higher for Asian Indians than for whites. However, a histogram implies that Asian Indians have virtually no income. This is because a histogram shows *number of people* in various income groups, and the population includes only 7 Asian Indians compared to 329 whites.

**2.** You might compare two different geographic regions and find that one has a high percentage of population under 10 years old and that another has a high percentage over age 70. The first community may decide to invest in day care and after-school programs, while the second may choose to support a senior center.

## EXTENSIONS

**A.** Results will vary.

**B.** Conjectures and explanations will vary.

## CHAPTER 2 REVIEW

### EXERCISES

**1.** Plot B has the greater standard deviation because the data have more spread. There is greater deviation from the center.

**2. a.** Each whisker represents 25% of the data values in each data set. Seven values are represented in each whisker of Group A. Six values are represented in each whisker of Group B.

**b.** Group B has the greater standard deviation because the data have more spread.

**c.** Possible answer:

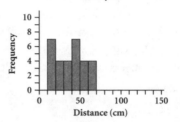

Group A

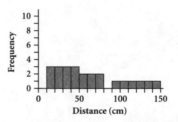

Group B

**3. a.** Mean: $\frac{8304}{15} = 553.6$ points; median: 460 points; mode: none

**b.** 5, 167, 460, 645, 2019

**c.** Points Scored by Los Angeles Lakers Players (2001–2002 Season)

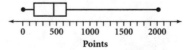

The box plot is skewed right.

**d.** $IQR = 645 - 167 = 478$ points

**e.** Outliers will be $1.5(478) = 717$ from an end of the box. Outliers will be less than $-550$ (not possible) or greater than 1362. There are two outliers: Kobe Bryant (2019 points) and Shaquille O'Neal (1822 points).

**4.** One strategy is to make Set A skewed and Set B symmetric. Possible answer: Set A: {1, 2, 3, 4, 5, 6, 47}; $s = \sqrt{\frac{1639.43}{6}} \approx 16.5$; $IQR = 6 - 2 = 4$. Set B: {1, 5, 7, 9, 11, 13, 17}; $s = \sqrt{\frac{168}{6}} \approx 5.3$; $IQR = 13 - 5 = 8$.

**5. a.** $\bar{x} = \frac{828}{7} \approx 118.3°F$; $s = \sqrt{\frac{4301.43}{6}} \approx 26.8°F$

   **b.** $\bar{x} = \frac{-420}{7} = -60.0°F$; $s = \sqrt{\frac{12530}{6}} \approx 45.7°F$

   **c.** Antarctica (59°F) is an outlier for the high temperatures. For outliers for the high temperatures, look for temperatures lower than $118 - 2(27) = 64°F$ or higher than $118 + 2(27) = 172°F$. Antarctica's high temperature is more than two standard deviations lower than the mean. For outliers for the low temperatures, look for temperatures lower than $-60 - 2(46) = -152°F$ or higher than $-60 + 2(46) = 32°F$. There are no outliers for the low temperatures.

**6. a.** $\bar{x} = \frac{1235}{32} \approx 38.6$; median = 35

   **b.** $\bar{x} = \frac{1450}{32} \approx 45.3$; median = 43

   **c.** Five-number summaries: Best Actress: 21, 32.5, 35, 41.5, 81; Best Actor: 30, 38, 43, 51.5, 76

**Academy Awards Winners**

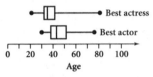

   **d.**

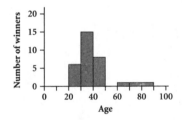

**Best Actress Winners**

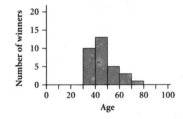

**Best Actor Winners**

   **e.** The Best Actress data set should have the greater standard deviation because it has more spread. Best Actress: $s = \sqrt{\frac{5251.72}{31}} \approx 13.0$; Best Actor: $s = \sqrt{\frac{3176.87}{31}} \approx 10.1$.

   **f.** 25th percentile. $\frac{8}{32}$, or 25%, of the Best Actress winners from 1970 to 2001 were younger than 33 when they won their award.

**7.** Answers will vary. In general, the theory is supported by the statistics and graphs. The mean age of Best Actor winners is about 6.7 years higher than that of Best Actress winners. No man under 30 won the award during these years, while 6 women under 30 did win. From the histograms, you can see that most men who won were between 30 and 60, while most women were between 20 and 50.

**8. a.**  2000 U.S. Passenger-Car Production

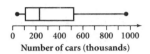

   Five-number summary: 39, 108, 228.5, 520, 965

   **b.**  2000 U.S. Passenger-Car Production

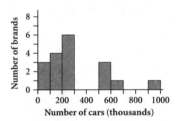

   **c.** The box plot will be shifted right, and some of the histogram's bins will change frequency as some brands fall into a different bin.

   **d.** 78th percentile. Pontiac car production is larger than $\frac{14}{18}$, or 78%, of the other car brands.

   **e.** 94th percentile. Ford car production is larger than $\frac{17}{18}$, or 94%, of the other car brands.

**TAKE ANOTHER LOOK**

**1.** Answers will vary, but you will probably find that many articles are not specific enough and possibly that most assume the arithmetic mean.

**2.** Answers should include one or more of these equations for the means:

$$geometric\ mean = \sqrt[n]{x_1 \cdot x_2 \cdot x_3 \cdot \ldots \cdot x_n}$$

$$harmonic\ mean = \frac{n}{\sum\limits_{i=1}^{n} \frac{1}{x_i}}$$

$$quadratic\ mean = \sqrt{\frac{\sum\limits_{i=1}^{n}(x_i)^2}{n}}$$

$$trimean = \frac{H_1 + 2M + H_2}{4}$$

where $M$ is the median, $H_1$ is the lower hinge (roughly equivalent to the first quartile but found by including the median as part of the lower half of data values), and $H_2$ is the upper hinge (roughly equivalent to the third quartile)

$$midmean = \frac{2 \cdot \sum\limits_{i=n/4}^{3n/4} x_i}{n}$$

You can also use an example to compare the means. Sample: For the mean monthly temperatures in New York City from the data table on page 92 of your book, the arithmetic mean is 53.8, the geometric mean is 51.4, the harmonic mean is 49.0, the quadratic mean is 55.9, the trimean is 54, and the midmean is 60.2. For these data the trimean is closest to the arithmetic mean, and the midmean, which ignores the extremes, differs most from the arithmetic mean. Both the geometric mean and the harmonic mean are below the arithmetic mean. The mean of these six means is 54.1, very close to the arithmetic mean.

3. One strategy for finding the mean begins with picking a representative value for each bin's interval, say the median. An estimate of the mean is calculated by summing the products of the bin heights and the representative values, then dividing by the number of data values.

Because individual data values are not shown in a histogram, you might say that it is impossible to find a mode. A mode can also be defined as the bin interval with the most data values.

4. Mean deviation, also called *mean absolute deviation*, is more descriptive but less commonly used than standard deviation.

Sample answer: For the rubber band data on page 87 of your book, the mean deviation is 1.14 for Group A and 16.6 for Group B. In both cases the mean deviation is less than the standard deviation. For the group with the larger deviations, the mean deviation and the standard deviation were farther apart than those for the group with the smaller deviations.

## CHAPTER 3

### LESSON 3.1

#### EXERCISES

1. a.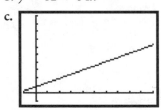

b. *slope* $= -3$. The common difference is the same as the slope.

c. *y*-intercept $= 18$. The *y*-intercept is the $u_0$-term of the sequence.

d. $y = 18 - 3x$

2. a. $u_0 = -1$ and $u_n = u_{n-1} + 5$ where $n \geq 1$; $d = 5$; $u_0 = -1$

b. *slope* $= 5$; *y*-intercept $= -1$

c. $y = -1 + 5x$

3. $y = 7 + 3x$. The sequence starts with 7, so that is the *y*-intercept. The common difference is 3, so that is the slope.

4. $u_0 = 6$ and $u_n = u_{n-1} - 0.5$ where $n \geq 1$. The *y*-intercept is 6, so that is the $u_0$-term of the sequence. The slope is $-0.5$, so that is the common difference.

5. The slope is the coefficient of the *x*-term.

a. *slope* $= 1.7$

b. *slope* $= 1$

c. *slope* $= -4.5$

d. *slope* $= 0$

6. a. $u_n = 6.3 + 2.5n$

b. The 29th term is 78.8. Substitute 78.8 for $u_n$. $78.8 = 6.3 + 2.5n$, so $72.5 = 2.5n$, and $n = 29$.

7. a. $82 + 54(2) = 190$ mi

b. $y = 82 + 54x$

c.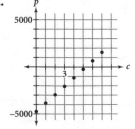

$[-1, 10, 1, -100, 1000, 100]$

d. The relationship is linear. If only distances on the hour are considered, it is an arithmetic sequence. Otherwise, the relationship is continuous rather than discrete.

8. a.

Two known points are $(3, -2050)$ and $(7, 1550)$. To calculate the common difference, find the difference between the 3rd and 7th terms and divide by 4, the distance between the known terms: $\frac{1550 - (-2050)}{4} = \frac{3600}{4} = 900$. The common difference is 900. Therefore, possible terms in the sequence are $-4750, -3850, -2950, -2050, -1150, -250, 650, 1550$.

**b.** The common difference, \$900, is the profit per car sold.

**c.** $u_n = -4750 + 900n$. Let $c$ represent the number of cars sold, and let $p$ represent the value of the sales in relation to the goal: $p = -4750 + 900c$.

**d.** The horizontal intercept, 5.28, represents the number of cars that must be sold to break even (six cars must be sold to surpass the goal). The vertical intercept, $-4750$, represents how far below the goal they are if no cars are sold.

**e.** The profit goal is the $y$-intercept, which is \$4750. Roy must sell two more cars. $2050 - 2(900) = \$250$, which is less than \$500.

**9. a.** $u_0 = 3 - 5 = -2$

**b.** 5 (count from the graph)

**c.** 50

**d.** You need to add 50 $d$'s to the original height of $u_0$.

**e.** $u_n = u_0 + nd$

**10. a.** 0.7 cm; $\frac{6.3 - 4.2}{3}$ or $\frac{9.1 - 6.3}{4} = 0.7$

**b.** $u_n = 4.2 + 0.7n$

**c.** 34 days. Substitute 28 for $u_n$ and solve the equation for $n$. $28 = 4.2 + 0.7n$, so $0.7n = 23.8$, and $n = 34$.

**11. a.** Possible answer: $(0, 7)$ and $(5, 27)$. The $x$-values should have a difference of 5.

**b.** $slope = \frac{27 - 7}{5} = 4$. Regardless of the points chosen in 11a, the slope should be 4.

**c.** The missing terms are found by adding 4 repeatedly to the initial term. The sequence becomes 7, 11, 15, 19, 23, 27.

**d.** $y = 7 + 4x$. The $y$-intercept will differ if the original points have different $x$-values.

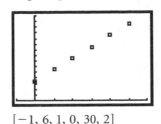

$[-1, 6, 1, 0, 30, 2]$

**12. a.** $u_1 = 16$ and $u_n = u_{n-1} + 32$ where $n \geq 2$

**b.** $u_n = 32n - 16$

**c.** 304 ft; $u_{10} = 32(10) - 16 = 304$

**d.** 304 ft/s

**e.** 13th second; $400 = 32n - 16$, so $32n = 416$, and $n = \frac{416}{32} = 13$.

**13.** Although the total earnings are different at the end of the odd-numbered six-month periods, at the end of each year the total income is always the same. *(See table at bottom of page.)*

**14. a.** $x = (1 - 0.4)x + 300$, so $0.4x = 300$, and $x = \frac{300}{0.4} = 750$ mL.

**b.** No, the long-run value is 750 mL, so eventually the level at the end of the day will approach 750 mL. Once the end-of-the-day level passes 700 mL, when 300 mL is added it will overflow.

**15. a.** *median* = \$93.49; $\bar{x} = \$96.80$; $s = \$7.55$

**b.** Knowing the median and mean prices informs a shopper of the mid-price and the average price. The standard deviation indicates whether there is price variation (and, therefore, it is worth shopping around for a good deal) or if all prices are pretty much the same. The median price is the better price to use as a frame of reference. The mean may be low or high if one store is having a sale or is unusually expensive (is an outlier).

**Lesson 3.1, Exercise 13**

| | Case 1 | | Case 2 | |
|---|---|---|---|---|
| | Earnings per 6 months (\$) | Total earnings (\$) | Earnings per 6 months (\$) | Total earnings (\$) |
| **0.5 yr** | 9,075 | 9,075 | 8,950 | 8,950 |
| **1 yr** | 9,075 | **18,150** | $8,950 + 250 = 9,200$ | **18,150** |
| **1.5 yr** | $\frac{18,150 + 1,000}{2} = 9,575$ | 27,725 | $9,200 + 250 = 9,450$ | 27,600 |
| **2 yr** | 9,575 | **37,300** | $9,450 + 250 = 9,700$ | **37,300** |
| **2.5 yr** | $\frac{19,150 + 1,000}{2} = 10,075$ | 47,375 | $9,700 + 250 = 9,950$ | 47,250 |
| **3 yr** | 10,075 | **57,450** | $9,950 + 250 = 10,200$ | **57,450** |

**16.** Answers will vary depending on bin width.

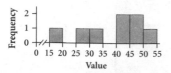

a. The left whisker will be longer because the data are skewed left. The range will be from 19 to 51. The median will be around 42.

b.

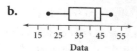

### IMPROVING YOUR REASONING SKILLS

The slope between any two points in the first sequence is $\frac{3}{2}$. The matches are a. B; b. C; c. F; d. D; e. A; f. E. For the rule $(x_n, y_n) = (x_{n-1} + h, y_{n-1} + k)$, the slope is $\frac{k}{h}$.

### EXTENSIONS

**A.** Here are generalizations of rules a–f.

a. $(x_n, y_n) = (x_{n-1} + a, y_{n-1} + a), a \neq 0$

b. $(x_n, y_n) = (x_{n-1} + a, y_{n-1} + 3a), a \neq 0$

c. $(x_n, y_n) = \left(x_{n-1} + a, y_{n-1} - \frac{4}{3}a\right), a \neq 0$

d. $(x_n, y_n) = (x_{n-1} + a, y_{n-1} - 5a), a \neq 0$

e. $(x_n, y_n) = (x_{n-1} + a, y_{n-1}), a \neq 0$

f. $(x_n, y_n) = \left(x_{n-1} + a, y_{n-1} + \frac{1}{3}a\right), a \neq 0$

**B.** If you consider each increment of $n$ to be 6 seconds and the units of $u_n$ to be cents, you can write the recursive formula

$u_0 = 0$

$u_n = 40$        where $0 < n \leq 10$

$u_n = u_{n-1} + 2$   where $n > 10$

In explicit form, this sequence is

$u_n = 40$            where $0 < n \leq 10$

$u_n = 2(n - 10) + 40$   where $n > 10$

The linear model for this sequence is

$y = 40$            where $0 < x \leq 10$

$y = 2(x - 10) + 40$   where $x > 10$

This linear model only gives the exact cost at six-second intervals. To find the cost for other values, round up to the nearest multiple of 6.

**C.** If $x_n = rx_{n-1} + h$ and $y_n = sy_{n-1} + k$, then the slope $\frac{y_n - y_{n-1}}{x_n - x_{n-1}} = \frac{(s-1)y_{n-1} + k}{(r-1)x_{n-1} + h}$ can be constant in two ways:

If $s = r = 1$, in which case both $x_n$ and $y_n$ are arithmetic sequences and the slope is $\frac{k}{h}$; or if $h = k = 0$

and $r = s \neq 1$, in which case both $x_n$ and $y_n$ are geometric sequences with the same common ratio and the slope is $\frac{y_0}{x_0}$. In this latter case, if $x_0 = 0$, then the line is vertical unless $y_0$ is also 0, in which case the sequence never leaves the origin.

## LESSON 3.2

### EXERCISES

**1. a.** $slope = \dfrac{2 - (-4)}{7 - 3} = \dfrac{6}{4} = \dfrac{3}{2} = 1.5$

   **b.** $slope = \dfrac{5 - 3}{2 - 5} = \dfrac{2}{-3} = -\dfrac{2}{3} \approx -0.67$

   **c.** $slope = \dfrac{-2.3 - 3.2}{0.08 - (-0.02)} = \dfrac{-5.5}{0.1} = -55$

**2. a.** $slope = 3$

   **b.** $slope = -2.8$

   **c.** $slope = 15$. Distribute the 5 to get $y = 15x - 15 + 2 = 15x - 13$.

   **d.** $slope = 2.4$. Rewrite the equation as $y = 2.4x + 5$.

   **e.** $slope = -\dfrac{47}{32}$, or $-1.46875$. Rewrite the equation as $y = \dfrac{-4.7x + 12.9}{3.2}$ or $y = -1.46875x + 4.03125$.

   **f.** $slope = 1$. Rewrite the equation as $y = x + \dfrac{3}{4}$.

**3. a.** $y = 4.7 + 3.2(3) = 4.7 + 9.6 = 14.3$

   **b.** $8 = -2.5 + 1.6x$, so $10.5 = 1.6x$, and $x = 6.5625$

   **c.** $-224 = a - 0.2(1000)$, so $a = -224 + 0.2(1000) = -24$

   **d.** $10 = 250 + b(960)$, so $b = \dfrac{10 - 250}{960} = -0.25$

**4. a.** **i.** $y = -2 - \dfrac{4}{3}x$. The $y$-intercept is $-2$ and the slope is $\dfrac{-2 - 0}{0 - \left(-\frac{3}{2}\right)} = -\dfrac{4}{3}$.

     **ii.** $y = -2 + \dfrac{3}{4}x$. The $y$-intercept is $-2$ and the slope is $\dfrac{-2 - 1}{0 - 4} = \dfrac{3}{4}$.

   **b.** **i.** $y = -1 - 1.5x$. The $y$-intercept is $-1$ and the slope is $\dfrac{-1 - (-4)}{0 - 2} = -1.5$.

     **ii.** $y = 3.5 - 1.5x$. The $y$-intercept is $3.5$ and the slope is $\dfrac{3.5 - (-1)}{0 - 3} = -1.5$.

**5. a.** The equations have the same constant, $-2$, therefore the lines share the same $y$-intercept. Their slopes are reciprocals with opposite signs, so the lines are perpendicular.

   **b.** The equations have the same $x$-coefficient, $-1.5$. The lines have the same slope, so they are parallel.

**6.** 0.5 m/s toward the motion sensor. At 0 s the rocket is 5 m from the sensor, and at 6 s the rocket is 2 m away. This is a rate of 3 m in 6 s, or 0.5 m/s.

**7. a.** Possible answer: Between the 2nd and 7th data points, the slope is approximately 1.47; $\dfrac{10.27 - 2.94}{7 - 2} \approx 1.47$ volts/battery.

*Discovering Advanced Algebra Solutions Manual*
©2004 Key Curriculum Press

**b.** Answers will vary. It is best to use points that are not too close together. The slope tells you that the voltage increases by about 1.47 volts for every additional battery.

**c.** Yes. There is no voltage produced from zero batteries, so the $y$-intercept should be 0.

**8. a.** Approximately 13. For each additional story, the building increases by about 13 ft.

**b.** Approximately 20. This is the additional height in feet that does not depend on the number of stories. Sometimes the stories of a building are not all the same height; the first story might be taller than the others or its floor could be higher than ground level.

**c.** Some of the buildings have more (or less) height per story.

**d.** Domain: $0 \leq x \leq 80$; range: $20 \leq y \leq 1100$

**9. a.** Fifth year: $847(4) + 17109 = \$20,497$. First year: $847(0) + 17109 = \$17,109$.

**b.** \$847 per year

**c.** $30000 = 847n + 17109$, so $847n = 12891$, and $n \approx 15.22$; round up to $n = 16$. Anita's salary will be more than \$30,000 after 16 years of experience, in her 17th year.

**10. a.** The length of the hall is the independent variable. The time the job takes will depend on this length.

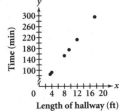

Length of hallway (ft)

**b.** $slope = \frac{212 - 92}{12.0 - 4.0} \approx 15$. This means it takes about 15 minutes to lay tile for each additional foot of hall beyond the first foot.

**c.** Possible answer: The 4th and 5th data points of the table. It is best to use points that are not too close together.

**d.** Approximately 32. You can find the $y$-intercept using the slope formula: $\frac{92 - y}{4 - 0} = 15$, so $y = 32$. This is the time in minutes that is not spent actually tiling, such as the time it takes to get the tools out before doing the job, put them away after the job is finished, or cut tile for the last row.

**11. a.** Possible answer: Using the 2nd and 7th data points, the slope is $\frac{4495.50 - 2353.50}{601 - 320} = \frac{2142}{281} \approx 7.62$. This means each additional ticket sold brings in about \$7.62 in revenue. This value is somewhere between the two different ticket prices offered.

**b.** Possible answer: The 2nd and 7th points. It is best to use points that are not too close together.

**12. a.**

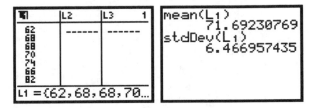

**b.** Using the 3rd and 7th points, the slope is $\frac{0.0646 - 0.0807}{152 - 32} = \frac{-0.0161}{120} \approx -0.000134$.

**c.** For each degree the temperature increases, the weight of a cubic foot of dry air decreases by about 0.000134 lb.

**13. a.** $2 + 3x - 12 = -10 + 3x$

**b.** $11 - 3x - 8x - 10 = 1 - 11x$

**c.** $5.1 - 2.7 + 2.7(2x + 9.7) = 2.4 + 5.4x + 26.19$
$= 28.59 + 5.4x$

**14. a.** $12 = 6 + 2x - 2$, so $8 = 2x$, and $x = 4$

**b.** $27 = 12 - 2x - 4$, so $2x = -19$, and $x = -9.5$

**15. a.** $\bar{x} = 71.7$ beats/min

**b.** $s = 6.47$ beats/min. The majority of the data falls within 6.47 beats/min of the mean.

| 🔲 | L2 | L3 | 1 |
|---|---|---|---|
| 62 | ------ | ------ | |
| 68 | | | |
| 68 | | | |
| 70 | | | |
| 74 | | | |
| 66 | | | |
| 82 | | | |
| L1 ={62,68,68,70… | | | |

```
mean(L1)
        71.69230769
stdDev(L1)
        6.466957435
```

**16.** $a$ is the $y$-intercept, $r$ is the common ratio, and $p$ is the common difference.

**a.** $a > 0$, $r = 0$, $p > 0$

**b.** $a > 0$, $r = 0$, $p = 0$ if it is an arithmetic sequence; or $a > 0$, $r = -1$, $p = a$ if it is a geometric sequence.

**17.** $a$ is the $y$-intercept and $b$ is the slope.

**a.** $a > 0$, $b < 0$

**b.** $a < 0$, $b > 0$

**c.** $a > 0$, $b = 0$

**d.** $a = 0$, $b < 0$

**EXTENSION**

Results will vary. The voltage of AA and AAA batteries is typically about 1.5 volts.

**LESSON 3.3**

**EXERCISES**

**1. a.** $y = 1 + \frac{2}{3}(x - 4)$. The slope of the line is $\frac{1 - (-3)}{4 - (-2)} = \frac{4}{6} = \frac{2}{3}$. It passes through point $(4, 1)$.

**b.** $y = 2 - \frac{1}{5}(x - 1)$. The slope of the line is $\frac{2-3}{1-(-4)} = -\frac{1}{5}$. It passes through point $(1, 2)$.

**2. a.** $y = -7 + \frac{2}{3}(x - 5)$

**b.** $y = 6 - 4(x - 1)$

**c.** Parallel lines have the same slope, so the slope is 3. The equation is $y = 8 + 3(x + 2)$.

**d.** Parallel lines have the same slope, so the slope is $-\frac{3}{5}$. The equation is $y = 11 - \frac{3}{5}(x + 4)$.

**3. a.** $u_n = 23 + 2(11 - 7) = 23 + 2(4) = 23 + 8 = 31$

**b.** $95 = -47 - 4(t + 6)$, so $142 = -4(t + 6)$, $-35.5 = t + 6$, and $t = -41.5$

**c.** $107 = 56 - 6(x - 10)$, so $51 = -6(x - 10)$, $-8.5 = x - 10$, and $x = 1.5$

**4. a.** Answers will vary, but the $y$-coordinate should always be 5. Possible answers: $(0, 5)$, $(1, 5)$, and $(2, 5)$.

**b.** $slope = \frac{5-5}{1-0} = \frac{0}{1} = 0$

**c.** $y = -4$

**d.** Sample answer: Horizontal lines have no $x$-intercepts (unless the horizontal line is the $x$-axis, or $y = 0$). They have a slope of 0. All points have the same $y$-coordinate.

**5. a.** Answers will vary, but the $x$-coordinate should always be $-3$. Possible answers: $(-3, 0)$, $(-3, 1)$, and $(-3, 2)$.

**b.** $slope = \frac{1-0}{-3-(-3)} = \frac{1}{0}$; undefined

**c.** $x = 3$. (*Note:* You can't use the point-slope form because the slope is undefined.)

**d.** Sample answer: Vertical lines have no $y$-intercepts (unless the vertical line is the $y$-axis, or $x = 0$). They have undefined slope. All points have the same $x$-coordinate.

**6.** In graph a, most of the points on the left are above the line; most of the points on the right are below the line. In graph b, most of the points on the left are below the line; most of the points on the right are above the line. Graph c is the best line of fit. In graph d, there are no points below the line.

**7.** Possible answers:

**a.** The $y$-intercept is about 1.7. Another point is at about $(5, 4.6)$. The slope of the line is $\frac{1.7-4.6}{0-5} = \frac{-2.9}{-5} = 0.58$. The equation of the line of fit is $\hat{y} = 1.7 + 0.58x$.

**b.** The $y$-intercept is about 7.5. Another point is at about $(5, 3.75)$. The slope of the line is $\frac{7.5-3.75}{0-5} = \frac{3.75}{-5} = -0.75$. The equation of the line of fit is $\hat{y} = 7.5 - 0.75x$.

**c.** The $y$-intercept is about 8.6. Another point is at about $(5, 3.9)$. The slope of the line is $\frac{8.6-3.9}{0-5} = \frac{4.7}{-5} = -0.94$. The equation of the line of fit is $\hat{y} = 8.6 - 0.94x$.

**8. a.** $\hat{y} = 19 + 0.3(x - 44)$, or $\hat{y} = 0.3x + 5.8$. The slope means that each picture increases the price by \$0.30.

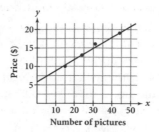

The sketched line of fit goes through two of the data points, $(44, 19)$ and $(24, 13)$, so you can use them to find the slope.

$$slope = \frac{19-13}{44-24} = 0.3$$

The equation of the line of fit is $\hat{y} = 19 + 0.3(x - 44)$.

**b.** Substitute 0 for $x$ and solve for $y$.

$y = 19 + 0.3(0 - 44) = 5.8$

In addition to the cost per picture, there is a fixed fee of \$5.80.

**c.** $5.8 + 0.3(75) = \$28.30$

**d.** Substitute 7.99 for $y$ and solve for $x$.

$5.8 + 0.3x = 7.99$

$0.3x = 2.19$

$x = 7.3$

The studio should include seven or eight prints. Seven prints would make more of a profit, but eight would be a better promotional discount.

**9. a.** $[145, 200, 5, 40, 52, 1]$

**b.** $\hat{y} = 50.5 + 0.26(x - 191.5)$, or $\hat{y} = 0.26x + 0.71$. Graph the data and sketch a line of fit.

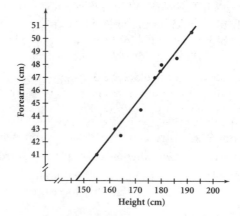

Using the points (191.5, 50.5) and (165, 43.5) from the sketched line, you can find the slope.

$$slope = \frac{50.5 - 43.5}{191.5 - 165} = 0.26$$

The equation of the line of fit is $\hat{y} = 50.5 + 0.26(x - 191.5)$.

**c.** On average, a student's forearm length increases by 0.26 cm for each additional 1 cm of height.

**d.** The $y$-intercept is meaningless because a height of 0 cm will not predict a forearm length of 0.71 cm. The domain should be specified.

**e.** 189.58 cm; 41.79 cm. Substitute 50 for $\hat{y}$ and solve for $x$. $50 = 0.26x + 0.71$, so $0.26x = 49.29$, and $x \approx 189.58$. Next, substitute 158 for $x$ and solve for $\hat{y}$. $\hat{y} = 0.26(158) + 0.71 = 41.79$.

**10. a.** Let $x$ represent the number of hours without sleep, and let $y$ represent the number of errors.

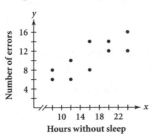

**b.** Possible answer: $\hat{y} = 3 + 0.5x$

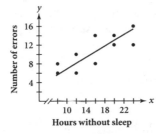

**c.** 14 errors; $0.5(22) + 3 = 14$

**d.** Interpolation, because you found a value between those given in the table

**11.** $u_{35} = 102$. The slope of the line between the two given points, (3, 54) and (21, 81), is $\frac{81 - 54}{21 - 3} = \frac{27}{18} = 1.5$. The zero term of the sequence is $54 - 3(1.5) = 49.5$. Write the explicit formula, $u_n = 49.5 + 1.5n$, and substitute 35 for $n$ to find the 35th term. $u_{35} = 49.5 + 1.5(35) = 102$.

Another way to calculate the 35th term is to multiply the common difference, 1.5, by the number of terms between $u_{21}$ and $u_{35}$, and add that to $u_{21}$. $u_{21} + 14(1.5) = 81 + 14(1.5) = 102$.

**12.** 56, 32, 20, 14. The long-run value of the sequence is 8.

$$u_1 = 56$$
$$u_2 = \frac{56}{2} + 4 = 28 + 4 = 32$$
$$u_3 = \frac{32}{2} + 4 = 16 + 4 = 20$$
$$u_4 = \frac{20}{2} + 4 = 10 + 4 = 14$$

To find the long-run value, set $u_n = u_{n-1} = c$ and solve the equation $c = \frac{c}{2} + 4$: $\frac{1}{2}c = 4$, so $c = 8$.

**13. a.** 16. Arrange the data in numerical order and find the middle value: {12, 14, 15, 15, **16**, 17, 20, 21, 30}.

**b.** Add 19.5 and any three numbers greater than 19.5 to the data set. For example, {12, 14, 15, 15, 16, 17, 19.5, 20, 21, 22, 23, 25, 30}.

**14. a.** $u_0 = 8$ and $u_n = u_{n-1} - 0.5$ where $n \geq 1$. $u_0 = 8$ because you start 8 m away. You move 0.5 m closer each second, so $u_n = u_{n-1} - 0.5$.

**b.** $u_n = 8 - 0.5n$. $n$ represents the number of seconds that have passed.

**c.** A negative value means that you have passed the marker.

**EXTENSIONS**

**A.** Answers will vary.

**B.** Research results will vary.

**C.** Research results will vary.

## LESSON 3.4

### EXERCISES

**1.** If a set cannot be divided into three equal groups, the first and last groups should be the same size.

**a.** 17, 17, 17      **b.** 17, 16, 17

**c.** 16, 15, 16      **d.** 13, 12, 13

**2. a.** The slope is $\frac{15.7 - 9.5}{8.1 - 17.3} = -\frac{6.2}{9.2}$, or $-0.6739$. The equation is $y = 15.7 - 0.6739(x - 8.1)$ or $y = 9.5 - 0.6739(x - 17.3)$.

**b.** The slope is $\frac{84 - 47}{18 - 3} = \frac{37}{15}$. The equation is $y = 47 + \frac{37}{15}(x - 3)$ or $y = 84 + \frac{37}{15}(x - 18)$.

**3.** Parallel lines have the same slope, so the slope is 0.75. The equation is $y = 0.9 + 0.75(x - 14.4)$.

**4.** The slope is $-1.8$. To find the $y$-intercept, average the three $y$-intercepts: $\frac{74.1 + 74.1 + 70.5}{3} = 72.9$. The equation of the line is $y = 72.9 - 1.8x$.

**5.** The slope is 4.7. The equation through the third point is $y = 64 + 4.7(x - 12.8)$ or $y = 3.84 + 4.7x$. To find the $y$-intercept, average the three $y$-intercepts: $\frac{2.8 + 2.8 + 3.84}{3} \approx 3.15$. The equation of the line is $y = 3.15 + 4.7x$.

**6. a.** 6, 5, 6

**b.** (1932.5, 58.75), (1960, 66.6), (1987.5, 71.5). For the first and third groups, you have to find the mean of the middle $x$- and $y$-values.

$M_1$ is $\left( \frac{1930 + 1935}{2}, \frac{58.1 + 59.4}{2} \right) =$ (1932.5, 58.75).

$M_2$ is (1960, 66.6).

$M_3$ is $\left( \frac{1985 + 1990}{2}, \frac{71.2 + 71.8}{2} \right) =$ (1987.5, 71.5).

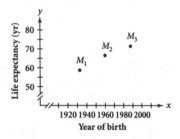

**c.**

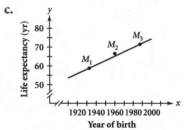

$slope = \frac{71.5 - 58.75}{87.5 - 32.5} \approx 0.232$. This means that each year the life expectancy for a male increases by 0.232 year.

**d.** $y = 58.75 + 0.232(x - 1932.5)$ or $y = 71.5 + 0.232(x - 1987.5)$; $y = -389.59 + 0.232x$

**e.**

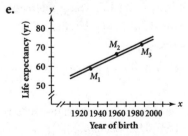

$y = 66.6 + 0.232(x - 1960)$; $y = -388.12 + 0.232x$

**f.** $\frac{-389.59 + (-389.59) + (-388.12)}{3} = -389.1$; $\hat{y} = -389.1 + 0.232x$

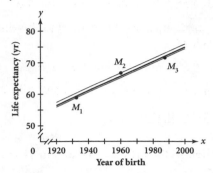

**g.** Substitute 1978 for $x$ to get $\hat{y} = -389.1 + 0.232(1978) \approx 69.8$ years.

**h.** Substitute 1991 for $x$ to get $\hat{y} = -389.1 + 0.232(1991) \approx 72.8$ years.

**i.** Around the year 2022. Substitute 80 for $y$ and solve for $x$. $80 = -389.1 + 0.232x$, so $469.1 = 0.232x$, and $x \approx 2021.98$. The life expectancy at birth for males in the United States should exceed 80 years in the year 2022.

**7.** Sample answer using the Investigation Spring Experiment: $-0.073, 0.047, 0.167, 0.087, 0.207, 0.127, 0.147, -0.033, -0.013, 0.007, -0.073, -0.053, -0.133, -0.113, -0.093, -0.073, 0.147, -0.133, -0.013, 0.107$. To find the residuals, substitute each mass ($x$-value) into the equation $\hat{y} = 3.173 + 0.038x$, and then subtract the $\hat{y}$-value from the actual $y$-value.

The model seems pretty good because the residuals have small magnitude and are randomly positive and negative.

**8.** Sample answer: $\hat{y} = 0.55x + 1.38$. The line of fit found in the investigation was $\hat{y} = 0.45x + 1.9$. The median-median line seems to be a better model for fewer people, while the line found before seems to be a better model for more people.

To find the median-median line, first divide the data into three groups of points. Then find the median $x$- and $y$-values of each group. The three summary points are $M_1(5, 4.4)$, $M_2(9, 5.8)$, and $M_3(16, 10.4)$.

Find the slope of the line through $M_1$ and $M_3$, which is the slope of the median-median line.

$slope = \frac{10.4 - 4.4}{16 - 5} = \frac{6}{11} = 0.55$

Now find the equation of the line through $M_1$ and $M_3$.

$y = 4.4 + 0.55(x − 5)$, or $y = 1.65 + 0.55x$

Find the equation of the line parallel to this line and through $M_2$.

$y = 5.8 + 0.55(x − 9)$, or $y = 0.85 + 0.55x$

Find the mean of the three $y$-intercepts.

$$\frac{1.65 + 1.65 + (0.85)}{3} \approx 1.38$$

The equation of the median-median line is $\hat{y} = 0.55x + 1.38$.

**9.** It is easiest to complete the calculations if you convert all the times to seconds.

**a.** $\hat{y} = 997.12 − 0.389x$. In order to obtain an accurate answer, it is best to avoid rounding until the final step. The three summary points are $M_1(1923, 250.4)$, $M_2(1951.5, 237.95)$, and $M_3(1985, 226.31)$. The slope of the line through $M_1$ and $M_3$ is $\frac{226.31 − 250.4}{1985 − 1923} \approx −0.3885483871$. The equation of this line is $y = 250.4 − 0.3885483871(x − 1923)$, or $y = 997.5785484 − 0.3885483871x$. The parallel line through $M_2$ has the equation $y = 237.95 − 0.3885483871 (x − 1951.5)$, or $y = 996.2021774 − 0.3885483871x$. The $y$-intercept of the median-median line is the mean of the three $y$-intercepts: $\frac{997.5785484 + 997.5785484 + 996.2021774}{3} \approx$ 997.1197581. Therefore the equation of the median-median line is approximately $\hat{y} = 997.12 − 0.389x$.

**b.** On average the world record for the 1-mile run is reduced by 0.389 s every year.

**c.** $\hat{y} = 997.12 − 0.389(1954) = 237.014$ s, or 3:57.014. This prediction is about 2.3 s faster than Roger Bannister actually ran.

**d.** $\hat{y} = 997.12 − 0.389(1875) = 267.745$ s, or 4:27.745. This prediction is about 3.2 s slower than Walter Slade actually ran.

**e.** This suggests that a world record for the mile in the year 0 would have been about 16.6 minutes. This is doubtful because a fast walker can walk a mile in about 15 minutes. The data are only approximately linear and only over a short domain.

**f.** A new record of 3:43.13 was set by Hicham El Guerrouj of Morocco in 1999. The model's prediction for 1999 is $997.12 − 0.389(1999) = 219.509$ s, or 3:39.509. This is about 3.6 s faster than the actual record.

**10.** Answers will vary. One possibility is to divide the data into three groups and then to use the mean $x$

and mean $y$ from each group and follow a similar procedure of writing three equations and finding the mean of the $y$-intercepts. Here is an example of the method, using the data from Exercise 9.

Divide the data set into three groups and find the mean $x$ and the mean $y$ of each group. The three summary points are $M_1(1925, 249.8)$, $M_2(1953, 238.3)$, and $M_3(1985.67, 226.57)$.

The slope through points $M_1$ and $M_3$ is $\frac{226.57 − 249.8}{1985.67 − 1925} \approx −0.383$. This will be the slope of the mean-mean line. The equation of the line through $M_1$ and $M_3$ is $y = 249.8 − 0.383(x − 1925)$, or $y = 987.075 − 0.383x$. The equation of the parallel line through $M_2$ is $y = 238.3 − 0.383(x − 1953)$, or $y = 1031.299 − 0.383x$.

The mean of the three $y$-intercepts is $\frac{987.075 + 987.075 + 1031.299}{3} = 1001.816$, and the equation of the mean-mean line is $\hat{y} = 1001.816 − 0.383x$.

In this case the mean-mean line is very similar to the median-median line. In other cases the mean-mean line might be affected too much by outliers to be accurate.

**11. a.**

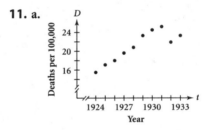

**b.** $M_1(1925, 17.1)$, $M_2(1928.5, 22.05)$, $M_3(1932, 23.3)$

**c.** $\hat{D} = −1687.83 + 0.886t$. The slope of the line through $M_1$ and $M_3$ is $\frac{23.3 − 17.1}{32 − 25} \approx 0.886$. The equation of this line is $D = 17.1 + 0.886(t − 1925)$, or $D = −1688.45 + 0.886t$. Using the same slope, the equation of the line through $M_2$ is $D = 22.05 + 0.886(t − 1928.5)$, or $D = −1686.601 + 0.886t$. The $y$-intercept of the median-median line is the mean of the three $y$-intercepts:

$$\frac{−1688.45 + (−1688.45) + (−1686.601)}{3} \approx −1687.83$$

Therefore the equation of the median-median line is $\hat{D} = −1687.83 + 0.886t$.

**d.** For each additional year, the number of deaths by automobile increases by 0.886 per hundred thousand population.

**e.** Answers might include the fact that the United States was in the Great Depression and fewer people were driving.

f. It probably would not be a good idea to extrapo-late because a lot has changed in the automotive industry in the past 75 years. Many safety features are now standard.

12. Possible answer: 11, 15, 18, 23, 28, 40, 50, 50, 50. Many answers are possible but must include the values 11, ?, ?, ?, 28, ?, $x$, $x$, $x$. The last three values must be equal.

13. $y = 7 - 3x$. The rate of change is $-3$, so that is the slope, and a point on the line is $(1, 4)$. The equation of the line is $y = 4 - 3(x - 1) = 7 - 3x$.

14. Ramon's score of 35 results in a percentile ranking between the 40th and 63rd percentile. $\frac{60}{150} = 0.4$, or 40%, of students scored lower than 30 and $\frac{95}{150} \approx$ 0.63, or 63%, of students scored lower than 40.

15. 2.3 g, 3.0 g, 3.0 g, 3.4 g, 3.6 g, 3.9 g. Because the mean is 3.2 and the largest deviation is $-0.9$, the smallest value is 2.3. There must be two values of 3.0 because that is the mode. There are now three values below 3.2, so to get a median of 3.2, the next value must be 3.4. Given the *IQR* of 0.6, the next value must be 3.6. To have a mean of 3.2, the last value has to be 3.9.

16. a. 58.3 mi/h
    b. 7.4 mi/h
    c. The standard deviation is rather large, with most of the data within a 14 mi/h range from about 51 mi/h to 65 mi/h. They had to drive a bit slower part of the time, possibly due to trucks, curves, or steep hills.

## EXTENSIONS

A. See the solution to Take Another Look activity 1 on page 53.

B. Results will vary. See Lesson 13.7 for details.

## LESSON 3.5

### EXERCISES

1. a. *residual* $= 8.2 - (2.4(2) + 3.6) = 8.2 - 8.4 = -0.2$
   b. *residual* $= 12.8 - (2.4(4) + 3.6) = 12.8 - 13.2 = -0.4$
   c. *residual* $= 28.2 - (2.4(10) + 3.6) = 28.2 - 27.6 = 0.6$

2. 82.3, 82.9, 74.5, 56.9. To find each $y$-value, solve the equation *residual* $= y - \hat{y}$, or $y = residual + \hat{y}$.

   For $x = 5$, $y = -2.7 + (-1.8(5) + 94) = -2.7 + 85 = 82.3$.

   For $x = 8$, $y = 3.3 + (-1.8(8) + 94) = 3.3 + 79.6 = 82.9$.

   For $x = 12$, $y = 2.1 + (-1.8(12) + 94) = 2.1 + 72.4 = 74.5$.

   For $x = 20$, $y = -1.1 + (-1.8(20) + 94) = -1.1 + 58 = 56.9$.

3. a. Set up a table that shows the actual $y$-value and the $\hat{y}$-value, and then subtract to find the residual. (*See table at bottom of page.*)
   b. About 1.23 yr. Sum the squares of the residuals and divide by 2 less than the number of data points. Finally, take the square root.
   $$s = \sqrt{\frac{22.5288}{17 - 2}} \approx 1.22$$
   c. In general, the life expectancy values predicted by the median-median line will be within 1.23 yr of the actual data values.

4. Approximately 0.28. Sum the squares of the resid-uals to get 0.48. Then divide by 6 (two less than the number of data points) to get 0.08. Finally, take the square root to get 0.28.

**Lesson 3.5, Exercise 3a**

| Year of birth | 1920 | 1925 | 1930 | 1935 | 1940 | 1945 | 1950 | 1955 |
|---|---|---|---|---|---|---|---|---|
| Male life expectancy (yr) | 53.6 | 56.3 | 58.1 | 59.4 | 60.8 | 62.8 | 65.6 | 66.2 |
| $\hat{y}$-value from line $\hat{y} = -389.1 + 0.232x$ | 56.34 | 57.5 | 58.66 | 59.82 | 60.98 | 62.14 | 63.3 | 64.46 |
| Residual | $-2.74$ | $-1.2$ | $-0.56$ | $-0.42$ | $-0.18$ | 0.66 | 2.3 | 1.74 |

| Year of birth | 1960 | 1965 | 1970 | 1975 | 1980 | 1985 | 1990 | 1995 | 1998 |
|---|---|---|---|---|---|---|---|---|---|
| Male life expectancy (yr) | 66.6 | 66.8 | 67.1 | 68.8 | 70.0 | 71.2 | 71.8 | 72.5 | 73.9 |
| $\hat{y}$-value from line $\hat{y} = -389.1 + 0.232x$ | 65.62 | 66.78 | 67.94 | 69.1 | 70.26 | 71.42 | 72.58 | 73.74 | 74.436 |
| Residual | 0.98 | 0.02 | $-0.84$ | $-0.3$ | $-0.26$ | $-0.22$ | $-0.78$ | $-1.24$ | $-0.536$ |

**5. a.** Let $x$ represent age in years, and let $y$ represent height in centimeters. The median-median line is $\hat{y} = 82.5 + 5.6x$. Use your calculator to find the equation of the median-median line.

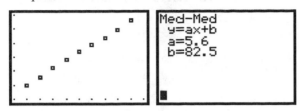

[4, 14, 1, 100, 160, 10]

**b.** The residuals are $-1.3$, $-0.4$, $0.3$, $0.8$, $0.8$, $0.3$, $-0.4$, $-0.4$, $1.1$. Use your calculator to find the residuals.

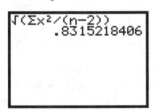

**c.** The root mean square error is $s = \sqrt{\frac{4.84}{7}} \approx$ 0.83 cm. Use your calculator to find the root mean square error.

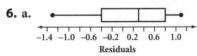

**d.** In general, the mean height of boys ages 5 to 13 will be within 0.83 cm of the values predicted by the median-median line.

**e.** Between 165.7 cm and 167.3 cm. The mean value is $\hat{y} = 82.5 + 5.6(15) = 166.5$. The range is the mean plus or minus the root mean square error: $166.5 \pm 0.83 = 167.33$ or $165.67$.

**6. a.**

![box plot with scale from -1.4 to 1.0 labeled Residuals]

$-1.4$ $-1.0$ $-0.6$ $-0.2$ $0.2$ $0.6$ $1.0$
Residuals

**b.** Possible answers: The median residual is positive. The lower half of the residuals have a larger spread than the upper half. Half of the residuals lie between $-0.4$ and $0.8$.

**7.** $\hat{y} = 29.8 + 2.4x$. You know the residual for the data point $(6, 47)$ and the slope of the line of fit, so you can use the equation for the residual and solve for the missing value.

$$residual = y - \hat{y}$$
$$= y - (ax + b)$$
$$2.8 = 47 - (2.4 \cdot 6 + b)$$
$$2.8 = 47 - 14.4 - b$$
$$2.8 = 32.6 - b$$
$$b = 29.8$$

The equation of the line of fit is $\hat{y} = 29.8 + 2.4x$.

**8. a.** Let $x$ represent temperature in degrees Fahrenheit, and let $y$ represent temperature in degrees Celsius. The median-median line is $\hat{y} = -14.21 + 0.4815x$.

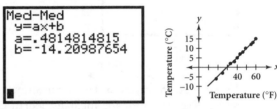

**b.** $-0.457$, $0.3205$, $-0.606$, $-0.8275$, $-0.05$, $0.061$, $0.5055$, $0.6165$, $-0.2725$, $0.32$, $-0.2355$. The points on the left end of the graph are generally below the line, and the points on the right end are generally above the line. (*See table at bottom of page.*)

**c.** The slope should increase and the $y$-intercept should decrease. Possible answer: $\hat{y} = -15 + 0.5x$.

**d.** For $\hat{y} = -14.21 + 0.4815x$, $s \approx 0.499$. For $\hat{y} = -15 + 0.5x$, $s \approx 0.441$. The smaller root mean square error for $\hat{y} = -15 + 0.5x$ indicates that this equation is a better fit for the data because it provides more accurate predictions.

**e. i.** 27.5°C. Substitute 85 for $x$ in the equation $\hat{y} = -15 + 0.5x$. $\hat{y} = -15 + 0.5(85) = 27.5$°C.

**ii.** 30°F. Substitute 0 for $\hat{y}$ in the equation $\hat{y} = -15 + 0.5x$. $0 = -15 + 0.5x$, so $0.5x = 15$, and $x = 30$°F.

**Lesson 3.5, Exercise 8b**

| °F (x-value) | 18 | 33 | 37 | 25 | 40 | 46 | 43 | 49 | 55 | 60 | 57 |
|---|---|---|---|---|---|---|---|---|---|---|---|
| °C (y-value) | −6 | 2 | 3 | −3 | 5 | 8 | 7 | 10 | 12 | 15 | 13 |
| $\hat{y}$-value | −5.543 | 1.6795 | 3.6055 | −2.1725 | 5.05 | 7.939 | 6.4945 | 9.3835 | 12.2725 | 14.68 | 13.2355 |
| Residual | −0.457 | 0.3205 | −0.606 | −0.8275 | −0.05 | 0.061 | 0.5055 | 0.6165 | −0.2725 | 0.32 | −0.2355 |

**9.** Alex's method: $\frac{2+1+3+4+1}{3} = 3.67$; root mean square error method: $\sqrt{\frac{4+1+9+16+1}{3}} \approx 3.21$.

Because both methods give values around 3, Alex's method could be used as an alternative measure of accuracy.

**10. a.** Let $x$ represent turns, and let $y$ represent distance in inches. The median-median line is $\hat{y} = 1.4667 + 73.2x$.

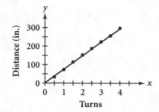

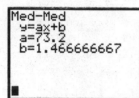

**b.** $s = \sqrt{\frac{79.8756}{6}} \approx 3.65$ in.

**c.** Between 363.8 in. and 371.1 in. Substitute 5 for $x$ in the equation for the median-median line: $\hat{y} = 1.4667 + 73.2(5) \approx 367.47$ in. The distance predicted by the median-median line will be within 3.65 in. of the actual distance. Because $367.47 \pm 3.65 = 371.12$ or 363.82, the actual distance should be between 363.8 in. and 371.1 in.

**11. a.**

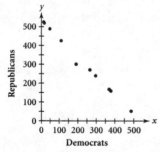

**b.** The points are nearly linear because the sum of electoral votes should be 538. The data are not perfectly linear because in a few of the elections, candidates other than the Democrats and Republicans received some electoral votes.

**c.** The points above the line are the elections in which the Republican Party's presidential candidate won.

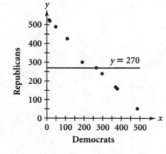

**d.** $-218, 31, 250, -30, 219, 255, 156, -102, -111, 1.$ Subtract 270 from each $y$-value to find these residuals. A negative residual means that the Democratic Party's presidential candidate won.

**e.** A close election

**12. a.** $y = 4.7 + 0.6(x - 2)$

**b.** $y = 0 - 7(x - 6)$, using the point $(6, 0)$.

**c.** The slope is $\frac{-18-11}{-6-3} = \frac{29}{9}$. Using the given points, $y = 11 + \frac{29}{9}(x - 3)$ or $y = -18 + \frac{29}{9}(x + 6)$.

**13.** Possible answer: 28, 38, 42, 47, 49, 50, 60. Answers should be in the pattern 28, $a$, ?, 47, ?, $a + 12$, ?.

**14. a.** $3 + 7x = 17$, so $7x = 14$, and $x = 2$.

**b.** $12 + 3t - 15 = 6t + 1$

$$3t - 3 = 6t + 1$$
$$3t = -4$$
$$t = -\frac{4}{3}$$

**15. a.** $u_0 = 30$ and $u_n = u_{n-1}\left(1 + \frac{0.07}{12}\right) + 30$ where $n \geq 1$

**b. i.** Deposited: \$360; interest: \$11.78

**ii.** Deposited: \$3,600; interest: \$1,592.54

**iii.** Deposited: \$9,000; interest: \$15,302.15

**iv.** Deposited: \$18,000; interest: \$145,442.13

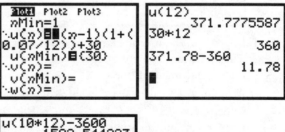

**c.** Sample answer: If you earn compound interest, in the long run the interest earned will far exceed the total amount deposited.

## EXTENSIONS

**A.** Results will vary. You can use Fathom to find the least squares line of fit: $\hat{y} = 82.8x + 426$. Residuals for this line are 3.2, 11.4, $-32.4$, and 17.8. The sum of the residuals is 0. See the Exploration Residual Plots and Least Squares on page 149.

**B.** Results will vary.

**C.** Opinions will vary.

## QUESTIONS

1. From the movable line, outliers are those points that have a vertical distance from the line far greater than the other points. From the residual plot, outliers are those residual points that have a vertical distance from the line $y = 0$ far greater than the other residuals. The residual plot usually makes it easier to identify outliers. Outliers are those points that have squares with area far greater than the other points. This is related to the other two approaches: the length of the side of each square is the vertical distance from the line, or the absolute value of the residual.

2. As the slope of the line of fit increases or decreases, the slope of the residual plot decreases or increases (inversely), but the residuals stay equidistant with respect to each other. As the $y$-intercept of the line moves up or down, the residual plot moves down or up (inversely). The residuals should have a sum approximately equal to zero, and be equally scattered positive and negative, so you can adjust the line of fit by watching how the residual plot changes.

3. The line of fit for Graph A needs to have its slope increased and its $y$-intercept decreased. The line of fit for Graph B needs to have its $y$-intercept decreased. The line of fit for Graph C is already a good line of fit and needs no adjustment.

4. A better fitting line will minimize the sum of the areas of the squares. The least squares line is so called because it absolutely minimizes the sum of the areas of the squares.

5. Answers will vary. For this data set at least, the median-median line and the least squares line differ slightly (*DriversThou* = 0.678*PopThou* + 18 and *DriversThou* = 0.655*PopThou* + 120, respectively). Outliers, and how each method of finding a line of fit deals with them, are the primary reason that the equations differ. If the data were perfectly linear, the median-median line and the least squares line would be equivalent.

## EXTENSION

The median-median line is more sensitive to extreme outliers than the least squares line.

## EXERCISES

1. a. The intersection point is $(1.8, -11.6)$. Use a table to see that the $y$-values are equal when $x = 1.8$.

| X | Y₁ | Y₂ |
|---|---|---|
| 0 | -17 | -8 |
| 1 | -14 | -10 |
| 2 | -11 | -12 |
| 1.5 | -12.5 | -11 |
| 1.6 | -12.2 | -11.2 |
| 1.7 | -11.9 | -11.4 |
| **1.8** | -11.6 | -11.6 |

X=1.8

   b. The intersection point is $(3.7, 31.9)$. Use a table to see that the $y$-values are equal when $x = 3.7$.

| X | Y₁ | Y₂ |
|---|---|---|
| 3.1 | 33.7 | 27.7 |
| 3.2 | 33.4 | 28.4 |
| 3.3 | 33.1 | 29.1 |
| 3.4 | 32.8 | 29.8 |
| 3.5 | 32.5 | 30.5 |
| 3.6 | 32.2 | 31.2 |
| **3.7** | 31.9 | 31.9 |

X=3.7

2. Possible answer: $\begin{cases} y = 7.5 + 4(x - 2) \\ y = 7.5 + 1.7(x - 2) \end{cases}$.

The equations should both pass through the point $(2, 7.5)$. Writing equations in point-slope form is one easy way to generate the desired lines. You can choose any two slopes.

3. $slope = -\left(\frac{1}{-2.5}\right) = 0.4$. Using the point-slope formula, the equation of the line is $y = 5 + 0.4(x - 1)$.

4. a. $x = \frac{32}{19} \approx 1.684$

$$4 - 2.5x + 15 = 3 + 7x$$
$$19 - 2.5x = 3 + 7x$$
$$9.5x = 16$$
$$x = \frac{16}{9.5} = \frac{32}{19} \approx 1.684$$

   b. $t = -\frac{61}{3} \approx -20.33$

$$11.5 + 4.1t = 6 + 3.2t - 12.8$$
$$11.5 + 4.1t = -6.8 + 3.2t$$
$$0.9t = -18.3$$
$$t = \frac{-18.3}{0.9} = -\frac{183}{9} = -\frac{61}{3} \approx -20.33$$

5. a. $(4.125, -10.625)$

| | |
|---|---|
| $y = 10 - 5x$ | Second equation. |
| $-2 + 3(x - 7) = 10 - 5x$ | Substitute the right side of the first equation for $y$. |
| $-2 + 3x - 21 = 10 - 5x$ | Distribute the 3. |
| $-23 + 3x = 10 - 5x$ | Add. |
| $8x = 33$ | Add 23 and $5x$ to both sides. |
| $x = 4.125$ | Divide both sides by 8. |

Substitute 4.125 for $x$ in either equation to find $y$.

$y = 10 - 5(4.125) = 10 - 20.625 = -10.625$

The lines intersect at $(4.125, -10.625)$.

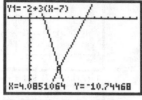

$[-3, 15, 1, -15, 3, 1]$

**b.** $(-3.16, 8.27)$

| | |
|---|---|
| $y = 4 - 1.35x$ | Second equation. |
| $0.23x + 9 = 4 - 1.35x$ | Substitute the right side of the first equation for $y$. |
| $1.58x = -5$ | Add $-9$ and $1.35x$ to both sides. |
| $x = \dfrac{-5}{1.58} \approx -3.16$ | Divide both sides by 1.58. |

Substitute $-3.16$ for $x$ in either equation to find $y$.

$y = 0.23(-3.16) + 9 \approx 8.27$

The lines intersect at $(-3.16, 8.27)$.

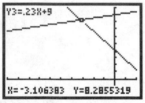

$[-10, 2, 1, -2, 10, 1]$

**c.** Multiply the first equation by 2. The result is $2y = -3x + 14$, the same as the second equation, so the equations represent the same line. They intersect at every point.

**6. a.** When you place 48.6 g on each spring, they will be the same length, 37.4 cm. Find $m$ when $s_1 = s_2$.

$18 + 0.4m = 11.2 + 0.54m$

$0.14m = 6.8$

$m = \dfrac{6.8}{0.14} \approx 48.57$

Substitute 48.6 for $m$ and solve for $s$.
$s = 18 + 0.4(48.6) = 37.4$.

**b.** When more than 120 g is placed on the springs, spring 2 will be at least 10 cm longer than spring 1. Spring 1 is 6.8 cm longer than spring 2, but it doesn't stretch as much for each added gram of mass, so you need to find when spring 2 is 10 cm longer than spring 1.

$11.2 + 0.54m > 10 + 18 + 0.4m$

$11.2 + 0.54m > 28 + 0.4m$

$0.14m > 16.8$

$m > 120$

**c.** Answers will vary but should include comments about spring 1 $\left(s_1\right)$ being longer than spring 2 $\left(s_2\right)$ in its unstretched condition and the fact that spring 2 stretches more for each added gram of mass than spring 1 does.

**7. a.** No. At $x = 25$, the cost line is above the income line.

**b.** Yes. When 200 pogo sticks are sold, the income line is above the cost line. The profit is approximately $120. This is the approximate difference between the $y$-values for the income line and the cost line at $x = 200$.

**c.** About 120 pogo sticks. Look for the point where the cost and income lines intersect.

**8. a.** Median-median line for men: $\hat{y} = 1040.04 - 0.4658x$; median-median line for women: $\hat{y} = 1670.70 - 0.7773x$. The point of intersection is $(2024.6, 97.0)$. This predicts that the men's and women's times will be about the same in the year 2024 or 2025.

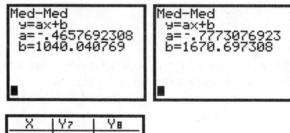

**b.** Answers will vary but probably should include a statement that there is a limit to how fast a person can skate and that eventually the winning times will approach a minimal value. It may or may not be as low as the predicted value.

**c.** Using the men's model, $\hat{y} = 1040.04 - 0.4658(2002) \approx 107.51$; the predicted time is 107.51 s, or 1:47.51. Using the women's model,

*Discovering Advanced Algebra Solutions Manual*
©2004 Key Curriculum Press

$\hat{y} = 1670.70 - 0.7773(2002) \approx 114.55$; the predicted time is 114.55 s, or 1:54.55. Actual times for 2002 Olympics: men: 1:43.95; women: 1:54.02.

**d.** No, because the data are linear only over a small domain.

**9. a.** Phrequent Phoner Plan: $y = 20 + 17([x] - 1)$; Small Business Plan: $y = 50 + 11([x] - 1)$.

**b.**

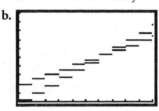

[0, 10, 1, 0, 200, 20]

**c.** If the time of the phone call is less than 6 min, PPP is less expensive. For times between 6 and 7 min, the plans charge the same rate. If the time of the phone call is greater than or equal to 7 min, PPP is more expensive than SBP. (You can look at the calculator table to see these results.)

**10. a.** Let $x$ represent the length of the humerus bone in centimeters, and let $y$ represent the person's height in centimeters.

[0, 60, 0, 50, 250, 0]

**b.** Male: $m = 3.08(42) + 70.45 = 199.81$, so approximately 199.81 cm. Female: $f = 3.36(42) + 58 = 199.12$, so approximately 199.12 cm.

**11. a.** $l = \frac{46}{3}$ cm, $w = \frac{20}{3}$ cm. Let $l$ represent length of a leg in centimeters, and let $w$ represent width in centimeters; $2l + 2w = 44$ and $l = 2 + 2w$.

| | |
|---|---|
| $2l + 2w = 44$ | First equation. |
| $l + w = 22$ | Divide both sides by 2. |
| $(2 + 2w) + w = 22$ | Substitute $2 + 2w$ for $l$. |
| $3w = 20$ | Combine terms. |
| $w = \frac{20}{3}$ | Divide both sides by 3. |
| $l = 2 + 2w$ | Second equation. |
| $l = 2 + 2\left(\frac{20}{3}\right)$ | Substitute $\frac{20}{3}$ for $w$. |
| $l = \frac{46}{3}$ | Combine terms. |

**b.** $l = 14$ cm, $b = 12$ cm. Let $l$ represent the length of a leg in centimeters, and let $b$ represent the length of the base in centimeters; $2l + b = 40$ and $b = l - 2$.

| | |
|---|---|
| $2l + b = 40$ | First equation. |
| $2l + (l - 2) = 40$ | Substitute $l - 2$ for $b$. |
| $3l = 42$ | Combine terms. |
| $l = 14$ | Divide both sides by 3. |
| $b = l - 2$ | Second equation. |
| $b = 14 - 2$ | Substitute 14 for $l$. |
| $b = 12$ | Combine terms. |

**c.** $c = 27°C$, $f = 80.6°F$. Let $f$ represent temperature in degrees Fahrenheit, and let $c$ represent temperature in degrees Celsius; $f = 3c - 0.4$ and $f = 1.8c + 32$.

| | |
|---|---|
| $f = 3c - 0.4$ | First equation. |
| $1.8c + 32 = 3c - 0.4$ | Substitute $1.8c + 32$ for $f$. |
| $1.2c = 32.4$ | Combine terms. |
| $c = 27$ | Divide both sides by 1.2. |
| $f = 1.8c + 32$ | Second equation. |
| $f = 1.8(27) + 32$ | Substitute 27 for $c$. |
| $f = 80.6$ | Combine terms. |

**12. a.** $343.5 + 1.55(1984 - 1984) = 343.5$ ppm

**b.** $343.5 + 1.55(2010 - 1984) = 383.8$ ppm

**c.** Approximately the year 2124

$$560 = 343.5 + 1.55(x - 1984)$$
$$560 = -2731.7 + 1.55x$$
$$3291.7 = 1.55x$$
$$x \approx 2123.68$$

**13. a.** Add the columns: $7 + 11 + 12 + 11 + 6 + 2 + 1 + 1 = 51$ jurisdictions.

**b.** 3rd bin

**c.** $\frac{18}{51} \approx 0.35$, or 35%

**14. a.** $8y = 3x - 12$

$$y = \frac{3x - 12}{8} = 0.375x + 1.5$$

**b.** $2y = 12 - 5x$

$$y = \frac{12 - 5x}{2} = 6 - 2.5x$$

**c.** $4y = 5 + 3x$

$$y = \frac{5 + 3x}{4} = 1.25 + 0.75x$$

Children have smaller feet and generally watch more cartoons than adults, but this does not mean that one trait causes the other.

## EXTENSIONS

**A.**

|      | Detroit   | San Jose |
|------|-----------|----------|
| 1995 | 1,003,701 | 821,467  |
| 1996 | 995,233   | 836,136  |
| 2000 | 951,270   | 894,943  |

(*U.S. Census Bureau*)

Using the median-median lines for the two cities, these are the predicted populations:

|      | Detroit  | San Jose |
|------|----------|----------|
| 1995 | 926,376  | 901,883  |
| 1996 | 904,903  | 920,418  |
| 2000 | 819,012  | 994,562  |

The residuals get higher and higher as the years go on, indicating that the data might not be as linear as it seemed from the data points given in the book.

**B.** Sample answer: For a human infant, some equations used are $l = 8.20u + 2.38$, $l = 6.44f + 4.51$, and $l = 7.24t + 4.90$, where $l$ is the length of the baby in centimeters, $u$ is the length of the ulna bone in centimeters, $f$ is the length of the femur bone in centimeters, and $t$ is the length of the tibia bone in centimeters. (*www.medal.org*)

## LESSON 3.7

### EXERCISES

**1. a.** $w = 11 + r$

**b.** $h = \dfrac{18 - 2p}{3} = 6 - \dfrac{2}{3}p$

**c.** $r = w - 11$

**d.** $p = \dfrac{18 - 3h}{2} = 9 - \dfrac{3}{2}p$

**2. a.** $-3j - 15k = -24$. The graphs are the same line.

**b.** $10p + 15h = 90$. The graphs are the same line.

**c.** $3f - 2g = 11$. The graphs are the same line.

**d.** $10a + 9b = 42$. The graphs are the same line.

**3. a.** $5x - 2y = 12$. The line of the new equation passes through the point of intersection of the original pair.

**b.** $-4y = 8$. The line of the new equation passes through the point of intersection of the original pair and is horizontal.

**4. a.** $(-4.7, 29.57)$. The graph shows the point of intersection is approximately $(-4.68, 29.12)$.

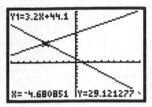

$[-10, 10, 1, -50, 75, 5]$

Both equations are in intercept form, so you can solve the system by substituting the right side of the first equation for $y$ in the second equation.

| | |
|---|---|
| $y = -5.1x + 5.60$ | Second equation. |
| $3.2x + 44.61 = -5.1x + 5.60$ | Substitute the right side of the first equation for $y$. |
| $8.3x = -39.01$ | Add $5.1x$ and $-44.61$ to both sides. |
| $x = -4.7$ | Divide both sides by $-4.7$. |

Substitute $-4.7$ for $x$ in either equation to find the value of $y$.

$$y = 3.2(-4.7) + 44.61 = 29.57$$

The solution to this system is $(-4.7, 29.57)$.

**b.** $\left(\dfrac{20}{3}, \dfrac{13}{9}\right)$. The graph shows that the solution is approximately $(6.7, 1.47)$.

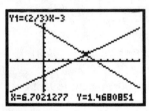

$[-5, 15, 1, -8, 10, 1]$

Use substitution.

| | |
|---|---|
| $y = -\dfrac{5}{6}x + 7$ | Second equation. |
| $\dfrac{2}{3}x - 3 = -\dfrac{5}{6}x + 7$ | Substitute the right side of the first equation for $y$. |
| $\dfrac{3}{2}x = 10$ | Add $\dfrac{5}{6}x$ and 3 to both sides. |
| $x = \dfrac{20}{3} = 6\dfrac{2}{3}$ | Multiply both sides by $\dfrac{2}{3}$. |

Substitute $\dfrac{20}{3}$ for $x$ in either equation to find the value of $y$.

$$y = \dfrac{2}{3}\left(\dfrac{20}{3}\right) - 3 = \dfrac{40 - 27}{9} = \dfrac{13}{9}$$

The solution to this system is $\left(\dfrac{20}{3}, \dfrac{13}{9}\right)$.

**c.** $(-3.36, 9.308)$. The graph shows that the solution is approximately $(-3.3, 9.6)$.

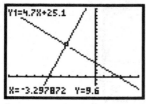

$[-10, 5, 1, -5, 20, 1]$

Use substitution.

| | |
|---|---|
| $3.1x + 2y = 8.2$ | Second equation. |
| $3.1x + 2(4.7x + 25.1) = 8.2$ | Substitute $4.7x + 25.1$ for $y$ in the second equation. |
| $3.1x + 9.4x + 50.2 = 8.2$ | Distribute 2. |
| $12.5x = -42$ | Subtract 50.2 from both sides and combine like terms. |
| $x = -3.36$ | Divide both sides by 12.5. |

Substitute $-3.36$ for $x$ in either equation to find the value of $y$.

$$y = 4.7(-3.36) + 25.1 = 9.308$$

The solution to this system is $(-3.36, 9.308)$.

**d.** $\left(-\frac{45}{59}, -\frac{130}{59}\right)$. Solve both equations for $y$ in terms of $x$: $y = \frac{-6x - 20}{7}$ and $y = \frac{5x - 5}{4}$. Graph these equations and locate the point of intersection at approximately $(-0.74, -2.22)$.

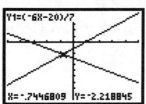

$[-5, 5, 1, -10, 5, 1]$

Solve the system using the elimination method. One approach is to multiply the first equation by 5 and the second equation by $-6$. Add the equations to eliminate $x$ and solve for $y$.

| | |
|---|---|
| $-30x - 35y = 100$ | Multiply both sides of the first equation by 5. |
| $30x - 24y = 30$ | Multiply both sides of the second equation by $-6$. |
| $-59y = 130$ | Add the equations. |
| $y = -\dfrac{130}{59}$ | Divide both sides by $-59$. |

Substitute $-\frac{130}{59}$ for $y$ in either equation to find the value of $x$.

$$-6x - 7\left(-\frac{130}{59}\right) = 20$$
$$-6x = 20 - \frac{910}{59}$$
$$-6x = \frac{1180 - 910}{59}$$
$$-6x = \frac{270}{59}$$
$$x = -\frac{45}{59}$$

The solution to this system is $\left(-\frac{45}{59}, -\frac{130}{59}\right)$.

**e.** $\left(-\frac{1126}{1239}, \frac{146}{59}\right)$. Solve both equations for $y$ in terms of $x$: $y = \frac{7 - 2.1x}{3.6}$ and $y = 8.2 + 6.3x$. Graph these equations and locate the point of intersection at approximately $(-0.96, 2.5)$.

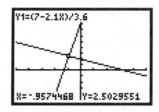

$[-5, 5, 1, -5, 10, 1]$

Solve the system using the elimination method. The easiest choice is to multiply the first equation by 3 and add the equations to eliminate $x$ and solve for $y$.

| | |
|---|---|
| $6.3x + 10.8y = 21$ | Multiply both sides of the first equation by 3. |
| $-6.3x + y = 8.2$ | The second equation. |
| $11.8y = 29.2$ | Add the equations. |
| $y = \dfrac{29.2}{11.8} = \dfrac{292}{118} = \dfrac{146}{59}$ | |

Substitute $\frac{146}{59}$ for $y$ in either equation to find the value of $x$.

$$2.1x + 3.6\left(\frac{146}{59}\right) = 7$$
$$21x + 36\left(\frac{146}{59}\right) = 70$$
$$21x = 70 - \frac{5256}{59}$$
$$21x = \frac{4130 - 5256}{59}$$
$$21x = -\frac{1126}{59}$$
$$x = -\frac{1126}{1239}$$

The solution to this system is $\left(-\frac{1126}{1239}, \frac{146}{59}\right)$.

**5. a.** $\left(-\frac{97}{182}, \frac{19}{7}\right) \approx (-0.5330, 2.7143)$. Add the equations to eliminate $x$ and solve for $y$.

$$\begin{array}{r} 5.2x + 3.6y = 7 \\ -5.2x + 2y = 8.2 \\ \hline 5.6y = 15.2 \end{array}$$

$$y = \frac{152}{56} = \frac{19}{7} \approx 2.7143$$

Substitute $\frac{19}{7}$ for $y$ in either equation to find the value of $x$.

$$5.2x + 3.6\left(\frac{19}{7}\right) = 7$$

$$52x + 36\left(\frac{19}{7}\right) = 70$$

$$52x = \frac{490}{7} - \frac{684}{7}$$

$$52x = -\frac{194}{7}$$

$$x = -\frac{194}{364} = -\frac{97}{182} \approx -0.5330$$

The solution to this system is $\left(-\frac{97}{182}, \frac{19}{7}\right) \approx$ $(-0.5330, 2.7143)$.

**b.** $\left(8, -\frac{5}{2}\right) = (8, -2.5)$. Add the equations to eliminate $y$ and solve for $x$.

$$\begin{array}{r} \frac{1}{4}x - \frac{2}{5}y = 3 \\ \frac{3}{8}x + \frac{2}{5}y = 2 \\ \hline \frac{5}{8}x = 5 \\ x = 8 \end{array}$$

Substitute 8 for $x$ in either equation to find the value of $y$.

$$\frac{1}{4}(8) - \frac{2}{5}y = 3$$

$$-\frac{2}{5}y = 3 - 2$$

$$-\frac{2}{5}y = 1$$

$$y = -\frac{5}{2}$$

The solution to this system is $\left(8, -\frac{5}{2}\right) =$ $(8, -2.5)$.

**c.** $\left(\frac{186}{59}, -\frac{4}{59}\right) \approx (3.1525, -0.0678)$. Multiply the first equation by 8 and the second equation by 9, then add the equations to eliminate the $y$ and solve for $x$.

$$\begin{array}{r} 32x + 72y = 96 \\ 27x - 72y = 90 \\ \hline 59x = 186 \end{array}$$

$$x = \frac{186}{59} \approx 3.1525$$

Substitute $\frac{186}{59}$ for $x$ in either equation to find the value of $y$.

$$4\left(\frac{186}{59}\right) + 9y = 12$$

$$9y = 12 - \frac{744}{59}$$

$$9y = \frac{708 - 744}{59}$$

$$9y = -\frac{36}{59}$$

$$y = -\frac{4}{59} \approx -0.0678$$

The solution to this system is $\left(\frac{186}{59}, -\frac{4}{59}\right) \approx$ $(3.1525, -0.0678)$.

**d.** $n = 26, s = -71$. Substitute $7 - 3n$ for $s$ and solve for $n$.

$$7n + 2(7 - 3n) = 40$$

$$7n + 14 - 6n = 40$$

$$n = 26$$

Substitute 26 for $n$ and find the value of $s$.

$$s = 7 - 3(26) = 7 - 78 = -71$$

The solution to this system is $n = 26$ and $s = -71$.

**e.** $d = -18, f = -49$. Substitute $3d + 5$ for $f$ and solve for $d$.

$$10d - 4(3d + 5) = 16$$

$$10d - 12d - 20 = 16$$

$$-2d = 36$$

$$d = -18$$

Substitute $-18$ for $d$ in either equation to find the value of $f$.

$$f = 3(-18) + 5 = -54 + 5 = -49$$

The solution to this system is $d = -18$ and $f = -49$.

**f.** $\left(\frac{44}{7}, -\frac{95}{14}\right) \approx (6.2857, -6.7857)$. Multiply the second equation by 2 and add the equations to eliminate $y$ and solve for $x$.

$$\begin{array}{r} \frac{1}{4}x - \frac{4}{5}y = 7 \\ \frac{6}{4}x + \frac{4}{5}y = 4 \\ \hline \frac{7}{4}x = 11 \end{array}$$

$$x = \frac{44}{7}$$

Substitute $\frac{44}{7}$ for $x$ in either equation to find the value of $y$.

$$\frac{3}{4}\left(\frac{44}{7}\right) + \frac{2}{5}y = 2$$

$$\frac{33}{7} + \frac{2}{5}y = 2$$

$$\frac{2}{5}y = -\frac{19}{7}$$

$$y = -\frac{95}{14}$$

The solution to this system is $\left(\frac{44}{7}, -\frac{95}{14}\right) \approx$ (6.2857, −6.7857).

**g.** No solution. Multiply the first equation by 1.2 and the second equation by −2, then add the equations to eliminate $y$ and solve for $x$.

$$\begin{array}{r} 2.4x + 3.6y = 4.8 \\ -2.4x - 3.6y = 5.2 \\ \hline 0 = 10 \end{array}$$

This is never true, so there is no solution to this system.

**6. a.** 9. Substitute 6 for $4x + y$ in the expression $(4x + y - 3)^2$. Then $(6 - 3)^2 = 9$.

**b.** 27. Add the two equations.

$$\begin{array}{r} 4x + 3y = 14 \\ 3x - 3y = 13 \\ \hline 7x = 27 \end{array}$$

**7.** 80°F. You are looking for the value of $F$ such that $F = 3C$. Substitute $3C$ for $F$ in the conversion formula.

$$C = \frac{5}{9}(3C - 32)$$

$$9C = 15C - 160$$

$$160 = 6C$$

$$C = \frac{80}{3}$$

$$F = 3C = 3\left(\frac{80}{3}\right) = 80°F$$

**8. a.** Cost for first camera: $y = 47 + 11.5x$; cost for second camera: $y = 59 + 4.95x$

**b.** The $47 camera; the $59 camera. Both equations are in intercept form, so you can find when the cost of the cameras are equal by substituting the right side of the first equation for $y$ in the second equation.

$$47 + 11.5x = 59 + 4.95x$$

$$6.55x = 12$$

$$x \approx 1.83$$

The cost is the same at approximately 2 yr.

**c.** You could graph each cost function and zoom in for the intersection point; you could use substitution to find the intersection point; or you could look at a table to find the point where the cost for both cameras is the same.

**9.** Possible answer: $\begin{cases} y = 3.6 + 2(x + 1.4) \\ y = 3.6 + 3(x + 1.4) \end{cases}$. It is simplest to use point-slope form. You can choose any two slopes.

**10.** $u_{31} = v_{31} = 21$. The first sequence has the equation $y = 11.7 + 0.3x$, and the second sequence has the equation $y = 14.8 + 0.2x$. Using substitution, $11.7 + 0.3x = 14.8 + 0.2x$, so $0.1x = 3.1$, and $x = 31$. For the 31st term, both sequences have the same value, which is $11.7 + 0.3(31) = 21$.

**11.** Solve for one variable and substitute.

**a.** $s = \frac{d}{\sqrt{2}}$, so $A = \left(\frac{d}{\sqrt{2}}\right)^2 = \frac{d^2}{2}$

**b.** $P = I(IR) = I^2R$

**c.** $r = \frac{C}{2\pi}$, so $A = \pi\left(\frac{C}{2\pi}\right)^2 = \frac{C^2}{4\pi}$

**12. a.** The fulcrum should be 16 in. from the 9 lb weight. $x + y = 40$ and $6x = 9y$. Solve the first equation for $x$: $x = 40 - y$. Substitute $40 - y$ for $x$ in the second equation and solve for $y$: $6(40 - y) = 9y$, so $240 - 6y = 9y$, $15y = 240$, and $y = 16$.

**b.** Justin weighs 100 lb and Alden weighs 80 lb.

$8J + 5A = 8(150)$ and $8A + 5.6J = 8(150)$. Solve for $A$ in the first equation: $A = \frac{1200 - 8J}{5}$. Substitute $\frac{1200 - 8J}{5}$ for $A$ in the second equation and solve.

$$8\left(\frac{1200 - 8J}{5}\right) + 5.6J = 1200$$

$$\frac{9600 - 64J}{5} + 5.6J = 1200$$

$$-36J = -3600$$

$$J = 100$$

Substitute 100 for $J$ in either equation and solve.

$$8A + 5.6(100) = 8(150)$$

$$8A + 560 = 1200$$

$$8A = 640$$

$$A = 80$$

**13. a.** True

**b.** False; $x^2 - 16 = (x - 4)(x + 4)$

**14. a.** $y = \dfrac{7 - 3x}{2} = \dfrac{7}{2} - \dfrac{3}{2}x = 3.5 - 1.5x$

**b.**

**c.** $-\dfrac{3}{2}$, or $-1.5$

**d.** $\dfrac{7}{2}$, or $3.5$

**e.** $slope = -\left(-\dfrac{2}{3}\right) = \dfrac{2}{3}$, so $y = \dfrac{7}{2} + \dfrac{2}{3}x$

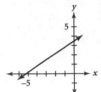

**15. a.**

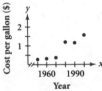

**b.** The median-median line is $\hat{y} = \dfrac{213}{8000}x - 51.78$, or $\hat{y} = 0.0266x - 51.78$.

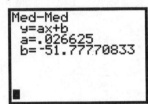

```
Med-Med
 y=ax+b
  a=.026625
  b=-51.77770833
```

**c.** If the same trend continues, the cost of gasoline in 2010 will be $\dfrac{213}{8000}(2010) - 51.78 \approx \$1.74$. It is best to use the equation with the nonrounded slope. If you use the equation with slope 0.0266, you will get $1.69. Possible answer: It's not likely that the cost of gasoline will continue in a linear pattern. Shortages and surpluses have a strong effect on gasoline prices.

**16. a.**

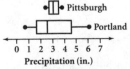

**b.** Pittsburgh: 2.4, 2.7, 3.05, 3.5, 3.8; Portland: 0.7, 1.65, 2.55, 4.6, 6.1

**c.** Sample answer: Pittsburgh has rather constant precipitation all year. Outdoor activities appropriate for one time of the year can be suitable

at any time if precipitation is the only consideration. (Of course, temperature may be a factor also.) Portland has a wet and a dry season. Wet and dry seasons affect outdoor activities like picnics, hiking, and outdoor sports. The wet season may bring floods and mud. The dry season may present fire concerns and concerns about drinking-water shortages.

**d.** Pittsburgh. Pittsburgh has a normal annual precipitation of 36.9 in. in comparison with Portland's 36.6 in.

**17. a.  i.** 768, $-1024$. Multiply each term by $-\dfrac{4}{3}$ to find the next term.

**ii.** 52, 61. The difference between consecutive terms increases by 1 each time.

**iii.** 32.75, 34.5. Add 1.75 to each term to find the next term.

**b.  i.** Geometric

**ii.** Other

**iii.** Arithmetic

**c.  i.** $u_1 = 243$ and $u_n = -\dfrac{4}{3}u_{n-1}$ where $n \geq 2$

**iii.** $u_1 = 24$ and $u_n = u_{n-1} + 1.75$ where $n \geq 2$

**d. iii.** $u_n = 1.75n + 22.25$

**18.** No, they don't qualify because $s \approx 0.059$ m.

### EXTENSIONS

**A.** See the solution to Take Another Look activity 3 on pages 53 and 54.

**B.** Results will vary. See Calculator Note 6D for the row commands on a calculator.

**C.** Results will vary.

## CHAPTER 3 REVIEW

### EXERCISES

**1.** $slope = \dfrac{3250 - 1300}{-22 - 16} = \dfrac{1950}{-38} = -\dfrac{975}{19}$

**2. a.** 23.45

**b.** Possible answer: $y = 23.45x$. Slope must be 23.45.

**c.** Possible answer: $y = -0.0426x$. Slope must be $-\left(\dfrac{1}{23.45}\right) \approx -0.0426$.

**3. a.** Approximately $(19.9, 740.0)$. $740 = 16.8x + 405$, so $16.8x = 335$, and $x \approx 19.9$.

**b.** Approximately $(177.01, 740.0)$. $740 = -7.4x + 4.3(x - 3.2)$, so $740 = -7.4 + 4.3x - 13.76$, $4.3x = 761.16$, and $x \approx 177.01$.

**4. a.** $3.2x - 4 = 3.1x - 3$. $0.1x = 1$, so $x = 10$.

**b.** $0 = 0.1x - 1$. $0.1x = 1$, and $x = 10$.

**c.** 4a uses the method of substitution to solve a system of equations, whereas 4b uses elimination. The lines intersect at only one place, so the system has only one solution.

**5. a.** Poor fit; there are too many points above the line.

  **b.** Reasonably good fit; the points are well-distributed above and below the line, and not clumped. The line follows the downward trend of the data.

  **c.** Poor fit; there are an equal number of points above and below the line, but they are clumped to the left and to the right, respectively. The line does not follow the trend of the data.

**6. a.** $\left(-\frac{110}{83}, \frac{4226}{415}\right) \approx (-1.3253, 10.1831)$. Substitute $6.2x + 18.4$ for $y$ in the second equation and solve for $x$: $6.2x + 18.4 = -2.1x + 7.40$, so $8.3x = -11$, and $x = -\frac{110}{83}$. Substitute $-\frac{110}{83}$ for $x$ in either equation to find the value of $y$:
$y = 6.2\left(-\frac{110}{83}\right) + 18.4 = \frac{-682 + 1527.2}{83} = \frac{845.2}{83} = \frac{4226}{415}$.

The solution to this system is $\left(-\frac{110}{83}, \frac{4226}{415}\right) \approx (-1.3253, 10.1831)$.

  **b.** $\left(\frac{42}{5}, \frac{53}{10}\right) = (8.4, 5.3)$. Substitute $\frac{3}{4}x - 1$ for $y$ in the second equation and solve for $x$.

$$\frac{7}{10}x + \frac{2}{5}\left(\frac{3}{4}x - 1\right) = 8$$
$$\frac{7}{10}x + \frac{3}{10}x - \frac{2}{5} = 8$$
$$x = \frac{10}{10}x = 8 + \frac{2}{5}$$
$$x = \frac{42}{5} = 8.4$$

Substitute 8.4 for $x$ and find the value of $y$:
$y = \frac{3}{4}(8.4) - 1 = 5.3$ or $\frac{53}{10}$. The solution to this system is $\left(\frac{42}{5}, \frac{53}{10}\right) = (8.4, 5.3)$.

  **c.** $\left(\frac{2}{3}, 1\right) = (0.\overline{6}, 1)$. Add the equations to eliminate $x$ and solve for $y$: $7y = 7$, so $y = 1$. Substitute 1 for $y$ in either equation to find the value of $x$: $3x + 2(1) = 4$, so $3x = 2$, and $x = \frac{2}{3}$. The solution to this system is $\left(\frac{2}{3}, 1\right) = (0.\overline{6}, 1)$.

**7. a.** $(1, 0)$. Divide the second equation by 2 and solve for $x$: $x + 5y = 1$, so $x = 1 - 5y$. Next, substitute $1 - 5y$ for $x$ in the first equation: $5(1 - 5y) - 4y = 5$, so $5 - 25y - 4y = 5$, $21y = 0$, and $y = 0$. Substitute 0 for $y$ in either equation to find the value of $x$. $5x - 4(0) = 5$, so $5x = 5$, and $x = 1$. The point of intersection is $(1, 0)$.

  **b.** Apply the distributive property in the first equation and evaluate to get $y = \frac{1}{4}x - 2 + 5 = \frac{1}{4}x + 3$. This is the same line as the second equation, so they intersect at every point.

  **c.** Rewrite both equations in intercept form. The lines have the same slope and different $y$-intercepts.

$$\begin{cases} y = -\frac{15}{2} + \frac{3}{2}x \\ y = 7.5 + 1.5x \end{cases}$$

Therefore, there is no point of intersection and the lines are parallel.

**8. a.** The ratio 0.38 represents the slope; that is, for each pound on Earth, you would weigh 0.38 pound on Mercury.

  **b.** $m = 0.38(160) = 60.8$. The student's weight on Mercury would be about 60.8 lb.

  **c.** Moon: D, $y_1 = 0.17x$; Mercury: C, $y_2 = 0.38x$; Earth: B, $y_3 = x$; Jupiter: A, $y_4 = 2.5x$. Larger ratios correspond to larger slopes of lines.

**9. a.**

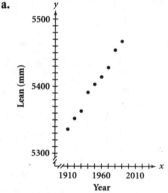

  **b.** $\hat{y} = 2088 + 1.7x$. The three summary points are $M_1(1920, 5352)$, $M_2(1950, 5403)$, and $M_3(1980, 5454)$.

The slope of the line through $M_1$ and $M_3$ is $\frac{5454 - 5352}{1980 - 1920} = 1.7$, so the equation of this line is $y = 5454 + 1.7(x - 1980)$, or $y = 2088 + 1.7x$. The equation of the parallel line through $M_2$ is $y = 5403 + 1.7(x - 1950)$, or $y = 2088 + 1.7x$. Therefore the equation of the median-median line is $\hat{y} = 2088 + 1.7x$.

  **c.** 1.7. For every additional year, the tower leans another 1.7 mm.

  **d.** $\hat{y} = 2088 + 1.7(1992) = 5474.4$ mm

  **e.** $s = \sqrt{\frac{195}{7}} \approx 5.3$ mm. The prediction in 9d is probably accurate within 5.3 mm. In other words, the actual value will probably be between 5469.1 and 5479.1.

  **f.** $1173 \le$ domain $\le 1992$ (year built to year retrofit began); $0 \le$ range $\le 5474.4$ mm

**10.** $u_{23} = 16.5$. First, find the common difference: $d = \frac{u_{54} - u_4}{54 - 4} = \frac{-61 - 64}{54 - 4} = -2.5$. Next, use the fourth term and the common difference to find the zero term in the sequence, $u_0 = 64 - 4(-2.5) = 74$. Finally, $u_{23} = 74 - 2.5(23) = 16.5$. Or, $u_{23} = 61 - 31(-2.5) = 16.5$.

**11. a.** Geometric because there is a common ratio; curved because the common ratio is 3; 4, 12, 36, 108, 324

 **b.** Shifted geometric because there is a common ratio and a common difference; curved because the common ratio is 2; 20, 47, 101, 209, 425

**12. a.** $u_0 = 500$ and $u_n = (1 + 0.059)u_{n-1}$ where $n \geq 1$

 **b.** 500, 529.50, 560.74. $u_0 = 500$, $u_1 = (1.059)(500) = 529.50$, and $u_2 = (1.059)(529.50) = 560.74$.

 **c.** The amount in the account after 3 years

 **d.** $u_{35} = \$3718.16$

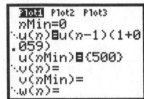

 **e.** $u_{35} = \$14,627.20$. The new recursive formula is $u_0 = 500$ and $u_n = (1 + 0.059)u_{n-1} + 100$ where $n \geq 1$.

**13. a.** Possible answer: $u_{2005} = 6{,}486{,}915{,}022$ and $u_n = (1 + 0.015)u_{n-1}$ where $n \geq 2006$. The sequence is geometric.

 **b.** Possible answer: $u_{2010} = 6{,}988{,}249{,}788$ people

 **c.** On January 1, 2035, the population will be just above 10 billion. So the population will first exceed 10 billion in late 2034.

 **d.** Sample answer: An increasing geometric sequence has no limit. The model will not work for the distant future because there is a physical limit to how many people will fit on Earth.

**14.** $u_0 = 25$ mg, $u_1 = 37.5$ mg, $u_2 = 43.75$ mg, $u_3 = 46.875$ mg, $u_4 = 48.4375$ mg. Using the equation $u_n = 25 + 0.5u_{n-1}$, replace the variables with $c$ to find the long-run amount of antibiotics remaining: $c = 25 + 0.5c$, so $0.5c = 25$, and $c = 50$. In the long run, he'll have about 50 mg of the antibiotic in his body.

**15.**

 0  5  10  15  20

 **a.** Skewed left      **b.** 12

 **c.** $IQR = 13 - 7 = 6$      **d.** 50%; 25%; 0%

**16. a.** $\bar{x} = 5.074$, $median = 4.6$, $mode = 4.5$, $s = 1.734$

 **b.** Louisiana lies more than 2 standard deviations above the mean.

 **c.** High School Dropout Rates, 1998–1999

 Number of states — Dropout rate

**17. a.** $\left(\frac{110}{71}, -\frac{53}{213}\right) \approx (1.5493, -0.2488)$. Add the equations to eliminate $y$ and solve for $x$.

 $$7.1x = 11$$
 $$x = \frac{11}{7.1} = \frac{110}{71}$$

 Substitute $\frac{110}{71}$ for $x$ in either equation to find the value of $y$.

 $$2.1\left(\frac{110}{71}\right) - 3y = 4$$
 $$3y = \frac{231}{71} - 4$$
 $$y = \frac{77}{71} - \frac{4}{3} = \frac{231 - 284}{213} = -\frac{53}{213}$$

 The solution to this system is $\left(\frac{110}{71}, -\frac{53}{213}\right) \approx (1.5493, -0.2488)$.

 **b.** $\left(-\frac{27}{20}, \frac{91}{20}\right) = (-1.35, 4.55)$. Substitute $\frac{1}{3}x + 5$ for $y$ in the second equation and solve for $x$.

 $$\frac{1}{3}x + 5 = -3x + \frac{1}{2}$$
 $$\frac{10}{3}x = -\frac{9}{2}$$
 $$x = -\frac{27}{20} = -1.35$$

 Substitute $-\frac{27}{20}$ for $x$ in either equation to find the value of $y$.

 $$y = \frac{1}{3}\left(-\frac{27}{20}\right) + 5 = -\frac{9}{20} + 5 = \frac{-9 + 100}{20}$$
 $$= \frac{91}{20}$$

 The solution to this system is $\left(-\frac{27}{20}, \frac{91}{20}\right) = (-1.35, 4.55)$.

 **c.** $\left(\frac{46}{13}, \frac{9}{26}\right) \approx (3.5385, 0.3462)$. Multiply the first equation by 2 and the second equation by $-3$. Then add the equations to eliminate the $x$ and solve for $y$.

 $$\begin{aligned} 6x + 8y &= 24 \\ -6x + 18y &= -15 \\ \hline 26y &= 9 \end{aligned}$$
 $$y = \frac{9}{26} \approx 0.3462$$

*Discovering Advanced Algebra Solutions Manual*
©2004 Key Curriculum Press

Substitute $\frac{9}{26}$ for $y$ in either equation to find the value of $x$.

$$3x + 4\left(\frac{9}{26}\right) = 12$$

$$3x = 12 - \frac{18}{13}$$

$$x = 4 - \frac{6}{13} = \frac{52 - 6}{13} = \frac{46}{13} \approx 3.5385$$

The solution to this system is $\left(\frac{46}{13}, \frac{9}{26}\right) \approx$ (3.5385, 0.3462).

**18. a.** The data may be linear.

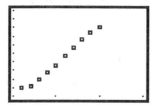

[1970, 2000, 10, 20, 25, 0.5]

**b.** $\hat{y} = -416.5333 + 0.2214x$. For the following, use the full unrounded slope. The three summary points for the data are $M_1$(1974, 20.6), $M_2$(1981, 22.05), and $M_3$(1988, 23.7). The slope of the line between $M_1$ and $M_3$, which is the slope of the median-median line, is $\frac{23.7 - 20.6}{1988 - 1974} \approx$ 0.2214. The equation of the line through $M_1$ and $M_3$ is $y = 23.7 + 0.2214(x - 1988)$, or $y = -416.5 + 0.2214x$. The parallel line through $M_2$ is $y = 22.05 + 0.2214(x - 1981)$, or $y = -416.6 + 0.2214x$.

The mean of the three $y$-intercepts is $\frac{-416.5 + (-416.5) + (-416.6)}{3} = -416.5333$. The median-median line is $\hat{y} = -416.5333 + 0.2214x$.

**c.** $\hat{y} = -416.5333 + 0.2214(2000) = 26.2667$; about 26.27 years old

**d.** $\hat{y} = -416.5333 + 0.2214(2100) = 48.4007$; about 48.41 years old. This is probably not realistic.

**e.** *(See table at bottom of page.)*

$s \approx 0.14$. This means that ages predicted by this equation are generally within 0.14 yr of the actual age.

**19. a.** $u_1 = 6$ and $u_n = u_{n-1} + 7$ where $n \geq 1$

**b.** $y = 6 + 7x$

**c.** The slope is 7. The slope of the line is the same as the common difference of the sequence.

**d.** $y = 6 + 7(32) = 230$. The first term is $u_1$, so the 32nd term is $u_{32}$. It is probably easier to use the equation from 19b.

**20. a.** $d = \frac{52.5 - 12}{10 - 1} = 4.5$

**b.** The slope is $\frac{52.5 - 12}{10 - 1} = 4.5$, so $y = 12 + 4.5(x - 1)$, or $y = 7.5 + 4.5x$.

**c.** The slope of the line is equal to the common difference of the sequence.

**TAKE ANOTHER LOOK**

**1.** The *centroid* $(\bar{x}, \bar{y})$ is (5, 28) because $\bar{x} = \frac{5 + 2 + 8}{3} = 5$ and $\bar{y} = \frac{11 + 32 + 41}{3} = 28$. The three representative points will always form a triangle unless all the data points are collinear. The median-median line has the equation $\hat{y} - 28 = 5(x - 5)$, or $\hat{y} = 5x + 3$. This line is the same as the parallel line through the centroid.

**2.** The median-median line, with equation $\hat{y} = 0.08326x - 162.02993$, does not fit the data well. A better model might be a piecewise function such as $\hat{y} = 0.01784x - 34.31991$ where $1935 \leq x \leq 1958$, $\hat{y} = 0.11947x - 233.70649$ where $1963 \leq x \leq 1990$, and $\hat{y} = 0.22143x - 437.53048$ where $1994 \leq x \leq 2010$. The third line of the piecewise function would predict the price of a ticket in 2010 better than any single line for all the data.

Perhaps a curve would fit the data better. A quadratic, logistic, or exponential function might be a better model than a linear or even a piecewise linear model. The data are not modeled best by a single linear equation because inflation is not linear.

**3.** $(\sqrt{2}, -2)$ and $(-\sqrt{2}, -2)$. First, graph the two equations. From the graph, it appears that the two parabolas intersect at $(-1.4, -2.04)$ and $(1.4, -2.04)$.

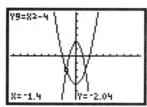

[−9.4, 9.4, 1, −6.2, 6.2, 1]

**Chapter 3 Review, Exercise 18e**

| Year | 1972 | 1974 | 1976 | 1978 | 1980 | 1982 | 1984 | 1986 | 1988 | 1990 |
|---|---|---|---|---|---|---|---|---|---|---|
| **Age** | 20.5 | 20.6 | 21.0 | 21.4 | 21.8 | 22.3 | 22.8 | 23.3 | 23.7 | 24.0 |
| **Age predicted by line** $\hat{y} = -416.5333 + 0.2214x$ | 20.124 | 20.567 | 21.01 | 21.452 | 21.895 | 22.338 | 22.781 | 23.224 | 23.667 | 24.110 |
| **Residual** | 0.376 | 0.033 | −0.01 | −0.052 | −0.095 | −0.038 | 0.019 | 0.076 | 0.033 | −0.110 |

Next, solve the system by substituting $x^2 - 4$ for $y$ in the second equation.

$$x^2 - 4 = -2x^2 + 2$$
$$3x^2 = 6$$
$$x^2 = 2$$
$$x = \pm\sqrt{2}$$

Substitute $\pm\sqrt{2}$ for $x$ in either equation.

$$y = \left(\pm\sqrt{2}\right)^2 - 4$$
$$y = -2$$

Finally, solve by elimination. Multiply the first equation by 2 and add the two equations.

$$2y = 2x^2 - 8$$
$$\underline{y = -2x^2 + 2}$$
$$3y = -6$$
$$y = -2$$

Now substitute $-2$ for $y$ in either equation.

$$-2 = x^2 - 4$$
$$x^2 = 2$$
$$x = \pm\sqrt{2}$$

The two algebraic methods arrived at the same answer, $\left(\pm\sqrt{2}, -2\right)$. The graphing method arrived at a very similar answer, $(\pm1.4, -2.04)$; it is difficult to be as accurate with graphing. The process is almost the same as with linear equations; the main difference is that there are two answers. The simplest method for this system is substitution. In other systems, elimination might be easier, especially if the equations aren't in intercept form.

# CHAPTER 4

## LESSON 4.1

### EXERCISES

1. a. The slope of the graph is positive throughout, starting small and then getting larger as the rate of change increases.

   b. The slope is negative, then more negative resulting in a curved graph, then suddenly the graph is horizontal as the slope becomes constant.

c. The slope of the graph oscillates between positive and negative. The graph is curved where the slope gradually changes from positive to negative.

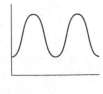

2. a. The graph decreases at a steady rate, suddenly becomes constant, and then suddenly increases at the same rate as before.

   b. The graph gradually decreases at an increasing rate, and then decreases more slowly until constant. Next, the graph increases at the same rates it was decreasing before; finally it levels off.

   c. The graph rapidly increases from zero, suddenly changes to rapidly decreasing until half the value is reached, and then suddenly becomes constant. It then suddenly rapidly decreases at a constant rate until reaching zero.

3. a. A. The slope is increasing at a faster and faster rate.

   b. C. The slope is positive but is getting smaller and smaller.

   c. D. The slope is decreasing at a faster and faster rate.

   d. B. The slope is negative but is getting larger.

4. a. Possible answer: The curve might describe the relationship between the amount of time the ball is in the air and how far away it is from the ground.

   b. Possible answer: seconds and feet

   c. Possible answer: domain: $0 \le t \le 10$ s; range: $0 \le h \le 200$ ft

   d. No, the horizontal distance traveled is not measured.

5. Sample answer: Zeke, the fish, swam slowly, then more rapidly to the bottom of his bowl and stayed there for a while. When Zeke's owner sprinkled fish food into the water, Zeke swam toward the surface to eat. The $y$-intercept represents the fish's depth at the start of the story. The $x$-intercept represents the time the fish reached the surface of the bowl.

6. a. Time in seconds is the independent variable, and the height of the basketball in feet is the dependent variable. The basketball is being dribbled toward the basket, a shot is made, and the basketball successfully passes

   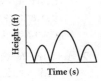

through the net and then hits the floor. The basketball rebounds at a decreased height before it hits the floor again.

**b.** The car's speed in miles per hour is the independent variable, and the braking distance in feet is the dependent variable. The faster the speed of the car, the longer braking distance is necessary for the car to come to a complete stop.

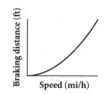

**c.** Time in minutes is the independent variable, and the drink's temperature in degrees Fahrenheit is the dependent variable. The initial temperature of the iced drink is below room temperature. The temperature of the drink increases slowly at first, then more rapidly, and then increases steadily until it reaches room temperature.

**d.** Time in seconds is the independent variable, and the acorn's speed in feet per second is the dependent variable. The acorn dropped from an oak tree picks up speed slowly at first until it is increasing at a steady rate before it hits the ground.

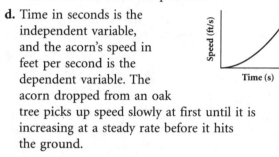

**e.** Time in minutes is the independent variable, and your height above the ground in feet is the dependent variable. When you first begin your ride on the Ferris wheel, you move a constant height above the ground at the base of the rotation, steadily increasing your height from the ground as the Ferris wheel rotates in counterclockwise direction. At frequent intervals new people get on the ride at which time the Ferris wheel stops momentarily. At the peak of the ride or at the top of the rotation, you move at a constant height from the ground briefly before your descent, decreasing your height in the same pattern as you did going up until you have completed one full rotation on the Ferris wheel.

**7. a.** Time in years is the independent variable, and the amount of money in dollars is the dependent variable. The graph will be a series of discontinuous segments.

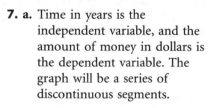

The money in your savings account is compounded only once a year, so the balance will remain constant each year until the new interest is added.

**b.** Time in years is the independent variable, and the amount of money in dollars is the dependent variable. The graph will be a continuous horizontal segment because the amount never changes.

**c.** Foot length in inches is the independent variable, and shoe size is the dependent variable. The graph will be a series of discontinuous horizontal segments because shoe sizes are discrete, not continuous.

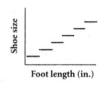

**d.** Time in hours is the independent variable, and distance in miles is the dependent variable. The graph will be continuous because the distance the airplane is from Detroit is changing continuously over time. The plane's distance from Detroit increases at a constant rate as the plane flies directly toward Newark, then gradually alternates between decreasing and increasing as the plane circles the airport.

**e.** The day of the month is the independent variable, and the maximum temperature in degrees Fahrenheit is the dependent variable. The graph will be discrete points because there is only one daily maximum temperature per day.

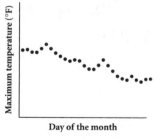

**8.** Sample answer: The cost of parking your car at a lot that charges a certain fixed price for up to an hour and then half as much for each additional hour or fraction thereof.

**9. a.** Car A speeds up quickly at first and then less quickly until it reaches 60 mi/h. Car B speeds up slowly at first and then quickly until it reaches 60 mi/h.

**b.** Car A will be in the lead because it is always going faster than Car B, which means it has covered more distance.

**10. a.** $l = 1.70 - 0.12k$. Let $l$ represent the length of the rope in meters, and let $k$ represent the number of knots. The number of knots is the independent variable, and the length of the rope is the dependent variable. The $y$-intercept is 1.70 and the slope is $-0.12$. Therefore the equation for the line that fits the situation is $l = 1.70 - 0.12k$.

**b.** $b = 7.00 + 9.50(c - 8)$ where $c \geq 8$. Let $b$ represent the bill in dollars, and let $c$ represent the number of CDs purchased. The number of CDs purchased is the independent variable, and the bill in dollars is the dependent variable. The slope is 9.50 and because $b = 7.00$ when $c = 8$, the first point on the graph is $(8, 7.00)$. Therefore the equation for the line that fits the situation is $b = 7.00 + 9.50(c - 8)$ where the domain of the function is $c \geq 8$.

**11. a.** $y = 155 + 15x$. Let $x$ represent the number of pictures, and let $y$ represent the amount of money (either cost or income) in dollars. The number of pictures is the independent variable, and the amount of money is the dependent variable. The $y$-intercept is 155 and the slope is 15, so $y = 155 + 15x$.

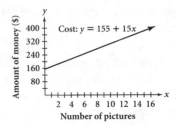

**b.** Albert's income will be $27 per picture sold, so $y = 27x$.

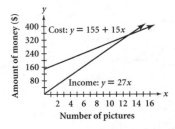

**c.** 13 pictures. One way to solve this problem is to locate the point of intersection of the cost and income equations. Once the income line is above the cost line, the next integer value on the $x$-axis is 13. You can also solve the problem using algebra. Solve the system of equations.

| | |
|---|---|
| $y = 155 + 15x$ | First equation. |
| $y = 27x$ | Second equation. |
| $27x = 155 + 15x$ | Substitute $27x$ for $y$ in the first equation. |
| $12x = 155$ | Subtract $15x$ from both sides. |
| $x = \dfrac{155}{12} = 12.91\overline{6}$ | Divide both sides by 12. |

Albert breaks even at $12.91\overline{6}$ pictures, so he needs to sell 13 pictures before he makes a profit.

**12. a.** $142,784.22$. The recursive formula is $u_0 = 200{,}000$ and $u_n = u_{n-1}\left(1 + \dfrac{0.065}{12}\right) - 1200$ where $n \geq 1$. Because interest is compounded 12 times yearly over 20 years, find $u(20 \cdot 12)$, or $u(240)$, which is 142,784.22.

**b.** $44,700.04$. The new recursive formula is $u_0 = 200{,}000$ and $u_n = u_{n-1}\left(1 + \dfrac{0.065}{12}\right) - 1400$ where $n \geq 1$. $u(240) = 44{,}700.04$. After 20 years, the balance remaining is $44,700.04.

**c.** The balance is $0. Adjust your recursive formula to $u_0 = 200{,}000$ and $u_n = u_{n-1}\left(1 + \dfrac{0.065}{12}\right) - 1500$ where $n \geq 1$. $u(240) = -\$4342.05$. The result is negative, so the loan balance is $0. (You actually pay off the loan after 19 yr 9 mo.)

**d.** Increasing your monthly payments from $1200 to $1500, an extra $300 per month for 20 years, or $72,000, saves hundreds of thousands of dollars in the long run.

**13. a.** $3x + 5y = -9$. Add Equation 1 and Equation 2 to eliminate $z$.

| | |
|---|---|
| $2x + 3y - 4z = -9$ | Equation 1. |
| $\underline{x + 2y + 4z = \phantom{-}0}$ | Equation 2. |
| $3x + 5y \phantom{- 4z} = -9$ | Add the equations. |

**b.** $6x - 3y = 21$. Multiply Equation 3 by 2 and then add it to Equation 1 to eliminate $z$.

| | |
|---|---|
| $4x - 6y + 4z = \phantom{-}30$ | Multiply Equation 3 by 2. |
| $\underline{2x + 3y - 4z = -9}$ | Equation 1. |
| $6x - 3y \phantom{- 4z} = \phantom{-}21$ | Add the equations. |

**c.** $x = 2$, $y = -3$. Multiply the resulting equation from 13a by $-2$, and then add it to the resulting equation from 13b to eliminate $x$ and solve for $y$.

| | |
|---|---|
| $-6x - 10y = 18$ | Multiply the equation from 13a by $-2$. |
| $\underline{\phantom{-}6x - \phantom{1}3y = 21}$ | Equation from 13b. |
| $-13y = 39$ | Add the equations. |
| $y = -3$ | Divide both sides by $-13$. |

*Discovering Advanced Algebra Solutions Manual*
©2004 Key Curriculum Press

Substitute $-3$ for $y$ in either of the equations from 13a or b and solve for $x$.

$$3x + 5(-3) = -9$$
$$3x - 15 = -9$$
$$3x = 6$$
$$x = 2$$

Therefore, $x = 2$ and $y = -3$.

**d.** $x = 2$, $y = -3$, $z = 1$. Substitute 2 for $x$ and $-3$ for $y$ in one of the original three equations and solve for $z$.

$$2 + 2(-3) + 4z = 0 \quad \text{Substitute 2 for } x \text{ and } -3 \text{ for } y \text{ in Equation 1.}$$
$$-4 + 4z = 0 \quad \text{Combine terms.}$$
$$4z = 4 \quad \text{Add 4 to both sides.}$$
$$z = 1 \quad \text{Divide both sides by 4.}$$

Therefore, $x = 2$, $y = -3$, and $z = 1$.

## LESSON 4.2

### EXERCISES

**1. a.** Function. No vertical line crosses the graph more than once; that is, each $x$-value corresponds to only one $y$-value.

**b.** Not a function. A vertical line crosses the graph more than once (at two points); that is, there are $x$-values that correspond to two $y$-values.

**c.** Function. No vertical line crosses the graph more than once; that is, each $x$-value corresponds to only one $y$-value.

**2. a.** $f(7) = 3(7) - 4 = 21 - 4 = 17$

**b.** $g(5) = (5)^2 + 2 = 25 + 2 = 27$

**c.** $f(-5) = 3(-5) - 4 = -15 - 4 = -19$

**d.** $g(-3) = (-3)^2 + 2 = 9 + 2 = 11$

**e.** $7 = 3x - 4$, so $3x = 11$, and $x = \frac{11}{3}$

**3.** B, $m(x) = 42 + 0.03x$. The $y$-intercept is 8(5.25), or 42, and the slope is 0.03, so the function that describes Miguel's earnings is $m(x) = 8(5.25) + 0.03x$, or $m(x) = 42 + 0.03x$.

**4.** René Descartes

**a.** $f(13) = 18 = R$

**b.** $f(25) + f(26) = 2 + 3 = 5 = E$

**c.** $2f(22) = 2 \cdot 7 = 14 = N$

**d.** $\dfrac{f(3) + 11}{\sqrt{f(3 + 1)}} = \dfrac{f(3) + 11}{\sqrt{f(4)}} = \dfrac{9 + 11}{\sqrt{16}} = \dfrac{20}{4} = 5 = E$

**e.** $\dfrac{f(1 + 4)}{f(1) + 4} - \dfrac{1}{4}\left(\dfrac{4}{f(1)}\right) = \dfrac{f(5)}{f(1) + 4} - \dfrac{1}{f(1)} =$

$\dfrac{25}{1 + 4} - \dfrac{1}{1} = 5 - 1 = 4 = D$

**f.** $f(6) = 26$, so $x + 1 = 6$, and $x = 5 = E$

**g.** $\sqrt[3]{f(21)} + f(14) = \sqrt[3]{8} + 17 = 2 + 17 = 19 = S$

**h.** $2f(x + 3) = 52$, so $f(x + 3) = 26$. Because $f(6) = 26$, $x + 3 = 6$, and $x = 3 = C$.

**i.** $f(2) = 4$, so $2x = 2$, and $x = 1 = A$

**j.** $f(f(2) + f(3)) = f(4 + 9) = f(13) = 18 = R$

**k.** $f(9) - f(25) = 22 - 2 = 20 = T$

**l.** $f(f(5) - f(1)) = f(25 - 1) = f(24) = 5 = E$

**m.** $f(4 \cdot 6) - f(4 \cdot 4) = f(24) - f(16) = 5 + 14 = 19 = S$

**5. a.** The tax depends on the price of the calculator, so the price of the graphing calculator is the independent variable. There cannot be two different amounts of sales tax for the same price, so the relation is a function.

**b.** The amount of money in your account depends on how long it is in the bank, so the time it is in the bank is the independent variable. You cannot have two different balances at the same time, so the relation is a function.

**c.** The length of your hair depends on how long it has been since you last got it cut, so the amount of time since your last haircut is the independent variable. At any moment in time, you will have a distinct length of hair, so the relation is a function.

**d.** The amount of gas in your tank depends on how far you drive, so the distance you have driven since your last fill-up is the independent variable. After driving a given distance, you can have only one gas level, so the relation is a function.

**6. a.** Let $x$ represent the price of the calculator in dollars, and let $y$ represent the sales tax in dollars.

**b.** Let $x$ represent the time in months, and let $y$ represent the account balance in dollars.

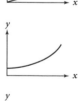

**c.** Let $x$ represent the time in days, and let $y$ represent the length of your hair.

**d.** Let $x$ represent the distance you have driven in miles, and let $y$ represent the amount of gasoline in your tank in gallons.

**7. a.** The slope is $-0.6$ and the $y$-intercept is 25. Use the slope and the $y$-intercept to sketch the graph.

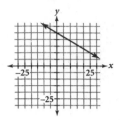

**b.** $f(7) = 25 - 0.6(7) = 20.8$

**c.**

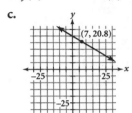

**d.** $27.4 = -0.6x + 25$, so $2.4 = -0.6x$, and $x = -4$.

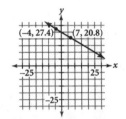

**8.** Domain: $-6 \le x \le 5$; range: $-2 \le y \le 4$

**9. a.** Possible answer:

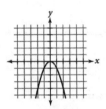

**b.** Possible answer:

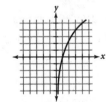

**c.**

**10. a.** $f(5) = 3(5 + 1)^2 - 4 = 3(6)^2 - 4 = 3(36) - 4 = 104$

**b.** $f(n) = 3(n + 1)^2 - 4$

**c.** $f(x + 2) = 3(x + 2 + 1)^2 - 4 = 3(x + 3)^2 - 4$

**d.**

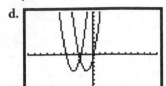

$[-10, 10, 1, -10, 10, 1]$

The graphs are the same shape (upward-facing parabolas). The graph of $f(x + 2)$ is translated 2 units to the left of the graph of $f(x)$.

**11.** Let $x$ represent the time since Kendall started moving, and let $y$ represent his distance from the motion sensor. The graph is a function. Kendall can be at only one position at each moment in time, so there is only one $y$-value for each $x$-value.

**12. a.** $L = 9.73(4)^2 = 155.68$ in.

**b.** Its period is approximately 16.5 seconds. $220(12) = 9.73t^2$, so $t^2 = \frac{2640}{9.73}$, and $t \approx 16.5$ s.

**13. a.** $d = \frac{12(12 - 3)}{2} = \frac{108}{2} = 54$ diagonals

**b.** 20 sides.

| | |
|---|---|
| $170 = \dfrac{n(n - 3)}{2}$ | Substitute 170 for $d$. |
| $340 = n(n - 3)$ | Multiply both sides by 2. |
| $340 = n^2 - 3n$ | Distribute. |
| $n^2 - 3n - 340 = 0$ | Subtract 340 from both sides. |
| $(n + 17)(n - 20) = 0$ | Factor. |
| $n = -17$ or $n = 20$ | Zero product property. |

It is impossible to have a negative number of sides, so the polygon would have 20 sides.

**14. a.** The bottle is cylindrical, so the water height increases at a steady rate.

**b.** The bottle has a spherical base and a cylindrical stem, so the water height increases quickly at first, then more slowly as water moves to the larger circumference

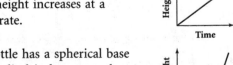

*Discovering Advanced Algebra Solutions Manual*
©2004 Key Curriculum Press

of the sphere. The water height again increases quickly as it gets to the top of the sphere, then more rapidly and at a steady rate at the cylindrical stem.

c. The bottle has a truncated cone base and a cylindrical stem, so the water height increases more and more rapidly and then increases at a steady rate at the stem.

**15.** Sample answer: Approximately $180.80. Divide the 32 students into four groups so that 8 students fall into each quartile. Assuming that the mean of each quartile is the midpoint of the quartile, the total will be

$$8\left(\frac{2.10 + 4.05}{2} + \frac{4.05 + 4.95}{2} + \frac{4.95 + 6.80}{2}\right.$$
$$\left. + \frac{6.80 + 11.50}{2}\right)$$
$$= 8(3.075 + 4.500 + 5.875 + 9.150)$$
$$= 8(22.6) = 180.80$$

Therefore the total amount of money raised is approximately $180.80.

**16.** (7, 25.5). Find the equations of the lines $\ell_1$ and $\ell_2$, and then use substitution to find the exact point of intersection. The slope of line $\ell_1$ is $\frac{13 - 8}{2 - 0} = \frac{5}{2}$ and the $y$-intercept is 8, so the equation of line $\ell_1$ is $y = \frac{5}{2}x + 8$. The slope of line $\ell_2$ is $\frac{20 - 14}{18 - 30} = \frac{6}{-12} = -\frac{1}{2}$. Using slope $-\frac{1}{2}$ and the point (18, 20), the equation of $\ell_2$ is $y = 20 - \frac{1}{2}(x - 18)$. Substitute $\frac{5}{2}x + 8$ for $y$ in the equation of line $\ell_2$ and solve for $x$.

$$\frac{5}{2}x + 8 = 20 - \frac{1}{2}(x - 18)$$
$$\frac{5}{2}x + 8 = 20 - \frac{1}{2}x + 9$$
$$\frac{5}{2}x = 21 - \frac{1}{2}x$$
$$3x = 21$$
$$x = 7$$

Substitute 7 for $x$ in either equation and solve for $y$.

$$y = \frac{5}{2}(7) + 8 = \frac{35}{2} + 8 = 17.5 + 8 = 25.5$$

The intersection point of lines $\ell_1$ and $\ell_2$ is (7, 25.5).

**17. a.** Possible answer:

**b.** Possible answer:

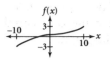

**c.** Possible answer:

**18. a.**

| | $x$ | 3 |
|---|---|---|
| $x$ | $x^2$ | $3x$ |
| 7 | $7x$ | 21 |

$(x + 3)(x + 7) = x^2 + 10x + 21$

**b.**

| | $x$ | 1 |
|---|---|---|
| $x$ | $x^2$ | $x$ |
| 2 | $2x$ | 2 |

$(x + 1)(x + 2) = x^2 + 3x + 2$

**c.**

| | $2x$ | 10 |
|---|---|---|
| $x$ | $2x^2$ | $10x$ |
| 10 | $20x$ | 100 |

$(2x + 10)(x + 10) = 2x^2 + 30x + 100$

## LESSON 4.3

### EXERCISES

**1.** $y = -3 + \frac{2}{3}(x - 5)$, or $y = \frac{2}{3}x - \frac{19}{3}$

**2.** The graph of $y = f(x - 3)$ is the graph of $y = f(x)$ translated right 3 units.

**3. a.** $f(x + 3) = -2(x + 3) = -2x - 6$

**b.** $-3 + f(x - 2) = -3 + (-2)(x - 2) = -2x + 1$

**c.** $5 + f(x + 1) = 5 + (-2)(x + 1) = -2x + 3$

**4. a.** $y = -4.4 - 1.1485(x - 1.4)$ or $y = 3.18 - 1.1485(x + 5.2)$. The slope is $\frac{-4.4 - 3.18}{1.4 - (-5.2)} = \frac{-7.58}{6.6} = -1.1485$. Use the point-slope form with one of the points.

**b.** Add 2 to $y_1$, $-4.4$ or 3.18, in either equation in 4a: $y = -2.4 - 1.1485(x - 1.4)$ or $y = 5.18 - 1.1485(x + 5.2)$. The slope, $-1.1485$, remains the same for the parallel line.

**5. a.** $y = -3 + 4.7x$

**b.** $y = -2.8(x - 2)$, or $y = -2.8x + 5.6$

**c.** $y = 4 - (x + 1.5)$, or $y = 2.5 - x$

**6. a.** $y = f(x + 3) - 2$. The graph passes through $(-3, 0)$. Consider this point to be the translated image of $(0, 2)$ on $y = f(x)$. Therefore the graph of $y = f(x)$ is translated left 3 units and down 2 units, so $y = f(x + 3) - 2$.

**b.** $y = f(x - 1) + 2$. The graph passes through $(1, 4)$. Consider this point to be the translated image of $(0, 2)$ on $y = f(x)$. The graph of $y = f(x)$ is translated right 1 unit and up 2 units, so $y = f(x - 1) + 2$.

**c.** $y = f(x + 2) - 5$. The graph passes through $(-2, -3)$. Consider this point to be the translated image of $(0, 2)$ on $y = f(x)$. The graph of $y = f(x)$ is translated left 2 units and down 5 units, so $y = f(x + 2) - 5$.

**d.** $y = f(x - 1) - 2$. The graph passes through $(1, 0)$. Consider this point to be the translated image of $(0, 2)$ on $y = f(x)$. The graph of $y = f(x)$ is translated right 1 unit and down 2 units, so $y = f(x - 1) - 2$.

**7.** $y = 47 - 6.3(x - 3)$. The two pieces came from the same original rope, so the equations will have the same slope. They are both translations of the equation $y = -6.3x$. Mitch should translate this equation right 3 units and up 47 units to get $y = 47 - 6.3(x - 3)$.

**8. a.** Brian was standing about 1.5 m behind Pete, and his sensor started 2 s later than Pete's sensor. Brian's distances are about 1.5 m more than Pete's, and the walk ended after 4 s on Brian's graph and after 6 s on Pete's graph.

**b.** $y = f(x + 2) + 1.5$. Brian's equation is a translation of Pete's equation, $y = f(x)$, left 2 units and up 1.5 units.

**9. a.** $(1400, 733.\overline{3})$. For each of the 15 steps, the change in $x$ is $\frac{7000 - 1000}{15} = 400$ and the change in $y$ is $\frac{4000 - 500}{15} = 233.\overline{3}$. The airplane's next position is $(1000 + 400, 500 + 233.\overline{3})$, or $(1400, 733.\overline{3})$.

**b.** $(x + 400, y + 233.\overline{3})$

**c.** 20 steps. Both $\frac{7000 - 1000}{300} = 20$ and $\frac{4000 - 500}{175} = 20$, so it will take 20 steps to reach the final position of $(7000, 4000)$.

**10. a.  i.** $a = 4$, $b = 3$, $c = 12$

**ii.** $a = -1$, $b = 1$, $c = 5$

**iii.** $a = 7$, $b = -1$, $c = 1$

**iv.** $a = -2$, $b = 4$, $c = -2$

**v.** $a = 0$, $b = 2$, $c = 10$

**vi.** $a = 3$, $b = 0$, $c = -6$

**b.** $y = \frac{c}{b} - \frac{a}{b}x$

$$ax + by = c \qquad \text{Equation in standard form.}$$

$$by = c - ax \qquad \text{Subtract } ax \text{ from both sides.}$$

$$y = \frac{c}{b} - \frac{a}{b}x \qquad \text{Divide both sides by } b.$$

The equation is in intercept form, where the $y$-intercept is $\frac{c}{b}$ and the slope is $-\frac{a}{b}$.

**c.  i.** $y$-intercept: $-\frac{c}{b} = -\frac{12}{3} = 4$; slope: $-\frac{a}{b} = -\frac{4}{3}$

**ii.** $y$-intercept: $\frac{5}{1} = 5$; slope: $-\frac{(-1)}{1} = 1$

**iii.** $y$-intercept: $\frac{1}{(-1)} = -1$; slope: $-\frac{7}{(-1)} = 7$

**iv.** $y$-intercept: $\frac{(-2)}{4} = -\frac{1}{2}$; slope: $-\frac{(-2)}{4} = \frac{1}{2}$

**v.** $y$-intercept: $\frac{10}{2} = 5$; slope: $-\frac{0}{2} = 0$

**vi.** $y$-intercept: $\frac{(-6)}{0} =$ undefined, no $y$-intercept; slope: $-\frac{3}{0} =$ undefined

**d.  i.** $4(x - 2) + 3y = 12$, so $4x + 3y = 20$

**ii.** $4(x + 5) + 3y = 12$, so $4x + 3y = -8$

**iii.** $4x + 3(y - 4) = 12$, so $4x + 3y = 24$

**iv.** $4x + 3(y + 1) = 12$, so $4x + 3y = 9$

**v.** $4(x - 1) + 3(y + 3) = 12$, so $4x + 3y = 7$

**vi.** $4(x + 2) + 3(y - 2) = 12$, so $4x + 3y = 10$

**e.** $a(x - h) + b(y - k) = c$, so $ax + by = c + ah + bk$

**11. a.** The $y$-intercept is 12,500. The original value of the equipment is $12,500.

**b.** The $x$-intercept is 10. After 10 years the equipment has no value.

**c.** The slope is $\frac{12500 - 0}{0 - 10} = -1250$. Every year the value of the equipment decreases by $1250.

**d.** $y = 12500 - 1250x$

**e.** After 4.8 yr the equipment will be worth $6500. Substitute 6500 for $y$ and solve for $x$.

$$6500 = 12500 - 1250x$$

$$1250x = 6000$$

$$x = 4.8$$

You can also find the point on the graph where $y = 6500$, which is $(4.8, 6500)$.

**12. a.** $\frac{(86 + 73 + 76 + 90 + 79)}{5} = 80.8$

**b.** $y = \frac{1}{5}x + 65$. Let $x$ represent the fifth-game score, and let $y$ represent the mean of the five scores.

$$y = \frac{89 + 73 + 76 + 90 + x}{5} = \frac{325 + x}{5} = 65 + \frac{x}{5}$$

In intercept form, $y = \frac{1}{5}x + 65$.

*Discovering Advanced Algebra Solutions Manual*
©2004 Key Curriculum Press

**c.** 95 points. Substitute 84 for $y$ in the equation $y = \frac{1}{5}x + 65$ and solve for $x$.

$$84 = \frac{1}{5}x + 65$$

$$\frac{1}{5}x = 19$$

$$x = 95$$

To average 84 points, the fifth-game score must be 95 points.

**13. a.** $x = 15$

$$2(x + 4) = 38$$

$$x + 4 = 19$$

$$x = 15$$

**b.** $x = 31$

$$7 + 0.5(x - 3) = 21$$

$$0.5(x - 3) = 14$$

$$x - 3 = 28$$

$$x = 31$$

**c.** $x = -21$

$$-2 + \frac{3}{4}(x + 1) = -17$$

$$\frac{3}{4}(x + 1) = -15$$

$$x + 1 = \frac{-60}{3}$$

$$x = -21$$

**d.** $x = 17.6$

$$4.7 + 2.8(x - 5.1) = 39.7$$

$$2.8(x - 5.1) = 35$$

$$x - 5.1 = 12.5$$

$$x = 17.6$$

**14.** $\hat{y} = \frac{29}{2} - \frac{3}{2}x$. The slope of the line through $M_1$ and $M_3$ is $\frac{11 - 2}{3 - 9} = \frac{9}{-6} = -\frac{3}{2}$, so the equation of this line is $y = 11 - \frac{3}{2}(x - 3)$, or $y = \frac{31}{2} - \frac{3}{2}x$. The equation of the parallel line through $M_2$ is $y = 5 - \frac{3}{2}(x - 5)$, or $y = -\frac{3}{2}x + \frac{25}{2}$. The $y$-intercept of the median-median line is the mean of the three $y$-intercepts.

$$\frac{\frac{31}{2} + \frac{31}{2} + \frac{25}{2}}{3} = \frac{\frac{87}{2}}{3} = \frac{87}{6} = \frac{29}{2}$$

Therefore the equation of the median-median line is $\hat{y} = \frac{29}{2} - \frac{3}{2}x$.

**EXTENSIONS**

**A.** Results will vary.

**B.** See the solution to Take Another Look activity 1 on page 83.

## LESSON 4.4

**EXERCISES**

**1. a.** $y = x^2 + 2$. $y = x^2$ is translated up 2 units.

**b.** $y = x^2 - 6$. $y = x^2$ is translated down 6 units.

**c.** $y = (x - 4)^2$. $y = x^2$ is translated right 4 units.

**d.** $y = (x + 8)^2$. $y = x^2$ is translated left 8 units.

**2. a.** $y = x^2 - 5$

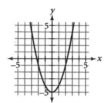

**b.** $y = x^2 + 3$

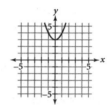

**c.** $y = (x - 3)^2$

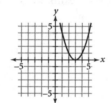

**d.** $y = (x + 4)^2$

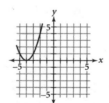

**3. a.** Translated down 3 units. Graph to check the answer.

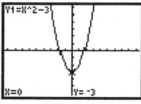

$[-9.4, 9.4, 1, -6.2, 6.2, 1]$

**b.** Translated up 4 units

**c.** Translated right 2 units

**d.** Translated left 4 units

**4. a.** Translated right 3 units

   **b.** Translated left 3 units

   **c.** Translated up 2 units

   **d.** Translated down 2 units

**5. a.** $x = 2$ or $x = -2$

   **b.** $x^2 = 16$, so $x = 4$ or $x = -4$

   **c.** $x - 2 = \pm 5$, so $x = 7$ or $x = -3$

**6.** Each parabola is a translation of the graph of the parent function $y = x^2$. If the vertex of the translated parabola is $(h, k)$, then the equation is $y = (x - h)^2 + k$.

   **a.** $y = (x - 2)^2$

   **b.** $y = (x - 2)^2 - 5$

   **c.** $y = (x + 6)^2$

   **d.** $y = (x + 6)^2 + 2$

**7. a.** $y = (x - 5)^2 - 3$

   **b.** $(5, -3)$. The equation of the translated parabola is in the form $y = (x - h)^2 + k$ with vertex $(h, k)$, so the vertex is $(5, -3)$. The vertex is the image of the origin translated right 5 units and down 3 units.

   **c.** $(6, -2)$, $(4, -2)$, $(7, 1)$, $(3, 1)$. Each point on the red parabola is translated right 5 units and down 3 units from the corresponding point on the black parabola. If $(x, y)$ are the coordinates of any point on the black parabola, then the coordinates of the corresponding point on the red parabola are $(x + 5, y - 3)$.

   **d.** Segment $b$ has length 1 unit and segment $c$ has length 4 units.

**8. a.** $y = f(x + 2)$ is the graph of $y = f(x)$ translated left 2 units. Choose the points $(-3, -1)$, $(-1, 1)$, $(2, 0)$, and $(3, 2)$ from the graph of $y = f(x)$, and subtract 2 from the $x$-coordinates. The corresponding points on the translated graph are $(-5, -1)$, $(-3, 1)$, $(0, 0)$, and $(1, 2)$.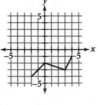

   **b.** $y = f(x - 1) - 3$ is the graph of $y = f(x)$ translated right 1 unit and down 3 units. Choose the points $(-3, -1)$, $(-1, 1)$, $(2, 0)$, and $(3, 2)$ from the graph of $y = f(x)$, and add 1 to the $x$-coordinates and subtract 3 from the $y$-coordinates. The corresponding points on the translated graph are $(-2, -4)$, $(0, -2)$, $(3, -3)$, and $(4, -1)$.

**9. a.**

| Number of teams $x$ | 4 | 5 | 6 | 7 | 8 | 9 | 10 |
|---|---|---|---|---|---|---|---|
| Number of games $y$ | 12 | 20 | 30 | 42 | 56 | 72 | 90 |

For each additional team, add double the previous number of teams to represent playing each of those teams twice. For example, $6 + 2(3) = 12$, $12 + 2(4) = 20$, $20 + 2(5) = 30$, and so on.

   **b.** Enter the values into two lists, set an appropriate window, and plot the points. The points appear to be part of a parabola.

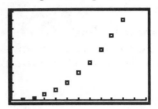

[0, 12, 1, 0, 100, 10]

   **c.** $y = (x - 0.5)^2 - 0.25$. Plot the function $y = x^2$ on top of the points, and experiment with translations until you find an explicit function that fits the points.

   **d.** 870 games. Substitute 30 for $x$ and solve for $y$.

$$y = (30 - 0.5)^2 - 0.25 = 870.25 - 0.25 = 870$$

There are 870 games required if there are 30 teams.

**10. a.** $(x - 5)^2 = 16$, so $x - 5 = \pm 4$, and $x = 9$ or $x = 1$.

   **b.** $(x + 3)^2 = 49$, so $x + 3 = \pm 7$, and $x = 4$ or $x = -10$.

   **c.** $-(x - 1) = -27$, so $x - 1 = 27$, and $x = 28$.

   **d.** $(x + 6)^2 = 8$, so $x + 6 = \pm\sqrt{8}$, and $x = -6 \pm \sqrt{8}$.

**11. a.** The histogram is translated right 5 units (1 bin).

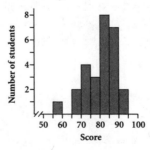

**b.** The histogram is translated left 10 units (2 bins).

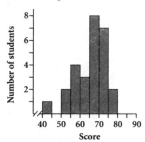

**12. a.** B. The common difference is 3, so the slope is 3; and $u_0 = 8$, so 8 is the $y$-intercept.

**b.** C. The common difference is $-8$, so the slope is $-8$. To find the $y$-intercept, you need to find $u_0$, so add 8 to $u_1$, or 3. The $y$-intercept is 11.

**13. a.** Let $m$ represent the miles driven, and let $C$ represent the cost of the one-day rental in dollars. Mertz: $C = 32 + 0.1m$; Saver: $C = 24 + 0.18m$; Luxury: $C = 51$.

**b.**
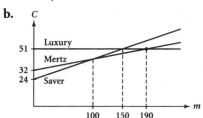

**c.** If you plan to drive less than 100 miles, then rent Saver. At exactly 100 miles, Mertz and Saver are the same. If you plan to drive between 100 miles and 190 miles, then rent Mertz. At exactly 190 miles, Mertz and Luxury are the same. If you plan to drive more than 190 miles, then rent Luxury.

**14.** The slope of the graph is negative and constant as the car drives straight toward point $X$. The graph changes direction, and the slope is positive and steady as the car takes a left at point $B$ and moves toward point $C$ and away from point $X$. The graph changes direction again at point $C$, and the slope is negative and then positive as the car passes point $D$ on its way to point $E$. From point $E$ to point $X$, the slope is negative and constant until the car reaches its destination.

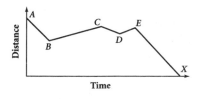

A very accurate graph would show $\overline{BC}$, $\overline{CD}$, and $\overline{DE}$ as slightly curved and then straight because the movement is actually hyperbolic in these cases. You might not have noticed this subtlety.

**15.** Sample answer using The Geometer's Sketchpad: To make a sequence of dilated segments, first construct a vertical segment and measure its length. Next, construct a horizontal segment to be used as a vector to move the transformed segments right. Make a horizontal slider and label it $r$ for common ratio. Select the calculation for $r$ and mark it as a scale factor. Then, select the bottom endpoint of the vertical segment and mark it as a center. Select the endpoints of the vertical segment and dilate it by the marked scale factor. Construct a segment between the bottom endpoint of the vertical segment and the dilated point. Select the endpoints of the horizontal segment left to right and mark it as a vector. Select the dilated segment including endpoints and translate it by the marked vector. Hide the original dilated segment, its top endpoint, and the horizontal segment used as a vector. Next, select the endpoints of the original vertical segment. Choose **Iterate** from the Transform menu. Select the corresponding endpoints of the shifted dilated segment and iterate. Use the "+" or "−" keys on the keyboard to increase or decrease the number of iterations.

The table given will include the terms of the sequence representing the lengths of the segments after each transformation. You can change the length of the original segment by sliding an endpoint, and you can adjust the $r$ slider to change the common ratio. These changes will automatically be reflected in the sequence of segments and in the table of values.

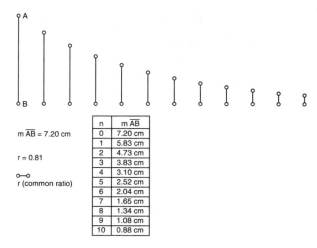

m $\overline{AB}$ = 7.20 cm

r = 0.81

r (common ratio)

| n | m $\overline{AB}$ |
|---|---|
| 0 | 7.20 cm |
| 1 | 5.83 cm |
| 2 | 4.73 cm |
| 3 | 3.83 cm |
| 4 | 3.10 cm |
| 5 | 2.52 cm |
| 6 | 2.04 cm |
| 7 | 1.65 cm |
| 8 | 1.34 cm |
| 9 | 1.08 cm |
| 10 | 0.88 cm |

**16. a.** The slopes vary, but the *y*-intercept is always 4. Sample answer: Create two sliders, *a* and *b*, and use them to plot the line $y = ax + b$. Adjust the *a* slider while keeping the *b* slider at length 4.

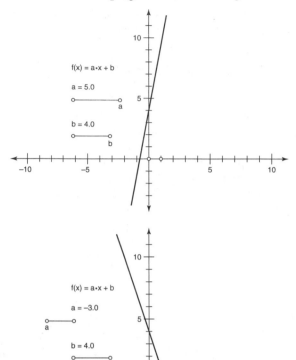

**b.** The lines move up or down, but they all have slope 2. Sample answer: Using the sketch from 16a, adjust the *b* slider while keeping the *a* slider at length 2.

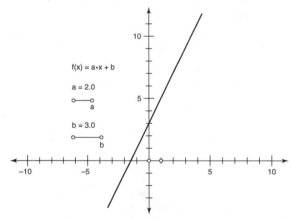

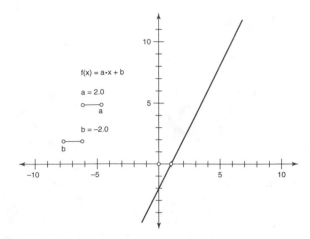

### IMPROVING YOUR REASONING SKILLS

For the constellation to appear the same from Earth, the stars that are farther away would move a greater distance. The stars would move along arcs of great circles on concentric spheres with Earth as the center. The stars farther from Earth would move along arcs with a greater radius, and therefore the arcs would have greater length. All of the arcs would, however, have the same degree measure.

### EXTENSION

Results will vary.

## LESSON 4.5

### EXERCISES

**1. a.** $y = \sqrt{x}$ is translated up 3 units, so $y = \sqrt{x} + 3$.

   **b.** $y = \sqrt{x}$ is translated left 5 units, so $y = \sqrt{x + 5}$.

   **c.** $y = \sqrt{x}$ is translated left 5 units and up 2 units, so $y = \sqrt{x + 5} + 2$.

   **d.** $y = \sqrt{x}$ is translated right 3 units and up 1 unit, so $y = \sqrt{x - 3} + 1$.

   **e.** $y = \sqrt{x}$ is translated right 1 unit and down 4 units, so $y = \sqrt{x - 1} - 4$.

**2. a.** Translated right 3 units

   **b.** Translated left 3 units

   **c.** Translated up 2 units

   **d.** Translated down 2 units

**3. a.** $y = -\sqrt{x}$. The graph of $y = \sqrt{x}$ is reflected across the *x*-axis.

   **b.** $y = -\sqrt{x} - 3$. The graph of $y = \sqrt{x}$ is reflected across the *x*-axis and then translated down 3 units.

*Discovering Advanced Algebra Solutions Manual*
©2004 Key Curriculum Press

**c.** $y = -\sqrt{x + 6} + 5$. The graph of $y = \sqrt{x}$ is reflected across the $x$-axis and then translated left 6 units and up 5 units.

**d.** $y = \sqrt{-x}$. The graph of $y = \sqrt{x}$ is reflected across the $y$-axis.

**e.** $y = \sqrt{-(x - 2)} - 3$, or $y = \sqrt{-x + 2} - 3$. The graph of $y = \sqrt{x}$ is reflected across the $y$-axis and then translated right 2 units and down 3 units.

**4. a.** The graph of $y = f(-x)$ is the graph of $y = f(x)$ reflected across the $y$-axis.

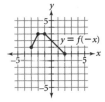

**b.** The graph of $y = -f(x)$ is the graph of $y = f(x)$ reflected across the $x$-axis.

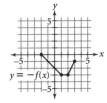

**c.** The graph of $y = -f(-x)$ is the graph of $y = f(x)$ reflected across both the $x$- and $y$-axes.

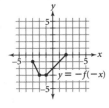

**5. a.** Possible answer: $(-4, -2)$, $(-3, -1)$, and $(0, 0)$. Select integer values to substitute for $x$ and solve for $y$. To ensure you find integer values of $y$, $x + 4$ must be a perfect square. For example, if $x = -4$ then $y = f(-4 + 4) - 2 = f(0) - 2 = \sqrt{0} - 2 = -2$, so one pair of integer coordinates is $(-4, -2)$.

**b.** $f(x + 4) = \sqrt{x + 4}$, so $y = \sqrt{x + 4} - 2$

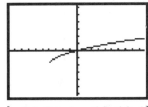

$[-9.4, 9.4, 1, -6.2, 6.2, 1]$

**c.** $f(x - 2) = \sqrt{x - 2}$, so $y = -\sqrt{x - 2} + 3$

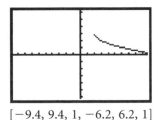

$[-9.4, 9.4, 1, -6.2, 6.2, 1]$

**6. a.** The functions are $y = \sqrt{x}$ and $y = -\sqrt{x}$. The parabola is not a function because it doesn't pass the vertical line test. In order to graph it, you need to enter two functions, one as a positive square root and one as a negative square root.

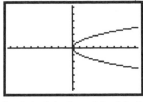

$[-9.4, 9.4, 1, -6.2, 6.2, 1]$

**b.** $y = \pm\sqrt{x}$; $y^2 = x$. Square both sides of $y = \pm\sqrt{x}$: $y^2 = (\pm\sqrt{x})^2$, and $y^2 = x$.

**7. a.** Neither parabola passes the vertical line test; or there are $x$-values that are paired with two $y$-values.

**b. i.** Graph i is the image of $y = \pm\sqrt{x}$ translated left 4 units, so $y = \pm\sqrt{x + 4}$.

**ii.** Graph ii is the image of $y = \pm\sqrt{x}$ translated up 2 units, so $y = \pm\sqrt{x} + 2$.

**c. i.** Square both sides of $y = \pm\sqrt{x + 4}$: $y^2 = (\pm\sqrt{x + 4})^2$, or $y^2 = x + 4$.

**ii.** Subtract 2 from both sides of $y = \pm\sqrt{x} + 2$ to get $y - 2 = \pm\sqrt{x}$, then square both sides: $(y - 2)^2 = (\pm\sqrt{x})^2$, or $(y - 2)^2 = x$.

**8. a.** Possible sketch:

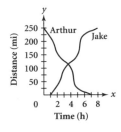

The graphs are first reflections of each other across the $x$-axis because the distance is decreasing for Arthur and increasing for Jake. Arthur's graph is also translated up 250 miles because of the difference between their reference points. Jake's graph is translated right by one hour because of the one-hour difference on their watches.

**b.** $y = -f(x + 1) + 250$. Arthur's graph is the image of Jake's graph, $y = f(x)$, reflected across the $x$-axis and then translated left 1 unit and up 250 units.

**c.** $y = -g(x - 1) + 250$. Jake's graph is the image of Arthur's graph, $y = g(x)$, reflected across the $x$-axis and then translated right 1 unit and up 250 units.

**9. a.** $y = -x^2$. The graph of the parent function $y = x^2$ is reflected across the $x$-axis.

**b.** $y = -x^2 + 2$. The graph of $y = x^2$ is reflected across the $x$-axis and translated up 2 units.

**c.** $y = -(x - 6)^2$. The graph of $y = x^2$ is reflected across the $x$-axis and translated right 6 units.

**d.** $y = -(x - 6)^2 - 3$. The graph of $y = x^2$ is reflected across the $x$-axis and translated right 6 units and down 3 units.

**10.** $y + 2 = -((x - 5) + 3)^2 + 4$, or $y = -(x - 2)^2 + 2$. Subtract 5 from $(x + 3)$ and add 2 to $y$.

**11. a.** Substitute 0.7 for $f$: $S = 5.5\sqrt{0.7D}$.

**b.**

**c.** Approximately 36 mi/h. Substitute 60 for $D$:
$S = 5.5\sqrt{0.7 \cdot 60} \approx 36$ mi/h.

**d.** $D = \dfrac{1}{0.7}\left(\dfrac{S}{5.5}\right)^2$

| | |
|---|---|
| $S = 5.5\sqrt{0.7D}$ | Original equation. |
| $\dfrac{S}{5.5} = \sqrt{0.7D}$ | Divide both sides by 5.5. |
| $\left(\dfrac{S}{5.5}\right)^2 = 0.7D$ | Square both sides. |
| $D = \dfrac{1}{0.7}\left(\dfrac{S}{5.5}\right)^2$ | Multiply both sides by $\dfrac{1}{0.7}$. |

The equation $D = \dfrac{1}{0.7}\left(\dfrac{S}{5.5}\right)^2$ can be used to determine the minimum braking distance when the speed is known.

**e.**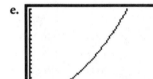

[0, 60, 5, 0, 100, 5]

It is a parabola, but the negative side is not used because the distance cannot be negative.

**f.** Approximately 199.5 ft. Substitute 65 for $S$ and solve for $D$.

$$D = \frac{1}{0.7}\left(\frac{65}{5.5}\right)^2 \approx 199.5$$

Your skid marks would be approximately 199.5 ft.

**12. a.** Not a function. Some large cities have more than one area code.

**b.** Function. There is only one greatest common factor for each pair of numbers.

**c.** Not a function. There are many common denominators for any pair of fractions.

**d.** Possible answers: It is a function if you consider only the days in one year at one location (at one location the sun rises at only one time for each day). It is not a function if you consider the day of any year (the sun could rise at different times on May 1, 2002 and May 1, 2003). It is also not a function if you consider different locations, such as neighboring towns separated by a time line.

**13. a.** $x = 293$

| | |
|---|---|
| $3 + \sqrt{x - 4} = 20$ | Original equation. |
| $\sqrt{x - 4} = 17$ | Subtract 3 from both sides. |
| $x - 4 = 289$ | Square both sides. |
| $x = 293$ | Add 4 to both sides. |

Check for an extraneous root by substituting 293 for $x$ in the original equation: $3 + \sqrt{293 - 4} = 20$, so $3 + \sqrt{289} = 20$, and $3 + 17 = 20$. The solution checks, so $x = 293$.

**b.** No solution

| | |
|---|---|
| $\sqrt{x + 7} = -3$ | Original equation. |
| $x + 7 = 9$ | Square both sides. |
| $x = 2$ | Subtract 7 from both sides. |

Check for an extraneous root by substituting 2 for $x$ in the original equation: $\sqrt{2 + 7} = \sqrt{9} = 3 \neq -3$. The solution doesn't check, so 2 is an extraneous root and there is no solution. You can also tell there is no solution because a radical always refers to the positive square root, so it could never equal $-3$.

**c.** $x = 7$ or $x = -3$

| | |
|---|---|
| $4 - (x - 2)^2 = -21$ | Original equation. |
| $-(x - 2)^2 = -25$ | Subtract 4 from both sides. |
| $(x - 2)^2 = 25$ | Divide both sides by $-1$. |
| $x - 2 = \pm 5$ | Take the square root of both sides. |
| $x = 7$ or $x = -3$ | Add 2 to both sides. |

Check for extraneous roots by substituting 7 and $-3$ for $x$ in the original equation.

Check $x = 7$: $4 - (7 - 2)^2 = 4 - 5^2 = 4 - 25 = -21$.

Check $x = -3$: $4 - (-3 - 2)^2 = 4 - (-5)^2 = 4 - 25 = -21$.

Both solutions check, so $x = 7$ or $x = -3$.

*Discovering Advanced Algebra Solutions Manual*
©2004 Key Curriculum Press

**d.** $x = -13$

$$5 - \sqrt{-(x+4)} = 2 \quad \text{Original equation.}$$
$$-\sqrt{-(x+4)} = -3 \quad \text{Subtract 5 from both sides.}$$
$$\sqrt{-(x+4)} = 3 \quad \text{Divide both sides by } -1.$$
$$-(x+4) = 9 \quad \text{Square both sides.}$$
$$(x+4) = -9 \quad \text{Divide both sides by } -1.$$
$$x = -13 \quad \text{Subtract 4 from both sides.}$$

Check for an extraneous root by substituting $-13$ for $x$ in the original equation: $5 - \sqrt{-(-13+4)} = 5 - \sqrt{9} = 5 - 3 = 2$. The solution checks, so $x = -13$.

**14.** $y = (x+6)^2 + 4$. Because the parabola has a vertical line of symmetry, use the vertex form, $y = (x-h)^2 + k$, with vertex $(h, k)$. Substitute the coordinates of the point $(-5, 5)$ in $y = (x+6)^2 + 4$ to make sure the graph is not reflected.

$$5 \stackrel{?}{=} (-5+6)^2 + 4$$
$$5 \stackrel{?}{=} (-1)^2 + 4$$
$$5 = 5$$

**15. a.** $y = \frac{1}{2}x + 5$. The slope is $\frac{6-1}{2-(-8)} = \frac{5}{10} = \frac{1}{2}$.
Using point-slope form, $y = 6 + \frac{1}{2}(x-2) = 6 + \frac{1}{2}x - 1 = \frac{1}{2}x + 5$, so the equation of the line is $y = \frac{1}{2}x + 5$.

**b.** Line $\ell_1$, or the graph of $y = \frac{1}{2}x + 5$, is translated right 8 units, so $y = \frac{1}{2}(x-8) + 5$.

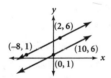

**c.** After the horizontal translation, line $\ell_2$ is translated down 4 units from line $\ell_1$, so $y = \left(\frac{1}{2}x + 5\right) - 4$, or $y + 4 = \frac{1}{2}x + 5$.

**d.** By removing parentheses and combining constants, both equations are equivalent to $y = \frac{1}{2}x + 1$.

15b: $y = \frac{1}{2}(x-8) + 5 = \frac{1}{2}x - 4 + 5 = \frac{1}{2}x + 1$

15c: $y = \left(\frac{1}{2}x + 5\right) - 4 = \frac{1}{2}x + 5 - 4 = \frac{1}{2}x + 1$

**16. a.** 35, 37.5, 41.5, 49, 73

**b.**

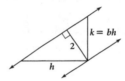

**c.** $IQR = 49 - 37.5 = 11.5$

**d.** 70 and 73 are outliers. $49 + 1.5(11.5) = 66.25$ and $37.5 - 1.5(11.5) = 20.25$. There are no values below 20.5 and there are two values above 66.25: 70 and 73. Therefore, 70 and 73 are outliers.

**IMPROVING YOUR GEOMETRY SKILLS**

The slope of the line is $b$.

$$h = \pm\frac{2}{b}\sqrt{b^2 + 1}; \quad k = \pm 2\sqrt{b^2 + 1}$$

The equations are $y = a - 2\sqrt{b^2 + 1} + bx$ and $y = a + 2\sqrt{b^2 + 1} + bx$.

There are several ways to derive the results algebraically. Because any translation of a line is equivalent to a horizontal translation, you might try to find the horizontal translation in terms of the slope, $b$. If you draw a perpendicular of length 2 to the two lines and then draw from one endpoint of the perpendicular to the other parallel line a horizontal segment (of length $h$) and a vertical segment (of length $k$), then $\frac{k}{h}$ is the slope, $b$, so $k = bh$.

You have constructed a right triangle whose legs have lengths $h$ and $k = bh$ and whose other altitude has length 2. The area of that triangle can be written two ways: $\frac{1}{2}h(bh)$ or, using the Pythagorean Theorem,

$$\frac{1}{2} \cdot 2\sqrt{b^2h^2 + h^2} = \pm h\sqrt{b^2 + 1}$$

Setting these area expressions equal, you get $h = \pm\frac{2}{b}\sqrt{b^2 + 1}$. The two values of $h$ correspond to the two directions in which the line could have been translated. The equations of the new lines are

$$y = a + b\left(x \mp \frac{2}{b}\sqrt{b^2 + 1}\right)$$
$$= \left(a \mp 2\sqrt{b^2 + 1}\right) + bx$$

**EXTENSIONS**

**A.** See the solution to Take Another Look activity 2 on page 83.

**B.** Investigations will vary.

## QUESTIONS

**1.** The coordinates of the 90° rotations are reversed (*x* and *y* are interchanged), and one of them is negated depending on the direction of the rotation. The coordinates of the 180° rotation are in the same order, but both are negated. The rules are the same even if the original figure is in a different quadrant.

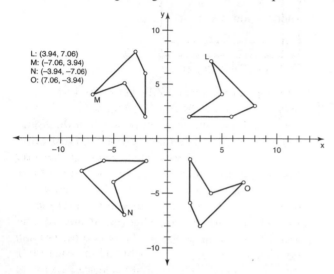

L: (3.94, 7.06)
M: (−7.06, 3.94)
N: (−3.94, −7.06)
O: (7.06, −3.94)

**2.** To transform the figure from the first to the third quadrant, use two reflections. A reflection across the *y*-axis negates the *x*-coordinate, and a reflection across the *x*-axis negates the *y*-coordinate. This combination of transformations follows the same rule as the 180° rotation.

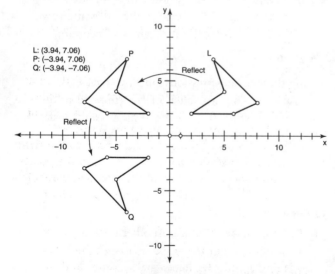

L: (3.94, 7.06)
P: (−3.94, 7.06)
Q: (−3.94, −7.06)

To transform the figure from the first to the second or fourth quadrants, reflect across the line $y = x$ (interchanging the coordinates), then reflect across one axis (negating one coordinate). This combination of transformations follows the same rule as the 90° rotations.

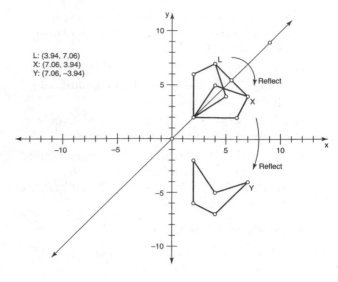

L: (3.94, 7.06)
X: (7.06, 3.94)
Y: (7.06, −3.94)

## LESSON 4.6

### EXERCISES

**1. a.** $y = |x| + 2$. The graph of $y = |x|$ is translated up 2 units.

**b.** $y = |x| - 5$. The graph of $y = |x|$ is translated down 5 units.

**c.** $y = |x + 4|$. The graph of $y = |x|$ is translated left 4 units.

**d.** $y = |x - 3|$. The graph of $y = |x|$ is translated right 3 units.

**e.** $y = |x| - 1$. The graph of $y = |x|$ is translated down 1 unit.

**f.** $y = |x - 4| + 1$. The graph of $y = |x|$ is translated right 4 units and up 1 unit.

**g.** $y = |x + 5| - 3$. The graph of $y = |x|$ is translated left 5 units and down 3 units.

**h.** $y = 3|x - 6|$. The graph of $y = |x|$ is translated right 6 units and is stretched vertically by a factor of 3. That is, every point on the graph has a *y*-coordinate that is 3 times the *y*-coordinate of the corresponding point on the parent function.

**i.** $y = -\left|\frac{x}{4}\right|$. The graph of $y = |x|$ is reflected across the *x*-axis and is stretched horizontally by a factor of 4. That is, every point on the graph has an *x*-coordinate that is 4 times the *x*-coordinate of the corresponding point on the parent function.

**j.** $y = (x - 5)^2$. The graph of $y = x^2$ is translated right 5 units.

**k.** $y = -\frac{1}{2}|x + 4|$. The graph of $y = |x|$ is reflected across the *x*-axis, translated left 4 units, and shrunk vertically by a factor of $\frac{1}{2}$. That is, every point on the graph has a *y*-coordinate that is $\frac{1}{2}$ the *y*-coordinate of the corresponding point on the parent function.

**l.** $y = -|x + 4| + 3$. The graph of $y = |x|$ is reflected across the $x$-axis and then translated left 4 units and up 3 units.

**m.** $y = -(x + 3)^2 + 5$. The graph of $y = x^2$ is reflected across the $x$-axis and then translated left 3 units and up 5 units.

**n.** $y = \pm\sqrt{x - 4} + 4$. The graph of $y = \pm\sqrt{x}$ is translated right 4 units and up 4 units.

**p.** $y = -2\left|\frac{x - 3}{3}\right|$. The graph of $y = |x|$ is reflected across the $x$-axis, translated right 3 units, stretched vertically by a factor of 2, and stretched horizontally by a factor of 3.

**2. a.** Horizontal stretch by a factor of 3

**b.** Reflection across the $y$-axis

**c.** Horizontal shrink by a factor of $\frac{1}{3}$

**d.** Vertical stretch by a factor of 2

**e.** Reflection across the $x$-axis

**f.** Vertical shrink by a factor of $\frac{1}{2}$

**3. a.** $y = 2(x - 5)^2 - 3$. Subtract 3 from both sides.

**b.** $y = 2\left|\frac{x + 1}{3}\right| - 5$. Multiply both sides by 2 and then subtract 5 from each side.

**c.** $y = -2\sqrt{\frac{x - 6}{-3}} - 7$. Multiply both sides by $-2$ and then subtract 7 from each side.

**4.** For $a > 0$, the graphs of $y = a|x|$ and $y = |ax|$ are equivalent. For $a < 0$, the graph of $y = a|x|$ is a reflection of $y = |ax|$ across the $x$-axis. For example, if $a = 2$, then $y = 2|x|$ and $y = |2x|$ are equivalent. However, if $a = -2$, then $y = -2|x|$, or $y = -|2x|$, is a reflection of $y = |-2x|$, which is equivalent to $y = |2x|$ or $y = 2|x|$.

**5. a.** 1 and 7; $x = 1$ and $x = 7$. $|x - 4| = 3$; $x - 4 = 3$ or $x - 4 = -3$; $x = 7$ or $x = 1$. The $x$-coordinates of the points of intersection of the graphs of $y = 3$ and $y = |x - 4|$ are the same as the solutions of $|x - 4| = 3$.

**b.** $x = -8$ and $x = 2$. Graph $y = |x + 3|$ and $y = 5$. The points of intersection are $(-8, 5)$ and $(2, 5)$. The solutions of $|x + 3| = 5$ are the $x$-coordinates of these points of intersection, $-8$ and 2.

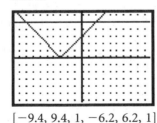

$[-9.4, 9.4, 1, -6.2, 6.2, 1]$

**6.** $\hat{y} = |x - 18.4|$. The transmitter is located on the road at about 18.4 mi from where you started. From the given data, several observations can be

made. The values are decreasing in a linear fashion from 0 to 20 mi and then appear to increase in the same linear fashion, so a mathematical model could be an absolute-value function. Graph the data points on your calculator to verify that the parent function is $y = |x|$. The parent function has been translated right and possibly stretched or shrunk.

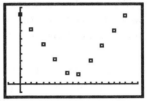

$[-4, 40, 2, -2, 20, 2]$

The slope of the graph to the left of the vertex, using points $(8, 10.5)$ and $(12, 6.6)$, is $\frac{6.6 - 10.5}{12 - 8} = \frac{-3.9}{4} \approx -1$, and the slope of the graph to the right of the vertex, using points $(24, 6)$ and $(28, 10)$, is $\frac{10 - 6}{28 - 24} = \frac{4}{4} = 1$, so the parent function has not been stretched or shrunk. Write the equation in the form $y = a\left|\frac{x - h}{b}\right| + k$ where $a = 1$ and $b = 1$ and $k = 0$, or $y = |x - h|$. Use guess-and-check to find the vertex, which appears to be between 16 and 20. The vertex seems to be at about $(18.4, 0)$, so the graph is translated 18.4 units to the right and the equation is $y = |x - 18.4|$. The transmitter is located on the road at about 18.4 mi from where you started.

**7. a.** $(6, -2)$. On the graph of $y = x^2$, the point 1 unit to the right of the vertex is located 1 unit above the vertex. If the graph is stretched vertically by a factor of 2, the point 1 unit to the right of the vertex is located 2 units above the vertex. The vertex is $(5, -4)$, so the point 1 unit to the right of the vertex of the stretched parabola is $(5 + 1, -4 + 2)$, or $(6, -2)$.

**b.** $(2, -3)$ and $(8, -3)$. On the graph of $y = x^2$, the points 1 unit above the vertex are located 1 unit to the left and 1 unit to the right of the vertex. If the graph is stretched horizontally by a factor of 3, the points 1 unit above the vertex are located 3 units to the left and 3 units to the right of the vertex. The vertex is $(5, -4)$, so the points 1 unit above the vertex of the stretched parabola are $(5 - 3, -4 + 1)$ and $(5 + 3, -4 + 1)$, or $(2, -3)$ and $(8, -3)$.

**c.** Possible answer: $(2, -2)$ and $(8, -2)$

Method 1: On the graph of $y = x^2$, the point $n$ units to the left of the vertex and the point $n$ units to the right of the vertex are located $n^2$ units above the vertex. If the graph is stretched horizontally by a factor of 3 and vertically by a factor of 2, then the point $3n$ units to the left and the point $3n$ units to the right are located $2n^2$ above the vertex. The vertex is

$(5, -4)$, so any two points symmetric with respect to the vertex are $(5 - 3n, -4 + 2n^2)$ and $(5 + 3n, -4 + 2n^2)$. Substitute any real value for $n$ in order to find the coordinates of two points. For example, if you let $n = 1$, then two symmetric points are $(5 - 3, -4 + 2)$ and $(5 + 3, -4 + 2)$, or $(2, -2)$ and $(8, -2)$.

Method 2: Notice that 7a gives the $y$-coordinate of the image of the point 1 unit above and 1 unit right of the vertex after a vertical stretch by a factor of 2. Also notice that 7b gives the $x$-coordinates of the image of the points 1 unit above and 1 unit left or right of the vertex after a horizontal stretch by a factor of 3. Combine the $y$-coordinate from 7a and the $x$-coordinates from 7b to get the image of the points 1 unit above and 1 unit right or left of the vertex after a vertical stretch by a factor of 2 and a horizontal stretch by a factor of 3: $(2, -2)$ and $(8, -2)$.

**8.** Rewrite the equation as $y = 3\left(\frac{x+7}{4}\right)^2 + 2$. Identify the values of $a$, $b$, $h$, and $k$. The parabola is stretched vertically by a factor of 3, stretched horizontally by a factor of 4, and translated left 7 units and up 2 units.

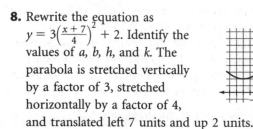

**9. a.** Possible answers: $x = 4.7$ or $y = 5$. The axis of symmetry always passes through the vertex. If the parabola is oriented vertically, then the equation of the axis of symmetry is in the form $x = h$, or $x = 4.7$. If it is oriented horizontally, then the equation of the axis of symmetry is in the form $y = k$, or $y = 5$.

**b.** Possible answer: $y = 4\left(\frac{x - 4.7}{1.9}\right)^2 + 5$, or $\left(\frac{y - 5}{4}\right)^2 = \frac{x - 4.7}{-1.9}$. The vertical scale factor is $a = 9 - 5 = 4$, and the horizontal scale factor is $b = 2.8 - 4.7 = -1.9$. The coordinates of the vertex tell you that $h = 4.7$ and $k = 5$. If you assume the parabola is oriented vertically, then the equation is $y = 4\left(\frac{x - 4.7}{1.9}\right)^2 + 5$. Because the horizontal scale factor, $-1.9$, is squared, the sign is not relevant. If you assume the parabola is oriented horizontally, then the equation is $y = 5 \pm 4\sqrt{\frac{x - 4.7}{-1.9}}$, or $\left(\frac{y - 5}{4}\right)^2 = \frac{x - 4.7}{-1.9}$.

**c.** There are at least two parabolas that meet the conditions. One is oriented horizontally, and another is oriented vertically. If you consider the possibility of a rotated parabola, there are infinitely many other possibilities.

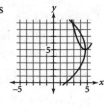

**10. a.** Rewrite the equation as $y = 3(x - 1)^2 + 2$. Identify the values of $a$, $b$, $h$, and $k$. The graph is a vertically oriented parabola with vertex $(1, 2)$ and a vertical stretch by a factor of 3.

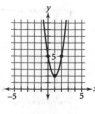

**b.** Rewrite the equation as
$$\frac{y + 1}{2} = \pm\sqrt{\frac{x - 2}{3}} \text{ or}$$
$$y = \pm 2\sqrt{\frac{x - 2}{3}} - 1$$

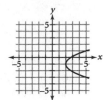

Identify the values of $a$, $b$, $h$, and $k$. The graph is a horizontally oriented parabola with vertex $(2, -1)$ $\big($the parent equation is $y = \pm\sqrt{x}\big)$, a vertical stretch by a factor of 2, and a horizontal stretch by a factor of 3.

**c.** Rewrite the equation as $y = 2\left|\frac{x + 1}{3}\right| + 2$. Identify the values of $a$, $b$, $h$, and $k$. The graph is an absolute-value function with vertex $(-1, 2)$, a vertical stretch by a factor of 2, and a horizontal stretch by a factor of 3.

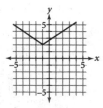

**11. a.** The graph of $\frac{y}{-2} = f(x)$, or $y = -2f(x)$, is a reflection across the $x$-axis and a vertical stretch by a factor of 2.

**b.** The graph of $y = f\left(\frac{x - 3}{2}\right)$ is a horizontal stretch by a factor of 2 and a translation right 3 units.

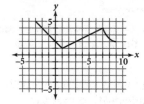

**c.** The graph of $\frac{y + 1}{\frac{1}{2}} = f(x + 1)$, or $y = \frac{1}{2}f(x + 1) - 1$, is a vertical shrink by a factor of $\frac{1}{2}$ and a translation left 1 unit and down 1 unit.

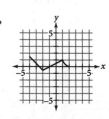

**12.** $y = 1050|x - 4| + 162$. Graph the data on your calculator. The graph appears to be an absolute-value function that has been translated and stretched. Start by determining the translation. The vertex has been translated from $(0, 0)$ to about $(4, 162)$. This is enough information to write the equation $y = |x - 4| + 162$.

*Discovering Advanced Algebra Solutions Manual*
©2004 Key Curriculum Press

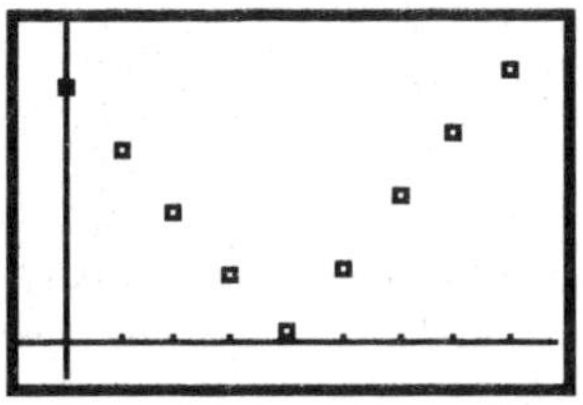

$[-1, 9, 1, -500, 4500, 5000]$

The graph of $y = |x - 4| + 162$ does not fit the data, because the function still needs to be stretched. Select one other point to determine the horizontal and vertical scale factors. For example, choose the data point (5, 1212). Assume this data point is the image of the point (1, 1) in the parent function, $y = |x|$. The data point (5, 1212) is 1 unit to the right and 1050 units above the vertex (4, 162). So the horizontal scale factor $b$ is 1 (no horizontal stretch) and the vertical scale factor $a$ is 1050. Include the scale factor with the translation to get the final equation, $y = 1050|x - 4| + 162$.

**13. a.** $\bar{x} = 83.75$, $s = 7.45$

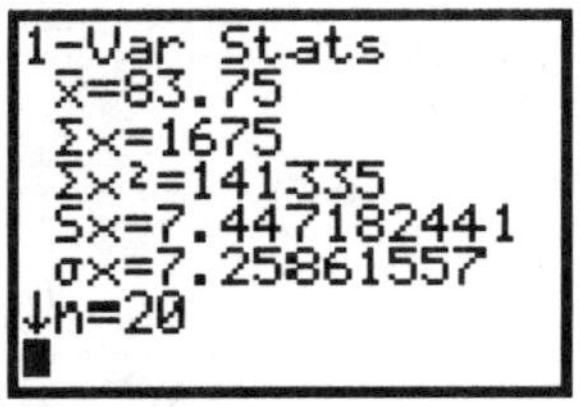


**b.** $\bar{x} = 89.75$, $s = 7.45$

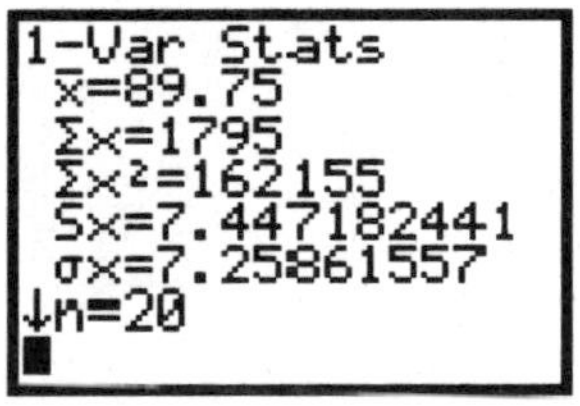


**c.** By adding 6 points to each rating, the mean increases by 6, but the standard deviation remains the same.

**14.** Let $x$ represent the year, and let $y$ represent the percentage of households with computers.

**a.**

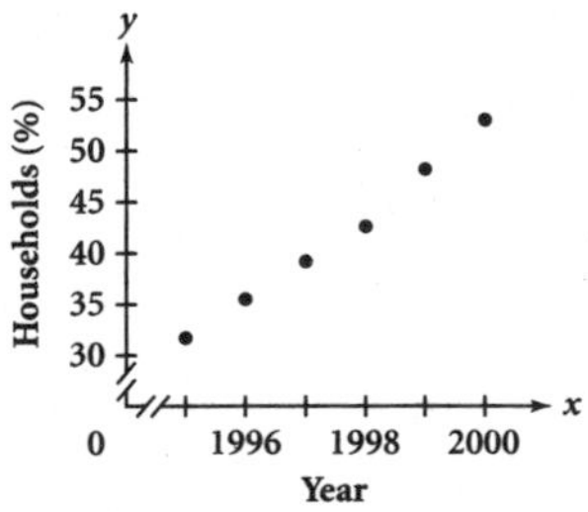


**b.** $\hat{y} = 4.25x - 8447.675$. To find the median-median line, first divide the data into three groups of points. The three summary points are $M_1(1995.5, 33.6)$, $M_2(1997.5, 40.9)$, and $M_3(1999.5, 50.6)$.

The slope of the line through $M_1$ and $M_3$ is $\frac{50.6 - 33.6}{1999.5 - 1995.5} = \frac{17}{4} = 4.25$, so the equation of this line is $y = 50.6 + 4.25(x - 1999.5)$, or $y = 4.25x - 8447.275$. The equation of the parallel line through $M_2$ is $y = 40.9 + 4.25(x - 1997.5)$, or $y = 4.25x - 8448.475$. The $y$-intercept of the median-median line is the mean of the three $y$-intercepts.

$$\frac{-8447.275 + (-8447.275) + (-8448.475)}{3}$$

$$= -8447.675$$

Therefore the equation of the median-median line is $\hat{y} = 4.25x - 8447.675$.

**c.** 60.8%. Substitute 2002 for $x$ in the equation of the median-median line. $\hat{y} = 4.25(2002) - 8447.675 \approx 60.8$. The prediction is that 60.8% of the households will have computers in 2002.

**d.** Sample answers: A linear model cannot work to predict results for years in the distant future because the percentage cannot increase beyond 100%. Realistically, there always will be some households without computers, so the long-run percentage will be less than 100%.

### Improving Your Visual Thinking Skills

Shannon's ball should hit the south wall at (10, 0), and Lori should aim at the point (9.8, 14) on the north wall. Because the angle of incidence is equal to the angle of reflection, the path of each ball is modeled by the graph of an absolute-value function. The vertex of each absolute-value function represents the point on the wall where the ball should hit. Shannon's ball is at (3, 8) and the hole is at (17, 8). Because the points are located the same distance above the vertex, the vertex of the absolute-value function through these two points is located on the south wall halfway between the points. The vertex is $\left(\frac{17+3}{2}, 0\right)$, or (10, 0); the absolute-value function that models the ball's path is $y = \frac{8}{7}|x - 10|$. Lori's ball is at (5, 10) and the hole is at (17, 8). The vertex of the absolute-value function through these points will be on the north wall, but because the points are not the same distance below the vertex, the vertex is not halfway between the points. Use guess-and-check to find the equation that models the ball's path, $y = -\frac{5}{6}|x - 9.8| + 14$; the vertex is (9.8, 14).

### Extensions

**A.** See the solutions to Take Another Look activities 1 and 3 on page 83.

**B.** Results will vary.

**C.** Answers will vary.

**1.**

| Equation | Transformation (translation, reflection, stretch, shrink) | Direction | Amount or scale factor |
|---|---|---|---|
| $-y = \lvert x \rvert$ | Reflection | Across $x$-axis | N/A |
| $y = \sqrt{\dfrac{x}{4}}$ | Stretch | Horizontal | 4 |
| $\dfrac{y}{0.4} = x^2$ | Shrink | Vertical | 0.4 |
| $y = \lvert x - 2 \rvert$ | Translation | Right | 2 |
| $y = \sqrt{-x}$ | Reflection | Across $y$-axis | N/A |

**2.** $y = 2\sqrt{1 - x^2}$. The graph of $y = \sqrt{1 - x^2}$ has been stretched vertically by a factor of 2.

**3. a.** The graph of $g(x) = -f(x)$, or $g(x) = -\sqrt{1 - x^2}$, is a reflection of the graph of $f(x) = \sqrt{1 - x^2}$ across the $x$-axis. It is the bottom half of a unit circle.

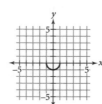

**b.** The graph of $h(x) = -2f(x)$, or $h(x) = -2\sqrt{1 - x^2}$, is a reflection of the graph of $f(x) = \sqrt{1 - x^2}$ across the $x$-axis and a vertical stretch by a factor of 2.

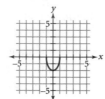

**c.** The graph of $j(x) = -3 + 2f(x)$, or $j(x) = -3 + 2\sqrt{1 - x^2}$, is a vertical stretch of the graph of $f(x) = \sqrt{1 - x^2}$ by a factor of 2 and a translation down 3 units.

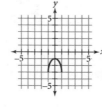

**4. a.** $y = 3\sqrt{1 - x^2}$. The graph of $y = \sqrt{1 - x^2}$ is stretched vertically by a factor of 3.

**b.** $y = 0.5\sqrt{1 - x^2}$. The graph of $y = \sqrt{1 - x^2}$ is shrunk vertically by a factor of 0.5.

**c.** $y = 2\sqrt{1 - x^2} + 1$. The graph of $y = \sqrt{1 - x^2}$ is stretched vertically by a factor of 2 and translated up 1 unit.

**d.** $y = 2\sqrt{1 - (x - 3)^2} + 1$. The graph of $y = \sqrt{1 - x^2}$ is stretched vertically by a factor of 2 and translated right 3 units and up 1 unit.

**e.** $y = -5\sqrt{1 - \left(\frac{x + 2}{2}\right)^2} + 3$.

The graph of $y = \sqrt{1 - x^2}$ is reflected across the $x$-axis, stretched vertically by a factor of 5 and horizontally by a factor of 2, and translated left 2 units and up 3 units.

**f.** $y = 4\sqrt{1 - (x - 3)^2} - 2$. The graph of $y = \sqrt{1 - x^2}$ is stretched vertically by a factor of 4 and translated right 3 units and down 2 units.

**5. a.** $y = \pm\sqrt{1 - x^2} + 2$, or $x^2 + (y - 2)^2 = 1$. The graph of $y = \pm\sqrt{1 - x^2}$ is translated up 2 units.

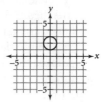

**b.** $y = \pm\sqrt{1 - (x + 3)^2}$, or $(x + 3)^2 + y^2 = 1$. The graph of $y = \pm\sqrt{1 - x^2}$ is translated left 3 units.

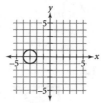

**c.** $y = \pm 2\sqrt{1 - x^2}$, or $x^2 + \left(\frac{y}{2}\right)^2 = 1$. The graph of $y = \pm\sqrt{1 - x^2}$ is stretched vertically by a factor of 2.

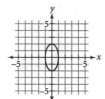

**d.** $y = \pm\sqrt{1 - \left(\frac{x}{2}\right)^2}$, or $\frac{x^2}{4} + y^2 = 1$. The graph of $y = \pm\sqrt{1 - x^2}$ is stretched horizontally by a factor of 2.

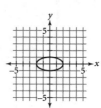

**6. a.** $\left(\frac{x}{3}\right)^2 + y^2 = 1$, or $y = \pm\sqrt{1 - \left(\frac{x}{3}\right)^2}$

**b.** $\dfrac{x}{3}$

**c.** $g(x) = f\left(\dfrac{x}{3}\right)$

**7. a.** $x^2 + (2y)^2 = 1$      **b.** $(2x)^2 + y^2 = 1$

**c.** $\left(\dfrac{x}{2}\right)^2 + (2y)^2 = 1$

**8. a.** $y = 3\sqrt{1 - \left(\frac{x}{0.5}\right)^2}$ and $y = -3\sqrt{1 - \left(\frac{x}{0.5}\right)^2}$.

The graph of the unit circle is horizontally shrunk by a factor of 0.5 and vertically stretched by a factor of 3.

**b.** $y = \pm 3\sqrt{1 - \left(\dfrac{x}{0.5}\right)^2}$
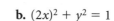

**c.** $y^2 = 9\left(1 - \left(\frac{x}{0.5}\right)^2\right)$, $\left(\frac{y}{3}\right)^2 = 1 - \left(\frac{x}{0.5}\right)^2$, or $\frac{x^2}{0.25} + \frac{y^2}{9} = 1$

$$y = \pm 3\sqrt{1 - \left(\frac{x}{0.5}\right)^2} \qquad \text{Equation in 8b.}$$

$$y^2 = \left(\pm 3\sqrt{1 - \left(\frac{x}{0.5}\right)^2}\right)^2 \qquad \text{Square both sides.}$$

$$y^2 = 9\left(1 - \left(\frac{x}{0.5}\right)^2\right) \qquad \text{Evaluate.}$$

Therefore other equations for the ellipse are $y^2 = 9\left(1 - \left(\frac{x}{0.5}\right)^2\right)$, $\left(\frac{y}{3}\right)^2 = 1 - \left(\frac{x}{0.5}\right)^2$, and $\frac{x^2}{0.25} + \frac{y^2}{9} = 1$.

**9. a.**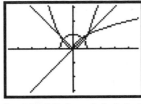

$[-4.7, 4.7, 1, -3.1, 3.1, 1]$

The first four functions intersect at $(0, 0)$ and $(1, 1)$.

**b.** The rectangle has width 1 and height 1. The width is the difference in $x$-coordinates, and the height is the difference in $y$-coordinates.

**c.** $y = \frac{1}{2}x$; $y = 2\left(\frac{x}{4}\right)^2$; $y = 2\sqrt{\frac{x}{4}}$; $y = 2\left|\frac{x}{4}\right|$;

$$y = 2\sqrt{1 - \left(\frac{x}{4}\right)^2}$$

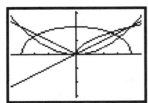

$[-4.7, 4.7, 1, -3.1, 3.1, 1]$

The first four functions intersect at $(0, 0)$ and $(4, 2)$.

**d.** The rectangle has width 4 and height 2. The width is the difference in $x$-coordinates, and the height is the difference in $y$-coordinates.

**e.** $y = 2\left(\frac{x-1}{4}\right) + 3$; $y = 2\left(\frac{x-1}{4}\right)^2 + 3$;

$y = 2\sqrt{\frac{x-1}{4}} + 3$; $y = 2\left|\frac{x-1}{4}\right| + 3$;

$$y = 2\sqrt{1 - \left(\frac{x-1}{4}\right)^2} + 3$$

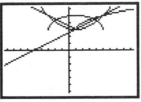

$[-9.4, 9.4, 1, -6.2, 6.2, 1]$

The first four functions intersect at $(1, 3)$ and $(5, 5)$.

**f.** The rectangle has width 4 and height 2. The width is the difference in $x$-coordinates, and the height is the difference in $y$-coordinates.

**g.** The $x$-coordinate is the location of the right endpoint, and the $y$-coordinate is the location of the top of the transformed semicircle.

**10. a.** $\frac{100}{94}$. They should multiply each rating by $\frac{100}{94}$ because $94 \cdot \frac{100}{94} = 100$.

**b.** The mean of the original ratings (from Lesson 4.6, Exercise 13) was 83.75, and the standard deviation was 7.45. For the new ratings, the mean is 89.10 and the standard deviation is 7.92.

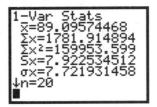

**c.**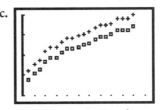

$[0, 22, 2, 60, 100, 10]$

The ratings have been stretched by a factor of $\frac{100}{94}$. All scores increased, so the mean increased. The high ratings differ from the original by more than the lower ones, so they are more spread out and the standard deviation is increased.

**d.** Sample answer: The judges should use the method of adding 6 points to each rating because the standard deviation remains the same and therefore will not change the relative standing of each exhibit. The method of multiplying the original ratings by a factor of $\frac{100}{94}$ increases the standard deviation and unfairly increases the high ratings more than the lower ratings.

**11.** 625, 1562.5, 3906.25. This is a geometric sequence with common ratio 2.5 and recursive formula $u_n = 2.5u_{n-1}$. $2.5(250) = 625$, $2.5(625) = 1562.5$, and $2.5(1562.5) = 3906.25$.

**12. a.** $a \approx 3.87$ or $a \approx 2.13$

| | |
|---|---|
| $\sqrt{1-(a-3)^2} = 0.5$ | Original equation. |
| $1-(a-3)^2 = 0.25$ | Square both sides. |
| $-(a-3)^2 = -0.75$ | Subtract 1 from both sides. |
| $(a-3)^2 = 0.75$ | Multiply both sides by $-1$. |
| $a-3 = \pm\sqrt{0.75}$ | Take the square root of both sides. |
| $a = \sqrt{0.75}+3$ or $a = -\sqrt{0.75}+3$ | Split into two equations. |
| $a \approx 3.87$ or $a \approx 2.13$ | Evaluate. |

Check for extraneous roots by substituting 3.87 and 2.13 for $a$ in the original equation. For accuracy, use the exact expressions, $\sqrt{0.75}+3$ and $-\sqrt{0.75}+3$, instead of the decimal approximations.

$$\sqrt{1-(\sqrt{0.75}+3-3)^2} \stackrel{?}{=} 0.5$$
$$\sqrt{1-0.75} \stackrel{?}{=} 0.5$$
$$\sqrt{0.25} \stackrel{?}{=} 0.5$$
$$0.5 = 0.5$$

$$\sqrt{1-(-\sqrt{0.75}+3-3)^2} \stackrel{?}{=} 0.5$$
$$\sqrt{1-0.75} \stackrel{?}{=} 0.5$$
$$\sqrt{0.25} \stackrel{?}{=} 0.5$$
$$0.5 = 0.5$$

The solutions check, so $a \approx 3.87$ or $a \approx 2.13$.

**b.** $b \approx -1.03$ or $b \approx -2.97$

| | |
|---|---|
| $-4\sqrt{1-(b+2)^2} = -1$ | Original equation. |
| $\sqrt{1-(b+2)^2} = 0.25$ | Divide both sides by $-4$. |
| $1-(b+2)^2 = 0.0625$ | Square both sides. |
| $-(b+2)^2 = -0.9375$ | Subtract 1 from both sides. |
| $(b+2)^2 = 0.9375$ | Multiply both sides by $-1$. |
| $b+2 = \pm\sqrt{0.9375}$ | Take the square root of both sides. |
| $b = \sqrt{0.9375}-2$ or $b = -\sqrt{0.9375}-2$ | Split into two equations. |
| $b \approx -1.03$ or $b \approx -2.97$ | Evaluate. |

Check for extraneous roots by substituting $-1.03$ and $-2.97$ for $b$ in the original equation. For accuracy, use the exact expressions, $\sqrt{0.9375}-2$ and $-\sqrt{0.9375}-2$, instead of the decimal approximations.

$$-4\sqrt{1-\left(\sqrt{0.9375}-2+2\right)^2} \stackrel{?}{=} -1$$
$$-4\sqrt{1-0.9375} \stackrel{?}{=} -1$$
$$-4\sqrt{0.0625} \stackrel{?}{=} -1$$
$$-1 = -1$$

$$-4\sqrt{1-\left(-\sqrt{0.9375}-2+2\right)^2} \stackrel{?}{=} -1$$
$$-4\sqrt{1-0.9375} \stackrel{?}{=} -1$$
$$-4\sqrt{0.0625} \stackrel{?}{=} -1$$
$$-1 = -1$$

The solutions check, so $b \approx -1.03$ or $b \approx -2.97$.

**c.** $c = 3.8$ or $c = 0.2$

| | |
|---|---|
| $\sqrt{1-\left(\dfrac{c-2}{3}\right)^2} = 0.8$ | Original equation. |
| $1-\left(\dfrac{c-2}{3}\right)^2 = 0.64$ | Square both sides. |
| $-\left(\dfrac{c-2}{3}\right)^2 = -0.36$ | Subtract 1 from both sides. |
| $\left(\dfrac{c-2}{3}\right)^2 = 0.36$ | Multiply both sides by $-1$. |
| $\dfrac{c-2}{3} = \pm\sqrt{0.36}$ | Take the square root of both sides. |
| $c = 3\sqrt{0.36}+2$ or $c = -3\sqrt{0.36}+2$ | Multiply both sides by 3, add 2 to both sides, and split into two equations. |
| $c = 3.8$ or $c = 0.2$ | Evaluate. |

Check for extraneous roots by substituting 3.8 and 0.2 for $c$ in the original equation.

$$\sqrt{1-\left(\frac{3.8-2}{3}\right)^2} \stackrel{?}{=} 0.8 \qquad \sqrt{1-\left(\frac{0.2-2}{3}\right)^2} \stackrel{?}{=} 0.8$$
$$\sqrt{0.64} \stackrel{?}{=} 0.8 \qquad\qquad\qquad \sqrt{0.64} \stackrel{?}{=} 0.8$$
$$0.8 = 0.8 \qquad\qquad\qquad\qquad 0.8 = 0.8$$

The solutions check, so $c = 3.8$ or $c = 0.2$.

**d.** $d = -1$

$$3 + 5\sqrt{1 - \left(\frac{d+1}{2}\right)^2} = 8 \qquad \text{Original equation.}$$

$$5\sqrt{1 - \left(\frac{d+1}{2}\right)^2} = 5 \qquad \text{Subtract 3 from both sides.}$$

$$\sqrt{1 - \left(\frac{d+1}{2}\right)^2} = 1 \qquad \text{Divide both sides by 5.}$$

$$1 - \left(\frac{d+1}{2}\right)^2 = 1 \qquad \text{Square both sides.}$$

$$-\left(\frac{d+1}{2}\right)^2 = 0 \qquad \text{Subtract 1 from both sides.}$$

$$\left(\frac{d+1}{2}\right)^2 = 0 \qquad \text{Multiply both sides by } -1.$$

$$\frac{d+1}{2} = 0 \qquad \text{Take the square root of both sides.}$$

$$d = -1 \qquad \text{Multiply both sides by 2 and then subtract 1 from both sides.}$$

Check for extraneous roots by substituting $-1$ for $d$ in the original equation.

$$3 + 5\sqrt{1 - \left(\frac{-1+1}{2}\right)^2} \stackrel{?}{=} 8$$

$$3 + 5 \stackrel{?}{=} 8$$

$$8 = 8$$

The solution checks, so $d = -1$.

**13. a.**

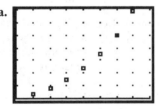

[0, 80, 10, 0, 350, 50]

**b.** Sample answer: $\hat{y} = 0.07(x - 3)^2 + 21$

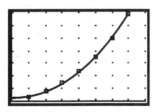

[0, 80, 10, 0, 350, 50]

The vertex of the parent parabola, $y = x^2$, has been translated from $(0, 0)$ to $(3, 21)$, so write the equation $y = (x - 3)^2 + 21$. The graph of

$y = (x - 3)^2 + 21$ does not fit the data because the function still needs to be shrunk. Pick a data point, such as $(50, 173)$. Because this point is $50 - 3$, or 47 units to the right of the vertex, if the graph were simply a translation of the graph of $y = x^2$, then the $y$-coordinate would be $47^2$, or 2209 units above the vertex. But $(50, 173)$ is only 152 units above the vertex, so the graph is shrunk vertically by a factor of $\frac{152}{2209}$, or approximately 0.07. Therefore the graph of $\hat{y} = 0.07(x - 3)^2 + 21$ fits the data nicely.

**c.** For the sample equation given in 13b, the residuals are $-5.43$, $0.77$, $0.97$, $-0.83$, $-2.63$, $-0.43$, and $7.77$, and the root mean square error is 4.45.

**d.** Approximately 221 ft. Substitute 56.5 for $x$ in the function in 13b: $\hat{y} = 0.07(56.5 - 3)^2 + 21 \approx 221$. The stopping distance for a car moving 56.5 mi/h is approximately 221 ft.

**e.** The root mean square error is 4.45, so from 13d, 221 ft should be correct within 4.45 ft ($\pm 4.45$ ft) of the actual stopping distance. That is, the actual stopping distance should fall between 216.55 and 225.45 ft.

**14. a.**

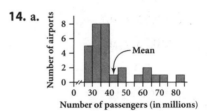

**b.** 1,240,000,000 passengers, assuming that all data occur at midpoints of bins. First find the midpoints of each bin, then multiply by the corresponding number of airports, and finally add the products to estimate the total number of passengers.

$27.5(5) + 32.5(8) + 37.5(8) + 42.5(1) +$
$47.5(2) + 57.5(1) + 62.5(2) + 67.5(1) +$
$72.5(1) + 82.5(1) = 1239.6 \approx 1240$

Therefore approximately 1,240,000,000 passengers used the 30 airports in the year 2000.

**c.** $\frac{1,240,000,000}{30} = 41,333,333$ passengers

**d.**

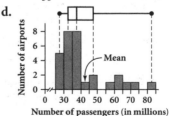

Five-number summary: 27.5, 32.5, 37.5, 47.5, 82.5. Assume that all data occur at midpoints of bins.

**15. a.** $y = -(3x + 1)$, or $y = -3x - 1$

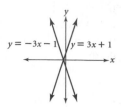

**b.** $y = 3(-x) + 1$, or $y = -3x + 1$

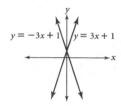

**c.** $y = -(3(-x) + 1)$, or $y = 3x - 1$

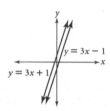

**d.** The two lines are parallel.

### IMPROVING YOUR VISUAL THINKING SKILLS

## LESSON 4.8

### EXERCISES

**1. a.** $f(4) = 3 + \sqrt{4 + 5} = 3 + \sqrt{9} = 3 + 3 = 6$

**b.** $f(g(4)) = 7$. First find $g(4)$, then find $f(g(4))$.

$g(4) = 2 + (4 - 1)^2 = 2 + 9 = 11$

$f(g(4)) = f(11) = 3 + \sqrt{11 + 5}$

$\qquad = 3 + \sqrt{16} = 3 + 4 = 7$

**c.** $g(-1) = 2 + (-1 - 1)^2 = 2 + 4 = 6$

**d.** $g(f(-1)) = 18$. First find $f(-1)$, then find $g(f(-1))$.

$f(-1) = 3 + \sqrt{-1 + 5} = 3 + 2 = 5$

$g(f(-1)) = g(5) = 2 + (5 - 1)^2 = 2 + 4^2$

$\qquad = 2 + 16 = 18$

**2. a.** $g(f(4)) = g(1) = 2$    **b.** $f(g(-2)) = f(4) = 1$

**c.** $f(g(f(3))) = f(g(5)) = f(5) = 0$

**3. a.** Approximately 1.5 m/s. On Graph A, locate 20 on the horizontal axis, move up to the curve, and move left to about 1.5 on the vertical axis.

**b.** Approximately 12 L/min. On Graph B, locate 1.5 on the horizontal axis, move up to the line, and move left to about 12 on the vertical axis.

**c.** Approximately 15 L/min. The swimmer's speed is approximately 1.8 m/s after 40 s of swimming, and the swimmer's oxygen consumption at a swimming speed of 1.8 m/s is approximately 15 L/min, so the swimmer's oxygen consumption after 40 s of swimming is approximately 15 L/min.

**4. a.** Product: $f(x) \cdot g(x)$ where $f(x) = 5$ and $g(x) = \sqrt{3 + 2x}$; or composition: $f(g(x))$ where $f(x) = 5\sqrt{x}$ and $g(x) = 3 + 2x$

**b.** Composition: $g(f(x))$ where $f(x) = |x + 5|$ and $g(x) = 3 + (x - 3)^2$

**c.** Product: $f(x) \cdot g(x)$ where $f(x) = (x - 5)^2$ and $g(x) = 2 - \sqrt{x}$

**5. a.** $y = |(x - 3)^2 - 1|$. The graph is a parabola whose range is limited to positive values, or $y \geq 0$. The portion of the graph that would be below the $x$-axis, from $(2, 0)$ to $(4, 0)$, is reflected across the $x$-axis, which is accomplished by taking the absolute value. The parabola is translated right 3 units and down 1 unit, yielding the equation $y = |(x - 3)^2 - 1|$.

**b.** $y = |(x - 3)^2 - 1|$ is a composition, $y = f(g(x))$, where $f(x) = |x|$ and $g(x) = (x - 3)^2 - 1$.

**6. a.** $g(f(2)) = g(1) = 2$

**b.** $f(g(6)) = f(-2) = 6$

**c.** Sample answer: Select 1 from $g$: $f(g(1)) = f(2) = 1$. Select 4 from $f$: $g(f(4)) = g(-2) = 4$. The composition of $f$ and $g$ will always give back the original number because $f$ and $g$ "undo" the effects of each other. This is because the coordinate pairs in function $g$ are the reverse of the coordinate pairs in function $f$.

**7. a.** For Gauges A and B, plot the points $(12, 13)$ and $(36, 29)$, and draw a line that contains these two points. For Gauges B and C, plot the points $(20, 57)$ and $(32, 84)$, and draw the line that contains these two points.

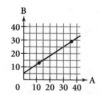
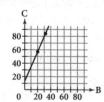

**b.** Approximately 41. When A measures 12, B measures 13 and, according to the graph of C as a function of B, when B measures 13, C measures about 41.

**c.** The slope between (12, 13) and (36, 29) is
$\frac{29-13}{36-12} = \frac{16}{24} = \frac{2}{3}$. Using either point and the slope, the function is $B = \frac{2}{3}(A - 12) + 13$, or $B = \frac{2}{3}A + 5$.

**d.** The slope between (20, 57) and (32, 84) is
$\frac{84-57}{32-20} = \frac{27}{12} = \frac{9}{4}$. Using either point and the slope, the function is $C = \frac{9}{4}(B - 20) + 57$, or $C = \frac{9}{4}B + 12$.

**e.** $C = 1.5A + 23.25$. Substitute $\frac{2}{3}A + 5$ for $B$ in the equation $C = \frac{9}{4}B + 12$.

$$C = \frac{9}{4}\left(\frac{2}{3}A + 5\right) + 12$$

$$C = \frac{3}{2}A + \frac{45}{4} + 12$$

$$C = 1.5A + 11.25 + 12$$

$$C = 1.5A + 23.25$$

**8.** The linear equation of the graph is $g(x) = \frac{1}{2}x + 1$.

**a.** The function is $y = \sqrt{\frac{1}{2}x + 1}$, or $y = \sqrt{\frac{x+2}{2}}$, whose graph is the image of $y = \sqrt{x}$ after a horizontal stretch by a factor of 2 and a translation left 2 units.

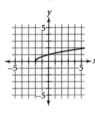

**b.** The function is $y = \left|\frac{1}{2}x + 1\right|$, or $y = \left|\frac{x+2}{2}\right|$, whose graph is the image of $y = |x|$ after a horizontal stretch by a factor of 2 and a translation left 2 units.

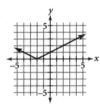

**c.** The function is $y = \left(\frac{1}{2}x + 1\right)^2$, or $y = \left(\frac{x+2}{2}\right)^2$, whose graph is the image of $y = x^2$ after a horizontal stretch by a factor of 2 and a translation left 2 units.

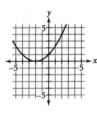

**9. a.** $g(f(2)) = g(3) = 2$

Solve graphically: When $x = 2$ the corresponding $y$-value on line $f$ is 3. Use the output value as the input value for $g$: When $x = 3$ the corresponding $y$-value on line $g$ is 2.

Solve numerically:

$$f(2) = 2(2) - 1 = 4 - 1 = 3$$

$$g(3) = \frac{1}{2}(3) + \frac{1}{2} = \frac{3}{2} + \frac{1}{2} = \frac{4}{2} = 2$$

**b.** $f(g(-1)) = f(0) = -1$

Solve graphically: When $x = -1$ the corresponding $y$-value on line $g$ is 0. Use the output value as the input value for $f$: When $x = 0$ the corresponding $y$-value on line $f$ is $-1$.

Solve numerically:

$$g(-1) = \frac{1}{2}(-1) + \frac{1}{2} = -\frac{1}{2} + \frac{1}{2} = 0$$

$$f(0) = 2(0) - 1 = -1$$

**c.** Possible answer: Choose $x = 3$.

Solve graphically: When $x = 3$ the corresponding $y$-value on line $f$ is 5. Use the output as the input value for $g$: When $x = 5$ the corresponding $y$-value on line $g$ is 3.

Solve numerically:

$$f(3) = 2(3) - 1 = 5$$

$$g(5) = \frac{1}{2}(5) + \frac{1}{2} = \frac{5}{2} + \frac{1}{2} = \frac{6}{2} = 3$$

**d.** Possible answer: Choose $x = 0$.

Solve graphically: When $x = 0$ the corresponding $y$-value on line $g$ is 0.5. Use the output as the input value for $f$: When $x = 0.5$ the corresponding $y$-value on line $f$ is 0.

Solve numerically:

$$g(0) = \frac{1}{2}(0) + \frac{1}{2} = 0.5$$

$$f(0.5) = 2(0.5) - 1 = 0$$

**e.** The two functions "undo" the effects of each other and thus give back the original value.

**10. a.** $f(g(3)) = 4$

$$g(3) = (3 - 2)^2 = 1^2 = 1$$

$$f(1) = -1^2 + 2(1) + 3 = -1 + 2 + 3 = 4$$

**b.** $f(g(2)) = 3$

$$g(2) = (2 - 2)^2 = 0^2 = 0$$

$$f(0) = -0^2 + 2(0) + 3 = 0 + 0 + 3 = 3$$

**c.** $g(f(0.5)) = 3.0625$

$$f(0.5) = -(0.5)^2 + 2(0.5) + 3$$

$$= -0.25 + 1 + 3 = 3.75$$

$$g(3.75) = (3.75 - 2)^2 = 1.75^2 = 3.0625$$

**d.** $g(f(1)) = 4$

$$f(1) = -1^2 + 2(1) + 3 = -1 + 2 + 3 = 4$$

$$g(4) = (4 - 2)^2 = 2^2 = 4$$

**e.** $f(g(x)) = -x^4 + 8x^3 - 22x^2 + 24x - 5$

$f(g(x)) = -\left((x-2)^2\right)^2 + 2(x-2)^2 + 3$

$\qquad = -(x-2)^4 + 2\left(x^2 - 4x + 4\right) + 3$

$\qquad = -\left(x^4 + 4x^3(-2) + 6x^2(-2)^2 + 4x(-2)^3 + 1(-2)^4\right) + 2x^2 - 8x + 8 + 3$

$\qquad = -\left(x^4 - 8x^3 + 24x^2 - 32x + 16\right) + 2x^2 - 8x + 11$

$\qquad = -x^4 + 8x^3 - 24x^2 + 32x - 16 + 2x^2 - 8x + 11$

$\qquad = -x^4 + 8x^3 - 22x^2 + 24x - 5$

**f.** $g(f(x)) = x^4 - 4x^3 + 2x^2 + 4x + 1$

$g(f(x)) = \left(\left(-x^2 + 2x + 3\right) - 2\right)^2$

$\qquad = \left(-x^2 + 2x + 1\right)^2$

$\qquad = \left(-x^2 + 2x + 1\right)\left(-x^2 + 2x + 1\right)$

$\qquad = x^4 - 2x^3 - x^2 - 2x^3 + 4x^2 + 2x - x^2 + 2x + 1$

$\qquad = x^4 - 4x^3 + 2x^2 + 4x + 1$

**11.** If the parent function is $y = x^2$, then the equation is $y = -3x^2 + 3$. If the parent function is $y = \sqrt{1 - x^2}$, then the equation is $y = 3\sqrt{1 - x^2}$. It appears that when $x = 0.5$, $y \approx 2.6$. Substitute 0.5 for $x$ in each equation and see which gives approximately 2.6 for $y$.

$y = -3(0.5)^2 + 3 = 2.25$

$y = 3\sqrt{1 - 0.5^2} \approx 2.598$

Thus the stretched semicircle is the better fit.

**12. a.** Jen: $5.49 - 0.50 = 4.99$; $(1 - 0.10)(4.99) = \$4.49$

Priya: $(1 - 0.10)(5.49) = 4.94$; $4.94 - 0.50 = \$4.44$

**b.** $C(x) = x - 0.50$

**c.** $D(x) = (1 - 0.10)x$, or $D(x) = 0.90x$

**d.** $C(D(x)) = 0.90x - 0.50$

**e.** The 10% discount was taken first, so it was Priya's server.

**f.** There is no price because $C(D(x)) = D(C(x))$, or $0.90x - 0.50 = 0.90(x - 0.50)$ has no solution. The lines $y = C(D(x))$ and $y = D(C(x))$ are parallel.

**13. a.** $x = -5$ or $x = 13$

| | |
|---|---|
| $\sqrt{\lvert x - 4 \rvert} = 3$ | Original equation. |
| $\lvert x - 4 \rvert = 9$ | Square both sides. |
| $x - 4 = 9$ or $x - 4 = -9$ | Split into two equations. |
| $x = 13$ or $\quad x = -5$ | Add 4 to both sides of both equations. |

Check for extraneous roots by substituting 13 and $-5$ for $x$ in the original equation:

$\sqrt{\lvert 13 - 4 \rvert} \overset{?}{=} 3 \qquad \sqrt{\lvert -5 - 4 \rvert} \overset{?}{=} 3$

$\sqrt{\lvert 9 \rvert} \overset{?}{=} 3 \qquad \sqrt{\lvert -9 \rvert} \overset{?}{=} 3$

$\sqrt{9} \overset{?}{=} 3 \qquad\qquad \sqrt{9} \overset{?}{=} 3$

$3 = 3 \qquad\qquad\qquad 3 = 3$

Both solutions check, so $x = -5$ or $x = 13$.

**b.** $x = -1$ or $x = 23$

| | |
|---|---|
| $\left(3 - \sqrt{x + 2}\right)^2 = 4$ | Original equation. |
| $3 - \sqrt{x + 2} = \pm 2$ | Take the square root of both sides. |
| $-\sqrt{x + 2} = -1$ or $-\sqrt{x + 2} = -5$ | Split into two equations and subtract 3 from both sides of both equations. |
| $x + 2 = 1$ or $x + 2 = 25$ | Square both sides of both equations. |
| $x = -1$ or $x = 23$ | Subtract 2 from both sides of both equations. |

Check for extraneous roots by substituting $-1$ and 23 for $x$ in the original equation:

$\left(3 - \sqrt{-1 + 2}\right)^2 \overset{?}{=} 4 \qquad \left(3 - \sqrt{23 + 2}\right)^2 \overset{?}{=} 4$

$\left(3 - \sqrt{1}\right)^2 \overset{?}{=} 4 \qquad\quad \left(3 - \sqrt{25}\right)^2 \overset{?}{=} 4$

$(3 - 1)^2 \overset{?}{=} 4 \qquad\qquad\quad (3 - 5)^2 \overset{?}{=} 4$

$2^2 \overset{?}{=} 4 \qquad\qquad\qquad\quad (-2)^2 \overset{?}{=} 4$

$4 = 4 \qquad\qquad\qquad\qquad 4 = 4$

Both solutions check, so $x = -1$ or $x = 23$.

**c.** $x = 64$

| | |
|---|---|
| $\lvert 3 - \sqrt{x} \rvert = 5$ | Original equation. |
| $3 - \sqrt{x} = 5$ or $3 - \sqrt{x} = -5$ | Split into two equations. |
| $-\sqrt{x} = 2$ or $-\sqrt{x} = -8$ | Subtract 3 from both sides of both equations. |
| $x = 4$ or $x = 64$ | Square both sides of both equations. |

Check for extraneous roots by substituting 4 and 64 for $x$ in the original equation:

$|3 - \sqrt{4}| \overset{?}{=} 5$ $\qquad$ $|3 - \sqrt{64}| \overset{?}{=} 5$

$|3 - 2| \overset{?}{=} 4$ $\qquad\qquad$ $|3 - 8| \overset{?}{=} 5$

$|1| \overset{?}{=} 4$ $\qquad\qquad$ $|-5| \overset{?}{=} 5$

$1 \neq 4$ $\qquad\qquad\qquad$ $5 = 5$

Only one solution checks, so $x = 64$.

You might have recognized the extraneous root earlier by noticing that $-\sqrt{x} = 2$ could never be true, because a negative value will never equal a positive value.

**d.** $x = \pm\sqrt{1.5} \approx \pm1.22$

| | |
|---|---|
| $3 + 5\sqrt{1 + 2x^2} = 13$ | Original equation. |
| $5\sqrt{1 + 2x^2} = 10$ | Subtract 3 from both sides. |
| $\sqrt{1 + 2x^2} = 2$ | Divide both sides by 5. |
| $1 + 2x^2 = 4$ | Square both sides of both equations. |
| $2x^2 = 3$ | Subtract 1 from both sides. |
| $x^2 = 1.5$ | Divide both sides by 2. |
| $x = \pm\sqrt{1.5}$ | Take the square root of both sides. |

Check for extraneous roots by substituting $\sqrt{1.5}$ and $-\sqrt{1.5}$ for $x$ in the original equation:

$3 + 5\sqrt{1 + 2(\sqrt{1.5})^2} \overset{?}{=} 13$

$3 + 5\sqrt{1 + 2(1.5)} \overset{?}{=} 13$

$3 + 5\sqrt{4} \overset{?}{=} 13$

$3 + 5(2) \overset{?}{=} 13$

$3 + 10 \overset{?}{=} 13$

$13 = 13$

$3 + 5\sqrt{1 + 2(-\sqrt{1.5})^2} \overset{?}{=} 13$

$3 + 5\sqrt{1 + 2(1.5)} \overset{?}{=} 13$

$3 + 5\sqrt{4} \overset{?}{=} 13$

$3 + 5(2) \overset{?}{=} 13$

$3 + 10 \overset{?}{=} 13$

$13 = 13$

Both solutions check, so $x = \pm\sqrt{1.5}$.

**14. a.** The independent variable, $x$, is potential difference (in volts). The dependent variable, $y$, is current (in amperes).

**b.**

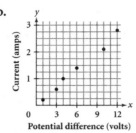

**c.** $\hat{y} = 0.2278x - 0.0167$. To find the median-median line, first divide the data set into three groups of points, and then find the median $x$- and $y$-values of each group. The three summary points are $M_1(2, 0.4)$, $M_2(5, 1.2)$, and $M_3(11, 2.45)$. The slope of the line through $M_1$ and $M_3$ is $\frac{2.45 - 0.4}{11 - 2} = \frac{2.05}{9} \approx 0.2278$, so the equation of this line is $y = 0.4 + 0.2278(x - 2)$, or $y = 0.2278x - 0.0556$. The equation of the parallel line through $M_2$ is $y = 1.2 + 0.2278(x - 5)$, or $y = 0.2278x + 0.061$. The $y$-intercept of the median-median line is the mean of the three $y$-intercepts.

$$\frac{-0.0556 + (-0.0556) + (0.061)}{3} \approx -0.0167$$

Therefore the equation of the median-median line is $\hat{y} = 0.2278x - 0.0167$.

**d.** The slope remains the same and the $y$-intercept is 0, so $\hat{y} = 0.2278x$.

**e.** The ohm rating is $\frac{potential\ difference}{current}$ and the slope of the median-median line measures the ratio $\frac{current}{potential\ difference}$. Therefore the ohm rating is the reciprocal of the slope of this line.

**f.** $\frac{1}{0.2278} \approx 4.4$ ohms

**15. a.** $\left(\frac{x}{3}\right)^2 + \left(\frac{y}{3}\right)^2 = 1$, or $x^2 + y^2 = 9$

**b.** The graph is a circle with center $(0, 0)$ and radius 3.

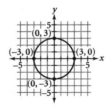

**16. a.** $g(x) = (x + 3)^2 + 5$

**b.** $(-3, 5)$. The equation for $g(x)$ is in the form $y = (x - h) + k$ with vertex $(h, k)$, so the vertex is $(-3, 5)$.

**c.** $(-1, 9)$. On the graph of $f(x) = x^2$, the point 2 units to the right of the vertex is $(2)^2$, or 4 units above the vertex. The same is true on the graph of $g(x) = (x - 3)^2 + 5$. The point is $(-3 + 2, 5 + 4)$, or $(-1, 9)$.

## EXTENSION

See the solution to Take Another Look activities 4 and 5 on page 84.

## CHAPTER 4 REVIEW

### EXERCISES

**1.** Sample answer: For a time there are no pops. Then the popping rate slowly increases. When the popping reaches a furious intensity, it seems to level out. Then the number of pops per second drops quickly until the last pop is heard.

**2. a.** $f(4) = -2(4) + 7 = -8 + 7 = -1$

**b.** $g(-3) = (-3)^2 - 2 = 9 - 2 = 7$

**c.** $h(x + 2) - 3 = ((x + 2) + 1)^2 - 3 = (x + 3)^2 - 3$

**d.** $f(g(3)) = -7$

$g(3) = 3^2 - 2 = 9 - 2 = 7$

$f(7) = -14 + 7 = -7$

**e.** $g(h(-2)) = -1$

$h(-2) = (-2 + 1)^2 = 1$

$g(1) = 1^2 - 2 = 1 - 2 = -1$

**f.** $h(f(-1)) = 100$

$f(-1) = -2(-1) + 7 = 2 + 7 = 9$

$h(9) = (9 + 1)^2 = 10^2 = 100$

**g.** $f(g(a)) = -2a^2 + 11$

$g(a) = a^2 - 2$

$f(a^2 - 2) = -2(a^2 - 2) + 7 = -2a^2 + 4 + 7$

$\qquad = -2a^2 + 11$

**h.** $g(f(a)) = 4a^2 - 28a + 47$

$f(a) = -2a + 7$

$g(-2a + 7) = (-2a + 7)^2 - 2$

$\qquad = 4a^2 - 28a + 49 - 2$

$\qquad = 4a^2 - 28a + 47$

**i.** $h(f(a)) = 4a^2 - 32a + 64$

$f(a) = -2a + 7$

$h(-2a + 7) = ((-2a + 7) + 1)^2$

$\qquad = (-2a + 8)^2 = 4a^2 - 32a + 64$

**3. a.** The graph of $y = f(x) - 3$ is a translation of the graph of $y = f(x)$ down 3 units.

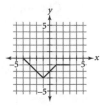

**b.** The graph of $y = f(x - 3)$ is a translation of the graph of $y = f(x)$ right 3 units.

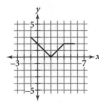

**c.** The graph of $y = 3f(x)$ is a vertical stretch of the graph of $y = f(x)$ by a factor of 3.

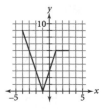

**d.** The graph of $y = f(-x)$ is a reflection of the graph of $y = f(x)$ across the $y$-axis.

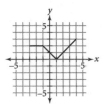

**4. a.** Translate left 2 units and down 3 units.

**b.** Rewrite the equation as $y = -f\left(\frac{x}{2}\right)$. Horizontally stretch by a factor of 2, and then reflect across the $x$-axis.

**c.** Horizontally shrink by a factor of $\frac{1}{2}$, vertically stretch by a factor of 2, translate right 1 unit, and translate up 3 units.

**5. a.** Rewrite the equation as $y = f(x - 2) + 1$. Translate the graph of $y = f(x)$ right 2 units and up 1 unit.

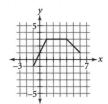

**b.** Rewrite the equation as $y = 2f(x + 1) - 3$. Vertically stretch the graph of $y = f(x)$ by a factor of 2, then translate left 1 unit and down 3 units.

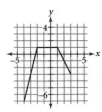

**c.** Reflect the graph of $y = f(x)$ across the $y$-axis and then translate up 1 unit.

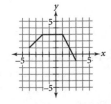

*Discovering Advanced Algebra Solutions Manual*
©2004 Key Curriculum Press

**d.** Rewrite the equation as $y = f\left(\frac{x}{2}\right) - 2$. Horizontally stretch the graph of $y = f(x)$ by a factor of 2 and then translate down 2 units.

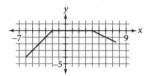

**e.** Reflect the graph of $y = f(x)$ across the $x$-axis and then translate right 3 units and up 1 unit.

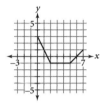

**f.** Rewrite the equation as $y = -2f\left(\frac{x-1}{1.5}\right) - 2$. Horizontally stretch the graph of $y = f(x)$ by a factor of 1.5, vertically stretch by a factor of 2, reflect across the $x$-axis, and translate right 1 unit and down 2 units.

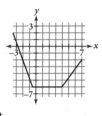

**6. a.** The graph is a transformed semicircle, so the parent function is $y = \sqrt{1 - x^2}$. The graph is stretched vertically by a factor of 3 and translated down 1 unit, so the equation is $y = 3\sqrt{1 - x^2} - 1$.

**b.** The parent function is $y = \sqrt{1 - x^2}$. The graph is stretched horizontally by a factor of 5, stretched vertically by a factor of 2, and translated up 3 units. The equation is $y = 2\sqrt{1 - \left(\frac{x}{5}\right)^2} + 3$.

**c.** The parent function is $y = \sqrt{1 - x^2}$. The graph is stretched horizontally by a factor of 4, stretched vertically by a factor of 4, and translated right 3 units and down 1 unit. The equation is $y = 4\sqrt{1 - \left(\frac{x-3}{4}\right)^2} - 1$.

**d.** The graph is a transformed parabola, so the parent function is $y = x^2$. The graph is translated right 2 units and down 4 units, so the equation is $y = (x - 2)^2 - 4$.

**e.** The parent function is $y = x^2$. The graph is stretched vertically by a factor of 2, reflected across the $y$-axis, and translated left 1 unit, so the equation is $y = -2(x + 1)^2$.

**f.** The graph is a transformed square root function, so the parent function is $y = \sqrt{x}$. The graph is reflected across the $y$-axis and the $x$-axis and translated right 1 unit and down 3 units, so the equation is $y = -\sqrt{-(x - 2)} - 3$.

**g.** The graph is a transformed absolute-value function, so the parent function is $y = |x|$.

The graph is shrunk vertically by a factor of 0.5 and translated left 2 units and down 2 units, so the equation is $y = 0.5|x + 2| - 2$.

**h.** The parent function is $y = |x|$. The graph is stretched vertically by a factor of 2, reflected across the $x$-axis, and translated right 3 units and up 2 units, so the equation is $y = -2|x - 3| + 2$.

**7. a.** $y = \frac{2}{3}x - 2$

| | |
|---|---|
| $2x - 3y = 6$ | Original equation. |
| $-3y = -2x + 6$ | Subtract $2x$ from both sides. |
| $y = \frac{2}{3}x - 2$ | Divide both sides by $-3$. |

**b.** $y = \pm\sqrt{x + 3} - 1$

| | |
|---|---|
| $(y + 1)^2 - 3 = x$ | Original equation. |
| $(y + 1)^2 = x + 3$ | Add 3 to both sides. |
| $y + 1 = \pm\sqrt{x + 3}$ | Take the square root of both sides. |
| $y = \pm\sqrt{x + 3} - 1$ | Subtract 1 from both sides. |

**c.** $y = \pm\sqrt{-(x - 2)^2 + 1}$

| | |
|---|---|
| $\sqrt{1 - y^2} + 2 = x$ | Original equation. |
| $\sqrt{1 - y^2} = x - 2$ | Subtract 2 from both sides. |
| $1 - y^2 = (x - 2)^2$ | Square both sides. |
| $-y^2 = (x - 2)^2 - 1$ | Subtract 1 from both sides. |
| $y^2 = -(x - 2)^2 + 1$ | Multiply both sides by $-1$. |
| $y = \pm\sqrt{-(x - 2)^2 + 1}$ | Take the square root of both sides. |

**8. a.** $x = 8.25$

| | |
|---|---|
| $4\sqrt{x - 2} = 10$ | Original equation. |
| $\sqrt{x - 2} = 2.5$ | Divide both sides by 4. |
| $x - 2 = 6.25$ | Square both sides. |
| $x = 8.25$ | Add 2 to both sides. |

Check for extraneous roots by substituting 8.25 for $x$.

$$4\sqrt{8.25 - 2} \stackrel{?}{=} 10$$
$$4\sqrt{6.25} \stackrel{?}{=} 10$$
$$\sqrt{6.25} \stackrel{?}{=} 2.5$$
$$2.5 = 2.5$$

The solution checks, so $x = 8.25$.

**b.** $x = \pm\sqrt{45} \approx \pm 6.7$

$$\left(\frac{x}{-3}\right)^2 = 5 \qquad \text{Original equation.}$$

$$\frac{x^2}{9} = 5 \qquad \text{Square } \frac{x}{-3}.$$

$$x^2 = 45 \qquad \text{Multiply both sides by 9.}$$

$$x = \pm\sqrt{45} \approx \pm 6.7 \quad \begin{array}{l}\text{Take the square root of}\\ \text{both sides.}\end{array}$$

Check for extraneous roots by substituting $\sqrt{45}$ and $-\sqrt{45}$ for $x$.

$$\left(\frac{\sqrt{45}}{-3}\right)^2 \overset{?}{=} 5 \qquad\qquad \left(\frac{-\sqrt{45}}{-3}\right)^2 \overset{?}{=} 5$$

$$\frac{45}{9} \overset{?}{=} 5 \qquad\qquad\qquad \frac{45}{9} \overset{?}{=} 5$$

$$5 = 5 \qquad\qquad\qquad\quad 5 = 5$$

The solutions check, so $x = \pm\sqrt{45}$.

**c.** $x = 11$ or $x = -5$

$$\left|\frac{x-3}{2}\right| = 4 \qquad \text{Original equation.}$$

$$\frac{x-3}{2} = 4 \text{ or } \frac{x-3}{2} = -4 \quad \begin{array}{l}\text{Split into two}\\ \text{equations.}\end{array}$$

$$x - 3 = 8 \text{ or } x - 3 = -8 \quad \begin{array}{l}\text{Multiply both sides of}\\ \text{both equations by 2.}\end{array}$$

$$x = 11 \text{ or } \quad x = -5 \quad \begin{array}{l}\text{Add 3 to both sides of}\\ \text{both equations.}\end{array}$$

**d.** No solution

$$3\sqrt{1 + \left(\frac{x}{5}\right)^2} = 2 \quad \text{Original equation.}$$

$$\sqrt{1 + \left(\frac{x}{5}\right)^2} = \frac{2}{3} \quad \text{Divide both sides by 3.}$$

$$1 + \left(\frac{x}{5}\right)^2 = \frac{4}{9} \quad \text{Square both sides.}$$

$$\left(\frac{x}{5}\right)^2 = -\frac{5}{9} \quad \text{Subtract 1 from both sides.}$$

The square of any real number is always positive, so there are no real solutions.

**9. a.** (*See table at bottom of page.*)

**b.**

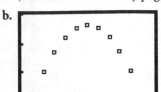

[0.8, 2, 0.1, 17000, 20000, 1000]

**c.** (1.40, 19600). By charging \$1.40 per ride, the company achieves the maximum revenue, \$19,600.

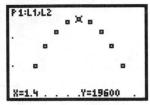

[0.8, 2, 0.1, 17000, 20000, 1000]

**d.** $\hat{y} = -10000(x - 1.4)^2 + 19600$. Using the form $y = a(x - h)^2 + k$ with vertex $(h, k)$ and vertical scale factor $a$, $y = a(x - 1.4)^2 + 19600$. Choose a point on the graph such as (1, 18000) and substitute for $x$ and $y$ to find the vertical scale factor.

$$18000 = a(1 - 1.4)^2 + 19600 \quad \begin{array}{l}\text{Substitute 1 for } x\\ \text{and 18000 for } y.\end{array}$$

$$-1600 = a(-0.4)^2 \quad \begin{array}{l}\text{Subtract 19600}\\ \text{from both sides.}\end{array}$$

$$a = \frac{-1600}{0.16} = -10000 \quad \begin{array}{l}\text{Divide both sides}\\ \text{by } (-0.4)^2, \text{ or}\\ 0.16.\end{array}$$

The function that models the data is $\hat{y} = -10000(x - 1.4)^2 + 19600$.

**i.** \$16,000. Substitute 2 for $x$.

$$y = -10000(2 - 1.4)^2 + 19600$$

$$= -10000(0.6)^2 + 19600 = -3600 + 19600$$

$$= 16000$$

If the fare is \$2.00, the revenue is \$16,000.

---

**Chapter 4 Review, Exercise 9a**

| Fare (\$) $x$ | 1.10 | 1.20 | 1.30 | 1.40 | 1.50 | 1.60 | 1.70 | 1.80 |
|---|---|---|---|---|---|---|---|---|
| Number of passengers | 17000 | 16000 | 15000 | 14000 | 13000 | 12000 | 11000 | 10000 |
| Revenue (\$) $y$ | 18700 | 19200 | 19500 | 19600 | 19500 | 19200 | 18700 | 18000 |

*Discovering Advanced Algebra Solutions Manual*
©2004 Key Curriculum Press

**ii.** $0 or $2.80. Substitute 0 for $y$ and solve for $x$.

$0 = -10000(x - 1.4)^2 + 19600$    Substitute 0 for $y$.

$-19600 = -10000(x - 1.4)^2$    Subtract 19600 from both sides.

$1.96 = (x - 1.4)^2$    Divide both sides by $-10,000$.

$\pm\sqrt{1.96} = x - 1.4$    Take the square root of both sides.

$x = \pm\sqrt{1.96} + 1.4$    Add 1.4 to both sides.

$x = \pm 1.4 + 1.4$    Evaluate $\sqrt{1.96}$.

$x = 2.8$ or $x = 0$

The fares that make no revenue are $0 and $2.80. The reason that neither of these fares would result in revenue is that for $0, you would be charging no fare so you would take in no revenue, and for $2.80, the fare is so expensive that no passenger would take the bus.

### TAKE ANOTHER LOOK

**1.** The parent functions $y = x^2$, $y = \sqrt{1 - x^2}$, and $y = |x|$ are even functions. They all have the $y$-axis as a line of symmetry.

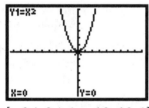

$[-9.4, 9.4, 1, -6.2, 6.2, 1]$

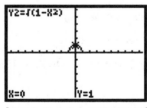

$[-9.4, 9.4, 1, -6.2, 6.2, 1]$

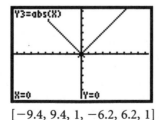

$[-9.4, 9.4, 1, -6.2, 6.2, 1]$

Here are the graphs of the odd functions $y = x^3$, $y = \frac{1}{x}$, and $y = \sqrt[3]{x}$.

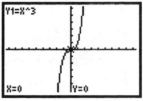

$[-9.4, 9.4, 1, -6.2, 6.2, 1]$

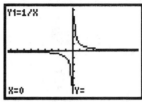

$[-9.4, 9.4, 1, -6.2, 6.2, 1]$

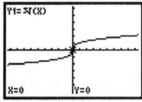

$[-9.4, 9.4, 1, -6.2, 6.2, 1]$

An odd function is said to have symmetry with respect to the origin. You can describe it as 2-fold rotational symmetry (through 180°). If the function $f$ is an odd function, then $-f(-x) = f(x)$ for all values of $x$ in the domain.

The linear function $y = a + bx$ is an example of a function that is neither even nor odd when $a \neq 0$ and $b \neq 0$.

**2.** $y = f(-x + 2a)$, $y = -f(x) + 2b$. Reflecting the graph across the vertical line $x = a$ is equivalent to translating the graph horizontally by the amount $a$ (to move the line $x = a$ to the $y$-axis), reflecting it across the $y$-axis, and then translating it back. This composition of transformations yields the equation $y = f(-(x - a) + a) = f(-x + 2a)$. By a similar composition, a reflection across the horizontal line $y = b$ is given by the equation $y = -(f(x) - b) + b = -f(x) + 2b$.

**3.** You cannot always think of a vertical stretch or shrink as an equivalent horizontal stretch or shrink. The semicircle function, $y = \sqrt{1 - x^2}$, and the circle relation, $x^2 + y^2 = 1$, are two examples where it does not hold true.

**4.**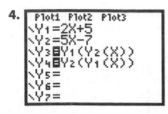

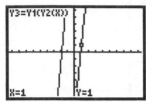

$[-9.4, 9.4, 1, -6.2, 6.2, 1]$

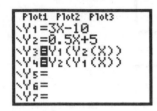

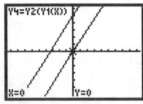

$[-9.4, 9.4, 1, -6.2, 6.2, 1]$

The graphs of the compositions of any two linear equations will be parallel. The linear equations resulting from the compositions will have the same slope, or $x$-coefficient. Algebraic proof:

Let $f(x) = ax + b$ and $g(x) = cx + d$.

$f(g(x)) = a(cx + d) + b = acx + ad + b$

$g(f(x)) = c(ax + b) + d = acx + cb + d$

**5.** Sample answer: Using the graphs of $y = f(x) = x^2$ and $y = g(x) = -x + 1$, you can find $f(g(2)) = 1$. Start at 2 on the $x$-axis, move to the corresponding point on the graph of $y = g(x)$, then move to $y = x$, then to the graph of $y = f(x)$, and lastly to 1 on the $y$-axis.

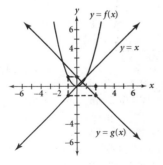

Compositions are essentially a series of input-output functions. Drawing a vertical line up to the graph of $y = g(x)$ gives the value of $g(x)$. Drawing a horizontal line to the graph of $y = x$ makes that $y$-value into an $x$-value. Drawing a vertical line to the graph of $y = f(x)$ evaluates $f(x)$ for that output value, and the horizontal line to the $y$-axis reveals the answer.

# CHAPTER 5

## LESSON 5.1

### EXERCISES

**1. a.** $f(5) = 4.753(0.9421)^5 \approx 3.52738$

  **b.** $g(14) = 238(1.37)^{14} \approx 19528.32$

  **c.** $h(24) = 47.3(0.835)^{24} + 22.3 \approx 22.9242$

  **d.** $j(37) = 225(1.0825)^{37-3} = 225(1.0825)^{34} \approx 3332.20$

**2. a.** 16, 12, 9; $y = 16(0.75)^x$. Starting with the initial value of 16, repeatedly multiply the previous term, $u_{n-1}$, by 0.75 to find the next term, $u_n$. Thus $u_0 = 16$, $u_1 = 0.75(16) = 12$, and $u_2 = 0.75u_1 = 0.75(12) = 9$. The explicit formula for the sequence is $u_n = 16(0.75)^n$. The exponent, $n$, represents the repeated multiplication of the common ratio, 0.75. The equation of the continuous function through the points of this sequence is $y = 16(0.75)^x$.

  **b.** 24, 36, 54; $y = 24(1.5)^x$. Starting with the initial value of 24, repeatedly multiply the previous term, $u_{n-1}$, by 1.5 to find the next term, $u_n$. Thus $u_0 = 24$, $u_1 = 1.5u_0 = 36$, and $u_2 = 1.5u_1 = 54$. The explicit formula for the sequence is given by $u_n = 24(1.5)^n$. The equation of the continuous function through the points of this sequence is $y = 24(1.5)^x$.

**3. a.** 125, 75, 45; $u_0 = 125$ and $u_n = 0.6u_{n-1}$ where $n \geq 1$. Starting with the initial value of 125, $f(0)$, repeatedly multiply the previous term by 0.6 to find the next term. Thus $f(0) = 125(0.6)^0 = 125$, $f(1) = 125(0.6)^1 = 75$, and $f(2) = 125(0.6)^2 = 45$. The recursive formula for the pattern is $u_0 = 125$ and $u_n = 0.6u_{n-1}$ where $n \geq 1$.

  **b.** 3, 6, 12; $u_0 = 3$ and $u_n = 2u_{n-1}$ where $n \geq 1$. Starting with the initial value of 3, $f(0)$, repeatedly multiply the previous term by 2 to find the next term. Thus $f(0) = 3(2)^0 = 3$, $f(1) = 3(2)^1 = 6$, and $f(2) = 3(2)^2 = 12$. The recursive formula for the pattern is given by $u_0 = 3$ and $u_n = 2u_{n-1}$ where $n \geq 1$.

*Discovering Advanced Algebra Solutions Manual*
©2004 Key Curriculum Press

**4. a.** The ratio of 36 to 48 is $\frac{36}{48} = 0.75$. $0.75 - 1 = -0.25$, so this is a 25% decrease.

**b.** The ratio of 72 to 54 is $\frac{72}{54} = 1.\overline{3}$. $1.\overline{3} - 1 = 0.\overline{3}$, so this is a 33.$\overline{3}$% increase.

**c.** The ratio of 47 to 50 is $\frac{47}{50} = 0.94$. $0.94 - 1 = -0.06$, so this is a 6% decrease.

**d.** The ratio of 50 to 47 is $\frac{50}{47} \approx 1.0638$. $1.0638 - 1 = 0.0638$, so this is approximately a 6.38% increase.

**5. a.** $u_0 = 1.151$ and $u_n = (1 + 0.015)u_{n-1}$ where $n \geq 1$. The starting population in 1991, $u_0$, is 1.151 billion. Each year the population is 1.5% greater than the population of the previous year. Multiply the previous year's population, $u_{n-1}$, by $(1 + 0.015)$ to calculate the current year's population, $u_n$. Thus the recursive formula is $u_0 = 1.151$ and $u_n = (1 + 0.015)u_{n-1}$ where $n \geq 1$.

**b.**

| Year | Population (in billions) |
|------|--------------------------|
| 1991 | 1.151 |
| 1992 | 1.168 |
| 1993 | 1.186 |
| 1994 | 1.204 |
| 1995 | 1.222 |
| 1996 | 1.240 |
| 1997 | 1.259 |
| 1998 | 1.277 |
| 1999 | 1.297 |
| 2000 | 1.316 |

Using the recursive formula in 5a, the population in 1991 is $u_0 = 1.151$. The population in 1992 is $u_1 = (1 + 0.015)u_0 = 1.015(1.151) \approx 1.168$. The population in 1993 is $u_2 = (1 + 0.015)u_1 = 1.015(1.168) \approx 1.186$. Continue to use this formula to complete the table.

**c.** $y = 1.151(1 + 0.015)^x$. Let $x$ represent the number of years since 1991, and let $y$ represent the population in billions. The starting population in 1991 is 1.151, and each year the population is multiplied by $(1 + 0.015)$. Express the population growth with the explicit formula $y = 1.151(1 + 0.015)^x$. The exponent, $x$, represents the repeated multiplication by $(1 + 0.015)$. To see that this formula works for your table of values, choose two data points, such as 1994 and 2000. In 1994 it had been 3 years since 1991. Check that the population (in billions) in 1994 equals $1.151(1 + 0.015)^3$. Calculate this to get $1.151(1 + 0.015)^3 \approx 1.204$, which is the same population calculated using the recursive formula. In 2000 it had been 9 years since 1991.

Check that the population (in billions) in 1994 equals $1.151(1 + 0.015)^9$. Calculate this to get $1.151(1 + 0.015)^9 \approx 1.316$, which also matches the table in 5b.

**d.** In 2001 it had been 10 years since 1991, so the exponential equation gives a population of $y = 1.151(1 + 0.015)^{10} \approx 1.336$, which is greater than the actual population. This shows that the growth rate of the Chinese population has decreased since 1991.

**6. a.** $y = 2.56(2.5)^x$; 250 cm; 625 cm. Calculate the ratio of the plant's height each day to its height the previous day: $\frac{6.4}{2.56} = 2.5$, $\frac{16}{6.4} = 2.5$, $\frac{40}{16} = 2.5$, and $\frac{100}{40} = 2.5$. Let $x$ represent the number of the day, and let $y$ represent the height in centimeters. The plant has height 2.56 cm on day 0 and its height increases by a factor of 2.5 every day, so the exponential equation is $y = 2.56(2.5)^x$. On the fifth day, $y = 2.56(2.5)^5 = 250$, so the plant's height is 250 cm. On the sixth day, $y = 2.56(2.5)^6 = 625$, so the plant's height is 625 cm.

**b.** $y = 2.56(2.5)^{3.5} \approx 63.25$ cm. Jack measured the height of the plant at 8:00 A.M. every day, so when Jack's brother measured the plant at 8:00 P.M. on the third day, it had been 3 days 12 hours, or 3.5 days. Use the equation $y = 2.56(2.5)^x$ to find the height of the plant. $y = 2.56(2.5)^{3.5} \approx 63.25$, so its height is approximately 63.25 cm at 8:00 P.M. on the third day.

**c.** Approximately 728 cm. At noon on the sixth day, it has been 6 days 4 hours, or approximately 6.167 days. The height is $y = 2.56(2.5)^{6.167} \approx 728.34$, or approximately 728 cm.

**d.** 0.76 day, or 18 hours. Using the equation $y = 2.56(2.5)^x$, find the value of $x$ when $y = 2 \cdot 2.56 = 5.12$. Using a table on a graphing calculator, you can see that $y \approx 5.1225$ when $x = 0.757$, so the doubling time is approximately 0.76 day, or 18 hours.

| X | Y1 |
|------|--------|
| .753 | 5.1037 |
| .754 | 5.1084 |
| .755 | 5.1131 |
| .756 | 5.1178 |
| .757 | 5.1225 |
| .758 | 5.1272 |
| .759 | 5.1319 |

Y1■2.56(2.5)^X

**e.** 11 days 13 hours, or 9 P.M. on day 11. To find the day and time when the stalk reached its final height of 1 km, or 100,000 cm, you can use guess-and-check, you can graph the equation and zoom in to find the time, or you can graph a second function, $y = 100000$, and find the intersection point of the two graphs. Multiply the decimal part of your answer by 24 to get the number of hours past 8 A.M.

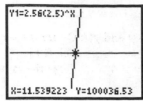

[11.0605, 11.9980, 1, 96411.29, 103911.29, 10000]

The plant will reach a height of 1 km at 11 days 13 hours, or at 9 P.M. on day 11.

**7. a–d.**

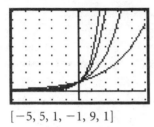

[−5, 5, 1, −1, 9, 1]

   **e.** As the base increases, the graph becomes steeper. The curves all intersect the $y$-axis at $(0, 1)$.

   **f.** The graph of $y = 6^x$ should be the steepest of all of these. It will contain the points $(0, 1)$ and $(1, 6)$.

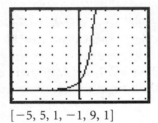

[−5, 5, 1, −1, 9, 1]

**8. a.** $y = 2^{x-3}$. This is the graph of $y = 2^x$ translated right 3 units.

   **b.** $y = 2^x + 2$, or $y - 2 = 2^x$. This is the graph of $y = 2^x$ translated up 2 units.

   **c.** $y = 3 \cdot 2^x$, or $\frac{y}{3} = 2^x$. This is the graph of $y = 2^x$ stretched vertically by a factor of 3.

   **d.** $y = 2^{x/3}$. This is the graph of $y = 2^x$ stretched horizontally by a factor of 3.

**9. a–d.**

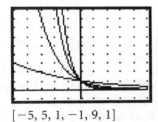

[−5, 5, 1, −1, 9, 1]

   **e.** As the base increases, the graph flattens out. The curves all intersect the $y$-axis at $(0, 1)$.

   **f.** The graph of $y = 0.1^x$ should be the steepest of all of these. It will contain the points $(0, 1)$ and $(−1, 10)$.

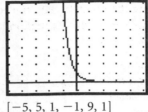

[−5, 5, 1, −1, 9, 1]

**10. a.** $y = 5 + 0.5^x$, or $y - 5 = 0.5^x$. This is the graph of $y = 0.5^x$ translated up 5 units.

   **b.** $y = -0.5^x + 5$, or $-(y - 5) = 0.5^x$. This is the graph of $y = 0.5^x$ reflected across the $x$-axis and then translated up 5 units.

   **c.** $y = -3(0.5^x) + 5$, or $\frac{y-5}{-3} = 0.5^x$. This is the graph of $y = 0.5^x$ reflected across the $x$-axis, stretched vertically by a factor of 3, and then translated up 5 units. The reflection gives the equation $-y = 0.5^x$. Then stretch vertically by a factor of 3 to get $\frac{-y}{3} = 0.5^x$, or $\frac{y}{-3} = 0.5^x$. Finally, translate up 5 units to get the equation $\frac{y-5}{-3} = 0.5^x$, or $y = -3(0.5^x) + 5$.

   **d.** $y = -3(0.5)^{x/2} + 5$, or $\frac{y-5}{-3} = 0.5^{x/2}$. This is the graph of $y = 0.5^x$ reflected across the $x$-axis, stretched vertically by a factor of 3, translated up 5 units, and stretched horizontally by a factor of 2. Starting with the equation $\frac{y-5}{-3} = 0.5^x$ or $y = -3(0.5)^x + 5$ from 10c, stretch the graph horizontally by a factor of 2 to get the equation $\frac{y-5}{-3} = 0.5^{x/2}$, or $y = -3(0.5^{x/2}) + 5$.

**11. a.** The common ratio is $\frac{f(1)}{f(0)} = \frac{27}{30} = 0.9$.

   **b.** $f(x) = 30(0.9)^x$. The general form of an exponential function is $f(x) = ab^x$, where $a$ is $f(0)$ and $b$ is the common ratio.

   **c.**

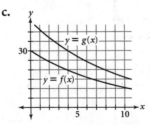

   **d.** $g(4) = f(4 - 4) = f(0) = 30$

   **e.** Because $g(x) = f(x - 4)$, $g(x) = 30(0.9)^{x-4}$.

   **f.** You can use the $x$- and $y$-values of any point on the curve, $(x_1, y_1)$, and the common ratio to write the equation.

**12. a.** The point $(3, 8.5)$ is on the graph of $f$, so $f(3) = 8.5$.

**b.** $y = 8.5 + 0.5(x - 3)$, $y = 10 + 0.5(x - 6)$, or $y = 7 + 0.5x$. The slope of the line is $\frac{10 - 8.5}{6 - 3}$, or 0.5. Using the point-slope form and the point $(3, 8.5)$, the equation of the line is $y = 8.5 + 0.5(x - 3)$. Or using the point $(6, 10)$, the equation is $y = 10 + 0.5(x - 6)$. Both equations are equivalent to $y = 7 + 0.5x$.

**13. a.** Let $x$ represent time in seconds, and let $y$ represent distance in meters. Janell starts 10 m from the motion sensor at time 0 s, so the graph starts at $(0, 10)$. Janell then moves at a constant rate of 2 m/s toward the motion sensor, so using the equation $d = rt$, or $t = \frac{d}{r}$, relating distance, rate, and time, it takes Janell $\frac{7}{2} = 3.5$ s to get 3 m from the sensor. Connect $(0, 10)$ to the new point, $(3.5, 3)$. When she turns around, it takes another 3.5 s for her to get back to where she started from, 10 m from the motion sensor. Connect $(3.5, 3)$ to the new point, $(7, 10)$.

**b.** The domain is $0 \leq x \leq 7$ because Janell starts at time 0 s and it takes 7 s for her round-trip walk. The range is $3 \leq y \leq 10$ because her distance from the motion sensor ranges between 3 m and 10 m.

**c.** $y = 2|x - 3.5| + 3$. This is the graph of $y = |x|$ stretched vertically by a factor of 2 and translated up 3 units and right 3.5 units.

**14. a, b.** The graphs of $f(g(x))$ and $g(f(x))$ are parallel lines or the same line. For example, using Y₁ = $2x + 2$ and Y₂ = $-x$, the graphs of Y₃ = Y₁(Y₂) and Y₄ = Y₂(Y₁) are parallel lines.

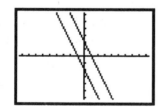

$[-9.4, 9.4, 1, -6.2, 6.2, 1]$

Using Y₁ = $x$ and Y₂ = $x + 1$, the graphs of Y₃ = Y₁(Y₂) and Y₄ = Y₂(Y₁) are the same line.

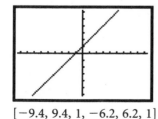

$[-9.4, 9.4, 1, -6.2, 6.2, 1]$

**c.** Let $f(x) = ax + b$ and $g(x) = cx + d$.

$f(g(x)) = a(cx + d) + b = acx + (ad + b)$

$g(f(x)) = c(ax + b) + d = cax + (cb + d)$

The slopes of $f(g(x))$ and $g(f(x))$ are the same ($ac = ca$), so the lines are parallel. If the $y$-intercepts, $ad + b$ and $cb + d$, are the same, the lines are identical.

**15.** Sample answers:

**Area ⊙M = 3.00 in.²**

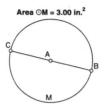

**a.**  **Area ⊙L = 6.00 in.²**

**b.  Area ⊙S = 1.50 in.²**

**c.** Duplicated the circle, measured the areas, dragged radii until areas were in the correct proportion

**d.** $\sqrt{2}$:1; $\sqrt{2}$:1; 2:1. The ratios of the areas must be the square of the ratios of the diameters. Therefore, if the ratio of the areas is 2:1, the ratio of the diameters will be $\sqrt{2}$:1, and if the ratio of the areas is 4:1, the ratio of the diameters will be 2:1.

**16. a.** The rectangle diagram shows that the area of a rectangle with side lengths $(x + 6)$ and $(x - 4)$ is $x^2 + 6x - 4x - 24$, or $x^2 + 2x - 24$.

|   | $x$ | $6$ |
|---|---|---|
| $x$ | $x^2$ | $6x$ |
| $-4$ | $-4x$ | $-24$ |

**b.** Distribute $(x - 4)$ across the sum $(x + 6)$.

$$(x - 4)(x + 6) = x(x + 6) - 4(x + 6)$$
$$= x^2 + 6x - 4x - 24$$
$$= x^2 + 2x - 24$$

**c.** Yes

**d.** A rectangle diagram also uses the distributive property. Each term in the first binomial is multiplied by each term in the second binomial.

## EXTENSIONS

**A.** Here are some examples of growth and decay in the real world:

Decay: the intensity of a star's light as it travels to Earth; the applause of a crowd after a show has ended

Growth: the intensity of the sound of an airplane as it flies toward you; the interest on an unpaid credit card balance

**B.** Research results will vary.

## LESSON 5.2

### EXERCISES

**1. a.** $5^{-3} = \frac{1}{5^3} = \frac{1}{5 \cdot 5 \cdot 5} = \frac{1}{125}$

**b.** $-6^2 = -(6 \cdot 6) = -36$

**c.** $-3^{-4} = -\frac{1}{3^4} = -\frac{1}{3 \cdot 3 \cdot 3 \cdot 3} = -\frac{1}{81}$

**d.** $(-12)^{-2} = \frac{1}{(-12)^2} = \frac{1}{(-12)(-12)} = \frac{1}{144}$

**e.** $\left(\frac{3}{4}\right)^{-2} = \left(\frac{4}{3}\right)^2 = \left(\frac{4}{3}\right)\left(\frac{4}{3}\right) = \frac{16}{9}$

**f.** $\left(\frac{2}{7}\right)^{-1} = \left(\frac{7}{2}\right)^1 = \frac{7}{2}$

**2. a.** By the product property of exponents, $a^8 \cdot a^{-3} = a^{8+(-3)} = a^5$

**b.** By the quotient property of exponents, $\frac{b^6}{b^2} = b^{6-2} = b^4$

**c.** By the power of a power property, $\left(c^4\right)^5 = c^{4 \cdot 5} = c^{20}$.

**d.** By the definition of zero exponent and the definition of negative exponents, $\frac{d^0}{e^{-3}} = \frac{1}{e^{-3}} = e^3$.

**3. a.** False. Valid reasons: You must have the same base for the product property of exponents; $243 \cdot 16 \neq 35831808$.

**b.** False. You must raise to the power before multiplying.

**c.** False. Valid reasons: You must raise to the power before dividing; only one factor can be divided out; it should be $\frac{4^x}{4} = 4^{x-1}$.

**d.** True. $\frac{6.6 \cdot 10^{12}}{8.8 \cdot 10^{-4}} = 0.75 \cdot 10^{12-(-4)} = 0.75 \cdot 10^{16} = 0.75 \cdot 10 \cdot 10^{15} = 7.5 \cdot 10^{15}$

**4. a.** $3^x = \frac{1}{9} = \frac{1}{3^2} = 3^{-2}$, so $x = -2$

**b.** $\left(\frac{5}{3}\right)^x = \frac{27}{125} = \left(\frac{3}{5}\right)^3 = \left(\frac{5}{3}\right)^{-3}$, so $x = -3$

**c.** $x = -5$

$\left(\frac{1}{3}\right)^x = 243 = 3^5$

$3^{-x} = 3^5$

$x = -5$

**d.** $x = 0$

$5\left(3^x\right) = 5$

$\frac{5\left(3^x\right)}{5} = \frac{5}{5}$

$3^x = 1$

$3^x = 3^0$

$x = 0$

**5. a.** $x \approx 3.27$

$x^7 = 4000$

$\left(x^7\right)^{1/7} = 4000^{1/7}$

$x = 4000^{1/7} \approx 3.27$

**b.** $x = 784$

$x^{0.5} = 28$

$\left(x^{0.5}\right)^2 = 28^2$

$x = 784$

**c.** $x \approx 0.16$

$x^{-3} = 247$

$\left(x^{-3}\right)^{-1/3} = 247^{-1/3}$

$x = 247^{-1/3} \approx 0.16$

**d.** $x \approx 0.50$

$5x^{1/4} + 6 = 10.2$

$5x^{1/4} = 4.2$

$x^{1/4} = 0.84$

$\left(x^{1/4}\right)^4 = (0.84)^4$

$x = 0.84^4 \approx 0.50$

**e.** $x \approx 1.07$

$3x^{-2} = 2x^4$

$3x^{-2} \cdot x^2 = 2x^4 \cdot x^2$

$3 = 2x^6$

$\frac{3}{2} = x^6$

$\left(\frac{3}{2}\right)^{1/6} = \left(x^6\right)^{1/6}$

$x = \left(\frac{3}{2}\right)^{1/6} \approx 1.07$

*Discovering Advanced Algebra Solutions Manual*
©2004 Key Curriculum Press

**f.** $x = 1$

$$-2x^{1/2} + (9x)^{1/2} = -1$$
$$-2x^{1/2} + 9^{1/2} \cdot \left(x^{1/2}\right) = -1$$
$$-2x^{1/2} + 3x^{1/2} = -1$$
$$x^{1/2} = -1$$
$$\left(x^{1/2}\right)^2 = (-1)^2$$
$$x = (-1)^2 = 1$$

**6. a.** $x^6 \cdot x^6 = x^{6+6} = x^{12}$

**b.** $4x^6 \cdot 2x^6 = (4 \cdot 2)\left(x^6 \cdot x^6\right) = 8x^{12}$

**c.** $\left(-5x^3\right) \cdot \left(-2x^4\right) = (-5)(-2)\left(x^3 \cdot x^4\right) = 10x^7$

**d.** $\dfrac{72x^7}{6x^2} = \dfrac{72}{6} \cdot \dfrac{x^7}{x^2} = 12x^5$

**e.** $\left(\dfrac{6x^5}{3x}\right)^3 = \left(2x^4\right)^3 = 2^3\left(x^4\right)^3 = 8x^{12}$

**f.** $\left(\dfrac{20x^7}{4x}\right)^{-2} = \left(5x^6\right)^{-2} = 5^{-2}\left(x^6\right)^{-2} = \dfrac{1}{5^2}x^{-12} =$
$\dfrac{1}{25}x^{-12}$

**7.** Sample answer: $(a + b)^n$ is not necessarily equivalent to $a^n + b^n$. For example, $(2 + 3)^2 = 25$ but $2^2 + 3^2 = 13$. However, they are equivalent when $n = 1$, or when $a + b = 0$ and $n$ is odd.

**8. a.** 49, 79.7023, 129.6418, 210.8723, 343

**b.** 30.7023; 49.9395; 81.2305; 132.1277. The sequence is not arithmetic because there is not a common difference.

**c.** 1.627; 1.627; 1.627; 1.627. The ratio of consecutive terms is always the same, so the difference is growing exponentially.

**d.** Possible answers: Non-integer powers may produce non-integer values. If the exponents form an arithmetic sequence, the decimal powers form a geometric sequence.

**9. a–d.**

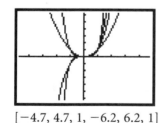

$[-4.7, 4.7, 1, -6.2, 6.2, 1]$

**e.** Sample answer: As the exponents increase, the graphs get narrower horizontally. The even-power functions are U-shaped and always in the first and second quadrants, whereas the odd-power

functions have only the right half of the U, with the left half pointed down in the third quadrant. They all pass through $(0, 0)$ and $(1, 1)$.

**f.** Sample answer: The graph of $y = x^6$ will be U-shaped, will be narrower than $y = x^4$, and will pass through $(0, 0)$, $(1, 1)$, $(-1, 1)$, $(2, 64)$, and $(-2, 64)$.

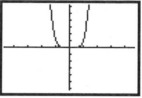

$[-4.7, 4.7, 1, -6.2, 6.2, 1]$

**g.** Sample answer: The graph of $y = x^7$ will be in the first and third quadrants, will be narrower than $y = x^3$, $y = x^5$, and will pass through $(0, 0)$, $(1, 1)$, $(-1, -1)$, $(2, 128)$, and $(-2, -128)$.

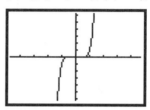

$[-4.7, 4.7, 1, -6.2, 6.2, 1]$

**10. a.** $y = x^3 + 4$, or $y - 4 = x^3$. This is the graph of $y = x^3$ translated up 4 units.

**b.** $y = (x + 2)^3$. This is the graph of $y = x^3$ translated left 2 units.

**c.** $y = \frac{1}{4}x^3$, or $4y = x^3$. This is the graph of $y = x^3$ shrunk vertically by a factor of 4.

**d.** $y = \frac{1}{8}x^3 - 2$, $8(y + 2) = x^3$, or $y + 2 = \left(\frac{1}{2}x\right)^3$. This is the graph of $y = x^3$ shrunk vertically by a factor of 8 and then translated down 2 units.

**11. a.** $47(0.9)^x = 47(0.9)^1(0.9)^{x-1} = 47(0.9)(0.9)^{x-1}$ by the product property of exponents; $47(0.9)(0.9)^{x-1} = (47(0.9))(0.9)^{x-1} = 42.3(0.9)^{x-1}$.

**b.** $47(0.9)(0.9)(0.9)^{x-2} = (47(0.9)(0.9))(0.9)^{x-2} = 38.07(0.9)^{x-2}$

**c.** The coefficients are equal to the values of $Y_1$ corresponding to the number subtracted from $x$ in the exponent. If $(x_1, y_1)$ is on the curve, then any equation $y = y_1 \cdot b^{(x-x_1)}$ is an exponential equation for the curve.

**12. a.** $y = 30.0r^{x-3}$; $y = 5.2r^{x-6}$. The ball rebounds to 30 cm on the third bounce, so $y_1 = 30$ and $x_1 = 3$. The ball rebounds to 5.2 cm on the sixth bounce, so $y_1 = 5.2$ and $x_1 = 6$.

**b.** $30.0r^{x-3} = 5.2r^{x-6}$; $r \approx 0.5576$

$$30.0r^{x-3} = 5.2r^{x-6}$$     Set the two equations as equal.

$$\frac{30.0}{5.2} = \frac{r^{x-6}}{r^{x-3}}$$     Divide both sides by 5.2 and $r^{x-3}$.

$$\frac{30.0}{5.2} = r^{x-6-x+3} = r^{-3}$$     Divide $r^{x-6}$ by $r^{x-3}$.

$$\left(\frac{30.0}{5.2}\right)^{-1/3} = \left(r^{-3}\right)^{-1/3}$$     Raise both sides to the power of $-\frac{1}{3}$.

$$r \approx 0.5576$$     Evaluate.

**c.** Approximately 173 cm. The equation for the rebound height is $y = 30.0(0.5576)^{x-3}$. Before the ball is dropped it is at the zero bounce, so set $x$ equal to 0.

$$y = 30.0(0.5576)^{0-3} \approx 173.0$$

The ball was dropped from approximately 173 cm.

**13. a.** $x = 7$

$$(x - 3)^3 = 64$$
$$x - 3 = 64^{1/3}$$
$$x - 3 = 4$$
$$x = 7$$

**b.** $x = -\frac{1}{2}$

$$256^x = \frac{1}{16}$$
$$\left(16^2\right)^x = 16^{-1}$$
$$16^{2x} = 16^{-1}$$
$$2x = -1$$
$$x = -\frac{1}{2}$$

**c.** $x = 0$

$$\frac{(x + 5)^3}{(x + 5)} = x^2 + 25$$
$$(x + 5)^2 = x^2 + 25$$
$$x^2 + 10x + 25 = x^2 + 25$$
$$10x = 0$$
$$x = 0$$

**14. a.** $\frac{39.8}{42} \approx 0.9476$

**b.** $y = 42(0.9476)^{x-2002}$

**c.** $y = 39.8(0.9476)^{x-2003}$

**d.** Using the first equation,

$$y = 42(0.9476)^{1980-2002} \approx 137.2$$

Using the second equation,

$$y = 39.8(0.9476)^{1980-2003} \approx 137.2$$

Both equations give approximately 137.2 rads.

**e.** Using the first equation,

$$y = 42(0.9476)^{2010-2002} \approx 27.3$$

Using the second equation,

$$y = 39.8(0.9476)^{2010-2003} \approx 27.3$$

Both equations give approximately 27.3 rads.

**f.** The first equation is $y = 42(0.9476)^{x-2002}$. By the product property, $y = 42(0.9476)(0.9476)^{x-2002-1}$. By multiplying $42(0.9476)$, $y = 39.8(0.9476)^{x-2003}$. This is the second equation.

**15. a.** $x = 7$. Move the decimal in 3.7 seven places to the right to get 37000000.

**b.** $x = -4$. Move the decimal in 8.01 four places to the left to get 0.000801.

**c.** $x = 4$. Move the decimal in 4.75 four places to the right to get 47500.

**d.** $x = 4.61$. Move the decimal in 4.61 two places to the left to get 0.0461.

**16.** $\frac{y + 3}{2} = (x + 4)^2$

$$y + 3 = 2(x + 4)^2$$
$$y = 2(x + 4)^2 - 3$$

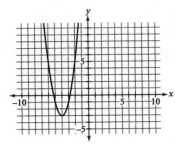

**17. a.** Let $x$ represent time in seconds, and let $y$ represent distance in meters.

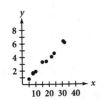

**b.** All you need is the slope of the median-median line, which is determined by $M_1(8, 1.6)$ and $M_3(31, 6.2)$. The slope is 0.2. The speed is approximately 0.2 m/s.

**IMPROVING YOUR REASONING SKILLS**

$$\frac{(Eas)^{-1}(ter)^0 Egg}{y} = \frac{(ter)^0 Egg}{(Eas)y} = \frac{1 Egg}{Easy},$$ or "one egg over easy."

**A.** $y = x^{-1}$

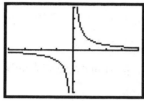

$[-4, 4, 1, -4, 4, 1]$

$y = x^{-2}$

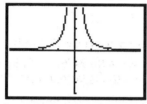

$[-4, 4, 1, -4, 4, 1]$

The even-power functions are in the first and second quadrants and go through $(-1, 1)$ and $(1, 1)$. The odd-power functions are in the first and third quadrants and go through $(-1, -1)$ and $(1, 1)$. The two parts of each graph get closer and closer to both axes. The smaller the absolute value of the exponent, the faster the graph approaches the axes.

**B.** See the solution to Take Another Look activity 1 on page 112.

## LESSON 5.3

### EXERCISES

**1.** a—e—j; $\sqrt[5]{x^2} = x^{2/5} = x^{0.4}$
   b—d—g; $\left(\sqrt{x}\right)^5 = \sqrt[2]{x^5} = x^{5/2} = x^{2.5}$
   c—i; $\sqrt[3]{x} = \sqrt[3]{x^1} = x^{1/3}$
   f—h; $\left(\dfrac{1}{x}\right)^{-3} = \left(x^{-1}\right)^{-3} = x^3$

**2. a.** Power; the base is a variable.

   **b.** Power; the base is a variable.

   **c.** Exponential; the exponent is a variable.

   **d.** Power; $x$ is equivalent to $x^1$, so the base is a variable.

   **e.** Power; a square root is equivalent to the power of $\frac{1}{2}$, so the base is a variable.

   **f.** Power; $f(t) = t^2 + 4t + 3 = t^2 + 4t + 4 - 1 = (t + 2)^2 - 1$, so it is a translation of $g(t) = t^2$.

   **g.** Exponential; $\dfrac{12}{3^t}$ is equivalent to $12(3)^{-t}$.

   **h.** Power; $\dfrac{28}{w - 5}$ is equivalent to $28(w - 5)^{-1}$.

   **i.** Power; $\dfrac{8}{y^4}$ is equivalent to $8y^{-4}$.

   **j.** Neither; the independent variable appears twice, raised to two different powers.

**k.** Power; $\sqrt[5]{4w^3}$ is equivalent to $4^{1/5}w^{3/5}$.

**l.** Exponential; the exponent contains a variable.

**3. a.** $a^{1/6}$

   **b.** $b^{8/10}$, $b^{4/5}$, or $b^{0.8}$

   **c.** $c^{-1/2}$, or $c^{-0.5}$

   **d.** $d^{7/5}$, or $d^{1.4}$

**4. a.** $a = 5489.031744$

$$a^{1/6} = 4.2 \qquad \sqrt[6]{a} = a^{1/6}$$
$$\left(a^{1/6}\right)^6 = 4.2^6 \qquad \text{Raise both sides to the power of 6.}$$
$$a = 5489.031744 \quad \text{Evaluate.}$$

   **b.** $b \approx 27.808$

$$b^{4/5} = 14.3 \qquad \sqrt[10]{b^8} = b^{4/5}$$
$$\left(b^{4/5}\right)^{5/4} = 14.3^{5/4} \qquad \text{Raise both sides to the power of } \tfrac{5}{4}.$$
$$b \approx 27.808 \qquad \text{Evaluate.}$$

   **c.** $c \approx 3.306$

$$c^{-1/2} = 0.55 \qquad \frac{1}{\sqrt{c}} = c^{-1/2}$$
$$\left(c^{-1/2}\right)^{-2} = 0.55^{-2} \qquad \text{Raise both sides to the power of } -2.$$
$$c \approx 3.306 \qquad \text{Evaluate.}$$

   **d.** $d \approx 9.390$

$$d^{7/5} = 23 \qquad \left(\sqrt[5]{d}\right)^7 = d^{7/5}$$
$$\left(d^{7/5}\right)^{5/7} = 23^{5/7} \qquad \text{Raise both sides to the power of } \tfrac{5}{7}.$$
$$d \approx 9.390 \qquad \text{Evaluate.}$$

**5.** 490 W/cm². Let $x$ represent the number of gels, and let $f(x)$ represent the intensity in W/cm². Express $f$ as an exponential function. Start with $f(x) = a \cdot r^{x-3}$. Using the point $f(3) = 900$, $a = 900$ and the equation is $f(x) = 900r^{x-3}$. Use the point $f(5) = 600$ to find $r$.

$$600 = 900r^{5-3} \qquad \text{Substitute 5 for } x \text{ and 600 for } f(x).$$
$$\frac{600}{900} = r^2 \qquad \text{Divide both sides by 900.}$$
$$\left(\frac{2}{3}\right)^{1/2} = \left(r^2\right)^{1/2} \qquad \text{Raise both sides to the power of } \tfrac{1}{2}.$$
$$r = \left(\frac{2}{3}\right)^{1/2} \qquad \left(r^2\right)^{1/2} = r$$

So, $f(x) = 900\left(\left(\dfrac{2}{3}\right)^{1/2}\right)^{x-3} = 900\left(\dfrac{2}{3}\right)^{(x-3)/2}$. Now find $f(6)$.

$$f(6) = 900\left(\frac{2}{3}\right)^{(6-3)/2} = 900\left(\frac{2}{3}\right)^{3/2} \approx 490$$

**6. a–d.**

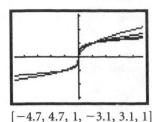

$[-4.7, 4.7, 1, -3.1, 3.1, 1]$

**e.** Each curve is less steep than the prior one. The graphs of $y = x^{1/2}$ and $y = x^{1/4}$ are only in the first quadrant, whereas the graphs of $y = x^{1/3}$ and $y = x^{1/5}$ are in the first and third quadrants. They all pass through the points $(0, 0)$ and $(1, 1)$, and the graphs of $y = x^{1/3}$ and $y = x^{1/5}$ both pass through the point $(-1, -1)$.

**f.** $y = x^{1/7}$ will be less steep than the others graphed and will be in the first and third quadrants. It will pass through the points $(0, 0)$, $(1, 1)$, and $(-1, -1)$.

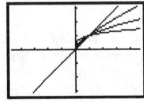

$[-4.7, 4.7, 1, -3.1, 3.1, 1]$

**g.** The domains of $y = x^{1/2}$ and $y = x^{1/4}$ are $x \geq 0$ because you can't take a square root or fourth root of a negative number. The domains of $y = x^{1/3}$ and $x^{1/5}$ are all real numbers.

**7. a–d.**

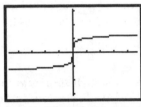

$[-4.7, 4.7, 1, -3.1, 3.1, 1]$

**e.** Each graph is steeper and less curved than the previous one. All of the functions go through $(0, 0)$ and $(1, 1)$.

**f.** $y = x^{5/4}$ should be steeper than the others and curve upward.

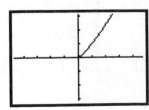

$[-4.7, 4.7, 1, -3.1, 3.1, 1]$

**8.** Sample answer: Power functions with rational exponents can have limited domain. When the exponent is between 0 and 1, the curve increases slowly with a shape similar to the graph of $y = \sqrt{x}$. Exponential curves always have a steadily increasing or decreasing slope, unlike power functions.

**9. a.** Exponential. The graph has a steadily increasing slope.

**b.** Neither. The graph looks like a parabola with the middle section reflected across a horizontal line. This is like neither an exponential function nor a power function.

**c.** Exponential. The graph has a steadily decreasing slope.

**d.** Power. The graph appears in the first and third quadrants. The shape in the first quadrant is similar to the graph of $y = \sqrt{x}$. The shape in the third quadrant is similar to the graph of $y = \sqrt{x}$ reflected across both axes.

**10. a.** $y = 3 + (x - 2)^{3/4}$. The black graph is translated right 2 units and up 3 units to get the red graph.

**b.** $y = 1 + (-(x - 5))^{3/4}$. The black graph is reflected across the $x$-axis, then translated right 5 units and up 1 unit to get the red graph.

**c.** $y = 4 + \left(\frac{x}{4}\right)^{3/4}$. The black graph is stretched horizontally by a factor of 4, and then translated up 4 units to get the red graph.

**d.** $\frac{y}{4} = \left(\frac{x-3}{2}\right)^{3/4}$, or $y = 4\left(\frac{x-3}{2}\right)^{3/4}$. The black graph is stretched horizontally by a factor of 2 and vertically by a factor of 4. Then it is translated right 3 units to get the red graph.

**11. a.** $x \approx 6.29$

| | |
|---|---|
| $9\sqrt[5]{x} + 4 = 17$ | Original equation. |
| $9\sqrt[5]{x} = 13$ | Subtract 4 from both sides. |
| $\sqrt[5]{x} = \frac{13}{9}$ | Divide both sides by 9. |
| $x = \left(\frac{13}{9}\right)^5 \approx 6.29$ | Raise both sides to the power of 5. |

**b.** $x \approx 3.66$

| | |
|---|---|
| $\sqrt{5x^4} = 30$ | Original equation. |
| $5x^4 = 30^2 = 900$ | Square both sides. |
| $x^4 = \frac{900}{5} = 180$ | Divide both sides by 5. |
| $x = 180^{1/4} \approx 3.66$ | Raise both sides by the power of $\frac{1}{4}$. |

*Discovering Advanced Algebra Solutions Manual*
©2004 Key Curriculum Press

**c.** $x \approx 180$

$$4\sqrt[3]{x^2} = \sqrt{35} \qquad \text{Original equation.}$$

$$\sqrt[3]{x^2} = \frac{\sqrt{35}}{4} \qquad \text{Divide both sides by 4.}$$

$$x^{2/3} = \frac{\sqrt{35}}{4} \qquad \sqrt[3]{x^2} = x^{2/3}.$$

$$x = \left(\frac{\sqrt{35}}{4}\right)^{3/2} \approx 1.80 \quad \text{Raise both sides to the power of } \tfrac{3}{2}.$$

**12. a.** Approximately 0.723 AU. Let $t$ represent the orbital time in years, and let $r$ represent the radius in AU. $r = t^{2/3}$. Substitute 0.615 for $t$ and solve for $r$. $r = (0.615)^{2/3} \approx 0.723$.

**b.** Approximately 29.475 yr. Substitute 9.542 for $r$ and solve for $t$.

$$9.542 = t^{2/3}$$

$$t = 9.542^{3/2} \approx 29.475$$

**c.** See 12a and b for examples of how to fill in the blanks.

| Planet | Mercury | Venus | Earth | Mars |
|---|---|---|---|---|
| Orbital radius (AU) | 0.387 | 0.7232 | 1.00 | 1.523 |
| Orbital time (yr) | 0.2408 | 0.615 | 1.00 | 1.8795 |

| Planet | Jupiter | Saturn | Uranus | Neptune |
|---|---|---|---|---|
| Orbital radius (AU) | 5.201 | 9.542 | 19.181 | 30.086 |
| Orbital time (yr) | 11.861 | 29.475 | 84.008 | 165.02 |

**13. a.** $P = kV^{-1}$    Original equation.

$$P = \frac{k}{V} \qquad V^{-1} = \frac{1}{V}$$

$$PV = k \qquad \text{Multiply both sides by } V.$$

**b.** $P = 40$ and $V = 12.3$, so using $PV = k$ from 13a, $k = (40)(12.3) = 492$.

**c.** 8.2 L. Substitute 60.0 for $P$ and 492 for $k$ in the equation $PV = K$.

$$60.0V = 492$$

$$V = \frac{492}{60} = 8.2$$

**d.** 32.8 mm Hg. Substitute 15 for $V$ and 492 for $k$ in the equation $P = kV^{-1}$.

$$P = 492(15)^{-1} = 32.8$$

**14. a.** $\left(3x^3\right)^3 = 3^3 \cdot \left(x^3\right)^3 = 27x^9$

**b.** $\left(2x^3\right)\left(2x^2\right)^3 = 2x^3\left(2^3 \cdot \left(x^2\right)^3\right) = 2x^3 \cdot 8x^6 = 16x^9$

**c.** $\dfrac{6x^4}{30x^5} = \dfrac{6}{30}x^{4-5} = 0.2x^{-1}$

**d.** $\left(4x^2\right)\left(3x^2\right)^3 = 4x^2\left(3^3 \cdot \left(x^2\right)^3\right) = 4x^2 \cdot 27x^6 = 108x^8$

**e.** $\dfrac{-72x^5y^5}{-4x^3y} = \dfrac{-72}{-4}x^{5-3}y^{5-1} = 18x^2y^4$

**15. a.** $y = (x + 4)^2$. This is $y = x^2$ translated left 4 units.

**b.** $y = x^2 + 1$. This is $y = x^2$ translated up 1 unit.

**c.** $y = -(x + 5)^2 + 2$. This is $y = x^2$ reflected across the $x$-axis and translated left 5 units and up 2 units.

**d.** $y = (x - 3)^2 - 4$. This is $y = x^2$ translated right 3 units and down 4 units.

**e.** $y = \sqrt{x + 3}$. This is $y = \sqrt{x}$ translated left 3 units.

**f.** $y = \sqrt{x} - 1$. This is $y = \sqrt{x}$ translated down 1 unit.

**g.** $y = \sqrt{x + 2} + 1$. This is $y = \sqrt{x}$ translated left 2 units and up 1 unit.

**h.** $y = -\sqrt{x - 1} - 1$. This is $y = \sqrt{x}$ reflected across the $x$-axis and translated right 1 unit and down 1 unit.

**16.** About 840. The dart players in at least the 98th percentile are the best 2% of all registered dart players. 2% of 42,000 is $0.02 \cdot 42{,}000 = 840$.

**17. a.** $u_1 = 20$ and $u_n = (1 + 0.2)u_{n-1} = 1.2u_{n-1}$ where $n \geq 2$

**b.** About 86 rats. You can use Home screen recursion or Sequence mode to find that $u_9 = 86$.

**c.** Follow the pattern in 17b to see that $u_n = 1.2^{n-1} \cdot 20$ where $n \geq 1$. Let $x$ represent the year number, and let $y$ represent the number of rats. $y = 20(1.2)^{x-1}$.

**EXTENSIONS**

**A.** See the Sketchpad demonstration Rational Exponents.

**B.** See the solution to Take Another Look activity 2 on page 112.

## LESSON 5.4

**EXERCISES**

**1. a.** $x^5 = 50$, so $x = 50^{1/5} \approx 2.187$

**b.** $\sqrt[3]{x} = 3.1$, so $x = 3.1^3 = 29.791$

**c.** No real solution. $x^2 = -121$ and the square of a number is never negative.

**2. a.** $x^{1/4} - 2 = 3$, so $x^{1/4} = 5$, and $x = 5^4 = 625$.

**b.** $x = 1$

$$4x^7 - 6 = -2$$

$$4x^7 = 4$$

$$x^7 = 1$$

$$x = 1^{1/7} = 1$$

**c.** $x = 512$

$$3(x^{2/3} + 5) = 207$$

$$x^{2/3} + 5 = 69$$

$$x^{2/3} = 64$$

$$x = 64^{3/2} = 512$$

**d.** $x \approx 0.951$

$$1450 = 800\left(1 + \frac{x}{12}\right)^{7.8}$$

$$1.8125 = \left(1 + \frac{x}{12}\right)^{7.8}$$

$$1.8125^{1/7.8} = 1 + \frac{x}{12}$$

$$x = 12(-1 + 1.8125^{1/7.8}) \approx 0.951$$

**e.** $x \approx 0.456$

$$14.2 = 222.1 \cdot x^{3.5}$$

$$\frac{14.2}{222.1} = x^{3.5}$$

$$x = \left(\frac{14.2}{222.1}\right)^{1/3.5} \approx 0.456$$

**3. a.** $\left(27x^6\right)^{2/3} = 27^{2/3} \cdot \left(x^6\right)^{2/3} = 9x^4$

**b.** $\left(16x^8\right)^{3/4} = 16^{3/4} \cdot \left(x^8\right)^{3/4} = 8x^6$

**c.** $\left(36x^{-12}\right)^{3/2} = 36^{3/2} \cdot \left(x^{-12}\right)^{3/2} = 216x^{-18}$

**4.** 10.9%. $y = a^x$ where $y$ is the light intensity coming through the glass and $x$ is the number of sheets of glass. To find $a$, substitute 0.50 for $y$ and 6 for $x$. $0.50 = a^6$; $0.50^{1/6} = a$; $a \approx 0.891$. Each sheet will allow 0.891, or 89.1%, of the light intensity through the glass, so it reduces it by a factor of 0.109, or 10.9%.

**5. a.** She must replace $y$ with $(y - 7)$ and replace $y_1$ with $(y_1 - 7)$; $y - 7 = (y_1 - 7) \cdot b^{x-x_1}$.

**b.**
$$y - 7 = (105 - 7)b^{x-1}$$

$$\frac{y - 7}{98} = b^{x-1}$$

$$\left(\frac{y - 7}{98}\right)^{1/(x-1)} = b$$

**c.**

| $x$ | 0 | 2 | 3 | 4 | 5 | 6 |
|---|---|---|---|---|---|---|
| $y$ | 200 | 57 | 31 | 18 | 14 | 12 |
| $b$ | 0.508 | 0.510 | 0.495 | 0.482 | 0.517 | 0.552 |

**d.** Possible answer: The mean of the $b$-values is 0.511. This gives the equation $\hat{y} = 7 + 98(0.511)^{x-1}$.

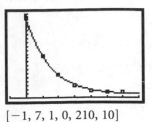

$[-1, 7, 1, 0, 210, 10]$

**6. a.**

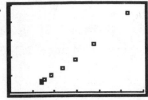

$[0, 6, 1, 0, 5, 1]$

**b.** Sample answer: $\hat{y} = 0.37x^{1.5}$. You might start by graphing the data with the line $y = x$.

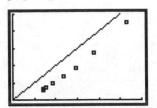

$[0, 6, 1, 0, 5, 1]$

The data curve upward slightly, so you know the exponent must be greater then 1, but the points lie below the line $y = x$, so you also need to apply a scale factor less than 1. The equation $\hat{y} = 0.37x^{1.5}$ appears to be a good fit.

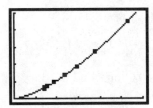

$[0, 6, 1, 0, 5, 1]$

**c.** Approximately 1,229,200 km. (Answers will vary depending on the equation found in 6b.) Substitute 15.945 for $y$ in the equation found in 6b.

$$15.945 = 0.37x^{1.5}$$

$$43.0946 = x^{1.5}$$

$$x = 43.0946^{1/1.5} \approx 12.292$$

This is in units of 100,000 km, so the orbit radius is approximately 1,229,200 km.

*Discovering Advanced Algebra Solutions Manual*
©2004 Key Curriculum Press

**d.** Approximately 545.390 days. (Answers will vary depending on the equation found in 6b.) Substitute 129.52 for $x$ in the equation found in 6b.

$$y = 0.37 \cdot (129.52)^{1.5} \approx 545.390$$

The orbital time is approximately 545.390 days.

**7. a.** Approximately 68.63 tons. Substitute 62 for $L$ in the given equation.

$$W = 0.000137 \cdot 62^{3.18} \approx 68.63$$

**b.** Approximately 63.75 ft. Substitute 75 for $W$ in the given equation.

$$75 = 0.000137L^{3.18}$$

$$547445.26 = L^{3.18}$$

$$L = 547445.25^{1/3.18} \approx 63.75$$

**8. a.** Approximately 19.58 cm. Substitute 18 for $h$ in the given equation.

$$18 = \frac{5}{3}d^{0.8}$$

$$\frac{54}{5} = d^{0.8}$$

$$d = \left(\frac{54}{5}\right)^{1/0.8} \approx 19.58$$

**b.** Approximately 23.75 m. The circumference and diameter are related by $C = \pi d$, so $d = \frac{87}{\pi}$. Substitute $\frac{87}{\pi}$ for $d$ in the given equation.

$$h = \frac{5}{3} \cdot \left(\frac{87}{\pi}\right)^{0.8} \approx 23.75$$

**9. a.** Approximately 1.9 g. Substitute 15 for $M$ in the given equation.

$$F = 0.033 \cdot 15^{1.5} \approx 1.9$$

**b.** Approximately 12.8%. Divide $(0.033 \cdot 15^{1.5})$ by 15. Use this unrounded number for better accuracy.

$$\frac{0.033 \cdot 15^{1.5}}{15} \approx 0.1278 \approx 12.8\%$$

**10.** Approximately 1%. Use the point-ratio equation, $y = 2.74(1 + r)^{x - 2002}$, where $r$ is the rate of inflation. A gallon of milk is predicted to be \$3.41 in 2024, so

$$3.41 = 2.74(1 + r)^{2024 - 2002}$$

$$1.2445 = (1 + r)^{22}$$

$$1 + r = 1.2355^{1/22} \approx 1.01$$

$$r \approx 0.01$$

**11. a.** 0.0466, or 4.66% per year. If $r$ is the decay rate, then use the two data points to write the equation $5.2 = 6.0(1 - r)^3$. Solve for $r$.

$$(1 - r)^3 = \frac{5.2}{6}$$

$$r = 1 - \left(\frac{5.2}{6}\right)^{1/3} \approx 0.0466$$

**b.** Approximately 6.6 g. If $y_0$ is the initial amount, then $6.0 = y_0 \cdot (1 - 0.0466)^2 = y_0 \cdot (0.9534)^2$. Solve for $y$.

$$y_0 = \frac{6.0}{0.9534^2} \approx 6.6$$

**c.** $y = 6.6(0.9534)^x$. The equation is in the form $y = y_0(1 - r)^x$.

**d.** Approximately 0.6 g. Substitute 50 for $x$ in the equation from 11c. $y = 6.6(0.9534)^{50} \approx 0.607$.

**e.** About 14.4 yr. Look for an $x$-value for which the corresponding $y$-value is 3.3. Trace the graph on a graphing calculator to estimate the time.

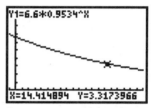

$[-1, 20, 1, -1, 10, 1]$

**12. a.**

Temperature (°F)

**b.** 18.7, 29.55, 39.1, 49.75, 56.8

**c.** $range = 56.8 - 18.7 = 38.1$;
$IQR = 49.75 - 29.55 = 20.2$

**d.** Sample answer: Because $Q_3 = 49.75$, less than 25% of the cities have mean January temperatures above 50°F. Because $Q_1 = 29.55$, more than 25% of the cities have mean January temperatures below 32°F. The data do not seem to support Juan's conjecture.

**13.** $x = -4.5$, $y = 2$, $z = 2.75$. Eliminate one variable and then solve a system of equations in two variables.

| | |
|---|---|
| $2x + y + 4z = 4$ | First equation. |
| $x + y + z = \frac{1}{4}$ | Second equation. |
| $x \quad + 3z = 3.75$ | Subtract. |
| $7x + 7y + 7z = 1.75$ | Multiply the second equation by 7. |
| $-3x - 7y + 2z = 5$ | Third equation. |
| $4x \quad + 9z = 6.75$ | Add. |

Now you have two equations without $y$.

$4x + 12z = 15$    Multiply the first equation without $y$ by 4.

$\underline{4x + \phantom{0}9z = 6.75}$    Second equation without $y$.

$\phantom{4x + }3z = 8.25$    Subtract.

$\phantom{4x + }z = 2.75$    Divide by 3.

Substitute 2.75 for $z$ in the first equation without $y$ and solve for $x$.

$x + 3(2.75) = 3.75$

$\phantom{x + 3(2.75)}x = -4.5$

Substitute $-4.5$ for $x$ and 2.75 for $z$ in the second original equation and solve for $y$.

$-4.5 + y + 2.75 = \dfrac{1}{4}$

$\phantom{-4.5 + }y = 2$

So $x = -4.5$, $y = 2$, and $z = 2.75$.

### IMPROVING YOUR REASONING SKILLS

To take the half root is the same as squaring.

$\sqrt[\frac{1}{2}]{cin}\ nati = (cin)^2 nati = cin\ cin\ nati$

He should look in Cincinnati, Ohio.

### EXTENSIONS

**A.** Answers will vary.

**B.** Answers will vary.

## LESSON 5.5

### EXERCISES

**1.** $(-3, -2)$, $(-1, 0)$, $(2, 2)$, $(6, 4)$. Switch the $x$- and $y$-coordinates of the known points.

**2. a.** $g(2) = 5 + 2(2) = 5 + 4 = 9$

**b.** $g^{-1}(9) = 2$. The inverse of $g(t) = 5 + 2t$ is $g^{-1}(t) = \dfrac{t-5}{2}$. $g^{-1}(9) = \dfrac{9-5}{2} = 2$. Or, from 2a, $g(2) = 9$, so $g^{-1}(9)$ must equal 2.

**c.** $g^{-1}(20) = \dfrac{20-5}{2} = \dfrac{15}{2} = 7.5$

**3.** Graph c is the inverse because the $x$- and $y$-coordinates have been switched from the original graph so that the graphs are symmetric across line $y = x$.

**4.** a and e are inverses; b and d are inverses; c and g are inverses; f and h are inverses.

To find the inverse of a, switch $x$ and $y$ and then solve for $y$.

$x = 6 - 2y$

$x - 6 = -2y$

$-\dfrac{1}{2}(x - 6) = y$. This is e.

To find the inverse of b, switch $x$ and $y$ and then solve for $y$.

$x = 2 - \dfrac{6}{y}$

$x - 2 = -\dfrac{6}{y}$

$y(x - 2) = -6$

$y = \dfrac{-6}{x - 2}$. This is d.

To find the inverse of c, switch $x$ and $y$ and then solve for $y$.

$x = -6(y - 2)$

$-\dfrac{1}{6}x = y - 2$

$2 - \dfrac{1}{6}x = y$. This is g.

To find the inverse of f, switch $x$ and $y$ and then solve for $y$.

$x = \dfrac{2}{y - 6}$

$x(y - 6) = 2$

$xy - 6x = 2$

$xy = 6x + 2$

$y = \dfrac{6x + 2}{x} = 6 + \dfrac{2}{x}$. This is h.

**5. a.** $f(7) = -4 + 0.5(7 - 3)^2 = -4 + 0.5 \cdot 16 = -4 + 8 = 4$

$g(4) = 3 + \sqrt{2(4 + 4)} = 3 + \sqrt{16} = 3 + 4 = 7$

**b.** They might be inverse functions.

**c.** $f(1) = -4 + 0.5(1 - 3)^2 = -4 + 0.5 \cdot 4 = -4 + 2 = -2$

$g(-2) = 3 + \sqrt{2(-2 + 4)} = 3 + \sqrt{4} = 3 + 2 = 5$

**d.** They are not inverse functions, at least not over their entire domains and ranges.

**e.** $f(x)$ for $x \geq 3$ and $g(x)$ for $x \geq -4$ are inverse functions. Sketch a graph of the two functions and the line $y = x$.

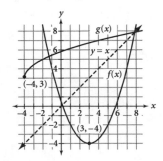

$f(x)$ is a whole vertically oriented parabola, but $g(x)$ is only the top half of a horizontally

oriented parabola. Only the right half of the
graph of $f(x)$ is the inverse of $g(x)$, so the
domain of $f(x)$ is $x \geq 3$. The domain of $g(x)$ is
$x \geq -4$.

**6. a.** $x = 34$

| | |
|---|---|
| $4 + (x - 2)^{3/5} = 12$ | Set $f(x)$ equal to 12. |
| $(x - 2)^{3/5} = 8$ | Subtract 4 from both sides. |
| $x - 2 = 8^{5/3} = 32$ | Raise both sides to the $\frac{5}{3}$ power and evaluate. |
| $x = 34$ | Add 2 to both sides. |

**b.** $f^{-1}(x) = 2 + (x - 4)^{5/3}$

| | |
|---|---|
| $4 + (y - 2)^{3/5} = x$ | Switch $x$ and $y$. |
| $(y - 2)^{3/5} = x - 4$ | Subtract 4 from both sides. |
| $y - 2 = (x - 4)^{5/3}$ | Raise both sides to the $\frac{5}{3}$ power. |
| $y = (x - 4)^{5/3} + 2$ | Add 2 to both sides. |

**c.** Sample answer: The steps are the same, but you
don't have to do the numerical calculations when
you find an inverse.

**7. a.**

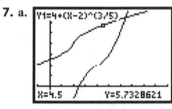

$[-1, 10, 1, -1, 7, 1]$

**b.** The inverse function from 6b should be the same
as the function drawn by your calculator.

**c.** Find the composition of $f^{-1}(f(x))$. If it equals $x$,
then you have the correct inverse.

**8. a.** Original function: $f(x) = 2x - 3$. Inverse
function: $f^{-1}(x) = \frac{x+3}{2}$, or $f^{-1}(x) = \frac{1}{2}x + \frac{3}{2}$.
To find the inverse, switch the $x$ and $y$ in the
original function and solve for $y$.

$$x = 2y - 3$$
$$x + 3 = 2y$$
$$y = \frac{x + 3}{2}$$

The inverse is a function, so $f^{-1}(x) = \frac{x+3}{2}$, or
$f^{-1}(x) = \frac{1}{2}x + \frac{3}{2}$.

**b.** Original function: $f(x) = \frac{-3x + 4}{2}$. Inverse function: $f^{-1}(x) = \frac{-2x + 4}{3}$, or $f^{-1}(x) = -\frac{2}{3}x + \frac{4}{3}$.

To find the inverse, switch the $x$ and $y$ in the
original function and solve for $y$.

$$3y + 2x = 4$$
$$3y = -2x + 4$$
$$y = \frac{-2x + 4}{3}$$

The inverse is a function, so $f^{-1}(x) = \frac{-2x + 4}{3}$, or
$f^{-1}(x) = -\frac{2}{3}x + \frac{4}{3}$.

**c.** Original function: $f(x) = \frac{-x^2 + 3}{2}$. Inverse:
$y = \pm\sqrt{-2x + 3}$; not a function. To find
the inverse, switch the $x$ and $y$ in the original
function and solve for $y$.

$$x = -\frac{1}{2}y^2 + \frac{3}{2}$$
$$-\frac{1}{2}y^2 = x - \frac{3}{2}$$
$$y^2 = -2\left(x - \frac{3}{2}\right) = -2x + 3$$
$$y = \pm\sqrt{-2x + 3}$$

The inverse isn't a function, so $f^{-1}(x)$ notation
doesn't apply.

**9. a.  i.** $f^{-1}(x) = \frac{x + 140}{6.34}$. To find $f^{-1}(x)$, switch the
dependent and independent variables.

$$x = 6.34y - 140$$
$$x + 140 = 6.34y$$
$$y = \frac{x + 140}{6.34}, \text{ or } f^{-1}(x) = \frac{x + 140}{6.34}$$

**ii.** $f\left(f^{-1}(15.75)\right) = 15.75$

**iii.** $f^{-1}(f(15.75)) = 15.75$

**iv.** $f\left(f^{-1}(x)\right) = f^{-1}(f(x)) = x$

$$f\left(f^{-1}(x)\right) = f\left(\frac{x + 140}{6.34}\right)$$
$$= 6.34\left(\frac{x + 140}{6.34}\right) - 140$$
$$= (x + 140) - 140 = x$$
$$f^{-1}(f(x)) = f^{-1}(6.34x - 140)$$
$$= \frac{(6.34x - 140) + 140}{6.34}$$
$$= \frac{6.34x}{6.34} = x$$

**b.  i.** $f^{-1}(x) = \frac{x - 32}{1.8}$. To find $f^{-1}(x)$, switch the
dependent and independent variables.

$$x = 1.8y + 32$$
$$x - 32 = 1.8y$$
$$y = \frac{x - 32}{1.8}, \text{ or } f^{-1}(x) = \frac{x - 32}{1.8}$$

**ii.** $f(f^{-1}(15.75)) = 15.75$

**iii.** $f^{-1}(f(15.75)) = 15.75$

**iv.** $f(f^{-1}(x)) = f^{-1}(f(x)) = x$

$$f(f^{-1}(x)) = f\left(\frac{x - 32}{1.8}\right)$$

$$= 1.8\left(\frac{x - 32}{1.32}\right) + 32$$

$$= (x - 32) + 32 = x$$

$$f^{-1}(f(x)) = f^{-1}(1.8x + 32)$$

$$= \frac{(1.8x + 32) - 32}{1.8}$$

$$= \frac{1.8x}{1.8} = x$$

**10. a.** Enter the data for altitude in meters and temperature in °C into lists in your calculator, and calculate the equation of the median-median line. The equation is $f(x) = -0.006546x + 14.75$.

**b.** $f^{-1}(x) = \frac{x - 14.75}{-0.006546x}$, or $f^{-1}(x) = -152.77x + 2253.28$. Exchange $x$ and $y$ to find the inverse and solve for $y$.

$$x = -0.006546y + 14.75$$

$$x - 14.75 = -0.006546y$$

$$y = \frac{x - 14.75}{-0.006546}, \text{ or}$$

$$f^{-1}(x) = -152.77x + 2253.28$$

**c.** Enter the data for altitude in feet and temperature in °F into lists in your calculator, and calculate the equation of the median-median line. The equation is $g(x) = -0.003545x + 58.814$.

**d.** $g^{-1}(x) = \frac{x - 58.814}{-0.003545}$, or $g^{-1}(x) = -282.1x + 16591$. Exchange $x$ and $y$ to find the inverse and solve for $y$.

$$x = -0.003545y + 58.814$$

$$x - 58.814 = -0.003545y$$

$$y = \frac{x - 58.814}{-0.003545}, \text{ or}$$

$$g^{-1}(x) = -282.1x + 16591$$

**e.** $-14.44°F$. Because the altitude is given in meters, use the function in 10a to find the temperature in °C first. $f(x) = -0.006546(6194) + 14.75 = -25.8°C$. Then use the function from 9b to change °C to °F: $y = 1.8x + 32$, so $y = 1.8(-25.8) + 32 = -14.44°F$.

**f.** $y = -0.01178x + 58.55$. Let $f(x) = -0.006546x + 14.75$ be the function that relates (*altitude in meters, temperature in °C*) and $h(x) = 1.8x + 32$ be the function that relates (°C, °F). Then, $h(f(x))$ with an input of altitude in

meters will give an output in °F. $h(f(x)) = 1.8(-0.006546x + 14.75) + 32$, or $y = -0.01178x + 58.55$.

**11. a.** $y = 100 - C$

**b.** $y = \frac{F - 212}{-1.8}$. The equation for converting °C to °F is $F = 1.8C + 32$. Solve the equation from 11a for $C$; $C = 100 - y$. Substitute this expression for $C$ into the equation for $F$ and solve for $y$.

$$F = 1.8(100 - y) + 32$$

$$F = 180 - 1.8y + 32$$

$$F = 212 - 1.8y$$

$$y = \frac{F - 212}{-1.8}$$

**12.** Your friend's score is 1. Sample answers are given for explanations of incorrect answers.

Problem 1 is correct.

Problem 2 is incorrect. The notation $f^{-1}(x)$ indicates the inverse function related to $f(x)$, not the exponent $-1$.

Problem 3 is incorrect. The expression $9^{-1/5}$ can be rewritten as $\frac{1}{9^{1/5}}$.

Problem 4 is incorrect. The expression $0^0$ is undefined.

**13. a.** $y = c(x) = 7.18 + 3.98x$, where $c(x)$ is the cost in dollars and $x$ is the number of thousand gallons.

**b.** $c(8) = 7.18 + 3.98(8) = \$39.02$

**c.** $y = g(x) = \frac{x - 7.18}{3.98}$, where $g(x)$ is the number of thousands of gallons and $x$ is the cost in dollars. This is the inverse function of $c$, so switch $x$ and $y$ in $y = 7.18 + 3.98x$ and solve for $y$.

$$x = 7.18 + 3.98y$$

$$x - 7.18 = 3.98y$$

$$\frac{x - 7.18}{3.98} = y, \text{ so } c^{-1}(x) = \frac{x - 7.18}{3.98}$$

**d.** 12,000 gallons. $g(54.94) = \frac{54.94 - 7.18}{3.98} = 12$

**e.** $g(c(x)) = g(7.18 + 3.98x) = \frac{7.18 + 3.98x - 7.18}{3.98}$

$$= \frac{3.98x}{3.98} = x$$

$$c(g(x)) = c\left(\frac{x - 7.18}{3.98}\right) = 7.18 + 3.98\left(\frac{x - 7.18}{3.98}\right)$$

$$= 7.18 + x - 7.18 = x$$

**f.** About $6. (50 gallons/day)(30 days) = 1500 gallons; $3.98(1.5) \approx 6.00$.

**g.** Answers will vary, but volume should equal $231 \cdot 1500$, or 346,500 in.³ (approximately 200 ft³). For example, the container could be 30 in. by 50 in. by 231 in.

**14.** Possible answers: $\sqrt[3]{125^2}$, $\left(\sqrt[3]{125}\right)^2$, $5^2$, $\sqrt[3]{15625}$, 25

**15.** $f(x) = 12.6(1.5)^{x-2}$, or $f(x) = 42.525(1.5)^{x-5}$. Use the point-ratio equation with the point (2, 12.6): $y = 12.6r^{x-2}$. Now use the second point, (5, 42.525), to solve for $r$.

$$42.525 = 12.6r^{5-2}$$

$$3.375 = r^3$$

$$r = 3.375^{1/3} = 1.5$$

**16. a.** $x = \dfrac{9}{2} = 4.5$

| | |
|---|---|
| $\left(2^2\right)^x = \left(2^3\right)^3$ | Replace 4 with $2^2$ and 8 with $2^3$. |
| $2^{2x} = 2^9$ | Power of a power property. |
| $2x = 9$ | Common base property of equality. |
| $x = \dfrac{9}{2} = 4.5$ | Divide both sides by 2. |

**b.** $x = -\dfrac{1}{2} = -0.5$

| | |
|---|---|
| $3^{4x+1} = \left(3^2\right)^x$ | Rewrite 9 as $3^2$. |
| $3^{4x+1} = 3^{2x}$ | Power of a power property. |
| $4x + 1 = 2x$ | Common base property of equality. |
| $2x = -1$ | Subtract $2x$ and 1 from both sides. |
| $x = -\dfrac{1}{2} = -0.5$ | Divide both sides by 2. |

**c.** $x = 1$

| | |
|---|---|
| $2^{x-3} = \left(2^{-2}\right)^x$ | Rewrite $\frac{1}{4}$ as $2^{-2}$. |
| $2^{x-3} = 2^{-2x}$ | Power of a power property. |
| $x - 3 = -2x$ | Common base property of equality. |
| $3x = 3$ | Add $2x$ and 3 to both sides. |
| $x = 1$ | Divide both sides by 3. |

**17.** $y = 3(x - 3)^2 + 2$ and $x = \frac{1}{9}(y - 2)^2 + 3$

The vertical parabola has equation $y = a(x - 3)^2 + 2$. Use the point (4, 5) to find $a$.

$$5 = a(4 - 3)^2 + 2$$

$$3 = a$$

The equation is $y = 3(x - 3)^2 + 2$.

The horizontal parabola has equation $x = b(y - 2)^2 + 3$. Use the point (4, 5) to find $b$.

$$4 = b(5 - 2)^2 + 3$$

$$b = \frac{1}{9}$$

The equation is $x = \frac{1}{9}(y - 2)^2 + 3$.

**18.** $x = -1$, $y = 1$, $z = 0$. Rewrite the second equation as $x + y - 2z = 0$, and then add it to the first equation to eliminate $x$. Also, divide the third equation by 2.2.

$$2z = x + y \qquad \text{Second equation.}$$

| | |
|---|---|
| $x + \phantom{3}y - 2z = 0$ | Subtract $2z$ from both sides. |
| $\underline{-x + 3y - \phantom{2}z = 4}$ | First equation. |
| $4y - 3z = 4$ | Add the two equations. |

Now use the third equation to solve for $y$ and $z$.

| | |
|---|---|
| $2.2y + 2.2z = 2.2$ | Third equation. |
| $y + z = 1$ | Divide both sides by 2.2. |
| $y = 1 - z$ | Subtract $z$ from both sides. |
| $4(1 - z) - 3z = 4$ | Substitute $(1 - z)$ for $y$ in $4y - 3z = 4$. |
| $4 - 4z - 3z = 4$ | Distribute 4. |
| $-7z = 0$ | Subtract 4 from both sides. |
| $z = 0$ | Divide both sides by $-7$. |

Substitute 0 for $z$ in the third equation.

$$2.2y + 2.2(0) = 2.2$$

$$y = 1$$

Substitute 0 for $z$ and 1 for $y$ in the first or second equation.

| | |
|---|---|
| $2(0) = x + 1$ | Second equation. |
| $x = -1$ | Subtract 1 from both sides. |

The solution is $x = -1$, $y = 1$, $z = 0$.

**EXTENSIONS**

**A.** Answers will vary.

**B.** Answers will vary.

## LESSON 5.6

### EXERCISES

**1. a.** $10^x = 1000$. Recall that $\log 1000 = \log_{10} 1000$, so $b = 10$ and $a = 1000$.

**b.** $5^x = 625$. $b = 5$ and $a = 625$.

**c.** $7^x = \sqrt{7}$. $b = 7$ and $a = \sqrt{7}$.

**d.** $8^x = 2$. $b = 8$ and $a = 2$.

**e.** $5^x = \frac{1}{25}$. $b = 5$ and $a = \frac{1}{25}$.

**f.** $6^x = 1$. $b = 6$ and $a = 1$.

**2. a.** $10^x = 1000 = 10^3$, so $x = 3$

**b.** $5^x = 625 = 5^4$, so $x = 4$

**c.** $7^x = \sqrt{7} = 7^{1/2}$, so $x = \frac{1}{2}$

**d.** $8^x = 2 = 8^{1/3}$, so $x = \frac{1}{3}$

**e.** $5^x = \frac{1}{25} = 5^{-2}$, so $x = -2$

**f.** $6^x = 1 = 6^0$, so $x = 0$

**3. a.** $x = \log_{10} 0.001$; $x = -3$

**b.** $x = \log_5 100$; $x = \log_5 100 = \dfrac{\log 100}{\log 5} \approx 2.8614$

**c.** $x = \log_{35} 8$; $x = \log_{35} 8 = \dfrac{\log 8}{\log 35} \approx 0.5849$

**d.** $x = \log_{0.4} 5$; $x = \log_{0.4} 5 = \dfrac{\log 5}{\log 0.4} \approx -1.7565$

**e.** $x = \log_{0.8} 0.03$; $x = \log_{0.8} 0.03 = \dfrac{\log 0.03}{\log 0.8} \approx 15.7144$

**f.** $x = \log_{17} 0.5$; $x = \log_{17} 0.5 = \dfrac{\log 0.5}{\log 17} \approx -0.2447$

**4. a.** This is a translation of $y = \log x$ left 2 units.

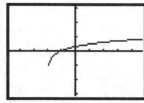

$[-4.7, 4.7, 1, -3.1, 3.1, 1]$

**b.** This is a vertical stretch of $y = \log x$ by a factor of 3.

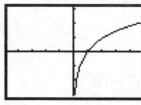

$[-4.7, 4.7, 1, -3.1, 3.1, 1]$

**c.** This is a reflection of $y = \log x$ across the $x$-axis, followed by a translation down 2 units.

$[-4.7, 4.7, 1, -3.1, 3.1, 1]$

**d.** This is a translation of $y = 10^x$ left 2 units.

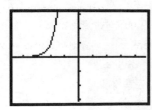

$[-4.7, 4.7, 1, -3.1, 3.1, 1]$

**e.** This is a vertical stretch of $y = 10^x$ by a factor of 3.

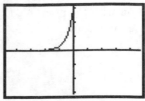

$[-4.7, 4.7, 1, -3.1, 3.1, 1]$

**f.** This is a reflection of $y = 10^x$ across the $x$-axis, followed by a translation down 2 units.

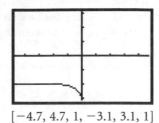

$[-4.7, 4.7, 1, -3.1, 3.1, 1]$

**5. a.** False; $x = \log_6 12$

**b.** False; $2^x = 5$

**c.** False; $x = \log_3 5.5 = \dfrac{\log 5.5}{\log 3}$ because $3^x = \frac{11}{2} = 5.5$.

**d.** False; $x = \log_3 7$

**6.** Approximately 25 min. Set $g(x)$ equal to 5 and solve for $x$.

$$5 = 23(0.94)^x$$

$$0.2174 = 0.94^x$$

$$x = \log_{0.94} 0.2174$$

$$x = \dfrac{\log 0.2174}{\log 0.94} \approx 24.66$$

**7. a.** 1980. Substitute 1000 for $y$ in the given equation and solve for $x$.

$$1000 = 0.051517(1.1306727)^x$$

$$19411.07 = 1.1306727^x$$

$$x = \log_{1.1306727} 19411.07$$

$$x = \dfrac{\log 19411.07}{\log 1.1306727}$$

$$x \approx 80.4$$

Because $x$ represents years after 1900, according to the model the debt passed \$1 trillion in 1980.

**b.** Approximately 13%. $(1 + r) = 1.1306727$, so $r \approx 0.13$.

**c.** Approximately 5.6 yr. The doubling time depends only on the ratio, so you can ignore the 0.051517 and assume the function doubles from $y = 1$ to $y = 2$. Set $y$ equal to 2, and solve for $x$.

$$2 = (1.1306727)^x$$

$$x = \log_{1.1306727} 2$$

$$x = \frac{\log 2}{\log 1.1306727}$$

$$x \approx 5.64$$

The doubling time is about 5.6 yr.

**8. a.** $y = 100(0.999879)^x$. Start with the equation $y = ab^x$, and use the data points $(0, 100)$ and $(5750, 50)$ to find $a$ and $b$. Using the first point, $100 = ab^0$, so $a = 100$. Now use the second point to find $b$.

$$50 = 100b^{5750}$$

$$0.5 = b^{5750}$$

$$b = 0.5^{1/5750} \approx 0.999879$$

The equation is $y = 100(0.999879)^x$.

**b.** About 6002 years ago. The technique is approximate and assumes that the carbon-14 concentration in the atmosphere has not changed over the last 6002 years.

$$48.37 = 100(0.999879)^x$$

$$0.4837 = 0.999879^x$$

$$x = \log_{0.999879} 0.4837$$

$$x = \frac{\log 0.4837}{\log 0.999879} \approx 6002$$

**9. a.** $y = 88.7(1.0077)^x$. Start with the equation $y = ab^x$, and use the data points $(0, 88.7)$ and $(6, 92.9)$ to find $a$ and $b$. Using the first point, $88.7 = ab^0$, so $a = 88.7$. Now use the second point to find $b$.

$$92.9 = 88.7b^6$$

$$1.0474 = b^6$$

$$b = 1.0474^{1/6} \approx 1.0077$$

The equation is $y = 88.7(1.0077)^x$.

**b.** 23 or 24 clicks

$$106.3 = 88.7(1.0077)^x$$

$$1.1984 = 1.0077^x$$

$$x = \log_{1.0077} 1.1984$$

$$x = \frac{\log 1.1984}{\log 1.0077} \approx 23.595$$

**10. a.** $x - 2 = 49^{3/2} = 343$, so $x = 345$

**b.** $x = 7^{1/2.4} \approx 2.25$

$$3x^{2.4} - 5 = 16$$

$$3x^{2.4} = 21$$

$$x^{2.4} = 7$$

$$x = 7^{1/24} \approx 2.25$$

**11. a.**

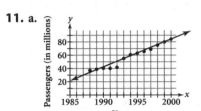

$$\hat{y} = \frac{38}{9}x - 8359.91$$

Divide the data points into the three sets. The three summary points are $M_1(1989.5, 39.45)$, $M_2(1994, 60.7)$, and $M_3(1998.5, 77.45)$. The slope of the line through $M_1$ and $M_3$ is $\frac{74.45 - 39.45}{1998.5 - 1989.5} = \frac{38}{9}$, so the equation of this line is $y = 39.45 + \frac{38}{9}(x - 1989.5)$, or $y = \frac{38}{9}x - 8360.66$. The line with this slope through $M_2$ is $y = 60.7 + \frac{38}{9}(x - 1994)$, or $y = \frac{38}{9}x - 8358.41$. The mean of the three $y$-intercepts is $-8359.91$, so the equation of the median-median line is $\hat{y} = \frac{38}{9}x - 8359.91$.

**b.** 3.03, 0.71, −2.11, −6.43, −9.16, 0.02, 1.50, −0.52, −2.05, −3.17, −0.99, −0.51, 0.43

| L1 | L2 | L3 | 11 |
|---|---|---|---|
| 1988 | 36.9 | 3.0322 | |
| 1989 | 38.8 | .71 | |
| 1990 | 40.2 | -2.112 | |
| 1991 | 40.1 | -6.434 | |
| 1992 | 41.6 | -9.157 | |
| 1993 | 55 | .02111 | |
| 1994 | 60.7 | 1.4989 | |

L3 =L2−Y1(L1)■

**c.** 3.78 million riders. Most data are within 3.78 million of the number predicted by the equation of the median-median line.

**d.** 126.8 million riders. $y = \frac{38}{9}(2010) - 8359.91 \approx 126.8$.

**12. a.** $C_1 = 32.7$, $C_2 = 65.4$, $C_3 = 130.8$, $C_6 = 1046.4$, $C_7 = 2092.8$, $C_8 = 4185.6$. To get the next frequency, multiply the previous term by 2, or to get a previous frequency divide by 2.

**b.** $y = 16.35(2)^x$ where $x$ represents C-note number and $y$ represents frequency in cycles per second. To find this equation, start with the point-ratio equation $y = 261.6(2)^{x-4}$. This is equivalent to $y = 261.6(2^{-4} \cdot 2^x) = 16.35(2)^x$.

**13. a.** $y + 1 = x - 3$, or $y = x - 4$. This is the graph of $y = x$ translated down 1 unit and right 3 units.

**b.** $y + 4 = (x + 5)^2$, or $y = (x + 5)^2 - 4$. This is the graph of $y = x^2$ translated down 4 units and left 5 units.

**c.** $y - 2 = |x + 6|$, or $y = |x + 6| + 2$. This is the graph of $y = |x|$ translated up 2 units and left 6 units.

**d.** $y - 7 = \sqrt{x - 2}$, or $y = \sqrt{x - 2} + 7$. This is the graph of $y = \sqrt{x}$ translated up 7 units and right 2 units.

**14. a.** $\begin{cases} 2l + 2w = 155 \\ l = 2w + 7 \end{cases}$

**b.** $l = 54$, $w = 23.5$; the length is 54 in. and the width is 23.5 in. Substitute the second equation into the first to get

$$2(2w + 7) + 2w = 155$$
$$4w + 14 + 2w = 155$$
$$6w = 141$$
$$w = 23.5$$

Substitute 23.5 for $w$ into the second equation to find $l$.

$$l = 2(23.5) + 7$$
$$l = 54$$

**15. a.** They are parallel.

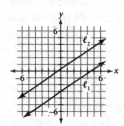

**b.** Possible answer: $A(0, -3)$; $P(1, 1)$; $Q(4, 3)$

**c.** Possible answer: Translate right 1 unit and up 4 units; $2(x - 1) - 3(y - 4) = 9$.

**d.** Possible answer: Translate right 4 units and up 6 units; $2(x - 4) - 3(y - 6) = 9$.

**e.** $2(x - 1) - 3(y - 4) = 9 \rightarrow 2x - 2 - 3y + 12 = 9 \rightarrow 2x - 3y = -1$, which is the equation of $\ell_2$.
$2(x - 4) - 3(y - 6) = 9 \rightarrow 2x - 8 - 3y + 18 = 9 \rightarrow 2x - 3y = -1$, which is the equation of $\ell_2$.

## EXTENSIONS

**A.** Answers will vary.

**B.** Answers will vary.

## LESSON 5.7

### EXERCISES

**1. a.** $g^h \cdot g^k$; product property of exponents

**b.** $\log st$; product property of logarithms

**c.** $f^{w-v}$; quotient property of exponents

**d.** $\log h - \log k$; quotient property of logarithms

**e.** $j^{st}$; power property of exponents

**f.** $g \log b$; power property of logarithms

**g.** $k^{m/n}$; definition of rational exponents

**h.** $\log_u t$; change-of-base property

**i.** $w^{t+s}$; product property of exponents

**j.** $\frac{1}{p^h}$; definition of negative exponents

**2. a.** $a \approx 1.255$

**b.** $b \approx 1.851$

**c.** $c \approx 3.107$

**d.** $d = 10^{3.107} \approx 1279$. If you use the unrounded value of $c$, you get $d = 1278$.

**e.** $e = 1278$

**f.** $f \approx 3.107$

**g.** $d = e$ and $c = f$

**h.** $\log a + \log b = \log ab$

**i.** The logarithm gives the exponent using a certain base. When numbers with the same base are multiplied, the exponents are added. Or, adding the logarithms of two numbers and then finding the antilog of the sum gives their product.

**3. a.** $a \approx 1.7634$

**b.** $b \approx 1.3424$

**c.** $c \approx 0.4210$

**d.** $d = 10^{0.421} \approx 2.6363$. If you use the unrounded value of $c$, you get $d \approx 2.6364$.

**e.** $e \approx 2.6364$

**f.** $f \approx 0.4210$

**g.** $c = f$ and $d = e$

**h.** $\log a - \log b = \log \frac{a}{b}$

**i.** The logarithm gives the exponent using a certain base. When numbers with the same base are divided, the exponents are subtracted. Or, subtracting the logarithms of two numbers and then finding the antilog of the difference gives their quotient.

**4. a.** $a \approx 1.1139$

**b.** $b \approx 4.0102$

**c.** $c = 10^{4.0102} \approx 10237.55$

**d.** $d \approx 10237.55$

**e.** $d = c$

**f.** $\log a^b = b \log a$

**g.** $\log \sqrt{a} = \log a^{0.5} = 0.5 \log a$

**5. a.** True; product property of logarithms

**b.** False; possible answer: $\log 5 + \log 3 = \log 15$

**c.** True; power property of logarithms

**d.** True; quotient property of logarithms

**e.** False; possible answer:
$\log 9 - \log 3 = \log \frac{9}{3} = \log 3$

**f.** False; possible answer:
$\log \sqrt{7} = \log 7^{1/2} = \frac{1}{2} \log 7$

**g.** False; possible answer: $\log 35 = \log 5 + \log 7$

**h.** True; $\log \frac{1}{4} = \log 1 - \log 4 = -\log 4$. ($\log 1 = 0$)

**i.** False; possible answer: $\log 3 - \log 4 = \log \frac{3}{4}$

**j.** True; $\log 64 = \log 2^6 = \log(2^4)^{6/4} = \log(16)^{3/2} = 1.5 \log 16$ by the power property of logarithms

**6. a.** $y = 100(0.999879)^x$. Start with the equation $y = ab^x$, and use the data points $(0, 100)$ and $(5750, 50)$ to find $a$ and $b$. Use the first point to find $a$. $100 = ab^0$, so $a = 100$. Now use the second point to find $b$.

$$50 = 100b^{5750}$$

$$0.5 = b^{5750}$$

$$b = 0.5^{1/5750} \approx 0.999879$$

The equation is $y = 100(0.999879)^x$.

**b.** Approximately 11,456 years old. Substitute 25 for $y$ and solve for $x$.

$$25 = 100(0.999879)^x$$

$$0.25 = 0.999879^x$$

$$x = \frac{\log 0.25}{\log 0.999879} \approx 11456.285$$

**c.** 1910 B.C.E. Substitute 62.45 for $y$ and solve for $x$.

$$62.45 = 100(0.999879)^x$$

$$0.6245 = 0.999879^x$$

$$x = \frac{\log 0.6245}{\log 0.999879} \approx 3890.706$$

Subtract this value from 1981 to get the year the ark was constructed: $1981 - 3890.706 = -1909.706$, or about 1910 B.C.E.

**d.** $y = 100(0.999879)^{100000000} \approx 0$. There is virtually nothing left to measure, so you could not use carbon-14 for dating coal unless you had very sensitive instruments to detect the radioactivity.

**7. a.** Let $x$ represent the note's number of steps above middle C, and let $y$ represent the note's frequency in hertz. $y = 261.6\left(2^{x/12}\right)$ because the starting value is 261.6 and there are 12 intermediate frequencies to get to the last C note, which has double that frequency.

**b.**

| | Note | Frequency (Hz) |
|---|---|---|
| Do | $C_4$ | 261.6 |
| | C# | 277.2 |
| Re | D | 293.6 |
| | D# | 311.1 |
| Mi | E | 329.6 |
| Fa | F | 349.2 |
| | F# | 370.0 |
| Sol | G | 392.0 |
| | G# | 415.3 |
| La | A | 440.0 |
| | A# | 466.1 |
| Ti | B | 493.8 |
| Do | $C_5$ | 523.2 |

**8. a.** $x \approx 3.3816$. Take the logarithm of both sides to get $\log 5.1^x = \log 247$. Use the power property of logarithms to get $x \log 5.1 = \log 247$. Then $x = \frac{\log 247}{\log 5.1} \approx 3.3816$.

**b.** $x \approx 11.495$. Subtract 17 from both sides to get $1.25^x = 13$. Take the logarithm of both sides to get $\log 1.25^x = \log 13$. Use the power property of logarithms to get $x \log 1.25 = \log 13$. Then $x = \frac{\log 13}{\log 1.25} \approx 11.495$.

**c.** $x \approx 11.174$. Divide both sides by 27 to get $0.93^x = \frac{12}{27} = \frac{4}{9}$. Take the logarithm of both sides to get $\log 0.93^x = \log \frac{4}{9}$. Use the power property of logarithms to get $x \log 0.93 = \log \frac{4}{9}$. Divide both sides by $\log 0.93$ to get $x \approx 11.174$.

**d.** $x \approx 42.739$. Subtract 23 from both sides and then divide both sides by 45 to get $1.024^x = \frac{124}{45}$. Take the logarithm of both sides to get $\log 1.024^x = \log \frac{124}{45}$. Use the power property of logarithms to get $x \log 1.024 = \log \frac{124}{45}$. Divide both sides by $\log 1.024$ to get $x \approx 42.739$.

**9. a.** $y = 14.7(0.8022078)^x$. The point-ratio equation is $y = 14.7 \cdot r^x$. Use the data point $(2, 9.46)$ to find $r$.

$$9.46 = 14.7 \cdot r^2$$

$$0.6435 = r^2$$

$$r = \sqrt{0.6435} \approx 0.8022078$$

**b.**

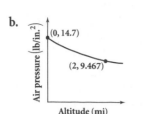
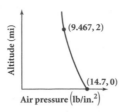

**c.** Approximately 8.91 lb/in.². Convert the altitude to miles and substitute that value in the equation from 9a. $\frac{12000 \text{ ft}}{5280 \text{ ft/mi}} = 2.27$ mi; $y = 14.7(0.8022078^{2.27}) \approx 8.91$.

**d.** Approximately 6.32 mi. Substitute 3.65 for $y$ and solve for $x$.

$$3.65 = 14.7(0.8022078^x)$$
$$0.248299 = 0.8022078^x$$
$$x = \frac{\log 0.248299}{\log 0.8022078} \approx 6.32$$

**10. a.** $100\% - 3.5\% = 96.5\%$ remains after 1 min.

**b.** $y = 100(0.965)^x$ where $x$ is time in minutes and $y$ is percentage of carbon-11 remaining. To find the equation, start with the point-ratio equation, $y = ab^x$, and use the data points (0, 100) and (1, 96.5) to find $a$ and $b$. $100 = ab^0$, so $a = 100$, and $y = 100b^x$. $96.5 = 100b^1$, so $b = 0.965$, and $y = 100(0.965)^x$.

**c.** Approximately 19.456 min

$$50 = 100(0.965)^x$$
$$0.5 = 0.965^x$$
$$x = \frac{\log 0.5}{\log 0.965} \approx 19.456$$

**d.** In one day the carbon-11 is virtually gone, so you could never date an archaeological find.

**11.** Graphs will vary. If a horizontal line intersects the graph in more than one point, its inverse is not a function.

**12. a.** $y = 5 + 3x$. The common difference, or slope, is 3, so the $y$-intercept is $8 - 3 = 5$. Therefore the equation is $y = 5 + 3x$.

**b.** $y = 2(3^x)$. The $y$-intercept is 2 and the common ratio is 3, so the equation is $y = 2(3^x)$.

**13. a.** The graph has been vertically stretched by a factor of 3, then translated right 1 unit and down 4 units.

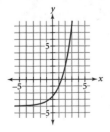

**b.** The graph has been horizontally stretched by a factor of 3, reflected across the $x$-axis, and translated up 2 units.

**14. a.** False. If everyone got a grade of 86% or better, one would have to have gotten a much higher grade to be in the 86th percentile.

**b.** False. Consider the data set {5, 6, 9, 10, 11}. The mean is 8.2; the median is 9.

**c.** False. Consider the data set {0, 2, 28}. The range is 28; the difference between the mean, 10, and the maximum, 28, is 18.

**d.** True

**15. a.** Let $h$ represent the length of time in hours, and let $c$ represent the driver's cost in dollars. $c = 14h + 20$. The domain is the set of possible values of the number of hours, $h > 0$. The range is the set of possible values of the cost paid to the driver, $c > 20$.

**b.** Let $c$ represent the driver's cost in dollars, and let $a$ represent the agency's charge in dollars. $a = 1.15c + 25$. The domain is the money paid to the driver if she had been booked directly, $c > 20$. The range is the amount charged by the agency, $a > 1.15(20) + 25 = 23 + 25$; $a > 48$.

**c.** $a = 1.15(14h + 20) + 25$, or $a = 16.1h + 48$

**EXTENSIONS**

**A.** See the solution to Take Another Look activity 3 on page 112.

**B.** Research results will vary.

**C.** Results will vary.

## LESSON 5.8

**EXERCISES**

**1. a.**

| | |
|---|---|
| $10^{n+p} = (10^n)(10^p)$ | Original equation. |
| $\log(10^{n+p}) = \log((10^n)(10^p))$ | Take the logarithm of both sides. |
| $(n + p)\log 10 = \log 10^n + \log 10^p$ | Power property and product property of logarithms. |
| $(n + p)\log 10 = n\log 10 + p\log 10$ | Power property of logarithms. |
| $(n + p)\log 10 = (n + p)\log 10$ | Combine terms. |

*Discovering Advanced Algebra Solutions Manual*
©2004 Key Curriculum Press

**b.**

$$\frac{10^d}{10^e} = 10^{d-e}$$  Original equation.

$$\log\left(\frac{10^d}{10^e}\right) = \log\left(10^{d-e}\right)$$  Take the logarithm of both sides.

$$\log 10^d - \log 10^e = \log\left(10^{d-e}\right)$$  Quotient property of logarithms.

$$d \log 10 - e \log 10 = (d - e)\log 10$$  Power property of logarithms.

$$(d - e)\log 10 = (d - e)\log 10$$  Combine terms.

**2. a.** $\log 800 = x \log 10$, so $x = \frac{\log 800}{\log 10} \approx 2.90309$

Check: $10^{2.90309} \approx 800$

**b.** $\log 2048 = x \log 2$, so $x = \frac{\log 2048}{\log 2} = 11$

Check: $2^{11} = 2048$

**c.** $\log 16 = x \log 0.5$, so $x = \frac{\log 16}{\log 0.5} = -4$

Check: $0.5^{-4} = 16$

**d.** $\frac{478}{18.5} = 10^x$, so $\log \frac{478}{18.5} = x \log 10$,

and $x = \frac{\log\left(\frac{478}{18.5}\right)}{\log 10} = \log\left(\frac{478}{18.5}\right) \approx 1.4123$

Check: $18.05\left(10^{1.4123}\right) \approx 478$

**e.** $\frac{155}{24.0} = 1.89^x$, so $\log\left(\frac{155}{24.0}\right) = x \log 1.89$, and

$x = \frac{\log\left(\frac{155}{24.0}\right)}{\log 1.89} \approx 2.9303$

Check: $24.0\left(1.89^{2.9303}\right) \approx 155$

**f.** $\frac{0.0047}{19.1} = 0.21^x$, so $\log\left(\frac{0.0047}{19.1}\right) = x \log 0.21$, and

$x = \frac{\log\left(\frac{0.0047}{19.1}\right)}{\log 0.21} \approx 5.3246$

Check: $19.1\left(0.21^{5.3246}\right) \approx 0.0047$

**3.** About 195.9 mo, or about 16 yr 4 mo. The equation for money invested at an annual rate $r$, compounded $n$ times per year, with initial amount $P$, is $A = P\left(1 + \frac{r}{n}\right)^t$, where $t$ is the number of compoundings. In this case it is $A = 3000\left(1 + \frac{0.0675}{12}\right)^t$, where $t$ is the number of months. Substitute 9000 for $A$ and solve for $t$.

$$9000 = 3000\left(1 + \frac{0.0675}{12}\right)^t$$

$$3 = 1.005625^t$$

$$t = \frac{\log 3}{\log 1.005625} \approx 195.9$$

195.9 months is $\frac{195.9 \text{ mo}}{12 \text{ mo/yr}} = 16.325$ yr, and 0.325 yr is $(0.325 \text{ yr})(12 \text{ mo/yr}) = 3.9$ mo. So, tripling your money will take about 195.9 months, or about 16 years 4 months.

**4. a.** $h = 146(0.9331226)^{T-4}$. Two points on the curve are (4, 146) and (22, 42). Use the point-ratio equation $h = y_1 \cdot b^{T-x_1}$, where $h$ represents the number of hours and $T$ represents the temperature. Using the first point, $h = 146b^{T-4}$. Substitute (22, 42) into the equation to find $b$; $42 = 146b^{18}$, so $\frac{42}{146} = b^{18}$, and $b = \left(\frac{42}{146}\right)^{1/18} \approx 0.9331226$. The function is $h = 146(0.9331226)^{T-4}$.

**b.** $h = 146(0.9331226)^{30-4} \approx 24.1$ hr at 30°C; $h = 146(0.9331226)^{16-4} \approx 63.6$ hr at 16°C.

**c.** Approximately 3.9°C

$$147 = 146(0.9331226)^{T-4}$$

$$1.00685 = 0.9331226^{T-4}$$

$$T - 4 = \frac{\log 1.00685}{\log 0.9331226}$$

$$T \approx -0.0986 + 4 \approx 3.9$$

**d.**

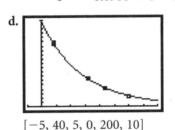

$[-5, 40, 5, 0, 200, 10]$

**e.** A realistic domain is 0° to 100°C; these are the freezing and boiling points of water.

**5. a.** $f(20) \approx 133.28$. After 20 days, 133 games have been sold.

**b.** $f(80) \approx 7969.17$. After 80 days, 7969 games have been sold.

**c.** $x \approx 72$. After 72 days, 6000 games have been sold. Make a table to approximate a value for $x$.

| X | Y₁ |
|---|---|
| 70 | 5461 |
| 71 | 5718.2 |
| 72 | 5976.6 |
| 73 | 6235 |
| 74 | 6492.5 |
| 75 | 6748.2 |
| 76 | 7001.2 |

X=72

$y = 6000$ when $x \approx 72$.

**d.**

$$6000 = \frac{12000}{1 + 499(1.09)^{-x}}$$

$$6000\left(1 + 499(1.09)^{-x}\right) = 12000$$

$$1 + 499(1.09)^{-x} = 2$$

$$499(1.09)^{-x} = 1$$

$$1.09^{-x} = \frac{1}{499}$$

$$-x \log 1.09 = \log \frac{1}{499}$$

$$x = -\frac{\log \frac{1}{499}}{\log 1.09} \approx 72.09$$

**e.**

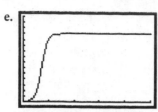

[0, 500, 100, 0, 15000, 1000]

Sample answer: The number of games sold starts out increasing slowly, then speeds up, then slows down as everyone who wants the game has purchased one.

**6. a.** $D = 10 \log\left(\dfrac{10^{-13}}{10^{-16}}\right) = 10 \log 10^3 = 10 \cdot 3 = 30$ dB

**b.** $D = 10 \log\left(\dfrac{3.16 \cdot 10^{-10}}{10^{-16}}\right) = 10 \log 3160000 \approx$ 65 dB

**c.** Approximately $5.01 \times 10^{-6}$ W/cm²

$$107 = 10 \log\left(\dfrac{I}{10^{-16}}\right)$$

$$10.7 = \log\left(\dfrac{I}{10^{-16}}\right)$$

$$10^{10.7} = \left(\dfrac{I}{10^{-16}}\right)$$

$$I = 10^{10.7-16} \approx 5.01 \times 10^{-6}$$

**d.** About 3.16 times as loud. Let $I_1$ be the power of the sound at 47 dB, and let $I_2$ be the power of the sound at 42 dB.

$$47 = 10 \log\left(\dfrac{I_1}{10^{-16}}\right) \qquad 42 = 10 \log\left(\dfrac{I_2}{10^{-16}}\right)$$

$$4.7 = \log\left(\dfrac{I_1}{10^{-16}}\right) \qquad 4.2 = \log\left(\dfrac{I_2}{10^{-16}}\right)$$

$$10^{4.7} = \dfrac{I_1}{10^{-16}} \qquad 10^{4.2} = \dfrac{I_2}{10^{-16}}$$

$$I_1 = 10^{4.7}\left(10^{-16}\right) = 10^{-11.3} \quad I_2 = 10^{4.2}\left(10^{-16}\right) = 10^{-11.8}$$

$$\dfrac{I_1}{I_2} = \dfrac{10^{-11.3}}{10^{-11.8}} = 10^{0.5} \approx 3.162$$

**7. a.**

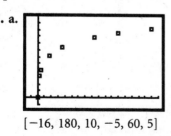

[−16, 180, 10, −5, 60, 5]

**b.** Points in the form $(\log x, y)$ give a linear graph.

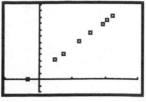

[−1, 3, 1, −10, 60, 5]

**c.** $\hat{y} = 6 + 20 \log x$. Use your calculator to approximate a line of fit.

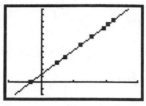

[−1, 3, 1, −10, 60, 5]

Two points on the line are (0.5, 16) and (2, 46), so the slope is 20. The $y$-intercept is 6, so the equation of the line is $y = 6 + 20x$. The $x$-values used to find this line were actually the logarithms of the $x$-values of the original data. Substitute $\log x$ for $x$. The final equation is $\hat{y} = 6 + 20 \log x$.

**d.**

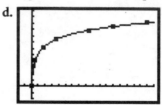

[−16, 180, 10, −10, 60, 5]

Sample answer: Yes; the graph shows that the equation is a good model for the data.

**8. a.** Let $x$ represent time in minutes, and let $y$ represent temperature in degrees Fahrenheit.

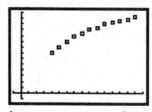

[−2, 32, 2, −5, 70, 5]

**b.** $\hat{y} = 74 - 68.55(0.9318)^x$. Because the curve is both reflected and translated, first graph points in the form $(x, -y)$ to account for the reflection. Then translate the points up so that the data approach a long-term value of zero. Then graph points in the form $(x, \log(-y + 74))$, which appear to be linear.

*Discovering Advanced Algebra Solutions Manual*
©2004 Key Curriculum Press

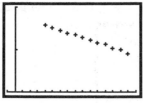

$[-2, 32, 2, 0, 2, 1]$

Use your calculator to find the median-median line through the points in the form $(x, \log(-y + 74))$, or approximately $\log(-y + 74) = 1.823 - 0.0298x$. Solving for $y$ gives the exponential equation $\hat{y} = 74 - 10^{1.823 - 0.0298x}$, or $\hat{y} = 74 - 66.53(0.9337)^x$.

Check that this equation fits the original data.

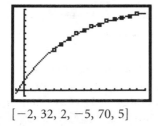

$[-2, 32, 2, -5, 70, 5]$

**9.** Let $x$ represent height in meters, and let $y$ represent viewing distance in kilometers.

**a.** The data are the most linear when plotted in the form $(\log x, \log y)$.

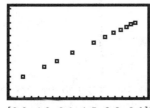

$[2.3, 4.2, 0.1, 1.5, 2.8, 0.1]$

**b.** $\hat{y} = 3.589x^{0.49909}$. Use your calculator to find that the median-median line through the points in the form $(\log x, \log y)$ is approximately $\log y = 0.555 + 0.49909 \log x$. Solving for $y$ gives

$$y = 10^{0.555 + 0.49909 \log x}$$

$$y = 10^{0.555} \cdot 10^{0.49909 \log x}$$

$$y = 3.589\left(10^{\log x}\right)^{0.49909}$$

$$\hat{y} = 3.589x^{0.49909}$$

Check that this equation fits the original data.

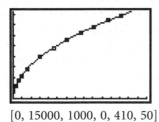

$[0, 15000, 1000, 0, 410, 50]$

**10. a.** After 1 day: $16(1 - 0.15) + 1 \approx 14.6$ qt.
After 2 days: $14.6(1 - 0.15) + 1 \approx 13.41$ qt.
The recursive formula is $u_0 = 16$ and $u_n = u_{n-1}(1 - 0.15) + 1$ where $n \geq 1$.

**b.**

| x | y | | x | y |
|---|---|---|---|---|
| 0 | 16 | | 11 | 8.23 |
| 1 | 14.6 | | 12 | 7.99 |
| 2 | 13.41 | | 13 | 7.80 |
| 3 | 12.40 | | 14 | 7.63 |
| 4 | 11.54 | | 15 | 7.48 |
| 5 | 10.81 | | 16 | 7.36 |
| 6 | 10.19 | | 17 | 7.26 |
| 7 | 9.66 | | 18 | 7.17 |
| 8 | 9.21 | | 19 | 7.09 |
| 9 | 8.83 | | 20 | 7.03 |
| 10 | 8.50 | | | |

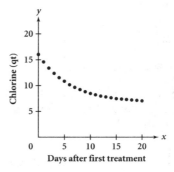

The sequence is a shifted geometric sequence, which corresponds to a translated exponential equation as an explicit model. To determine the amount of translation, find the long-run value of the sequence. Recall that you do this by assigning the same variable to $u_n$ and $u_{n-1}$.

| | |
|---|---|
| $c = 0.85c + 1$ | Substitute $c$ for both $u_n$ and $u_{n-1}$, and rewrite $(1 - 0.15)$ as $0.85$. |
| $c - 0.85c = 1$ | Subtract $0.85c$ from both sides. |
| $0.15c = 1$ | Subtract. |
| $c \approx 6.67$ | Divide both sides by $0.15$. |

On your calculator, plot points in the form $(x, y - 6.67)$. These points form an exponential curve with long-run value 0.

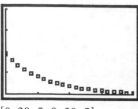

[0, 20, 5, 0, 20, 5]

The explicit exponential equation through these points will be in the form $y = ab^x$. The points still decay at the same rate, so $b$ is still $(1 - 0.15)$, or 0.85. The starting value has been translated, so $a$ is $(16 - 6.67)$, or 9.33. The equation through the points in the form $(x, y - 6.67)$ is $y - 6.67 = 9.33(0.85)^x$. Solving for $y$ gives $y = 9.33(0.85)^x + 6.67$.

Check that this equation fits the original data.

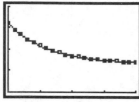

[0, 20, 5, 0, 20, 5]

**11. a.** $y = 18(\sqrt{2})^{x-4}$, $y = 144(\sqrt{2})^{x-10}$, or $y = 4.5(\sqrt{2})^x$. Start by using the point-ratio equation with the first point, $y = 18b^{x-4}$, and use the second point to find $b$.

$$144 = 18b^{10-4}$$

$$8 = b^6$$

$$b = 8^{1/6} = (2^3)^{1/6} = 2^{1/2} = \sqrt{2}$$

The equation is $y = 18(\sqrt{2})^{x-4}$.

**b.** $y = \dfrac{\log x - \log 18}{\log \sqrt{2}} + 4$, $y = \dfrac{\log x - \log 144}{\log \sqrt{2}} + 10$, or $y = \dfrac{\log x - \log 4.5}{\log \sqrt{2}}$.

Notice that the points (18, 4) and (144, 10) are on the graph of the inverse of the function from 11a.

Start with $y = 18(\sqrt{2})^{x-4}$, switch $x$ and $y$, and solve for $y$.

$$x = 18(\sqrt{2})^{y-4}$$

$$\frac{x}{18} = (\sqrt{2})^{y-4}$$

$$\log \frac{x}{18} = (y - 4) \log \sqrt{2}$$

$$\frac{\log \frac{x}{18}}{\log \sqrt{2}} = y - 4$$

$$y = \frac{\log \frac{x}{18}}{\log \sqrt{2}} + 4 = \frac{\log x - \log 18}{\log \sqrt{2}} + 4$$

**12. a.** Let $x$ represent the amount of fish sticks in pounds, and let $y$ represent cost or income in dollars. Cost: $y = 1.75x + 19000$; income: $y = 1.92x$.

**b.**

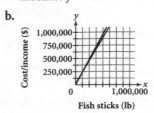

**c.** 111,765 pounds. Find the point where the two lines intersect. $y = 1.75x + 19000$ and $y = 1.92x$, so $1.75x + 19000 = 1.92x$. Therefore $19000 = 0.17x$, and $x \approx 111765$.

**d.** \$66,000. The profit is the income minus the cost: $profit = 1.92x - (1.75x + 19000) = 0.17x - 19000$. At 500,000 fish, $profit = 0.17(500000) - 19000 = 66000$.

**13.**

This is the ellipse $(4x)^2 + \left(\dfrac{y}{2}\right)^2 = 1$ translated left 5 units and up 8 units. A horizontal line segment from the center to either side of the ellipse is $\frac{1}{4}$ unit long, so two points are $\left(-5\frac{1}{4}, 8\right)$ and $\left(-4\frac{3}{4}, 8\right)$. A vertical line segment from the center to either the top or bottom of the ellipse is 2 units long, so the ellipse also contains the points $(-5, 10)$ and $(-5, 6)$.

**14. a.** $x \approx 5.09$

| | |
|---|---|
| $x^5 = 3418$ | Original equation. |
| $(x^5)^{1/5} = 3418^{1/5}$ | Use the power property of equality and raise both sides to the power of $\frac{1}{5}$. |
| $x = 3418^{1/5} \approx 5.09$ | Power of a power property. |

*Discovering Advanced Algebra Solutions Manual*
©2004 Key Curriculum Press

**b.** $x \approx 9.1$

$(x - 5.1)^4 = 256$      Original equation.

$((x - 5.1)^4)^{1/4} = 256^{1/4}$      Use the power property of equality and raise both sides to the power of $\frac{1}{4}$.

$x - 5.1 = 256^{1/4}$      Power of a power property.

$x = 256^{1/4} + 5.1$      Add 5.1 to both sides.

$x = 9.1$      Evaluate

*Note:* $x = 1.1$ is also a valid solution. You would find this solution by recognizing that the 4th root of 256 could be 4 or $-4$. However, because the properties of exponents are defined for positive bases, this solution may be missed.

**c.** $x \approx 1.40$

$7.3x^6 + 14.4 = 69.4$      Original equation.

$7.3x^6 = 55$      Subtract 14.4 from both sides.

$x^6 = \dfrac{55}{7.3}$      Divide both sides by 7.3.

$\left(x^6\right)^{1/6} = \left(\dfrac{55}{7.3}\right)^{1/6}$      Use the power property of equality and raise both sides to the power of $\frac{1}{6}$.

$x = \left(\dfrac{55}{7.3}\right)^{1/6} \approx 1.40$      Power of a power property.

*Note:* $x = -\left(\frac{55}{7.3}\right)^{1/6} \approx -1.40$ is also a valid solution. You would find this solution by recognizing that a 6th root can be positive or negative. However, because the properties of exponents are defined for positive bases, this solution may be missed.

## EXPLORATION · THE NUMBER *e*

### QUESTIONS

**1.** Using the new equation, answers will probably be slightly more accurate than before.

**2. a.** $k \approx 0.0045$

$0.80 = 1e^{-k(50)}$

$\log 0.80 = -k(50)\log e$

$k = \dfrac{\log 0.80}{-50 \log e} \approx 0.0045$

**b.** Approximately 10.23 m

$0.01 = 1e^{-0.0045t}$

$\log 0.01 = -0.0045t \log e$

$t = \dfrac{\log 0.01}{-0.0045 \log e} \approx 1023.37$

The depth was approximately 1023 cm, or 10.23 m. If you use the unrounded value of $k$, you get 1031.89 cm $\approx$ 10.32 m.

## CHAPTER 5 REVIEW

### EXERCISES

**1. a.** $4^{-2} = \dfrac{1}{4^2} = \dfrac{1}{16}$

   **b.** $(-3)^{-1} = \dfrac{1}{-3} = -\dfrac{1}{3}$

   **c.** $\left(\dfrac{1}{5}\right)^{-3} = \left(\dfrac{5}{1}\right)^3 = 125$

   **d.** $49^{1/2} = \sqrt{49} = 7$

   **e.** $64^{-1/3} = \dfrac{1}{\sqrt[3]{64}} = \dfrac{1}{4}$

   **f.** $\left(\dfrac{9}{16}\right)^{3/2} = \left(\left(\dfrac{9}{16}\right)^{1/2}\right)^3 = \left(\sqrt{\dfrac{9}{16}}\right)^3 = \left(\dfrac{3}{4}\right)^3 = \dfrac{27}{64}$

   **g.** $-7^0 = -1$. Calculate the exponent before multiplying.

   **h.** $(3)(2)^2 = (3)(4) = 12$

   **i.** $\left(0.6^{-2}\right)^{-1/2} = 0.6^{(-2)(-1/2)} = 0.6^1 = 0.6$

**2. a.** $\log xy$ by the product property of logarithms

   **b.** $\log z - \log v$ by the quotient property of logarithms

   **c.** $\left(7x^{2.1}\right)\left(0.3x^{4.7}\right) = 2.1x^{2.1+4.7} = 2.1x^{6.8}$ by the associative property and the product property of exponents

   **d.** $k \log w$ by the power property of logarithms

   **e.** $x^{1/5}$ by definition of rational exponents

   **f.** $\dfrac{\log t}{\log 5}$ by the change-of-base property

**3. a.** $x = \dfrac{\log 28}{\log 4.7} \approx 2.153$

$4.7^x = 28$

$\log 4.7^x = \log 28$

$x \log 4.7 = \log 28$

$x = \dfrac{\log 28}{\log 4.7} \approx 2.153$

Check: $4.7^{2.153} \approx 28$

**b.** $x = \pm\sqrt{\dfrac{\log 2209}{\log 4.7}} \approx \pm 2.231$

$$4.7^{x^2} = 2209$$

$$x^2 \log 4.7 = \log 2209$$

$$x^2 = \frac{\log 2209}{\log 4.7}$$

$$x = \pm\sqrt{\frac{\log 2209}{\log 4.7}} \approx \pm 2.231$$

Check: $4.7^{\pm 2.231^2} \approx 2209$

**c.** $x = 2.9^{1/1.25} = 2.9^{0.8} \approx 2.344$. Start by writing the logarithmic equation in exponential form.

Check: $\log_{2.344} 2.9 = \dfrac{\log 2.9}{\log 2.344} \approx 1.25$

**d.** $x = 3.1^{47} \approx 1.242 \times 10^{23}$. Start by writing the logarithmic equation $\log_{3.1} x = 47$ in exponential form.

Check:

$$\log_{3.1}\left(1.242 \times 10^{23}\right) = \frac{\log\left(1.242 \times 10^{23}\right)}{\log 3.1} \approx 47$$

**e.** $x = \left(\dfrac{101}{7}\right)^{1/2.4} \approx 3.041$

$$7x^{2.4} = 101$$

$$x^{2.4} = \frac{101}{7}$$

$$x = \left(\frac{101}{7}\right)^{1/2 \cdot 4} \approx 3.041$$

Check: $7(3.041)^{2.4} \approx 101$

**f.** $18 = 1.065^x$, so $x = \log_{1.065} 18 = \dfrac{\log 18}{\log 1.065} \approx 45.897$

Check: $500(1.065)^{45.897} \approx 9000$

**g.** $x = 10^{3.771} \approx 5902$. Start by writing the logarithmic equation in exponential form.

Check: $\log 5902 \approx 3.771$

**h.** $x = 47^{5/3} \approx 612$

$$\sqrt[5]{x^3} = 47$$

$$x^{3/5} = 47$$

$$x = 47^{5/3} \approx 612$$

Check: $\sqrt[5]{612^3} \approx 47$

**4. a.** $x \approx 0.825$

$$\sqrt[8]{2432} = 2x + 1$$

$$\sqrt[8]{2432} - 1 = 2x$$

$$x = \frac{\sqrt[8]{2432} - 1}{2} \approx 0.825$$

**b.** $x \approx 5.779$

$$4x^{2.7} = 456$$

$$x^{2.7} = 114$$

$$x = 114^{1/2.7} \approx 5.779$$

**c.** $x \approx 9.406$

$$734 = 11.2(1.56)^x$$

$$\frac{734}{11.2} = 1.56^x$$

$$\log\left(\frac{734}{11.2}\right) = x \log 1.56$$

$$x = \frac{\log\left(\dfrac{734}{11.2}\right)}{\log 1.56} \approx 9.406$$

**d.** $x = 20.2$ because $f\left(f^{-1}(x)\right) = x$.

**e.** $x \approx 1.962$

$$147 = 12.1(1 + x)^{2.3}$$

$$\frac{147}{12.1} = (1 + x)^{2.3}$$

$$\left(\frac{147}{12.1}\right)^{1/2.3} = 1 + x$$

$$x = \left(\frac{147}{12.1}\right)^{1/2.3} - 1 \approx 1.962$$

**f.** $x \approx 36.063$

$$2\sqrt{x - 3} + 4.5 = 16$$

$$2\sqrt{x - 3} = 11.5$$

$$\sqrt{x - 3} = 5.75$$

$$x - 3 = 5.75^2$$

$$x = 5.75^2 + 3 \approx 36.063$$

**5.** About 39.9 h. Start with the equation $y = 45b^x$ by using the point-ratio equation with the initial point $(0, 45)$. The half-life of 16 h gives $22.5 = 45b^{16}$. Solve this equation for $b$. $0.5 = b^{16}$, so $b = 0.5^{1/16}$. Thus the equation is $y = 45\left(0.5^{1/16}\right)^x = 45\left(0.5^{x/16}\right)$. Now solve $8 = 45\left(0.5^{x/16}\right)$ for $x$.

$$\frac{8}{45} = 0.5^{x/16}$$

$$\log\frac{8}{45} = \frac{x}{16}\log 0.5$$

$$x = \frac{16\log\left(\dfrac{8}{45}\right)}{\log 0.5} \approx 39.9$$

**6. a.** $f(2.5) = (4 \cdot 2.5 - 2)^{1/3} - 1 = 8^{1/3} - 1 = 2 - 1 = 1$

**b.** $f^{-1}(x) = \dfrac{(x+1)^3 + 2}{4}$. Switch $x$ and $y$, and then solve for $y$.

$$x = (4y - 2)^{1/3} - 1$$

$$x + 1 = (4y - 2)^{1/3}$$

$$(x + 1)^3 = 4y - 2$$

$$(x + 1)^3 + 2 = 4y$$

$$y = \dfrac{(x+1)^3 + 2}{4}$$

**c.** $f^{-1}(-1) = \dfrac{(-1+1)^3 + 2}{4} = \dfrac{2}{4} = \dfrac{1}{2}$

**d.** $f\big(f^{-1}(12)\big) = 12$ because $f\big(f^{-1}(x)\big)$ is always $x$.

**7.** $y = 5\left(\dfrac{32}{5}\right)^{(x-1)/6}$. Start with the point-ratio equation using the first point, $y = 5b^{x-1}$. Use the second point to find $b$.

$$32 = 5b^{7-1}$$

$$\dfrac{32}{5} = b^6$$

$$b = \left(\dfrac{32}{5}\right)^{1/6}$$

The equation is $y = 5\left(\left(\dfrac{32}{5}\right)^{1/6}\right)^{x-1}$, or $y = 5\left(\dfrac{32}{5}\right)^{(x-1)/6}$.

**8.** Identify the coordinates of several points on the graph of $y = f(x)$. Switch the $x$- and $y$-coordinates to find several points on the graph of $y = f^{-1}(x)$, and then connect them. Alternatively, imagine reflecting the graph across the line $y = x$.

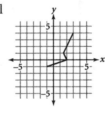

**9. a.**

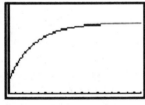

[0, 18, 1, 0, 125, 0]

**b.** Domain: $0 \le x \le 120$; range: $20 \le y \le 100$. The domain is limited to positive values because your age can only be a positive real value. A reasonable maximum for age is 120 yr. The range is limited between the size of your head as a newborn and the long-run size as an adult.

**c.** Vertically stretch by a factor of 80; reflect across the $x$-axis; translate up 100.

**d.** 55% of the average adult size.
$y = 100 - 80(0.75)^2 = 55$.

**e.** About 4 years old

$$75 = 100 - 80(0.75)^x$$

$$-25 = -80(0.75)^x$$

$$\dfrac{5}{16} = 0.75^x$$

$$\log \dfrac{5}{16} = x \log 0.75$$

$$x = \dfrac{\log \dfrac{5}{16}}{\log 0.75} \approx 4.04$$

**10. a.** $a = 0.50$

$$cost = a + b \log t$$

$$0.50 = a + b \log 1$$

$$0.50 = a + b(0)$$

$$a = 0.50$$

**b.** $b = \dfrac{2.94}{\log 15} \approx 2.4998$

$$cost = 0.50 + b \log t$$

$$3.44 = 0.50 + b \log 15$$

$$2.94 = b \log 15$$

$$b = \dfrac{2.94}{\log 15} \approx 2.4998$$

**c.** The $t$-intercept is about 0.63. The real-world meaning of the $t$-intercept is that the first 0.63 of a minute of calling is free.

From the work in 10a and b, the equation is $cost = 0.50 + 2.4998 \log t$. To find the $t$-intercept, set $cost = 0$ and solve for $t$.

$$0 = 0.50 + 2.4998 \log t$$

$$-0.50 = 2.4998 \log t$$

$$\log t = -0.2$$

$$t = 10^{-0.2} \approx 0.63$$

**d.** $cost = 0.50 + 2.4998 \log 30 \approx \$4.19$

**e.** About 4 min

$$2.00 = 0.50 + 2.4998 \log t$$

$$1.5 = 2.4998 \log t$$

$$0.6 = \log t$$

$$t = 10^{0.6} \approx 3.98$$

**11. a.** Approximately 37 sessions

$$t = -144 \log\left(1 - \dfrac{40}{90}\right) \approx 37$$

**b.** Approximately 47.52 wpm

$$47 = -144 \log\left(1 - \frac{N}{90}\right)$$

$$-0.326 = \log\left(1 - \frac{N}{90}\right)$$

$$10^{-0.326} = 1 - \frac{N}{90}$$

$$0.472 = 1 - \frac{N}{90}$$

$$-0.528 = -\frac{N}{90}$$

$$N \approx 47.52$$

**c.** Sample answer: It takes much longer to improve your typing speed as you reach higher levels. 60 wpm is a good typing speed, and very few people type more than 90 wpm, so $0 \leq x \leq 90$ is a reasonable domain.

**12. a.** $u_0 = 1$ and $u_n = \left(u_{n-1}\right) \cdot 2$ where $n \geq 1$. All humans start as one cell, so $u_0 = 1$. After each cell division, the number of cells doubles, so $u_n = \left(u_{n-1}\right) \cdot 2$ where $n \geq 1$.

**b.** $y = 2^x$. To get from any term in the sequence to the next, you multiply by a factor of 2. Thus the explicit equation is $y = 2^x$.

**c.**

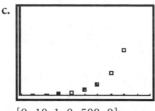

[0, 10, 1, 0, 500, 0]

**d.** Answers will vary but can include curving upward, increasing, increasing at an increasing rate, and discrete.

**e.** After 20 cell divisions

$$1000000 = 2^x$$

$$\log 1000000 = x \log 2$$

$$x = \frac{\log 1000000}{\log 2} \approx 19.93$$

**f.** After 29 divisions. The number of cells doubles after each division, so one division before there were 1 billion cells, there were 500 million cells.

**TAKE ANOTHER LOOK**

**1.** When $m$ is even, you are taking an even root. You can take the even root only of a nonnegative number; therefore the domain of $y = \left(x^{1/m}\right)^n$ is

$x \geq 0$ for all values of $n$. In the expression $\left(x^n\right)^{1/m}$, if $n$ is even, then $x^n$ is positive for all $x$; you can take an even or an odd root, so the domain is all values of $x$, no matter the value of $m$. When $m$ is odd, or when $m$ is even and $n$ is odd, the domain of both equations will be all real numbers, and all $y$-values will be the same.

Here is an example of different graphs when both $m$ and $n$ are even:

$y = \left(x^{1/6}\right)^2$

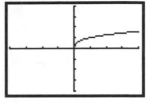

$[-4, 4, 1, -4, 4, 1]$

$y = \left(x^2\right)^{1/6}$

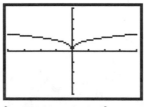

$[-4, 4, 1, -4, 4, 1]$

**2.** $y = 695.04(0.4898)^x$. It is easier to solve for $a$ in each equation. The first equation yields $a = \frac{40}{b^4}$, and the second equation yields $a = \frac{4.7}{b^7}$. Use substitution to set these two expressions as equal and solve for $b$.

$$\frac{40}{b^4} = \frac{4.7}{b^7}$$

$$\frac{b^7}{b^4} = \frac{4.7}{40}$$

$$b^3 = .1175$$

$$b = .1175^{1/3} \approx 0.4898$$

Now find $a$: $a = \frac{40}{b^4} = \frac{40}{.1175^{4/3}} \approx 695.04$. The equation of the function is $y = ab^x = 695.04(0.4898)^x$.

**3.** The shortcut works because lining up the 5 with the 10 is the same as dividing 5 by 10. (The answer 0.5 would be apparent if the top scale extended farther to the left.) The number above 7 is then the product of 0.5 and 7. Multiplying by 10 gives the correct product. The process also works lining up 7 with 10, which gives 0.7, and looking up the number above 5, which gives 0.7 times 5.

*Discovering Advanced Algebra Solutions Manual*
©2004 Key Curriculum Press

# CHAPTER 6

## LESSON 6.1

### EXERCISES

**1. a.**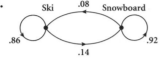

**b.** $\begin{bmatrix} .86 & .14 \\ .08 & .92 \end{bmatrix}$

**2.**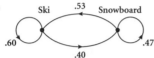

The sum of the percentages coming out of each node must equal 1; $.60 + .40 = 1.0$ and $.47 + .53 = 1.0$.

**3.** $\begin{bmatrix} .60 & .40 \\ .53 & .47 \end{bmatrix}$

**4. a.** $A(-3, 2)$, $B(1, 3)$, and $C(2, -2)$

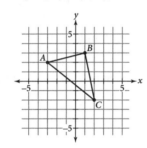

**b.** $\begin{bmatrix} -3 & 1 & 2 \\ -2 & -1 & -6 \end{bmatrix}$

Subtract 4 units from each entry in row 2, which represents the $y$-coordinates.

**c.** $\begin{bmatrix} 1 & 5 & 6 \\ 2 & 3 & -2 \end{bmatrix}$

Add 4 units to each entry in row 1, which represents the $x$-coordinates.

**5. a.** 20 girls and 25 boys. For girls, add the entries in row 1. For boys, add the entries in row 2.

**b.** 18 boys. The entry in row 2, column 2, is 18.

**c.** 13 girls batted right-handed. In matrix $[A]$, $a_{12} = 13$ because 13 is the entry in row 1, column 2.

**6. a.**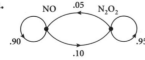

**b.** $\begin{bmatrix} .90 & .10 \\ .05 & .95 \end{bmatrix}$

**c.** After 1 s: [46    194]; after 2 s: [51.1    188.9]. After 1 second, 90% of the NO remains the same and 5% of the $N_2O_2$ changes to NO, so NO $= 40(.90) + 200(.05) = 46$. After 1 second, 10% of the NO changes to $N_2O_2$ and 90% of the $N_2O_2$ remains the same, so $N_2O_2 = 40(.10) + 200(.90) = 194$.

Use the matrix [46    194] to find the amount in milliliters of NO and $N_2O_2$ after 2 seconds.

NO $= 46(.90) + 194(.05) = 51.1$

$N_2O_2 = 46(.10) + 194(.90) = 188.9$

In matrix form: $\begin{bmatrix} NO & N_2O_2 \end{bmatrix} = [46 \quad 194]$ after 1 s and $\begin{bmatrix} NO & N_2O_2 \end{bmatrix} = [51.1 \quad 188.9]$ after 2 s.

**7. a.**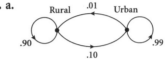

**b.** $\begin{bmatrix} .99 & .01 \\ .10 & .90 \end{bmatrix}$

**c.** After 1 yr: [16.74    8.26]; after 2 yr: [17.3986    7.6014]

After 1 year:

$urban = 16(.99) + 9(.10) = 16.74$

To find the rural population, subtract 16.74 from the total population, 25.

$rural = 25 - 16.74 = 8.26$

After 2 years:

$urban = 16.74(.99) + 8.26(.10) = 17.3986$

$rural = 25 - 17.3986 = 7.6014$

In matrix form: after 1 yr, $[urban \quad rural] = [16.74 \quad 8.26]$; after 2 yr, $[urban \quad rural] = [17.3986 \quad 7.6014]$.

**8. a.** There were 50 history books sold at the branch bookstore. In matrix $[A]$, $a_{32} = 50$ because 50 is the entry in row 3, column 2, where row 3 represents history and column 2 represents the branch bookstore.

**b.** There were 65 science books sold at the main bookstore. In matrix $[A]$, $a_{21} = 65$ because 65 is the entry in row 2, column 1, where row 2 represents science and column 1 represents the main bookstore.

**c.** This week there were 3 more math books sold at the main bookstore and 8 more math books sold at the branch bookstore. The entries in row 1, column 1, for matrices $[A]$ and $[B]$ represent the number of math books sold at the main bookstore this week and last week, respectively. The difference between $a_{11} = 83$ and $b_{11} = 80$ is 3, so 3 more math books were sold at the main bookstore this week. Similarly, the entries in row 1, column 2, for matrices $[A]$ and $[B]$ represent the number of math books sold at the branch bookstore this week and last week, respectively. The difference between $a_{12} = 33$ and $b_{12} = 25$ is 8, so 8 more math books were sold at the branch bookstore this week.

**d.** Because the rows and columns have the same meaning in both matrices, you can add the corresponding entries in matrices $[A]$ and $[B]$.

$$\begin{bmatrix} 83 + 80 & 33 + 25 \\ 65 + 65 & 20 + 15 \\ 98 + 105 & 50 + 55 \end{bmatrix} = \begin{bmatrix} 163 & 58 \\ 130 & 35 \\ 203 & 105 \end{bmatrix}$$

**9. a.**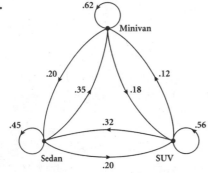

**b.** $\begin{bmatrix} .62 & .20 & .18 \\ .35 & .45 & .20 \\ .12 & .32 & .56 \end{bmatrix}$

**c.** The sum of each row is 1. The percentages should add to 100%.

**10. a.**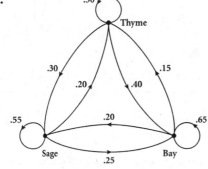

**b.** $\begin{bmatrix} .65 & .20 & .15 \\ .25 & .55 & .20 \\ .40 & .30 & .30 \end{bmatrix}$

**c.** The sum of each row is 1. The percentages should add to 100%.

**d.** 47 trucks in Bay County, 33 trucks in Sage County, and 20 trucks in Thyme County.

Bay: $45(.65) + 30(.25) + 25(.40) = 46.75 \approx 47$

Sage: $45(.20) + 30(.55) + 25(.30) = 33$

Thyme: $45(.15) + 30(.20) + 25(.30) = 20.25 \approx 20$

**11. a.** $5 \times 5$; matrix $[M]$ has five rows and five columns.

**b.** $m_{32} = 1$ because 1 is the entry in row 3, column 2. There is one round-trip flight between City C and City B.

**c.** City A has the most flights. From the route map, more paths have A as an endpoint than any other city. From the matrix, the sum of row 1 (or column 1) is greater than the sum of any other row (or column).

**d.** Start with four points, J, K, L, and M. Then use the numbers in the matrix to tell you how many paths to draw between endpoints. For example, $n_{13} = 2$ tells you to draw 2 paths between J and L.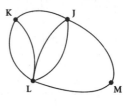

**12.** $\left(\frac{37}{9}, -\frac{10}{9}\right)$. To solve by substitution, solve the second equation for $x$: $x = 3 - y$. Substitute $(3 - y)$ into the first equation and solve for $y$.

$$5(3 - y) - 4y = 25$$
$$15 - 5y - 4y = 25$$
$$-9y = 10$$
$$y = -\frac{10}{9}$$

Substitute $-\frac{10}{9}$ for $y$ in either equation and solve for $x$: $x = 3 - \left(-\frac{10}{9}\right) = \frac{37}{9}$.

To solve by elimination, multiply the second equation by 4 and add the two equations. Once $y$ is eliminated, solve for $x$. Then substitute the value of $x$ into either equation and solve for $y$.

**13.** $7.4p + 4.7s = 100$

**14.** $3y = 12 - 2x$, so $y = 4 - \frac{2}{3}x$. The $x$-intercept is 4 and the slope is $-\frac{2}{3}$.

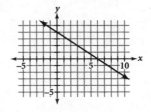

**15. a.** Let $x$ represent the year, and let $y$ represent the number of subscribers.

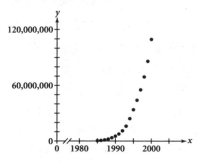

**b.** $\hat{y} = 1231000(1.44)^{x-1987}$. Use the point-ratio method with the points (1987, 1231000) and (1998, 69209000). Substitute the coordinates of the points into point-ratio form, $y = y_1 \cdot b^{x-x_1}$.

$y = 1231000b^{x-1987}$ and $y = 69209000b^{x-1998}$

Use substitution to combine the two equations and solve for $b$.

$$1231000b^{x-1987} = 69209000b^{x-1998}$$

$$\frac{b^{x-1987}}{b^{x-1998}} = \frac{69209000}{1231000}$$

$$b^{(x-1987)-(x-1998)} = \frac{69209000}{1231000}$$

$$b^{11} = \frac{69209000}{1231000}$$

$$b = \left(\frac{69209000}{1231000}\right)^{1/11} \approx 1.44$$

Substitute 1.44 for $b$ in either of the two original equations. The exponential equation is $\hat{y} = 1231000(1.44)^{x-1987}$.

**c.** About 420,782,749 subscribers. Substitute 2003 for $x$ in the equation from 15b: $\hat{y} = 1231000(1.44)^{2003-1987} \approx 420{,}782{,}749$. Therefore there are about 420,782,749 subscribers in 2003. This is not a realistic prediction because it far exceeds the 2003 population of the United States. (The population was about 288 million in 2002.) It is unlikely that there will ever be more than one cellular phone for every person in the country. The number of cell phones cannot possibly continue to increase at a rate of 44% a year. Because the number of cell phones will level off rather than continue to increase exponentially, an exponential model is not appropriate.

**16. a.** $y = 20 \log\left(\dfrac{0.00356}{0.00002}\right) \approx 45$ dB

**b.** $y = 20 \log\left(\dfrac{20}{0.00002}\right) = 120$ dB

**c.** $y = (0.00002)(10)^{x/20}$. To find the inverse function, switch $x$ and $y$ and then solve for $y$.

$$x = 20 \log\left(\frac{y}{0.00002}\right)$$

$$10^x = \left(\frac{y}{0.00002}\right)^{20}$$

$$(10^x)^{1/20} = \frac{y}{0.00002}$$

$$y = (0.00002)(10)^{x/20}$$

Therefore the inverse function is $y = (0.00002)(10)^{x/20}$, where $x$ represents the intensity in decibels and $y$ represents pressure in Pascals.

**d.** 0.63246 Pa. Substitute 90 for $x$ in the inverse function: $y = (0.00002)(10)^{90/20} \approx 0.63246$ Pa.

**EXTENSION**

Answers will vary.

## LESSON 6.2

**EXERCISES**

**1.** 197 students will choose ice cream and 43 will choose frozen yogurt.

$$[203.35 \quad 36.65]\begin{bmatrix} .95 & .05 \\ .10 & .90 \end{bmatrix} =$$

$$[196.8475 \quad 43.1525]$$

Multiply row 1 by column 1:

$$203.35(.95) + 36.65(.10) = 196.8475 \approx 197$$

Multiply row 1 by column 2:

$$203.35(.05) + 36.65(.90) = 43.1525 \approx 43$$

**2. a.** $x = 7$, $y = 54$

$$[13 \quad 23] + [-6 \quad 31] = [13 + (-6) \quad 23 + 31]$$
$$= [7 \quad 54]$$

**b.** $c_{11} = 0.815$, $c_{12} = 0.185$, $c_{21} = 0.0925$, $c_{22} = 0.9075$

$$\begin{bmatrix} .90 & .10 \\ .05 & .95 \end{bmatrix}\begin{bmatrix} .90 & .10 \\ .05 & .95 \end{bmatrix} =$$

$$\begin{bmatrix} .90(.90) + .10(.05) & .90(.10) + .10(.95) \\ .05(.90) + .95(.05) & .05(.10) + .95(.95) \end{bmatrix} =$$

$$\begin{bmatrix} .815 & .185 \\ .0925 & .9075 \end{bmatrix}$$

**c.** $a = 15.6$, $b = -10.8$, $c = 10.7$, $d = 42.2$

$$\begin{bmatrix} 18 & -23 \\ 5.4 & 32.2 \end{bmatrix} + \begin{bmatrix} -2.4 & 12.2 \\ 5.3 & 10 \end{bmatrix} =$$

$$\begin{bmatrix} 18 + (-2.4) & -23 + 12.2 \\ 5.4 + 5.3 & 32.2 + 10 \end{bmatrix} =$$

$$\begin{bmatrix} 15.6 & -10.8 \\ 10.7 & 42.2 \end{bmatrix}$$

**d.** $m_{11} = 180$, $m_{12} = -230$, $m_{21} = 54$, $m_{22} = 322$

$$10 \begin{bmatrix} 18 & -23 \\ 5.4 & 32.2 \end{bmatrix} = \begin{bmatrix} 10 \cdot 18 & 10 \cdot -23 \\ 10 \cdot 5.4 & 10 \cdot 32.2 \end{bmatrix}$$

$$= \begin{bmatrix} 180 & -230 \\ 54 & 322 \end{bmatrix}$$

**e.** $a = -5$, $b = 57$, $c = 44.5$, $d = 78$

$$\begin{bmatrix} 7 & -4 \\ 18 & 28 \end{bmatrix} + 5 \begin{bmatrix} -2.4 & 12.2 \\ 5.3 & 10 \end{bmatrix} =$$

$$\begin{bmatrix} 7 & -4 \\ 18 & 28 \end{bmatrix} + \begin{bmatrix} -12 & 61 \\ 26.5 & 50 \end{bmatrix} =$$

$$\begin{bmatrix} 7 - 12 & -4 + 61 \\ 18 + 26.5 & 28 + 50 \end{bmatrix} = \begin{bmatrix} -5 & 57 \\ 44.5 & 78 \end{bmatrix}$$

**3. a.** $\begin{bmatrix} 1 & 2 \\ 3 & -2 \\ 0 & 1 \end{bmatrix} \begin{bmatrix} -3 & -1 & 2 \\ 5 & 2 & -1 \end{bmatrix} =$

$$\begin{bmatrix} 1(-3) + 2(5) & 1(-1) + 2(2) & 1(2) + 2(-1) \\ 3(-3) + -2(5) & 3(-1) + -2(2) & 3(2) + -2(-1) \\ 0(-3) + 1(5) & 0(-1) + 1(2) & 0(2) + 1(-1) \end{bmatrix} =$$

$$\begin{bmatrix} 7 & 3 & 0 \\ -19 & -7 & 8 \\ 5 & 2 & -1 \end{bmatrix}$$

**b.** $\begin{bmatrix} 1 & -2 \\ 6 & 3 \end{bmatrix} + \begin{bmatrix} -3 & 7 \\ 2 & 4 \end{bmatrix} = \begin{bmatrix} 1 - 3 & -2 + 7 \\ 6 + 2 & 3 + 4 \end{bmatrix}$

$$= \begin{bmatrix} -2 & 5 \\ 8 & 7 \end{bmatrix}$$

**c.** $\begin{bmatrix} 5 & -2 & 7 \end{bmatrix} \begin{bmatrix} -2 & 3 \\ -1 & 0 \\ 3 & 2 \end{bmatrix} =$

$$\begin{bmatrix} 5(-2) + (-2)(-1) + 7(3) & 5(3) + (-2)(0) + 7(2) \end{bmatrix} =$$

$$\begin{bmatrix} 13 & 29 \end{bmatrix}$$

**d.** Not possible; the inside dimensions do not match. The four rows of the first matrix do not match up with the two columns of the second matrix.

**e.** $\begin{bmatrix} 3 & 6 \\ -4 & 1 \end{bmatrix} - \begin{bmatrix} -1 & 7 \\ -8 & 3 \end{bmatrix} =$

$$\begin{bmatrix} 3 - (-1) & 6 - 7 \\ -4 - (-8) & 1 - 3 \end{bmatrix} = \begin{bmatrix} 4 & -1 \\ 4 & -2 \end{bmatrix}$$

**f.** Not possible; the dimensions aren't the same. The entries in the first matrix do not match up with the entries in the second matrix.

**4.** $\begin{bmatrix} 3 & -4 & 2.5 \\ -2 & 6 & 4 \end{bmatrix}$. You can solve this matrix equation similar to solving an algebraic equation. First subtract $\begin{bmatrix} 8 & -5 & 4.5 \\ -6 & 9.5 & 5 \end{bmatrix}$ from both sides.

$$-[B] = \begin{bmatrix} 5 & -1 & 2 \\ -4 & 3.5 & 1 \end{bmatrix} - \begin{bmatrix} 8 & -5 & 4.5 \\ -6 & 9.5 & 5 \end{bmatrix}$$

$$= \begin{bmatrix} -3 & 4 & -2.5 \\ 2 & -6 & -4 \end{bmatrix}$$

Then multiply both sides by the scalar $-1$.

$$[B] = -1 \begin{bmatrix} -3 & 4 & -2.5 \\ 2 & -6 & -4 \end{bmatrix}$$

$$= \begin{bmatrix} 3 & -4 & 2.5 \\ -2 & 6 & 4 \end{bmatrix}$$

**5. a.** The coordinates of the vertices are organized in columns.

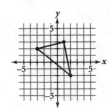

**b.** $\begin{bmatrix} -1 & 0 \\ 0 & 1 \end{bmatrix} \begin{bmatrix} -3 & 1 & 2 \\ 2 & 3 & -2 \end{bmatrix} =$

$$\begin{bmatrix} -1(-3) + 0(2) & -1(1) + 0(3) & -1(2) + 0(-2) \\ 0(-3) + 1(2) & 0(1) + 1(3) & 0(2) + 1(-2) \end{bmatrix} =$$

$$\begin{bmatrix} 3 & -1 & -2 \\ 2 & 3 & -2 \end{bmatrix}$$

**c.**

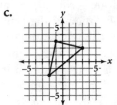

**d.** The original triangle is reflected across the $y$-axis. After the matrix multiplication, the signs of the $x$-values are changed.

**6.** $[A] = \begin{bmatrix} 1 & 0 \\ 0 & -1 \end{bmatrix}$; $[C] = \begin{bmatrix} -3 & 1 & 2 \\ -2 & -3 & 2 \end{bmatrix}$

To find matrix $[C]$, change the signs of the $y$-value of the original matrix. $[A] = \begin{bmatrix} 1 & 0 \\ 0 & -1 \end{bmatrix}$, because this matrix will keep the $x$-values the same but change the sign of the $y$-values.

**7. a.**

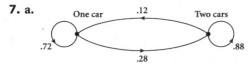

One car   .12   Two cars
.72   .28   .88

**b.** $[4800 \quad 4200]$

**c.** $\begin{bmatrix} .72 & .28 \\ .12 & .88 \end{bmatrix}$

**d.** $[4800 \quad 4200] \begin{bmatrix} .72 & .28 \\ .12 & .88 \end{bmatrix} =$

$[4800(.72) + 4200(.12) \quad 4800(.28) + 4200(.88)] =$

$[3960 \quad 5040]$

**e.** $[3960 \quad 5040] \begin{bmatrix} .72 & .28 \\ .12 & .88 \end{bmatrix} =$

$[3960(.72) + 5040(.12) \quad 3960(.28) + 5040(.88)] =$

$[3456 \quad 5544]$

**8. a.** $[A][B] = \begin{bmatrix} 6 & 2 \\ -3 & -6 \end{bmatrix}$; $[B][A] = \begin{bmatrix} 2 & 13 \\ 2 & -2 \end{bmatrix}$.
They are not the same.

**b.** $[A][C] = \begin{bmatrix} -7 & 21 & 12 \\ 1 & 2 & 4 \end{bmatrix}$. You cannot multiply $[C][A]$ because the inside dimensions are not the same. In order for both $[A][C]$ and $[C][A]$ to exist, both have to be square matrices.

**c.** $[A][D] = \begin{bmatrix} 2 & 3 \\ -1 & 1 \end{bmatrix}$; $[D][A] = \begin{bmatrix} 2 & 3 \\ -1 & 1 \end{bmatrix}$.
They are the same and equal to $[A]$. Multiplying by $[D]$ does not change $[A]$.

**d.** No, matrix multiplication is generally not commutative. Order does matter. In 8c, multiplying by matrix $[D]$ is an exception.

**9. a.** $a = 3, b = 4$

$\begin{bmatrix} 2 & a \\ b & -1 \end{bmatrix}\begin{bmatrix} 5 \\ 3 \end{bmatrix} = \begin{bmatrix} 19 \\ 17 \end{bmatrix}$

$2(5) + a(3) = 19$, so $3a = 9$, and $a = 3$

$b(5) + (-1)(3) = 17$, so $5b = 20$, and $b = 4$

**b.** $a = 7, b = 4$

$\begin{bmatrix} a & -2 \\ 3 & 1 \end{bmatrix}\begin{bmatrix} -3 \\ b \end{bmatrix} = \begin{bmatrix} -29 \\ -5 \end{bmatrix}$

$a(-3) + (-2)(b) = -29$, so $-3a - 2b = -29$

$3(-3) + 1(b) = -5$, so $b = -5 + 9$, and $b = 4$

Substitute 4 for $b$ in $-3a - 2b = -29$ and solve for $a$.

$-3a - 2(4) = -29$, so $-3a = -21$, and $a = 7$

**10.** $[160 \quad 80]$. An equilibrium is reached because 10% of 80 students is the same as 5% of 160 students.

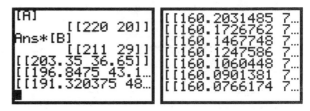

**11.** The probability that the spider is in room 1 after four room changes is .375. The long-run probabilities for rooms 1, 2, and 3 are $[.\overline{3} \quad .\overline{3} \quad .\overline{3}]$.

Use this transition matrix, where rows and columns represent room 1, room 2, and room 3, in order.

$\begin{bmatrix} 0 & .5 & .5 \\ .5 & 0 & .5 \\ .5 & .5 & 0 \end{bmatrix}$

After one room change:

$[1 \quad 0 \quad 0]\begin{bmatrix} 0 & .5 & .5 \\ .5 & 0 & .5 \\ .5 & .5 & 0 \end{bmatrix} = [0 \quad .5 \quad .5]$

After two room changes:

$[0 \quad .5 \quad .5]\begin{bmatrix} 0 & .5 & .5 \\ .5 & 0 & .5 \\ .5 & .5 & 0 \end{bmatrix} = [.5 \quad .25 \quad .25]$

After three room changes:

$[.5 \quad .25 \quad .25]\begin{bmatrix} 0 & .5 & .5 \\ .5 & 0 & .5 \\ .5 & .5 & 0 \end{bmatrix} =$

$[.25 \quad .375 \quad .375]$

After four room changes:

$[.25 \quad .375 \quad .375]\begin{bmatrix} 0 & .5 & .5 \\ .5 & 0 & .5 \\ .5 & .5 & 0 \end{bmatrix} =$

$[.375 \quad .3125 \quad .3125]$

Multiplying the initial condition by the transition matrix four times, or alternatively multiplying by the transition matrix raised to the power of 4, gives [.375   .3125   .3125]. Therefore the probability that the spider is in room 1 after four room changes is .375.

By raising the matrix to a higher power, such as 40, you will see that the long-run probabilities are [$.\overline{3}$   $.\overline{3}$   $.\overline{3}$].

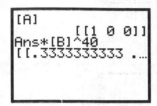

**12. a.** $\begin{bmatrix} .5 & .45 & .05 \\ .25 & .5 & .25 \\ .3 & .3 & .4 \end{bmatrix}$

**b.** After one generation: [32%   45.75%   22.25%]

After two generations:
[34.1125%   43.95%   21.9375%]

After three generations:
[34.625%   43.906875%   21.468125%]

In the long run:
[34.74903475%   44.01544402%   21.23552124%]

For each generation, multiply the matrix representing the percentages in each category by the transition matrix.

After one generation:

$[.25 \quad .60 \quad .15] \begin{bmatrix} .5 & .45 & .05 \\ .25 & .5 & .25 \\ .3 & .3 & .4 \end{bmatrix} =$

[.32   .4575   .2225]

After two generations:

$[.32 \quad .4575 \quad .2225] \begin{bmatrix} .5 & .45 & .05 \\ .25 & .5 & .25 \\ .3 & .3 & .4 \end{bmatrix} =$

[.341125   .4395   .219375]

After three generations:

$[.341125 \quad .4395 \quad .219375] \begin{bmatrix} .5 & .45 & .05 \\ .25 & .5 & .25 \\ .3 & .3 & .4 \end{bmatrix} =$

[.34625   .43906875   .21468125]

By raising the matrix to a higher power, such as 15, you will see that the long-run percentages are [.3474903475   .4401544402   .2123552124].

**13. a.** $\begin{bmatrix} 3 \\ 1 \\ 3 \\ 1 \\ 3 \\ 1 \\ 3 \\ 1 \\ 3 \\ 1 \\ 3 \\ 1 \end{bmatrix}$

**b.** The first and last UPCs are valid. Multiply the UPCs matrix by the matrix in 13a.

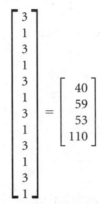

$\begin{bmatrix} 0 & 3 & 6 & 2 & 0 & 0 & 0 & 0 & 4 & 0 & 0 & 5 \\ 0 & 7 & 6 & 1 & 0 & 7 & 0 & 2 & 2 & 3 & 3 & 6 \\ 0 & 7 & 4 & 2 & 2 & 0 & 0 & 0 & 2 & 9 & 1 & 8 \\ 0 & 8 & 5 & 3 & 9 & 1 & 7 & 8 & 6 & 2 & 2 & 1 \end{bmatrix} \cdot \begin{bmatrix} 3 \\ 1 \\ 3 \\ 1 \\ 3 \\ 1 \\ 3 \\ 1 \\ 3 \\ 1 \\ 3 \\ 1 \end{bmatrix} = \begin{bmatrix} 40 \\ 59 \\ 53 \\ 110 \end{bmatrix}$

The first and last UPC codes resulted in multiples of 10, so they are valid.

**c.** For the second code, the check digit should be 7. For the third code, the check digit should be 5. For the second code, the check digit needs to be raised by 1 for a product of 60, so it should be 6 + 1, or 7. For the third code, the check digit needs to be reduced by 3 for a product of 50, so it should be 8 − 3, or 5.

**14. a.  i.** Consistent and independent because there is exactly one solution.

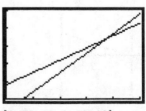

[0, 50, 10, 0, 50, 10]

*Discovering Advanced Algebra Solutions Manual*
©2004 Key Curriculum Press

**ii.** Inconsistent because there are no solutions. The lines are parallel.

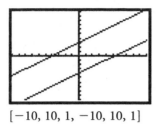

$[-10, 10, 1, -10, 10, 1]$

**iii.** Inconsistent because there are no solutions. The lines are parallel.

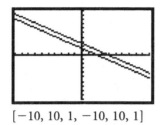

$[-10, 10, 1, -10, 10, 1]$

**iv.** Consistent and independent because there is exactly one solution.

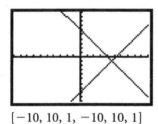

$[-10, 10, 1, -10, 10, 1]$

**v.** Inconsistent because there are no solutions. The lines are parallel.

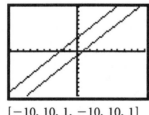

$[-10, 10, 1, -10, 10, 1]$

**vi.** Consistent and dependent because there are infinitely many solutions. The two lines are the same.

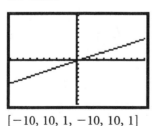

$[-10, 10, 1, -10, 10, 1]$

**vii.** Consistent and dependent because there are infinitely many solutions. The two lines are the same.

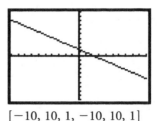

$[-10, 10, 1, -10, 10, 1]$

**viii.** Consistent and independent because there is exactly one solution.

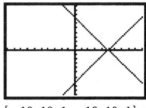

$[-10, 10, 1, -10, 10, 1]$

**ix.** Consistent and dependent because there are infinitely many solutions. The two lines are the same.

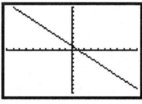

$[-10, 10, 1, -10, 10, 1]$

**b.** The graphs of inconsistent linear systems are parallel lines.

**c.** When you try to solve an inconsistent system, you reach a false statement, such as $0 = 7$.

  **ii.** By substitution, $\frac{3}{4}x - 4 = 0.75x + 3$, so $0 = 7$, which is false.

  **iii.** Multiply the first equation by 1.2 and the second equation by $-4$, and use elimination.

$$\begin{array}{r} 4.8x + 7.2y = 10.8 \\ -4.8x - 7.2y = -18.8 \\ \hline 0 = -10 \end{array}$$

  The statement $0 = -10$ is false.

  **v.** By substitution, $1.2x + 3 = 1.2x - 1$, so $0 = -4$, which is false.

**d.** You can recognize an inconsistent linear system without graphing it because the equations have the same slope but different $y$-intercepts.

**e.** The graphs of consistent and dependent linear systems are the same line.

**f.** When you try to solve a consistent and dependent system, you get a true but useless statement, such as $0 = 0$.

**vi.** By substitution,

$$\frac{1}{4}(2x - 1) = 0.5x - 0.25$$

$$\frac{1}{2}x - \frac{1}{4} = 0.5x - 0.25$$

$$\frac{1}{2}x - 0.5x = \frac{1}{4} - 0.25$$

$$0 = 0$$

**vii.** Multiply the first equation by 1.2 and the second equation by $-4$, and then use elimination.

$$\begin{array}{r} 4.8x + 7.2y = 10.8 \\ -4.8x - 7.2y = -10.8 \\ \hline 0 = 0 \end{array}$$

**g.** The lines in a consistent and dependent linear system have the same slope and the same $y$-intercept, or the equations are multiples of each other.

**15.** Find the slope of each segment and then use either endpoint to write an equation in point-slope form, $y = y_1 + b(x - x_1)$.

$\overline{CD}$: $y = -3 + \frac{2}{3}(x - 1)$ or $y = -1 + \frac{2}{3}(x - 4)$

$\overline{AB}$: $y = 2 + \frac{2}{3}(x + 2)$ or $y = 4 + \frac{2}{3}(x - 1)$

$\overline{AD}$: $y = 2 - \frac{5}{3}(x + 2)$ or $y = -3 - \frac{5}{3}(x - 1)$

$\overline{BC}$: $y = 4 - \frac{5}{3}(x - 1)$ or $y = -1 - \frac{5}{3}(x - 4)$

$[-9.4, 9.4, 1, -6.2, 6.2, 1]$

**16. a.** $\log_p xy = \log_p x + \log_p y = a + b$

**b.** $\log_p x^3 = 3\log_p x = 3a$

**c.** $\log_p \frac{y^2}{x} = \log_p y^2 - \log_p x = 2\log_p y - \log_p x = 2b - a$

**d.** $\frac{1}{2}b$. Let $\log_{p^2} y = z$, so $p^{2z} = y$. Given that $\log_p y = b$, then $p^b = y$. By substitution, $p^{2z} = p^b$, so $2z = b$, and $z = \frac{1}{2}b$. Therefore, $\log_{p^2} y = \frac{1}{2}b$.

**e.** $\log_p \sqrt{x} = \log_p x^{1/2} = \frac{1}{2}\log_p x = \frac{1}{2}a$

**f.** $\log_m xy = \log_m x + \log_m y = \frac{\log_p x}{\log_p m} + \frac{\log_p y}{\log_p m} = \frac{a + b}{\log_p m}$

**17.** $x = 2$, $y = \frac{1}{2}$, $z = -3$. First, eliminate one variable entirely to get two equations with two unknowns.

Multiply the first equation by 2 and then add it to the second equation to eliminate $y$.

$$\begin{array}{r} 2x + 4y + 2z = 0 \\ 3x - 4y + 5z = -11 \\ \hline 5x \quad\quad + 7z = -11 \end{array}$$

Multiply the second equation by $-2$ and then add it to the third equation to eliminate $y$.

$$\begin{array}{r} -6x + 8y - 10z = 22 \\ -2x - 8y - 3z = 1 \\ \hline -8x \quad\quad - 13z = 23 \end{array}$$

Now you have two equations in $x$ and $z$. Multiply the first equation by 8 and the second equation by 5, and then add to eliminate $x$ and solve for $z$.

$$\begin{array}{r} 40x + 56z = -88 \\ -40x - 65z = 115 \\ \hline -9z = 27 \end{array}$$

$$z = -3$$

Substitute $-3$ for $z$ in either of the two equations in $x$ and $z$ and solve for $x$.

$$5x + 7(-3) = -11$$

$$5x - 21 = -11$$

$$5x = 10$$

$$x = 2$$

Substitute 2 for $x$ and $-3$ for $z$ in any of the original equations to solve for $y$.

$$(2) + 2y + (-3) = 0$$

$$2y - 1 = 0$$

$$2y = 1$$

$$y = \frac{1}{2}$$

The solution to the system of equations is $x = 2$, $y = \frac{1}{2}$, and $z = -3$.

## EXTENSIONS

**A.** Answers will vary.

**B.** Matrix multiplication is distributive over matrix addition.

For example, if $[A] = \begin{bmatrix} a_1 & a_2 \end{bmatrix}$,

$[B] = \begin{bmatrix} b_{11} & b_{12} \\ b_{21} & b_{22} \end{bmatrix}$, and $[C] = \begin{bmatrix} c_{11} & c_{12} \\ c_{21} & c_{22} \end{bmatrix}$,

then $[A]([B] + [C]) = \begin{bmatrix} a_1 & a_2 \end{bmatrix} \cdot$

$\begin{bmatrix} b_{11} + c_{11} & b_{12} + c_{12} \\ b_{21} + c_{21} & b_{22} + c_{22} \end{bmatrix} = \begin{bmatrix} a_1(b_{11} + c_{11}) + \end{bmatrix}$

$a_2(b_{21} + c_{21}) \quad a_1(b_{12} + c_{12}) + a_2(b_{22} + c_{22})\big]$

and $[A][B] + [A][C] =$

$$\begin{bmatrix} a_1b_{11} + a_2b_{21} & a_1b_{12} + a_2b_{22} \end{bmatrix} +$$
$$\begin{bmatrix} a_1c_{11} + a_2c_{21} & a_1c_{12} + a_2c_{22} \end{bmatrix} =$$
$$\begin{bmatrix} a_1b_{11} + a_2b_{21} + a_1c_{11} + a_2c_{21} & a_1b_{12} + a_2b_{22} + \end{bmatrix}$$
$$a_1c_{12} + a_2c_{22} \end{bmatrix}.$$

These are the same matrices by the distributive property.

## LESSON 6.3

### EXERCISES

**1. a.** $\begin{cases} 2x + 5y = 8 \\ 4x - y = 6 \end{cases}$

**b.** $\begin{cases} x - y + 2z = 3 \\ x + 2y - 3z = 1 \\ 2x + y - z = 2 \end{cases}$

**2. a.** $\begin{bmatrix} 1 & 2 & -1 & | & 1 \\ 2 & -1 & 3 & | & 2 \\ 2 & 1 & 1 & | & -1 \end{bmatrix}$

**b.** $\begin{bmatrix} 2 & 1 & -1 & | & 12 \\ 2 & 0 & 1 & | & 4 \\ 2 & -1 & 3 & | & -4 \end{bmatrix}$

**3. a.**
$$\begin{bmatrix} 1 & -1 & 2 & | & 3 \\ -1(1)+1 & -1(-1)+2 & -1(2)+(-3) & | & -1(3)+1 \\ 2 & 1 & -1 & | & 2 \end{bmatrix}$$
$$= \begin{bmatrix} 1 & -1 & 2 & | & 3 \\ 0 & 3 & -5 & | & -2 \\ 2 & 1 & -1 & | & 2 \end{bmatrix}$$

**b.**
$$\begin{bmatrix} 1 & -1 & 2 & | & 3 \\ 1 & 2 & -3 & | & 1 \\ -2(1)+2 & -2(-1)+1 & -2(2)+(-1) & | & -2(3)+2 \end{bmatrix}$$
$$= \begin{bmatrix} 1 & -1 & 2 & | & 3 \\ 1 & 2 & -3 & | & 1 \\ 0 & 3 & -5 & | & -4 \end{bmatrix}$$

**4. a.** $\begin{bmatrix} 2 & 5 & | & 8 \\ 4 & -1 & | & 6 \end{bmatrix}$

**b.** $\begin{bmatrix} 2 & 5 & | & 8 \\ -2(2)+4 & -2(5)+(-1) & | & -2(8)+6 \end{bmatrix} =$
$$\begin{bmatrix} 2 & 5 & | & 8 \\ 0 & -11 & | & -10 \end{bmatrix}$$

**c.** $\frac{R_2}{-11} \to R_2$ because
$$\begin{bmatrix} 2 & 5 & | & 8 \\ \frac{0}{-11} & \frac{-11}{-11} & | & \frac{-10}{-11} \end{bmatrix} = \begin{bmatrix} 2 & 5 & | & 8 \\ 0 & 1 & | & \frac{10}{11} \end{bmatrix}$$

**d.** $-5R_2 + R_1 \to R_1$ because
$$\begin{bmatrix} -5(0)+2 & -5(1)+5 & | & -5\left(\frac{10}{11}\right)+8 \\ 0 & 1 & | & \frac{10}{11} \end{bmatrix} =$$
$$\begin{bmatrix} 2 & 0 & | & \frac{38}{11} \\ 0 & 1 & | & \frac{10}{11} \end{bmatrix}$$

**e.** $\frac{R_1}{2} \to R_1$ because
$$\begin{bmatrix} \frac{2}{2} & \frac{0}{2} & | & \frac{38}{11(2)} \\ 0 & 1 & | & \frac{10}{11} \end{bmatrix} = \begin{bmatrix} 1 & 0 & | & \frac{19}{11} \\ 0 & 1 & | & \frac{10}{11} \end{bmatrix}$$

**5. a.** $\begin{bmatrix} 1 & 2 & 3 & | & 5 \\ 2 & 3 & 2 & | & 2 \\ -1 & -2 & -4 & | & -1 \end{bmatrix}; \begin{bmatrix} 1 & 0 & 0 & | & -31 \\ 0 & 1 & 0 & | & 24 \\ 0 & 0 & 1 & | & -4 \end{bmatrix}$

Here is one possible sequence of row operations to obtain a solution matrix.

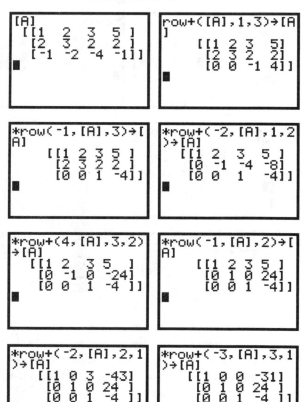

The solution to the system is $x = -31$, $y = 24$, and $z = -4$.

**b.** $\begin{bmatrix} -1 & 3 & -1 & 4 \\ 1 & 1 & -2 & 0 \\ 0 & 2.2 & 2.2 & 2.2 \end{bmatrix}; \begin{bmatrix} 1 & 0 & 0 & -1 \\ 0 & 1 & 0 & 1 \\ 0 & 0 & 1 & 0 \end{bmatrix}$

Here is one possible sequence of row operations to obtain a solution matrix.

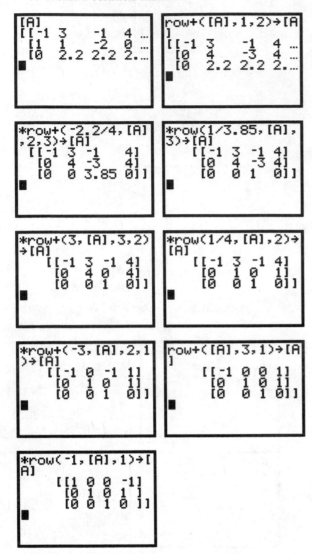

The solution to the system is $x = -1$, $y = 1$, and $z = 0$.

**c.** $\begin{bmatrix} 3 & -1 & 1 & 7 \\ 1 & -2 & 5 & 1 \\ 6 & -2 & 2 & 14 \end{bmatrix}$.

The augmented matrix cannot be reduced to row-echelon form (dependent system). In the process of finding a possible sequence of row operations to obtain a solution matrix, you will see that not all augmented matrices can be reduced to row-echelon form. Here, the row operation used yields an entire row of 0's in row 3. This means that the first equation is a multiple of the third; therefore, not enough information was given to find a single solution, and there are infinitely many solutions.

A system with infinitely many solutions is a dependent system.

**d.** $\begin{bmatrix} 3 & -7 & 1 & 5 \\ 1 & -2 & 5 & 1 \\ 6 & -2 & 2 & 14 \end{bmatrix}; \begin{bmatrix} 1 & 0 & 0 & \frac{5}{2} \\ 0 & 1 & 0 & \frac{1}{3} \\ 0 & 0 & 1 & -\frac{1}{6} \end{bmatrix}$

Here is one possible sequence of row operations to obtain a solution matrix.

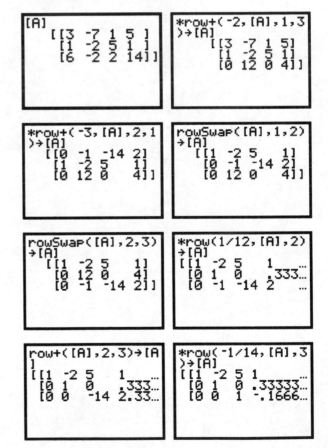

*Discovering Advanced Algebra Solutions Manual*
©2004 Key Curriculum Press

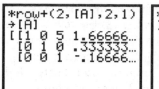
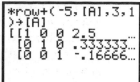

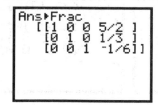

The solution to the system is $x = \frac{5}{2}$, $y = \frac{1}{3}$, and $z = -\frac{1}{6}$.

**6. a.** Let $x$ represent the number of goats, and let $y$ represent the number of chickens.

$$\begin{cases} x + y = 47 \\ 4x + 2y = 118 \end{cases}; \begin{bmatrix} 1 & 1 & | & 47 \\ 4 & 2 & | & 118 \end{bmatrix}$$

He has 12 goats and 35 chickens.

Enter the augmented matrix into your calculator and use the reduced row-echelon command.

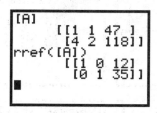

The reduced row-echelon matrix represents that there are 12 goats and 35 chickens.

**b.** $\begin{cases} x + y = 118 \\ 4x + 2y = 47 \end{cases}; \begin{bmatrix} 1 & 1 & | & 118 \\ 4 & 2 & | & 47 \end{bmatrix}$

She has $-94.5$ goats and 212.5 chickens, which is impossible. She must have made an error in reporting her numbers.

```
[A]
     [[1 1 118]
      [4 2 47 ]]
rref([A])
     [[1 0 -94.5]
      [0 1 212.5]]
■
```

**7.** 38°, 62°, 80°. Let $x$ represent the measure of the smallest angle, let $y$ represent the measure of the midsize angle, and let $z$ represent the measure of the largest angle. Write a system of three linear equations and then rewrite it as an augmented matrix.

$$\begin{cases} x + y + z = 180 \\ z = 2x + 4 \\ y - x = 24 \end{cases} \rightarrow \begin{bmatrix} 1 & 1 & 1 & | & 180 \\ -2 & 0 & 1 & | & 4 \\ -1 & 1 & 0 & | & 24 \end{bmatrix}$$

Solve the system using the reduced row-echelon command.

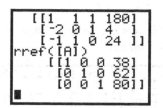

The angle measures are 38°, 62°, and 80°.

**8. a.** Supply: $\hat{y} = 158.96x - 11412.4$; demand: $\hat{y} = -54.36x + 7617.27$. Use your calculator to find these median-median lines.

**b.** Approximately $(89, 2768)$.

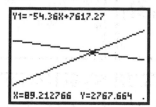

[88, 90, 10, 2500, 3000, 1000]

**c.** $\begin{bmatrix} 54.36 & 1 & | & 7617.27 \\ 158.96 & -1 & | & 11412.4 \end{bmatrix}; \begin{bmatrix} 1 & 0 & | & 89.2 \\ 0 & 1 & | & 2768.0 \end{bmatrix};$

this verifies the answer to 8b. Use row reduction to solve the augmented matrix.

$R_2 + R_1 \rightarrow R_1 \qquad \begin{bmatrix} 213.32 & 0 & | & 19029.67 \\ 158.96 & -1 & | & 11412.4 \end{bmatrix}$

$\dfrac{R_1}{213.32} \rightarrow R_1 \qquad \begin{bmatrix} 1 & 0 & | & 89.20... \\ 158.96 & -1 & | & 11412.4 \end{bmatrix}$

$-158.96R_1 + R_2 \rightarrow R_2 \quad \begin{bmatrix} 1 & 0 & | & 89.20... \\ 0 & -1 & | & -2767.96... \end{bmatrix}$

$\dfrac{R_2}{-1} \rightarrow R_2 \qquad \begin{bmatrix} 1 & 0 & | & 89.2 \\ 0 & 1 & | & 2768.0 \end{bmatrix}$

The solution matrix verifies that $x \approx 89.2$ and $y \approx 2768.0$.

**9.** $y = 2x^2 - 3x + 4$. Write three equations with the variables $a$, $b$, and $c$ by substituting the three pairs of coordinates.

$a(1)^2 + b(1) + c = 3$, so $a + b + c = 3$

$a(4)^2 + b(4) + c = 24$, so $16a + 4b + c = 24$

$a(-2)^2 + b(-2) + c = 18$, so $4a - 2b + c = 18$

Create a system of three equations and write it as an augmented matrix.

$$\begin{cases} a + b + c = 3 \\ 16a + 4b + c = 24 \\ 4a - 2b + c = 18 \end{cases} \rightarrow \begin{bmatrix} 1 & 1 & 1 & | & 3 \\ 16 & 4 & 1 & | & 24 \\ 4 & -2 & 1 & | & 18 \end{bmatrix}$$

Use the calculator's reduced row-echelon command to solve.

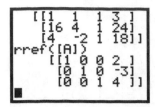

The solution is $a = 2$, $b = -3$, and $c = 4$, so the equation is $y = 2x^2 - 3x + 4$.

10. 3 full-page ads, 7 half-page ads, and 12 business-card-size ads. Let $x$ represent the number of full-page ads, let $y$ represent the number of half-page ads, and let $z$ represent the number of business-card-size ads. There were 22 ads sold, so $x + y + z = 22$. Full-size ads sell for \$200, half-page ads sell for \$125, business-card-size ads sell for \$20, and the total income was \$1715, so $200x + 125y + 20z = 1715$. There were four times as many business-card-size ads as full-page ads, so $4x = z$, or $4x - z = 0$. Write this system of three equations as an augmented matrix.

$$\begin{cases} x + y + z = 22 \\ 200x + 125y + 20z = 1715 \\ 4x - z = 0 \end{cases} \rightarrow$$

$$\begin{bmatrix} 1 & 1 & 1 & | & 22 \\ 200 & 125 & 20 & | & 1715 \\ 4 & 0 & -1 & | & 0 \end{bmatrix}$$

Use the calculator's reduced row-echelon command to solve.

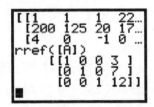

The solution is $x = 3$, $y = 7$, and $z = 12$, or 3 full-page ads, 7 half-page ads, and 12 business-card-size ads.

11. a. First plan: $12{,}500 + 0.05(12)(3500) = \$14{,}600$
    Second plan: $6800 + 0.15(12)(3500) = \$13{,}100$

    b. Let $x$ represent the number of tickets sold, and let $y$ represent the income in dollars; $y = 12500 + 0.05(12)x = 12500 + 0.6x$.

    c. $y = 6800 + 0.15(12)x = 6800 + 1.8x$

    d. More than 4750 tickets. Find the number of tickets sold at which the two plans generate the same amount of pay. By substitution,

$12500 + 0.6x = 6800 + 1.8x$, so $5700 = 1.2x$, and $x = 4750$. The second plan will be the better choice if they sell more than 4750 tickets.

    e. The company should choose the first plan if they expect to sell fewer than 4750 tickets and the second if they expect to sell more than 4750 tickets.

12. a. $(4, 2)$. The intersection point for the two linear equations is $(4, 2)$.

    b. Using point-slope form, $y_1 = 2 + 2(x - 4)$, or $y_1 = 2(x - 3)$, and $y_2 = 2 - 0.75(x - 4)$, or $y_2 = -1 - 0.75(x - 8)$. The slope of line $y_1$ is 2 and the slope of line $y_2$ is $-\frac{3}{4}$, or $-0.75$. Line $y_1$ contains the point $(3, 0)$, line $y_2$ contains the point $(8, -1)$, and both lines contain the point $(4, 2)$.

13. $\overline{AB}$: $y = 6 + \frac{2}{3}(x - 4)$ or $y = 4 + \frac{2}{3}(x - 1)$

$\overline{BC}$: $y = 4 - \frac{2}{3}(x - 7)$ or $y = 6 - \frac{2}{3}(x - 4)$

$\overline{CD}$: $y = 1 + 3(x - 6)$ or $y = 4 + 3(x - 7)$

$\overline{DE}$: $y = 1$

$\overline{AE}$: $y = 4 - 3(x - 1)$ or $y = 1 - 3(x - 2)$

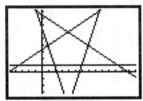

$[-4.7, 14.1, 1, -3.1, 9.3, 1]$

14. a. $[M] = \begin{bmatrix} 2 & 6 & 6 \\ 1 & 1 & 3 \end{bmatrix}$. The vertices of the triangle are at $(2, 1)$, $(6, 1)$, and $(6, 3)$.

    b. i. $\begin{bmatrix} 1 & 1 & 3 \\ 2 & 6 & 6 \end{bmatrix}$. $\triangle ABC$ is reflected across the line $y = x$.

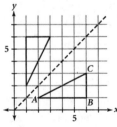

$$\begin{bmatrix} 0 & 1 \\ 1 & 0 \end{bmatrix} \begin{bmatrix} 2 & 6 & 6 \\ 1 & 1 & 3 \end{bmatrix} = \begin{bmatrix} 1 & 1 & 3 \\ 2 & 6 & 6 \end{bmatrix}$$

**ii.** $\begin{bmatrix} -1 & -1 & -3 \\ 2 & 6 & 6 \end{bmatrix}$. $\triangle ABC$ is rotated 90°
counterclockwise about the origin.

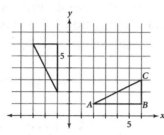

$$\begin{bmatrix} 0 & -1 \\ 1 & 0 \end{bmatrix}\begin{bmatrix} 2 & 6 & 6 \\ 1 & 1 & 3 \end{bmatrix} = \begin{bmatrix} -1 & -1 & -3 \\ 2 & 6 & 6 \end{bmatrix}$$

## IMPROVING YOUR VISUAL THINKING SKILLS

There are eight possible outcomes. For one outcome, the
three planes are coincident, a consistent and dependent
case. For two other outcomes, exactly two of the planes
are coincident. If the third plane intersects these two in
a line, the system is consistent and dependent. If the
third plane is parallel to these two, then the system
is inconsistent. The outcomes with no coincident
planes are shown below.

Consistent and independent          Inconsistent

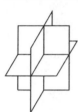

Inconsistent          Inconsistent

Consistent and dependent

## EXTENSIONS

**A.** See the solution to Take Another Look activity 2 on
page 148.

**B.** Models should appear similar to the representations
given in the solution to Improving Your Visual
Thinking Skills.

### EXERCISES

**1. a.** $\begin{bmatrix} 3 & 4 \\ 2 & -5 \end{bmatrix}\begin{bmatrix} x \\ y \end{bmatrix} = \begin{bmatrix} 11 \\ -8 \end{bmatrix}$

**b.** $\begin{bmatrix} 1 & 2 & 1 \\ 3 & -4 & 5 \\ -2 & -8 & -3 \end{bmatrix}\begin{bmatrix} x \\ y \\ z \end{bmatrix} = \begin{bmatrix} 0 \\ -11 \\ 1 \end{bmatrix}$

**c.** $\begin{bmatrix} 5.2 & 3.6 \\ -5.2 & 2 \end{bmatrix}\begin{bmatrix} x \\ y \end{bmatrix} = \begin{bmatrix} 7 \\ 8.2 \end{bmatrix}$

**d.** $\begin{bmatrix} \frac{1}{4} & -\frac{2}{5} \\ \frac{3}{8} & \frac{2}{5} \end{bmatrix}\begin{bmatrix} x \\ y \end{bmatrix} = \begin{bmatrix} 3 \\ 2 \end{bmatrix}$

**2. a.** $\begin{bmatrix} 5 & 2 \\ 7 & 3 \end{bmatrix}\begin{bmatrix} 1 & -3 \\ 5 & -2 \end{bmatrix} =$

$\begin{bmatrix} 5(1) + 2(5) & 5(-3) + 2(-2) \\ 7(1) + 3(5) & 7(-3) + 3(-2) \end{bmatrix} =$

$\begin{bmatrix} 15 & -19 \\ 22 & -27 \end{bmatrix}$

**b.** $\begin{bmatrix} 4 & -1 \\ 3 & 6 \\ 2 & -3 \end{bmatrix}\begin{bmatrix} 2 & -5 & 0 \\ 1 & -2 & 7 \end{bmatrix} =$

$\begin{bmatrix} 4(2) + -1(1) & 4(-5) + -1(-2) & 4(0) + -1(7) \\ 3(2) + 6(1) & 3(-5) + 6(-2) & 3(0) + 6(7) \\ 2(2) + -3(1) & 2(-5) + -3(-2) & 2(0) + -3(7) \end{bmatrix} =$

$\begin{bmatrix} 7 & -18 & -7 \\ 12 & -27 & 42 \\ 1 & -4 & -21 \end{bmatrix}$

**c.** Not possible; the dimensions of the matrices are
$1 \times 2$ and $3 \times 2$, so the inside dimensions are
not the same.

**3. a.** $\begin{bmatrix} a & b \\ c & d \end{bmatrix} = \begin{bmatrix} 3 & -7 \\ -2 & 8 \end{bmatrix}$

$\begin{bmatrix} 1 & 5 \\ 6 & 2 \end{bmatrix}\begin{bmatrix} a & b \\ c & d \end{bmatrix} = \begin{bmatrix} 1a + 5c & 1b + 5d \\ 6a + 2c & 6b + 2d \end{bmatrix} =$

$\begin{bmatrix} -7 & 33 \\ 14 & -26 \end{bmatrix}$

Set corresponding entries equal.

$a + 5c = -7$      $b + 5d = 33$

$6a + 2c = 14$      $6b + 2d = -26$

Treat the equations as two systems of equations. Use either substitution or elimination to solve each system.

$$\begin{cases} a + 5c = -7 \\ 6a + 2c = 14 \end{cases}$$   A system in two variables, $a$ and $c$.

$2a + 10c = -14$   Multiply the first equation by 2.

$-30a - 10c = -70$   Multiply the second equation by $-5$.

$-28a \quad = -84$   Add the equations to eliminate $c$.

$a = 3$   Divide both sides by $-28$.

$(3) + 5c = -7$   Substitute 3 for $a$ in the first equation to find $c$.

$5c = -10$   Subtract 3 from both sides.

$c = -2$   Divide both sides by 2.

The solution is $a = 3$ and $c = -2$. Use a similar procedure to find $b$ and $d$.

$$\begin{cases} b + 5d = 33 \\ 6b + 2d = -26 \end{cases}$$   A system in two variables, $b$ and $d$.

$2b + 10d = 66$   Multiply the first equation by 2.

$-30b - 10d = 130$   Multiply the second equation by $-5$.

$-28b = 196$   Add the equations to eliminate $d$.

$b = -7$   Divide both sides by $-28$.

$(-7) + 5d = 33$   Substitute $-7$ for $b$ in the first equation to find $d$.

$5d = 40$   Add 7 to both sides.

$d = 8$   Divide both sides by 5.

The solution is $b = -7$ and $d = 8$.

The four variables are $a = 3$, $b = -7$, $c = -2$, and $d = 8$.

**b.** $\begin{bmatrix} a & b \\ c & d \end{bmatrix} = \begin{bmatrix} -\dfrac{1}{14} & \dfrac{5}{28} \\ \dfrac{3}{14} & -\dfrac{1}{28} \end{bmatrix}$

$\begin{bmatrix} 1 & 5 \\ 6 & 2 \end{bmatrix}\begin{bmatrix} a & b \\ c & d \end{bmatrix} = \begin{bmatrix} 1a + 5c & 1b + 5d \\ 6a + 2c & 6b + 2d \end{bmatrix} =$

$\begin{bmatrix} 1 & 0 \\ 0 & 1 \end{bmatrix}$

Set corresponding entries equal.

$a + 5c = 1$       $b + 5d = 0$

$6a + 2c = 0$       $6b + 2d = 1$

Treat the equations as two systems of equations. Use either substitution or elimination to solve each system.

$$\begin{cases} a + 5c = 1 \\ 6a + 2c = 0 \end{cases}$$   A system in two variables, $a$ and $c$.

$a = 1 - 5c$   Solve the first equation for $a$.

$6(1 - 5c) + 2c = 0$   Substitute $(1 - 5c)$ for $a$ in the second equation.

$6 - 30c + 2c = 0$   Distribute.

$-28c = -6$   Add $-30c$ and $2c$, and subtract 6 from both sides.

$c = \dfrac{3}{14}$   Divide both sides by $-28$.

$a + 5\left(\dfrac{3}{14}\right) = 1$   Substitute $\dfrac{3}{14}$ for $c$ in the first equation.

$a + \dfrac{15}{14} = 1$   Multiply $5\left(\dfrac{3}{14}\right)$.

$a = -\dfrac{1}{14}$   Subtract $\dfrac{15}{14}$ from both sides.

The solution is $a = -\dfrac{1}{14}$ and $c = \dfrac{3}{14}$. Use a similar procedure to find $b$ and $d$.

$$\begin{cases} b + 5d = 0 \\ 6b + 2d = 1 \end{cases}$$   A system in two variables, $b$ and $d$.

$b = -5d$   Solve the first equation for $b$.

$6(-5d) + 2d = 1$   Substitute $-5d$ for $b$ in the second equation.

$-30d + 2d = 1$   Multiply $6(-5d)$.

$-28d = 1$   Add $-30d$ and $2d$.

$d = -\dfrac{1}{28}$   Divide both sides by $-28$.

$b + 5\left(-\dfrac{1}{28}\right) = 0$   Substitute $-\dfrac{1}{28}$ for $d$ in the first equation.

$b - \dfrac{5}{28} = 0$   Multiply $5\left(-\dfrac{1}{28}\right)$.

$b = \dfrac{5}{28}$   Add $\dfrac{5}{28}$ to both sides.

The solution is $b = \dfrac{5}{28}$ and $d = -\dfrac{1}{28}$.

The four variables are $a = -\dfrac{1}{14}$, $b = \dfrac{5}{28}$, $c = \dfrac{3}{14}$, and $d = -\dfrac{1}{28}$.

**4. a.** Yes, the matrices are inverses of each other because the product is the identity matrix.

$$\begin{bmatrix} 5 & 2 \\ 7 & 3 \end{bmatrix}\begin{bmatrix} 3 & -2 \\ -7 & 5 \end{bmatrix} =$$

$$\begin{bmatrix} 5(3) + 2(-7) & 5(-2) + 2(5) \\ 7(3) + 3(-7) & 7(-2) + 3(5) \end{bmatrix} =$$

$$\begin{bmatrix} 1 & 0 \\ 0 & 1 \end{bmatrix}$$

**b.** Yes, the matrices are inverses of each other because the product is the identity matrix. *(See equation at bottom of page.)*

**5. a.** $\begin{bmatrix} 4 & -3 \\ -5 & 4 \end{bmatrix}$. Write a matrix equation in the form $[A][A]^{-1} = [I]$. Let $[A]^{-1} = \begin{bmatrix} a & b \\ c & d \end{bmatrix}$.

$$\begin{bmatrix} 4 & 3 \\ 5 & 4 \end{bmatrix}\begin{bmatrix} a & b \\ c & d \end{bmatrix} = \begin{bmatrix} 4a + 3c & 4b + 3d \\ 5a + 4c & 5b + 4d \end{bmatrix} =$$

$$\begin{bmatrix} 1 & 0 \\ 0 & 1 \end{bmatrix}$$

Set corresponding entries equal.

$4a + 3c = 1 \qquad 4b + 3d = 0$

$5a + 4c = 0 \qquad 5b + 4d = 1$

Treat the equations as two systems of equations. Use substitution, elimination, or row reduction to solve each system.

$\begin{cases} 4a + 3c = 1 \\ 5a + 4c = 0 \end{cases}; a = 4$ and $c = -5$

$\begin{cases} 4b + 3d = 0 \\ 5b + 4d = 1 \end{cases}; b = -3$ and $d = 4$

The four variables are $a = 4$, $b = -3$, $c = -5$, and $d = 4$, so $[A]^{-1} = \begin{bmatrix} 4 & -3 \\ -5 & 4 \end{bmatrix}$.

Use your calculator to find $[A]^{-1}$ and check your answer.

```
[A]
              [[4 3]
               [5 4]]
[A]⁻¹
             [[4  -3]
              [-5  4]]
■
```

**b.** $\begin{bmatrix} -\frac{1}{6} & \frac{2}{3} & \frac{1}{9} \\ \frac{1}{2} & -1 & 0 \\ 0 & 0 & \frac{1}{3} \end{bmatrix}$, or $\begin{bmatrix} -0.1\overline{6} & 0.\overline{6} & 0.\overline{1} \\ 0.5 & -1 & 0 \\ 0 & 0 & 0.\overline{3} \end{bmatrix}$

Write a matrix equation in the form

$$[A][A]^{-1} = [I]. \text{ Let } [A]^{-1} = \begin{bmatrix} a & b & c \\ d & e & f \\ g & h & i \end{bmatrix}.$$

$$\begin{bmatrix} 6 & 4 & -2 \\ 3 & 1 & -1 \\ 0 & 0 & 3 \end{bmatrix}\begin{bmatrix} a & b & c \\ d & e & f \\ g & h & i \end{bmatrix} =$$

$$\begin{bmatrix} 6a + 4d - 2g & 6b + 4e - 2h & 6c + 4f - 2i \\ 3a + 1d - 1g & 3b + 1e - 1h & 3c + 1f - 1i \\ 0a + 0d + 3g & 0b + 0e + 3h & 0c + 0f + 3i \end{bmatrix} =$$

$$\begin{bmatrix} 1 & 0 & 0 \\ 0 & 1 & 0 \\ 0 & 0 & 1 \end{bmatrix}$$

Set corresponding entries equal.

$6a + 4d - 2g = 1 \quad 6b + 4e - 2h = 0 \quad 6c + 4f - 2i = 0$

$3a + 1d - 1g = 0 \quad 3b + 1e - 1h = 1 \quad 3c + 1f - 1i = 0$

$0a + 0d + 3g = 0 \quad 0b + 0e + 3h = 0 \quad 0c + 0f + 3i = 1$

---

**Lesson 6.4, Exercise 4b**

$$\begin{bmatrix} 1 & 5 & 4 \\ 6 & 2 & -2 \\ 0 & 3 & 1 \end{bmatrix}\begin{bmatrix} 0.16 & 0.14 & -0.36 \\ -0.12 & 0.02 & 0.52 \\ 0.36 & -0.06 & -0.56 \end{bmatrix} =$$

$$\begin{bmatrix} 1(0.16) + 5(-0.12) + 4(0.36) & 1(0.14) + 5(0.02) + 4(-0.06) & 1(-0.36) + 5(0.52) + 4(-0.56) \\ 6(0.16) + 2(-0.12) - 2(0.36) & 6(0.14) + 2(0.02) - 2(-0.06) & 6(-0.36) + 2(0.52) - 2(-0.56) \\ 0(0.16) + 3(-0.12) + 1(0.36) & 0(0.14) + 3(0.02) + 1(-0.06) & 0(-0.36) + 3(0.52) + 1(-0.56) \end{bmatrix} =$$

$$\begin{bmatrix} 1 & 0 & 0 \\ 0 & 1 & 0 \\ 0 & 0 & 1 \end{bmatrix}$$

Treat the equations as three systems of three equations. Use substitution, elimination, or row reduction to solve each system.

$$\begin{cases} 6a + 4d - 2g = 1 \\ 3a + 1d - 1g = 0; \ a = -\frac{1}{6}, \ d = \frac{1}{2}, \text{ and } g = 0 \\ 3g = 0 \end{cases}$$

$$\begin{cases} 6b + 4e - 2h = 0 \\ 3b + 1e - 1h = 1; \ b = \frac{2}{3}, \ e = -1, \text{ and } h = 0 \\ 3h = 0 \end{cases}$$

$$\begin{cases} 3c + 1f - 1i = 0 \\ 6c + 4f - 2i = 0; \ c = \frac{1}{9}, \ f = 0, \text{ and } i = \frac{1}{3} \\ 3i = 1 \end{cases}$$

The nine variables are $a = -\frac{1}{6}$, $b = \frac{2}{3}$, $c = \frac{1}{9}$, $d = \frac{1}{2}$, $e = -1$, $f = 0$, $g = 0$, $h = 0$, and $i = \frac{1}{3}$, so

$$[A]^{-1} = \begin{bmatrix} -\frac{1}{6} & \frac{2}{3} & \frac{1}{9} \\ \frac{1}{2} & -1 & 0 \\ 0 & 0 & \frac{1}{3} \end{bmatrix}$$

Use your calculator to find $[A]^{-1}$ and check your answer.

**c.** $\begin{bmatrix} \frac{7}{5} & -\frac{3}{5} \\ -2 & 1 \end{bmatrix}$, or $\begin{bmatrix} 1.4 & -0.6 \\ -2 & 1 \end{bmatrix}$

Write a matrix equation in the form $[A][A]^{-1} = [I]$. Let $[A]^{-1} = \begin{bmatrix} a & b \\ c & d \end{bmatrix}$.

$$\begin{bmatrix} 5 & 3 \\ 10 & 7 \end{bmatrix} \begin{bmatrix} a & b \\ c & d \end{bmatrix} = \begin{bmatrix} 5a + 3c & 5b + 3d \\ 10c + 7c & 10 + 7d \end{bmatrix} = \begin{bmatrix} 1 & 0 \\ 0 & 1 \end{bmatrix}$$

Set corresponding entries equal.

$5a + 3c = 1 \quad 5b - 3d = 0$

$10a + 7c = 0 \quad 10b + 7d = 1$

Treat the equations as two systems of equations. Use substitution, elimination, or row reduction to solve each system.

$$\begin{cases} 5a + 3c = 1 \\ 10a + 7c = 0 \end{cases}; \ a = \frac{7}{5} \text{ and } c = -2$$

$$\begin{cases} 5b + 3d = 0 \\ 10b + 7d = 1 \end{cases}; \ b = -\frac{3}{5} \text{ and } d = 1$$

The four variables are $a = \frac{7}{5}$, $b = -\frac{3}{5}$, $c = -2$, and $d = 1$, so

$$[A]^{-1} = \begin{bmatrix} \frac{7}{5} & -\frac{3}{5} \\ -2 & 1 \end{bmatrix}$$

Use your calculator to find $[A]^{-1}$ and check your answer.

**d.** Inverse does not exist. Write a matrix equation in the form $[A][A]^{-1} = [I]$. Let $[A]^{-1} = \begin{bmatrix} a & b \\ c & d \end{bmatrix}$.

$$\begin{bmatrix} 1 & 2 \\ 2 & 4 \end{bmatrix} \begin{bmatrix} a & b \\ c & d \end{bmatrix} = \begin{bmatrix} 1a + 2c & 1b + 2d \\ 2a + 4c & 2b + 4d \end{bmatrix} = \begin{bmatrix} 1 & 0 \\ 0 & 1 \end{bmatrix}$$

Set corresponding entries equal.

$1a + 2c = 1 \qquad 1b + 2d = 0$

$2a + 4c = 0 \qquad 2b + 4d = 1$

Treat the equations as two systems of equations. When you attempt to solve either system by elimination, you reach $0 = 1$ because the second row is a multiple of the first row. Therefore the inverse does not exist; when you enter $[A]^{-1}$ into your calculator, you will get an error message.

**6.** For 6a–d, let matrix $[A]$ represent the coefficients of the variables, matrix $[X]$ represent the variables, and matrix $[B]$ represent the constant terms. To find the solution to each system, multiply $[A]^{-1}[B]$.

**a.** $\begin{bmatrix} 8 & 3 \\ 6 & 5 \end{bmatrix}\begin{bmatrix} x \\ y \end{bmatrix} = \begin{bmatrix} 41 \\ 39 \end{bmatrix}$; $x = 4$, $y = 3$

Use your calculator to find the inverse of $[A]$.

$$[A]^{-1} = \begin{bmatrix} \dfrac{5}{22} & -\dfrac{3}{22} \\ -\dfrac{3}{11} & \dfrac{4}{11} \end{bmatrix}$$

Left-multiply both sides of the equation by the inverse to find the solution to the system of equations.

$$\begin{bmatrix} 8 & 3 \\ 6 & 5 \end{bmatrix}\begin{bmatrix} x \\ y \end{bmatrix} = \begin{bmatrix} 41 \\ 39 \end{bmatrix}$$

$$\begin{bmatrix} \dfrac{5}{22} & -\dfrac{3}{22} \\ -\dfrac{3}{11} & \dfrac{4}{11} \end{bmatrix}\begin{bmatrix} 8 & 3 \\ 6 & 5 \end{bmatrix}\begin{bmatrix} x \\ y \end{bmatrix} = \begin{bmatrix} \dfrac{5}{22} & -\dfrac{3}{22} \\ -\dfrac{3}{11} & \dfrac{4}{11} \end{bmatrix}\begin{bmatrix} 41 \\ 39 \end{bmatrix}$$

By the definitions of inverse and identity matrix, you are left with only matrix $[X]$ on the left side of the equation. Complete the matrix multiplication to find the solution.

$$\begin{bmatrix} 1 & 0 \\ 0 & 1 \end{bmatrix}\begin{bmatrix} x \\ y \end{bmatrix} = \begin{bmatrix} \dfrac{5}{22} & -\dfrac{3}{22} \\ -\dfrac{3}{11} & \dfrac{4}{11} \end{bmatrix}\begin{bmatrix} 41 \\ 39 \end{bmatrix}$$

$$\begin{bmatrix} x \\ y \end{bmatrix} = \begin{bmatrix} \dfrac{5}{22} & -\dfrac{3}{22} \\ -\dfrac{3}{11} & \dfrac{4}{11} \end{bmatrix}\begin{bmatrix} 41 \\ 39 \end{bmatrix}$$

$$\begin{bmatrix} x \\ y \end{bmatrix} = \begin{bmatrix} 4 \\ 3 \end{bmatrix}$$

The solution to the system is $x = 4$ and $y = 3$. Substitute values back into the original equations to check the solution.

$$8x + 3y = 41 \qquad\qquad 6x + 5y = 39$$
$$8(4) + 3(3) \overset{?}{=} 41 \qquad 6(4) + 5(3) \overset{?}{=} 39$$
$$32 + 9 \overset{?}{=} 41 \qquad\qquad 34 + 15 \overset{?}{=} 39$$
$$41 = 41 \qquad\qquad\qquad 39 = 39$$

The solution checks.

**b.** $\begin{bmatrix} 11 & -5 \\ 9 & 2 \end{bmatrix}\begin{bmatrix} x \\ y \end{bmatrix} = \begin{bmatrix} -38 \\ -25 \end{bmatrix}$; $x = -3$, $y = 1$

Use your calculator to find $[A]^{-1}$.

$$[A]^{-1} = \begin{bmatrix} \dfrac{2}{67} & \dfrac{5}{67} \\ -\dfrac{9}{67} & \dfrac{11}{67} \end{bmatrix}$$

To find the solution to the system, multiply $[A]^{-1}[B]$.

$$\begin{bmatrix} x \\ y \end{bmatrix} = \begin{bmatrix} \dfrac{2}{67} & \dfrac{5}{67} \\ -\dfrac{9}{67} & \dfrac{11}{67} \end{bmatrix}\begin{bmatrix} -38 \\ -25 \end{bmatrix}$$

$$\begin{bmatrix} x \\ y \end{bmatrix} = \begin{bmatrix} -3 \\ 1 \end{bmatrix}$$

The solution to the system is $x = -3$ and $y = 1$. Substitute values back into the original equations to check the solution.

$$11x - 5y = -38 \qquad\qquad 9x + 2y = -25$$
$$11(-3) - 5(1) \overset{?}{=} -38 \qquad 9(-3) + 2(1) \overset{?}{=} -25$$
$$-33 - 5 \overset{?}{=} -38 \qquad\qquad -27 + 2 \overset{?}{=} -25$$
$$-38 = -38 \qquad\qquad\qquad -25 = -25$$

The solution checks.

**c.** $\begin{bmatrix} 2 & 1 & -2 \\ 6 & 2 & -4 \\ 4 & -1 & 3 \end{bmatrix}\begin{bmatrix} x \\ y \\ z \end{bmatrix} = \begin{bmatrix} 1 \\ 3 \\ 5 \end{bmatrix}$; $x = 0.5$, $y = 6$, $z = 3$

Find $[A]^{-1}$ on your calculator.

$$[A]^{-1} = \begin{bmatrix} -1 & 0.5 & 0 \\ 17 & -7 & 2 \\ 7 & -3 & 1 \end{bmatrix}$$

To find the solution to the system, multiply $[A]^{-1}[B]$.

$$\begin{bmatrix} x \\ y \\ z \end{bmatrix} = \begin{bmatrix} -1 & 0.5 & 0 \\ 17 & -7 & 2 \\ 7 & -3 & 1 \end{bmatrix}\begin{bmatrix} 1 \\ 3 \\ 5 \end{bmatrix}$$

$$\begin{bmatrix} x \\ y \\ z \end{bmatrix} = \begin{bmatrix} 0.5 \\ 6 \\ 3 \end{bmatrix}$$

The solution to the system is $x = 0.5$, $y = 6$, and $z = 3$. Substitute values back into the original equations to check the solution.

$$2x + y - 2z = 1$$
$$2(0.5) + 6 - 2(3) \overset{?}{=} 1$$
$$1 + 6 - 6 \overset{?}{=} 1$$
$$1 = 1$$

$$6x + 2y - 4z = 3$$
$$6(0.5) + 2(6) - 4(3) \overset{?}{=} 3$$
$$3 + 12 - 12 \overset{?}{=} 3$$
$$3 = 3$$

$$4x - y + 3z = 5$$

$$4(0.5) - 6 + 3(3) \overset{?}{=} 5$$

$$2 - 6 + 9 \overset{?}{=} 5$$

$$5 = 5$$

The solution checks.

**d.** $\begin{bmatrix} 4 & 1 & 2 & -3 \\ -3 & 3 & -1 & 4 \\ 5 & 4 & 3 & -1 \\ -1 & 2 & 5 & 1 \end{bmatrix} \begin{bmatrix} w \\ x \\ y \\ z \end{bmatrix} = \begin{bmatrix} -16 \\ 20 \\ -10 \\ -4 \end{bmatrix};$

$w = -1, x = 1, y = -2, z = 3$

Find $[A]^{-1}$ on your calculator.

$$[A]^{-1} = \begin{bmatrix} -\dfrac{43}{58} & -\dfrac{23}{58} & \dfrac{31}{58} & -\dfrac{3}{29} \\ \dfrac{23}{29} & \dfrac{15}{29} & -\dfrac{19}{58} & -\dfrac{1}{58} \\ -\dfrac{13}{58} & -\dfrac{11}{58} & \dfrac{3}{29} & \dfrac{11}{58} \\ -\dfrac{35}{29} & -\dfrac{14}{29} & \dfrac{39}{58} & -\dfrac{1}{58} \end{bmatrix}$$

To find the solution to the system, multiply $[A]^{-1}[B]$.

$$\begin{bmatrix} w \\ x \\ y \\ z \end{bmatrix} = \begin{bmatrix} -\dfrac{43}{58} & -\dfrac{23}{58} & \dfrac{31}{58} & -\dfrac{3}{29} \\ \dfrac{23}{29} & \dfrac{15}{29} & -\dfrac{19}{58} & -\dfrac{1}{58} \\ -\dfrac{13}{58} & -\dfrac{11}{58} & \dfrac{3}{29} & \dfrac{11}{58} \\ -\dfrac{35}{29} & -\dfrac{14}{29} & \dfrac{39}{58} & -\dfrac{1}{58} \end{bmatrix} \begin{bmatrix} -16 \\ 20 \\ -10 \\ -4 \end{bmatrix}$$

$$\begin{bmatrix} w \\ x \\ y \\ z \end{bmatrix} = \begin{bmatrix} -1 \\ 1 \\ -2 \\ 3 \end{bmatrix}$$

The solution to the system is $w = -1$, $x = 1$, $y = -2$, and $z = 3$. Substitute values back into the original equations to check the solution.

$$4w + x + 2y - 3z = -16$$

$$4(-1) + 1 + 2(-2) - 3(3) \overset{?}{=} -16$$

$$-4 + 1 - 4 - 9 \overset{?}{=} -16$$

$$-16 = -16$$

$$5w + 4x + 3y - z = -10$$

$$5(-1) + 4(1) + 3(-2) - 3 \overset{?}{=} -10$$

$$-5 + 4 - 6 - 3 \overset{?}{=} -10$$

$$-10 = -10$$

$$-3w + 3x - y + 4z = 20$$

$$-3(-1) + 3(1) - (-2) + 4(3) \overset{?}{=} 20$$

$$3 + 3 + 2 + 12 \overset{?}{=} 20$$

$$20 = 20$$

$$-w + 2x + 5y + z = -4$$

$$-(-1) + 2(1) + 5(-2) + 3 \overset{?}{=} -4$$

$$1 + 2 - 10 + 3 \overset{?}{=} -4$$

$$-4 = -4$$

The solution checks.

**7. a.** Jolly rides cost $0.50, Adventure rides cost $0.85, and Thrill rides cost $1.50. Let $j$ represent the cost in dollars of each Jolly ride, let $a$ represent the cost in dollars of each Adventure ride, and let $t$ represent the cost in dollars of each Thrill ride. Use the numbers of tickets and the prices paid by each person to write a system of three equations in three variables.

$$\begin{cases} 7j + 3a + 9t = 19.55 \\ 9j + 10a = 13 \\ 8j + 7a + 10t = 24.95 \end{cases} \rightarrow [A][X] = [B] \rightarrow$$

$$\begin{bmatrix} 7 & 3 & 9 \\ 9 & 10 & 0 \\ 8 & 7 & 10 \end{bmatrix} \begin{bmatrix} j \\ a \\ t \end{bmatrix} = \begin{bmatrix} 19.55 \\ 13 \\ 24.95 \end{bmatrix}$$

Solve the system by multiplying $[A]^{-1}[B]$.

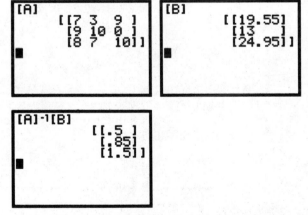

The solution is $j = 0.5$, $a = 0.85$, and $t = 1.5$. Therefore Jolly rides cost $0.50, Adventure rides cost $0.85, and Thrill rides cost $1.50.

**b.** $10(0.5 + 0.85 + 1.5) = 28.50$

**c.** Carey would have been better off buying a ticket book because without it, the cost was $24.95 + $5.00, or $29.95.

*Discovering Advanced Algebra Solutions Manual*
©2004 Key Curriculum Press

**8.** $2300 at 6% and $2700 at 7.5%. Let $x$ represent the amount in dollars invested at 6%, and let $y$ represent the amount in dollars invested at 7.5%. The total amount invested was $5000, so $x + y = 5000$. The total interest after one year was $340.50, so $0.06x + 0.075y = 340.50$. Write the system of two equations as a matrix equation.

$$[A][X] = [B]$$

$$\begin{bmatrix} 1 & 1 \\ 0.06 & 0.075 \end{bmatrix} \begin{bmatrix} x \\ y \end{bmatrix} = \begin{bmatrix} 5000 \\ 340.5 \end{bmatrix}$$

Solve the system by multiplying $[A]^{-1}[B]$.

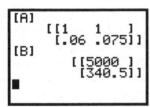
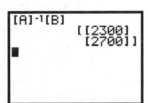

The solution is (2300, 2700). Therefore the family invested $2300 at 6% and $2700 at 7.5%.

**9.** 20°, 50°, 110°. Let $x$ represent the measure of the smallest angle, let $y$ represent the measure of the midsize angle, and let $z$ represent the measure of the largest angle. Write a system of three equations and then rewrite it as a matrix equation.

$$\begin{cases} x + y + z = 180 \\ y = 30 + x \\ z = 2y + 10 \end{cases} \rightarrow [A][X] = [B] \rightarrow$$

$$\begin{bmatrix} 1 & 1 & 1 \\ -1 & 1 & 0 \\ 0 & -2 & 1 \end{bmatrix} \begin{bmatrix} x \\ y \\ z \end{bmatrix} = \begin{bmatrix} 180 \\ 30 \\ 10 \end{bmatrix}$$

Solve the system by multiplying $[A]^{-1}[B]$.

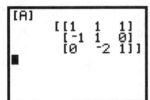
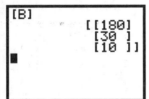

The solution is $x = 20$, $y = 50$, and $z = 110$. Therefore the angle measures are 20°, 50°, and 110°.

**10.** The price of a citron is 8; the price of a fragrant wood apple is 5. Let $c$ represent the price of a citron, and let $w$ represent the price of a wood apple. Write a system of two equations and a matrix equation.

$$\begin{cases} 9c + 7w = 107 \\ 7c + 9w = 101 \end{cases} \rightarrow \begin{bmatrix} 9 & 7 \\ 7 & 9 \end{bmatrix} \begin{bmatrix} c \\ w \end{bmatrix} = \begin{bmatrix} 107 \\ 101 \end{bmatrix}$$

Solve the system by multiplying $[A]^{-1}[B]$. Find $[A]^{-1}$ on your calculator.

$$[X] = [A]^{-1}[B]$$

$$\begin{bmatrix} c \\ w \end{bmatrix} = \begin{bmatrix} \dfrac{9}{32} & -\dfrac{7}{32} \\ -\dfrac{7}{32} & \dfrac{9}{32} \end{bmatrix} \begin{bmatrix} 107 \\ 101 \end{bmatrix}$$

$$\begin{bmatrix} c \\ w \end{bmatrix} = \begin{bmatrix} 8 \\ 5 \end{bmatrix}$$

The solution is (8, 5). Therefore the price of a citron is 8 and the price of a fragrant wood apple is 5.

**11.** $x = 0.0016$, $y = 0.0126$, $z = 0.0110$. Write a system of three equations and a matrix equation.

$$\begin{cases} 47x + 470y = 6 \\ 280z + 470y = 9 \\ x + z - y = 0 \end{cases} \rightarrow$$

$$\begin{bmatrix} 47 & 470 & 0 \\ 0 & 470 & 280 \\ 1 & -1 & 1 \end{bmatrix} \begin{bmatrix} x \\ y \\ z \end{bmatrix} = \begin{bmatrix} 6 \\ 9 \\ 0 \end{bmatrix}$$

Solve the system by multiplying $[A]^{-1}[B]$. Find $[A]^{-1}$ on your calculator.

$$[X] = [A]^{-1}[B]$$

$$\begin{bmatrix} x \\ y \\ z \end{bmatrix} = \begin{bmatrix} \dfrac{15}{3337} & -\dfrac{1}{355} & \dfrac{56}{71} \\ 0.0017 & 0.0003 & -\dfrac{28}{355} \\ -\dfrac{1}{355} & \dfrac{11}{3550} & \dfrac{47}{355} \end{bmatrix} \begin{bmatrix} 6 \\ 9 \\ 0 \end{bmatrix}$$

$$\begin{bmatrix} x \\ y \\ z \end{bmatrix} = \begin{bmatrix} 0.0016 \\ 0.0126 \\ 0.0110 \end{bmatrix}$$

The solution is $x = 0.0016$, $y = 0.0126$, and $z = 0.0110$. Therefore the current flowing through each resistor is 0.0016, 0.0126, and 0.0110 amps.

**12.** An error message means the system is either dependent or inconsistent. In this system, the lines are the same because the first equation is a multiple of the second equation, so the system is dependent. You can multiply the second equation by 1.6 to get the first equation.

**13. a.** $\begin{bmatrix} 4 & -3 \\ -5 & 4 \end{bmatrix}$

Here are possible row operations on the augmented matrix for finding the inverse.

Augmented matrix $\begin{bmatrix} 4 & 3 & | & 1 & 0 \\ 5 & 4 & | & 0 & 1 \end{bmatrix}$

$-R_1 + R_2 \rightarrow R_1 \quad \begin{bmatrix} 1 & 1 & | & -1 & 1 \\ 5 & 4 & | & 0 & 1 \end{bmatrix}$

$-5R_1 + R_2 \rightarrow R_2 \quad \begin{bmatrix} 1 & 1 & | & -1 & 1 \\ 0 & -1 & | & 5 & -4 \end{bmatrix}$

$R_2 + R_1 \rightarrow R_1 \quad \begin{bmatrix} 1 & 0 & | & 4 & -3 \\ 0 & -1 & | & 5 & -4 \end{bmatrix}$

$\dfrac{R_2}{-1} \rightarrow R_2 \quad \begin{bmatrix} 1 & 0 & | & 4 & -3 \\ 0 & 1 & | & -5 & 4 \end{bmatrix}$

Therefore, $\begin{bmatrix} 4 & -3 \\ -5 & 4 \end{bmatrix}$ is the inverse.

**b.** $\begin{bmatrix} -0.\overline{5} & 1.\overline{4} & 0.\overline{1} \\ 0.5 & -1 & 0 \\ -1.\overline{6} & 2.\overline{3} & 0.\overline{3} \end{bmatrix}$, or $\begin{bmatrix} -\dfrac{5}{9} & \dfrac{13}{9} & \dfrac{1}{9} \\ \dfrac{1}{2} & -1 & 0 \\ -\dfrac{7}{6} & \dfrac{7}{3} & \dfrac{1}{3} \end{bmatrix}$

Here are the possible row operations on the augmented matrix for finding the inverse.

Augmented matrix $\begin{bmatrix} 6 & 4 & -2 & | & 1 & 0 & 0 \\ 3 & 1 & -1 & | & 0 & 1 & 0 \\ 0 & 7 & 3 & | & 0 & 0 & 1 \end{bmatrix}$

$\dfrac{R_1}{2} \rightarrow R_1 \quad \begin{bmatrix} 3 & 2 & -1 & | & \dfrac{1}{2} & 0 & 0 \\ 3 & 1 & -1 & | & 0 & 1 & 0 \\ 0 & 7 & 3 & | & 0 & 0 & 1 \end{bmatrix}$

$-R_2 + R_1 \rightarrow R_1 \quad \begin{bmatrix} 0 & 1 & 0 & | & \dfrac{1}{2} & -1 & 0 \\ 3 & 1 & -1 & | & 0 & 1 & 0 \\ 0 & 7 & 3 & | & 0 & 0 & 1 \end{bmatrix}$

$-7R_1 + R_3 \rightarrow R_3 \quad \begin{bmatrix} 0 & 1 & 0 & | & \dfrac{1}{2} & -1 & 0 \\ 3 & 1 & -1 & | & 0 & 1 & 0 \\ 0 & 0 & 3 & | & -\dfrac{7}{2} & 7 & 1 \end{bmatrix}$

$\dfrac{R_3}{3} \rightarrow R_3 \quad \begin{bmatrix} 0 & 1 & 0 & | & \dfrac{1}{2} & -1 & 0 \\ 3 & 1 & -1 & | & 0 & 1 & 0 \\ 0 & 0 & 1 & | & -\dfrac{7}{6} & \dfrac{7}{3} & \dfrac{1}{3} \end{bmatrix}$

$R_1 \leftrightarrow R_2 \quad \begin{bmatrix} 3 & 1 & -1 & | & 0 & 1 & 0 \\ 0 & 1 & 0 & | & \dfrac{1}{2} & -1 & 0 \\ 0 & 0 & 1 & | & -\dfrac{7}{6} & \dfrac{7}{3} & \dfrac{1}{3} \end{bmatrix}$

$-R_3 + R_1 \rightarrow R_1 \quad \begin{bmatrix} 3 & 0 & 0 & | & -\dfrac{10}{6} & \dfrac{13}{3} & \dfrac{1}{3} \\ 0 & 1 & 0 & | & \dfrac{1}{2} & -1 & 0 \\ 0 & 0 & 1 & | & -\dfrac{7}{6} & \dfrac{7}{3} & \dfrac{1}{3} \end{bmatrix}$

$\dfrac{R_1}{3} \rightarrow R_1 \quad \begin{bmatrix} 1 & 0 & 0 & | & -\dfrac{5}{9} & \dfrac{13}{9} & \dfrac{1}{9} \\ 0 & 1 & 0 & | & \dfrac{1}{2} & -1 & 0 \\ 0 & 0 & 1 & | & -\dfrac{7}{6} & \dfrac{7}{3} & \dfrac{1}{3} \end{bmatrix}$

Therefore, $\begin{bmatrix} -\dfrac{5}{9} & \dfrac{13}{9} & \dfrac{1}{9} \\ \dfrac{1}{2} & -1 & 0 \\ -\dfrac{7}{6} & \dfrac{7}{3} & \dfrac{1}{3} \end{bmatrix}$,

or $\begin{bmatrix} -0.\overline{5} & 1.\overline{4} & 0.\overline{1} \\ 0.5 & -1 & 0 \\ -1.\overline{6} & 2.\overline{3} & 0.\overline{3} \end{bmatrix}$, is the inverse.

**14.** $[X] = \begin{bmatrix} 202.9 \\ 228.6 \\ 165.7 \end{bmatrix}$

First, factor $[X]$ from the right side of the equation $[X] - [A][X] = [D]$ to get $([I] - [A])[X] = [D]$. Solve the equation $([I] - [A])[X] = [D]$ by left-multiplying by the inverse of $([I] - [A])$, or $[X] = ([I] - [A])^{-1}[D]$.

$[I] - [A] = \begin{bmatrix} 1 & 0 & 0 \\ 0 & 1 & 0 \\ 0 & 0 & 1 \end{bmatrix} - \begin{bmatrix} 0.2 & 0.2 & 0.1 \\ 0.2 & 0.4 & 0.1 \\ 0.1 & 0.2 & 0.3 \end{bmatrix}$

$= \begin{bmatrix} 0.8 & -0.2 & -0.1 \\ -0.2 & 0.6 & -0.1 \\ -0.1 & -0.8 & 0.7 \end{bmatrix}$

$([I] - [A])^{-1} = \begin{bmatrix} 1.43 & 0.57 & 0.29 \\ 0.54 & 1.96 & 0.36 \\ 0.36 & 0.64 & 1.57 \end{bmatrix}$

$[X] = \begin{bmatrix} 1.43 & 0.57 & 0.29 \\ 0.54 & 1.96 & 0.36 \\ 0.36 & 0.64 & 1.57 \end{bmatrix} \begin{bmatrix} 100 \\ 80 \\ 50 \end{bmatrix} = \begin{bmatrix} 202.9 \\ 228.6 \\ 165.7 \end{bmatrix}$

To fulfill consumer demand, \$202.9 million worth of agriculture products, \$228.6 million worth of manufacturing, and \$165.7 million worth of services should be produced.

**15.** In each case, you can multiply the original equation by any number to create a consistent and dependent system. Possible answers:

**a.** $2y = 4x + 8$

**b.** $3y = -x - 9$

**c.** $4x + 10y = 20$

**d.** $2x - 4y = -12$

**16.** In each case, you can choose a different constant term and leave all other terms the same to create an inconsistent system. Possible answers:

**a.** $y = 2x + 6$

**b.** $y = -\frac{1}{3}x + 2$

**c.** $2x + 5y = 0$

**d.** $x - 2y = 6$

**17. a.** $[A] = \begin{bmatrix} 0 & 2 & 0 & 1 \\ 2 & 0 & 1 & 0 \\ 0 & 1 & 0 & 1 \\ 1 & 0 & 1 & 0 \end{bmatrix}$

**b.** The value of $a_{22}$ is 0 because there are zero roads connecting Murray to itself.

**c.** The matrix has reflection symmetry across the main diagonal.

**d.** 5; 10. The matrix sum is twice the number of roads. Each road is counted twice in the matrix because it can be traveled in either direction.

**e.** For example, if the road between Davis and Terre is one-way toward Davis, $a_{34}$ changes from 1 to 0. The matrix is no longer symmetric.

**18.** 2. Given that $u_3 = 28$ and $u_7 = 80$, the common difference is $\frac{u_7 - u_3}{7 - 3} = \frac{80 - 28}{4} = \frac{52}{4} = 13$. So the first term, $u_1$, is $u_3 - 2(13) = 28 - 26 = 2$.

### IMPROVING YOUR REASONING SKILLS

Because the cards in the deck are evenly divided (red or black), about half of the 60 people answered each question. About 50% of phone numbers have even last digits, so, of the 30 respondents who answered Question 1, roughly 15 answered yes and 15 answered no. The remainder of the respondents were answering Question 2, so approximately $37 - 15$, or 22, of their responses must have been yes and 8 no. Therefore, of those who answered Question 2, about $\frac{22}{30}$, or 73%, answered yes.

You can also solve this problem with a probability tree diagram.

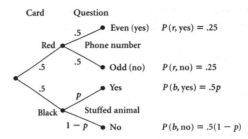

There are 37 yes answers, so $P(\text{yes}) = \frac{37}{60}$.

The tree diagram shows $P(\text{yes}) = .25 + .5p$.

$$\frac{37}{60} = .25 + .5p$$

$$p \approx .73$$

### EXTENSIONS

**A.** See the solution to Take Another Look activity 1 on page 148.

**B.** Research results will vary.

## LESSON 6.5

### EXERCISES

**1. a.** $y < \frac{10 - 2x}{-5}$, or $y < -2 + 0.4x$

$$2x - 5y > 10$$
$$-5y > 10 - 2x$$
$$y < \frac{10 - 2x}{-5}, \text{ or } y < -2 + 0.4x$$

**b.** $y < \frac{6 - 2x}{-12}$, or $y < -\frac{1}{2} + \frac{1}{6}x$

$$4(2 - 3y) + 2x > 14$$
$$8 - 12y + 2x > 14$$
$$-12y > 6 - 2x$$
$$y < \frac{6 - 2x}{-12}, \text{ or } y < -\frac{1}{2} + \frac{1}{6}x$$

**2. a.**

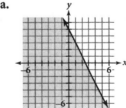

**b.** Rewrite the linear inequality as $y > \frac{5}{2} - x$.

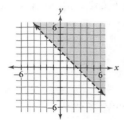

**c.**

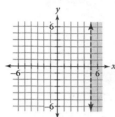

**3. a.** $y < 2 - 0.5x$. The $y$-intercept is 2, the slope is $-0.5$, and the graph is shaded below the dotted boundary line.

**b.** $y \geq 3 + 1.5x$. The $y$-intercept is 3, the slope is 1.5, and the graph is shaded above the solid boundary line.

**c.** $y > 1 - 0.75x$. The $y$-intercept is 1, the slope is $-0.75$, and the graph is shaded above the dotted boundary line.

**d.** $y \leq 1.5 + 0.5x$. The $y$-intercept is 1.5, the slope is 0.5, and the graph is shaded below the solid boundary line.

**4.** $y \geq 2.4x + 2$ and $y \leq -x^2 - 2x + 6.4$. The graph is shaded above the solid boundary line, $y = 2.4x + 2$, and below the solid boundary of the parabola, $y = -x^2 - 2x + 6.4$.

**5.** Vertices: $(0, 2)$, $(0, 5)$, $(2.752, 3.596)$, and $(3.529, 2.353)$. Find the vertices by finding the intersection point of each pair of equations using substitution, elimination, or matrices, or by graphing the lines on your calculator and tracing to the intersection points. You only need to find the intersection points that are vertices of the feasible region.

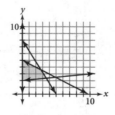

| Equations | Intersection Points |
|---|---|
| $y = 0.1x + 2$ and $x = 0$ | $(0, 2)$ |
| $y = -0.51x + 5$ and $x = 0$ | $(0, 5)$ |
| $y = -0.51x + 5$ and $y = -1.6x + 8$ | $(2.752, 3.596)$ |
| $y = -1.6x + 8$ and $y = 0.1x + 2$ | $(3.529, 2.354)$ |

**6.** Vertices: $(1, 0)$, $(1.875, 0)$, $(3.307, 2.291)$, $(0.209, 0.791)$. Find the vertices by finding the intersection point of each pair of equations using substitution, elimination, or matrices, or by graphing the lines on your calculator and tracing to the intersection points. You only need to find the intersection points that are vertices of the feasible region.

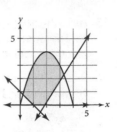

| Equations | Intersection Points |
|---|---|
| $y = 1 - x$ and $y = 0$ | $(1, 0)$ |
| $y = 1.6x - 3$ and $y = 0$ | $(1.875, 0)$ |
| $y = 1.6x - 3$ and $y = -(x - 2)^2 + 4$ | $(3.307, 2.291)$ |
| $y = -(x - 2)^2 + 4$ and $y = 1 - x$ | $(0.209, 0.791)$ |

**7.** Vertices: $(0, 4)$, $(3, 0)$, $(1, 0)$, $(0, 2)$. Find the vertices by finding the intersection point of each pair of equations using substitution, elimination, or matrices, or by graphing the lines on your calculator and tracing to the intersection points. You only need to find the intersection points that are vertices of the feasible region.

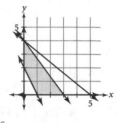

In slope-intercept form, the inequalities are $y \leq \frac{12 - 4x}{3}$, $y \leq \frac{8 - 1.6x}{2}$, and $y \geq 2 - 2x$.

| Equations | Intersection Points |
|---|---|
| $4x + 3y = 12$ and $x = 0$ | $(0, 4)$ |
| $4x + 3y = 12$ and $y = 0$ | $(3, 0)$ |
| $2x + y = 2$ and $y = 0$ | $(1, 0)$ |
| $2x + y = 2$ and $x = 0$ | $(0, 2)$ |

**8.** Vertices: $(1, 0)$, $(2.562, 1.562)$, $(1.658, 2.5)$, $(-1.5, 2.5)$. Find the vertices by finding the intersection point of each pair of equations using substitution, elimination, or matrices, or by graphing the lines on your calculator and tracing to the intersection points. You only need to find the intersection points that are vertices of the feasible region.

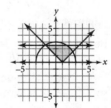

| Equations | Intersection Points |
|---|---|
| $y = |x - 1|$ and $y = 0$ | $(1, 0)$ |
| $y = |x - 1|$ and $y = \sqrt{9 - x^2}$ | $(2.562, 1.562)$ |
| $y = \sqrt{9 - x^2}$ and $y = 2.5$ | $(1.658, 2.5)$ |
| $y = |x - 1|$ and $y = 2.5$ | $(-1.5, 2.5)$ |

*Discovering Advanced Algebra Solutions Manual*
©2004 Key Curriculum Press

You may have noticed you don't actually have to find the intersection point of $y = |x - 1|$ and $y = 0$ because the vertex of $y = |x - 1|$ is $(1, 0)$.

**9. a.** Let $x$ represent length in inches, and let $y$ represent width in inches.

$$\begin{cases} xy \geq 200 \\ xy \leq 300 \\ x + y \geq 33 \\ x + y \leq 40 \end{cases}$$

**b.**

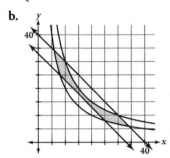

**c. i.** No. Neither $(12.4, 16.3)$ nor $(16.3, 12.4)$ is in the feasible region.

  **ii.** Yes. $(16, 17.5)$ and $(17.5, 16)$ are in the feasible region.

  **iii.** No. Neither $(14.3, 17.5)$ nor $(17.5, 14.3)$ is in the feasible region.

**10. a.** $x > 27767$ km. Substitute 2 for $W$ and solve for $x$.

$$2 = 57 \cdot \frac{6400^2}{(6400 + x)^2}$$

$$2(6400 + x)^2 = 57 \cdot 6400^2$$

$$(6400 + x)^2 = \frac{57 \cdot 6400^2}{2}$$

$$6400^2 + 2(6400)x + x^2 = 1167360000$$

$$40960000 + 12800x + x^2 = 1167360000$$

$$x^2 + 12800x - 1126400000 = 0$$

Use the quadratic formula where $a = 1$, $b = 12800$, and $c = -1126400000$.

$$x = \frac{-(12800) \pm \sqrt{(12800)^2 - 4(1)(-1126400000)}}{2(1)}$$

$x \approx 27767$ or $x \approx -40567$

The altitude cannot be negative, so the astronaut will weigh less than 2 kg at altitudes greater than 27,767 km.

**b.** 50.5 kg. Substitute 400 for $x$ and solve for $W$.

$$W = 57 \cdot \frac{6400^2}{(6400 + 400)^2} \approx 57(0.8858) \approx 50.5 \text{ kg}$$

**c.** In theory no, because as the denominator grows larger, the value of the fraction approaches zero but never gets to zero.

**11. a.** $5x + 2y > 100$

  **b.** $y < 10$

  **c.** $x + y \leq 40$

  **d.** Commonsense constraints: $x \geq 0$, $y \geq 0$

  **e.** $(20, 0)$, $(40, 0)$, $(30, 10)$, $(16, 10)$

**12. a.** $a = 3$, $b = 16$, $c = -12$. First, substitute the coordinate pairs in the quadratic equation $y = ax^2 + bx + c$ to create a system of three equations in three unknowns, $a$, $b$, and $c$. Set up a matrix equation in the form $[A][X] = [B]$.

$$\begin{cases} -32 = 4a - 2b + c \\ 7 = a + b + c \\ 63 = 9a + 3b + c \end{cases} \rightarrow$$

$$\begin{bmatrix} 4 & -2 & 1 \\ 1 & 1 & 1 \\ 9 & 3 & 1 \end{bmatrix} \begin{bmatrix} a \\ b \\ c \end{bmatrix} = \begin{bmatrix} -32 \\ 7 \\ 63 \end{bmatrix}$$

To find the solution to the system, multiply $[A]^{-1}[B]$.

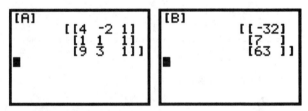

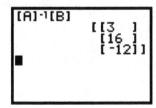

Therefore, $a = 3$, $b = 16$, and $c = -12$.

**b.** $y = 3x^2 + 16x - 12$

**c.** Sample answer: Substitute each point into the equation to verify that it lies on the parabola. Or use a calculator table to make sure all the points fit the equation.

**13.** $a = 100$, $b \approx 0.7$. Substitute the given values for $x$ and $y$ in the exponential equation, $y = ab^x$.

There will be two equations with two variables, $a$ and $b$. Solve the first equation for $a$ in terms of $b$, and use substitution to find the values of $a$ and $b$.

$34.3 = ab^3$, so $a = \dfrac{34.3}{b^3}$

$8.2 = ab^7$

$8.2 = \left(\dfrac{34.3}{b^3}\right)b^7$

$8.2 = 34.3b^4$

$b^4 = \dfrac{8.2}{34.3}$

$b \approx 0.7$

Substitute 0.7 for $b$ in either equation to solve for $a$.

$a = \dfrac{34.3}{(0.7)^3} = 100$

Therefore, $a = 100$ and $b \approx 0.7$.

**14.** $\begin{bmatrix} 3 & -1 & | & 5 \\ -4 & 2 & | & 1 \end{bmatrix}$, $\dfrac{1}{3}R_1 \to R_1$, $\begin{bmatrix} 1 & -\dfrac{1}{3} & | & \dfrac{5}{3} \\ -4 & 2 & | & 1 \end{bmatrix}$,

$4R_1 + R_2 \to R_2$, $\begin{bmatrix} 1 & -\dfrac{1}{3} & | & \dfrac{5}{3} \\ 0 & \dfrac{2}{3} & | & \dfrac{23}{3} \end{bmatrix}$,

$\dfrac{3}{2}R_2 \to R_2$, $\begin{bmatrix} 1 & -\dfrac{1}{3} & | & \dfrac{5}{3} \\ 0 & 1 & | & \dfrac{23}{2} \end{bmatrix}$,

$\dfrac{1}{3}R_2 + R_1 \to R_1$, $\begin{bmatrix} 1 & 0 & | & \dfrac{11}{2} \\ 0 & 1 & | & \dfrac{23}{2} \end{bmatrix}$

**15. a.** 2 or 3 spores. Substitute 0 for $x$:
$y = f(0) = (2.68)(3.84)^0 = 2.68$.

**b.** About 1,868,302 spores. Substitute 10 for $x$:
$y = f(10) = (2.68)(3.84)^{10} = 1868301.824 \approx 1868302$.

**c.** $x = \dfrac{\log \frac{y}{2.68}}{\log 3.84}$. Solve for $x$ in terms of $y$ to find the inverse function.

$y = (2.68)(3.84)^x$

$\dfrac{y}{2.68} = (3.84)^x$

$\log \dfrac{y}{2.68} = \log(3.84)^x$

$\log \dfrac{y}{2.68} = x\log(3.84)$

$x = \dfrac{\log \frac{y}{2.68}}{\log 3.84}$

**d.** After 14 hr 40 min. Substitute $1.0 \times 10^9$ for $y$.

$y = \dfrac{\log \frac{1.0 \times 10^9}{2.68}}{\log 3.84} \approx 14.67$

0.67, or $\frac{2}{3}$, of an hour is 40 minutes, so the number of spores will exceed 1 billion after 14 hours 40 minutes.

**IMPROVING YOUR REASONING SKILLS**

The message says, "If eyes have no tears the soul can have no rainbow."

This coded message uses the same coding matrix $[E]$, so to decode, use the inverse, $\begin{bmatrix} 2 & 1 \\ 1 & 1 \end{bmatrix}$.

Begin by breaking the letters into groups of four letters each.

CCFS LGGT QNYP OPII YUCB DKIC BYFB EQQW WURQ LPRE

Convert the letters to numbers and multiply by the inverse of the coding matrix, $[E]^{-1} = \begin{bmatrix} 2 & 1 \\ 1 & 1 \end{bmatrix}$, and then convert back into the corresponding letter in the alphabet.

CCFS: $\begin{bmatrix} 3 & 3 \\ 6 & 19 \end{bmatrix} [E]^{-1} = \begin{bmatrix} 9 & 6 \\ 31 & 25 \end{bmatrix} \to$

$\begin{bmatrix} 9 & 6 \\ 5 & 25 \end{bmatrix} \to \begin{bmatrix} I & F \\ E & Y \end{bmatrix}$

LGGT: $\begin{bmatrix} 12 & 7 \\ 7 & 20 \end{bmatrix} [E]^{-1} = \begin{bmatrix} 31 & 19 \\ 34 & 27 \end{bmatrix} \to$

$\begin{bmatrix} 5 & 19 \\ 8 & 1 \end{bmatrix} \to \begin{bmatrix} E & S \\ H & A \end{bmatrix}$

QNYP: $\begin{bmatrix} 17 & 14 \\ 25 & 16 \end{bmatrix} [E]^{-1} = \begin{bmatrix} 48 & 31 \\ 66 & 41 \end{bmatrix} \to$

$\begin{bmatrix} 22 & 5 \\ 14 & 15 \end{bmatrix} \to \begin{bmatrix} V & E \\ N & O \end{bmatrix}$

OPII: $\begin{bmatrix} 15 & 16 \\ 9 & 9 \end{bmatrix} [E]^{-1} = \begin{bmatrix} 46 & 31 \\ 27 & 18 \end{bmatrix} \to$

$\begin{bmatrix} 20 & 5 \\ 1 & 18 \end{bmatrix} \to \begin{bmatrix} T & E \\ A & R \end{bmatrix}$

YUCB: $\begin{bmatrix} 25 & 21 \\ 3 & 2 \end{bmatrix} [E]^{-1} = \begin{bmatrix} 71 & 46 \\ 8 & 5 \end{bmatrix} \to$

$\begin{bmatrix} 19 & 20 \\ 8 & 5 \end{bmatrix} \to \begin{bmatrix} S & T \\ H & E \end{bmatrix}$

DKIC: $\begin{bmatrix} 4 & 11 \\ 9 & 3 \end{bmatrix} [E]^{-1} = \begin{bmatrix} 19 & 15 \\ 21 & 12 \end{bmatrix} \to$

$\begin{bmatrix} S & O \\ U & L \end{bmatrix}$

BYFB: $\begin{bmatrix} 2 & 25 \\ 6 & 2 \end{bmatrix} [E]^{-1} = \begin{bmatrix} 29 & 27 \\ 14 & 8 \end{bmatrix} \rightarrow$

$\begin{bmatrix} 3 & 1 \\ 14 & 8 \end{bmatrix} \rightarrow \begin{bmatrix} C & A \\ N & H \end{bmatrix}$

EQQW: $\begin{bmatrix} 5 & 17 \\ 17 & 23 \end{bmatrix} [E]^{-1} = \begin{bmatrix} 27 & 22 \\ 57 & 40 \end{bmatrix} \rightarrow$

$\begin{bmatrix} 1 & 22 \\ 5 & 14 \end{bmatrix} \rightarrow \begin{bmatrix} A & V \\ E & N \end{bmatrix}$

WURQ: $\begin{bmatrix} 23 & 21 \\ 18 & 17 \end{bmatrix} [E]^{-1} = \begin{bmatrix} 67 & 44 \\ 53 & 35 \end{bmatrix} \rightarrow$

$\begin{bmatrix} 15 & 18 \\ 1 & 9 \end{bmatrix} \rightarrow \begin{bmatrix} O & R \\ A & I \end{bmatrix}$

LPRE: $\begin{bmatrix} 12 & 16 \\ 18 & 5 \end{bmatrix} [E]^{-1} = \begin{bmatrix} 40 & 28 \\ 41 & 23 \end{bmatrix} \rightarrow$

$\begin{bmatrix} 14 & 2 \\ 15 & 23 \end{bmatrix} \begin{bmatrix} N & B \\ O & W \end{bmatrix}$

Arrange the letters in order and decipher the encoded message.

IFEY ESHA VENO TEAR STHE SOUL CANH AVEN ORAI NBOW

## LESSON 6.6

### EXERCISES

**1.**

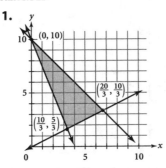

**2.** In 2a–d, substitute the coordinates of the vertices of the feasible region for $x$ and $y$ in each expression to find the maximum or minimum value.

**a.** $\left( \dfrac{20}{3}, \dfrac{10}{3} \right)$

$(0, 10)$: $5(0) + 2(10) = 20$

$\left( \dfrac{10}{3}, \dfrac{5}{3} \right)$: $5\left( \dfrac{10}{3} \right) + 2\left( \dfrac{5}{3} \right) = \dfrac{60}{3} = 20$

$\left( \dfrac{20}{3}, \dfrac{10}{3} \right)$: $5\left( \dfrac{20}{3} \right) + 2\left( \dfrac{10}{3} \right) = \dfrac{120}{3} = 40$

The vertex $\left( \dfrac{20}{3}, \dfrac{10}{3} \right)$ gives the largest value and thus maximizes the expression.

**b.** $\left( \dfrac{10}{3}, \dfrac{5}{3} \right)$

$(0, 10)$: $0 + 3(10) = 30$

$\left( \dfrac{10}{3}, \dfrac{5}{3} \right)$: $\dfrac{10}{3} + 3\left( \dfrac{5}{3} \right) = \dfrac{25}{3}$

$\left( \dfrac{20}{3}, \dfrac{10}{3} \right)$: $\dfrac{20}{3} + 3\left( \dfrac{10}{3} \right) = \dfrac{50}{3}$

The vertex $\left( \dfrac{10}{3}, \dfrac{5}{3} \right)$ gives the smallest value and thus minimizes the expression.

**c.** $(0, 10)$

$(0, 10)$: $0 + 4(10) = 40$

$\left( \dfrac{10}{3}, \dfrac{5}{3} \right)$: $\dfrac{10}{3} + 4\left( \dfrac{5}{3} \right) = \dfrac{30}{3} = 10$

$\left( \dfrac{20}{3}, \dfrac{10}{3} \right)$: $\dfrac{20}{3} + 4\left( \dfrac{10}{3} \right) = \dfrac{60}{3} = 20$

The vertex $(0, 10)$ gives the largest value and thus maximizes the expression.

**d.** $(0, 10)$

$(0, 10)$: $5(0) + 10 = 10$

$\left( \dfrac{10}{3}, \dfrac{5}{3} \right)$: $5\left( \dfrac{10}{3} \right) + \dfrac{5}{3} = \dfrac{55}{3}$

$\left( \dfrac{20}{3}, \dfrac{10}{3} \right)$: $5\left( \dfrac{20}{3} \right) + \dfrac{10}{3} = \dfrac{110}{3}$

The vertex $(0, 10)$ gives the smallest value and thus minimizes the expression.

**e.** It is not always obvious which point provides a maximum or minimum value.

**3.**

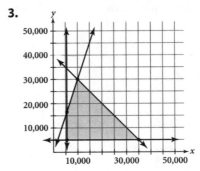

Vertices: $(5500, 5000)$, $(5500, 16500)$, $(10000, 30000)$, $(35000, 5000)$. The vertex $(10000, 30000)$ maximizes the function at $P = 3800$. Substitute the coordinates of each vertex into the function $P = 0.08x + 0.10y$.

$(5500, 5000)$: $P = 0.08(5500) + 0.10(5000) = 940$

$(5500, 16500)$: $P = 0.08(5500) + 0.10(16500) = 2090$

$(10000, 30000)$: $P = 0.08(10000) + 0.10(30000) = 3800$

$(35000, 5000)$: $P = 0.08(35000) + 0.10(5000) = 3300$

The integer coordinates of the vertex $(10000, 30000)$ maximize the function.

**4. a.** There are zero or more pairs of each species in the region.

**b.** The area required by species X plus the area required by species Y is no more than 180,000 m².

**c.** The total food requirement of species X plus the total food requirement of species Y is no more than 72,000 kg.

**d.**

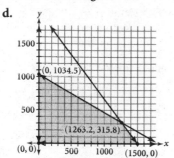

**e.** The maximum number of nesting pairs is 1578. Evaluate the function $N = x + y$ at each of the vertices.

$(0, 1034.5)$: $N = 0 + 1034.5 = 1034.5$

$(1263.2, 315.8)$: $N = 1263.2 + 315.8 = 1579$

$(1500, 0)$: $N = 1500 + 0 = 1500$

The vertex $(1263.2, 315.8)$ gives the largest value, but you need integer points because $x$ and $y$ represent the number of nesting pairs of birds. Any of the integer points around $(1263.2, 315.8)$, which are $(1261, 317)$, $(1262, 316)$, $(1263, 315)$, $(1264, 314)$, and $(1265, 313)$, give the maximum number of nesting pairs, 1578.

**5. a.** Possible answer:

$$\begin{cases} y \geq 7 \\ y \leq \dfrac{7}{5}(x - 3) + 6 \\ y \leq -\dfrac{7}{12}x + 13 \end{cases}$$

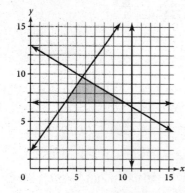

**b.** Possible answer:

$$\begin{cases} x \geq 0 \\ y \geq 7 \\ y \geq \dfrac{7}{5}(x - 3) + 6 \\ y \leq -\dfrac{7}{12}x + 13 \end{cases}$$

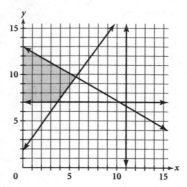

**c.** Possible answer:

$$\begin{cases} x \geq 0 \\ y \geq 0 \\ x \leq 11 \\ y \leq \dfrac{7}{5}(x - 3) + 6 \\ y \leq 7 \end{cases}$$

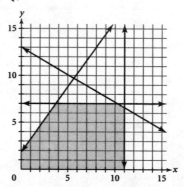

**6.** 12 sled dogs and 12 poodles for a maximum profit of $3360. Let $x$ represent the number of sled dogs, and let $y$ represent the number of poodles. Organize the constraint information into a table, and then write inequalities that reflect the constraints. Be sure to include commonsense constraints.

| | Number of sled dogs, $x$ | Number of poodles, $y$ | Limiting value |
|---|---|---|---|
| **Maximum poodles** | | $y$ | $\leq 20$ |
| **Maximum sled dogs** | $x$ | | $\leq 15$ |
| **Food** | 6 | 2 | $\leq 100$ |
| **Training** | 250 | 1000 | $\leq 15000$ |
| **Profit** | 80 | 200 | Maximize |

*Discovering Advanced Algebra Solutions Manual*
©2004 Key Curriculum Press

$$\begin{cases} y \le 20 \\ x \le 15 \\ 6x + 2y \le 100 \\ 250x + 1000y \le 15000 \\ x \ge 0 \\ y \ge 0 \end{cases}$$

$profit = 80x + 200y$

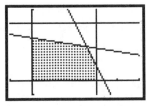

$[-5, 25, 5, -5, 25, 5]$

The vertices of the feasible region are $(0, 0)$, $(15, 0)$, $(15, 5)$, $(12.7273, 11.8182)$, and $(0, 15)$. Evaluate the function $profit = 80x + 200y$ at each of the vertices.

$(0, 0)$: $profit = 80(0) + 200(0) = 0$

$(15, 0)$: $profit = 80(15) + 200(0) = 1200$

$(15, 5)$: $profit = 80(15) + 200(5) = 1120$

$(12.7273, 11.8182)$: $profit = 80(12.7273) + 200(11.8182) = 3381.82$

$(0, 15)$: $profit = 80(0) + 200(15) = 3000$

The vertex $(12.7273, 11.8182)$ maximizes the function but does not represent whole values for dogs. The closest integer point to $(12.7273, 11.8182)$ in the feasible region, which has the largest profit, is $(12, 12)$: $profit = 80(12) + 200(12) = \$3360$. Therefore, to maximize profits, they should raise 12 sled dogs and 12 poodles.

7. 5 radio minutes and 10 newspaper ads to reach a maximum of 155,000 people. This requires the assumption that people who listen to the radio are independent of people who read the newspaper, which is probably not realistic, and that the shop must buy both radio minutes and newspaper ads.

Let $x$ represent the number of newspaper ads and $y$ represent the number of minutes of radio advertising. Use the constraints to write this system of inequalities:

$$\begin{cases} x \ge 4 \\ y \ge 5 \\ 50x + 100y \le 1000 \end{cases}$$

$people = 8000x + 15000y$

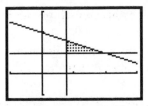

$[-5, 15, 5, -5, 15, 5]$

The vertices of the feasible region are $(4, 5)$, $(4, 8)$, and $(10, 5)$. Test which point gives the largest number of people reached. Evaluate the function $people = 8000x + 15000y$ at each of the vertices.

$(4, 5)$: $people = 8000(4) + 15000(5) = 107{,}000$

$(4, 8)$: $people = 8000(4) + 15000(8) = 152{,}000$

$(10, 5)$: $people = 8000(10) + 15000(5) = 155{,}000$

Therefore, place 10 radio ads and 5 newspaper ads to reach a maximum of 155,000 people.

If the store places 20 radio ads and 0 newspaper ads, 160,000 people are reached. If it places 0 radio ads and 10 newspaper ads, 150,000 people are reached. Therefore the store could place 20 radio ads and no newspaper ads to reach the most people.

8. 600 barrels each of low-sulfur oil and high-sulfur oil for a minimum total cost of \$19,920. Let $x$ represent the number of barrels of low-sulfur oil, and let $y$ represent the number of barrels of high-sulfur oil. Use the constraints to create this system of inequalities:

$$\begin{cases} x + y \ge 1200 \\ 0.02x + 0.06y \le 0.04(x + y) \\ x \ge 0 \\ y \ge 0 \end{cases}$$

$cost = 18.50x + 14.70y$

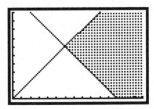

$[0, 1500, 100, 0, 1000, 100]$

The vertices of the feasible region are $(1200, 0)$ and $(600, 600)$. Test which points minimize cost.

$(1200, 0)$: $cost = 18.50(1200) + 14.70(0) = 22200$

$(600, 600)$: $cost = 18.50(600) + 14.70(600) = 19920$

Therefore the minimum cost of \$19,920 occurs when you use 600 barrels of low-sulfur oil and 600 barrels of high-sulfur oil.

**9.** 3000 acres of coffee and 4500 acres of cocoa for a maximum total income of \$289,800. Let $x$ represent the number of acres of coffee, and let $y$ represent the number of acres of cocoa. Use the constraints to write this system:

$$\begin{cases} x + y \leq 7500 \\ x \geq 2450 \\ y \geq 1230 \\ 30x + 40y \leq 270000 \end{cases}$$

$profit = 1.26(30x) + .98(40y) = 37.8x + 39.2y$

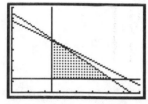

[0, 8000, 1000, 0, 8000, 1000]

The vertices of the feasible region are (2450, 1230), (2450, 4912.5), (3000, 4500), and (6270, 1230). Test which point maximizes profit.

(2450, 1230): $profit = 37.8(2450) + 39.2(1230) = 140826$

(2450, 4912.5): $profit = 37.8(2450) + 39.2(4912.5) = 92610 + 192570 = 285180$

(3000, 4500): $profit = 37.8(3000) + 39.2(4500) = 113400 + 176400 = 289800$

(6270, 1230): $profit = 37.8(6270) + 39.2(1230) = 237006 + 48216 = 285222$

Therefore the maximum profit of \$289,000 occurs when you plant 3000 acres of coffee and 4500 acres of cocoa.

**10. a.** Let $x$ represent the length in inches, and let $y$ represent the girth in inches.

$$\begin{cases} x + y \leq 130 \\ x \leq 108 \\ x > 0 \\ y > 0 \end{cases}$$

**b.**

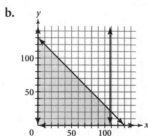

**c.** Yes. For this box, $x = 20$ and $y = 2 \cdot 14 + 2 \cdot 8 = 44$. The point (20, 14) is in the feasible region.

**11. a.** $x = -\frac{7}{11}, y = \frac{169}{11}$

First, solve by using elimination.

$16x + 6y = 82$  Multiply the first equation by 2.

$-27x - 6y = -75$  Multiply the second equation by $-3$.

$-11x = 7$  Add the two equations.

$x = -\frac{7}{11}$  Divide both sides by $-11$.

Substitute $-\frac{7}{11}$ for $x$ in the first equation and solve for $y$.

$8\left(-\frac{7}{11}\right) + 3y = 41$

$3y = 41 + \frac{56}{11} = \frac{451 + 56}{11} = \frac{507}{11}$

$y = \frac{169}{11}$

By elimination, $x = -\frac{7}{11}$ and $y = \frac{169}{11}$.

Second, solve the system using matrices. Enter the coefficients of the variables into matrix $[A]$, the variables into matrix $[X]$, and the constant terms into matrix $[B]$.

To find the solution to the system, find $[A]^{-1}[B]$.

$$\begin{bmatrix} 8 & 3 \\ 9 & 2 \end{bmatrix}\begin{bmatrix} x \\ y \end{bmatrix} = \begin{bmatrix} 41 \\ 25 \end{bmatrix}$$

$$[A]^{-1} = \begin{bmatrix} -\frac{2}{11} & \frac{3}{11} \\ \frac{9}{11} & -\frac{8}{11} \end{bmatrix}$$

$$\begin{bmatrix} x \\ y \end{bmatrix} = \begin{bmatrix} -\frac{2}{11} & \frac{3}{11} \\ \frac{9}{11} & -\frac{8}{11} \end{bmatrix}\begin{bmatrix} 41 \\ 25 \end{bmatrix}$$

$$\begin{bmatrix} x \\ y \end{bmatrix} = \begin{bmatrix} -\frac{7}{11} \\ \frac{169}{11} \end{bmatrix}$$

By the matrix method, $x = -\frac{7}{11}$ and $y = \frac{169}{11}$.

*Discovering Advanced Algebra Solutions Manual*
©2004 Key Curriculum Press

**b.** $x = -3.5$, $y = 74$, $z = 31$. First, solve by using elimination.

| | |
|---|---|
| $-4x - 2y + 4z = -10$ | Multiply the first equation by $-2$. |
| $\underline{6x + 2y - 4z = \quad 3}$ | The second equation. |
| $2x \qquad\qquad = -7$ | Add the two equations. |
| $x = -3.5$ | Divide both sides by 2. |

| | |
|---|---|
| $2x + y - 2z = 5$ | The first equation. |
| $\underline{4x - y + 3z = 5}$ | The third equation. |
| $6x \qquad + z = 10$ | Add the first and third equations. |
| $6(-3.5) + z = 10$ | Substitute $-3.5$ for $x$ in the resulting equation and solve for $z$. |
| $z = 31$ | Add 21 to both sides. |

| | |
|---|---|
| $2(-3.5) + y - 2(31) = 5$ | Substitute $-3.5$ for $x$ and 31 for $z$ in the first equation and solve for $y$. |
| $-7 + y - 62 = 5$ | Multiply. |
| $y = 74$ | Add 69 to both sides. |

By elimination, $x = -3.5$, $y = 74$, and $z = 31$.

Second, solve the system by using matrices. Write the system in matrix form and multiply $[A]^{-1}[B]$ to find the solution.

$$[A][X] = [B]$$

$$\begin{bmatrix} 2 & 1 & -2 \\ 6 & 2 & -4 \\ 4 & -1 & 3 \end{bmatrix} \begin{bmatrix} x \\ y \\ z \end{bmatrix} = \begin{bmatrix} 5 \\ 3 \\ 5 \end{bmatrix}$$

$$\begin{bmatrix} x \\ y \\ z \end{bmatrix} = \begin{bmatrix} -1 & 0.5 & 0 \\ 17 & -7 & 2 \\ 7 & -3 & 1 \end{bmatrix} \begin{bmatrix} 5 \\ 3 \\ 5 \end{bmatrix}$$

$$\begin{bmatrix} x \\ y \\ z \end{bmatrix} = \begin{bmatrix} -3.5 \\ 74 \\ 31 \end{bmatrix}$$

By the matrix method, $x = -3.5$, $y = 74$, and $z = 31$.

**12.**

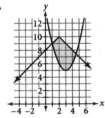

**13.** $\begin{cases} x \geq 2 \\ y \leq 5 \\ x + y \geq 3 \\ 2x - y \leq 9 \end{cases}$

**14. a.** $\begin{bmatrix} 2 & -1 & \bigg| & \frac{1}{2} \\ 5 & -2 & \bigg| & -5 \end{bmatrix}$

**b.** $\begin{bmatrix} 1 & 0 & \bigg| & -6 \\ 0 & 1 & \bigg| & -12.5 \end{bmatrix}$; $(-6, -12.5)$

```
[A]
      [[2 -1 .5]
       [5 -2 -5]]
rref([A])
      [[1 0 -6   ]
       [0 1 -12.5]]
■
```

**c.**

$$y = 2x - \frac{1}{2}$$
$$-12.5 \overset{?}{=} 2(-6) - \frac{1}{2}$$
$$-12.5 = -12.5$$

$$5x - 2y + 5 = 0$$
$$5(-6) - 2(-12.5) + 5 \overset{?}{=} 0$$
$$-30 + 25 + 5 \overset{?}{=} 0$$
$$0 = 0$$

The solution checks.

**15.** $y = -\left(\frac{x}{2}\right)^2 - \frac{3}{2}$ or $y = -\frac{1}{4}x^2 - \frac{3}{2}$. The parabola, with parent function $y = x^2$, is reflected across the $x$-axis, shrunk vertically by a factor of $\frac{1}{4}$, and translated down $\frac{3}{2}$ units.

**EXTENSIONS**

**A.** See the solution to Take Another Look activity 3 on page 148.

**B.** Research results will vary.

## CHAPTER 6 REVIEW

**EXERCISES**

**1. a.** The matrices are impossible to add because the dimensions are not the same.

**b.** $\begin{bmatrix} -3 - 1 & 7 - 0 \\ 6 - 5 & 4 - 2 \end{bmatrix} = \begin{bmatrix} -4 & 7 \\ 1 & 2 \end{bmatrix}$

**c.** $\begin{bmatrix} 4(-3) & 4(1) & 4(2) \\ 4(2) & 4(3) & 4(-2) \end{bmatrix} =$

$\begin{bmatrix} -12 & 4 & 8 \\ 8 & 12 & -8 \end{bmatrix}$

**d.** $\begin{bmatrix} 1(-3) + 0(2) & 1(1) + 0(3) & 1(2) + 0(-2) \\ 5(-3) + 2(2) & 5(1) + 2(3) & 5(2) + 2(-2) \end{bmatrix} =$

$\begin{bmatrix} -3 & 1 & 2 \\ -11 & 11 & 6 \end{bmatrix}$

**e.** The matrices are impossible to multiply because the inside dimensions do not match.

**f.** $[1(-3) + (-2)(2) \quad 1(1) + (-2)(3) \quad 1(2) + (-2)(-2)] = [-7 \quad -5 \quad 6]$

**2. a.** $\begin{bmatrix} 0.8 & -0.6 \\ 0.2 & -0.4 \end{bmatrix}$

Write an equation in the form $[A][A]^{-1} = [I]$.

Let $[A]^{-1} = \begin{bmatrix} a & b \\ c & d \end{bmatrix}$.

$\begin{bmatrix} 2 & -3 \\ 1 & -4 \end{bmatrix}\begin{bmatrix} a & b \\ c & d \end{bmatrix} = \begin{bmatrix} 2a - 3c & 2b - 3d \\ 1a - 4c & 1b - 4d \end{bmatrix}$

$= \begin{bmatrix} 1 & 0 \\ 0 & 1 \end{bmatrix}$

Set corresponding entries equal.

$2a - 3c = 1 \quad 2b - 3d = 0$

$a - 4c = 0 \quad b - 4d = 1$

Treat the equation as two systems of equations. Use substitution or elimination to solve.

$\begin{cases} 2a - 3c = 1 \\ a - 4c = 0 \end{cases}$; $a = 0.8$ and $c = 0.2$

$\begin{cases} 2b - 3d = 0 \\ b - 4d = 1 \end{cases}$; $b = -0.6$ and $d = -0.4$

Use the four variables to write the inverse.

$[A]^{-1} = \begin{bmatrix} a & b \\ c & d \end{bmatrix} = \begin{bmatrix} 0.8 & -0.6 \\ 0.2 & -0.4 \end{bmatrix}$

**b.** $\begin{bmatrix} -\dfrac{3}{85} & \dfrac{16}{85} & -\dfrac{2}{85} \\ \dfrac{18}{85} & -\dfrac{11}{85} & \dfrac{12}{85} \\ -\dfrac{32}{85} & \dfrac{29}{85} & \dfrac{7}{85} \end{bmatrix}$, or

$\begin{bmatrix} -0.0353 & 0.1882 & -0.0235 \\ 0.2118 & -0.1294 & 0.1412 \\ -0.3765 & 0.3412 & 0.0824 \end{bmatrix}$

Use your calculator to find $[A]^{-1}$.

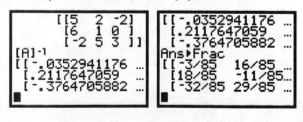

**c.** Does not exist because the second row is a multiple of the first.

**d.** $\begin{bmatrix} -\dfrac{5}{56} & \dfrac{1}{7} & \dfrac{1}{8} \\ -\dfrac{3}{56} & \dfrac{2}{7} & -\dfrac{1}{8} \\ -\dfrac{29}{56} & \dfrac{3}{7} & \dfrac{1}{8} \end{bmatrix}$, or

$\begin{bmatrix} -0.0893 & 0.1429 & 0.125 \\ -0.0536 & 0.2857 & -0.125 \\ -0.5179 & 0.4286 & 0.125 \end{bmatrix}$

Write the matrix augmented by an identity matrix.

$\begin{bmatrix} 5 & 2 & -3 & | & 1 & 0 & 0 \\ 5 & 3 & -1 & | & 0 & 1 & 0 \\ 7 & -2 & -1 & | & 0 & 0 & 1 \end{bmatrix}$

Use your calculator's reduced row-echelon command to get the inverse on the right.

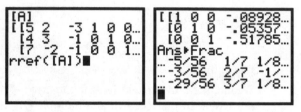

**3. a.** $x = 2.5$, $y = 7$. Write the system as an augmented matrix.

$\begin{cases} 8x - 5y = -15 \\ 6x + 4y = 43 \end{cases} \rightarrow \begin{bmatrix} 8 & -5 & | & -15 \\ 6 & 4 & | & 43 \end{bmatrix}$

Here is one possible sequence of row operations to obtain a solution matrix.

$4R_1 + 5R_2 \rightarrow R_1 \quad \begin{bmatrix} 62 & 0 & | & 155 \\ 6 & 4 & | & 43 \end{bmatrix}$

$\dfrac{R_1}{62} \rightarrow R_1 \quad \begin{bmatrix} 1 & 0 & | & 2.5 \\ 6 & 4 & | & 43 \end{bmatrix}$

$-6R_1 + R_2 \rightarrow R_2 \quad \begin{bmatrix} 1 & 0 & | & 2.5 \\ 0 & 4 & | & 28 \end{bmatrix}$

$\dfrac{R_2}{4} \rightarrow R_2 \quad \begin{bmatrix} 1 & 0 & | & 2.5 \\ 0 & 1 & | & 7 \end{bmatrix}$

The solution is $x = 2.5$ and $y = 7$.

**b.** $x = 1.22$, $y = 6.9$, $z = 3.4$. Write the system as an augmented matrix.

$\begin{cases} 5x + 3y - 7z = 3 \\ 10x - 4y + 6z = 5 \\ 15x + y - 8z = -2 \end{cases} \rightarrow \begin{bmatrix} 5 & 3 & -7 & | & 3 \\ 10 & -4 & 6 & | & 5 \\ 15 & 1 & -8 & | & -2 \end{bmatrix}$

Here is one possible sequence of row operations to obtain a solution matrix.

$-2R_1 + R_2 \to R_2 \quad \begin{bmatrix} 5 & 3 & -7 & | & 3 \\ 0 & -10 & 20 & | & -1 \\ 15 & 1 & -8 & | & -2 \end{bmatrix}$

$-3R_1 + R_3 \to R_3 \quad \begin{bmatrix} 5 & 3 & -7 & | & 3 \\ 0 & -10 & 20 & | & -1 \\ 0 & -8 & 13 & | & -11 \end{bmatrix}$

$\dfrac{R_2}{-10} \to R_2 \quad \begin{bmatrix} 5 & 3 & -7 & | & 3 \\ 0 & 1 & -2 & | & 0.1 \\ 0 & -8 & 13 & | & -11 \end{bmatrix}$

$8R_2 + R_3 \to R_3 \quad \begin{bmatrix} 5 & 3 & -7 & | & 3 \\ 0 & 1 & -2 & | & 0.1 \\ 0 & 0 & -3 & | & -10.2 \end{bmatrix}$

$\dfrac{R_3}{-3} \to R_3 \quad \begin{bmatrix} 5 & 3 & -7 & | & 3 \\ 0 & 1 & -2 & | & 0.1 \\ 0 & 0 & 1 & | & 3.4 \end{bmatrix}$

$-3R_2 + R_1 \to R_1 \quad \begin{bmatrix} 5 & 0 & -1 & | & 2.7 \\ 0 & 1 & -2 & | & 0.1 \\ 0 & 0 & 1 & | & 3.4 \end{bmatrix}$

$2R_3 + R_2 \to R_2 \quad \begin{bmatrix} 5 & 0 & -1 & | & 2.7 \\ 0 & 1 & 0 & | & 6.9 \\ 0 & 0 & 1 & | & 3.4 \end{bmatrix}$

$R_3 + R_1 \to R_1 \quad \begin{bmatrix} 5 & 0 & 0 & | & 6.1 \\ 0 & 1 & 0 & | & 6.9 \\ 0 & 0 & 1 & | & 3.4 \end{bmatrix}$

$\dfrac{R_1}{5} \to R_1 \quad \begin{bmatrix} 1 & 0 & 0 & | & 1.22 \\ 0 & 1 & 0 & | & 6.9 \\ 0 & 0 & 1 & | & 3.4 \end{bmatrix}$

The solution is $x = 1.22$, $y = 6.9$, and $z = 3.4$.

4. In each problem, enter the coefficients of the variables into matrix $[A]$, the variables into matrix $[X]$, and the constant terms into matrix $[B]$. To find the solution to the system, multiply $[A]^{-1}[B]$.

a. $x = 2.5$, $y = 7$

$$[A][X] = [B]$$

$$\begin{bmatrix} 8 & -5 \\ 6 & 4 \end{bmatrix}\begin{bmatrix} x \\ y \end{bmatrix} = \begin{bmatrix} -15 \\ 43 \end{bmatrix}$$

$$\begin{bmatrix} x \\ y \end{bmatrix} = \begin{bmatrix} \dfrac{2}{31} & \dfrac{5}{62} \\ -\dfrac{3}{31} & \dfrac{4}{31} \end{bmatrix}\begin{bmatrix} -15 \\ 43 \end{bmatrix}$$

$$\begin{bmatrix} x \\ y \end{bmatrix} = \begin{bmatrix} 2.5 \\ 7 \end{bmatrix}$$

The solution to the system is $x = 2.5$ and $y = 7$.

b. $x = 1.22$, $y = 6.9$, $z = 3.4$

$$[A][X] = [B]$$

$$\begin{bmatrix} 5 & 3 & -7 \\ 10 & -4 & 6 \\ 15 & 1 & -8 \end{bmatrix}\begin{bmatrix} x \\ y \\ z \end{bmatrix} = \begin{bmatrix} 3 \\ 5 \\ -2 \end{bmatrix}$$

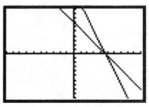

$$\begin{bmatrix} x \\ y \\ z \end{bmatrix} = \begin{bmatrix} \dfrac{13}{75} & \dfrac{17}{150} & -\dfrac{1}{15} \\ \dfrac{17}{15} & \dfrac{13}{30} & -\dfrac{2}{3} \\ \dfrac{7}{15} & \dfrac{4}{15} & -\dfrac{1}{3} \end{bmatrix}\begin{bmatrix} 3 \\ 5 \\ -2 \end{bmatrix}$$

$$\begin{bmatrix} x \\ y \\ z \end{bmatrix} = \begin{bmatrix} 1.22 \\ 6.9 \\ 3.4 \end{bmatrix}$$

The solution to the system is $x = 1.22$, $y = 6.9$, and $z = 3.4$.

5. a. Consistent and independent. By graphing, you can see that the system of equations has only one solution.

[−10, 10, 1, −10, 10, 1]

b. Consistent and dependent. Rewrite the first equation as $y = \frac{1}{4}x + 3$ by distributing $\frac{1}{4}$ and combining like terms. You can see that it is the same as the second equation, $y = 0.25x + 3$. If you graph the two equations, there will be only one line.

c. Inconsistent. Rewrite the equations in intercept form: $y = \frac{4}{3} - \frac{2}{3}x$ and $y = \frac{13}{9} - \frac{2}{3}x$. The slopes of both lines are $-\frac{2}{3}$ and the $y$-intercepts are different. By graphing, you can verify that the lines are parallel.

d. Inconsistent. If you rewrite the first equation using decimals or the second equation using fractions, you will see that the coefficients of the variables are the same but the constant term is different. Therefore the lines are parallel.

**6. a.**

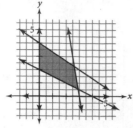

Vertices: $(0, 4)$, $(2.625, 2.25)$, $(3, 0)$, $(0, 2)$

Find the vertex that maximizes $1.65x + 5.2y$.

$(0, 4)$: $1.65(0) + 5.2(4) = 20.8$

$(2.625, 2.25)$: $1.65(2.625) + 5.2(2.25) = 16.03125$

$(3, 0)$: $1.65(3) + 5.2(0) = 4.95$

$(0, 2)$: $1.65(0) + 5.2(2) = 12.05$

The maximum occurs at $(0, 4)$.

**b.**

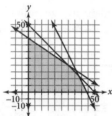

Vertices: $(0, 0)$, $(0, 40)$, $(30, 20)$, $(38, 12)$, $(44, 0)$

Find the vertex that maximizes $6x + 7y$.

$(0, 0)$: $6(0) + 7(0) = 0$

$(0, 40)$: $6(0) + 7(40) = 280$

$(30, 20)$: $6(30) + 7(20) = 320$

$(38, 12)$: $6(38) + 7(12) = 312$

$(44, 0)$: $6(44) + 7(0) = 264$

The maximum occurs at $(30, 20)$.

**7.** About 4.4 yr, or about 4 yr 5 mo. Let $x$ represent the number of years, and let $y$ represent the cost of the water heater.

Cost for old unit: $y = 300 + 75x$

Cost for new unit: $y = 500 + 0.40(75x)$

Write the system as an augmented matrix.

$$\begin{bmatrix} -75 & 1 & | & 300 \\ -30 & 1 & | & 500 \end{bmatrix}$$

Use your calculator to find the reduced row-echelon form.

$$\begin{bmatrix} 1 & 0 & | & 4.\overline{4} \\ 0 & 1 & | & 633.\overline{3} \end{bmatrix}$$

The solution to the system indicates that after 4.4 yr, both water heaters will cost the same, $633.33. Therefore a new heater will pay for itself in about 4.4 yr.

**8. a.** Let $x$ represent the number of parts of the first pre-mixed color, let $y$ represent the number of parts of the second pre-mixed color, and let $z$ represent the number of parts of the third pre-mixed color. The correct portion of red is given by the equation $2x + 1y + 3z = 5$.

**b.** $4x + 0y + 1z = 6$ for yellow; $0x + 2y + 1z = 2$ for black

**c.** $x = \frac{11}{8}$, $y = \frac{3}{4}$, $z = \frac{1}{2}$. Solve the system of equations using matrices.

$$\begin{cases} 2x + 1y + 3z = 5 \\ 4x + 0y + 1z = 6 \to \\ 0x + 2y + 1z = 2 \end{cases} \begin{bmatrix} 2 & 1 & 3 \\ 4 & 0 & 1 \\ 0 & 2 & 1 \end{bmatrix} \begin{bmatrix} x \\ y \\ z \end{bmatrix} = \begin{bmatrix} 5 \\ 6 \\ 2 \end{bmatrix}$$

Use your calculator to find $[A]^{-1}[B]$.

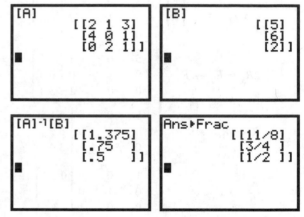

The solution to the system is $x = \frac{11}{8}$, $y = \frac{3}{4}$, and $z = \frac{1}{2}$.

**d.** 8. The least common denominator of the fractions $\frac{11}{8}$, $\frac{3}{4}$, and $\frac{1}{2}$ is 8. Using 8 as a scalar multiplier, $8\left(\frac{11}{8}\right) = 11$, $8\left(\frac{3}{4}\right) = 6$, and $8\left(\frac{1}{2}\right) = 4$.

**e.** 11 parts of the first pre-mixed color, 6 parts of the second pre-mixed color, and 4 parts of the third pre-mixed color will yield the particular color needed.

**9. a.** $\begin{bmatrix} .92 & .08 & 0 \\ .12 & .82 & .06 \\ 0 & .15 & .85 \end{bmatrix}$

**b.** Set up a matrix equation using $[80 \quad 60 \quad 70]$ as the initial matrix to find the populations in the dorms after each month. Recursively multiply by the transition matrix to find the populations in the dorms in the given month.

**i.** October:

$$[80 \quad 60 \quad 70] \begin{bmatrix} .92 & .08 & 0 \\ .12 & .82 & .06 \\ 0 & .15 & .85 \end{bmatrix} =$$

$$[Mozart \quad Picasso \quad Hemingway]$$

Mozart: $80(.92) + 60(.12) = 80.8 \approx 81$

Picasso: $80(.08) + 60(.82) + 70(.15) = 66.1 \approx 66$

Hemingway: $60(.06) + 70(.85) = 63.1 \approx 63$

**ii.** November:

$$[81 \quad 60 \quad 70] \begin{bmatrix} .92 & .08 & 0 \\ .12 & .82 & .06 \\ 0 & .15 & .85 \end{bmatrix} =$$

$$[Mozart \quad Picasso \quad Hemingway]$$

Mozart: $81(.92) + 66(.12) = 82.44 \approx 82$

Picasso: $81(.08) + 66(.82) + 63(.15) = 70.05 \approx 70$

Hemingway: $66(.06) + 63(.85) = 57.51 \approx 58$

**iii.** May: Because May is eight months later, raise the transition matrix to the eighth power and multiply it by the initial matrix.

$$[80 \quad 60 \quad 70] \begin{bmatrix} .92 & .08 & 0 \\ .12 & .82 & .06 \\ 0 & .15 & .85 \end{bmatrix}^8 \approx$$

$$[94 \quad 76 \quad 40]$$

Therefore, in May, the dorm population is 94 students in Mozart, 76 students in Picasso, and 40 students in Hemingway.

**10.** They should make 4 shawls and 2 blankets to make the maximum profit of \$104. Let $x$ represent the number of shawls, and let $y$ represent the number of blankets. Use the constraints to write this system:

$$\begin{cases} 1x + 2y \le 8 \\ 1x + 1y \le 6 \\ 1x + 4y \le 14 \\ x \ge 0 \\ y \ge 0 \end{cases}$$

Maximize: $16x + 20y$

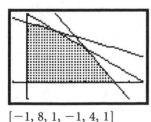

$[-1, 8, 1, -1, 4, 1]$

Vertices: $(0, 0), (6, 0), (4, 2), (2, 3), (0, 3.5)$. Test which point maximizes profit.

$(0, 0)$: $16(0) + 20(0) = 0$

$(6, 0)$: $16(6) + 20(0) = 96$

$(4, 2)$: $16(4) + 20(2) = 64 + 40 = 104$

$(2, 3)$: $16(2) + 20(3) = 92$

$(0, 3.5)$: $16(0) + 20(3.5) = 70$

The maximum occurs at $(4, 2)$.

**11. a.** $a < 0$; $p < 0$; $d > 0$

   **b.** $a > 0$; $p > 0$; $d$ cannot be determined.

   **c.** $a > 0$; $p = 0$; $d < 0$

**12. a.** $f(-3) = 3$

   **b.** $-5$ or approximately 3.5

   **c.** It is a function because no vertical line crosses the graph in more than one place.

   **d.** $-6 \le x \le 5$

   **e.** $-2 \le y \le 4$

**13.** 20 students in second period, 18 students in third period, and 24 students in seventh period. Let $x$ represent the number of students in second period, let $y$ represent the number of students in third period, and let $z$ represent the number of students in seventh period. Write a system of equations from the information given and solve it by any method. For example, rewrite the system of three equations in matrix form and multiply $[A]^{-1}[B]$ to find the solution to the system.

$$\begin{cases} \frac{1}{2}x + \frac{1}{3}y + \frac{1}{4}z = 22 \\ \frac{1}{4}x + \frac{1}{2}y + \frac{1}{6}z = 18 \\ \frac{1}{4}x + \frac{1}{6}y + \frac{7}{12}z = 22 \end{cases} \rightarrow [A][X] = [B]$$

$$\begin{bmatrix} \frac{1}{2} & \frac{1}{3} & \frac{1}{4} \\ \frac{1}{4} & \frac{1}{2} & \frac{1}{6} \\ \frac{1}{4} & \frac{1}{6} & \frac{7}{12} \end{bmatrix} \begin{bmatrix} x \\ y \\ z \end{bmatrix} = \begin{bmatrix} 22 \\ 18 \\ 22 \end{bmatrix}$$

$$\begin{bmatrix} x \\ y \\ z \end{bmatrix} = \begin{bmatrix} \frac{38}{11} & -2 & -\frac{10}{11} \\ -\frac{15}{11} & 3 & -\frac{3}{11} \\ -\frac{12}{11} & 0 & \frac{24}{11} \end{bmatrix} \begin{bmatrix} 22 \\ 18 \\ 22 \end{bmatrix}$$

$$\begin{bmatrix} x \\ y \\ z \end{bmatrix} = \begin{bmatrix} 20 \\ 18 \\ 24 \end{bmatrix}$$

The solution is $x = 20$, $y = 18$, and $z = 24$. There are 20 students in second period, 18 students in third period, and 24 students in seventh period.

**14. a.** Let $x$ represent the year, and let $y$ represent the number of barrels per day in millions.

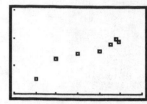

[1950, 2010, 10, 0, 3, 1]

**b.** $M_1(1965, 0.89)$, $M_2(1990, 1.55)$, $M_3(1998.5, 1.945)$; $\hat{y} = 0.0315x - 61.04$. To find $M_1$, $M_2$, and $M_3$, divide the data into three groups (2-3-2), and find the median of each group. Use your calculator to find the best approximation for the median-median line.

**c.** 2.023 million barrels per day. Using the median-median line, substitute 2002 for $x$: $\hat{y} = 0.0315(2002) - 61.04 = 2.023$.

**15. a.** $x = 245$

$$\log 35 + \log 7 = \log x$$
$$\log(35 \cdot 7) = \log x$$
$$35 \cdot 7 = x$$
$$x = 245$$

**b.** $x = 20$

$$\log 500 - \log 25 = \log x$$
$$\log \frac{500}{25} = \log x$$
$$\frac{500}{25} = x$$
$$x = 20$$

**c.** $x = -\dfrac{1}{2}$

$$\log \sqrt{\frac{1}{8}} = x \log 8$$
$$\log \sqrt{\frac{1}{8}} = \log 8^x$$
$$\sqrt{\frac{1}{8}} = 8^x$$
$$\left(8^{-1}\right)^{1/2} = 8^x$$
$$8^{-1/2} = 8^x$$
$$x = -\frac{1}{2}$$

**d.** $x = \dfrac{\log\left(\frac{37000}{15}\right)}{\log 9.4} \approx 3.4858$

$$15(9.4)^x = 37000$$
$$(9.4)^x = \frac{37000}{15}$$
$$\log(9.4)^x = \log\left(\frac{37000}{15}\right)$$
$$x \log(9.4) = \log\left(\frac{37000}{15}\right)$$
$$x = \frac{\log\left(\frac{37000}{15}\right)}{\log 9.4} \approx 3.4858$$

**e.** $x = 21$

$$\sqrt[3]{(x + 6)} + 18.6 = 21.6$$
$$\sqrt[3]{(x + 6)} = 3$$
$$(x + 6)^{1/3} = 3$$
$$\left((x + 6)^{1/3}\right)^3 = 3^3$$
$$x + 6 = 27$$
$$x = 21$$

**f.** $x = \dfrac{\log 342}{\log 36} \approx 1.6282$

$$\log_6 342 = 2x$$
$$6^{2x} = 342$$
$$\log 6^{2x} = \log 342$$
$$x \log 6^2 = \log 342$$
$$x = \frac{\log 342}{\log 6^2}$$
$$x = \frac{\log 342}{\log 36} \approx 1.6282$$

**16. a.** $100\% - 15\% = 85\%$

**b.**

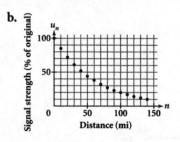

*Discovering Advanced Algebra Solutions Manual*
©2004 Key Curriculum Press

| Distance (mi) | Percentage of original signal |
|---|---|
| 0 | 100 |
| 10 | 85 |
| 20 | 72.3 |
| 30 | 61.4 |
| 40 | 52.2 |
| 50 | 44.4 |
| 60 | 37.7 |
| 70 | 32.1 |
| 80 | 27.29 |
| 90 | 23.19 |
| 100 | 19.71 |
| 110 | 16.76 |
| 120 | 14.24 |
| 130 | 12.11 |
| 140 | 10.29 |

c. 280 mi. Use Home screen recursion to find that at a distance of 280 mi, 1.06% of the original signal strength is left.

**17. a.** $y = 50(0.72)^{x-4}$ or $y = 25.92(0.72)^{x-6}$. Using the point-ratio method, substitute the coordinates of the points into the point ratio form, $y = y_1 \cdot b^{x-x_1}$.

$y = 50b^{x-4}$ and $y = 25.92b^{x-6}$

Use substitution to combine the two equations and solve for $b$.

$$50b^{x-4} = 25.92b^{x-6}$$

$$b^{x-4} = \frac{25.92b^{x-6}}{50}$$

$$\frac{b^{x-4}}{b^{x-6}} = \frac{25.92}{50}$$

$$b^{(x-4)-(x-6)} = 0.5184$$

$$b^2 = 0.5184$$

$$\left(b^2\right)^{1/2} = (0.5184)^{1/2}$$

$$b = 0.72$$

Substitute 0.72 for $b$ in either of the two original equations.

$y = 50(0.72)^{x-4}$ or $y = 25.92(0.72)^{x-6}$

**b.** 0.72; decay

**c.** Approximately 186; $y = 50(0.72)^{0-4} \approx 186.0544315$

**d.** 0

**18. a.** Sample answer using a bin width of 10:

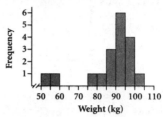

**b.** Skewed left

**c.** Using the 1.5 · *IQR* method, 54, 55, and 79 are outliers. Using the 2*s* method, only 54 and 55 are outliers.

$1.5\left(Q_3 - Q_1\right) = 1.5(95 - 89) = 1.5(6) = 9$, so $Q_3 + 9 = 95 + 9 = 104$, and $Q_1 - 9 = 89 - 9 = 90$. There are no values greater than 104, and there are three values, 54, 55, and 79, below 90, which are therefore outliers.

The standard deviation is 13. Adding 2*s*, or 26, to the mean, 87.4, gives 113.4, and subtracting 26 from the mean gives 61.4. Therefore only 54 and 55 are outliers below 61.4.

**d.** 67th percentile. There are 12 weights that are lower than 94 kg when the data are put in increasing order, so $\frac{12}{18} \approx .67$, or 67%.

**19. a.** A translation right 5 units and down 2 units

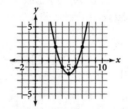

**b.** A reflection across the *x*-axis and a vertical stretch by a factor of 2

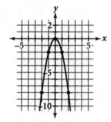

**c.** $-1 \cdot [P] = \begin{bmatrix} 2 & 1 & 0 & -1 & -2 \\ -4 & -1 & 0 & -1 & -4 \end{bmatrix}$

This is a reflection across the $x$-axis and a reflection across the $y$-axis. However, because the graph is symmetric with respect to the $y$-axis, a reflection across the $y$-axis does not change the graph.

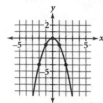

**d.** $[P] + \begin{bmatrix} -2 & -2 & -2 & -2 & -2 \\ 3 & 3 & 3 & 3 & 3 \end{bmatrix} =$

$\begin{bmatrix} -4 & -3 & -2 & -1 & 0 \\ 7 & 4 & 3 & 4 & 7 \end{bmatrix}$

**20. a.** Let $x$ represent the year and $y$ represent mean household population. Sample answer using the calculator's median-median command: $\hat{y} = -0.0247x + 51.71$.

**b.** Sample answer: What was the mean household population in 1965? Substitute 1965 for $x$: $\hat{y} = -0.0247(1965) + 51.71 = 3.1745$. In 1965, the mean household population was approximately 3.17.

**c.** Sample answer: In what year will the mean household population be 2.00? Substitute 2.00 for $\hat{y}$: $2.00 = -0.0247x + 51.71$, so $0.0247x = 49.71$, and $x = \frac{49.71}{0.0247} \approx 2013$. The mean household population will be 2.00 in the year 2013.

**TAKE ANOTHER LOOK**

**1.** When det = 1, $\begin{bmatrix} a & b \\ c & d \end{bmatrix}^{-1} = \begin{bmatrix} d & -b \\ -c & a \end{bmatrix}$.

When det = 2, $\begin{bmatrix} a & b \\ c & d \end{bmatrix}^{-1} = \begin{bmatrix} \frac{d}{2} & \frac{-b}{2} \\ \frac{-c}{2} & \frac{a}{2} \end{bmatrix}$.

Conjecture: $\begin{bmatrix} a & b \\ c & d \end{bmatrix}^{-1} = \frac{1}{\det}\begin{bmatrix} d & -b \\ -c & a \end{bmatrix}$

If a matrix is thought of as a transformation, the determinant gives the area of the image of the unit square, thus capturing the amount of stretching or shrinking. That's why the inverse matrix can be expressed with the determinant being divided.

**2.** Yes; it is a 90° counterclockwise rotation of all points and figures in the plane.

For other rotations:

$\begin{bmatrix} -1 & 0 \\ 0 & -1 \end{bmatrix}$ produces a 180° rotation, and

$\begin{bmatrix} 0 & 1 \\ -1 & 0 \end{bmatrix}$ produces a 90° clockwise rotation.

If you recall the exploration from Chapter 4 (or a theorem from geometry), you may think of these rotations as compositions of reflections.

For example, $\begin{bmatrix} 0 & -1 \\ 1 & 0 \end{bmatrix}$ interchanges $x$ and $y$ (a reflection across the line $y = x$) and then negates the first coordinate (a reflection across the $y$-axis).

**3.**

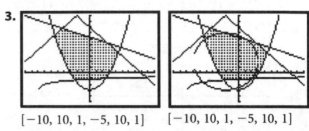

$[-10, 10, 1, -5, 10, 1]$    $[-10, 10, 1, -5, 10, 1]$

Vertices: (2.8, 5.2), (4.437, 3.563), (2.461, −0.980), (−5.373, 6.626), (−4.182, 7.818), (−2.295, −1.244)

Graph the equation for any value of $P$ (the second graph shows the circle with $P = 25$) and imagine increasing the value of $P$, enlarging the circle, until the last point within the feasible region is hit. This will show that the vertex on the far right provides the maximum value.

The maximum value of $P$ occurs at (4.437, 3.563), where $P = 43.878$.

**4.** The matrix $\begin{bmatrix} a & b & | & 1 & 0 \\ c & d & | & 0 & 1 \end{bmatrix}$ reduces to

$\begin{bmatrix} 1 & 0 & | & \frac{d}{ad - bc} & \frac{-b}{ad - bc} \\ 0 & 1 & | & \frac{-c}{ad - bc} & \frac{a}{ad - bc} \end{bmatrix}$

which means the inverse is

$\frac{1}{ad - bc}\begin{bmatrix} d & -b \\ -c & a \end{bmatrix}$

Because the determinant is defined as det = $ad - bc$, this is the same result as in Take Another Look activity 1.

*Discovering Advanced Algebra Solutions Manual*
©2004 Key Curriculum Press

**EXERCISES**

**1. a.** 3. The term with greatest exponent is $x^3$.

   **b.** 2. The term with greatest exponent is $7x^2$.

   **c.** 7. The term with greatest exponent is $x^7$.

   **d.** 5. The term with greatest exponent is $9x^5$.

**2. a.** Polynomial; 3rd degree; $\frac{5}{9}x^3 - 3.5x^2 + 4x - 3$

   **b.** Not a polynomial because $\frac{4}{p^2} = 4p^{-2}$ has a negative exponent

   **c.** Not a polynomial because $4\sqrt{x^3} = 4x^{3/2}$ has a non-integer exponent

   **d.** Polynomial; 2nd degree; already in general form

**3. a.** No; $\{2.2, 2.6, 1.8, -0.2, -3.4\}$

   **b.** No; $\{0.006, 0.007, 0.008, 0.009\}$

   **c.** No; $\{150, 150, 150\}$

**4.** 3. Use the finite differences method to see that the third set of differences is constant.

| $x$ | $y$ | $D_1$ | $D_2$ | $D_3$ |
|---|---|---|---|---|
| 0 | 12 | | | |
| | | −16 | | |
| 2 | −4 | | −144 | |
| | | −160 | | −144 |
| 4 | −164 | | −288 | |
| | | −448 | | −144 |
| 6 | −612 | | −432 | |
| | | −880 | | −144 |
| 8 | −1492 | | −576 | |
| | | −1456 | | −144 |
| 10 | −2948 | | −720 | |
| | | −2176 | | |
| 12 | −5124 | | | |

**5. a.** $D_1 = \{2, 3, 4, 5, 6\}$, $D_2 = \{1, 1, 1, 1\}$; 2nd degree

| $n$ | 1 | 2 | 3 | 4 | 5 | 6 |
|---|---|---|---|---|---|---|
| $s$ | 1 | 3 | 6 | 10 | 15 | 21 |

$D_1$    2   3   4   5   6

$D_2$    1   1   1   1

   **b.** The polynomial is 2nd degree, and the $D_2$ values are constant.

   **c.** 4 points. You have to find the finite differences twice, so you need at least four data points to calculate two $D_2$ values that can be compared.

   **d.** $s = 0.5n^2 + 0.5n$; $s = 78$ when $n = 12$. Because the function is quadratic, start with $s = an^2 + bn + c$.

Use three data points to get three equations and solve for the constants $a$, $b$, and $c$.

$$\begin{cases} a + b + c = 1 & \text{Using the data point } (1, 1). \\ 4a + 2b + c = 3 & \text{Using the data point } (2, 3). \\ 9a + 3b + c = 6 & \text{Using the data point } (3, 6). \end{cases}$$

Solve this system to get $a = 0.5$, $b = 0.5$, and $c = 0$. The equation is $s = 0.5n^2 + 0.5n$.

Now substitute 12 for $n$, and solve for $s$: $s = 0.5(12)^2 + 0.5(12) = 72 + 6 = 78$.

   **e.** The pennies can be arranged to form triangles, where each row of a triangle has one more penny than the previous row. Using the polynomial $s = 0.5n^2 + 0.5n$ found in 5d, if you form a triangle with $n$ rows, it will contain $s$ pennies.

**6. a.**

| Layers $x$ | 1 | 2 | 3 | 4 | 5 | 6 |
|---|---|---|---|---|---|---|
| Blocks $y$ | 1 | 5 | 14 | 30 | 55 | 91 |

   **b.** $y = \frac{1}{3}x^3 + \frac{1}{2}x^2 + \frac{1}{6}x$. Use the finite differences method to find that the polynomial is 3rd degree.

| $x$ | 1 | 2 | 3 | 4 | 5 | 6 |
|---|---|---|---|---|---|---|
| $y$ | 1 | 5 | 14 | 30 | 55 | 91 |

$D_1$    4   9   16   25   36

$D_2$    5   7   9   11

$D_3$    2   2   2

The function is a 3rd-degree polynomial, so start with $y = ax^3 + bx^2 + cx + d$. Use four data points to get four equations and solve for the constants $a$, $b$, $c$, and $d$.

$$\begin{cases} a + b + c + d = 1 & \text{Using the data point } (1, 1). \\ 8a + 4b + 2c + d = 5 & \text{Using the data point } (2, 5). \\ 27a + 9b + 3c + d = 14 & \text{Using the data point } (3, 14). \\ 64a + 16b + 4c + d = 30 & \text{Using the data point } (4, 30). \end{cases}$$

Solve this system to get $a = \frac{1}{3}$, $b = \frac{1}{2}$, $c = \frac{1}{6}$, and $d = 0$. The fastest way to solve the system is with a reduced row-echelon matrix.

The equation is $y = \frac{1}{3}x^3 + \frac{1}{2}x^2 + \frac{1}{6}x$.

**c.** 204 blocks. Substitute 8 for $x$ and solve for $y$:
$y = \frac{1}{3}(8)^3 + \frac{1}{2}(8)^2 + \frac{1}{6}(8) = \frac{512}{3} + 32 + \frac{4}{3} = 204$.

**d.** 12 layers. Substitute integer values for $x$ until $y$ equals 650. Because $x = 8$ results in $y = 204$ in 6c, start with $x = 9$. When $x = 12$, $y = \frac{1}{3}(12)^3 + \frac{1}{2}(12)^2 + \frac{1}{6}(12) = 576 + 72 + 2 = 650$.

**7. a.  i.** $D_1 = \{15.1, 5.3, -4.5, -14.3, -24.1, -33.9\}$;
$D_2 = \{-9.8, -9.8, -9.8, -9.8, -9.8\}$

**ii.** $D_1 = \{59.1, 49.3, 39.5, 29.7, 19.9, 10.1\}$;
$D_2 = \{-9.8, -9.8, -9.8, -9.8, -9.8\}$

**b.** Both are 2nd-degree polynomials because the second differences are constant in each case.

**c.  i.** $h = -4.9t^2 + 20t + 80$. The function is quadratic, so start with $h = at^2 + bt + c$. Use three data points to get three equations and solve for the constants $a$, $b$, and $c$.

$$\begin{cases} c = 80 & \text{Using the data point } (0, 80). \\ 9a + 3b + c = 95.9 & \text{Using the data point } (3, 95.9). \\ 36a + 6b + c = 23.6 & \text{Using the data point } (6, 23.6). \end{cases}$$

Solve this system to get $a = -4.9$, $b = 20$, and $c = 80$. The equation is $h = -4.9t^2 + 20t + 80$. Check that the point $(3, 95.9)$ satisfies this equation.

$$95.9 \overset{?}{=} -4.9(3)^2 + 20(3) + 80$$

$$95.9 = 95.9$$

**ii.** $h = -4.9t^2 + 64t + 4$. The function is quadratic, so start with $h = at^2 + bt + c$. Use three data points to get three equations and solve for the constants $a$, $b$, and $c$.

$$\begin{cases} c = 4 & \text{Using the data point } (0, 4). \\ 9a + 3b + c = 151.9 & \text{Using the data point } (3, 151.9). \\ 36a + 6b + c = 211.6 & \text{Using the data point } (6, 211.6). \end{cases}$$

Solve this system to get $a = -4.9$, $b = 64$, and $c = 4$. The equation is $h = -4.9t^2 + 64t + 4$. Check that the point $(3, 151.9)$ satisfies this equation.

$$151.9 \overset{?}{=} -4.9(3)^2 + 64(3) + 4$$

$$151.9 = 151.9$$

**8. a.** $D_1 = \{0.07, 0.06, 0.04, 0.02, 0.01, 0.01, 0, 0, 0, 0.01, 0.01, 0.02, 0.03, 0.05, 0.07\}$. The graph is approximately parabolic.

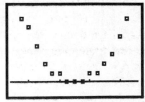

$[9.5, 13.5, 1, -0.02, 0.08, 1]$

**b.** $D_2 = \{-0.01, -0.02, -0.02, -0.01, 0, -0.01, 0, 0, 0.01, 0, 0.01, 0.01, 0.02, 0.02\}$. These points are approximately linear.

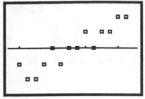

$[9.5, 13.5, 1, -0.03, 0.03, 1]$

$D_3 = \{-0.01, 0, 0.01, 0.01, -0.01, 0.01, 0, 0.01, -0.01, 0.01, 0, 0.01, 0\}$. There is no pattern to these numbers.

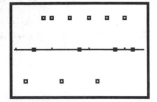

$[9.5, 13.5, 1, -0.013, 0.013, 1]$

**c.** 3rd-degree polynomial; the third differences are nearly constant and show no pattern.

**d.** Possible answer: Let $x$ represent Andy's age in years, and let $y$ represent his height in meters; $y = 0.029x^3 - 0.993x^2 + 11.34x - 41.818$. Start with the function $y = ax^3 + bx^2 + cx + d$ and use four data points, such as $(9.5, 1.14)$, $(10.75, 1.34)$, $(12, 1.36)$, and $(13.25, 1.54)$. Then solve the system to find values for $a$, $b$, $c$, and $d$, as in Exercise 7c. *Note:* When using this method, it is best to use four data points that are spread throughout the domain, rather than just using, for example, the first four points. The model appears to be reasonable for about $8.5 \le x \le 14$.

**9.** The data are represented by the quadratic function $y = 2x^2$. $D_1 = \{6, 10, 14, 18, 22, 26\}$; $D_2 = \{4, 4, 4, 4, 4\}$. The second differences are constant, so a quadratic function expresses the relationship. Let $x$ represent the energy level, and let $y$ represent the maximum number of electrons. Start with the equation $y = ax^2 + bx + c$, and use three data points to find the constants $a$, $b$, and $c$.

$$\begin{cases} a + b + c = 2 & \text{Using the data point } (1, 2). \\ 16a + 4b + c = 7 & \text{Using the data point } (4, 7). \\ 49a + 7b + c = 98 & \text{Using the data point } (7, 98). \end{cases}$$

Solve this system to get $a = 2$, $b = 0$, and $c = 0$, so $y = 2x^2$.

*Discovering Advanced Algebra Solutions Manual*
©2004 Key Curriculum Press

**10. a.** This is the image of the graph of $y = x^2$ translated right 2 units.

**b.** This is the image of the graph of $y = x^2$ translated down 4 units.

**c.** This is the image of the graph of $y = x^2$ translated left 4 units and up 1 unit.

**11. a.** $x = 2.5$

$$12x - 17 = 13$$
$$12x = 30$$
$$x = \frac{30}{12}$$
$$x = 2.5$$

**b.** $x = 3$ or $x = -1$

$$2(x - 1)^2 + 3 = 11$$
$$2(x - 1)^2 = 8$$
$$(x - 1)^2 = 4$$
$$x - 1 = \pm 2$$
$$x = 2 + 1 \text{ or } x = -2 + 1$$
$$x = 3 \quad \text{ or } x = -1$$

**c.** $x = \dfrac{\log 16}{\log 5} \approx 1.7227$

$$3(5^x) = 48$$
$$5^x = 16$$
$$x \log 5 = \log 16$$
$$x = \frac{\log 16}{\log 5} \approx 1.7227$$

**12. a.**

|      | 2x     | 3  |
|------|--------|----|
| 3x   | $6x^2$ | 9x |
| 1    | 2x     | 3  |

**b.** $(2x + 3)(3x + 1) = 6x^2 + 2x + 9x + 3 = 6x^2 + 11x + 3$

**c.**

|   | x      | 5  |
|---|--------|----|
| x | $x^2$  | 5x |
| 3 | 3x     | 15 |

Use the fact that $x^2 + 8x + 15 = x^2 + 5x + 3x + 5(3)$.

**d.** $(x + 3)(x + 5)$

**13.**
$$\begin{cases} y \geq -\frac{1}{2}x + \frac{3}{2} \\ y \leq \frac{1}{2}x + \frac{9}{2} \\ y \leq -\frac{11}{6}x + \frac{97}{6} \end{cases}$$

The line connecting points $A$ and $B$ has slope $\frac{3 - (-4)}{-3 - 11} = -\frac{1}{2}$. Use the point-slope equation with $(-3, 3)$ to get $y = -\frac{1}{2}(x + 3) + 3 = -\frac{1}{2}x + \frac{3}{2}$. The feasible region is above the solid line, so the inequality is $y \geq -\frac{1}{2}x + \frac{3}{2}$.

The line connecting points $A$ and $C$ has slope $\frac{7 - 3}{5 - (-3)} = \frac{1}{2}$. Use the point-slope equation with $(5, 7)$ to get $y = \frac{1}{2}(x - 5) + 7 = \frac{1}{2}x + \frac{9}{2}$. The feasible region is below the solid line, so the inequality is $y \leq \frac{1}{2}x + \frac{9}{2}$.

The line connecting points $B$ and $C$ has slope $\frac{7 - (-4)}{5 - 11} = -\frac{11}{6}$. Use the point-slope equation with $(5, 7)$ to get $y = -\frac{11}{6}(x - 5) + 7 = -\frac{11}{6}x + \frac{97}{6}$. The feasible region is below the solid line, so the inequality is $y \leq -\frac{11}{6}x + \frac{97}{6}$.

**14.** $(x + 3)(x + 4)(x + 2) = (x^2 + 7x + 12)(x + 2) = x^2(x + 2) + 7x(x + 2) + 12(x + 2) = x^3 + 2x^2 + 7x^2 + 14x + 12x + 24 = x^3 + 9x^2 + 26x + 24$

### EXTENSIONS

**A.** Results will vary depending on the initial velocity at which the pillow is tossed upward, but the model should still be quadratic. Specifically, the model will be in the form $y = -4.9x^2 + v_0x + s_0$, where $v_0$ is the initial velocity and $s_0$ is the initial height. The model for tossing the pillow upward has an $x$-term, whereas the model for free fall does not.

**B.** See the solution to Take Another Look activity 1 on page 178.

**C.** The finite differences never become constant for $y = e^x$, because it is not a polynomial function. Enter $\{1, 2, 3, 4, 5, 6, 7, 8, 9, 10\}$ into list L1 and define list L2 as e^(L1). Then define list L3 as $\Delta$List(L2) to find the first finite differences, define list L4 as $\Delta$List(L3) to find the second finite differences, and so on. You will find that the finite differences never become constant.

**EXERCISES**

**1. a.** Factored form and vertex form

**b.** None of these forms

**c.** Factored form

**d.** General form

**2.** In 2a–c, identify the values of $h$ and $k$ for the equations in the form $y = a(x - h)^2 + k$.

**a.** (2, 3)

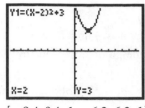

$[-9.4, 9.4, 1, -6.2, 6.2, 1]$

**b.** (−4, −2)

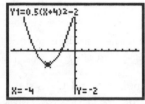

$[-9.4, 9.4, 1, -6.2, 6.2, 1]$

**c.** (5, 4)

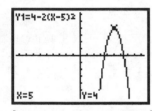

$[-9.4, 9.4, 1, -6.2, 6.2, 1]$

**3.** In 3a–c, identify the values of $r_1$ and $r_2$ for the equations in the form $y = a(x - r_1)(x - r_2)$.

**a.** −1 and 2

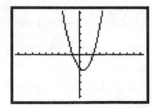

$[-9.4, 9.4, 1, -6.2, 6.2, 1]$

**b.** −3 and 2

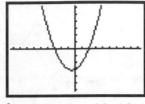

$[-9.4, 9.4, 1, -6.2, 6.2, 1]$

**c.** 2 and 5

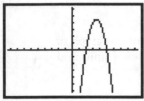

$[-9.4, 9.4, 1, -6.2, 6.2, 1]$

**4.** Because the equations are equivalent, the graphs for each part should look like only one parabola.

**a.** $y = (x - 2)^2 + 3 = x^2 - 4x + 4 + 3 = x^2 - 4x + 7$

**b.** $y = 0.5(x + 4)^2 - 2 = 0.5(x^2 + 8x + 16) - 2 = 0.5x^2 + 4x + 8 - 2 = 0.5x^2 + 4x + 6$

**c.** $y = 4 - 2(x - 5)^2 = 4 - 2(x^2 - 10x + 25) = 4 - 2x^2 + 20x - 50 = -2x^2 + 20x - 46$

**5.** Because the equations are equivalent, the graphs for each part should look like only one parabola.

**a.** $y = x^2 - x - 2$

**b.** $y = 0.5(x - 2)(x + 3) = 0.5(x^2 + x - 6) = 0.5x^2 + 0.5x - 3$

**c.** $y = -2(x - 2)(x - 5) = -2(x^2 - 7x + 10) = -2x^2 + 14x - 20$

**6. a.** $x = 4.5$. Notice that the values in the table have symmetry about (4.5, 19).

**b.** (4.5, 19); maximum. The line of symmetry passes through the vertex, so (4.5, 19) is the vertex. It is a maximum because all other $y$-values are less than 19.

**c.** $y = -3(x - 4.5)^2 + 19$. The vertex is (4.5, 19), so start with the equation $y = a(x - 4.5)^2 + 19$ and substitute another data point to find $a$. For example, substitute the coordinates (1.5, −8) to get

$$-8 = a(1.5 - 4.5)^2 + 19$$

$$-27 = a(-3)^2$$

$$-27 = 9a$$

$$a = -3$$

The equation is $y = -3(x - 4.5)^2 + 19$.

**7. a.** $y = 4 - 0.5(x + h)^2 = 4 - 0.5(x^2 + 2hx + h^2) = 4 - 0.5x^2 - hx - 0.5h^2 = -0.5x^2 - hx - 0.5h^2 + 4$

**b.** $y = a(x - 4)^2 = a(x^2 - 8x + 16) = ax^2 - 8ax + 16a$

**c.** $y = a(x - h)^2 + k = a(x^2 - 2hx + h^2) + k = ax^2 - 2ahx + ah^2 + k$

**d.** $y = -0.5(x + r)(x + 4) = -0.5(x^2 + rx + 4x + 4r) = -0.5x^2 - 0.5rx - 2x - 2r$

**e.** $y = a(x - 4)(x + 2) = a(x^2 - 2x - 8) = ax^2 - 2ax - 8a$

**f.** $y = a(x - r)(x - s) = a(x^2 - rx - sx + rs) = a(x^2 - (r + s)x + rs) = ax^2 - a(r + s)x + ars$

**8. a.** $y = a(x + 2.4)(x - 0.8)$. Substitute the $x$-intercepts, $-2.4$ and $0.8$, for $r_1$ and $r_2$ in the form $y = a(x - r_1)(x - r_2)$.

**b.** $y = -1.8(x + 2.4)(x - 0.8)$. Substitute 1.2 for $x$ and $-2.592$ for $y$ and solve for $a$.

$$-2.592 = a(1.2 + 2.4)(1.2 - 0.8)$$

$$-2.592 = a(3.6)(0.4)$$

$$a = \frac{-2.592}{1.44} = -1.8$$

**c.** $x = -0.8$, $y = 4.608$. First, find the mean of the $x$-intercepts to get the $x$-coordinate of the vertex. $x = \frac{-2.4 + 0.8}{2} = -0.8$. Then use the equation of the graph to find the $y$-coordinate. $y = -1.8(-0.8 + 2.4)(-0.8 - 0.8) = 4.608$.

**d.** $y = -1.8(x + 0.8)^2 + 4.608$. Substitute the values of $h$ and $k$ from the vertex, $h = -0.8$ and $k = 4.608$, and the value of $a$ from 8b in the form $y = a(x - h) + k$.

**9.** In 9a–c, use the graph to identify the $x$- and $y$-intercepts.

**a.** $y = (x + 2)(x - 1)$. The $x$-intercepts are $-2$ and 1, so start with the equation $y = a(x + 2)(x - 1)$. Use the $y$-intercept point, $(0, -2)$, to solve for $a$.

$$-2 = a(0 + 2)(0 - 1)$$

$$-2 = -2a$$

$$a = 1$$

The equation is $y = (x + 2)(x - 1)$.

**b.** $y = -0.5(x + 2)(x - 3)$. The $x$-intercepts are $-2$ and 3, so start with the equation $y = a(x + 2)(x - 3)$. Use the $y$-intercept point, $(0, 3)$, to solve for $a$.

$$3 = a(0 + 2)(0 - 3)$$

$$3 = -6a$$

$$a = -0.5$$

The equation is $y = -0.5(x + 2)(x - 3)$.

**c.** $y = \frac{1}{3}(x + 2)(x - 1)(x - 3)$. The $x$-intercepts are $-2$, 1, and 3, so start with the equation $y = a(x + 2)(x - 1)(x - 3)$. Use the $y$-intercept point, $(0, 2)$, to solve for $a$.

$$2 = a(0 + 2)(0 - 1)(0 - 3)$$

$$2 = 6a$$

$$a = \frac{1}{3}$$

The equation is $y = \frac{1}{3}(x + 2)(x - 1)(x - 3)$.

**10. a.** Use the projection that the sales decrease by 5 packs per day with each \$0.10 increase in selling price to get the number sold. Multiply the selling price by the number sold to get the revenue.

| Selling price ($) | 2.00 | 2.10 | 2.20 | 2.30 | 2.40 |
|---|---|---|---|---|---|
| Number sold | 200 | 195 | 190 | 185 | 180 |
| Revenue ($) | 400 | 409.50 | 418 | 425.50 | 432 |

**b.** $D_1 = \{9.5, 8.5, 7.5, 6.5\}$; $D_2 = \{-1, -1, -1\}$

| Number sold | 200 | 195 | 190 | 185 | 180 |
|---|---|---|---|---|---|
| Revenue ($) | 400 | 409.50 | 418 | 425.50 | 432 |

$D_1$      9.5    8.5   7.5    6.5

$D_2$        $-1$    $-1$    $-1$

**c.** $y = -50x^2 + 300x$. The second differences are constant, so this is a quadratic function. Start with the equation $y = ax^2 + bx + c$ and use three data points to solve for $a$, $b$, and $c$.

$$\begin{cases} 4.00a + 2.00b + c = 400 & \text{Using the data point } (2.00, 400). \\ 4.84a + 2.20b + c = 418 & \text{Using the data point } (2.20, 418). \\ 5.76a + 2.40b + c = 432 & \text{Using the data point } (2.40, 432). \end{cases}$$

Solve this system to get $a = -50$, $b = 300$, and $c = 0$, so the equation is $y = -50x^2 + 300x$.

**d.** The maximum revenue is \$450 at a selling price of \$3. Graph the function and trace to find the maximum.

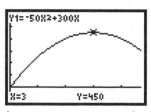

$[0, 4.7, 1, -100, 600, 1]$

**11. a.**

| Width (m) | 5 | 10 | 15 | 20 | 25 |
|---|---|---|---|---|---|
| Length (m) | 35 | 30 | 25 | 20 | 15 |
| Area (m²) | 175 | 300 | 375 | 400 | 375 |

Use the formula *Perimeter* = 80 = 2(*length*) + 2(*width*), or 40 = *length* + *width*, to get the second row. Use the formula *Area* = *length*(*width*) to get the third row.

**b.** $y = x(40 - x)$, or $y = -x^2 + 40x$. Because *Perimeter* = 2(*length*) + 2(*width*), 80 = 2(*length*) + 2*x*. Therefore, *length* = 40 − *x*. Use the formula *Area* = *length*(*width*) to obtain $y = x(40 - x)$.

**c.** A width of 20 m (and length of 20 m) maximizes the area at 400 m². Graph the function and trace to find the maximum, which is also the vertex.

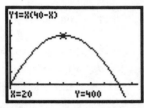

[0, 47, 5, −100, 600, 100]

**d.** 0 m and 40 m. The equation $y = x(40 - x)$ is in factored form and shows that the zeros are 0 and 40.

**12. a.** The graph is parabolic. As the temperature increases, the rate of photosynthesis also increases until a maximum rate is reached; then the rate decreases.

**b.** At approximately 23°C, the rate of photosynthesis is maximized at 100%. The vertex of the parabola is approximately (23, 100).

**c.** 0°C and 46°C. The *x*-intercepts of the parabola are 0 and 46.

**d.** $y = -0.19x(x - 46)$; $y = -0.19(x - 23)^2 + 100$. For the factored form, substitute the *x*-intercepts to start with the equation $y = a(x - 0)(x - 46)$. Then use the vertex, (23, 100), to find *a*.

$$100 = a(23)(23 - 46)$$

$$100 = -529a$$

$$a = -\frac{100}{529} \approx -0.19$$

The function in factored form is $y = -0.19x(x - 46)$.

For the vertex form, substitute the vertex to start with the equation $y = a(x - 23)^2 + 100$. Then use the same value of *a* as above, so the equation in vertex form is $y = -0.19(x - 23)^2 + 100$.

**13. a.** $12x^2 - 15x$

|  | 4x | −5 |
|---|---|---|
| 3x | 12x² | −15x |

**b.** $x^2 - 2x - 15$

|  | x | −5 |
|---|---|---|
| x | x² | −5x |
| 3 | 3x | −15 |

**c.** $x^2 - 49$

|  | x | 7 |
|---|---|---|
| x | x² | 7x |
| −7 | −7x | −49 |

**d.** $9x^2 - 6x + 1$

|  | 3x | −1 |
|---|---|---|
| 3x | 9x² | −3x |
| −1 | −3x | 1 |

**14. a.** $3x(4x) - 3x(5) = 12x^2 - 15x$

**b.** $x(x - 5) + 3(x - 5) = x^2 - 5x + 3x - 15 = x^2 - 2x - 15$

**c.** $x(x - 7) + 7(x - 7) = x^2 - 7x + 7x - 49 = x^2 - 49$

**d.** $(3x + 1)(3x + 1) = 3x(3x + 1) + 1(3x + 1) = 9x^2 + 3x + 3x + 1 = 9x^2 - 6x + 1$

**15. a.** $(x + 5)(x - 2)$. The numbers that multiply to −10 and add to 3 are 5 and −2.

|  | x | 5 |
|---|---|---|
| x | x² | 5x |
| −2 | −2x | −10 |

**b.** $(x + 4)(x + 4)$. The numbers that multiply to 16 and add to 8 are 4 and 4.

|  | x | 4 |
|---|---|---|
| x | x² | 4x |
| 4 | 4x | 16 |

**c.** $(x + 5)(x - 5)$. The numbers that multiply to −25 and add to 0 are 5 and −5.

|  | x | 5 |
|---|---|---|
| x | x² | 5x |
| −5 | −5x | −25 |

**16. a.** $f(2) = 3(2)^3 - 5(2)^2 + 2 - 6 = 3(8) - 5(4) - 4 = 0$

**b.** $f(-1) = 3(-1)^3 - 5(-1)^2 - 1 - 6 = 3(-1) - 5(1) - 7 = -15$

**c.** $f(0) = 3(0)^3 - 5(0)^2 + 0 - 6 = -6$

**d.** $f\left(\frac{1}{2}\right) = 3\left(\frac{1}{2}\right)^3 - 5\left(\frac{1}{2}\right)^2 + \frac{1}{2} - 6 = 3\left(\frac{1}{8}\right) - 5\left(\frac{1}{4}\right) - \frac{11}{2} = -\frac{51}{8} = -6\frac{3}{8}$

*Discovering Advanced Algebra Solutions Manual*
©2004 Key Curriculum Press

**e.** $f\left(-\frac{4}{3}\right) = 3\left(-\frac{4}{3}\right)^3 - 5\left(-\frac{4}{3}\right)^2 - \frac{4}{3} - 6 =$

$3\left(-\frac{64}{27}\right) - 5\left(\frac{16}{9}\right) - \frac{22}{3} = -\frac{210}{9} = -23\frac{1}{3}$

### IMPROVING YOUR REASONING SKILLS

Let $S$ represent the sum of the first $n$ terms.

$S = \frac{1}{2}n^2 + \frac{1}{2}n$; $S = n^2$; $S = \frac{3}{2}n^2 - \frac{1}{2}n$;

$S = \frac{d}{2}n^2 + \left(1 - \frac{d}{2}\right)n$

For the first sequence, start with a table of values, and use the finite differences method.

| $n$ | 1 | 2 | 3 | 4 | 5 |
|-----|---|---|---|---|---|
| $S$ | 1 | 3 | 6 | 10 | 15 |

$D_1$    2    3    4    5

$D_2$    1    1    1

The second differences are constant, so the formula is a quadratic equation. Start with the equation $S = an^2 + bn + c$, and use the three points $(1, 1)$, $(2, 3)$, and $(3, 6)$ to find $a$, $b$, and $c$.

$\begin{cases} a + b + c = 1 & \text{Using the point } (1, 1). \\ 9a + 3b + c = 6 & \text{Using the point } (3, 6). \\ 25a + 5b + c = 15 & \text{Using the point } (5, 15). \end{cases}$

Solve this system to get $a = \frac{1}{2}$, $b = \frac{1}{2}$, and $c = 0$.

Use a similar process for the second and third sequences. For any arithmetic sequence, note that the terms are $1, 1 + d, 1 + 2d, 1 + 3d, \ldots, 1 + (n - 1)d$.

Another way to find a formula for the sum of the first $n$ terms of any arithmetic sequence is to write $S$ first in one order and then in the reverse order of summation.

$S = 1 + (1 + d) + (1 + 2d) + \cdots +$
$(1 + (n - 3)d) + (1 + (n - 2)d) + (1 + (n - 1)d)$

$S = (1 + (n - 1)d) + (1 + (n - 2)d) + (1 + (n - 3)d)$
$+ \cdots + (1 + 2d) + (1 + d) + 1$

Now add $S$ to itself, using these two orders of summation:

$2S = (2 + (n - 1)d) + (2 + (n - 1)d) +$
$(2 + (n - 1)d) + \cdots + (2 + (n - 1)d) +$
$(2 + (n - 1)d) + (2 + (n - 1)d)$

Each term in the sum of $2S$ is the same, and there are $n$ terms, so

$2S = n(2 + (n - 1)d)$

$S = \frac{n(2 + (n - 1)d)}{2}$

This is equivalent to $S = \frac{d}{2}n^2 + \left(1 - \frac{d}{2}\right)n$.

---

## LESSON 7.3

### EXERCISES

**1. a.** $(x - 5)^2$

    **b.** $\left(x + \frac{5}{2}\right)^2$

    **c.** $(2x - 3)^2$, or $4\left(x - \frac{3}{2}\right)^2$

    **d.** $(x - y)^2$

**2. a.** $\left(\frac{20}{2}\right)^2 = 10^2 = 100$

    **b.** $\left(\frac{-7}{2}\right)^2 = \frac{49}{4}$, or 12.25

    **c.** 16. First, factor out the 4.

       $4x^2 - 16x = 4\left(x^2 - 4x\right)$

       $\left(\frac{-4}{2}\right)^2 = 4$

    So you need to add a 4 inside the parentheses to complete the square. Everything inside the parentheses is multiplied by 4, so you actually **add 16.**

    **d.** $-3$. First, factor out the $-3$.

       $-3x^2 - 6x = -3\left(x^2 + 2x\right)$

       $\left(\frac{2}{2}\right)^2 = 1$

    So you need to add a 1 inside the parentheses to complete the square. Everything inside the parentheses is multiplied by $-3$, so you actually **add $-3$.**

**3. a.** $y = (x + 10)^2 - 6$. As in 2a, you need to add 100 to $x^2 + 20x$ to complete the square.

       $y = \left(x^2 + 20x + 100\right) + 94 - 100$
       $= (x + 10)^2 - 6$

    **b.** $y = (x - 3.5)^2 + 3.75$. As in 2b, you need to add 12.25 to $x^2 - 7x$ to complete the square.

       $y = \left(x^2 - 7x + 12.25\right) + 16 - 12.25$
       $= (x - 3.5)^2 + 3.75$

    **c.** $y = 6(x - 2)^2 + 123$. As an alternative to completing the square, identify the values of $a$, $b$, and $c$ in general form, and use the formulas for $h$ and $k$ to write the vertex form.

       $a = 6, b = -24, c = 147$

       $h = -\frac{b}{2a} = \frac{24}{12} = 2$

       $k = c - \frac{b^2}{4a} = 147 - \frac{576}{24} = 123$

    The vertex form is $y = 6(x - 2)^2 + 123$.

**d.** $y = 5(x + 0.8)^2 - 3.2$. Identify the coefficients and then calculate $h$ and $k$:

$a = 5$, $b = 8$, $c = 0$

$$h = \frac{-b}{2a} = \frac{-8}{10} = -0.8$$

$$k = c - \frac{b^2}{4a} = 0 - \frac{64}{20} = -3.2$$

Use the values of $a$, $h$, and $k$ in the vertex form: $y = 5(x + 0.8)^2 - 3.2$.

**4. a.** No rewriting necessary; $a = 3$, $b = 2$, $c = -5$

**b.** $2x^2 + 14$; $a = 2$, $b = 0$, $c = 14$

**c.** $4x^2 + 6x - 3$; $a = 4$, $b = 6$, $c = -3$

**d.** $-x^2 + 3x$; $a = -1$, $b = 3$, $c = 0$

**5.** $(-4, 12)$

$a = -2$, $b = -16$, $c = -20$

$$h = -\frac{b}{2a} = -\left(\frac{-16}{-4}\right) = -4$$

$$k = c - \frac{b^2}{4a} = -20 - \frac{(-16)^2}{-8} = 12$$

**6.** $y = 7.51(x - 3.15)^2 + 54.93$

$$h = -\frac{b}{2a} = \frac{47.32}{2(7.51)} \approx 3.15$$

$$k = c - \frac{b^2}{4a} = 129.47 - \frac{(47.32)^2}{4(7.51)} \approx 54.93$$

Rewrite the equation in vertex form:
$y = 7.51(x - 3.15)^2 + 54.93$.

Use a calculator table to verify that the functions are approximately equivalent.

| Plot1 Plot2 Plot3 | | X | Y1 | Y2 |
|---|---|---|---|---|
| \Y1■7.51X²-47.32 | | -3 | 339.02 | 338.98 |
| X+129.47 | | -2 | 254.15 | 254.11 |
| \Y2■7.51(X-3.15) | | -1 | 184.3 | 184.27 |
| ²+54.93 | | 0 | 129.47 | 129.45 |
| \Y3=■ | | 1 | 89.66 | 89.645 |
| \Y4= | | 2 | 64.87 | 64.862 |
| \Y5= | | 3 | 55.1 | 55.099 |
| | | X=-3 | | |

**7. a.** Let $x$ represent time in seconds, and let $y$ represent height in meters; $y = -4.9(x - 1.1)(x - 4.7)$, or $y = -4.9x^2 + 28.42x - 25.333$. Use the factored form because you are given the zeros, 1.1 and 4.7. Start with $y = a(x - 1.1)(x - 4.7)$. The acceleration due to gravity is $-4.9$ m/s², so $a = -4.9$.

**b.** 28.42 m/s. This is the coefficient of the $x$-term.

**c.** 25.333 m. At 0 s, the arrow starts at the bottom of the well. Substitute 0 for $x$, or identify the constant term as the $y$-intercept. The height at time 0 s is $-25.333$ m, so the well is 25.333 m deep.

**8. a.** Possible table, where $x$ represents the sides perpendicular to the building:

| x | 5 | 10 | 15 | 20 | 25 | 30 | 35 |
|---|---|---|---|---|---|---|---|
| y | 350 | 600 | 750 | 800 | 750 | 600 | 350 |

$y = -2x^2 + 80x$. If $l$ is the length of the rectangle, then the amount of fencing needed to build a fence using the building as one side is $2x + l$. You have 80 ft of fencing, so $80 = 2x + l$, or $l = 80 - 2x$. The area is $y = xl = x(80 - 2x)$, or $y = -2x^2 + 80x$.

**b.** 20 ft; 800 ft². Complete the square for the function $y = -2x^2 + 80x$.

$$y = -2(x^2 - 40x)$$

$$y = -2(x^2 - 40x + 400 - 400)$$

$$y = -2(x^2 - 40x + 400) + 800$$

$$y = -2(x^2 - 20)^2 + 800$$

The vertex is (20, 800), indicating a maximum area of 800 ft² when the width is 20 ft.

**9.** Let $x$ represent time in seconds, and let $y$ represent height in meters; $y = -4.9x^2 + 17.2x + 50$. The acceleration due to gravity is $-4.9$ m/s², the initial velocity is 17.2 m/s, and the initial height is 50 m. Substitute these values in the projectile motion function, $y = ax^2 + v_0x + s_0$.

**10. a.** $y = -4.9t^2 + 100t + 25$. Start with the equation $y = -4.9t^2 + v_0t + s_0$, and use two data points to find $v_0$ and $s_0$.

$$\begin{cases} -4.9 + v_0 + s_0 = 120.1 & \text{Using the point (1, 120.1).} \\ -78.4 + 4v_0 + s_0 = 346.6 & \text{Using the point (4, 346.6).} \end{cases}$$

Solve this system to get $v_0 = 100$ and $s_0 = 25$, so $y = -4.9t^2 + 100t + 25$.

**b.** $s_0 = 25$ m; $v_0 = 100$ m/s

**c.** 10.2 s; 535 m. $h = -\dfrac{100}{2(-4.9)} \approx 10.2$ and $k = 25 - \dfrac{100^2}{4(-4.9)} \approx 535$, so the vertex is approximately (10.2, 535). This indicates a maximum height of 535 m at 10.2 s.

**11. a.** $n = -2p + 100$. Write the equation of the line that passes through the points (20, 60) and (25, 50). Obtain the second point, (25, 50), from the information that a \$5 increase in price results in 10 fewer sales. The slope of the line is $\frac{50 - 60}{25 - 20} = -2$. Use the point-slope equation to get $n = -2(p - 20) + 60$, or $n = -2p + 100$.

**b.** $R(p) = -2p^2 + 100p$. The revenue is the price per T-shirt times the number of T-shirts sold, $R(p) = pn = p(-2p + 100)$, or $R(p) = -2p^2 + 100p$.

**c.** Vertex form: $R(p) = -2(p - 25)^2 + 1250$. The vertex is $(25, 1250)$. This means that the maximum revenue is \$1250 when the price is \$25.

$h = -\dfrac{100}{2(-2)} = 25$ and $k = 0 - \dfrac{100^2}{4(-2)} = 1250$, so the vertex form is $R(p) = -2(p - 25)^2 + 1250$ and the vertex is $(25, 1250)$.

**d.** Between \$15 and \$35. Find the points where $R(p) = 1050$, or $-2p^2 + 100p = 1050$.

$$-2p^2 + 100p - 1050 = 0$$

$$-2\left(p^2 - 50p + 525\right) = 0$$

$$-2(p - 15)(p - 35) = 0$$

$$p = 15 \text{ or } p = 35$$

Any price between \$15 and \$35 will yield at least \$1050 in revenue.

**12. a.** $x(2x + 4) - 3(2x + 4) = 2x^2 + 4x - 6x - 12 = 2x^2 - 2x - 12$

**b.** $x^2(x + 2) + 1(x + 2) = x^3 + 2x^2 + x + 2$

**13.** $x = 2$, $x = -3$, or $x = \frac{1}{2}$. By the zero-product property, $x - 2 = 0$, $x + 3 = 0$, or $2x - 1 = 0$, so $x = 2$, $x = -3$, or $x = \frac{1}{2}$.

**14. a.** $(x + 5)^2 + \left(\dfrac{y - 7}{3}\right)^2 = 1$; ellipse. For the vertical stretch, replace $y$ with $\frac{y}{3}$ to get the equation $x^2 + \left(\dfrac{y}{3}\right)^2 = 1$. For the translation, replace $x$ with $(x + 5)$ and $y$ with $(y - 7)$ to get the equation $(x + 5)^2 + \left(\dfrac{y - 7}{3}\right)^2 = 1$.

**b.**

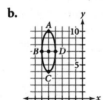

$A(-5, 10)$, $B(-6, 7)$, $C(-5, 4)$, $D(-4, 7)$; center: $(-5, 7)$

**15. a.** Let $x$ represent the year, and let $y$ represent the number of endangered species.

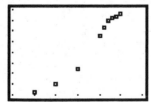

[1975, 2005, 5, 200, 1000, 100]

**b.** $\hat{y} = 45.64x - 90289$. Use your calculator to find the median-median line.

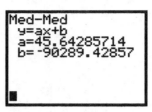

**c.** Approximately 1219 species in 2005; 3273 species in 2050.

Substitute 2005 for $x$:
$\hat{y} = 45.64(2005) - 90289 = 1219.2$.

Substitute 2050 for $x$:
$\hat{y} = 45.64(2050) - 90289 = 3273$.

## LESSON 7.4

### EXERCISES

**1. a.** $x - 2.3 = \pm 5$, so $x = 7.3$ or $x = -2.7$

**b.** $x + 4.45 = \pm 3.5$, so $x = -0.95$ or $x = -7.95$

**c.** $x - \dfrac{3}{4} = \pm \dfrac{5}{4}$, so $x = 2$ or $x = -\dfrac{1}{2}$

**2. a.** $3x^2 - 13x - 10 = 0$; $a = 3$, $b = -13$, $c = 10$

**b.** $x^2 - 5x - 13 = 0$; $a = 1$, $b = -5$, $c = -13$

**c.** $3x^2 + 5x + 1 = 0$; $a = 3$, $b = 5$, $c = 1$

**d.** $3x^2 - 3x - 2 = 0$; $a = 3$, $b = -3$, $c = -2$

**e.** $x^2 - 15x + 50 = 0$; $a = 1$, $b = -15$, $c = 50$

$$14(x - 4) - (x + 2) = (x + 2)(x - 4)$$

$$14x - 56 - x - 2 = x^2 - 4x + 2x - 8$$

$$13x - 58 = x^2 - 2x - 8$$

$$0 = x^2 - 15x + 50$$

**3.** In 3a–d, be sure to use parentheses as necessary. Here's the correct entry for 3a.

**a.** $-0.102$      **b.** $-5.898$

**c.** $-0.243$      **d.** $8.243$

**4. a.** $x = 1$ or $x = 5$. Use factoring and the zero-product property.

$$x^2 - 6x + 5 = 0$$

$$(x - 1)(x - 5) = 0$$

$$x = 1 \text{ or } x = 5$$

Alternatively, you can use the quadratic formula.

**b.** $x = -2$ or $x = 9$. Use factoring and the zero-product property.

$$x^2 - 7x - 18 = 0$$

$$(x + 2)(x - 9) = 0$$

$$x = -2 \text{ or } x = 9$$

Alternatively, you can use the quadratic formula.

**c.** $x = -1$ or $x = -1.4$. Use the quadratic formula; $a = 5$, $b = 12$, $c = 7$.

$$x = \frac{-12 \pm \sqrt{12^2 - 4 \cdot 5 \cdot 7}}{2 \cdot 5}$$

$$x = -1 \text{ or } x = -1.4$$

**5. a.** $y = (x - 1)(x - 5)$

**b.** $y = (x + 2)(x - 9)$

**c.** $y = 5(x + 1)(x + 1.4)$

**6. a.** $x^2 + 9x + 10 = 0$. The quadratic formula shows that $a = 1$, $b = 9$, and $c = 10$.

**b.** $x = \dfrac{-9 \pm \sqrt{41}}{2}$

**c.** $\dfrac{-9 + \sqrt{41}}{2}$ and $\dfrac{-9 - \sqrt{41}}{2}$

**7.** In 7a–c, substitute the $x$-intercepts for $r_1$ and $r_2$ in the factored form, $y = a(x - r_1)(x - r_2)$. In each, $a$ can be any nonzero value, or you can leave it as a variable.

**a.** $y = a(x - 3)(x + 3)$ for $a \neq 0$

**b.** $y = a(x - 4)\left(x + \frac{2}{5}\right)$, or $y = a(x - 4)(5x + 2)$, for $a \neq 0$. The second equation is found by multiplying the factor $x + \frac{2}{5}$ by the denominator of the root, 5. Note that $x + \frac{2}{5} = 0$ and $5x + 2 = 0$ both have the solution $x = -\frac{2}{5}$.

**c.** $y = a(x - r_1)(x - r_2)$ for $a \neq 0$

**8.** The solution includes the square root of $-36$, so there are no real solutions. The graph shows no $x$-intercepts. Before using the quadratic function, evaluate $b^2 - 4ac$. If $b^2 - 4ac < 0$, then there will be no real solutions.

**9.** The function can be any quadratic function for which $b^2 - 4ac$ is negative, as shown in Exercise 8. Sample answer: $y = x^2 + x + 1$.

**10.** The mean of the two solutions is

$$\frac{1}{2}\left( \frac{-b + \sqrt{b^2 - 4ac}}{2a} + \frac{-b - \sqrt{b^2 - 4ac}}{2a} \right) =$$

$$\frac{1}{2}\left( \frac{-2b}{2a} \right) = -\frac{b}{2a}$$

The $x$-coordinate of the vertex, $-\frac{b}{2a}$, is midway between the two $x$-intercepts.

**11. a.** $y = -4x^2 - 6.8x + 49.2$

| Time (min) $x$ | 1 | 1.5 | 2 | 2.5 |
|---|---|---|---|---|
| Amount of water (L) $y$ | 38.4 | 30.0 | 19.6 | 7.2 |

$D_1$     $-8.4$   $-10.4$   $-12.4$

$D_2$     $-2$   $-2$

The model appears to be quadratic because the second differences are constant. Start with the equation $y = ax^2 + bx + c$, and use three data points to solve for the coefficients $a$, $b$, and $c$.

$$\begin{cases} a + b + c = 38.4 & \text{Using the point } (1, 3.8). \\ 2.25a + 1.5b + c = 30.0 & \text{Using the point } (1.5, 30.0). \\ 4a + 2b + c = 19.6 & \text{Using the point } (2, 19.6). \end{cases}$$

Solve this system to get $a = -4$, $b = -6.8$, and $c = 49.2$, so the equation is $y = -4x^2 - 6.8x + 49.2$.

**b.** 49.2 L. The plug was pulled at 0 min, so substitute 0 for $x$: $y = -4(0)^2 - 6.8(0) + 49.2 = 49.2$. Alternatively, identify the constant term, 49.2, as the $y$-intercept.

**c.** 2.76 min. Use the quadratic formula to find the time when there is 0 L of water in the tub.

$$x = \frac{6.8 \pm \sqrt{(-6.8)^2 - 4(-4)(49.2)}}{2(-4)}$$

$$x \approx -4.46 \text{ or } x \approx 2.76$$

Because $x$ represents time, the only solution that makes sense is the positive one, $x \approx 2.76$. The tub empties in 2.76 min.

**12.** $\dfrac{a}{a + 1} = \dfrac{1}{a}$, $a = \dfrac{1 \pm \sqrt{5}}{2}$

$$\frac{a}{a + 1} = \frac{1}{a} \qquad \text{Original equation.}$$

$$a^2 = a + 1 \qquad \text{Multiply both sides by } a(a + 1).$$

$$a^2 - a - 1 = 0 \qquad \text{Subtract } a + 1 \text{ from both sides.}$$

$$a = \frac{1 \pm \sqrt{5}}{2} \qquad \text{Use the quadratic formula.}$$

Because only a positive value makes sense in the context of the rectangle, $a = \frac{1 + \sqrt{5}}{2}$.

**13. a.** $x^2 + 14x + 49 = (x + 7)^2$. Take the square root of the constant, $\sqrt{49} = 7$, and then multiply by 2 to get 14. This is the $x$-coefficient of the perfect square $(x + 7)^2$.

**b.** $x^2 - 10x + 25 = (x - 5)^2$. $\left(\frac{-10}{2}\right)^2 = 25$, so add 25 to $x^2 - 10x$ to complete the square.

**c.** $x^2 + 3x + \frac{9}{4} = \left(x + \frac{3}{2}\right)^2$. $\left(\frac{3}{2}\right)^2 = \frac{9}{4}$, so add $\frac{9}{4}$ to $x^2 + 3x$ to complete the square.

*Discovering Advanced Algebra Solutions Manual*
©2004 Key Curriculum Press

**d.** $2x^2 + 8x + 8 = 2(x^2 + 4x + 4) = 2(x + 2)^2$. It's easiest to first fill in the third and fourth blanks. When you factor 2 from 8, you get 4 in the third blank. The factor of 2 carries over to the last expression, so put 2 in the fourth blank.

$$2x^2 + ? + 8 = 2(x^2 + ? + \mathbf{4}) = 2(x + ?)^2$$

Now look at the middle expression and determine what to add to make it a perfect square. Take the square root of 4, $\sqrt{4} = 2$, and then double it. This gives 4 in the second blank and 2 in the fifth blank.

$$2x^2 + ? + 8 = 2(x^2 + \mathbf{4x} + 4) = 2(x + \mathbf{2})^2$$

Finally, distribute the 2 through the middle expression to fill in the first blank with $2(4x)$, or $8x$.

$$2x^2 + \mathbf{8x} + 8 = 2(x^2 + 4x + 4) = 2(x + 2)^2$$

**14. a.** $y = \pm\sqrt{x} - 1$. Switch $x$ and $y$, and then solve for $y$.

$$x = (y + 1)^2$$
$$\pm\sqrt{x} = y + 1$$
$$y = \pm\sqrt{x} - 1$$

**b.** $y = \pm\sqrt{x - 4} - 1$. Switch $x$ and $y$, and then solve for $y$.

$$x = (y + 1)^2 + 4$$
$$x - 4 = (y + 1)^2$$
$$\pm\sqrt{x - 4} = y + 1$$
$$y = \pm\sqrt{x - 4} - 1$$

**c.** $y = \pm\sqrt{x + 6} - 1$. Switch $x$ and $y$, and then solve for $y$.

$$x = y^2 + 2y - 5$$
$$x = (y^2 + 2y + 1) - 5 - 1$$
$$x = (y + 1)^2 - 6$$
$$x + 6 = (y + 1)^2$$
$$\pm\sqrt{x + 6} = y + 1$$
$$y = \pm\sqrt{x + 6} - 1$$

**15. a.** $y = 2x^2 - x - 15$

| | |
|---|---|
| $y = (x - 3)(2x + 5)$ | Original equation. |
| $y = 2x^2 + 5x - 6x - 15$ | Use the distributive property. |
| $y = 2x^2 - x - 15$ | Combine terms. |

**b.** $y = -2x^2 + 4x + 2$

| | |
|---|---|
| $y = -2(x - 1)^2 + 4$ | Original equation. |
| $y = -2x + 4x - 2 + 4$ | Use the distributive property. |
| $y = -2x^2 + 4x + 2$ | Combine terms. |

**16. a.** $y = \sqrt{400 - x^2}$. By the Pythagorean Theorem, $x^2 + y^2 = 20^2$.

$$y^2 = 400 - x^2$$
$$y = \pm\sqrt{400 - x^2}$$

The function is $y = \sqrt{400 - x^2}$ because only positive values of $y$ make sense in the context of this problem.

**b.** Approximately 17.32 ft. Substitute 10 for $x$ in the equation for 16a: $y = \sqrt{400 - 10^2} \approx 17.32$ ft.

**c.** Approximately 8.72 ft. Solve the equation $x^2 + y^2 = 20^2$ from 16a for $x$: $x = \sqrt{400 - y^2}$. Substitute 18 for $y$: $x = \sqrt{400 - 18^2} \approx 8.72$ ft.

**17.** $a$ and $k$ have length 52.08$\overline{3}$ ft, $b$ and $j$ have length 33.$\overline{3}$ ft, $c$ and $i$ have length 18.75 ft, $d$ and $h$ have length 8.$\overline{3}$ ft, $e$ and $g$ have length 2.08$\overline{3}$ ft, and $f$ has length 0 ft. The total length of support cable needed for the portion of the bridge between two towers is 229.1$\overline{6}$ ft. *Note:* If you consider that there is a support cable on each side of the bridge, your answer will be 458.32 ft.

Start by putting the bridge on a coordinate plane with the vertex of the parabola at (0, 0) and the tips of the towers at the points (−80, 75) and (80, 75).

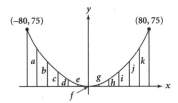

The equation in vertex form of this parabola is $y = ax^2$ because the vertex is (0, 0). Substitute the coordinates of the point (80, 75) to find $a$: $75 = a \cdot 80^2$, so $a = \frac{75}{80^2} = \frac{3}{256}$. Hence the equation of the parabola is $y = \frac{3}{256}x^2$. The support cables break up the interval from the vertex to one of the towers into six equal intervals, each of length $\frac{80}{6} = \frac{40}{3} = 13.\overline{3}$. Now use the equation $y = \frac{3}{256}x^2$ to compute the lengths of the support cables.

| Support cable | Distance from center (ft) $x$ | Support cable length (ft) $y$ |
|---|---|---|
| $a$ | $-66.\overline{6}$ | $52.08\overline{3}$ |
| $b$ | $-53.\overline{3}$ | $33.\overline{3}$ |
| $c$ | $-40$ | $18.75$ |
| $d$ | $-26.\overline{6}$ | $8.\overline{3}$ |
| $e$ | $-13.\overline{3}$ | $2.08\overline{3}$ |
| $f$ | $0$ | $0$ |
| $g$ | $13.\overline{3}$ | $2.08\overline{3}$ |
| $h$ | $26.\overline{6}$ | $8.\overline{3}$ |
| $i$ | $40$ | $18.75$ |
| $j$ | $53.\overline{3}$ | $33.\overline{3}$ |
| $k$ | $66.\overline{6}$ | $52.08\overline{3}$ |

The total length of support cables needed between two towers is the sum of the lengths, $229.1\overline{6}$ ft.

## EXTENSION

See the Sketchpad demonstration Quadratic Functions for a pre-made sketch and guided instructions. You should find that as $a$ changes, the vertex follows a linear path, specifically $y = \frac{b}{2}x + c$. As $b$ changes, the vertex follows a parabolic path, specifically $y = -ax^2 + c$. As $c$ changes, the vertex follows a linear path, specifically $x = -\frac{b}{2a}$.

## LESSON 7.5

## EXERCISES

**1. a.** $(5 - 1i) + (3 + 5i) = (5 + 3) + (-1 + 5)i = 8 + 4i$

   **b.** $(6 + 2i) - (-1 + 2i) = (6 - (-1)) + (2 - 2)i = 7$

   **c.** $(2 + 3i) + (2 - 5i) = (2 + 2) + (3 - 5)i = 4 - 2i$

   **d.** $(2.35 + 2.71i) - (4.91 + 3.32i) = (2.35 - 4.91) + (2.71 - 3.32)i = -2.56 - 0.61i$

**2. a.** $(5 - 1i)(3 + 5i) = 15 + 25i - 3i - 5i^2 = 15 + 22i - 5(-1) = 20 + 22i$

   **b.** $-6 + 12i$

   **c.** $3i(2 - 5i) = 6i - 15i^2 = 6i - 15(-1) = 15 + 6i$

   **d.** $(2.35 + 2.71i)(4.91 + 3.32i) = 11.5385 + 7.802i + 13.3061i + 8.9972i^2 = 11.5385 + 21.1081i + 8.9972(-1) = 2.5413 + 21.1081i$

**3.** To find the conjugate, negate the imaginary part.

   **a.** $5 + i$  **b.** $-1 - 2i$

   **c.** $2 - 3i$  **d.** $-2.35 + 2.71i$

**4.** A: $5 - 4i$, B: $-3i$, C: $-3 - i$, D: $-6$, E: $-2 + 4i$, F: $1$, G: $1 + i$

**5. a.**

All real numbers are also complex.

   **b.**

No number is both rational and irrational.

   **c.**

All imaginary numbers are also complex.

   **d.**

No number is both real and imaginary.

   **e.**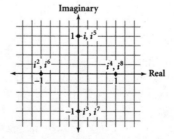

All real numbers are complex and all imaginary numbers are complex, but no number is both real and imaginary.

**6.** $x^2 - 4x + 5 = 0$. Any product in the form $(x - a)(x - b)$ expands to $x^2 - (a + b)x + ab$. Letting $a = 2 + i$ and $b = 2 - i$, note that $a$ and $b$ are complex conjugates and that $a + b = 4$ and $ab = 5$. So, $(x - (2 + i))(x - (2 - i)) = x^2 - 4x + 5$.

**7. a.** $i^3 = i^2 \cdot i = -1 \cdot i = -i$

   **b.** $i^4 = i^2 \cdot i^2 = -1 \cdot -1 = 1$

   **c.** $i^5 = i^4 \cdot i = 1 \cdot i = i$

   **d.** $i^{10} = i^5 \cdot i^5 = i \cdot i = i^2 = -1$

**8.** $i^{17} = i$

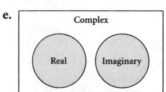

Each multiplication by $i$ rotates another 90° counterclockwise. They all correspond to 1, $i$, $-1$, or $-i$. To find $i^{17}$, use the fact that $i^4 = 1$.

$i^{17} = i^{16} \cdot i = \left(i^4\right)^4 \cdot i = 1^4 \cdot i = i$. In general, divide the exponent by 4 and raise $i$ to the power of the remainder.

**9.** $0.2 + 1.6i$. Multiply the numerator and denominator by the complex conjugate of the denominator, $2 + i$.

$$\frac{2 + 3i}{2 - i} \cdot \frac{2 + i}{2 + i} = \frac{1 + 8i}{5} = 0.2 + 1.6i$$

**10. a.** $2 \pm i\sqrt{2}$; complex. Using the quadratic formula, the solutions are

$$\frac{4 \pm \sqrt{(-4)^2 - 4 \cdot 1 \cdot 6}}{2(1)} = \frac{4 \pm \sqrt{-8}}{2}$$

$$= \frac{4 \pm 2i\sqrt{2}}{2}$$

$$= 2 \pm i\sqrt{2}$$

**b.** $\pm i$; complex and imaginary

$$x^2 = -1$$

$$x = \pm\sqrt{-1} = \pm i$$

**c.** $-\frac{1}{2} \pm i\frac{\sqrt{3}}{2}$; complex. Rewrite the equation as $x^2 + x + 1 = 0$. Using the quadratic formula, the solutions are

$$\frac{-1 \pm \sqrt{1^2 - 4 \cdot 1 \cdot 1}}{2.1} = \frac{-1 \pm \sqrt{-3}}{2}$$

$$= \frac{1}{2} \pm i\frac{\sqrt{3}}{2}$$

**d.** $\pm 1$; complex and real

$$x^2 = 1$$

$$x = \pm\sqrt{1}$$

$$x = \pm 1$$

**11.** For 11a–d, substitute the values of the zeros into the factored form $y = \left(x - r_1\right)\left(x - r_2\right)$, and then convert to general form.

**a.** $y = (x + 3)(x - 5) = x^2 - 2x - 15$

**b.** $y = (x + 3.5)(x + 3.5) = x^2 + 7x + 12.25$

**c.** $y = (x - 5i)(x + 5i) = x^2 - 25i^2 = x^2 + 25$

**d.** $y = (x - (2 + i))(x - (2 - i)) =$
$x^2 - (2 - i)x - (2 + i)x + (2 + i)(2 - i) =$
$x^2 - (2 - i + 2 + i)x + \left(4 - i^2\right) = x^2 - 4x + 5$

**12.** $y = 2x^2 - 16x + 50$. Start with a quadratic equation whose zeros are $4 + 3i$ and its complex conjugate, $4 - 3i$.

$$y = (x - (4 + 3i))(x - (4 - 3i))$$

$$= x^2 - (4 - 3i)x - (4 + 3i)x + (4 + 3i)(4 - 3i)$$

$$= x^2 - 8x + 25$$

The function $y = x^2 - 8x + 25$ has the correct roots, but its $y$-intercept is 25, half of 50. Stretch it vertically by a factor of 2 to get the desired function, $y = 2\left(x^2 - 8x + 25\right) = 2x^2 - 16x + 50$.

**13. a.** $x = \left(5 + \sqrt{34}\right)i \approx 10.83i$ or $x = \left(5 - \sqrt{34}\right)i \approx -0.83i$. Use the quadratic formula with $a = 1$, $b = -10i$, and $c = -9i^2 = 9$.

$$x = \frac{10i \pm \sqrt{100i^2 - 4(1)(9)}}{2(i)} = \frac{10i \pm \sqrt{-136}}{2}$$

$$= \frac{10i \pm i\sqrt{136}}{2} = \frac{10 \pm 2\sqrt{34}}{2}i$$

$$x = \left(5 \pm \sqrt{34}\right)i \approx 10.83i \text{ or } -0.83i$$

**b.** $x = 2i$ or $x = i$

$x^2 - 3ix - 2 = 0$. Use the quadratic formula with $a = 1$, $b = -3i$, and $c = -2$.

$$x = \frac{3i \pm \sqrt{9i^2 - 4 \cdot 1 \cdot (-2)}}{2(1)} = \frac{3i \pm \sqrt{-9 + 8}}{2}$$

$$= \frac{3i \pm i}{2} = 2i \text{ or } i$$

**c.** The coefficients of the quadratic equations are nonreal.

**14. a.** $b^2 - 4ac < 0$. The solutions are nonreal when $b^2 - 4ac < 0$, or when $b^2 < 4ac$. In this case, when you use the quadratic formula, you are taking the square root of a negative number.

**b.** $b^2 - 4ac \geq 0$. The solutions are real when $b^2 - 4ac \geq 0$, or when $b^2 \geq 4ac$.

**c.** $b^2 - 4ac = 0$. In the quadratic formula, the two solutions are equal when $b^2 - 4ac = 0$, or when $b^2 = 4ac$, because the square root of zero is zero.

**15.** For 15a–d, use recursion on your calculator to evaluate $z_0$ to $z_5$ and to verify the long-run value.

**a.** 0, 0, 0, 0, 0, 0; remains constant at 0

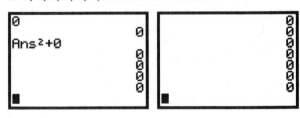

**b.** 0, $i$, $-1 + i$, $-i$, $-1 + i$, $-i$; alternates between $-1 + i$ and $-i$

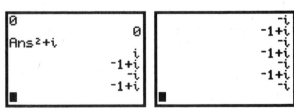

**c.** 0, $1 - i$, $1 - 3i$, $-7 - 7i$, $1 + 97i$, $-9407 + 193i$; no recognizable pattern in the long run.

```
0
                0
Ans²+1-i
              1-i
              1-3i
             -7-7i
             1+97i
```

```
            -7-7i
            1+97i
       -9407+193i
88454401-363110…
7.810996147ᴇ15-…
6.059901635ᴇ31-…
3.571536287ᴇ63-…
```

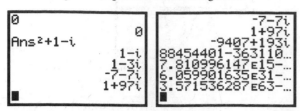

**d.** 0, $0.2 + 0.2i$, $0.2 + 0.28i$, $0.1616 + 0.312i$, $0.12877056 + 0.3008384i$, $0.1260781142 + 0.2774782585i$; approaches $0.142120634 + 0.2794237653i$ in the long run

```
0
                0
Ans²+0.2+0.2i
           .2+.2i
          .2+.28i
      .1616+.312i
.12877056+.3008…
```

```
.1260781142+.27…
.138901507+.269…
.1464109772+.27…
.1458123357+.28…
.1425667265+.28…
.1409094476+.28…
.1412577093+.27…
```

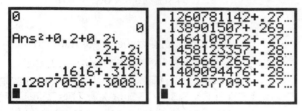

After many recursions:

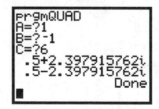

```
.142120634+.279…
.142120634+.279…
.142120634+.279…
.142120634+.279…
.142120634+.279…
.142120634+.279…
…34+.2794237653i
```

**16. a.** $x = \frac{-3 \pm \sqrt{15}}{2}$; $x = -3.44$ or $x = 0.44$. Use the quadratic formula with $a = 2$, $b = 6$, and $c = -3$.

$$x = \frac{-6 \pm \sqrt{6^2 - 4 \cdot 2 \cdot (-3)}}{2 \cdot 2} = \frac{-6 \pm 2\sqrt{15}}{4}$$

$$= \frac{-3 \pm \sqrt{15}}{2} \approx -3.44 \text{ or } 0.44$$

**b.**

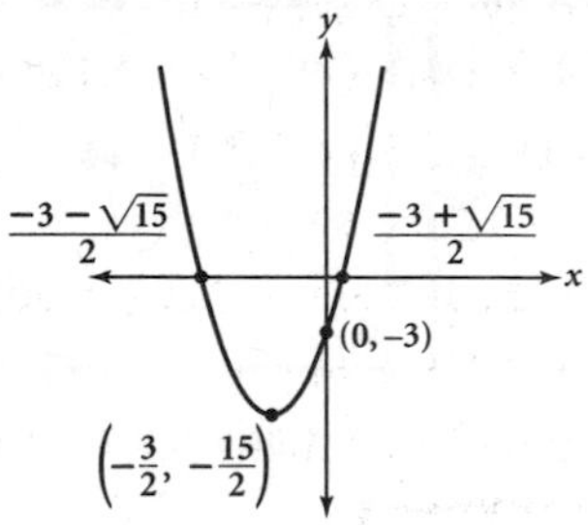

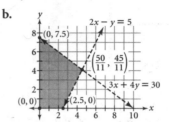

The graph crosses the $y$-axis at $(0, -3)$ because the constant term is $-3$, which is also the $y$-intercept. To find the vertex, complete the square.

$$y = 2x^2 + 6x - 3$$

$$y = 2(x^2 + 3x) - 3$$

$$y = 2\left(x^2 + 3x + \frac{9}{4} - \frac{9}{4}\right) - 3$$

$$y = 2\left(x^2 + 3x + \frac{9}{4}\right) - \frac{9}{2} - 3$$

$$y = 2\left(x + \frac{3}{2}\right)^2 - \frac{15}{2}$$

The vertex is $\left(-\frac{3}{2}, \frac{15}{2}\right)$.

**17. a.** Let $x$ represent the first integer, and let $y$ represent the second integer.

$$\begin{cases} x > 0 \\ y > 0 \\ 3x + 4y < 30 \\ 2x < y + 5 \end{cases}$$

**b.**

**c.** (1, 1), (2, 1), (1, 2), (2, 2), (3, 2), (1, 3), (2, 3), (3, 3), (1, 4), (2, 4), (3, 4), (4, 4), (1, 5), (2, 5), (3, 5), (1, 6)

## Extensions

**A.** See the solutions to Take Another Look activities 3 and 4 on page 178.

**B.** The program should be modified to switch to the appropriate complex mode. For example, a simple program for the TI-83 Plus is

```
prgmQUAD
a+bi
Prompt A,B,C
(-B+√(B²-4AC))/(2A)→R
(-B-√(B²-4AC))/(2A)→S
Disp R,S
```

```
prgmQUAD
A=?1
B=?-1
C=?6
 .5+2.397915762i
 .5-2.397915762i
            Done
```

**C.** Sample answer: In electronics, the state of an element in a circuit is described by two real numbers: voltage and current. These two states can be combined with a complex number in the form *voltage* + (*current*)*i*. Similarly, inductance and capacitance can be represented with a complex number. The laws of electricity, therefore, can be expressed using complex arithmetic.

**D.** Results will vary.

**EXERCISES**

**1. a.** $x$-intercepts: $-1.5, -6$; $y$-intercept: $-2.25$. To find the $x$-intercepts, identify the values of $r_1$ and $r_2$ in factored form. $r_1 = -1.5$ and $r_2 = -6$. To find the $y$-intercept, substitute 0 for $x$ and solve for $y$.

$$y = -0.25(0 + 1.5)(0 + 6) = -2.25$$

Check by graphing.

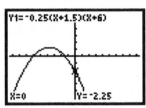

$[-9.4, 9.4, 1, -6.2, 6.2, 1]$

**b.** $x$-intercept: 4; $y$-intercept: 48. To find the $x$-intercepts, identify the values of $r_1$ and $r_2$ in factored form. $r_1 = r_2 = 4$. To find the $y$-intercept, substitute 0 for $x$ and solve for $y$.

$$y = 3(0 - 4)(0 - 4) = 48$$

Check by graphing.

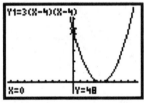

$[-9.4, 9.4, 1, -10, 70, 10]$

**c.** $x$-intercepts: 3, $-2$, $-5$; $y$-intercept: 60. To find the $x$-intercepts, identify $r_1 = 3$, $r_2 = -2$, and $r_3 = -5$ from the factored form. To find the $y$-intercept, substitute 0 for $x$ and solve for $y$.

$$y = -2(0 - 3)(0 + 2)(0 + 5) = 60$$

Check by graphing.

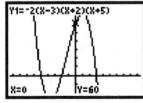

$[-9.4, 9.4, 1, -20, 80, 10]$

**d.** $x$-intercepts: $-3, 3$; $y$-intercept: $-135$. To find the $x$-intercepts, identify $r_1 = r_2 = -3$ and $r_3 = 3$ from the factored form. To find the $y$-intercept, substitute 0 for $x$ and solve for $y$.

$$y = 5(0 + 3)(0 + 3)(0 - 3) = -135$$

Check by graphing.

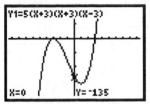

$[-9.4, 9.4, 1, -200, 100, 50]$

**2. a.** $y = 2(x - 2)(x - 4)$. Start with the factored equation $y = a(x - 2)(x - 4)$, using the $x$-intercepts, 2 and 4. Then substitute the coordinates of the vertex, $(3, -2)$, to find $a$.

$$-2 = a(3 - 2)(3 - 4) = -a$$

$$a = 2$$

The equation is $y = 2(x - 2)(x - 4)$.

**b.** $y = -0.25(x + 1.5)(x + 6)$. Start with the factored equation $y = a(x + 1.5)(x + 6)$, using the $x$-intercepts, $-1.5$ and $-6$. Then substitute the coordinates of the $y$-intercept, $(0, -2.25)$, to find $a$.

$$-2.25 = a(0 + 1.5)(0 + 6) = 9a$$

$$a = -0.25$$

The equation is $y = -0.25(x + 1.5)(x + 6)$.

**3. a.** $y = (x - 4)(x - 6) = x^2 - 6x - 4x + 24 = x^2 - 10x + 24$

**b.** $y = (x - 3)(x - 3) = x^2 - 3x - 3x + 9 = x^2 - 6x + 9$

**c.** $y = x(x + 8)(x - 8) = x(x^2 - 64) = x^3 - 64x$

**d.** $y = 3(x + 2)(x - 2)(x + 5) = 3(x^2 - 4)(x + 5) = 3(x^3 + 5x^2 - 4x - 20) = 3x^3 + 15x^2 - 12x - 60$

**4. a.** 7.5, $-2.5$, 3.2. Identify the values of $r_1$, $r_2$, and $r_3$ from the factored form.

**b.** 150. Substitute 0 for $x$ and solve for $y$: $y = 2.5(0 - 7.5)(0 + 2.5)(0 - 3.2) = 150$.

**c.** $y = 2.5(x - 7.5)(x + 2.5)(x - 3.2) = 2.5(x - 7.5)(x^2 - 0.7x - 8) = 2.5(x^3 - 0.7x^2 - 8x - 7.5x^2 + 5.25x + 60) = 2.5(x^3 - 8.2x^2 - 2.75x + 60) = 2.5x^3 - 20.5x^2 - 6.875x + 150$

**d.**

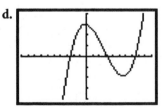

$[-10, 10, 1, -200, 200, 50]$

If the functions are equivalent, you should see only one curve.

**5. a.** Approximately 2.94 units; approximately 420 cubic units. Graph the function $y = x(16 - 2x)(20 - 2x)$, zoom in on the peak, and then trace the function to approximate the maximum volume.

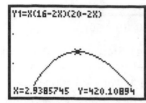

[1.279, 4.529, 1, 351.411, 488.911, 50]

**b.** 5 and approximately 1.28. Graph the linear function $y = 300$ along with $y = x(16 - 2x)(20 - 2x)$ and trace to approximate the intersections.

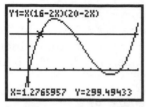

[−2, 12, 1, −200, 500, 100]

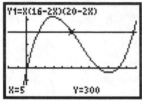

[−2, 12, 1, −200, 500, 100]

**c.** The graph exists, but these $x$- and $y$-values make no physical sense in this context. If $x \geq 8$, there will be no box left after you take out two 8-unit square corners from the 16-unit width.

**d.** The graph exists, but these $x$- and $y$-values make no physical sense in this context.

**6. a.** $4(x - 12)(x - 10)$. First, factor out the common factor, 4: $4x^2 - 88x + 480 = 4(x^2 - 22x + 120) = 4(x - 12)(x - 10)$.

**b.** $6\left(x - \frac{5}{3}\right)\left(x + \frac{1}{2}\right)$, or $(3x - 5)(2x + 1)$. Use the quadratic formula: The zeros of the polynomial are $\frac{7 \pm \sqrt{(-7)^2 - 4 \cdot 6 \cdot (-5)}}{2 \cdot 6} = \frac{7 \pm 13}{12}$, or $\frac{5}{3}$ and $-\frac{1}{2}$. Hence the polynomial factors as $6\left(x - \frac{5}{3}\right)\left(x + \frac{1}{2}\right) = 3\left(x - \frac{5}{3}\right) \cdot 2\left(x + \frac{1}{2}\right) = (3x - 5)(2x + 1)$.

**c.** $(x + 2)(x - 2)(x + 5)$

$x^3 + 5x^2 - 4x - 20$     Original equation.

$x^2(x + 5) - 4(x + 5)$     Factor out the common factor $x^2$ from $x^3 + 5x^2$, and factor out the common factor $-4$ from $-4x - 20$.

$(x^2 - 4)(x + 5)$     Factor out the common factor, $(x + 5)$.

$(x + 2)(x - 2)(x + 5)$     Factor $x^2 - 4$ into $(x + 2)(x - 2)$.

**d.** $2(x + 1)(x + 3)(x + 4)$. Graph the function $y = 2x^3 + 16x^2 + 38x + 24$ on your calculator. It has $x$-intercepts $-1$, $-3$, and $-4$. Use these values for $r_1$, $r_2$, and $r_3$ in the factored form along with the value of $a$ from the leading coefficient, $a = 2$. So the factored form is $2(x + 1)(x + 3)(x + 4)$.

**e.** $(a + b)(a + b)$, or $(a + b)^2$. This is the general form of a perfect square.

**f.** $(x - 8)(x + 8)$. The roots of the polynomial $x^2 - 64$ are $\pm 8$, so it can be factored as $(x - 8)(x + 8)$.

**g.** $(x + 8i)(x - 8i)$. The roots of the polynomial $x^2 + 64$ are $\pm 8i$, so it can be factored as $(x + 8i)(x - 8i)$.

**h.** $\left(x - \sqrt{7}\right)\left(x + \sqrt{7}\right)$. The roots of the polynomial $x^2 - 7$ are $\pm\sqrt{7}$, so it can be factored as $\left(x - \sqrt{7}\right)\left(x + \sqrt{7}\right)$.

**i.** $x(x - 3)$. Factor out the common factor, $x$.

**7. a.** Sample answer:

Any parabola with its vertex on the $x$-axis has one real zero.

**b.** Sample answer:

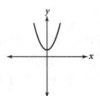

Any parabola that does not cross the $x$-axis has no real zeros.

**c.** Not possible. Any parabola intersects the $x$-axis at most twice.

**d.** Sample answer:

Any cubic curve that crosses the $x$-axis once has one real zero.

**e.** Sample answer:

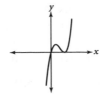

Any cubic curve that crosses the *x*-axis once and then touches the *x*-axis (has a double root) has two real zeros.

**f.** Not possible. Any cubic curve intersects the *x*-axis at least once.

**8. a.** $y = a(x + 5)(x - 3)(x - 6)$

**b.** $y = 2(x + 5)(x - 3)(x - 6)$. Substitute the coordinates of the *y*-intercept, (0, 180), and solve for *a*.

$$180 = a(0 + 5)(0 - 3)(0 - 6)$$

$$180 = 90a$$

$$a = 2$$

**c.** Replace *y* with $y - 100$:

$$y = 2(x + 5)(x - 3)(x - 6) + 100$$

**d.** Replace *x* with $x + 4$:

$$y = 2((x + 4) + 5)((x + 4) - 3)((x + 4) - 6)$$

$$= 2(x + 9)(x + 1)(x - 2)$$

**9. a.** $(T + t)^2$, or $T^2 + 2Tt + t^2$

|     | *T*  | *t*  |
|-----|------|------|
| *T* | *TT* | *Tt* |
| *t* | *Tt* | *tt* |

**b.** $(T + t)^2 = 1$, or $T^2 + 2Tt + t^2 = 1$

**c.** $0.70 + t^2 = 1$. Because *T* is the dominant gene, the people who have either *TT* or *Tt* constitute 70% of the population. Looking at the equation in 9b, this means $T^2 + 2Tt = 0.70$, so $0.70 + t^2 = 1$.

**d.** $t \approx 0.548$. Use the equation from 9c to solve for *t*.

$$t^2 = 1 - 0.70$$

$$t^2 = 0.30$$

$$t = \pm\sqrt{0.30} \approx 0.548$$

Only the positive root makes sense.

**e.** Subtract *t* from 1 to find *T*: $T \approx 1 - 0.548 \approx 0.452$.

**f.** $TT \approx 0.452 \cdot 0.452 \approx 0.204$, or about 20% of the population.

**10.** No. These points are collinear. Any attempt to find a 2nd-degree polynomial function will give $a = 0$.

**11.** $y = 0.25(x + 2)^2 + 3$. Start with the vertex form of the equation, $y = a(x + 2) + 3$, and use the point (4, 12) to find *a*.

$$12 = a(4 + 2)^2 + 3$$

$$9 = 36a$$

$$a = 0.25$$

So the equation is $y = 0.25(x + 2)^2 + 3$.

**12. a.** $x = \pm\sqrt{50.4} \approx \pm7.1$

**b.** $x = \pm\sqrt{13} \approx \pm3.6$

$$x^4 = 169$$

$$x^2 = 13 \text{ or } x^2 = -13$$

$$x = \pm\sqrt{13}$$

The equation $x^2 = -13$ has no real solution.

**c.** $x = 2.4 \pm \sqrt{40.2} \approx 2.4 \pm 6.3$; $x \approx 8.7$ or $x \approx -3.9$

$$(x - 2.4)^2 = 40.2$$

$$x - 2.4 = \pm\sqrt{40.2}$$

$$x = 2.4 \pm \sqrt{40.2}$$

**d.** $x = \sqrt[3]{-64} = -4$

**13. a.** $f^{-1}(x) = \frac{3}{2}x - 5$. Write the function as $y = \frac{2}{3}(x + 5)$, then switch *x* and *y* and solve for *y*.

$$x = \frac{2}{3}(y + 5)$$

$$\frac{3}{2}x = y + 5$$

$$\frac{3}{2}x - 5 = y$$

So, $f^{-1}(x) = \frac{3}{2}x - 5$. Check your answer: $f(4) = \frac{2}{3}(4 + 5) = 6$; $f^{-1}(6) = \frac{3}{2}(6) - 5 = 4$.

**b.** $g^{-1}(x) = -3 + (x + 6)^{3/2}$. Write the function as $y = -6 + (x + 3)^{2/3}$, then switch *x* and *y* and solve for *y*.

$$x = -6 + (y + 3)^{2/3}$$

$$x + 6 = (y + 3)^{2/3}$$

$$(x + 6)^{3/2} = y + 3$$

$$(x + 6)^{3/2} - 3 = y$$

So, $g^{-1}(x) = -3 + (x + 6)^{3/2}$. Check your answer: $g(5) = -6 + (5 + 3)^{2/3} = -6 + 4 = -2$; $g^{-1}(-2) = -3 + (-2 + 6)^{3/2} = -3 + 8 = 5$.

**c.** $h^{-1}(x) = \log_2(7 - x)$. Write the function as $y = 7 - 2^x$, then switch $x$ and $y$ and solve for $y$.

$$x = 7 - 2^y$$

$$x - 7 = -2^y$$

$$7 - x = 2^y$$

$$\log_2(7 - x) = y$$

So, $h^{-1}(x) = \log_2(7 - x)$. Check your answer: $h(2) = 7 - 2^2 = 7 - 4 = 3$; $h^{-1}(3) = \log_2(7 - 3) = \log_2 4 = \log_2 2^2 = 2$.

**14.** $f(x) = -2.5x + 1$. The first differences are all $-1$, so the function is linear. Find an equation for the line through any two of the points. The slope of the line through the points $(2.2, -4.5)$ and $(2.6, -5.5)$ is $\frac{-5.5 + 4.5}{2.6 - 2.2} = -2.5$. Use point-slope form to find the equation: $f(x) = -2.5(x - 2.2) - 4.5 = -2.5x + 1$.

## LESSON 7.7

### EXERCISES

**1.** For 1a–d, identify the $x$-intercepts.

  **a.** $x = -5$, $x = 3$, and $x = 7$

  **b.** $x = -6$, $x = -3$, $x = 2$, and $x = 6$

  **c.** $x = -5$ and $x = 2$

  **d.** $x = -5$, $x = -3$, $x = 1$, $x = 4$, and $x = 6$

**2. a.** $(0, 105)$

  **b.** $(0, 108)$

  **c.** $(0, -100)$

  **d.** $(0, -90)$

**3. a.** 3, because it has 3 $x$-intercepts

  **b.** 4, because it has 4 $x$-intercepts

  **c.** 2, because it has 2 $x$-intercepts

  **d.** 5, because it has 5 $x$-intercepts

**4. a.** $y = (x + 5)(x - 3)(x - 7)$. First use the zeros to start with the factored form $y = a(x + 5)(x - 3)(x - 7)$, and then use the $y$-intercept point, $(0, 105)$, to find $a$.

$$105 = a(0 + 5)(0 - 3)(0 - 7)$$

$$105 = 105a$$

$$a = 1$$

**b.** $y = 0.5(x + 6)(x + 3)(x - 2)(x - 6)$. First use the zeros to start with the factored form $y = a(x + 6)(x + 3)(x - 2)(x - 6)$, and then use the $y$-intercept, $(0, 108)$, to find $a$.

$$108 = a(0 + 6)(0 + 3)(0 - 2)(0 - 6)$$

$$108 = 216a$$

$$a = 0.5$$

**c.** $y = 10(x + 5)(x - 2)$. First use the zeros to start with the factored form $y = a(x + 5)(x - 2)$, and then use the $y$-intercept, $(0, -100)$, to find $a$.

$$-100 = a(0 + 5)(0 - 2)$$

$$-100 = -10a$$

$$a = 10$$

**d.** $y = 0.25(x + 5)(x + 3)(x - 1)(x - 4)(x - 6)$. First use the zeros to start with the factored form $y = a(x + 5)(x + 3)(x - 1)(x - 4)(x - 6)$, and then use the $y$-intercept, $(0, -90)$, to find $a$.

$$-90 = a(0 + 5)(0 + 3)(0 - 1)(0 - 4)(0 - 6)$$

$$-90 = -360a$$

$$a = 0.25$$

**5. a.** $y = a(x - 4)$ where $a \neq 0$

  **b.** $y = a(x - 4)^2$ where $a \neq 0$

  **c.** $y = a(x - 4)^3$ where $a \neq 0$; or $y = a(x - 4)(x - r_1)(x - r_2)$ where $a \neq 0$, and $r_1$ and $r_2$ are nonreal complex conjugates

**6. a.**

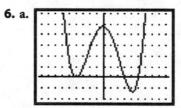

$[-9.4, 9.4, 1, -200, 600, 100]$

**b.**

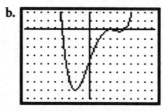

$[-9.4, 9.4, 1, -800, 200, 100]$

**c.**

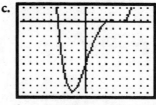

$[-9.4, 9.4, 1, -1000, 200, 100]$

*Discovering Advanced Algebra Solutions Manual*
©2004 Key Curriculum Press

**d.**

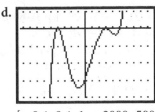

$[-9.4, 9.4, 1, -2000, 500, 500]$

**e.**

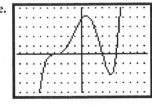

$[-9.4, 9.4, 1, -2000, 2500, 500]$

**f.**

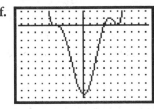

$[-9.4, 9.4, 1, -10000, 2000, 1000]$

**g.** A factor raised to the power of 1 results in an $x$-intercept that crosses the $x$-axis. A factor raised to the power of 2 results in an $x$-intercept that touches but does not cross the $x$-axis. A factor raised to the power of 3 results in an $x$-intercept that crosses the $x$-axis in a curved fashion. It appears that if the power of the factor is odd, the graph crosses the $x$-axis, whereas if the power of the factor is even, it touches but does not cross the $x$-axis.

**7. a.** 4

**b.** 5. There are only 4 $x$-intercepts, but $x = -5$ is a double root because the graph touches the $x$-axis at $(-5, 0)$ but does not cross it.

**c.** $y = -x(x + 5)^2(x + 1)(x - 4)$. Use the zeros $x = 0$, $x = -5$ (double root), $x = -1$, and $x = 4$ to start with the factored form $y = a(x - 0)(x + 5)^2(x + 1)(x - 4)$. Then use the point $(1, 216)$ to find $a$.

$216 = a(1 + 5)^2(1 + 1)(1 - 0)(1 - 4)$

$216 = -216a$

$a = -1$

**8. a.** $y = (x + 4)(x - 5)(x + 2)^2$. Start with the factored form $y = a(x + 4)(x - 5)(x + 2)^2$. Use the $y$-intercept point, $(0, -80)$, to find $a$.

$-80 = a(4)(-5)(2)^2$

$-80 = -80a$

$a = 1$

**b.** $y = -2(x + 4)(x - 5)(x + 2)^2$. Start with the factored form $y = a(x + 4)(x - 5)(x + 2)^2$. Use the $y$-intercept point, $(0, 160)$, to find $a$.

$160 = a(4)(-5)(2)^2$

$160 = -80a$

$a = -2$

**c.** $y = ax\left(x - \frac{1}{3}\right)\left(x + \frac{2}{5}\right)$, or $y = ax(3x - 1)(5x + 2)$ where $a \neq 0$. Start with the factored form $y = ax(3x - 1)(5x + 2)$. Use the $y$-intercept point, $(0, 0)$, to find $a$.

$0 = a(0)(-1)(2)$

$0 = 0$

In this case, the $a$-value is not uniquely defined. Any nonzero value for $a$ will give the same $x$-intercepts.

**d.** $y = (x + 5i)(x - 5i)(x + 1)^3(x - 4)$, or $y = (x^2 + 25)(x + 1)^3(x - 4)$. Complex roots always come in conjugate pairs, so $5i$ is also a root. Start with the factored form $y = a(x + 5i)(x - 5i)(x + 1)^3(x - 4)$. Use the $y$-intercept point, $(0, -100)$, to find $a$.

$-100 = a(5i)(-5i)(1)^3(-4)$

$-100 = 100i^2a$

$-100 = -100a$

$a = 1$

**9.** The leading coefficient is equal to the $y$-intercept divided by the product of the zeros if the degree of the function is even. The leading coefficient is equal to the $y$-intercept divided by $-1$ times the product of the zeros if the degree of the function is odd.

**10.** Graphs will be a basic "W" shape, pointed either up or down. The points of the "W" can vary in relative length or be basically the same. In the extreme case, $y = x^4$ or $y = -x^4$, the "W" flattens to a "U." Sample graphs:

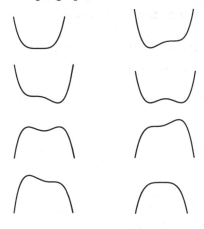

**11. a.  i.** $y = (x + 5)^2(x + 2)(x - 1)$. $x = -5$ is a double root because the graph only touches the $x$-axis at $(-5, 0)$. The other roots are $x = -2$ and $x = 1$. The graph opens upward, so the leading coefficient must be 1.

**ii.** $y = -(x + 5)^2(x + 2)(x - 1)$. This is the image of graph i after a reflection across the $x$-axis, so replace $y$ with $-y$.

$$-y = (x + 5)^2(x + 2)(x - 1)$$
$$y = -(x + 5)^2(x + 2)(x - 1)$$

**iii.** $y = (x + 5)^2(x + 2)(x - 1)^2$. $x = -5$ and $x = 1$ are double roots because the graph only touches the $x$-axis at those $x$-values. The other root is $x = -2$. The $y$-values increase as the $x$-values get increasingly more positive, and the $y$-values decrease as the $x$-values get decreasingly more negative, so the leading coefficient must be 1.

**iv.** $y = -(x + 5)(x + 2)^3(x - 1)$. $x = -2$ is a triple root because the graph curves a bit as it crosses the $x$-axis at $(-2, 0)$. The other roots are $x = -5$ and $x = 1$. The $y$-values decrease as the $x$-values get increasingly more positive, and the $y$-values increase as the $x$-values get decreasingly more negative, so the leading coefficient must be $-1$.

**b.  i.** $x = -5$, $x = -5$, $x = -2$, and $x = 1$

**ii.** $x = -5$, $x = -5$, $x = -2$, and $x = 1$

**iii.** $x = -5$, $x = -5$, $x = -2$, $x = 1$, and $x = 1$

**iv.** $x = -5$, $x = -2$, $x = -2$, $x = -2$, and $x = 1$

**12. a.  i.** 4

**ii.** 4

**iii.** 5

**iv.** 5

**b.  i.** 3. The graph has two local minimums, at $(-5, 0)$ and about $(0, -50)$, and one local maximum, at about $(-3, 15)$.

**ii.** 3. The graph has one local minimum, at about $(-3, -15)$, and two local maximums, at $(-5, 0)$ and about $(0, 50)$.

**iii.** 4. The graph has two local minimums, at about $(-3.5, -70)$ and $(1, 0)$, and two local maximums, at $(-5, 0)$ and about $(-0.7, 70)$.

**iv.** 2. The graph has one local minimum, at about $(-4.3, -45)$, and one local maximum, at about $(0.3, 45)$.

**c.** The number of extreme values of a polynomial function of degree $n$ is at most $n - 1$.

**d.  i.** $n$

**ii.** $n$

**iii.** $n$

**iv.** $n - 1$

**13. a.** Sample answer:

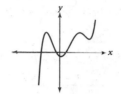

The graph should have at most five $x$-intercepts and at most four extreme values.

**b.** Sample answer:

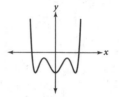

The graph should have at most six $x$-intercepts and at most five extreme values.

**c.** Sample answer:

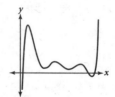

The graph should have at most seven $x$-intercepts and at most six extreme values.

**14. a.** $x = -\frac{2}{3}$ or $x = 5$. Use the quadratic formula.

$$x = \frac{13 \pm \sqrt{169 + 120}}{6} = \frac{13 \pm 17}{6} = \frac{30}{6} \text{ or } \frac{-4}{6}$$
$$x = -\frac{2}{3} \text{ or } x = 5$$

**b.** $x = \frac{3}{2}$ or $x = \frac{1}{3}$. Use the quadratic formula.

$$x = \frac{11 \pm \sqrt{121 - 72}}{12} = \frac{11 \pm 7}{12} = \frac{18}{12} \text{ or } \frac{4}{12}$$
$$x = \frac{3}{2} \text{ or } x = \frac{1}{3}$$

**c.** For 14a, the factors of the constant term are $\pm 1$, $\pm 2$, $\pm 5$, $\pm 10$, and the factors of the leading coefficient are $\pm 1$, $\pm 3$. For 14b, the factors of the constant term are $\pm 1$, $\pm 3$, and the factors of the leading coefficient are $\pm 1$, $\pm 2$, $\pm 3$, $\pm 6$. Each root is the quotient of a factor of the constant term and a factor of the leading coefficient.

**15.** $3 - 5\sqrt{2}$; $0 = a(x^2 - 6x - 41)$ where $a \neq 0$. Using the quadratic formula, the solutions to the equation $ax^2 + bx + c = 0$ are

$$x = \frac{-b \pm \sqrt{b^2 - 4ac}}{2a} = \frac{-b}{2a} \pm \frac{\sqrt{b^2 - 4ac}}{2a}$$

This shows that if $3 + 5\sqrt{2}$ is a root of a quadratic equation with rational coefficients, then the other root must be $3 - 5\sqrt{2}$. Any quadratic equation with these roots must be of the form

$$0 = a\left(x - \left(3 + 5\sqrt{2}\right)\right)\left(x - \left(3 - 5\sqrt{2}\right)\right)$$
$$= a\left(x^2 - \left(3 - 5\sqrt{2}\right)x - \left(3 + 5\sqrt{2}\right)x + \left(3 + 5\sqrt{2}\right)\left(3 - 5\sqrt{2}\right)\right)$$
$$= a\left(x^2 - \left(3 - 5\sqrt{2} + 3 + 5\sqrt{2}\right)x + \left(9 - 15\sqrt{2} + 15\sqrt{2} - 25(2)\right)\right)$$
$$0 = a\left(x^2 - 6x - 41\right)$$

**16. a.** $Q(-3) = (-3)^2 + 2(-3) + 10 =$
$9 - 6 + 10 = 13$

**b.** $Q\left(-\frac{1}{5}\right) = \left(-\frac{1}{5}\right)^2 + 2\left(-\frac{1}{5}\right) + 10 =$
$\frac{1}{25} - \frac{2}{5} + 10 = \frac{241}{25}$

**c.** $Q\left(2 - 3\sqrt{2}\right) = \left(2 - 3\sqrt{2}\right)^2 + 2\left(2 - 3\sqrt{2}\right) +$
$10 = 4 - 12\sqrt{2} + 18 + 4 - 6\sqrt{2} + 10 =$
$36 - 18\sqrt{2}$

**d.** $Q(-1 + 3i) = (-1 + 3i)^2 + 2(-1 + 3i) +$
$10 = 1 - 6i + 9i^2 - 2 + 6i + 10 = 0$

**17. a.** $x = \frac{5}{2}$, $y = -\frac{2}{3}$. Let matrix $[A]$ represent the coefficients, matrix $[X]$ represent the variables, and matrix $[B]$ represent the constant terms.

$$\begin{bmatrix} 4 & 9 \\ 2 & -3 \end{bmatrix}\begin{bmatrix} x \\ y \end{bmatrix} = \begin{bmatrix} 4 \\ 7 \end{bmatrix}$$

Find the inverse of matrix $[A]$ on your calculator.

$$[A]^{-1} = \begin{bmatrix} \frac{1}{10} & \frac{3}{10} \\ \frac{1}{15} & -\frac{2}{15} \end{bmatrix}$$

Multiply $[A]^{-1}[B]$ to solve the system.

$$\begin{bmatrix} x \\ y \end{bmatrix} = \begin{bmatrix} \frac{1}{10} & \frac{3}{10} \\ \frac{1}{15} & -\frac{2}{15} \end{bmatrix}\begin{bmatrix} 4 \\ 7 \end{bmatrix} = \begin{bmatrix} \frac{4}{10} + \frac{21}{10} \\ \frac{4}{15} - \frac{14}{15} \end{bmatrix} = \begin{bmatrix} \frac{5}{2} \\ -\frac{2}{3} \end{bmatrix}$$

The solution to the system is $x = \frac{5}{2}$ and $y = -\frac{2}{3}$.

**b.** $x = \frac{5}{2}$, $y = -\frac{2}{3}$

Augmented matrix $\begin{bmatrix} 4 & 9 & | & 4 \\ 2 & -3 & | & 7 \end{bmatrix}$

$-2R_2 + R_1 \rightarrow R_2$ $\begin{bmatrix} 4 & 9 & | & 4 \\ 0 & 15 & | & -10 \end{bmatrix}$

$-\frac{3}{5}R_2 + R_1 \rightarrow R_1$ $\begin{bmatrix} 4 & 0 & | & 10 \\ 0 & 15 & | & -10 \end{bmatrix}$

$\frac{1}{4}R_1 \rightarrow R_1$ $\begin{bmatrix} 1 & 0 & | & \frac{5}{2} \\ 0 & 15 & | & -10 \end{bmatrix}$

$\frac{1}{15}R_2 \rightarrow R_2$ $\begin{bmatrix} 1 & 0 & | & \frac{5}{2} \\ 0 & 1 & | & -\frac{2}{3} \end{bmatrix}$

**18.** Approximately 17.9 knots. Let $l$ represent the blue whale's length in feet, and let $S$ represent its speed in knots. Froude's Law states that $S = k\sqrt{l}$ for some constant $k$. Use the point $(75, 20)$ to find $k$. $20 = k\sqrt{75} = k \cdot 5\sqrt{3}$, so $k = \frac{20}{5\sqrt{3}} = \frac{4\sqrt{3}}{3}$. Thus the function relating a blue whale's length to its speed is $S = \frac{4\sqrt{3}}{3}\sqrt{l}$, or $S = \frac{4\sqrt{3l}}{3}$. To find out how fast a 60-foot-long blue whale would swim, substitute 60 for $l$: $S = \frac{4\sqrt{3(60)}}{3} \approx 17.9$. So a 60-ft blue whale would swim about 17.9 knots.

### EXTENSIONS

**A.** See the solution to Take Another Look activity 2 on page 178.

**B.** Answers will vary.

## LESSON 7.8

### EXERCISES

**1. a.** $a = 3x^2 + 7x + 3$. You first divide $3x^3$ by $x$ to get $3x^2$, and then you divide $7x^2$ by $x$ to get $7x$, and finally divide $3x$ by $x$ to get 3.

**b.** $b = 6x^3 - 4x^2$. In the first step of the long division, you multiply $2x^2$ by the divisor, $3x - 2$, to get $6x^3 - 4x^2$.

**2. a.** $3x^3 + 22x^2 + 38x + 15 = (x + 5)\left(3x^2 + 7x + 3\right)$

**b.** $6x^3 + 11x^2 - 19x + 6 = (3x - 2)\left(2x^2 + 5x - 3\right)$

**3. a.** $a = 12$. Multiply the divisor, 4, by 3 to get 12.

**b.** $b = 2$. Add the column: $5 + (-3) = 2$.

**c.** $c = 7$. The column must sum to 4: $c - 3 = 4$, so $c = 7$.

**d.** $d = -4$. The divisor, $d$, times the numbers in the bottom row must equal the next entry in the middle row. $d \cdot 1 = -4$, $d \cdot 3 = -12$, and $d \cdot (-1) = 4$, so $d = -4$.

**4.** For 4a–d, the dividend comes from the first line, the divisor comes from the upper left corner, and the quotient comes from the last line.

   **a.** $3x^3 - 11x^2 + 7x - 44 = (x - 4)(3x^2 + x + 11)$

   **b.** $x^3 + 5x^2 - x - 21 = (x + 3)(x^2 + 2x - 7)$

   **c.** $4x^3 - 8x^2 + 7x - 6 = (x - 1.5)(4x^2 - 2x + 4)$

   **d.** $x^3 + 7x^2 + 11x - 4 = (x + 4)(x^2 + 3x - 1)$

**5.** $\pm 15, \pm 5, \pm 3, \pm 1, \pm\frac{15}{2}, \pm\frac{5}{2}, \pm\frac{3}{2}, \pm\frac{1}{2}$. The numerator must be a factor of 15 and the denominator must be a factor of 2.

**6. a.** $47 = 11 \cdot 4 + 3$

   **b.** $P(x) = (x - 1)(6x^3 + x^2 + 8x - 4) + 11$. Use synthetic division to divide $6x^4 - 5^3 + 7x^2 - 12x + 15$ by $x - 1$. It shows a remainder of 11.

$$\begin{array}{r|rrrrr} 1 & 6 & -5 & 7 & -12 & 15 \\ & & 6 & 1 & 8 & -4 \\ \hline & 6 & 1 & 8 & -4 & \boxed{11} \end{array}$$

   **c.** $P(x) = (x - 2)(x^2 + x - 8) + 0$. Use synthetic division to divide $x^3 - x^2 - 10x + 16$ by $x - 2$. It shows a remainder of 0.

$$\begin{array}{r|rrrr} 2 & 1 & -1 & -10 & 16 \\ & & 2 & 2 & -16 \\ \hline & 1 & 1 & -8 & \boxed{0} \end{array}$$

**7. a.** $2(3i)^3 - (3i)^2 + 18(3i) - 9 = -54i + 9 + 54i - 9 = 0$ (Remember that $i^2 = -1$ and $i^3 = -i$.)

   **b.** $x = -3i$ and $x = \frac{1}{2}$. The conjugate pair $(x - 3i)$ and $(x + 3i)$ will be factors, so their product, $x^2 + 9$, will also be a factor. Use long division to find the other factor.

$$\begin{array}{r} 2x - 1 \phantom{xxxxx} \\ x^2 + 9 \overline{)\, 2x^3 - \phantom{x} x^2 + 18x - 9} \\ \underline{2x^3 + 0x^2 + 18x} \phantom{xxxxx} \\ -x^2 \phantom{xxxx} - 9 \\ \underline{-x^2 \phantom{xxxx} - 9} \\ 0 \end{array}$$

   This shows $2x^3 - x^2 + 18x - 9 = (x^2 + 9)(2x - 1)$, so the zeros are $\pm 3i$ and $\frac{1}{2}$.

**8. a.** 4. There are four zeros because the function is a 4th-degree polynomial.

   **b.** $x = 1$, $x = 2$, $x = -5$, and $x = -1$. First look for rational zeros. Their denominators must be factors of the leading coefficient, 1, so any rational zeros are in fact integers that are factors of 10. The possibilities are $\pm 1$, $\pm 2$, $\pm 5$, and $\pm 10$.

Try dividing by one of these possibilities, such as 1.

$$\begin{array}{r|rrrrr} 1 & 1 & 3 & -11 & -3 & 10 \\ & & 1 & 4 & -7 & -10 \\ \hline & 1 & 4 & -7 & -10 & \boxed{0} \end{array}$$

The remainder is 0, so $(x - 1)$ is a factor. Now try dividing the quotient, $x^3 + 4x^2 - 7x - 10$, by another possibility, such as 2.

$$\begin{array}{r|rrrr} 2 & 1 & 4 & -7 & -10 \\ & & 2 & 12 & 10 \\ \hline & 1 & 6 & 5 & \boxed{0} \end{array}$$

The remainder is 0, so $(x - 2)$ is also a factor. Now factor the quotient, $x^2 + 6x + 5 = (x + 5)(x + 1)$. The zeros are 1, 2, $-5$, and $-1$.

   **c.** $y = (x - 1)(x - 2)(x + 5)(x + 1)$

**9.** $y = (x - 3)(x + 5)(2x - 1)$, or $y = 2(x - 3)(x + 5)\left(x - \frac{1}{2}\right)$. Use trial and error to find a zero from the list of possible rational zeros. Try an integer first, such as 3.

$$\begin{array}{r|rrrr} 3 & 2 & 3 & -32 & 15 \\ & & 6 & 27 & -15 \\ \hline & 2 & 9 & -5 & \boxed{0} \end{array}$$

Now try 5.

$$\begin{array}{r|rrr} 5 & 2 & 9 & -5 \\ & & -10 & 5 \\ \hline & 2 & -1 & \boxed{0} \end{array}$$

These synthetic divisions show that 3 and $-5$ are zeros and that $2x^3 + 3x^2 - 32x + 15 = (x - 3)(x + 5)(2x - 1)$.

**10.** For 10a–d, first graph the function and approximate the x-intercepts. Then use the BISECTN program given in Calculator Note 7I to verify all real roots. If there are any nonreal roots (and you'll know this because the graph has fewer x-intercepts than the degree of the polynomial), use synthetic division to factor the polynomial. Finally, use the quadratic formula, or any other solution method, to find the zeros of any remaining quadratic factor.

   **a.** $x = \pm 2$, $x = 1$, and $x = \pm 2i$. The graph shows x-intercepts at approximately $-2$, 1, and 2.

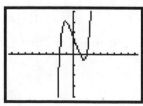

$[-9.4, 9.4, 1, -40, 40, 10]$

*Discovering Advanced Algebra Solutions Manual*
©2004 Key Curriculum Press

Use the BISECTN program to confirm these zeros.

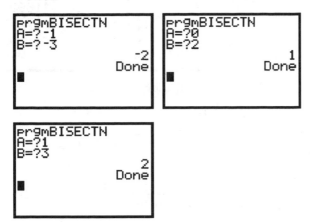

Now do synthetic division with these zeros to factor the polynomial.

$$
\begin{array}{r|rrrrr}
-2 & 1 & -1 & 0 & 0 & -16 & 16 \\
   &   & -2 & 6 & -12 & 24 & -16 \\
\hline
   & 1 & -3 & 6 & -12 & 8 & \phantom{-}0
\end{array}
$$

$$
\begin{array}{r|rrrrr}
1 & 1 & -3 & 6 & -12 & 8 \\
  &   & 1 & -2 & 4 & -8 \\
\hline
  & 1 & -2 & 4 & -8 & \phantom{-}0
\end{array}
$$

$$
\begin{array}{r|rrrr}
2 & 1 & -2 & 4 & -8 \\
  &   & 2 & 0 & 8 \\
\hline
  & 1 & 0 & 4 & \phantom{-}0
\end{array}
$$

So the factored form of the polynomial function is $y = (x + 2)(x - 1)(x - 2)(x^2 + 4)$. Find the zeros of the quadratic factor: $x^2 + 4 = 0$, so $x^2 = -4$, and $x = \pm 2i$. The five zeros are $\pm 2$, 1, and $\pm 2i$.

**b.** $x \approx -7.01$, $x \approx -0.943$, and $x \approx 0.454$. In graphing the function, it looks like one of the $x$-intercepts is between $-8$ and $-6$, one is between $-2$ and 0, and one is between 0 and 1.

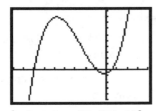

$[-9, 4, 1, -50, 100, 10]$

Use the BISECTN program to find the zeros.

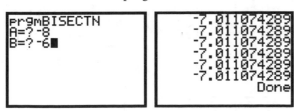

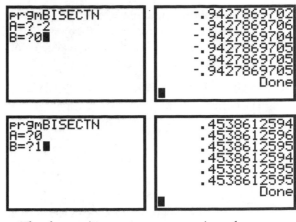

The three $x$-intercepts are approximately $-7.01$, $-0.943$, and 0.454.

**c.** $x \approx 6.605$, $x \approx 12.501$, $x \approx 17.556$, and $x \approx 11.675 \pm 0.380i$. In graphing the function, it looks like one of the $x$-intercepts is between 6 and 8, one is between 10 and 14, and one is between 16 and 18.

$[-1, 20, 2, -200, 180, 50]$

Use the BISECTN program to find the zeros.

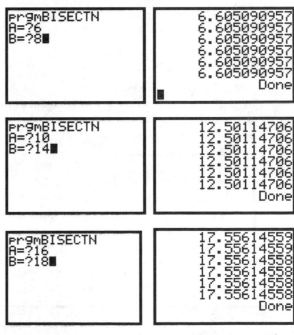

Multiplying out $y = 0.2(x - 12)^5 - 6(x - 12)^3 - (x - 12)^2 + 1$ will be cumbersome. Instead, notice that $y = 0.2(x - 12)^5 - 6(x - 12)^3 - (x - 12)^2 + 1$ is a translation right 12 units of the polynomial function $y = 0.2x^5 - 6x^3 - x^2 + 1$. The real zeros of $y = 0.2x^5 - 6x^3 - x^2 + 1$ are each 12 less than the real zeros of $y = 0.2(x - 12)^5 - 6(x - 12)^3 - (x - 12)^2 + 1$.

$6.605 - 12 = -5.395$

$12.501 - 12 = 0.501$

$17.556 - 12 = 5.556$

Use synthetic division to factor $y = 0.2x^5 - 6x^3 - x^2 + 1$.

$$
\begin{array}{r|rrrrrr}
-5.395 & 0.2 & 0 & -6 & -1 & 0 & 1 \\
& & -1.08 & 5.82 & 0.97 & 0.16 & -0.86 \\
\hline
& 0.2 & -1.08 & -0.18 & -0.03 & 0.16 & \boxed{\approx 0}
\end{array}
$$

$$
\begin{array}{r|rrrrr}
0.501 & 0.2 & -1.08 & -0.18 & -0.03 & 0.16 \\
& & 0.10 & -0.49 & -0.34 & -0.18 \\
\hline
& 0.2 & -0.98 & -0.67 & -0.37 & \boxed{\approx 0}
\end{array}
$$

$$
\begin{array}{r|rrrr}
5.556 & 0.2 & -0.98 & -0.67 & -0.37 \\
& & 1.11 & 0.72 & 0.28 \\
\hline
& 0.2 & 0.13 & 0.05 & \boxed{\approx 0}
\end{array}
$$

So, $y = 0.2x^5 - 6x^3 - x^2 + 1 \approx (x + 5.395) \cdot (x - 0.501)(x - 5.556)(0.2x^2 + 0.13x + 0.05)$.

Now use the quadratic formula to find the zeros of the quadratic factor.

$$x = \frac{-0.13 \pm \sqrt{(0.13)^2 - 4(0.2)(0.05)}}{2(0.2)}$$

$$= -0.325 \pm 0.380i$$

Now add 12 to each of these zeros to account for the translation: $x = 11.675 \pm 0.380i$.

The five zeros are approximately 6.605, 12.501, 17.556, and $11.675 \pm 0.380i$.

**d.** $x \approx -3.033$, $x \approx 2.634$, and $x \approx -0.3 \pm 0.812i$. In graphing the function, it looks like one of the $x$-intercepts is between $-3.5$ and $-2.5$ and that one is between 2 and 3.

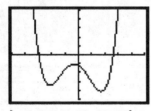

$[-5, 5, 1, -50, 50, 10]$

Use the BISECTN program to find the zeros.

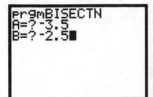

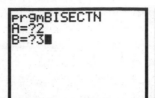

Use synthetic division to factor.

$$
\begin{array}{r|rrrrr}
-3.033 & 2 & 2 & -14 & -9 & -12 \\
& & -6.07 & 12.34 & 5.04 & 14 \\
\hline
& 2 & -4.07 & -1.66 & -3.96 & \boxed{\approx 0}
\end{array}
$$

$$
\begin{array}{r|rrrr}
2.634 & 2 & -4.07 & -1.66 & -3.96 \\
& & 5.26 & 3.16 & 3.94 \\
\hline
& 2 & 1.20 & 1.50 & \boxed{\approx 0}
\end{array}
$$

So, $y = 2x^4 + 2x^3 - 14x^2 - 9x - 12 \approx (x + 3.033)(x - 2.634)(2x^2 + 1.20x + 1.50)$.

Now use the quadratic formula to find the zeros of the quadratic factor.

$$x = \frac{-1.2 \pm \sqrt{(1.2)^2 - 4(2)(1.5)}}{2(2)} \approx -0.3 \pm 0.812i$$

The four zeros are $-3.033$, $2.634$, and $-0.3 \pm 0.812i$.

**11. a.** $f(x) = 0.00639x^{3/2}$. Use the data point $(221, 21)$ to find the constant $k$ for the British Columbian pine. $21 = k(221)^{3/2}$, so $k = \frac{21}{221^{3/2}} \approx 0.00639$. Hence the function is $f(x) = 0.00639x^{3/2}$.

**b.** $f^{-1}(x) \approx (156x)^{2/3}$. Start with $y = 0.00639x^{3/2}$, and then switch $x$ and $y$ and solve for $y$.

$$x = 0.00639y^{3/2}$$

$$156.4477x = y^{3/2}$$

$$(156.4477x)^{2/3} = y, \text{ or } y \approx (156x)^{2/3}$$

$$f^{-1}(x) \approx (156x)^{2/3}$$

**c.** $f(300) = 0.00639(300)^{3/2} \approx 33.21$, so the diameter is approximately 33 in.

**d.** $f^{-1}(15) = (156 \cdot 15)^{2/3} = 2340^{2/3} \approx 176.26$, so the tree would be approximately 176 ft tall.

**12.** $y = 2.1x^3 - 2.1x^2 - 6x + 5$. Use finite differences to find the degree of the polynomial.

| $x$ | $y$ | $D_1$ | $D_2$ | $D_3$ |
|-----|-----|-------|-------|-------|
| $-2$ | $-8.2$ | | | |
| | | $15$ | | |
| $-1$ | $6.8$ | | $-16.8$ | |
| | | $-1.8$ | | $12.6$ |
| $0$ | $5$ | | $-4.2$ | |
| | | $-6$ | | $12.6$ |
| $1$ | $-1$ | | $8.4$ | |
| | | $2.4$ | | $12.6$ |
| $2$ | $1.4$ | | $21$ | |
| | | $23.4$ | | |
| $3$ | $24.8$ | | | |

The polynomial of lowest degree whose graph passes through the given points is 3rd degree. Start with the general form $y = ax^3 + bx^2 + cx + d$, and use four data points to find $a$, $b$, $c$, and $d$.

$$\begin{cases} -8a + 4b - 2c + d = -8.2 & \text{Using } (-2, -8.2). \\ d = 5 & \text{Using } (0, 5). \\ a + b + c + d = -1 & \text{Using } (1, -1). \\ 27a + 9b + 3c + d = 24.8 & \text{Using } (3, 24.8). \end{cases}$$

Now solve this system of linear equations to get $a = 2.1$, $b = -2.1$, $c = -6$, and $d = 5$, so $y = 2.1x^3 - 2.1x^2 - 6x + 5$.

**13. a.**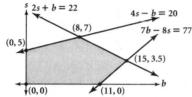

**b.** 14 baseball caps and 4 sun hats; $32. Maximize the profit function, $P = 2b + s$, within the feasible region. Check the value of $P$ at each of the vertices of the feasible region; the point that maximizes it is $(15, 3.5)$. Sam and Beth can only make integer numbers of each type of hat, so you need to find an integer point inside the feasible region near $(15, 3.5)$. $(14, 4)$ satisfies all of the constraints and gives the maximum profit of $32.

**14. a.** $y = x^2 - 4x - 12$, $y = (x - 6)(x + 2)$; vertex: $(2, -16)$; $y$-intercept: $-12$; $x$-intercepts: $6, -2$. $y = (x - 2)^2 - 16$ is in vertex form, and it shows that the vertex is $(2, -16)$. Multiply out the right side to get $y = x^2 - 4x + 4 - 16$, or $y = x^2 - 4x - 12$, the general form; the constant term shows that the $y$-intercept is $-12$. This factors as $y = (x - 6)(x + 2)$, which shows that the $x$-intercepts are $6$ and $-2$.

**b.** $y = 3x^2 + 6x - 24$, $y = 3(x - 2)(x + 4)$; vertex: $(-1, -27)$; $y$-intercept: $-24$; $x$-intercepts: $2, -4$. $y = 3(x + 1)^2 - 27$ is in vertex form, and it shows that the vertex is $(-1, -27)$. Multiply out the right side to get $y = 3(x^2 + 2x + 1) - 27$, or $y = 3x^2 + 6x - 24$, the general form; the constant term shows that the $y$-intercept is $-24$. This factors as $y = 3(x^2 + 2x - 8) = 3(x - 2)(x + 4)$, which shows that the $x$-intercepts are $2$ and $-4$.

**c.** $y = -\frac{1}{2}x^2 + 5x + 12$, $y = -\frac{1}{2}(x - 12)(x + 2)$; vertex: $\left(5, \frac{49}{2}\right)$; $y$-intercept: $12$; $x$-intercepts: $12$, $-2$. $y = -\frac{1}{2}(x - 5)^2 + \frac{49}{2}$ is in vertex form, and it shows that the vertex is $\left(5, \frac{49}{2}\right)$. Multiply out the right side to get $y = -\frac{1}{2}(x^2 - 10x + 25) + \frac{49}{2}$, or $y = -\frac{1}{2}x^2 + 5x + 12$, the general form; the

constant term shows that the $y$-intercept is 12. This factors as $y = -\frac{1}{2}(x^2 - 10x - 24) = -\frac{1}{2}(x - 12)(x + 2)$, which shows that the $x$-intercepts are 12 and $-2$.

**d.** $y = 2x^2 - 12x + 21$, $y = 2\left(x - \frac{6 + i\sqrt{6}}{2}\right)\left(x - \frac{6 - i\sqrt{6}}{2}\right)$; vertex: $(3, 3)$; $y$-intercept: 21; $x$-intercept: none. $y = 2(x - 3)^2 + 3$ is in vertex form, and it shows that the vertex is $(3, 3)$. Multiply out the right side to get $y = 2(x^2 - 6x + 9) + 3$, or $y = 2x^2 - 12x + 21$, the general form; the constant term shows that the $y$-intercept is 21.

Use the quadratic formula to find the zeros of $y = 2x^2 - 12x + 21$.

$$x = \frac{12 \pm \sqrt{144 - 168}}{4} = \frac{12 \pm 2i\sqrt{6}}{4}$$

$$= \frac{6 \pm i\sqrt{6}}{2}$$

Use the zeros and the value of $a$ from the general form to write the factored form, $y = 2\left(x - \frac{6 + i\sqrt{6}}{2}\right)\left(x - \frac{6 - i\sqrt{6}}{2}\right)$. The zeros of the polynomial are not real, so the graph of the function has no $x$-intercepts.

**15. a.** $x = -3$ or $x = 1$

$$6x + x^2 + 5 = -4 + 4(x + 3)$$
$$x^2 + 6x + 5 = 4x + 8$$
$$x^2 + 2x - 3 = 0$$
$$(x + 3)(x - 1) = 0$$
$$x + 3 = 0 \quad \text{or } x - 1 = 0$$
$$x = -3 \text{ or} \quad x = 1$$

**b.** $x = \frac{-3 \pm \sqrt{37}}{2}$

$$7 = x(x + 3)$$
$$0 = x^2 + 3x - 7$$

Use the quadratic formula.

$$x = \frac{-3 \pm \sqrt{3^2 - 4(1)(-7)}}{2(1)} = \frac{-3 \pm \sqrt{37}}{2}$$

**c.** $x = 1 \pm 2i$

$$2x^2 - 3x + 1 = x^2 - x - 4$$
$$x^2 - 2x + 1 = -4$$
$$(x - 1)^2 = -4$$
$$x - 1 = \pm 2i$$
$$x = 1 \pm 2i$$

## EXTENSION

First, note that 1 is a zero of any function in the form $y = x^n - 1$. Start with $y = x^3 - 1$. Because 1 is a zero, you can factor the right side as $(x - 1)$ times some polynomial. Long or synthetic division shows that $x^3 - 1 = (x - 1)(x^2 + x + 1)$.

Using the quadratic formula, the second factor has zeros $-\frac{1}{2} \pm i\frac{\sqrt{3}}{2}$. So the zeros of $y = x^3 - 1$ are $x = 1$, $x = -\frac{1}{2} + i\frac{\sqrt{3}}{2}$, and $x = -\frac{1}{2} - i\frac{\sqrt{3}}{2}$. Graph these numbers on a complex plane. The points appear to form an equilateral triangle centered at $(0, 0)$.

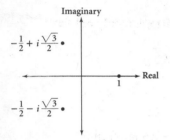

Now find the zeros of $y = x^4 - 1$. This factors as $y = (x^2 + 1)(x^2 - 1) = (x^2 + 1)(x + 1)(x - 1)$. The zeros of $x^2 + 1$ are $\pm i$, so the function factors completely as $y = (x + i)(x - i)(x + 1)(x - 1)$, and the zeros are $x = \pm i$, $x = \pm 1$. Graph these numbers on a complex plane. The points form a square centered at 0.

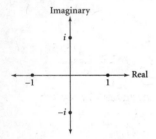

Find the zeros of $y = x^6 - 1$. This factors as $y = (x^3 + 1)(x^3 - 1)$. The zeros of the second factor were already found to be $x = 1$, $x = -\frac{1}{2} \pm i\frac{\sqrt{3}}{2}$. Use a similar method to find the zeros of $x^3 + 1$. First note that $-1$ is a zero, and then use long division to get $x^3 + 1 = (x + 1)(x^2 - x + 1)$. Use the quadratic formula to find the zeros of the second factor, $\frac{1}{2} \pm i\frac{\sqrt{3}}{2}$. In all, the zeros of $y = x^6 - 1$ are $x = \pm 1$ and $x = \pm\frac{1}{2} \pm i\frac{\sqrt{3}}{2}$. Graph these numbers on a complex plane. The points appear to form a regular hexagon centered at 0.

Conjecture: The zeros of the function $y = x^n - 1$ are vertices of a regular $n$-gon centered at 0.

## CHAPTER 7 REVIEW

### EXERCISES

**1. a.** First factor out the common factor, 2, to get $2(x^2 - 5x + 6)$. Then, $2(x - 2)(x - 3)$.

　**b.** $(2x + 1)(x + 3)$, or $2(x + 0.5)(x + 3)$

　**c.** First factor out the common factor, $x$, to get $x(x^2 - 10x - 24)$. Then, $x(x - 12)(x + 2)$.

**2. a.** $x = 9$ or $x = -1$

$$x^2 - 8x - 9 = 0$$
$$(x - 9)(x + 1) = 0$$
$$x - 9 = 0 \text{ or } x + 1 = 0$$
$$x = 9 \text{ or } \qquad x = 1$$

　**b.** $x = 0$, $x = 3$, or $x = -5$

$$x^4 + 2x^3 - 15x^2 = 0$$
$$x^2(x^2 + 2x - 15) = 0$$
$$x^2(x - 3)(x + 5) = 0$$
$$x^2 = 0 \text{ or } x - 3 = 0 \text{ or } x + 5 = 0$$
$$x = 0 \text{ or } \qquad x = 3 \text{ or } \qquad x = -5$$

**3.** Three points: 1; four points: 4; five points: 10; $n$ points: $\frac{1}{6}n^3 - \frac{1}{2}n^2 + \frac{1}{3}n$. Use finite differences to find the model for $n$ points.

| Points $n$ | 3 | 4 | 5 | 6 | 7 |
|---|---|---|---|---|---|
| Triangles $t$ | 1 | 4 | 10 | 20 | 35 |

$D_1$ 　　　3　　6　　10　　15

$D_2$ 　　　　3　　4　　5

$D_3$ 　　　　　1　　1

The model must be cubic. Start with the equation $t = an^3 + bn^2 + cn + d$, where $n$ is the number of points and $t$ is the number of triangles you can draw with those points. Use four data points, such as (3, 1), (4, 4), (5, 10), and (6, 20), to obtain a linear system to solve for $a$, $b$, $c$, and $d$.

$$\begin{cases} 27a + 9b + 3c + d = 1 \\ 64a + 16b + 4 + d = 4 \\ 125a + 25b + 5 + d = 10 \\ 216a + 36b + 6 + d = 20 \end{cases}$$

Use your calculator to reduce an augmented matrix to reduced row-echelon form.

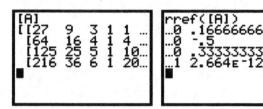

$a = \frac{1}{6}$, $b = -\frac{1}{2}$, $c = \frac{1}{3}$, and $d = 0$, so for $n$ points, the number of triangles you can draw is $t = \frac{1}{6}n^3 - \frac{1}{2}n^2 + \frac{1}{3}n$.

**4. a.** It is in vertex form. General form:
$y = 2x^2 - 8x - 8$; factored form:
$y = 2\left(x - \left(2 + 2\sqrt{2}\right)\right)\left(x - \left(2 - 2\sqrt{2}\right)\right)$.

To find the general form, multiply out the right side.

$$y = -16 + 2(x - 2)^2$$
$$= -16 + 2\left(x^2 - 4x + 4\right)$$
$$= -16 + 2x^2 - 8x + 8$$
$$= 2x^2 - 8x - 8$$

To find the factored form, use the quadratic formula to find the zeros.

$$x = \frac{-(-8) \pm \sqrt{(-8)^2 - 4(2)(-8)}}{2(2)}$$
$$= \frac{8 \pm \sqrt{128}}{4} = \frac{8 \pm 8\sqrt{2}}{4} = 2 \pm 2\sqrt{2}$$

So the factored form is
$y = 2\left(x - \left(2 + 2\sqrt{2}\right)\right)\left(x - \left(2 - 2\sqrt{2}\right)\right)$.

**b.** It is in factored form. General form: $y = -3x^2 + 12x + 15$; vertex form: $y = -3(x - 2)^2 - 27$.

To find the general form, multiply out the right side.

$$y = -3(x - 5)(x + 1) = -3\left(x^2 - 4x - 5\right)$$
$$= -3x^2 + 12x + 15$$

To find the vertex form, calculate $h$ and $k$.

$$h = -\frac{b}{2a} = -\frac{12}{-6} = 2$$

$$k = c - \frac{b^2}{4a} = 15 - \frac{144}{-12} = 27$$

So the vertex form is $y = -3(x - 2)^2 - 27$.

**c.** It is in general form. Factored form:
$y = (x + 2)(x + 1)$; vertex form: $y = (x + 1.5)^2 - 0.25$.

To find the factored form, factor $x^2 + 3x + 2$: $(x + 2)(x + 1)$.

To find the vertex form, complete the square.

$$y = x^2 + 3x + 1.5^2 - 1.5^2 + 2$$
$$= (x + 1.5)^2 - 2.25 + 2$$
$$= (x + 1.5)^2 - 0.25$$

**d.** It is in factored form. General form: $y = x^3 + 2x^2 - 11x - 12$. There is no vertex form for a cubic equation.

To find the general form, multiply out the right side.

$$y = (x + 1)(x - 3)(x + 4)$$
$$= \left(x^2 - 2x - 3\right)(x + 4)$$
$$= x^3 + 2x^2 - 11x - 12$$

**e.** It is in general form. Factored form:
$y = 2\left(x - \frac{-5 + \sqrt{73}}{4}\right)\left(x - \frac{-5 - \sqrt{73}}{4}\right)$;
vertex form: $y = 2(x + 1.25)^2 - 9.125$.

To find the factored form, use the quadratic formula to find the zeros.

$$x = \frac{-5 \pm \sqrt{5^2 - 4(2)(-6)}}{2(2)} = \frac{-5 \pm \sqrt{73}}{4}$$

The factored form is

$$y = 2\left(x - \frac{-5 + \sqrt{73}}{4}\right)\left(x - \frac{-5 - \sqrt{73}}{4}\right)$$

To find the vertex form, complete the square.

$$y = 2\left(x^2 + \frac{5}{2}x + \left(\frac{5}{4}\right)^2 - \left(\frac{5}{4}\right)^2\right) - 6$$
$$= 2\left(\left(x + \frac{5}{4}\right)^2 - \frac{25}{16}\right) - 6$$
$$= 2\left(x + \frac{5}{4}\right)^2 - \frac{25}{8} - 6$$
$$y = 2\left(x + \frac{5}{4}\right)^2 - \frac{73}{8} = 2(x + 1.25)^2 - 9.125$$

**f.** It is in vertex form. General form:
$y = -x^2 - 14x - 51$; factored form:
$y = -\left(x - \left(-7 + i\sqrt{2}\right)\right)\left(x - \left(-7 - i\sqrt{2}\right)\right)$

To find the general form, multiply out the right side of the equation.

$$y = -2 - (x + 7)^2$$
$$= -2 - \left(x^2 + 14x + 49\right)$$
$$= -x^2 - 14x - 51$$

To find the factored form, use the quadratic formula to find the zeros.

$$x = \frac{14 \pm \sqrt{(-14)^2 - 4(-1)(-51)}}{2(-1)}$$

$$= \frac{14 \pm \sqrt{196 - 204}}{-2} = \frac{14 \pm i\sqrt{8}}{-2}$$

$$= -7 \pm i\sqrt{2}$$

So the factored form is
$$y = -\left(x - \left(-7 + i\sqrt{2}\right)\right)\left(x - \left(-7 - i\sqrt{2}\right)\right).$$

**5. a.**

Zeros: $x = -0.83$ and $x = 4.83$

**b.**

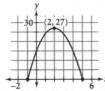

Zeros: $x = -1$ and $x = 5$

**c.**

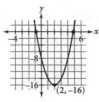

Zeros: $x = 1$ and $x = 2$

**d.**

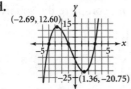

Zeros: $x = -4$, $x = -1$, and $x = 3$

**e.**

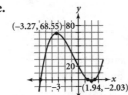

Zeros: $x = -5.84$, $x = 1.41$, and $x = 2.43$

**f.**

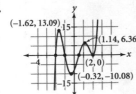

Zeros: $x = -2$, $x = -1$, $x = 0.5$, and $x = 2$

**6. a.** $y = 2(x + 1)(x - 4)$. The $x$-intercepts are $x = -1$ and $x = 4$. Start with $y = a(x + 1)(x - 4)$ and use the $y$-intercept point, $(0, -8)$, to find $a$.

$$-8 = a(0 + 1)(0 - 4) = -4a$$

$$a = 2$$

**b.** $y = 2(x + 3)^2(x - 1)$. The $x$-intercepts are $x = -3$ (double root) and $x = 1$. Start with $y = a(x + 3)^2(x - 1)$ and use the $y$-intercept point, $(0, -18)$, to find $a$.

$$-18 = a(0 + 3)^2(0 - 1) = -9a$$

$$a = 2$$

**c.** $y = -(x + 2)(x - 3)^3$. The $x$-intercepts are $x = -2$ and $x = 3$. $x = 3$ is a triple root because the graph curves as it crosses the $x$-axis. Start with $y = a(x + 2)(x - 3)^3$ and use the $y$-intercept point, $(0, 54)$, to find $a$.

$$54 = a(0 + 2)(0 - 3)^3 = -54a$$

$$a = -1$$

**d.** $y = 0.5(x + 4)(x - 2)(x - 3i)(x + 3i)$. The $x$-intercepts are $x = -4$ and $x = 2$. One of the zeros is $3i$, so its complex conjugate, $-3i$, must also be a zero. Start with $y = a(x + 4)(x - 2)(x - 3i)(x + 3i) = a(x + 4)(x - 2)(x^2 + 9)$ and use the $y$-intercept point, $(0, -36)$, to find $a$.

$$-36 = a(0 + 4)(0 - 2)(0^2 + 9) = -72$$

$$a = 0.5$$

$$y = 0.5(x + 4)(x - 2)(x^2 + 9)$$

$$= 0.5(x + 4)(x - 2)(x - 3i)(x + 3i)$$

**7.** 18 in. by 18 in. by 36 in. Let $V$ represent the volume of the package in cubic inches. Then, by the postal regulations, $4x + y = 108$, so $y = 108 - 4x$. The volume of the box is $V = x^2y = x^2(108 - 4x)$.

Trace the graph on your calculator to see that a local maximum occurs near $x = 18$. Then, $y = 108 - 4(18) = 36$ and the volume is $V = 18^2(36) = 11664$.

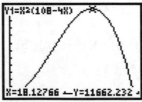

$[-1, 28, 2, -100, 12000, 1000]$

**8.** Approximately 227 m, or 740 ft. The function representing the height in meters of a free-falling object is $h = -4.9t^2 + v_0t + s_0$, where $h$ is the height in meters, $t$ is the time in seconds, $v_0$ is the initial velocity, and $s_0$ is the initial height. The initial velocity is 0 because the object was at rest before it was dropped. The object hits the water at 6.8 s, so $0 = -4.9(6.8)^2 + s_0$. Hence, $s_0 = 4.9(6.8)^2 = 226.576$; the object was dropped from approximately 227 m.

The same process can be carried out in units of feet. The function representing the height in feet of a free-falling object is $h = -16t^2 + v_0 t + s_0$, where $h$ is now the height in feet. Again, $v_0 = 0$, so the equation is $h = -16t^2 + s_0$. The object hit the water at 6.8 s, so $0 = -16(6.8)^2 + s_0$. Hence, $s_0 = 16(6.8)^2 = 739.84$; the object was dropped from approximately 740 ft.

**9. a.** $y = 0.5x^2 + 0.5x + 1$. Use finite differences to find the degree of the model.

| Number of cuts $x$ | Maximum number of pieces $y$ | $D_1$ | $D_2$ |
|---|---|---|---|
| 0 | 1 | | |
| 1 | 2 | 1 | |
| 2 | 4 | 2 | 1 |
| 3 | 7 | 3 | 1 |
| 4 | 11 | 4 | 1 |

The model is quadratic. Start with $y = ax^2 + bx + c$ and use three points to find $a$, $b$, and $c$.

$$\begin{cases} c = 1 \\ a + b + c = 2 \\ 4a + 2b + c = 4 \end{cases}$$

Substitute $c = 1$ into the second equation, so $1 = a + b$, and $b = 1 - a$. Now substitute $b = 1 - a$ and $c = 1$ into the third equation.

$4 = 4a + 2(1 - a) + 1$

$4 = 2a + 3$

$1 = 2a$

$a = 0.5$

$b = 1 - 0.5 = 0.5$

The equation is $y = 0.5x^2 + 0.5x + 1$.

**b.** 16 pieces; 56 pieces. Substitute 5 and 10 for $x$ in the equation from 9a.

$y = 0.5(5)^2 + 0.5(5) + 1 = 16$

$y = 0.5(10)^2 + 0.5(10) + 1 = 56$

**10. a.** $y = (26 - 2x)(21 - 2x)$

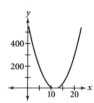

**b.** Domain: $0 < x < 10.5$; range: $0 < y < 546$. Find the zeros of the function.

$$0 = (26 - 2x)(21 - 2x)$$

$26 - 2x = 0$  or  $21 - 2x = 0$

$x = 13$ or  $x = 10.5$

For values of $x$ between 10.5 and 13, the function is negative, which doesn't make sense in the context of the problem. This is why the domain is $0 < x < 10.5$.

Within this domain, the maximum area is at the $y$-intercept. Substitute 0 for $x$ to find the $y$-intercept: $y = (26)(21) = 546$. So the range is $0 < y < 546$.

**c.** $x \approx 3.395$ cm. The area of the large rectangle is $26(21) = 546$. To make the two areas equal, the area of the shaded region and the area of the unshaded region should both be $\frac{546}{2} = 273$. The area of the shaded region is $y = (26 - 2x)(21 - 2x)$, so solve the equation $273 = (26 - 2x)(21 - 2x)$.

$273 = (26 - 2x)(21 - 2x)$

$273 = 546 - 94x + 4x^2$

$0 = 4x^2 - 94x + 273$

$x = \dfrac{94 \pm \sqrt{(-94)^2 - 4(4)(273)}}{2(4)}$

$x \approx 3.395$ or $x \approx 20.105$

The only solution between 0 and 10.5 is $x \approx 3.395$, so the areas are equal when $x$ is about 3.395 cm.

**11. a.** $\pm 1, \pm 3, \pm 13, \pm 39, \pm\frac{1}{3}, \pm\frac{13}{3}$. The numerator must be a factor of the constant term, $-39$, and the denominator must be a factor of the leading coefficient, 3.

**b.** $x = -\frac{1}{3}$, $x = 3$, $x = 2 + 3i$, and $x = 2 - 3i$. By trial and error, test the possible rational roots found in 11a to find that $x = -\frac{1}{3}$ and $x = 3$ are both roots.

$$3\overline{)\,3\;-20\quad 68\quad -92\quad -39}$$
$$\underline{\phantom{3\;}\;9\;-33\quad 105\quad 39}$$
$$3\;-11\quad 35\quad 13\;\boxed{0}$$

$$-\tfrac{1}{3}\overline{)\,3\;-11\quad 35\quad 13}$$
$$\underline{\phantom{3\;}\;-1\quad 4\;-13}$$
$$3\;-12\quad 39\;\boxed{0}$$

So, $3x^4 - 20x^3 + 68x^2 - 92x - 39 =$
$(x - 3)\left(x + \tfrac{1}{3}\right)\left(3x^2 - 12x + 39\right) =$
$(x - 3)(3x + 1)\left(x^2 - 4x + 13\right)$. To find the
zeros of the quadratic factor, use the quadratic
formula.

$$x = \frac{4 \pm \sqrt{16 - 52}}{2} = \frac{4 \pm 6i}{2} = 2 \pm 3i$$

The four roots of the polynomial equation are
$x = -\tfrac{1}{3}$, $x = 3$, $x = 2 + 3i$, and $x = 2 - 3i$.

**12. a.** $(4 - 2i)(-3 + 6i) = -12 + 24i + 6i - 12i^2 =$
$-12 + 30i - 12(-1) = 30i$

**b.** $(-3 + 4i) - (3 + 13i) = -3 + 4i - 3 -$
$13i = -6 - 9i$

**c.** $\dfrac{2 - i}{3 - 4i} \cdot \dfrac{3 + 4i}{3 + 4i} = \dfrac{6 + 5i - 4i^2}{9 + 16} =$
$\dfrac{10 + 5i}{25} = 0.4 + 0.2i$

**13.** $2x^2 + 4x + 3$

$$3x - 2\overline{)6x^3 + 8x^2 + x - 6}$$
$$\underline{6x^3 - 4x^2}$$
$$12x^2 + x$$
$$\underline{12x^2 - 8x}$$
$$9x - 6$$
$$\underline{9x - 6}$$
$$0$$

**TAKE ANOTHER LOOK**

**1.** Using the method of finite differences, you never
reach a constant difference, so no polynomial function perfectly fits these data. Based on the graph, it
appears that an exponential decay curve may fit
these data.

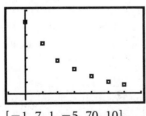

$[-1, 7, 1, -5, 70, 10]$

**2.** A line is determined by two points. A quadratic
curve (parabola) is determined by three points.
Continuing the pattern, four points determine a
cubic curve, and five points determine a quartic
(4th-degree) curve. In this chapter you used a

system of three equations in three variables to find
the coefficients $a$, $b$, and $c$ in a quadratic equation.
The number of points you need is one more than
the degree of the equation.

**3.** If you connect the origin and the three points in a
particular order, you can construct a parallelogram.
The only difference between the parallelograms
formed by adding or subtracting is the order in
which the points are connected.

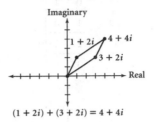

$(1 + 2i) + (3 + 2i) = 4 + 4i$

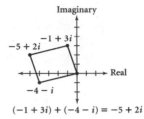

$(-1 + 3i) + (-4 - i) = -5 + 2i$

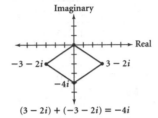

$(3 - 2i) + (-3 - 2i) = -4i$

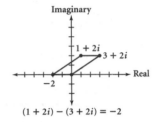

$(1 + 2i) - (3 + 2i) = -2$

**4.**

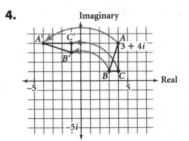

$i \cdot (3 + 4i) = 3i + 4i^2 = -4 + 3i$

$i \cdot (2 + i) = 2i + i^2 = -1 + 2i$

$i \cdot (3 + i) = 3i + i^2 = -1 + 3i$

Plotting the complex numbers associated with the
image of $\triangle ABC$ suggests that multiplying by $i$
provides a 90° counterclockwise rotation about the
origin.

Multiplying by $i^2$ rotates the point 180° counterclockwise. Multiplying by $i^3$ rotates it 270° counterclockwise. Multiplying by $i^n$ rotates it $n \cdot 90°$
counterclockwise.

In general, multiplying a point by a complex
number rotates that point counterclockwise by the
angle formed between a segment from the complex
number to the origin and the positive $x$-axis, and
multiplies the distance of the point from the origin
by the distance of the complex number from the
origin. For imaginary number $i^n$, the angle is $n(90°)$
and the distance from the origin is 1.

*Discovering Advanced Algebra Solutions Manual*
©2004 Key Curriculum Press

# CHAPTER 8

## LESSON 8.1

### EXERCISES

**1. a.**

| t | x | y |
|---|---|---|
| −2 | −7 | −3 |
| −1 | −4 | −1 |
| 0 | −1 | 1 |
| 1 | 2 | 3 |
| 2 | 5 | 5 |

**b.**

| t | x | y |
|---|---|---|
| −2 | −1 | 4 |
| −1 | 0 | 1 |
| 0 | 1 | 0 |
| 1 | 2 | 1 |
| 2 | 3 | 4 |

**c.**

| t | x | y |
|---|---|---|
| −2 | 4 | 1 |
| −1 | 1 | 2 |
| 0 | 0 | 3 |
| 1 | 1 | 4 |
| 2 | 4 | 5 |

**d.**

| t | x | y |
|---|---|---|
| −2 | −3 | 0 |
| −1 | −2 | 1.73 |
| 0 | −1 | 2 |
| 1 | 0 | 1.73 |
| 2 | 1 | 0 |

**2. a.**

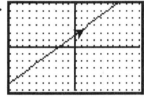

$[−9.4, 9.4, 1, −6.2, 6.2, 1]$
$−3 \leq t \leq 2.5$

**b.**

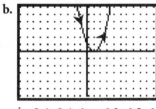

$[−9.4, 9.4, 1, −6.2, 6.2, 1]$
$−2.5 \leq t \leq 2.5$

**c.**

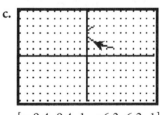

$[−9.4, 9.4, 1, −6.2, 6.2, 1]$
$−2 \leq t \leq 1$

**d.**

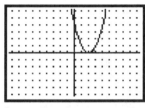

$[−9.4, 9.4, 1, −6.2, 6.2, 1]$
$−2 \leq t \leq 2$

**3. a.**

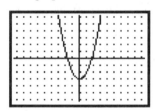

$[−9.4, 9.4, 1, −6.2, 6.2, 1]$
$−10 \leq t \leq 10$

**b.** The graph is translated right 2 units.

$[−9.4, 9.4, 1, −6.2, 6.2, 1]$
$−10 \leq t \leq 10$

**c.** The graph is translated down 3 units.

$[−9.4, 9.4, 1, −6.2, 6.2, 1]$
$−10 \leq t \leq 10$

**d.** The graph is translated right 5 units and up 2 units.

$[−9.4, 9.4, 1, −6.2, 6.2, 1]$
$−10 \leq t \leq 10$

**e.** The graph is translated horizontally *a* units and vertically *b* units.

**4. a.**

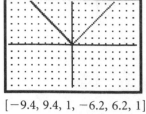

$[-9.4, 9.4, 1, -6.2, 6.2, 1]$
$-10 \leq t \leq 10$

**b.** The graph is translated left 1 unit and up 2 units.

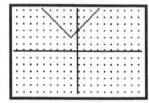

$[-9.4, 9.4, 1, -6.2, 6.2, 1]$
$-10 \leq t \leq 10$

**c.** $x = t - 4, y = |t| - 3$

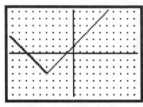

$[-9.4, 9.4, 1, -6.2, 6.2, 1]$
$-10 \leq t \leq 10$

**d.** The graph is stretched horizontally by a factor of 2.

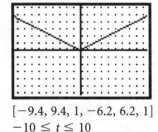

$[-9.4, 9.4, 1, -6.2, 6.2, 1]$
$-10 \leq t \leq 10$

**e.** The graph is stretched vertically by a factor of 3.

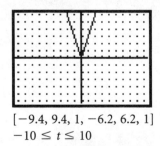

$[-9.4, 9.4, 1, -6.2, 6.2, 1]$
$-10 \leq t \leq 10$

**f.** The 3 stretches the graph vertically, the 2 translates it right 2 units, and the 4 being subtracted translates it down 4 units.

**5. a.** $t = 15$, so 15 s has elapsed.

**b.** 30 yd. The mascot starts at $x = 65$ and stops at $x = 35$, so $65 - 35 = 30$.

**c.** The average velocity is $\frac{30 \text{ yd}}{15 \text{ s}} = 2$ yd/s west, or $-2$ yd/s.

**d.** 65 yd is her starting position, $-2$ yd/s is her velocity, and 50 yd is her position relative to the sideline.

**e.** The graph simulation produces the graphs pictured in the problem. A good window is $[0, 100, 10, 0, 60, 10]$ with $0 \leq t \leq 15$.

**f.** Select increasing maximum $t$-values to find an $x$-value that is equal to or less than 10. When $t = 27.5$, $x = 10$, so the mascot crosses the 10 yd line after 27.5 s.

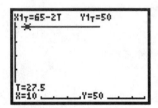

$[0, 100, 10, 0, 60, 10]$
$0 \leq t \leq 30$

**g.** $65 - 2t = 10$; $t = 27.5$ s. This verifies that the mascot crosses the 10 yd line after 27.5 s.

**6. a.** Possible answer: $x = t, y = 2\sqrt{1 - \left(\frac{t}{2}\right)^2}$. The equation for a circle with the center at the origin and radius 2 is $x^2 + y^2 = 4$, or $\left(\frac{x}{2}\right)^2 + \left(\frac{y}{2}\right)^2 = 1$. Solve for $y$ in terms of $x$.

$$\left(\frac{y}{2}\right)^2 = 1 - \left(\frac{x}{2}\right)^2$$

$$\frac{y}{2} = \pm\sqrt{1 - \left(\frac{x}{2}\right)^2}$$

$$y = \pm 2\sqrt{1 - \left(\frac{x}{2}\right)^2}$$

The semicircle is above the $x$-axis, so the equation for the graph is $y = +2\sqrt{1 - \left(\frac{x}{2}\right)^2}$. Let $x = t$ and change $y$ to a function of $t$ by substituting $t$ for $x$. The parametric equations for the graph are $x = t$ and $y = 2\sqrt{1 - \left(\frac{t}{2}\right)^2}$.

**b.** Possible answer: $x = t + 2$, $y = 2\sqrt{1 - \left(\frac{t}{2}\right)^2}$. The graph is the graph of the semicircle in 6a translated right 2 units, so the parametric equations are $x = t + 2$ and $y = 2\sqrt{1 - \left(\frac{t}{2}\right)^2}$.

**c.** Possible answer: $x = t$, $y = -2\sqrt{1 - \left(\frac{t}{2}\right)^2} + 1$. The graph is the graph of the semicircle in 6a reflected across the $x$-axis and translated up 1 unit, so the parametric equations are $x = t$ and $y = -2\sqrt{1 - \left(\frac{t}{2}\right)^2} + 1$.

**d.** Possible answer: $x = 2t$, $y = 2\sqrt{1 - \left(\frac{t}{2}\right)^2} + 1$. The graph is the graph of the semicircle in 6a stretched horizontally by a factor of 2 and translated up 1 unit, so the parametric equations are $x = 2t$ and $y = 2\sqrt{1 - \left(\frac{t}{2}\right)^2} + 1$.

**7. a.** The graph is reflected across the $x$-axis.

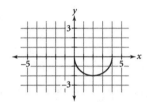

**b.** The graph is reflected across the $y$-axis.

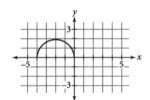

**8. a.** $x = r(t) - 2$, $y = s(t) + 2$. The graph of the parametric equations $x = r(t)$ and $y = s(t)$ is translated left 2 units and up 2 units, so the parametric equations for the transformed graph are $x = r(t) - 2$ and $y = s(t) + 2$.

**b.** $x = r(t)$, $y = 2s(t)$. The graph of the parametric equations is stretched vertically by a factor of 2.

**c.** $x = 2r(t)$, $y = s(t)$. The graph of the parametric equations is stretched horizontally by a factor of 2.

**d.** $x = r(t) - 1$, $y = -s(t)$. The graph of the parametric equations is translated left 1 unit and reflected across the $x$-axis.

**9. a.** $x = 0.4t$, $y = 1$

**b.** $[0, 50, 5, 0, 3, 1]$; $0 \le t \le 125$. To find the range of $t$-values, set $x$ equal to 50 and solve for $t$: $50 = 0.4t$, so $t = 125$.

**c.** $x = 1.8(t - 100)$, $y = 2$

**d.** At 125 s, the tortoise finishes the race, and the hare has gone $1.8(125 - 100)$, or 45 m. Therefore the tortoise wins the race.

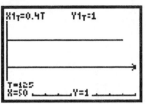

$[0, 50, 5, 0, 3, 1]$
$0 \le t \le 125$

**e.** The tortoise takes 125 s and the hare takes approximately 28 s, but because the hare starts 100 s later, he finishes at 128 s.

**10. a.** The Los Angeles to Honolulu plane flies west at 450 mi/h and leaves 2 h later than the Honolulu to Los Angeles plane. The Honolulu to Los Angeles plane flies east at 525 mi/h and starts 2500 mi west of Los Angeles.

**b.** 3.5 h; 675 mi west of Los Angeles. Let $x_1$ and $x_2$ represent the distance west of Los Angeles for the first and second planes where $x_1 = 450(t - 2)$ and $x_2 = 2500 - 525t$.

| $t$ | $x_1$ | $x_2$ |
|-----|-------|-------|
| 0 | 0 (−900) | 2500 |
| 1 | 0 (−450) | 1975 |
| 2 | 0 | 1450 |
| 3 | 450 | 925 |
| 3.5 | 675 | 662.5 |
| 4 | 900 | 400 |

The table shows that the planes pass each other between 3 and 4 hours. Testing values between $t = 3$ and $t = 4$ for a more accurate approximation shows that $t = 3.5$ results in similar distances west of Los Angeles. Therefore the planes pass each other after approximately 3.5 h, 675 mi west of Los Angeles.

**c.** $450(t - 2) = 2500 - 525t$; 3.5 h, 675 mi west of Los Angeles. The planes pass each other when they are at the same distance west of Los Angeles, so set $x_1 = x_2$. Use substitution to write the equation $450(t - 2) = 2500 - 525t$. Then solve for $t$ to find the time and location that the planes pass each other.

$$450(t - 2) = 2500 - 525t$$

$$450t - 900 = 2500 - 525t$$

$$t = \frac{3400}{975} \approx 3.5$$

Substitute 3.5 for $t$ to find $x_1$ or $x_2$.

$$450(3.5 - 2) = 675 \text{ or } 2500 - 525(3.5) = 662.5$$

The planes pass each other after approximately 3.5 hours, 675 miles west of Los Angeles.

**11. a.**

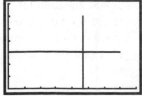

[0, 8, 1, 0, 7, 1]
$0 \leq t \leq 5$

**b.** 1.4 m/s is the velocity of the first walker, 3.1 m is the vertical distance between the walkers when they start, 4.7 m is the horizontal distance between the walkers when they start, and 1.2 m/s is the velocity of the second walker.

**c.** (4.7, 3.1)

**d.** No, the first walker arrives at (4.7, 3.1) at 3.357 s, and the second walker arrives at 2.583 s.

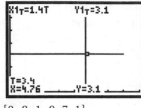 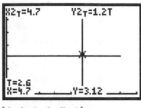

[0, 8, 1, 0, 7, 1]        [0, 8, 1, 0, 7, 1]
$0 \leq t \leq 5$          $0 \leq t \leq 5$

**12. a.** Possible answer: air: $x = 0.3t$, $y = 1$; ground: $x = 6.1t$, $y = 2$

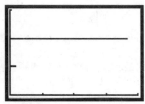

[0, 20, 5, 0, 3, 1]
$0 \leq t \leq 3$

**b.** 18.3 km; 61 s. Trace your graph to find that when $t = 3$, $x = 18.3$. Or substitute 3 for $t$ in the equation $x = 6.1t$ to find that $x = 6.1(3) = 18.3$. Next, substitute 18.3 for $x$ in the equation $x = 0.3t$: $18.3 = 0.3t$, so $t = 61$. It takes 61 s for the sound wave to travel the same distance in the air.

**c.** 3.2 km. Let $t$ represent the time it takes the researcher's equipment to detect the sound vibration in the ground and let $(t + 10)$ represent the time it takes the researcher's equipment to detect the sound waves in the air. The distances the sound waves travel in the air and in the ground from the elephant to the detection equipment are the same, so $0.3(t + 10) = 6.1t$. Solve for $t$.

$$0.3t + 3 = 6.1t$$

$$5.8t = 3$$

$$t = 0.5172$$

Substitute 0.5172 for $t$ in either of the equations $x = 0.3(t + 10)$ or $x = 6.1t$ to find the distance the sound waves travel.

$$x = 6.1(0.5172) = 3.15492 \approx 3.2$$

The elephant was about 3.2 km from the researcher.

**13.** $(7, -3)$. Solve the second equation for $x$ in terms of $y$: $x = 4y + 19$. Then solve the system by substituting $4y + 19$ for $x$ in the first equation.

$$3(4y + 19) + 5y = 6$$

$$12y + 57 + 5y = 6$$

$$17y = -51$$

$$y = -3$$

Substitute $-3$ for $y$ in either equation to find the value of $x$.

$$4(-3) = x - 19$$

$$x = -12 + 19 = 7$$

The solution to the system is $x = 7$ and $y = -3$, or $(7, -3)$.

**14.** $2, \left(1 - \sqrt{3}\right), \left(1 + \sqrt{3}\right)$. The possible rational roots are $\pm 1$, $\pm 2$, and $\pm 4$. Try substituting the values into the original polynomial to find a rational root.

$$P(1) = 1^3 - 4(1)^2 + 2(1) + 4 = 3 \neq 0$$

$$P(-1) = (-1)^3 - 4(-1)^2 + 2(-1) + 4 = -3 \neq 0$$

$$P(2) = 2^3 - 4(2)^2 + 2(2) + 4 = 0$$

Because $P(2) = 0$, you know that 2 is a root of the equation and that $(x - 2)$ is a factor. Use long division to divide out this factor.

$$
\begin{array}{r}
x^2 - 2x - 2 \\
x - 2 \overline{\smash{)}\, x^3 - 4x^2 + 2x + 4} \\
\underline{x^3 - 2x^2} \phantom{+ 2x + 4} \\
-2x^2 + 2x \phantom{+ 4} \\
\underline{-2x^2 + 4x} \phantom{+ 4} \\
-2x + 4 \\
\underline{-2x + 4} \\
0
\end{array}
$$

So, $x^3 - x^2 + 2x + 4 = 0$ is equivalent to $(x - 2)(x^2 - 2x - 2) = 0$. You already know that 2 is a root. Now solve $x^2 - 2x - 2 = 0$. This equation does not have any rational roots, so use the quadratic formula.

$$x = \frac{-(-2) \pm \sqrt{(-2)^2 - 4(1)(-2)}}{2(1)}$$

$$= \frac{2 \pm \sqrt{12}}{2} = \frac{2 \pm 2\sqrt{3}}{2} = 1 \pm \sqrt{3}$$

The three roots are $2$, $\left(1 - \sqrt{3}\right)$, and $\left(1 + \sqrt{3}\right)$.

*Discovering Advanced Algebra Solutions Manual*
©2004 Key Curriculum Press

**15. a.** $u_n = 2.5n^2 - 5.5n - 3$. Use the finite differences method to find that the second set of differences, $D_2$, are constant, so you can model the data with a 2nd-degree polynomial function in the form $u_n = an^2 + bn + c$.

| $n$ | 1 | 2 | 3 | 4 | 5 |
|---|---|---|---|---|---|
| $u_n$ | $-6$ | $-4$ | 3 | 15 | 32 |

$D_1$  2    7    12    17

$D_2$        5    5    5

To find the values of $a$, $b$, and $c$, you need a system of three equations. Choose three points from your table, for example $(1, -6)$, $(3, 3)$, and $(5, 32)$, and substitute the coordinates into $u_n = an^2 + bn + c$ to create a system of three equations in three variables.

$$\begin{cases} a + b + c = -6 \\ 9a + 3b + c = 3 \\ 25a + 5b + c = 32 \end{cases}$$

Solve the system by any method to find that $a = 2.5$, $b = -5.5$, and $c = -3$. Use the values of the coefficients to write the function for the $n$th term: $u_n = 2.5n^2 - 5.5n - 3$.

**b.** 887. Substitute 20 for $n$ to find $u_{20}$: $2.5(20)^2 - 5.5(20) - 3 = 887$.

**16.** $y = -\frac{5}{3}x + 5$. The slope of the line is $\frac{-5 - 10}{6 - (-3)} = \frac{-15}{9} = -\frac{5}{3}$. Using the point-slope form, $y - 10 = -\frac{5}{3}(x + 3)$, or $y = -\frac{5}{3}x + 5$.

**17.** $y = -2x^2 + 5x - 2$. Using the standard form of the equation, $y = ax^2 + bx + c$, substitute the values of the points given for $x$ and $y$ to write a system of three equations in three variables.

$$\begin{cases} 4a - 2b + c = -20 \\ 4a + 2b + c = 0 \\ 16a + 4a + c = -14 \end{cases}$$

Solve the system of equations by any method to find that $a = -2$, $b = 5$, and $c = -2$. The equation of the parabola is $y = -2x^2 + 5x - 2$.

## LESSON 8.2

### EXERCISES

**1. a.** $t = x - 1$  **b.** $t = \dfrac{x + 1}{3}$

   **c.** $t = \pm\sqrt{x}$  **d.** $t = x + 1$

**2.** To eliminate the parameter in 2a–d, solve one of the parametric equations for $t$ and substitute it into the other parametric equation.

**a.** $y = (x - 1)^2$. Solve the first equation for $t$ to get $t = x - 1$. Substitute $x - 1$ for $t$ in the second equation to get $y = (x - 1)^2$. Graph to verify that the new equation and the pair of parametric equations are the same.

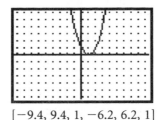

$[-9.4, 9.4, 1, -6.2, 6.2, 1]$

**b.** $y = \frac{2}{3}x + \frac{5}{3}$. Solve the first equation for $t$ to get $t = \frac{x + 1}{3}$. Substitute $\frac{x + 1}{3}$ for $t$ in the second equation to get $y = 2\left(\frac{x + 1}{3}\right) + 1 = \frac{2}{3}x + \frac{5}{3}$. Graph to verify that the new equation and the pair of parametric equations are the same.

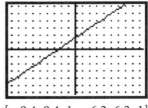

$[-9.4, 9.4, 1, -6.2, 6.2, 1]$

**c.** $y = \pm\sqrt{x} + 3$. Solve the first equation for $t$ to get $t = \pm\sqrt{x}$. Substitute $\pm\sqrt{x}$ for $t$ in the second equation to get $y = \pm\sqrt{x} + 3$. Graph to verify that the new equation and the pair of parametric equations are the same.

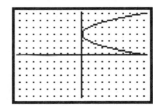

$[-9.4, 9.4, 1, -6.2, 6.2, 1]$

**d.** $y = \sqrt{4 - (x + 1)^2}$. Solve the first equation for $t$ to get $t = x + 1$. Substitute $x + 1$ for $t$ in the second equation to get $y = \sqrt{4 - (x + 1)^2}$. Graph to verify that the graph of the new equation and the pair of parametric equations are the same.

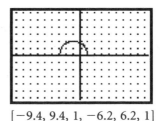

$[-9.4, 9.4, 1, -6.2, 6.2, 1]$

**3. a.** $y = \frac{x+7}{2}$. Solve the first equation for $t$ to get $t = \frac{x+3}{2}$. Substitute $\frac{x+3}{2}$ for $t$ in the second equation to get $y = \frac{x+3}{2} + 2 = \frac{x+3}{2} + \frac{4}{2} = \frac{x+7}{2}$.

**b.** $y = \pm\sqrt{x} + 1$. Solve the first equation for $t$ to get $t = \pm\sqrt{x}$. Substitute $\pm\sqrt{x}$ for $t$ in the second equation to get $y = \pm\sqrt{x} + 1$.

**c.** $y = \frac{2x-4}{3}$. Solve the first equation for $t$ to get $t = 2x - 2$. Substitute $(2x - 2)$ for $t$ in the second equation to get $y = \frac{(2x-2)-2}{3} = \frac{2x-4}{3}$.

**d.** $y = 2(x+2)^2$. Solve the first equation for $t$ to get $t = x + 3$. Substitute $(x + 3)$ for $t$ in the second equation to get $y = 2((x+3)-1)^2 = 2(x+2)^2$.

**4. a.** $x = t + 2$. Each $x$-value is 2 more than the corresponding value of $t$.

**b.** $y = |t - 3| - 1$. Plot the values of $t$ and $y$ to show that the graph is of an absolute-value function translated right 3 units and down 1 unit.

**c.** $y = |x - 5| - 1$. Solve the equation in 4a for $t$ to get $t = x - 2$. Substitute $(x - 2)$ for $t$ in the equation from 4b to get $y = |(x - 2) - 3| - 1 = |x - 5| - 1$.

**5.** Make a table that gives $x$- and $y$-values for values of $t$. Use the $x$- and $y$-values to create a graph of $y$ as a function of $x$.

| $t$ | $x$ | $y$ |
|-----|-----|-----|
| 0   | 4   | 1   |
| 3   | 2   | 3   |
| 6   | 0   | 4.5 |

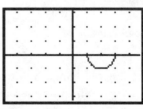

**6.** $x = -\frac{2}{3}t + 4$, $y = \frac{3}{5}t + 1$; $y = -\frac{9}{10}x + \frac{23}{5}$. The graph of $x = f(t)$ has slope $-\frac{2}{3}$ and $y$-intercept 4, so $x = -\frac{2}{3}t + 4$. The graph of $y = g(t)$ has slope $\frac{3}{5}$ and $y$-intercept 1, so $y = \frac{3}{5}t + 1$. Eliminate the parameter by solving for $t$ in terms of $x$.

$$x = -\frac{2}{3}t + 4$$
$$-\frac{2}{3}t = x - 4$$
$$t = -\frac{3}{2}(x - 4) = -\frac{3}{2}x + 6$$

Substitute $\left(-\frac{3}{2}x + 6\right)$ for $t$ in the parametric equation for $y$.

$$y = \frac{3}{5}\left(-\frac{3}{2}x + 6\right) + 1$$
$$= -\frac{9}{10}x + \frac{18}{5} + 1 = -\frac{9}{10}x + \frac{23}{5}$$

The ratio of the slopes of the parametric equations is

$$\frac{\frac{3}{5}}{-\frac{2}{3}} = \frac{3}{5}\left(-\frac{3}{2}\right) = -\frac{9}{10}$$

Therefore the slope of the equation in $x$ and $y$ is equal to the ratio of the two slopes of the parametric equations.

**7.** $-2.5 \le t \le 2.5$. Test values in your calculator to find the smallest interval that just fits the given window.

**8. a.**

$[-4.7, 4.7, 1, -3.1, 3.1, 1]$

**b.** The graph is reflected across the $x$-axis; $y = -\sqrt{1 - (x - 2)^2}$. Solve the first equation for $t$ to get $t = x - 2$. Substitute $x - 2$ for $t$ in the second equation to get $y = -\sqrt{1 - (x - 2)^2}$.

$[-4.7, 4.7, 1, -3.1, 3.1, 1]$

**c.** The graph is reflected across the $y$-axis; $y = \sqrt{1 - (x + 2)^2}$. Solve the first equation for $t$ to get $t = -x - 2$. Substitute $-x - 2$ for $t$ in the second equation to get $y = \sqrt{1 - (-x - 2)^2} = \sqrt{1 - (-(x + 2))^2} = \sqrt{1 - (x + 2)^2}$.

$[-4.7, 4.7, 1, -3.1, 3.1, 1]$

**d.** The graph is reflected across the $x$- and $y$-axes. Combine the transformations of the original equation in 8b and c to get $y = -\sqrt{1 - (x + 2)^2}$.

*Discovering Advanced Algebra Solutions Manual*
©2004 Key Curriculum Press

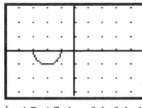

[−4.7, 4.7, 1, −3.1, 3.1, 1]

**9. a.** $x = 20 + 2t$, $y = 5 + t$. The slope of the parametric equation for $x$ is $\frac{24 - 20}{2 - 0} = \frac{4}{2}$ and the $y$-intercept is 20, so $x = 20 + 2t$. The slope of the parametric equation for $y$ is $\frac{7 - 5}{2 - 0} = \frac{2}{2} = 1$ and the $y$-intercept is 5, so $y = 5 + t$.

**b.** The points lie on the line.

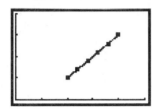

[0, 50, 10, 0, 20, 5]
$0 \le t \le 10$

**c.** $y = \frac{1}{2}x - 5$. Using the points $(20, 5)$ and $(24, 7)$, the slope of the line that passes through the data points $(x, y)$ is $\frac{7 - 5}{24 - 20} = \frac{2}{4} = \frac{1}{2}$ and the equation of the line is $y - 5 = \frac{1}{2}(x - 20)$, or $y - 7 = \frac{1}{2}(x - 24)$, so $y = \frac{1}{2}x - 5$.

**d.** The slope of the line in 9c is the ratio of the $y$-slope over the $x$-slope in the parametric equations.

**10.** Possible answer: $x = 3 + 2t$, $y = 2 - t$ and $x = 3 + t$, $y = 2 + 2t$. One line has to have slope $-0.5$. In the parametric equations, this is the ratio of the $y$-slope to the $x$-slope. Start with the equations $x = 2t$, $y = -t$ and then translate the line right 2 units and up 3 units to go through $(3, 2)$. The equations are $x = 3 + 2t$, $y = 2 - t$. The other line is perpendicular to this one, so its slope is the negative reciprocal of $-0.5$, or 2. Use the same method to find the equations for this line.

**11. a.** $x = 1$, $y = 1.5t$          **b.** $x = 1.1$, $y = 12 - 2.5t$

**c.** Possible answer: $[0, 2, 1, 0, 12, 1]$, $0 \le t \le 3$

**d.** They meet after hiking 3 h, when both are 4.5 mi north of the trailhead.

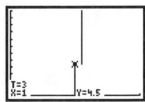

[0, 2, 1, 0, 12, 1]
$0 \le t \le 3$

**e.** $1.5t = 12 - 2.5t$; $t = 3$. They meet when $d_1 = d_2$, so $1.5t = 12 - 2.5t$. Solve for $t$: $4t = 12$, so $t = 3$. Substitute 3 for $t$ in either $y$-equation to get $y = 1.5(3) = 4.5$.

**12. a.** 4.47 s. Use the projectile motion function, $y = -4.9x^2 + v_0x + s_0$, where the initial velocity, $v_0$, is 0 (because the egg is dropped) and the initial height, $s_0$, is 98 m, to get the equation $y = -4.9x^2 + 98$. The egg hits the ground when the height is 0, so set $y$ equal to 0 and solve for $x$.

$$0 = -4.9x^2 + 98$$
$$4.9x^2 = 98$$
$$x^2 = 20$$
$$x \approx \pm 4.47$$

It takes the egg approximately 4.47 s to reach the ground.

**b.** Possible answer: $x = 1$, $y = 98 - 4.9t^2$. The direction of this motion is vertical and downward, so the horizontal component is 0 and $x$ can be set to any constant value.

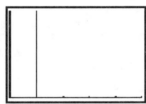

[0, 5, 1, 0, 100, 100]
$0 \le t \le 5$

**c.** 4.43 s. Substitute 1.75 for $y$ and solve for $t$.

$$1.75 = 98 - 4.9t^2$$
$$4.9t^2 = 96.25$$
$$t^2 = 19.64$$
$$t \approx \pm 4.43$$

The egg will reach a height of 1.75 m at approximately 4.43 s.

**d.** About 5.32 m. Multiply the rate of 1.2 m/s by the time it takes the egg to reach a height of 1.75 m: $(1.2 \text{ m/s})(4.43 \text{ s}) \approx 5.32$ m.

**e.** Possible answer: egg: $x = 5.32$, $y = 98 - 4.9t^2$; trampoline: $x = 1.2t$, $y = 1.75$; $0 \le t \le 5$

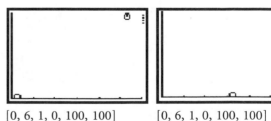

[0, 6, 1, 0, 100, 100]          [0, 6, 1, 0, 100, 100]

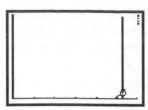

[0, 6, 1, 0, 100, 100]

**13.** $x = t^2$, $y = t$. To reflect the parabola across the line $y = x$, switch $x$ and $y$ in the equations: $x = t$ and $y = t^2$ becomes $x = t^2$ and $y = t$.

**14. a.** Tanker A: $x = 18t$, $y = 1$; Tanker B: $x = 22(t - 5)$, $y = 2$

**b.** Possible answer: [0, 900, 100, −1, 3, 1]; $0 \le t \le 50$

**c.** After 27.5 h, 495 mi east of Corpus Christi. Use the graph or table to find when Tanker B is in the same position as Tanker A.

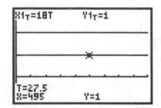 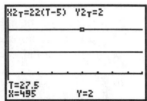

For both tankers, $t = 27.5$ when $x = 495$, so Tanker B passes Tanker A at 27.5 h, 495 mi east of Corpus Christi.

**d.** Tanker A: $x = 18t$, $y = 1$; Tanker B: $x = 900 - 22t$, $y = 2$; they are within 50 mi of each other for $21.50 \le t \le 23.75$. Use a table or a graph to find when Tanker A is within 50 mi of Tanker B.

**15.** $y = \left(\frac{2}{3}(x - 5) - 2\right) + 3$, or $y = \frac{2}{3}x - \frac{7}{3}$

**16. a.  i.** $f(9) = 3 + \sqrt[3]{((9) - 1)^2} = 3 + \sqrt[3]{64} = 3 + 4 = 7$

**ii.** $f(1) = 3 + \sqrt[3]{((1) - 1)^2} = 3 + \sqrt[3]{0} = 3 + 0 = 3$

**iii.** $f(0) = 3 + \sqrt[3]{((0) - 1)^2} = 3 + \sqrt[3]{1} = 3 + 1 = 4$

**iv.** $f(-7) = 3 + \sqrt[3]{((-7) - 1)^2} = 3 + \sqrt[3]{64} = 3 + 4 = 7$

**b.** $y = 1 \pm \sqrt{(x - 3)^3}$; not a function. Find the equation of the inverse of $f(x)$ by switching $x$ and $y$ and then solving for $y$.

$$y = 3 + \sqrt[3]{(x - 1)^2}$$
$$x = 3 + \sqrt[3]{(y - 1)^2}$$
$$x - 3 = \sqrt[3]{(y - 1)^2}$$
$$(x - 3)^3 = (y - 1)^2$$
$$\pm\sqrt{(x - 3)^3} = y - 1$$
$$y = 1 \pm \sqrt{(x - 3)^3}$$
$$f^{-1}(x) = 1 \pm \sqrt{(x - 3)^3}$$

The graph of $f^{-1}(x) = 1 \pm \sqrt{(x - 3)^3}$ does not pass the vertical line test, so it is not a function.

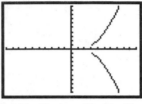

[−10, 10, 1, −10, 10, 1]

**c.** Substitute each $y$-value found in 16a for $x$ in the inverse. Check that the output is equivalent to the original $x$-value. For example, $f^{-1}(7) = 1 \pm \sqrt{(7 - 3)^3} = 1 \pm 8 = 9$ or $-7$.

**d.**

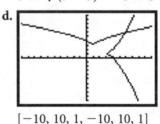

[−10, 10, 1, −10, 10, 1]

**EXTENSIONS**

**A.** See the solution to Take Another Look activity 1 on page 205.

**B.** Investigations will vary.

## LESSON 8.3

**EXERCISES**

**1.** $\sin A = \frac{k}{j}$; $\sin B = \frac{h}{j}$; $\sin^{-1}\left(\frac{k}{j}\right) = A$; $\sin^{-1}\left(\frac{h}{j}\right) = B$;

$\cos B = \frac{k}{j}$; $\cos A = \frac{h}{j}$; $\cos^{-1}\left(\frac{k}{j}\right) = B$; $\cos^{-1}\left(\frac{h}{j}\right) = A$;

$\tan A = \frac{k}{h}$; $\tan B = \frac{h}{k}$; $\tan^{-1}\left(\frac{k}{h}\right) = A$; $\tan^{-1}\left(\frac{h}{k}\right) = B$

**2. a.** $a = 12 \sin 20° \approx 4.1$   **b.** $b = \dfrac{25}{\cos 80°} \approx 144.0$

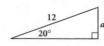

**c.** $\tan 55° = 1 + \frac{4}{c}$, so $c(\tan 55° - 1) = 4$, and $c = \frac{4}{\tan 55° - 1} \approx 9.3$

**d.** $D \approx 34.5°$

**3. a.** $\cos 32° = \frac{14.7}{a}$, so $a = \frac{14.7}{\cos 32°} \approx 17.3$

    **b.** $\tan 47.2° = \frac{24.6}{b}$, so $b = \frac{24.6}{\tan 47.2°} \approx 22.8$

    **c.** $\sin 47° = \frac{58}{c}$, so $c = \frac{58}{\sin 47°} \approx 79.3$

**4. a.** $\sin A = \frac{36}{125}$, so $A = \sin^{-1}\left(\frac{36}{125}\right) \approx 17°$

    **b.** $\tan B = \frac{4.2}{7.3}$, so $B = \tan^{-1}\left(\frac{4.2}{7.3}\right) \approx 30°$

    **c.** $\tan C = \frac{12}{60}$, so $C = \tan^{-1}\left(\frac{12}{60}\right) \approx 11°$

**5.**

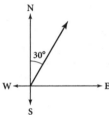

    **a.** $90° - 30° = 60°$

    **b.**

    **c.** 180 mi east, 311.8 mi north. The plane travels 180(2), or 360 mi in 2 h, so the length of the hypotenuse of the right triangle in 5b is 360. Use this to find $x$ and $y$.

$$\cos 60° = \frac{x}{360}, \text{ so } x = 360\cos 60° = 180$$

$$\sin 60° = \frac{y}{360}, \text{ so } y = 360\sin 60° \approx 311.8$$

The plane travels 180 mi east and 311.8 mi north.

**6. a.**

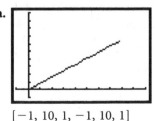

    $[-1, 10, 1, -1, 10, 1]$
    $0 \le t \le 10$

**b.** The graph is a line segment 10 units long, at an angle of 39° with the horizontal axis. Changing the range of $t$-values changes the length (starting and ending points) of the segment.

**c.** 39°. Trace to the point (7.77, 6.29), at $t = 10$. Create a right triangle where the length of the horizontal leg, $x$, is 7.77 and the length of the vertical leg, $y$, is 6.29. Find the angle between the line and the $x$-axis by solving $\tan A = \frac{6.29}{7.77}$ for $A$.

$$A = \tan^{-1}\left(\frac{6.29}{7.77}\right) \approx 39°$$

**7. a.**

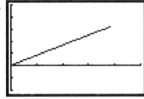

    $[0, 5, 1, -2, 5, 1]$
    $0 \le t \le 1$

**b.** It is a segment 5 units long, at an angle of 40° above the $x$-axis.

**c.** This is the value of the angle in the equations.

**d.** The 5 in each equation makes the segment 5 units long when $t = 1$. Changing 5 to 1 in the first equation makes the graph become steeper and the segment become shorter. Changing 5 to 1 in both equations makes the graph become shorter, but the slope stays the same.

**8. a.** $x = t\cos 47°$, $y = t\sin 47°$

    **b.** $x = t\cos 115°$, $y = t\sin 115°$

**9. a.** $x = 100t\cos 30°$, $y = 100t\sin 30°$

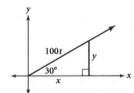

    **b.** $0 \le t \le 5$. Use guess-and-check on your calculator or solve the equation $100t = 500$ for $t$ to find the maximum value of $t$.

    **c.** 100 represents the speed of the plane in miles per hour, $t$ represents time in hours, 30° is the angle the plane is making with the $x$-axis, $x$ is the horizontal position at any time, and $y$ is the vertical position at any time.

**10. a.**

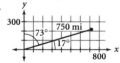

    **b.** $\frac{750 \text{ m}}{18 \text{ m/h}} \approx 41.7$ h

**c.** 717.2 mi east, 219.3 mi north. Create a right triangle to find the horizontal and vertical positions of Panama City from Corpus Christi. Tanker A makes a 17° angle with the $x$-axis and the hypotenuse is 750 mi.

$\cos 17° = \dfrac{x}{750}$, so $x = 750 \cos 17° \approx 717.2$

$\sin 17° = \dfrac{y}{750}$, so $y = 750 \sin 17° \approx 219.3$

Panama City is 717.2 mi east and 219.3 mi north of Corpus Christi.

**11. a.**

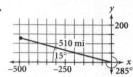

**b.** $\dfrac{510 \text{ m}}{22 \text{ m/h}} \approx 23.2$ h

**c.** 492.6 mi west, 132.0 mi north. Create a right triangle to find the horizontal and vertical positions of New Orleans from St. Petersburg. Tanker B makes a 15° angle with the $x$-axis and the hypotenuse is 510 mi.

$\cos 15° = \dfrac{x}{510}$, so $x = 510 \cos 15° \approx 492.6$

$\sin 15° = \dfrac{y}{510}$, so $y = 510 \sin 15° \approx 132.0$

New Orleans is 492.6 mi west and 132.0 mi north of St. Petersburg.

**d.** The paths cross at approximately 480 mi west and 129 mi north of St. Petersburg. No, the ships do not collide, because Tanker A reaches this point at 24.4 h and Tanker B reaches this point at 22.6 h.

**12. a.** 12°. Convert 40 km/h to $\dfrac{100}{9}$ m/s to use the formula.

$$\tan \theta = \frac{\left(\dfrac{100}{9}\right)^2}{60 \cdot 9.8} = \frac{\left(\dfrac{10000}{81}\right)}{588}$$

$$\theta = \tan^{-1}\left(\frac{\dfrac{10000}{81}}{588}\right) \approx 12°$$

The curb should be banked at 12°.

**b.** 396 km/h. Convert 1.7 km to 1700 m to use the formula.

$$\tan 36° = \frac{v^2}{1700 \cdot 9.8}$$

$$v^2 = 16660 \tan 36°$$

$$v = \sqrt{16660 \tan 36°} \approx 110 \text{ m/s}$$

Convert back to km/h: 110 m/s = 396 km/h. The curve is designed for 396 km/h.

**13. a.** $y = 5 + \frac{3}{4}(x - 6)$, or $y = \frac{1}{2} + \frac{3}{4}x$. The slope of the data is $\frac{11 - 5}{14 - 6} = \frac{6}{8} = \frac{3}{4}$. Use the point-slope form.

**b.** $y = 5 + \dfrac{3(x - 6)}{4}$. They are the same equation. Eliminate the parameter by solving the $x$-equation for $t$ to get $t = \frac{x - 6}{4}$. Substitute $\frac{x - 6}{4}$ for $t$ in the $y$-equation to get $y = 5 + \frac{3(x - 6)}{4}$, which is the same as $y = 5 + \frac{3}{4}(x - 6)$.

**14.**

$[-1, 7, 1, -3, 38, 5]$

**a.** (3.2, 35)

**b.** $x = 3.2 + \sqrt{\frac{35}{4.9}} \approx 5.873$ and $x = 3.2 - \sqrt{\frac{35}{4.9}} \approx 0.527$. To find the $x$-intercepts, let $y = 0$ and solve for $x$.

$$0 = 35 - 4.9(x - 3.2)^2$$
$$(x - 3.2)^2 = \frac{35}{4.9}$$
$$x - 3.2 = \pm\sqrt{\frac{35}{4.9}}$$
$$x = 3.2 \pm \sqrt{\frac{35}{4.9}}$$

**c.** $x = 3.2 + \sqrt{\frac{20}{4.9}} \approx 5.220$ and $x = 3.2 - \sqrt{\frac{20}{4.9}} \approx 1.180$. Substitute 15 for $y$ and solve for $x$.

$$15 = 35 - 4.9(x - 3.2)^2$$
$$-20 = -4.9(x - 3.2)^2$$
$$\frac{20}{4.9} = (x - 3.2)^2$$
$$\pm\sqrt{\frac{20}{4.9}} = x - 3.2$$
$$x = 3.2 \pm \sqrt{\frac{20}{4.9}}$$

**15.** $(x - 2.6)^2 + (y + 4.5)^2 = 12.96$. The standard equation for a circle with radius $r$ and center $(h, k)$ is $(x - h)^2 + (y - k)^2 = r^2$.

**16. a.** Constructions will vary, but for any graph scale and any setting of $a$, $h$, and $k$, the graph should have vertex $(h, k)$ and scale factor $a$.

**b.** Constructions will vary, but for any graph scale and any setting of $a$, $r_1$, and $r_2$, the graph should have $x$-intercepts $r_1$ and $r_2$ and scale factor $a$.

**EXTENSIONS**

**A.** See the solution to Take Another Look activity 3 on page 205.

**B.** Answers will vary.

## QUESTIONS

**1.** The parametric equations $x = 3\cos t$ and $y = 3\sin t$ are the equations for a circle if the domain of $t$ is continuous. The graph of a polygon, such as a square or hexagon, is the result of changing the $t$-step and connecting the discrete points with line segments. Mathematically, the continuous curve is always a circle.

**2. a.** $x = 2\cos t + 2$, $y = 2\sin t$. The circle with radius 2 is translated right 2 units.

**b.** $x = 2\cos t - 3$, $y = 2\sin t$. The circle with radius 2 is translated left 3 units.

**c.** $x = 2\cos t$, $y = 2\sin t + 4$. The circle with radius 2 is translated up 4 units.

**d.** $x = 2\cos t + 3$, $y = 2\sin t + 2$. The circle with radius 2 is translated right 3 units and up 2 units.

**3. a.** $0° \le t \le 360°$, $t$-step $45°$

**b.** $90° \le t \le 450°$, $t$-step $72°$

**c.** $-90° \le t \le 270°$, $t$-step $120°$

**d.** $0° \le t \le 1080°$, $t$-step $108°$

**4. a.** $x = \cos t$, $y = \sin t$

**b.** $(\cos t)^2 + (\sin t)^2 = 1$. This can also be written as $\sin^2 t + \cos^2 t = 1$.

**c.** $(\cos 47°)^2 + (\sin 47°)^2 = 1$. The equation from 4b is true for $t = 47°$.

**5. a.** $x = 2\cos t$, $y = 3\sin t$. The unit circle is stretched horizontally by a factor of 2 and vertically by a factor of 3.

**b.** $x = 3.5\cos t$, $y = \sin t$. The unit circle is stretched horizontally by a factor of 3.5.

**c.** $x = 2\cos t$, $y = 4\sin t$. The unit circle is stretched horizontally by a factor of 2 and vertically by a factor of 4.

**d.** $x = 3\cos t + 2$, $y = 2\sin t + 2$. The unit circle is stretched horizontally by a factor of 3 and vertically by a factor of 2. It is then translated right 2 units and up 2 units.

## LESSON 8.4

### EXERCISES

**1.** $x = 10t\cos 30°$, $y = 10t\sin 30°$

**2. a.** 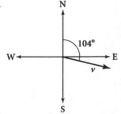   **b.**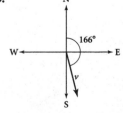

**c.** 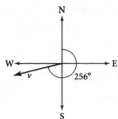   **d.**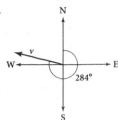

**3. a.** 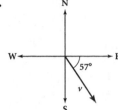   **b.**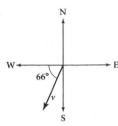

**c.** 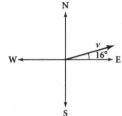   **d.**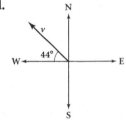

**4. a.** $x$ is positive, $y$ is negative

**b.** $x$ is negative, $y$ is negative

**c.** $x$ is positive, $y$ is positive

**d.** $x$ is negative, $y$ is positive

**5. a.** $(-0.3, 0.5)$

**b.** $x = -0.3 + 4t$. The velocity of the boat is positive because it is aiming directly east.

**c.** $y = 0.5 - 7t$. The velocity of the current is negative because it is flowing south.

**d.**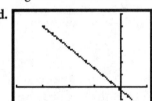

$[-0.4, 0.1, 0.1, -0.1, 0.6, 0.1]$
$0 \le t \le 0.1$

**e.** At 0.075 h, the boat meets the river's east bank 0.025 km south of the dock. Find the $y$-value when $x = 0$ by substituting 0 for $x$ in the equation for $x$ to get $0 = -0.3 + 4t$, and $t = \frac{0.3}{4} = 0.075$. Substitute 0.075 for $t$ in the equation for $y$ to find that $y = 0.5 - 7(0.075) = -0.025$, which corresponds to 0.025 km south of the dock.

**f.** 0.605 km. Create a right triangle so that the horizontal leg is 0.3 km, the vertical leg is (0.5 + 0.025) km, and the hypotenuse is the distance you have traveled. Using the Pythagorean Theorem, you have traveled $\sqrt{0.3^2 + 0.525^2}$, or about 0.605 km.

**6. a.** $y = 25t$. The wind's velocity is positive because it is blowing toward the north.

**b.** $x = -120t$. The velocity is negative because the plane is flying west.

**c.**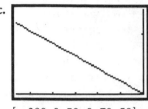

$[-280, 0, 50, 0, 70, 50]$
$0 \le t \le 3$

**d.** 58.3 mi north. Solve by tracing the graph or by eliminating the parameter in the $y$-equation by substituting $-\frac{x}{120}$ for $t$ to get $y = 25\left(-\frac{x}{120}\right)$. When $x = -280$, $y = 25\left(-\frac{(-280)}{120}\right) \approx 58.3$, so the plane is 58.3 mi north after traveling 280 mi west.

**e.** 286 mi. Using the Pythagorean Theorem, the plane has actually traveled $\sqrt{280^2 + 58.3^2}$, or about 286 mi.

**f.** 122.6 mi/h. Find the time the plane traveled: $\frac{280 \text{ mi}}{120 \text{ mi/h}} \approx 2.3$ h. Divide the actual distance traveled by the time: $\frac{286 \text{ mi}}{2.3 \text{ h}} = 122.6$ mi/h.

**7. a.** $y = -5t$. If you orient the river with the positive $y$-axis pointing upstream, then the velocity of the river current goes in the direction of the negative $y$-axis.

**b.** $x = st$

**c.** $s = 10$ mi/h. The boat traveled 2 mi down the river, so $-2 = -5t$ gives the component of motion down the river. The boat traveled 4 mi across the river, so the other equation in the system is $4 = st$. Solve the first equation for $t$ to get $t = \frac{2}{5}$. Substitute $\frac{2}{5}$ for $t$ in the second equation and solve for $s$: $4 = s\left(\frac{2}{5}\right)$, and $s = 10$. Therefore Fred reaches the point 2 mi downstream by traveling 10 mi/h.

**d.** 4.47 mi. Using the Pythagorean Theorem, Fred traveled $\sqrt{4^2 + 2^2}$, or about 4.47 mi.

**e.** 0.4 h. From 7c, $t = \frac{2}{5}$, or 0.4, so it took Fred 0.4 h, or 24 min.

**f.** 11.18 mi/h. Divide the actual distance traveled by the time: $\frac{4.47 \text{ mi}}{0.4 \text{ h}} \approx 11.18$ mi/h.

**g.** 63.4°. The angle the boat makes with the riverbank is $\tan^{-1}\left(\frac{4}{2}\right)$, or about 63.4°.

**8. a.** 97.5 mi east of Cleveland. The plane's motion can be described by the equation $y = 250t$. The velocity is positive because the plane is flying north. The effect of the wind on the plane's motion can be described by the equation $x = 25t$. The wind's velocity is positive because the wind is blowing east. Substitute 975 for $y$ to get $975 = 250t$, and $t = 3.9$. The plane has flown 975 mi north after 3.9 h. Then substitute 3.9 for $t$ to get $x = 25(3.9) = 97.5$ to find the planes' horizontal distance from Cleveland. The plane is 97.5 mi east of Cleveland after traveling 975 mi north.

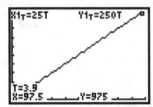

$[0, 100, 10, 0, 1000, 100]$
$0 \le t \le 4$

**b.** 979.9 mi. Using the Pythagorean Theorem, the plane has actually traveled $\sqrt{97.5^2 + 975^2}$, or about 979.9 mi.

**c.** The plane's actual speed was $\frac{979.9 \text{ mi}}{3.9 \text{ h}} \approx 251.3$ mi/h.

**d.** The angle from the horizontal is $\tan^{-1}\left(\frac{975}{97.5}\right)$, or about 84.3°.

**e.** The plane traveled east of north, so its bearing was $90° - 84.3°$, or 5.7°.

**9. a.** $y = -20t \sin 45°$

**b.** $x = 20t \cos 45°$

**c.** Both the plane's motion and the wind contribute to the actual path of the plane, so you add the $x$-components and add the $y$-components to form the final equations.

**d.** Possible answer: $[-1000, 0, 100, -100, 0, 10]$; $0 \le t \le 5$

**e.** $t = 4.24$. It takes the plane 4.24 h to fly 1000 mi west. Solve the given equation for $t$.

$$-1000 = -250t + 20t \cos 45°$$

$$-1000 = t(-250 + 20 \cos 45°)$$

$$t = \frac{-1000}{(-250 + 20 \cos 45°)} \approx 4.24$$

*Discovering Advanced Algebra Solutions Manual*
©2004 Key Curriculum Press

**f.** 60 mi. Substitute 4.24 for $t$ and solve for $y$.

$$y = -20(4.24) \sin 45° \approx -60$$

The plane ended up 60 mi south of Albuquerque.

**10. a.** $A = 3.24°$. Write an equation and solve for $A$.

$250t \sin A - 20t \sin 45° = 0$ — The sum of the north-south velocities of the plane and the wind is 0.

$250t \sin A = 20t \sin 45°$ — Add $20t \sin 45°$ to both sides.

$250 \sin A = 20 \sin 45°$ — Divide by $t$ (assume $t \neq 0$).

$\sin A = \dfrac{20 \sin 45°}{250}$ — Divide both sides by 250.

$A = \sin^{-1}\left(\dfrac{20 \sin 45°}{250}\right)$ — Take the inverse sine of both sides.

$A \approx 3.24°$ — Evaluate.

The plane must head 3.24° north of west to head directly to Albuquerque.

**b.** $x = -250t \cos 3.24° + 20t \cos 45°$,
$y = 250t \sin 3.24° - 20t \sin 45°$

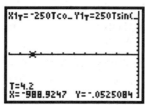

$[-1200, 0, 100, -10, 10, 1]$
$0 \leq t \leq 5$

**c.** 273.243°. The plane must head 3.243° north of west, which is equivalent to a bearing of $270° + 3.243°$, or 273.243°.

**11. a.**

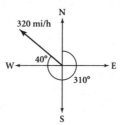

**b.** $x = -320t \cos 40°$, $y = 320t \sin 40°$

**c.**

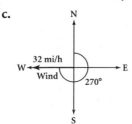

**d.** $x = -32t$, $y = 0$

**e.** $x = -320t \cos 40° - 32t$, $y = 320t \sin 40°$. Both the plane's motion and the wind contribute to the actual path of the plane, so you add the $x$-components and add the $y$-components to form the final equations.

**f.** 1385.7 mi west and 1028.5 mi north. Substitute 5 for $t$ in both the $x$- and $y$-equations.

$$x = -320(5) \cos 40° - 32(5) \approx -1385.7$$

$$y = 320(5) \sin 40° \approx 1028.5$$

**12.** 48.59°. Sketch Angelina's path. The boat moves 4 mi/h, so its distance along this path is $4t$. This distance is broken into two separate components. The east-west component is $x = 4t \cos A$, and the north-south component is $y = 4t \sin A$ where $A$ is the angle toward the north that Angelina should aim the boat. The effect of the river current on the boat's motion can be described by the equation $y = -3t$. The sum of the north-south components must be 0 if Angelina wants her boat to go straight across the Wyde River. Solve for $A$.

$$4t \sin A - 3t = 0$$
$$4t \sin A = 3t$$
$$\sin A = 0.75$$
$$A = \sin^{-1} 0.75 \approx 48.59°$$

Angelina must aim her boat at 48.59° north of east to end up going straight across the Wyde River.

**13. a.** $x$-component: $50 \cos 40° \approx 38.3$;
$y$-component: $50 \sin 40° \approx 32.1$

**b.** $x$-component: $90 \cos 140° \approx -68.9$;
$y$-component: $90 \sin 140° \approx 57.9$

**c.** $x$-component: $38.3 - 68.9 = -30.6$;
$y$-component: $32.1 + 57.9 = 90.0$

**d.** 95.1 N. Using the Pythagorean Theorem, $\sqrt{30.6^2 + 90^2} \approx 95.1$, so 95.1 N is the resulting magnitude.

**e.** 109°. The angle of the resulting force is $\tan^{-1}\left(\dfrac{90}{-30.6}\right)$, or about $-71°$. Add 180° to $-71°$ to get 109°.

**f.** 95.1 N at 289°. The magnitude of the additional force is 95.1 N, the same as the magnitude of the sum of Forces A and B from 13d. To find the angle of the opposing force, add 180° to 109° to get 289°.

**14.** 143° and 37°. Sketch the rectangle. Draw a perpendicular bisector from the vertex of the triangle to its base to form two congruent right triangles.

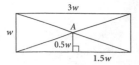

Find the measure of angle $A$.

$\tan A = \dfrac{1.5w}{0.5w} = 3$, so $A = \tan^{-1} 3 \approx 71.565°$

Double the measure of angle $A$ to find one of the angles formed where the diagonals intersect, and then subtract this angle from 180° to find the other angle.

$2(71.565°) \approx 143°$ and $180° - 143° = 37°$

The diagonals intersect at 143° and 37° angles.

**15. a.** Two real, rational roots.

$b^2 - 4ac = (-5)^2 - 4(2)(-3) = 49 > 0$

The roots are real when $b^2 - 4ac > 0$ because when you use the quadratic formula, you take the square root of 49, so there are two rational roots.

**b.** Two real, irrational roots.

$b^2 - 4ac = (4)^2 - 4(1)(-1) = 20 > 0$

The roots are real when $b^2 - 4ac > 0$ because when you use the quadratic formula, you take the square root of 20, so there are two irrational roots.

**c.** No real roots.

$b^2 - 4ac = (-3)^2 - 4(3)(4) = -39 < 0$

The roots are nonreal when $b^2 - 4ac < 0$ because when you use the quadratic formula, you take the square root of a negative number.

**d.** One real, rational root.

$b^2 - 4ac = (-12)^2 - 4(9)(4) = 0$

In the quadratic formula, the two solutions are equal when $b^2 - 4ac = 0$ because the square root of 0 is 0, so there is one real, rational root.

**16. a.** $\begin{bmatrix} 5 & -3 & | & -1 \\ 2 & 4 & | & 5 \end{bmatrix}$

**b.** $\begin{bmatrix} 5 & -3 & | & -1 \\ 2 & 5 & | & 5 \end{bmatrix} \xrightarrow{\frac{1}{5}R_1 \to R_1} \begin{bmatrix} 1 & -\frac{3}{5} & | & -\frac{1}{5} \\ 2 & 4 & | & 5 \end{bmatrix}$

$\xrightarrow{-2R_1+R_2 \to R_2} \begin{bmatrix} 1 & -\frac{3}{5} & | & -\frac{1}{5} \\ 0 & \frac{26}{5} & | & \frac{27}{5} \end{bmatrix}$

$\xrightarrow{\frac{5}{26}R_2 \to R_2} \begin{bmatrix} 1 & -\frac{3}{5} & | & -\frac{1}{5} \\ 0 & 1 & | & \frac{27}{26} \end{bmatrix}$

$\xrightarrow{\frac{3}{5}R_2+R_1 \to R_1} \begin{bmatrix} 1 & 0 & | & \frac{11}{26} \\ 0 & 1 & | & \frac{27}{26} \end{bmatrix}$

**c.** $\left(\dfrac{11}{26}, \dfrac{27}{26}\right)$. Check your answer by substituting $\dfrac{11}{26}$ for $x$ and $\dfrac{26}{27}$ for $y$ in both of the original equations.

$5\left(\dfrac{11}{26}\right) - 3\left(\dfrac{27}{26}\right) \overset{?}{=} -1 \qquad 2\left(\dfrac{11}{26}\right) + 4\left(\dfrac{27}{26}\right) \overset{?}{=} 5$

$\dfrac{55}{26} - \dfrac{81}{26} \overset{?}{=} -1 \qquad\qquad \dfrac{11}{13} + \dfrac{54}{13} \overset{?}{=} 5$

$-\dfrac{26}{26} = -1 \qquad\qquad\qquad \dfrac{65}{13} = 5$

The solution checks.

## LESSON 8.5

### EXERCISES

**1. a.** The Moon; centimeters and seconds. From the projectile motion equation, $-\frac{1}{2}g = -81$, so $g = 162$. This is the gravitational constant for the Moon in cm/s$^2$.

**b.** Right 400 cm and up 700 cm. Substitute 0 for $t$ in both equations.

**c.** Up-left. The vertical component of the initial velocity is upward and therefore positive ($50 \sin 30°$), and the horizontal component is leftward and therefore negative ($-50 \cos 30°$).

**d.** 50 cm/s. From the projectile motion equation, $v_0 = 50$.

**2. a.** Right 40 cm and up 60 cm. When $t = 0$, $x = -50(0) \cos 30° + 40 = 40$ and $y = -81(0)^2 + 50(0) \sin 30° + 60 = 60$.

**b.** Left 3.3 cm and up 4 cm. When $t = 1$, $x = -50(1) \cos 30° + 40 \approx -3.3$ and $y = -81(1)^2 + 50(1) \sin 30° + 60 = 4$.

**c.** Left 46.6 cm and down 214 cm. When $t = 2$, $x = -50(2) \cos 30° + 40 \approx -46.6$ and $y = -81(2)^2 + 50(2) \sin 30° + 60 = -214$.

**d.** Left 133.2 cm and down 1136 cm. When $t = 4$, $x = -50(4) \cos 30° + 40 \approx -133.2$ and $y = -81(4)^2 + 50(4) \sin 30° + 60 = -1136$.

**3. a.** $x = 2t$, $y = -4.9t^2 + 12$

**b.** $-4.9t^2 + 12 = 0$. The ball hits the ground at the point where $y = 0$.

*Discovering Advanced Algebra Solutions Manual*
©2004 Key Curriculum Press

**c.** 1.56 s, 3.13 m from the cliff. Solve the equation $-4.9t^2 + 12 = 0$ for $t$.

$$-4.9t^2 + 12 = 0$$

$$-4.9t^2 = -12$$

$$t^2 = \frac{12}{4.9}$$

$$t = \pm\sqrt{\frac{12}{4.9}}$$

$$t \approx \pm 1.5649$$

Only the positive answer makes sense in this situation, so the ball hits the ground at approximately 1.56 s. To find where this occurs, substitute this $t$-value into the equation for $x$.

$$x = 2(1.5649) \approx 3.13$$

The ball hits the ground at a horizontal distance of approximately 3.13 m from the cliff.

**d.** Possible answer: [0, 4, 1, 0, 12, 1]; $0 \le t \le 2$

**4. a.** 3.87 s, 7.75 m from the cliff. Replace the gravitational constant, $g$, with 1.6 m/s$^2$ to get $0 = -0.8t^2 + 12$. Solve the equation for $t$.

$$0 = -0.8t^2 + 12$$

$$0.8t^2 = 12$$

$$t^2 = \frac{12}{0.8}$$

$$t = \pm\sqrt{\frac{12}{0.8}} \approx \pm 3.873$$

Using only the positive answer, the ball hits the ground at approximately 3.87 s. To find where this occurs, substitute this $t$-value into the equation for $x$.

$$x = 2(3.873) \approx 7.75$$

The ball hits the ground at a horizontal distance of approximately 7.75 m from the cliff.

**b.** 2.55 s, 5.09 m from the cliff. Replace the gravitational constant, $g$, with 3.7 m/s$^2$ to get $0 = -1.85t^2 + 12$. Solve the equation for $t$.

$$0 = -1.85t^2 + 12$$

$$1.85t^2 = 12$$

$$t^2 = \frac{12}{1.85}$$

$$t = \pm\sqrt{\frac{12}{1.85}} \approx \pm 2.547$$

Using only the positive answer, the ball hits the ground at approximately 2.55 s. To find where this occurs, substitute this $t$-value into the equation for $x$.

$$x = 2(2.547) \approx 5.09$$

The ball hits the ground at a horizontal distance of approximately 5.09 m from the cliff.

**5. a.** Possible answer: [0, 5, 1, 0, 4, 1], $0 \le t \le 1.5$

**b.** Sample answer: This projectile was launched from 2 m above Earth with a velocity of 6 m/s at an inclination of 52°.

**6. a.** 0.43 s. Write parametric equations to model the motion of the ball. Let $v$ represent the velocity of the ball.

$$x = vt$$
$$y = -16t^2 + 3$$

The ball hits the floor at the point where $y = 0$. Solve the equation $0 = -16t^2 + 3$.

$$0 = -16t^2 + 3$$

$$16t^2 = 3$$

$$t^2 = \frac{3}{16}$$

$$t = \pm\sqrt{\frac{3}{16}} \approx \pm 0.433$$

Only the positive answer makes sense, so the ball hits the ground at approximately 0.43 s.

**b.** 4.16 ft/s. The ball hits the ground at a point 1.8 ft from the table at 0.43 s. Substitute 0.433 and 1.8 into the equation for $x$ and solve for $v$.

$$1.8 = v(0.433), \text{ so } v = \frac{1.8}{0.433} \approx 4.16$$

The ball was traveling at a velocity of about 4.16 ft/s when it left the table.

**7. a.** $x = 83t\cos 0°$, $y = -4.9t^2 + 83t\sin 0° + 1.2$ (or $x = 83t$, $y = -4.9t^2 + 1.2$)

**b.** No; it will hit the ground 28.93 m before reaching the target. Graph the equations $x = 83t\cos 0°$ and $y = -4.9t^2 + 83t\sin 0° + 1.2$ with $0 \le t \le 1$ and $t$-step 0.01. You can see that the arrow doesn't make the target. Find when the arrow hits the ground by solving the equation $0 = -4.9t^2 + 83t\sin 0° + 1.2$.

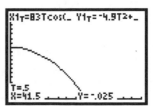

[0, 70, 5, 0, 2, 1]
$0 \le t \le 1$

$$0 = -4.9t^2 + 83t \sin 0° + 1.2$$
$$-1.2 = -4.9t^2$$
$$t^2 = \frac{1.2}{4.9}$$
$$t = \pm\sqrt{\frac{1.2}{4.9}} \approx \pm 0.49487$$

Using only the positive answer, the arrow hits the ground at approximately 0.49 s. To find when this occurs, substitute this $t$-value into the equation for $x$.

$$x = 83(0.49487) \cos 0° \approx 41.07$$

The arrow will hit the ground $70 - 41.07$, or 28.93 m before reaching the target.

c. The angle must be between 2.44° and 3.43°. The bottom of the target is $1.3 - 0.5(1.22)$, or 0.69 m above the ground, and the top is $1.3 + 0.5(1.22)$, or 1.91 m above the ground. Experiment with different values for angle $A$ in the parametric equations with $x$ equal to 70 and $y$ between 0.69 m and 1.91 m $(0.69 \leq y \leq 1.91)$.

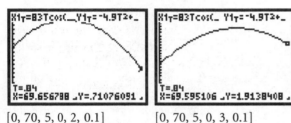

$[0, 70, 5, 0, 2, 0.1]$   $[0, 70, 5, 0, 3, 0.1]$

d. At least 217 m/s. Experiment with different values for the initial velocity in the original parametric equation for $x$ so that the arrow travels 70 m $(x = 70)$ and the height of the arrow is at least 0.69 m $(y \geq 0.69)$.

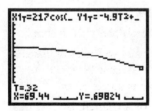

$[0, 70, 5, 0, 2, 0.1]$

8. The ball does not clear the fence. Convert 8 mi/h to ft/s.

$$(8 \text{ mi/h})\left(\frac{5280 \text{ ft}}{1 \text{ mi}}\right)\left(\frac{1 \text{ h}}{60 \text{ min}}\right)\left(\frac{1 \text{ min}}{60 \text{ s}}\right) \approx 11.73 \text{ ft/s}$$

Change the parametric equation for $x$ to $x = 120t \cos 30° - 11.73t$ to account for the wind blowing at 11.73 ft/s directly toward Carolina from the fence. Graph the equations $x = 120t \cos 30° - 11.73t$ and $y = -16t^2 + 120t \sin 30° + 3$. Trace the graph to show that the ball hits the ground at approximately 3.8 s, 350 ft away from where the

ball is hit, so the ball does not clear a 10 ft fence 365 ft away.

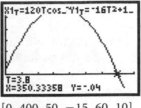

$[0, 400, 50, -15, 60, 10]$
$0 \leq t \leq 4$

9. 46 ft from the end of the cannon. The equations $x = 40t \cos 60°$ and $y = -16t^2 + 40t \sin 60° + 10$ model Gonzo's motion. Substitute 5 for $y$ and solve for $t$ to find when he hits the net.

$$5 = -16t^2 + 40t \sin 60° + 10$$
$$0 = -16t^2 + 40t \sin 60° + 5$$
$$t = \frac{-40(\sin 60°) \pm \sqrt{(-40 \sin 60°)^2 - 4(-16)(5)}}{2(-16)}$$
$$t \approx -0.136 \text{ or } t \approx 2.301$$

A negative value for $t$ doesn't make sense, so Gonzo hits the net about 2.3 s after being fired out of the cannon. To determine how far the net needs to be from the cannon, substitute this $t$-value into the equation for $x$: $x = 40(2.301) \cos 60° \approx 46.01$. The net needs to be about 46 ft from the end of the cannon.

10. The ball will bounce on the fourth step (3 steps down from the top step). Let the point $(0, 0)$ be the initial position of the golf ball at time $t = 0$. The projectile motion of the golf ball is modeled by the parametric equations $x = -5t$ and $y = -16t^2$, or in inches, $x = -60t$ and $y = -192t^2$. The edge of the second step (1 step down from the top step) is at the point $(-8, -8)$, the third step (2 steps down) is at $(-16, -16)$, the fourth step is at $(-24, -24)$, and so on. Check the $y$-values for $x \approx -8, -16$, and so on. When $t = 0.14$ at the point $(-8.4, -3.76)$, the golf ball will not bounce on the second step because the $y$-coordinate, $-3.76$, is not less than $-8$. Similarly, when $t = 0.27$ at the point $(-16.2, -14.0)$, the golf ball will not bounce on the third step because the $y$-coordinate is not less than $-16$. The point $(-24, -30.72)$ on the graph shows that the golf ball will bounce on the fourth step.

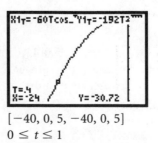

$[-40, 0, 5, -40, 0, 5]$
$0 \leq t \leq 1$

**11. a.** $x = 122t \cos 38°$, $y = -16t^2 + 122t \sin 38°$

**b.** 451 ft. To find when the ball first hits the ground, find when $y = 0$. Graph the equations $x = 122t \cos 38°$ and $y = -16t^2 + 122t \sin 38°$. Trace the graph to show that the ball hits the ground at approximately 4.7 s, 451 ft away from where it was hit.

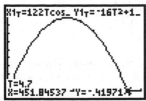

$[0, 500, 50, -5, 100, 10]$
$0 \le t \le 5$

**c.** 378 ft. The parametric equations that model this shot are $x = 110t \cos 46°$ and $y = -16t^2 + 110t \sin 46°$. To find when the ball first hits the ground, find when $y = 0$. Graph the equations and trace the graph to show that the ball hits the ground at approximately 4.95 s, 378 ft away from where it was hit.

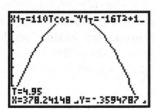

$[0, 400, 50, 0, 100, 10]$
$0 \le t \le 5$

**12. a.** The tip starts at $(0, 1)$ and moves back and forth along a circular arc from $(0.7, 0.714)$ to $(-0.7, 0.714)$.

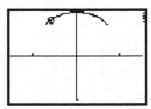

$[-1.5, 1.5, 1, -1, 1, 1]$
$0° \le t \le 360°$

**b.** $y = \sqrt{1 - x^2}$. Eliminate the parameter, $t$, by substituting $x^2$ for $(0.7 \sin t)^2$ in the $y$-equation to get $y = \sqrt{1 - x^2}$.

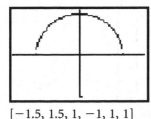

$[-1.5, 1.5, 1, -1, 1, 1]$

**c.** The single equation is an entire semicircle, whereas the parametric equation is the part of the circle from $x = -0.7$ to $x = 0.7$.

**d.** $x = 0.7 \sin t$ and $y = -\sqrt{1 - (0.7 \sin t)^2}$

**e.** The graph appears the same, but the number of back-and-forth movements is increased.

**13. a.** $x = 2.3t + 4$, $y = 3.8t + 3$

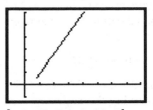

$[-5, 40, 5, -5, 30, 5]$

**b.** 4.44 m/s on a bearing of 31°. To determine the ball's velocity, find the distance the ball has moved over a specified time. For example, at 5 s the ball has moved from the position $(4, 3)$ to $(15.5, 22)$. Create a right triangle where the horizontal leg measures $15.5 - 4$, or 11.5 m and the vertical leg measures $22 - 3$, or 19 m. By the Pythagorean Theorem, the ball moves $\sqrt{11.5^2 + 19^2}$, or about 22.2 m in 5 s, so the velocity of the ball is $\frac{22.5 \text{ m}}{5 \text{ s}} = 4.44$ m/s. The ball's angle of motion is $\tan^{-1}\left(\frac{19}{11.5}\right) = 59°$, so its bearing is $90° - 59° = 31°$.

**14. a.** 20 ft 1 in. Let $x$ represent the height of the tree less the 5 ft 2 in. trunk.

$$\tan 36° = \left(\frac{x}{20.5}\right)$$
$$x = 20.5 \tan 36° \approx 14.894, \text{ or 14 ft 11 in.}$$

Add 14 ft 11 in. to 5 ft 2 in. to find that the total height of the tree is about 20 ft 1 in.

**b.** 33 m. Let $x$ represent the width of the lake. $\sin 29° = \frac{x}{68.4}$, so $x = 68.4 \sin 29° \approx 33$ m. The width of the lake is about 33 m.

**c.** 930.9 cm². The area of a triangle is $A = \frac{1}{2}base \cdot height$. The height of the triangle is 48 cm. To find the base, draw the altitude from the vertex of the triangle to the midpoint of the base of the isosceles triangle to divide the original triangle into two right triangles. Let $x$ represent the length of the base of one of the right triangles. $\tan 68° = \frac{48}{x}$, so $x = \frac{48}{\tan 68°} \approx 19.393$. The base of the original triangle is $2(19.393)$, or 38.786 cm. The area of the triangle is then $\frac{1}{2}(38.786)(48) \approx 930.9$ cm².

**d.** 315.96 ft. Let $x$ represent the distance from the boat to the lighthouse. $\tan 20° = \frac{115}{x}$, so $x = \frac{115}{\tan 20°} \approx 314.96$ ft. The distance from the boat to the lighthouse is about 315.96 ft.

**15.** $a\left(4x^3 + 8x^2 - 23x - 33\right)$, where $a$ is an integer, $a \neq 0$. If $\left(\frac{1}{2} - \sqrt{3}\right)$ is a root, then the other root must be $\left(\frac{1}{2} + \sqrt{3}\right)$. Any polynomial with these roots must be in this form. Multiply the factors together.

$$0 = a(x + 3)\left(x - \left(\frac{1}{2} - \sqrt{3}\right)\right)\left(x - \left(\frac{1}{2} + \sqrt{3}\right)\right)$$

$$= a(x + 3)\left(x^2 - \left(\frac{1}{2} - \sqrt{3}\right)x - \left(\frac{1}{2} + \sqrt{3}\right)x + \left(\frac{1}{2} - \sqrt{3}\right)\left(\frac{1}{2} + \sqrt{3}\right)\right)$$

$$= a(x + 3)\left(x^2 - \left(\frac{1}{2} - \sqrt{3} + \frac{1}{2} + \sqrt{3}\right)x + \left(\frac{1}{4} - \frac{\sqrt{3}}{2} + \frac{\sqrt{3}}{2} - 3\right)\right)$$

$$= a(x + 3)\left(x^2 - x - \frac{11}{4}\right)$$

$$= a\left(x^3 - x^2 - \frac{11}{4}x + 3x^2 - 3x - \frac{33}{4}\right)$$

$$= a\left(x^3 + 2x^2 - \frac{23}{4}x - \frac{33}{4}\right)$$

$$= a\left(4x^3 + 8x^2 - 23x - 33\right)$$

$$= a\left(4x^3 + 8x^2 - 23x - 33\right)$$

**16.** $x = 2\cos t - 3$, $y = 5\sin t + 4$; $\left(\frac{x + 3}{2}\right)^2 + \left(\frac{y - 4}{5}\right)^2 = 1$. The center of the ellipse is $(-3, 4)$, and the distance from the center to the vertices along the minor axis is 2 and along the major axis is 5.

**EXTENSIONS**

**A.** See the solution to Take Another Look activity 2 on page 205.

**B.** Answers will vary.

## LESSON 8.6

**EXERCISES**

**1.** 9.7 cm. Use the Law of Sines to find the length of side $\overline{AC}$.

$$\frac{\sin A}{a} = \frac{\sin B}{b} \qquad \text{Select the proportion for the given angles and sides.}$$

$$\frac{\sin 85.4°}{12.5} = \frac{\sin 50.6°}{b} \qquad \text{Substitute the angle measures and the known side lengths.}$$

$$b\sin 85.4° = 12.5 \sin 50.6° \qquad \text{Multiply both sides by } 12.5b.$$

$$b = \frac{12.5 \sin 50.6°}{\sin 85.4°} \qquad \text{Divide both sides by } \sin 85.4°.$$

$$b \approx 9.7 \qquad \text{Evaluate.}$$

The length of $\overline{AC}$ is approximately 9.7 cm.

**2.** 63.2°. Use the Law of Sines to find the measure of $\angle P$.

$$\frac{\sin 55.3°}{8.13} = \frac{\sin P}{8.83} \qquad \text{Set up a proportion using opposite sides and angles.}$$

$$\sin P = \frac{8.83 \sin 55.3°}{8.13} \qquad \text{Solve for } \sin P.$$

$$P = \sin^{-1}\left(\frac{8.83 \sin 55.3°}{8.13}\right) \qquad \text{Take the inverse sine of both sides.}$$

$$P \approx 63.2° \qquad \text{Evaluate.}$$

Assuming $\angle P$ is acute, it measures approximately 63.2°.

**3.** $X \approx 50.2°$ and $Z \approx 92.8°$. Use the Law of Sines to find the measure of $\angle X$.

$$\frac{\sin X}{6} = \frac{\sin 37°}{4.7}$$

$$\sin X = \frac{6 \sin 37°}{4.7}$$

$$X = \sin^{-1}\left(\frac{6 \sin 37°}{4.7}\right)$$

$$X \approx 50.2°$$

The measure of $\angle X$ is about 50.2°. To find the measure of the third angle, $\angle Z$, use the fact that the sum of the measure of the angles in a triangle is 180°: $Z \approx 180° - (50.2° + 37°) = 92.8°$.

**4.** 7.8 cm. Use the Law of Sines and $Z \approx 92.8°$ from Exercise 3 to find the length of $\overline{XY}$.

$$\frac{\sin 37°}{4.7} = \frac{\sin 92.8°}{c}$$

$$c\sin 37° = 4.7 \sin 92.8°$$

$$c = \frac{4.7 \sin 92.8°}{\sin 37°}$$

$$c \approx 7.8$$

The length of $\overline{XY}$ is approximately 7.8 cm.

**5. a.** $B = 25.5°$; $BC \approx 6.4$ cm; $AB \approx 8.35$ cm. The sum of the measures of the angles in a triangle is 180°, so the measure of $\angle B$ is $180° - (47° + 107.5°)$, or 25.5°. Use the Law of Sines to find the lengths of $\overline{AB}$ and $\overline{BC}$. Let $c$ represent $AB$ and let $a$ represent $BC$.

$$\frac{\sin 25.5°}{3.77} = \frac{\sin 107.5°}{c}$$

$$c\sin 25.5° = 3.77 \sin 107.5°$$

$$c = \frac{3.77 \sin 107.5°}{\sin 25.5°}$$

$$c \approx 8.35$$

The length of $\overline{AB}$ is approximately 8.35 cm.

$$\frac{\sin 25.5°}{3.77} = \frac{\sin 47°}{a}$$

$$a \sin 25.5° = 3.77 \sin 47°$$

$$a = \frac{3.77 \sin 47°}{\sin 25.5°}$$

$$a \approx 6.4$$

The length of $\overline{BC}$ is approximately 6.4 cm.

**b.** $J \approx 38.8°$; $L \approx 33.3°$; $KJ \approx 4.77$ cm. Use the Law of Sines to find the measure of $\angle J$.

$$\frac{\sin 107.9°}{8.26} = \frac{\sin J}{5.44}$$

$$\sin J = \frac{5.44 \sin 107.9°}{8.26}$$

$$J = \sin^{-1}\left(\frac{5.44 \sin 107.9°}{8.26}\right)$$

$$J \approx 38.8°$$

The measure of $\angle J$ is approximately 38.8°. The angle measures sum to 180°, so the measure of $\angle L$ is approximately $180° - (107.9° + 38.8°)$, or 33.3°. Use the Law of Sines to find the length of $\overline{KJ}$. Let $l$ represent $KJ$.

$$\frac{\sin 107.9°}{8.26} = \frac{\sin 33.3°}{l}$$

$$l \sin 107.9° = 8.26 \sin 33.3°$$

$$l = \frac{8.26 \sin 33.3°}{\sin 107.9°}$$

$$l \approx 4.77$$

The length of $\overline{KJ}$ is approximately 4.77 cm.

**6.** 160.7 ft. The angle measures sum to 180°, so the measure of the third angle is $180° - (93° + 70°)$, or 17°. Let $h$ represent the height of the cliff and solve for $h$ using the Law of Sines.

$$\frac{\sin 17°}{50} = \frac{\sin 70°}{h}$$

$$h \sin 17° = 50 \sin 70°$$

$$h = \frac{50 \sin 70°}{\sin 17°}$$

$$h \approx 160.7$$

The cliff is about 160.7 ft high.

**7. a.** 12.19 cm. In an isosceles triangle, if one of the base angles measures 42°, then the other base angle also measures 42°. The sum of the angle measures is 180°, so the measure of the angle opposite the base is $180° - (42° + 42°)$, or 96°. Let $b$ represent the length of the base and use the Law of Sines to find $b$.

$$\frac{\sin 42°}{8.2} = \frac{\sin 96°}{b}$$

$$b \sin 42° = 8.2 \sin 96°$$

$$b = \frac{8.2 \sin 96°}{\sin 42°}$$

$$b \approx 12.19$$

The length of the base of the isosceles triangle is approximately 12.19 cm.

**b.** Because the triangle is isosceles, knowing the measures of one angle allows you to determine the measures of all three angles.

**8.** Approximately 27 million mi or approximately 153 million mi. Sketch a triangle to represent the situation. This is an ambiguous case because knowing two sides and a non-included angle does not allow you to know if the triangle is acute or obtuse.

Use the Law of Sines to find one possible measure of $\angle V$.

$$\frac{\sin 14°}{67} = \frac{\sin V}{93}$$

$$\sin V = \frac{93 \sin 14°}{67}$$

$$V = \sin^{-1}\left(\frac{93 \sin 14°}{67}\right)$$

$$V \approx 19.6°$$

If $\angle V$ is acute, it measures approximately 19.6°. The other possibility for the measure of $\angle V$ is the supplement of 19.6°, or 160.4°. To find the distance between Venus and Earth, you need to find the measure of the third angle.

$$180° - (14° + 19.6°) = 146.4° \text{ or}$$
$$180° - (14° + 160.4°) = 5.6°$$

Use the Law of Sines to find the two possible distances, $s$, between Venus and Earth.

$$\frac{\sin 14°}{67} = \frac{\sin 146.4°}{s} \qquad \frac{\sin 14°}{67} = \frac{\sin 5.6°}{s}$$

$$s \sin 14° = 67 \sin 146.4° \qquad s \sin 14° = 67 \sin 5.6°$$

$$s = \frac{67 \sin 146.4°}{\sin 14°} \qquad s = \frac{67 \sin 5.6°}{\sin 14°}$$

$$s \approx 153 \qquad s \approx 27$$

At this moment in time, Venus is approximately 27 million mi or 153 million mi from Earth.

**9.** 2.5 km. The angle measure of the triangle at the point of the first sighting is $107° - 60°$, or 47°. When two parallel lines are crossed by a transversal, the interior angles on the same side of the transversal are supplementary, so part of the angle measure of the triangle at the point of the second sighting is $180° - 107°$, or $73°$. Adding $73°$ to $34°$, you get $107°$, the angle measure of the triangle at the point of the second sighting. The sum of the angles of the triangle is $180°$, so the measure of the angle at the point of the light is $180° - (47° + 107°)$, or $26°$. Use the Law of Sines to find the distance the boat is from the light at the time of the second sighting.

$$\frac{\sin 26°}{1.5} = \frac{\sin 47°}{d}$$
$$d \sin 26° = 1.5 \sin 47°$$
$$d = \frac{1.5 \sin 47°}{\sin 26°}$$
$$d \approx 2.5$$

The boat is 2.5 km from the source of the light at the time of the second sighting.

10. 5.4685 light-years at the first reading and 5.4684 light-years at the second reading. Draw a diagram to represent the situation. The first measure of the angle between the star and the ecliptic is $42.13204°$. The measure of the angle of the triangle at the second reading is the supplement of $42.13226°$, or $180° - 42.13226° = 137.86774°$. The sum of the angles of the triangle is $180°$, so the measure of the angle at the point of the star is $180° - (42.13204° + 137.86774°)$, or $(2.2 \times 10^{-4})°$.

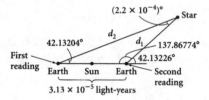

Use the Law of Sines to find the distances, $d_1$ and $d_2$, to the star.

$$\frac{\sin(2.2 \times 10^{-4})°}{3.13 \times 10^{-5}} = \frac{\sin 42.13204°}{d_1}$$
$$d_1 \sin(2.2 \times 10^{-4})° = (3.13 \times 10^{-5}) \sin 42.13204°$$
$$d_1 = \frac{(3.13 \times 10^{-5}) \sin 42.13204°}{\sin(2.2 \times 10^{-4})°}$$
$$d_1 \approx 5.4684$$
$$\frac{\sin(2.2 \times 10^{-4})°}{3.13 \times 10^{-5}} = \frac{\sin 137.86774°}{d_2}$$
$$d_2 \sin(2.2 \times 10^{-4})° = (3.13 \times 10^{-5}) \sin 137.86774°$$
$$d_2 = \frac{(3.13 \times 10^{-5}) \sin 137.86774°}{\sin(2.2 \times 10^{-4})°}$$
$$d_2 \approx 5.4685$$

Earth is approximately 5.4685 light-years from the star at the first reading and 5.4684 light-years from the star at the second reading.

11. a. $41°$. Substitute $60°$ for $\theta_1$ and solve for $\theta_2$.
$$\frac{\sin 60°}{1.33} = \frac{\sin \theta_2}{1}$$
$$\sin \theta_2 = \frac{\sin 60°}{1.33}$$
$$\theta_2 = \sin^{-1}\left(\frac{\sin 60°}{1.33}\right) \approx 41°$$

The angle of refraction in water is $41°$.

b. $70°$. Substitute $45°$ for $\theta_2$ and solve for $\theta_1$.
$$\frac{\sin \theta_1}{1.33} = \frac{\sin 45°}{1}$$
$$\sin \theta_1 = 1.33 \sin 45°$$
$$\theta_1 = \sin^{-1}(1.33 \sin 45°) \approx 70°$$

The ray entered the water at a $70°$ angle.

c. $0°$. Substitute $0°$ for $\theta_1$ and solve for $\theta_2$.
$$\frac{\sin 0°}{1.33} = \frac{\sin \theta_2}{1}$$
$$\frac{0}{1.33} = \sin \theta_2$$
$$\sin \theta_2 = 0$$
$$\theta_2 = \sin^{-1} 0 = 0°$$

The angle of refraction is $0°$.

12. a. $x = \frac{4 \pm \sqrt{6}}{2}$. $a = 2$, $b = -8$, and $c = 5$. Substitute $a$, $b$, and $c$ into the quadratic formula to solve for $x$.
$$x = \frac{-(-8) \pm \sqrt{(-8)^2 - 4(2)(5)}}{2(2)}$$
$$x = \frac{8 \pm \sqrt{24}}{4}$$
$$x = \frac{4 \pm \sqrt{6}}{2}$$

b. $x = \frac{-2 \pm \sqrt{31}}{3}$. $a = 3$, $b = 4$, and $c = -9$. Substitute $a$, $b$, and $c$ into the quadratic formula to solve for $x$.
$$x = \frac{-4 \pm \sqrt{4^2 - 4(3)(-9)}}{2(3)}$$
$$x = \frac{-4 \pm \sqrt{124}}{6} = \frac{-2 \pm \sqrt{31}}{3}$$

13. a. $x$-component: $12 \cos 78° \approx 2.5$; $y$-component: $-12 \sin 78° \approx -11.7$

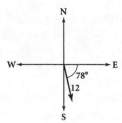

*Discovering Advanced Algebra Solutions Manual*
©2004 Key Curriculum Press

**b.** $x$-component: $-16 \cos 49° \approx -10.5$;
$y$-component: $-16 \sin 49° \approx -12.1$

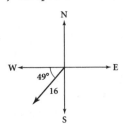

**14. a.** 10 units on a bearing of 294°. By the Pythagorean Theorem, the magnitude of the vector is $\sqrt{9.1^2 + 4.1^2}$, or about 10 units. The angle of the vector with the $x$-axis is $\tan^{-1}\left(\frac{4.1}{9.1}\right)$, or about 24°. Because the $x$-coordinate is negative and the $y$-coordinate is positive, the vector is in Quadrant II. So its bearing is $270° + 24°$, or 294°.

**b.** 22 units on a bearing of 49°. By the Pythagorean Theorem, the magnitude of the vector is $\sqrt{16.6^2 + 14.4^2}$, or about 22 units. The angle of the vector with the $x$-axis is $\tan^{-1}\left(\frac{14.4}{16.6}\right)$, or about 41°. The vector is in Quadrant I, so its bearing is $90° - 41°$, or 49°.

**15. a.** $value = 36{,}500(1 - 0.06)^{5.25} \approx \$26{,}376.31$

**b.** 20 years 11 months. Substitute 10,000 for $value$. Let $t$ represent time and solve for $t$ in the equation from 15a.

$$10000 = 36500(1 - 0.06)^t$$

$$\frac{10000}{36500} = 0.94^t$$

$$\log\left(\frac{10000}{36500}\right) = t \log 0.94$$

$$t = \frac{\log\left(\frac{10000}{36500}\right)}{\log 0.94} \approx 20.92$$

The building will be worth less than $10,000 at 20 years 11 months.

**16.** 13,824 ft³. The body of the greenhouse is a rectangular prism and the roof is a triangular prism. The volumes of the rectangular and triangular prisms are given by (*area of base*)(*height*). The volume of the rectangular prism is $(32 \cdot 24)(12) = 9216$ ft³. To find the volume of the triangular prism, first calculate the side lengths of the isosceles right triangle that is the base. Each length is $\sqrt{288}$ ft by the Pythagorean Theorem. So the volume of the prism is

$$\left(\frac{\sqrt{288} \cdot \sqrt{288}}{2}\right)(32) = 4608 \text{ ft}^3$$

The total volume of the greenhouse is $9216 + 4608 = 13824$ ft³.

---

**IMPROVING YOUR GEOMETRY SKILLS**

The area of the triangle is given by $\frac{1}{2}ah$, where $h$ is the height of the triangle to base $\overline{BC}$. Then $\sin C = \frac{h}{b}$, or $b \sin C = h$. Substituting $b \sin C$ for $h$ in the area formula gives the equation $Area = \frac{1}{2}ab \sin C$. The symmetry of this expression shows that $\overline{AC}$ could have been considered the base as well.

**EXTENSION**

Answers will vary.

## LESSON 8.7

**EXERCISES**

**1.** Approximately 6.1 km. Use the Law of Cosines to find the length of $\overline{AC}$. Let $a$ represent $BC$ and let $c$ represent $AB$.

| | |
|---|---|
| $b^2 = a^2 + c^2 - 2ac \cos B$ | The Law of Cosines for finding $b$. |
| $b^2 = 5.1^2 + 9.2^2 - 2(5.1)(9.2) \cos 38°$ | Substitute 5.1 for $a$, 9.2 for $c$, and 38° for $B$. |
| $b^2 = 26.01 + 84.64 - 93.84 \cos 38°$ | Multiply. |
| $b = \sqrt{26.01 + 84.64 - 93.84 \cos 38°}$ | Take the positive square root of both sides. |
| $b \approx 6.1$ | Evaluate. |

The length of $\overline{AC}$ is approximately 6.1 km.

**2.** Approximately 35.33°. Use the Law of Cosines to find the measure of $\angle T$. Let $t$ represent $RS$, let $r$ represent $ST$, and let $S$ represent $TR$.

$$t^2 = r^2 + s^2 - 2rs \cos T$$

$$6.64^2 = 6.14^2 + 10.62^2 - 2(6.14)(10.62) \cos T$$

$$44.0896 = 37.6996 + 112.7844 - 130.4136 \cos T$$

$$44.0896 = 150.484 - 130.4136 \cos T$$

$$-106.3944 = -130.4136 \cos T$$

$$\cos T = \frac{-106.3944}{-130.4136}$$

$$T \approx \cos^{-1}\left(\frac{-106.3944}{-130.4136}\right)$$

$$T \approx 35.33°$$

$\angle T$ measures approximately 35.33°.

**3. a.** $\cos A = \frac{16 - 25 - 36}{-2(5)(6)}$, so $A = \cos^{-1}\left(\frac{3}{4}\right) \approx 41.4°$

   **b.** $b = 8$. $b^2 - 40 - 6b(0.5) = 0$, so $b^2 - 3b - 40 = 0$, $(b - 8)(b + 5) = 0$, and $b = 8$ (assuming $b$ is positive).

**4. a.** $AC \approx 6.4$, $A \approx 78°$, $C \approx 53°$. Use the Law of Cosines to find the length of $\overline{AC}$.

$b^2 = 8.3^2 + 6.8^2 - 2(8.3)(6.8) \cos 49°$

$b^2 = 68.89 + 46.24 - 112.88 \cos 49°$

$b = \sqrt{68.89 + 46.24 - 112.88 \cos 49°}$

$b \approx 6.4$

The length of $\overline{AC}$ is approximately 6.4 units. Now use the Law of Cosines to find the measure of $\angle A$.

$8.3^2 = 6.4^2 + 6.8^2 - 2(6.4)(6.8) \cos A$

$68.89 = 87.2 - 87.04 \cos A$

$-18.31 = -87.04 \cos A$

$\cos A = \frac{-18.31}{-87.04}$

$A = \cos^{-1}\left(\frac{-18.31}{-87.04}\right)$

$A \approx 78°$

$\angle A$ measures approximately 78°. To find the measure of $\angle C$, use the fact that the measures of the three angles in any triangle sum to 180°. The measure of $\angle C$ is approximately 180° − (49° + 78°), or 53°.

**b.** $D = 72°$, $F = 36°$, $DE \approx 7.7$. $\triangle EFD$ is an isosceles triangle where the angles opposite the congruent sides are congruent, so $\angle D$ measures 72°. The measures of the three angles in any triangle sum to 180°, so the measure of $\angle F$ is 180° − 2(72°), or 36°. Use the Law of Cosines to find the length of $\overline{DE}$.

$f^2 = 12.4^2 + 12.4^2 - 2(12.4)(12.4) \cos 36°$

$f^2 = 153.76 + 153.76 - 307.52 \cos 36°$

$f = \sqrt{153.76 + 153.76 - 307.52 \cos 36°}$

$f \approx 7.7$

The length of $\overline{DE}$ is approximately 7.7 units.

**c.** $G \approx 114°$, $H \approx 38°$, $I \approx 28°$. Use the Law of Cosines to find the measure of $\angle G$.

$9.1^2 = 6.1^2 + 4.7^2 - 2(6.1)(4.7) \cos G$

$82.81 = 37.21 + 22.09 - 57.34 \cos G$

$82.81 = 59.3 - 57.34 \cos G$

$23.51 = -57.34 \cos G$

$\cos G = \frac{23.51}{-57.34}$

$G = \cos^{-1}\left(\frac{23.51}{-57.34}\right)$

$G \approx 114°$

$\angle G$ measures approximately 114°. Now use the Law of Sines to find the measure of $\angle H$.

$\frac{\sin 114°}{9.1} = \frac{\sin H}{6.1}$

$9.1 \sin H = 6.1 \sin 114°$

$\sin H = \frac{6.1 \sin 114°}{9.1}$

$H = \sin^{-1}\left(\frac{6.1 \sin 114°}{9.1}\right)$

$H \approx 38°$

$\angle H$ measures approximately 38°. The measures of the three angles sum to 180°, so the measure of $\angle I$ is approximately 180° − (114° + 38°), or 28°.

**5.** 1659.8 mi. The distances the planes have traveled after 2 h are 400(2), or 800 mi, and 450(2), or 900 mi, and the included angle is 260° − 105°, or 155°.

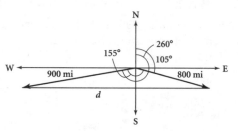

Use the Law of Cosines to find the distance between the planes after 2 h.

$d^2 = 900^2 + 800^2 - 2(900)(800) \cos 155°$

$d = \sqrt{900^2 + 800^2 - 2(900)(800) \cos 155°}$

$d \approx 1659.8$

The airplanes will be approximately 1659.8 mi apart after 2 h.

**6.** 112.3°. Use the Law of Cosines to find the measure of $\angle S$.

$10.62^2 = 6.14^2 + 6.64^2 - 2(6.14)(6.64) \cos S$

$112.7844 = 37.6996 + 44.0896 - 81.5392 \cos S$

$112.7844 = 81.7892 - 81.5392 \cos S$

$30.9952 = -81.5392 \cos S$

$\cos S = \frac{30.9952}{-81.5392}$

$S = \cos^{-1}\left(\frac{30.9952}{-81.5392}\right)$

$S \approx 112.3°$

**7.** From point $A$, the underground chamber is at a 22° angle from the ground between $A$ and $B$. From point $B$, the chamber is at a 60° angle from the ground. If the truck goes 1.5 km farther in the same direction, the chamber will be approximately 2.6 km directly beneath the truck. Draw a diagram. Call the chamber $C$ and the point directly above the chamber $D$.

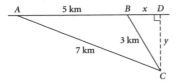

Use the Law of Cosines to find the measure of $\angle A$.

$$3^2 = 7^2 + 5^2 - 2(7)(5) \cos A$$

$$9 = 49 + 25 - 70 \cos A$$

$$9 = 74 - 70 \cos A$$

$$-65 = -70 \cos A$$

$$\cos A = \frac{65}{70}$$

$$A = \cos^{-1}\left(\frac{65}{70}\right) \approx 22°$$

From point $A$, the chamber is at a 22° angle from the ground between $A$ and $B$. Let $X$ represent the measure of $\angle ABC$ and use the Law of Cosines to find $X$.

$$7^2 = 3^2 + 5^2 - 2(3)(5) \cos X$$

$$49 = 9 + 25 - 30 \cos X$$

$$49 = 34 - 30 \cos X$$

$$15 = -30 \cos X$$

$$\cos X = \frac{15}{-30}$$

$$X = \cos^{-1}\left(\frac{15}{-30}\right) = 120°$$

$\angle ABC$ measures 120°. $\angle DBC$ is the supplement of $\angle ABC$, so it measures 60°, and then $\angle BCD$ measures 30°. Use the Law of Sines to find $x$ and $y$.

$$\frac{\sin 90°}{3} = \frac{\sin 30°}{x} \qquad \frac{\sin 90°}{3} = \frac{\sin 60°}{y}$$

$$x \sin 90° = 3 \sin 30° \qquad y \sin 90° = 3 \sin 60°$$

$$x = \frac{3 \sin 30°}{\sin 90°} = 1.5 \qquad y = \frac{3 \sin 60°}{\sin 90°} \approx 2.6$$

From point $B$, the chamber is at a 60° angle from the ground. If the truck goes 1.5 km farther in the same direction, the chamber will be about 2.6 km directly beneath it.

**8.** Approximately 58 cm. Use the Law of Cosines to find the distance, $d$, between front and rear legs at the floor.

$$d^2 = 75^2 + 55^2 - 2(75)(55) \cos 50°$$

$$d = \sqrt{75^2 + 55^2 - 2(75)(55) \cos 50°}$$

$$d \approx 58$$

The front and rear legs are approximately 58 cm apart at the floor.

**9.** 2.02 mi. The angle at the Pleasant Beach point, between the cell tower and the point of maximum distance, is the same as the bearing of 60° because alternate interior angles are congruent when parallel lines are cut by a transversal. Use the Law of Cosines to find the distance, $d$, between Pleasant Beach and the point of maximum distance.

$$1.75^2 = (1)^2 + d^2 - 2(1)(d) \cos 60°$$

$$3.0625 = 1 + d^2 - 2d(0.5)$$

$$0 = d^2 - d - 2.0625$$

$$d = \frac{-(-1) \pm \sqrt{(-1)^2 - 4(1)(-2.0625)}}{2(1)}$$

$$d \approx 2.02 \text{ or } d \approx -1.02$$

The customers of Pleasant Beach will be able to use their cell phones approximately 2.02 mi south. The solution $d \approx -1.02$ means that the signal will also reach approximately 1.02 mi north of Pleasant Beach.

**10.** Approximately 148° to 149°. Make a scale drawing of the situation. Call the source $S$.

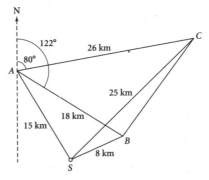

You should find that you can't locate point $S$ exactly; you get one location using points $A$ and $B$ and a different location using points $A$ and $C$. Calculate the bearing using both locations to get a range of values.

Consider $\triangle ABS$. Let $X$ represent $\angle SAB$ and use the Law of Cosines to find $X$.

$$8^2 = 15^2 + 18^2 - 2(15)(18) \cos X$$

$$64 = 225 + 324 - 540 \cos X$$

$$\cos X = \frac{-485}{-540}$$

$$X = \cos^{-1}\left(\frac{-485}{-540}\right) \approx 26.08°$$

The bearing of the source from Receiver A using $\triangle ABS$ is $122° + 26.08°$, or about $148.08°$. Now consider $\triangle ACS$. Let $Y$ represent $\angle SAC$ and use the Law of Cosines to find $Y$.

$$25^2 = 26^2 + 15^2 - 2(26)(15)\cos Y$$

$$625 = 676 + 224 - 780 \cos Y$$

$$\cos Y = \frac{-276}{-780}$$

$$Y = \cos^{-1}\left(\frac{-276}{-780}\right) \approx 69.28°$$

The bearing of the source from Receiver A using $\triangle ACS$ is $80° + 69.28°$, or about $149.28°$. So the bearing is approximately $148°$ to $149°$.

**11.** 10.3 nautical mi. Sketch a diagram of the situation.

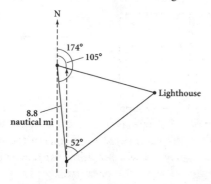

The measure of the angle of the triangle at the point of the first sighting is $174° - 105°$, or $69°$, and the angle at the second sighting measures $52° + 6°$, or $58°$. Because the measures of the three angles in a triangle sum to $180°$, the measure of the angle at the lighthouse is $180° - (69° + 58°)$, or $53°$. Use the Law of Sines to find the distance of the ship from the lighthouse.

$$\frac{\sin 53°}{8.8} = \frac{\sin 69°}{d}$$

$$\sin 53° \, d = 8.8 \sin 69°$$

$$d = \frac{8.8 \sin 69°}{\sin 53°}$$

$$d \approx 10.3$$

The ship is approximately 10.3 nautical mi from the lighthouse.

**12. a.**

[0.25, 0.4, 0.01, 0, 1, 0]

**b.** .281, .2905, .314, .330, .368

**c.** range = $.368 - .281 = .087$,
   IQR = $.330 - .2905 = .0395$

**d.** $\bar{x} \approx .315$, $s \approx .025$

**13.** 1751 cm². To find the total surface area, find the area of the two bases, which are each $\frac{300°}{360°}$, or $\frac{5}{6}$ the area of a circle; the area of the two rectangles that form the indentation; and the surface area of the remaining body, which when flattened out is a rectangle. The area of the bases is $2\left(\frac{5}{6}\right)(36\pi)$, or $60\pi$ cm². The area of the two rectangles is $2(6)(36)$, or 432 cm². The area of the rectangular body of the figure is the product of the length, which is $\frac{5}{6}$ the circumference of a circle, and the width, also the height of the figure, which is 36 cm, so $\frac{5}{6}(12\pi)(36) = 360\pi$ cm². Therefore the total surface area is $60\pi + 432 + 360\pi \approx 1751$ cm².

**14.** $ST = 3\sqrt{2}$ units. Ray $ST$ is tangent to circle $B$ at $S$, so $\triangle RST$ is a right triangle where $\angle S$ measures $90°$. Ray $RU$ is tangent to circle $B$ at $U$, so $\triangle RUB$ is also a right triangle where $\angle RUB$ is a right angle. $\angle R$ is shared by $\triangle RST$ and $\triangle RUB$, and they are both right triangles, so the third angles of the triangles are congruent. By the AAA Similarity Theorem from geometry, $\triangle RST$ is similar to $\triangle RUB$. Set up equal ratios and substitute measurements to find the length of $\overline{ST}$.

$$\frac{RU}{RS} = \frac{BU}{ST}$$

$$\frac{\sqrt{9^2 - 3^2}}{12} = \frac{3}{ST}$$

$$(6\sqrt{2})ST = 36$$

$$ST = \frac{36}{6\sqrt{2}} = \frac{6}{\sqrt{2}} = \frac{6\sqrt{2}}{2} = 3\sqrt{2}$$

The length of $\overline{ST}$ is $3\sqrt{2}$ units.

**EXTENSION**

Answers will vary.

**CHAPTER 8 REVIEW**

**EXERCISES**

**1. a.** When $t = 3$, $x = -8$ and $y = 0.5$. When $t = 0$, $x = 1$ and $y = 2$. When $t = -3$, $x = 10$ and $y = -1$.

$$t = 3: x = -3(3) + 1 = -8$$
$$y = \frac{2}{(3) + 1} = \frac{2}{4} = 0.5$$
$$t = 0: x = -3(0) + 1 = 1$$
$$y = \frac{2}{(0) + 1} = \frac{2}{1} = 2$$
$$t = -3: x = -3(-3) + 1 = 10$$
$$y = \frac{2}{(-3) + 1} = \frac{2}{-2} = -1$$

**b.** $y = \frac{6}{11}$. Substitute $-7$ for $x$ and solve for $t$.

$-7 = -3t + 1$, so $-3t = -8$, and $t = \frac{8}{3}$

Now substitute $\frac{8}{3}$ for $t$ in the equation for $y$ and solve.

$$y = \frac{2}{\left(\frac{8}{3}\right) + 1} = \frac{2}{\frac{11}{3}} = \frac{6}{11}$$

**c.** $x = \frac{5}{2}$. Substitute 4 for $y$ and solve for $t$.

$$4 = \frac{2}{t + 1}$$

$$4(t + 1) = 2$$

$$t + 1 = \frac{1}{2}$$

$$t = -\frac{1}{2}$$

Now substitute $-\frac{1}{2}$ for $t$ in the equation for $x$ and solve.

$$x = -3\left(-\frac{1}{2}\right) + 1 = \frac{3}{2} + \frac{2}{2} = \frac{5}{2}$$

**d.** When $t = -1$, the $y$-value is undefined.

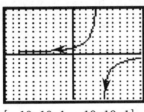

$[-10, 10, 1, -10, 10, 1]$

**2. a.** 160 m east and 240 m south. After 8 s, the raft has moved (20 m/s)(8 s), or 160 m east and (30 m/s)(8 s), or 240 m south.

**b.** $x = 20t$, $y = -30t$. The velocity is negative in the equation for $y$ because the current is flowing south.

**3. a.** $y = \frac{x + 7}{2}$. The graph is the same. Eliminate the parameter by solving the $x$-equation for $t$ and substituting in the equation for $y$.

$2t = x + 5$, so $t = \frac{x + 5}{2}$, and $y = \left(\frac{x + 5}{2}\right) + 1 = \frac{x + 7}{2}$

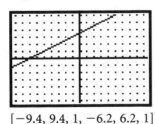

$[-9.4, 9.4, 1, -6.2, 6.2, 1]$

**b.** $y = \pm\sqrt{x - 1} - 2$. The graph is the same except for the restrictions on $t$. Eliminate the parameter: $t^2 = x - 1$, so $t = \pm\sqrt{x - 1}$, and $y = \pm\sqrt{x - 1} - 2$.

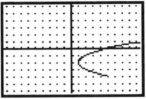

$[-9.4, 9.4, 1, -6.2, 6.2, 1]$

**c.** $y = (2x - 1)^2$. The graph is the same. The values of $t$ are restricted, but endpoints are not visible within the calculator screen given. Eliminate the parameter: $t + 1 = 2x$, so $t = 2x - 1$, and $y = (2x - 1)^2$.

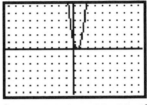

$[-9.4, 9.4, 1, -6.2, 6.2, 1]$

**d.** $y = x^2 - 5$. The graph is the same, except the parametric equations will not allow for negative values for $x$. Eliminate the parameter: $t + 2 = x^2$, so $t = x^2 - 2$, and $y = x^2 - 2 - 3 = x^2 - 5$.

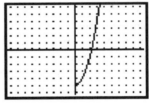

$[-9.4, 9.4, 1, -6.2, 6.2, 1]$

**4. a.** $x = -(2t - 5)$, $y = t + 1$. $x = -(2t - 5)$ is a reflection of $x = 2t - 5$ across the $y$-axis.

**b.** $x = 2t - 5$, $y = -(t + 1)$. $y = -(t + 1)$ is a reflection of $y = t + 1$ across the $x$-axis.

**c.** $x = 2t - 5$, $y = t + 4$. Add 3 units to the $y$-equation to get $y = t + 1 + 3 = t + 4$.

**d.** $x = 2t - 9$, $y = t - 1$. Subtract 4 units from the $x$-equation to get $x = 2t - 5 - 4 = 2t - 9$ and subtract 2 units from the $y$-equation to get $y = t + 1 - 2 = t - 1$.

**5. a.** $\cos A = \frac{11}{15}$, so $A = \cos^{-1}\left(\frac{11}{15}\right) \approx 43°$

**b.** $\tan B = \frac{7}{13}$, so $B = \tan^{-1}\left(\frac{7}{13}\right) \approx 28°$

**c.** $16^2 + c^2 = 28^2$, so $c^2 = 28^2 - 16^2$, and $c = \sqrt{28^2 - 16^2} \approx 23.0$

**d.** $\cos 31° = \frac{d}{15}$, so $d = 15 \cos 31° \approx 12.9$

**e.** $\sin 22° = \frac{8}{e}$, so $e = \frac{8}{\sin 22°} \approx 21.4$

**f.** $\tan 42° = \frac{f}{19}$, so $f = 19 \tan 42° \approx 17.1$

**6.** 28°. The slope of the line is $\frac{\sin 28°}{\cos 28°}$, so the angle between the graph and the $x$-axis is $\tan^{-1}\left(\frac{\sin 28°}{\cos 28°}\right)$, or 28°.

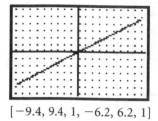

$[-9.4, 9.4, 1, -6.2, 6.2, 1]$

**7.** 7.2 m. The parametric equations that model the motion of the diver are $x = 4t + 1.5$ and $y = -4.9t^2 + 10$. Graph the equations to find that when $y = 0$, $x \approx 7.2$. The diver hits the water at approximately 7.2 m from the edge of the pool.

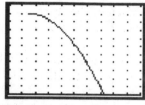

$[0, 10, 1, 0, 11, 1]$

**8.** 1.43 ft/s. The parametric equations that model the movement of the duck are $x = 2.4t$ and $y = vt$ where $v$ is the speed of the current. Consider the duck's original location as the origin and the landing location as $(47, -28)$. Substitute 47 for $x$ into the equation for $x$ and solve for $t$, to get $47 = 2.4t$, and $t \approx 19.58$. Now substitute $-28$ for $y$ and 19.58 for $t$ into the equation for $y$, to get $-28 = v(19.58)$, and $v = -1.43$. Therefore the speed of the current is 1.43 ft/s downstream.

**9.** She will miss it by 11.16 ft. The parametric equations that model the motion of the rock are $x = 100t\cos 72°$ and $y = -16t^2 + 100t\sin 72°$. Substitute 20 for $x$ to find when the rock reaches this horizontal distance, and then substitute this $t$-value in the equation for $y$ to find how high the rock is at this time.

$20 = 100t\cos 72°$

$t = \dfrac{20}{100\cos 72°} \approx 0.647$

$y = -16(0.65)^2 + 100(0.65)\sin 72° \approx 54.84$

At about 0.65 s, the rock is 20 ft away from Aliya and has reached a height of about 55.1 ft. Therefore she will miss the coconut by about $66 - 54.84$, or 11.16 ft.

**10.** She should fly at a bearing of 107.77° if the wind averages 25 mi/h. Assume that the average wind velocity is 25 mi/h and draw a diagram.

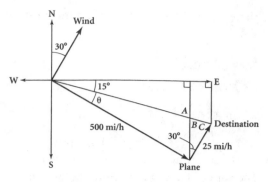

To find the angle the pilot needs to adjust her plane, find $C$ and then use the Law of Sines to find $\theta$. Using the fact that the measures of the angles of a triangle sum to 180°, $A = 180° - (90° + 15°) = 75°$. Then $B = 75°$ because $A$ and $B$ are vertical angles, and $C = 180° - (30° + 75°) = 75°$.

$\dfrac{\sin \theta}{25} = \dfrac{\sin 75°}{500}$

$500 \sin \theta = 25 \sin 75°$

$\sin \theta = \dfrac{25 \sin 75°}{500}$

$\theta = \sin^{-1}\left(\dfrac{25 \sin 75°}{500}\right) \approx 2.77°$

So the pilot should aim her plane at an angle of $-15° + (-2.77°)$, or $-17.77°$, which corresponds to a bearing of 107.77°.

**11. a.** $a \approx 7.8$ m, $c \approx 6.7$ m, $C = 42°$. Use the Law of Sines to find $a$.

$\dfrac{\sin 87°}{10} = \dfrac{\sin 51°}{a}$

$a \sin 87° = 10 \sin 51°$

$a = \dfrac{10 \sin 51°}{\sin 87°} \approx 7.8$

The sum of the angle measures is 180°, so $\angle C$ measures $180° - (51° + 87°)$, or 42°. Now use the Law of Sines to find $c$.

$\dfrac{\sin 87°}{10} = \dfrac{\sin 42°}{c}$

$c \sin 87° = 10 \sin 42°$

$c = \dfrac{10 \sin 42°}{\sin 87°} \approx 6.7$

So $a \approx 7.8$ m, $c \approx 6.7$ m, and $C = 42°$.

**b.** $A \approx 41°$, $b \approx 3.5$ cm, $C \approx 57°$. Use the Law of Cosines to find $b$.

$b^2 = 2.3^2 + 3^2 - 2(2.3)(3)\cos 82°$

$b = \sqrt{2.3^2 + 3^2 - 2(2.3)(3)\cos 82°}$

$b \approx 3.5$

*Discovering Advanced Algebra Solutions Manual*
©2004 Key Curriculum Press

Now use the Law of Sines to find the measure of $\angle A$.

$$\frac{\sin A}{2.3} = \frac{\sin 82°}{3.5}$$

$$3.5 \sin A = 2.3 \sin 82°$$

$$\sin A = \frac{2.3 \sin 82°}{3.5}$$

$$A = \sin^{-1}\left(\frac{2.3 \sin 82°}{3.5}\right) \approx 41°$$

The sum of the angle measures is 180°, so $\angle C$ measures $180° - (41° + 82°)$, or 57°. So $A \approx 41°$, $b \approx 3.5$ cm, and $C \approx 57°$.

### TAKE ANOTHER LOOK

**1.** Sample answers:

If both equations are constant, with $x = c$ and $y = d$, the graph is a single point at $(c, d)$.

If the equation for $x$ is constant and the equation for $y$ is linear, with $x = c$ and $y = a + bt$ $(b \neq 0)$, the graph is a vertical line at $x = c$.

If the equation for $x$ is linear and the equation for $y$ is constant, with $x = a + bt$ $(b \neq 0)$ and $y = c$, the graph is a horizontal line at $y = c$.

If both equations are linear, with $x = a + bt$ and $y = c + dt$ $(bd \neq 0)$, the graph is a line that is neither vertical nor horizontal.

If the equation for $x$ is constant and the equation for $y$ is quadratic, with $x = d$ and $y = at^2 + bt + c$, the graph is a vertical ray along the line $x = d$, starting at point $\left(d, \frac{-b}{4a} + c\right)$ and heading in the direction of the sign of $a$.

If the equation for $x$ is quadratic and the equation for $y$ is constant, with $x = at^2 + bt + c$ and $y = d$, the graph is a horizontal ray along the line $y = d$, starting at point $\left(\frac{-b}{4a} + c, d\right)$ and heading in the direction of the sign of $a$.

If the equation for $x$ is linear and the equation for $y$ is quadratic, with $x = d + et$ and $y = at^2 + bt + c$, the graph is a vertically oriented parabola.

If the equation for $x$ is quadratic and the equation for $y$ is linear, with $x = at^2 + bt + c$ and $y = d + et$, the graph is a horizontally oriented parabola.

If both equations are quadratic, with $x = at^2 + bt + c$ and $y = dt^2 + et + f$, the graph can be a line (for example, the equations $x = t^2$ and $y = -t^2 + 1$ give the line $y = -x + 1$) but is usually a parabola that is oriented neither vertically nor horizontally.

**2.** $x = 3t \cos 240°$ $(t \leq 2.5) + (-3.75 + 3(t - 2.5) \cos 0°)$ $(t > 2.5)$ $(t \leq 4.25) + (1.5 + 3(t - 4.25) \cos 103°)$ $(t > 4.25)$

$y = 3t \sin 240°$ $(t \leq 2.5) + (-6.50 + 3(t - 2.5) \sin 0°)$ $(t > 2.5)(t \leq 4.25) + (-6.50 + 3(t - 4.25) \sin 103°)$ $(t > 4.25)$

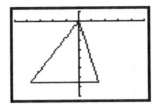

$[-5, 5, 1, -8, 1, 1]$
$0 \leq t \leq 6.47$, $t$-step 0.05

Todd starts on the path given by the equations $x = 3t \cos 240°$, $y = 3t \sin 240°$, or $x = -1.5t$, $y = -1.5t\sqrt{3}$. At 2.5 h, he is at point $(-3.75, -3.75\sqrt{3})$, or about $(-3.75, -6.50)$. The path starting from this point and going due east starting at time 2.5 h is given by the equations $x = -3.75 + 3(t - 2.5) \cos 0°$, $y = -6.50 + 3(t - 2.5) \sin 0°$, or $x = -3.75 + 3(t - 2.5)$, $y = -6.50$. After going in this direction for 1.75 h, the total time is $t = 2.5 + 1.75 = 4.25$ h, and Todd is at point $(1.5, -6.50)$. The angle this creates with the $x$-axis is $\tan^{-1}\left(\frac{-6.50}{1.5}\right) \approx -77°$, or 283°. Therefore, to walk back to where he started from, Todd is walking at an angle of about $283° - 180°$, or about 103°. This final leg of his walk is given by the equations $x = 1.5 + 3(t - 4.25) \cos 103°$, $y = -6.495 + 3(t - 4.25) \sin 103°$. To find out when he reaches his starting point, set either $x$ or $y$ equal to 0 and solve for $t$.

$$0 = 1.5 + 3(t - 4.25) \cos 103°$$

$$t = \frac{-1.5}{3 \cos 103°} + 4.25 \approx 6.47$$

Todd returns to his starting point at about 6.47 h, so use the domain $0 \leq t \leq 6.47$.

**3.** For a supplementary pair, $\angle A$ and $\angle B$, $\sin A = \sin B$, $\cos A = -\cos B$, and $\tan A = -\tan B$.

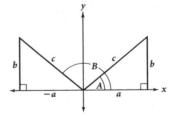

For a complementary pair, $\angle C$ and $\angle D$, $\sin C = \cos D$, $\cos C = \sin D$, and $\tan C = \frac{1}{\tan D}$. (In fact, the word *cosine* means "complement's sine.")

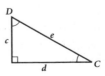

# CHAPTER 9

## LESSON 9.1

### Exercises

**1. a.** $\sqrt{(8-2)^2 + (13-5)^2} = \sqrt{6^2 + 8^2} = \sqrt{100} = 10$ units

**b.** $\sqrt{(5-0)^2 + (10-3)^2} = \sqrt{5^2 + 7^2} = \sqrt{74}$ units

**c.** $\sqrt{(-2-(-4))^2 + (-3-6)^2} = \sqrt{2^2 + (-9)^2} = \sqrt{85}$ units

**d.** $\sqrt{(-6-3)^2 + (3d-d)^2} = \sqrt{(-9)^2 + (2d)^2} = \sqrt{81 + 4d^2}$ units

**2.** $y = 11$ or $y = 3$. The distance between $(5, y)$ and $(2, 7)$ is 5 units, so $\sqrt{(5-2)^2 + (y-7)^2} = 5$. Solve this equation for $y$.

$$\sqrt{9 + (y-7)^2} = 5$$
$$9 + (y-7)^2 = 25$$
$$(y-7)^2 = 16$$
$$y - 7 = \pm 4$$
$$y = 11 \text{ or } y = 3$$

**3.** $x = -1 \pm \sqrt{2160}$, or $x = -1 \pm 12\sqrt{15}$. The distance between $(-1, 5)$ and $(x, -2)$ is 47 units, so $\sqrt{(-1-x)^2 + (5-(-2))^2} = 47$. Solve this equation for $x$.

$$\sqrt{(-1-x)^2 + 49} = 47$$
$$(-1-x)^2 + 49 = 2209$$
$$(-1-x)^2 = 2160$$
$$-1 - x = \pm\sqrt{2160}$$
$$x = -1 \pm \sqrt{2160}$$
$$= -1 \pm 12\sqrt{15}$$

**4.** $\overline{BC}$ is the longest side.

$$AB = \sqrt{(3-1)^2 + (-1-2)^2} = \sqrt{4+9} = \sqrt{13}$$
$$AC = \sqrt{(5-1)^2 + (3-2)^2} = \sqrt{16+1} = \sqrt{17}$$
$$BC = \sqrt{(5-3)^2 + (3-(-1))^2} = \sqrt{4+16}$$
$$= \sqrt{20}$$

**5.** Approximately 25.34 units

$$AB = \sqrt{(1-8)^2 + (5-(-2))^2} = \sqrt{98} = 7\sqrt{2}$$
$$AC = \sqrt{(4-8)^2 + ((-5)-(-2))^2} = \sqrt{25} = 5$$
$$BC = \sqrt{(4-1)^2 + ((-5)-5)^2} = \sqrt{109}$$

The perimeter is $7\sqrt{2} + 5 + \sqrt{109} \approx 25.34$ units.

**6.** $x^2 - 12x + y^2 = -32$, or $y = \pm\sqrt{-x^2 + 12x - 32}$. A point $(x, y)$ is twice as far from $(2, 0)$ as it is from $(5, 0)$ if $\sqrt{(x-2)^2 + (y-0)^2} = 2\sqrt{(x-5)^2 + (y-0)^2}$, or $(x-2)^2 + y^2 = 4((x-5)^2 + y^2)$. Expand the binomials and collect terms.

$$x^2 - 4x + 4 + y^2 = 4(x^2 - 10x + 25 + y^2)$$
$$x^2 - 4x + 4 + y^2 = 4x^2 - 40x + 100 + 4y^2$$
$$-3x^2 + 36x - 3y^2 = 96$$
$$x^2 - 12x + y^2 = -32, \text{ or}$$
$$y = \pm\sqrt{-x^2 + 12x - 32}$$

**7.** $\frac{6-\sqrt{3}}{2} < y < \frac{6+\sqrt{3}}{2}$, or approximately between the points $(2.5, 2.134)$ and $(2.5, 3.866)$. You are looking for a point $(2.5, y)$ on the line $x = 2.5$ that is 1 unit away from the point $(2, 3)$. Write an equation and solve for $y$.

$$\sqrt{(2.5-2)^2 + (y-3)^2} = 1$$
$$0.5^2 + (y-3)^2 = 1$$
$$(y-3)^2 = 0.75$$
$$y - 3 = \pm\sqrt{0.75}$$
$$y = 3 \pm \sqrt{0.75}$$
$$= 3 \pm 0.5\sqrt{3} = \frac{6 \pm \sqrt{3}}{2}$$

The points where the distance is less than 1 mi are between the $y$-values $\frac{6-\sqrt{3}}{2}$ and $\frac{6+\sqrt{3}}{2}$, so $\frac{6-\sqrt{3}}{2} < y < \frac{6+\sqrt{3}}{2}$.

**8. a.** In miles, $\sqrt{x^2 + 4}$ through the field and $(3 - x)$ on the road

**b.** In hours, $\frac{\sqrt{x^2 + 4}}{9}$ through the field and $\frac{3-x}{22}$ on the road. Use the formula *distance* = *rate* · *time*, or *time* = $\frac{distance}{rate}$.

**c.** When $x$ is approximately 0.897 mi, Josh gets home in approximately 0.339 h, a little over 20 min. The total time it takes Josh to get home is $\frac{\sqrt{x^2 + 4}}{9} + \frac{3-x}{22}$. Use the minimum function on your calculator to find the value of $x$ for which the time is minimized. Time is minimized when $x \approx 0.8966$, and in this case it takes Josh approximately 0.339 h, or 20.35 min, to bike home.

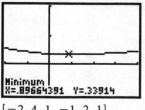

$[-2, 4, 1, -1, 2, 1]$

*Discovering Advanced Algebra Solutions Manual*
©2004 Key Curriculum Press

**9. a.** $y = \sqrt{10^2 + x^2} + \sqrt{(20 - x)^2 + 13^2}$. The distance from the top of the 10 m pole to where the wire touches the ground is $\sqrt{10^2 + x^2}$, and the distance from where the wire touches the ground to the top of the 20 m pole is $\sqrt{(20 - x)^2 + 13^2}$.

**b.** Domain: $0 \le x \le 20$; range: $30 < y < 36$. The value of $x$ must be between 0 and 20 from the context of the problem. Enter the equation in your calculator, and use the table of values to see that the $y$-values are between 30 and 36 for $x$ in this domain.

**c.** Graph the function on your calculator and use the trace function or the minimum function to find the value of $x$ to minimize the length of the wire. The length of the wire is minimized when $x \approx 8.696$ m, in which case the wire is approximately 30.48 m long.

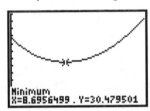

$[0, 21, 2, 25, 37, 1]$

**10. a.** After $t$ seconds, the base of the ladder is $2t$ ft away from the wall (because it is moving away from the wall at a rate of 2 ft/s) and the top of the ladder is at a height of $\sqrt{24^2 - (2t)^2}$.

| Time (s) | Height (ft) |
|---|---|
| 0 | 24 |
| 1 | 23.92 |
| 2 | 23.66 |
| 3 | 23.24 |
| 4 | 22.63 |
| 5 | 21.82 |
| 6 | 20.78 |
| 7 | 19.49 |
| 8 | 17.89 |
| 9 | 15.87 |
| 10 | 13.27 |
| 11 | 9.59 |
| 12 | 0 |

**b.** 12 s. *distance = rate · time,* and the base of the ladder has 24 ft to go at 2 ft/s, so $24 = 2t$, and $t = 12$.

**c.** No, the distance the ladder slides down increases each second.

**d.** $x = 2t$, $y = \sqrt{24^2 - (2t)^2}$. By the formula *distance = rate · time, x = 2t.* Using the Pythagorean Theorem, $y = \sqrt{24^2 - x^2}$, or $y = \sqrt{24^2 - (2t)^2}$.

**e.** The rate at which the ladder is sliding down the wall increases as the ladder is pulled out. If you graph this function on your calculator, the $y$-values decrease slowly at first and then much more rapidly until $t$ reaches 12.

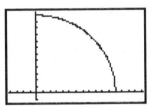

$[-8.47, 32.47, 2, -2, 25, 2]$

**11. a.** $d = \sqrt{(x - 5)^2 + (0.5x^2 + 4)^2}$. The distance from any point $(x, y)$ to the point $(5, -3)$ is $d = \sqrt{(x - 5)^2 + (y + 3)^2}$. Any point on the parabola must satisfy the equation $y = 0.5x^2 + 1$, so substitute this expression for $y$ in the formula for distance.

**b.** Approximately 6.02 units; approximately $(0.92, 1.42)$. Graph the function for $d$ from 11a on your calculator and use the minimum function to find the minimum distance. The distance is minimized when $x \approx 0.92$, in which case the distance is approximately 6.02 units. Find the $y$-coordinate of the point by substituting 0.92 for $x$ in the equation for the parabola: $y = 0.5(0.92)^2 + 1 \approx 1.42$.

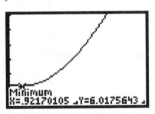

$[0, 10, 1, 0, 30, 5]$

**12. a.** $\left(\frac{37}{6}, \frac{11}{2}\right)$, or approximately $(6.17, 5.50)$. Let $(x, y)$ be the point at which the recreation center should be built. The distances from $(x, y)$ to Ashton, Bradburg, and Carlville are, respectively, $\sqrt{x^2 + (y - 4)^2}$, $\sqrt{(x - 3)^2 + y^2}$, and $\sqrt{(x - 12)^2 + (y - 8)^2}$. These distances should all be equal to each other, which is the same as the squares of the distances being equal, so you get these three equations:

$$x^2 + (y - 4)^2 = (x - 3)^2 + y^2$$

$$x^2 + (y - 4)^2 = (x - 12)^2 + (y - 8)^2$$

$$(x - 3)^2 + y^2 = (x - 12)^2 + (y - 8)^2$$

Expand the first equation and collect terms:
$x^2 + y^2 - 8y + 16 = x^2 - 6x + 9 + y^2$, so
$6x - 8y = -7$.

Similarly, the second equation becomes
$24x + 8y = 192$, or $3x + y = 24$, and the third
equation becomes $18x + 16y = 199$. Find the
intersection point of the first two equations,
$6x - 8y = -7$ and $3x + y = 24$.

| | |
|---|---|
| $6x - 8y = -7$ | The first equation. |
| $y = -3x + 24$ | Solve the second equation for $y$. |
| $6x - 8(-3x + 24) = -7$ | Substitute $(-3x + 24)$ for $y$ in the first equation. |
| $30x - 192 = -7$ | Distribute and combine terms. |
| $x = \dfrac{185}{30} = \dfrac{37}{6}$ | Add 192 to both sides and divide both sides by 5. |
| $y = -3\left(\dfrac{37}{6}\right) + 24 = \dfrac{11}{2}$ | Substitute $\frac{37}{6}$ for $x$ in the second equation. |

The point $\left(\frac{37}{6}, \frac{11}{2}\right)$ also lies on the third line
because $18\left(\frac{37}{6}\right) + 16\left(\frac{11}{2}\right) = 199$. Therefore this
is the solution point.

**b.** The city councils couldn't build the recreation
center equidistant from the towns if they are
collinear because the perpendicular bisectors of
$\overline{AB}$, $\overline{BC}$, and $\overline{AC}$ would have the same slope,
making them parallel. There would be no
intersection.

**c.** Possible factors: the population of each town or
the arrangement of roads between the towns.

**13. a.–d.**

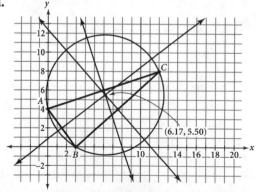

**b.** All three perpendicular bisectors intersect at the
same point. No, you could find the intersection
by constructing only two perpendicular bisectors.

**c.** Approximately (6.17, 5.50); this agrees with 12a.

**d.** Regardless of which point is chosen, the circle
passes through points $A$, $B$, and $C$. The radius of
the circle is constant, so the distance from the
recreation center to all three towns is the same.

**14. a.** $x^2 + 6x + 9 = 5 + 9$, or $(x + 3)^2 = 14$

  **b.** $y^2 - 4y + 4 = -1 + 4$, or $(y - 2)^2 = 3$

  **c.** $x^2 + 6x + 9 + y^2 - 4y + 4 = 4 + 9 + 4$, or
  $(x + 3)^2 + (y - 2)^2 = 17$

**15. a.** The midpoint of each side has coordinates that
are the averages of the coordinates of the
endpoints.

midpoint of $\overline{AB}$: $\left(\dfrac{8 + 1}{2}, \dfrac{-2 + 5}{2}\right) = (4.5, 1.5)$

midpoint of $\overline{BC}$: $\left(\dfrac{1 + 4}{2}, \dfrac{5 - 5}{2}\right) = (2.5, 0)$

midpoint of $\overline{AC}$: $\left(\dfrac{8 + 4}{2}, \dfrac{-2 - 5}{2}\right) = (6, -3.5)$

  **b.** Median from $A$ to $\overline{BC}$: $y = -\frac{4}{11}x + \frac{10}{11}$,
  or $y = -0.\overline{36}x + 0.\overline{90}$; median from $B$ to
  $\overline{AC}$: $y = -1.7x + 6.7$; median from $C$ to
  $\overline{AB}$: $y = 13x - 57$.

  The line from $A$ to the midpoint of $\overline{BC}$
  has slope $\frac{0 + 2}{2.5 - 8} = -\frac{4}{11}$, so its equation is
  $y = -\frac{4}{11}(x - 2.5)$, or $y = -\frac{4}{11}x + \frac{10}{11}$.
  The line from $B$ to the midpoint of $\overline{AC}$ has
  slope $\frac{-3.5 - 5}{6 - 1} = -1.7$, so its equation is
  $y = -1.7(x - 6) - 3.5$, or $y = -1.7x + 6.7$.
  The line from $C$ to the midpoint of $\overline{AB}$ has slope
  $\frac{1.5 + 5}{4.5 - 4} = 13$, so its equation is $y = 13(x - 4.5) +$
  $1.5$, or $y = 13x - 57$.

  **c.** $\left(4\frac{1}{3}, -\frac{2}{3}\right)$, or $(4.\overline{3}, -0.\overline{6})$. Find the intersection
  of the last two lines, $y = -1.7x + 6.7$ and
  $y = 13x - 57$, using substitution.

$$-1.7x + 6.7 = 13x - 57$$
$$-14.7x = -63.7$$
$$x = \frac{13}{3}$$

  So $y = 13\left(\frac{13}{3}\right) - 57 = -\frac{2}{3}$. The point $\left(4\frac{1}{3}, -\frac{2}{3}\right)$ is
  also on the first median line, so it is the intersec-
  tion point of all three median lines.

**16.** Domain: all real numbers; range: $y \geq -2$. Write the
function in vertex form:

$$f(x) = x^2 + 6x + 9 - 9 + 7$$
$$f(x) = (x + 3)^2 - 2$$

$x$ can be anything, but $f(x)$ will always be at
least $-2$.

*Discovering Advanced Algebra Solutions Manual*
©2004 Key Curriculum Press

**17.** About 44.6 nautical mi. Find the distance the ship traveled on each bearing: (2.5 h)(8 knots) = 20 nautical mi and (3 h)(10 knots) = 30 nautical mi. The diagram shows the ship's travel. To find the direct distance from the port to the ship, use the Law of Cosines. The distance is $d = \sqrt{20^2 + 30^2 - 2 \cdot 20 \cdot 30 \cos 125°} \approx 44.6$.

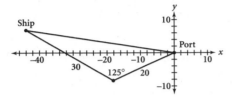

**18.** 9.56 cm. When the linear dimensions of a solid are all scaled by a factor of $k$, its volume is scaled by a factor of $k^3$. Consider the dimensions of the top unfilled part of this cone. The height and the base radius are in the same proportions, as they are in the original cone (because the triangles are similar), so the unfilled part of the cone has dimensions that are all $\frac{1}{2}$ of the dimensions of the original cone. So the volume of the unfilled tip of the cone is $\frac{1}{8}$ of the volume of the full cone and the liquid takes up $\frac{7}{8}$ of the volume of the full cone. When the cone is turned upside down, the liquid still fills $\frac{7}{8}$ of the cone's volume, so the linear dimensions are scaled by $\sqrt[3]{\frac{7}{8}} \approx 0.956$. Therefore the liquid's height is approximately $0.956 \cdot 10 = 9.56$ cm.

**19.** $w = 74°$, $x = 50°$. Draw a diagram to help you find the missing measures.

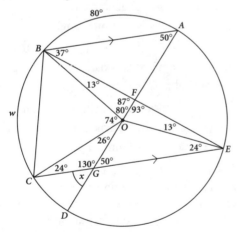

$\triangle AOB$ is isosceles, so $\angle OBA$ and $\angle OAB$ both have measure 50°. $\overline{AB}$ is parallel to $\overline{CE}$, so $\angle OAB$ is congruent to $\angle OGE$, which is also congruent to $\angle CGD$. Therefore $x = 50°$. $\angle AOB$ is intercepted by arc $AB$ with measure 80°, so $\angle AOB$ has measure 80°. $\angle OFB$ is the supplement of $\angle EFG$, so it has measure 87°. Then $\angle OBE$ has measure 180° −

$(80° + 87°) = 13°$. $\triangle BOE$ is isosceles because $\overline{OB}$ and $\overline{OE}$ are both radii, so $\angle OEB$ also has measure 13°. $\angle FEG$ has measure $180° - (93° + 50°) = 37°$, so $\angle OEG$ has measure 24°. $\triangle COE$ is isosceles because $\overline{OC}$ and $\overline{OE}$ are both radii, so $\angle OCE$ also has measure 24°. Therefore $\angle COG$ has measure 26° and $\angle COB$ has measure 74°, so $w = 74°$.

## LESSON 9.2

### EXERCISES

**1. a.** Center: (0, 0); radius: 2; $y = \pm\sqrt{4 - x^2}$

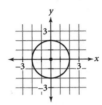

**b.** Center: (3, 0); radius: 1; $y = \pm\sqrt{1 - (x - 3)^2}$

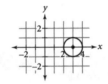

**c.** Center: (−1, 2); radius: 3;
$y = \pm\sqrt{9 - (x + 1)^2} + 2$

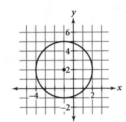

**d.** Center: (0, 1.5); radius: 0.5;
$y = \pm\sqrt{0.25 - x^2} + 1.5$

**e.** Center: (1, 2); radius: 2

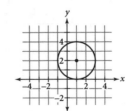

**f.** Center: $(-3, 0)$; radius: 4

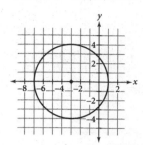

**2. a.** The circle has center $(3, 0)$ and radius 5, so its equation is $(x - 3)^2 + (y - 0)^2 = 5^2$, or $(x - 3)^2 + y^2 = 25$.

**b.** The circle has center $(-1, 2)$ and radius 3, so its equation is $(x + 1)^2 + (y - 2)^2 = 9$.

**c.** The circle has center $(2.5, 0.75)$ and radius 4, so its equation is $(x - 2.5)^2 + (y - 0.75)^2 = 16$.

**d.** The circle has center $(2.5, 1.25)$ and radius 0.5, so its equation is $(x - 2.5)^2 + (y - 1.25)^2 = 0.25$.

**3. a.** $x = 5 \cos t + 3$, $y = 5 \sin t$

**b.** $x = 3 \cos t - 1$, $y = 3 \sin t + 2$

**c.** $x = 4 \cos t + 2.5$, $y = 4 \sin t + 0.75$

**d.** $x = 0.5 \cos t + 2.5$, $y = 0.5 \sin t + 1.25$

**4. a.** Endpoints: $(2, 0)$, $(-2, 0)$, $(0, 4)$, $(0, -4)$. The ellipse is centered at $(0, 0)$; the horizontal axis is $4 = 2 \cdot 2$ units long, and the vertical axis is $8 = 2 \cdot 4$ units long.

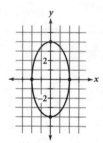

**b.** Endpoints: $(5, -2)$, $(-1, -2)$, $(2, -1)$, $(2, -3)$. The ellipse is centered at $(2, -2)$; the horizontal axis is $6 = 2 \cdot 3$ units long, and the vertical axis is $2 = 2 \cdot 1$ units long.

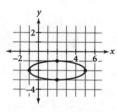

**c.** Endpoints: $(1, 1)$, $(7, 1)$, $(4, 4)$, $(4, -2)$. Endpoints may vary because the graph is a circle. The circle is centered at $(4, 1)$ and has radius 3.

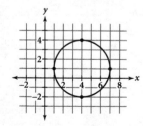

**d.** Endpoints: $(-5, -1)$, $(1, -1)$, $(-2, 1)$, $(-2, -3)$. The ellipse is centered at $(-2, -1)$; the horizontal axis is $6 = 2 \cdot 3$ units long, and the vertical axis is $4 = 2 \cdot 2$ units long.

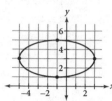

**e.** Endpoints: $(-5, 3)$, $(3, 3)$, $(-1, 5)$, $(-1, 1)$. The ellipse is centered at $(-1, 3)$; the horizontal axis is $8 = 2 \cdot 4$ units long, and the vertical axis is $4 = 2 \cdot 2$ units long.

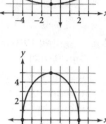

**f.** Endpoints: $(0, 0)$, $(6, 0)$, $(3, 5)$, $(3, -5)$. The ellipse is centered at $(3, 0)$; the horizontal axis is $6 = 2 \cdot 3$ units long, and the vertical axis is $10 = 2 \cdot 5$ units long.

**5. a.** $x = 2 \cos t$, $y = 2 \sin t + 3$

**b.** $x = 6 \cos t - 1$, $y = 6 \sin t + 2$

**6. a.** $\left(\frac{x}{6}\right)^2 + \left(\frac{y}{3}\right)^2 = 1$. The ellipse is centered at $(0, 0)$; the horizontal axis is 12 units long, and the vertical axis is 6 units long.

**b.** $\left(\frac{x - 3}{2}\right)^2 + \left(\frac{y}{5}\right)^2 = 1$. The ellipse is centered at $(3, 0)$; the horizontal axis is 4 units long, and the vertical axis is 10 units long.

**c.** $\left(\frac{x + 1}{4}\right)^2 + \left(\frac{y - 2}{3}\right)^2 = 1$. The ellipse is centered at $(-1, 2)$; the horizontal axis is 8 units long, and the vertical axis is 6 units long.

**d.** $\left(\frac{x - 3}{6}\right)^2 + \left(\frac{y + 1}{3}\right)^2 = 1$. The ellipse is centered at $(3, -1)$; the horizontal axis is 12 units long, and the vertical axis is 6 units long.

**7. a.** $\left(\sqrt{27}, 0\right)$, $\left(-\sqrt{27}, 0\right)$. The major axis is horizontal, so use the relation $b^2 + c^2 = a^2$. Hence $3^2 + c^2 = 6^2$ and $c = \pm\sqrt{27}$. The ellipse is centered at $(0, 0)$, so the foci are at $\left(\sqrt{27}, 0\right)$ and $\left(-\sqrt{27}, 0\right)$.

**b.** $\left(3, \sqrt{21}\right)$, $\left(3, -\sqrt{21}\right)$. The major axis is vertical, so use the relation $a^2 + c^2 = b^2$. Hence $2^2 + c^2 = 5^2$ and $c = \pm\sqrt{21}$. The ellipse is centered at $(3, 0)$, so the foci are at $\left(3, \sqrt{21}\right)$ and $\left(3, -\sqrt{21}\right)$.

*Discovering Advanced Algebra Solutions Manual*
©2004 Key Curriculum Press

**c.** $\left(-1 + \sqrt{7}, 2\right), \left(-1 - \sqrt{7}, 2\right)$. The major axis is horizontal, so use the relation $b^2 + c^2 = a^2$. Hence $3^2 + c^2 = 4^2$ and $c = \pm\sqrt{7}$. The ellipse is centered at $(-1, 2)$, so the foci are at $\left(-1 + \sqrt{7}, 2\right)$ and $\left(-1 - \sqrt{7}, 2\right)$.

**d.** $\left(3 + \sqrt{27}, -1\right), \left(3 - \sqrt{27}, -1\right)$. The major axis is horizontal, so use the relation $b^2 + c^2 = a^2$. Hence $3^2 + c^2 = 6^2$ and $c = \pm\sqrt{27}$. The ellipse is centered at $(3, -1)$, so the foci are at $\left(3 + \sqrt{27}, -1\right)$ and $\left(3 - \sqrt{27}, -1\right)$.

**8. a.** Possible answer: $\left(\frac{x - 493}{497}\right)^2 + \left(\frac{y}{63}\right)^2 = 1$

Draw a scatter plot of the data. Sketch a smooth curve through the points and estimate the $x$-intercepts. The left intercept should be slightly less than $-2.1$ and the right intercept should be slightly greater than $982.4$.

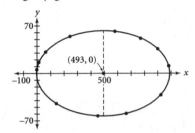

For estimates of $(990, 0)$ and $(-4, 0)$, the center is at $(493, 0)$. To find $b$, plot the center point and estimate the length of the minor axis or use the equation $b^2 + c^2 = a^2$ with $c = 493$ and $a = 497$.

Using either method, $b \approx 63$, so the equation of the ellipse is $\left(\frac{x - 493}{497}\right)^2 + \left(\frac{y}{63}\right)^2 = 1$. Graph the data with the two equations $y = \pm 63\sqrt{1 - \left(\frac{x - 493}{497}\right)^2}$ to check your answer.

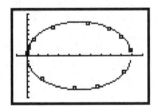

$[-100, 1100, 100, -80, 80, 10]$

The equation fits the data well.

**b.** Substitute $x = 493$ into the equation from 8a: $y = 63$ AU or $y = -63$ AU.

**c.** 990 AU. The distance is greatest at the $x$-intercept, $(990, 0)$.

**d.** $(0, 0)$ and $(986, 0)$. The Sun is one focus of the ellipse. It is 493 AU from the center. The other focus is 493 AU from the center in the opposite direction, at $(986, 0)$.

**9. a.** 1.0 m. Find the foci of the ellipse using $62.4^2 + c^2 = \left(\frac{160}{2}\right)^2$: $c = \pm\sqrt{2506.24} \approx \pm 50$. Therefore the foci are approximately 100 cm, or 1 m, apart.

**b.** 1.6 m. This is the same as the length of the major axis.

**10. a.** The whisperers should stand at the two foci, approximately 5.2 m from the center of the room, along the major axis. Find the foci of the ellipse using $\left(\frac{6}{2}\right)^2 + c^2 = \left(\frac{12}{2}\right)^2$: $c = \pm\sqrt{27} \approx 5.2$.

**b.** The sound travels 12 m, the length of the major axis.

**11. a.** 240 r/min. The rear wheel makes four revolutions for every one revolution the pedal makes, so when Matthew is pedaling 60 r/min, the rear wheel is spinning at $4 \cdot 60 = 240$ r/min.

**b.** 18.6 mi/h. The circumference of the tire is $26\pi \approx 81.68$ in., which is how far Matthew travels with each revolution of his rear tire. In in./min, Matthew's speed is $(240 \text{ r/min})(26\pi \text{ in./r}) \approx 19603.53$ in./min. Convert this speed to mi/h.

$(19603.53 \text{ in./min})\left(\frac{60 \text{ min}}{1 \text{ h}}\right)\left(\frac{1 \text{ ft}}{12 \text{ in.}}\right)\left(\frac{1 \text{ mi}}{5280 \text{ ft}}\right) \approx 18.56$ mi/h

**c.** 6.3 mi/h. Matthew's new gear ratio is 22:30 rather than 1:4, so when he pedals 60 r/min, his rear tire is spinning at $60 \cdot \frac{30}{22} \approx 81.82$ r/min. Convert this speed to mi/h.

$(81.82 \text{ r/min})\left(\frac{26\pi \text{ in.}}{1 \text{ r}}\right)\left(\frac{60 \text{ min}}{1 \text{ h}}\right)\left(\frac{1 \text{ ft}}{12 \text{ in.}}\right)\left(\frac{1 \text{ mi}}{5280 \text{ ft}}\right) \approx 6.3$ mi/h

**12.** Let $x$ represent distance in miles measured parallel to the major axis and measured from the intersection of the major and minor axes. Let $y$ represent distance in miles measured parallel to the minor axis and measured from the intersection of the axes.

$$\left(\frac{x}{237176.5}\right)^2 + \left(\frac{y}{236667.3}\right)^2 = 1$$

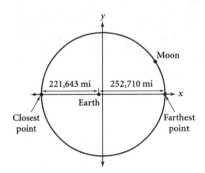

Orient the ellipse so that it is centered at the origin, with the major axis horizontal. Earth must be on the $x$-axis because it is at a focus. The point on the ellipse farthest from Earth is at the opposite end of the major axis. The sum of the distances from the two foci to any point on the ellipse is a constant, so the point on the ellipse closest to Earth is on the closer end of the major axis. Therefore the major axis is $221643 + 252710 = 474353$ mi long, so $a = \frac{1}{2}(474353) = 237176.5$. Use Earth's distance from each end of the major axis to calculate its coordinates as $(-15533.5, 0)$.

Use the relation $b^2 + c^2 = a^2$ to find $b$: $b = \sqrt{237176.5^2 - (-15533.5)^2} \approx 236667.3$. Thus the equation is $\left(\frac{x}{237176.5}\right)^2 + \left(\frac{y}{236667.3}\right)^2 = 1$. Notice that the orbit of the Moon around Earth is almost circular.

**13.** $y = -(x + 3)^2 + 2$

**14.** $\frac{y - 4}{0.5} = \left(\frac{x + 2}{3}\right)^2$, so $y - 4 = 0.5\left(\frac{x + 2}{3}\right)^2$, and $y = 0.5\left(\frac{x + 2}{3}\right)^2 + 4$.

**15.** $y = 2x^2 - 24x + 117$. Start with the equation $y = ax^2 + bx + c$ and use three data points, for example $(0, 117)$, $(3, 63)$, and $(5, 47)$, to get three linear equations in $a$, $b$, and $c$.

$$\begin{cases} c = 117 \\ 9a + 3b + c = 63 \\ 25a + 5b + c = 47 \end{cases}$$

Solve this system to find $a = 2$, $b = -24$, and $c = 117$. The quadratic equation fitting the given data points is $y = 2x^2 - 24x + 117$.

**16.** About 34.45 units

$AB = \sqrt{(2 + 4)^2 + (5 - 2)^2} = \sqrt{45}$

$AC = \sqrt{(6 + 4)^2 + (-8 - 2)^2} = \sqrt{200}$

$BC = \sqrt{(6 - 2)^2 + (-8 - 5)^2} = \sqrt{185}$

The perimeter of the triangle is $\sqrt{45} + \sqrt{200} + \sqrt{185} \approx 34.45$ units.

## IMPROVING YOUR REASONING SKILLS

Hit ball 1 through the focus without the pocket. It will bounce off the side and go in the pocket at the other focus. Or hit ball 1 harder directly away from the pocket. It will bounce off the side, go through the other focus, bounce off the other side again, and go in the pocket.

## EXTENSIONS

**A.** See the solution to Take Another Look activity 1 on pages 236 and 237.

**B.** Answers will vary.    **C.** Answers will vary.

## LESSON 9.3

### EXERCISES

**1. a.** $(1, 0.5)$. The vertex is halfway between the focus and the directrix, so its $x$-coordinate is 1 and its $y$-coordinate is $\frac{-3 + 4}{2} = 0.5$.

**b.** $y = 8$. The focus is 6 units below the vertex, so the directrix must be horizontal and 6 units above the vertex.

**c.** $(9, 2)$. The directrix is vertical and 3 units to the left of the vertex, so the focus must be 3 units to the right of the vertex.

**2. a.** Line of symmetry: $x = 0$

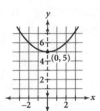

**b.** Line of symmetry: $y = -2$

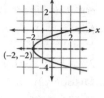

**c.** Line of symmetry: $x = -3$

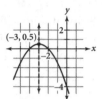

**d.** Line of symmetry: $y = 0$

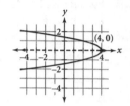

**e.** Line of symmetry: $x = -1$

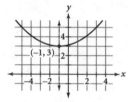

**f.** Line of symmetry: $y = 0$

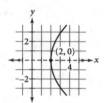

**3. a.** Focus: $(0, 6)$; directrix: $y = 4$. The equation in standard form is $\left(\frac{x}{2}\right)^2 = \frac{y - 5}{1}$, so $a = 2$, $b = 1$, and $f = \frac{2^2}{1 \cdot 4} = 1$. The vertex is $(0, 5)$. Add 1 to the $y$-coordinate of the vertex to get the focus, $(0, 6)$. Subtract 1 from the $y$-coordinate of the vertex to get the equation of the directrix, $y = 4$.

**b.** Focus: $(-1.75, -2)$; directrix: $x = -2.25$. The equation in standard form is $(y + 2)^2 = x + 2$, so $a = b = 1$, and $f = \frac{1^2}{1 \cdot 4} = 0.25$. The vertex is $(-2, -2)$. Add 0.25 to the $x$-coordinate of the vertex to get the focus, $(-1.75, -2)$. Subtract 0.25 from the $x$-coordinate of the vertex to get the equation of the directrix, $x = -2.25$.

**c.** Focus: $(-3, 0)$; directrix: $y = 1$. The equation in standard form is $(x + 3)^2 = \frac{y - 0.5}{-0.5}$, so $a = 1$, $b = -0.5$, and $f = \frac{1^2}{-0.5 \cdot 4} = -0.5$. The vertex is $(-3, 0.5)$. Subtract 0.5 from the $y$-coordinate of the vertex to get the focus, $(-3, 0)$. Add 0.5 to the $y$-coordinate of the vertex to get the equation of the directrix, $y = 1$.

**d.** Focus: $(3.875, 0)$; directrix: $x = 4.125$. The equation in standard form is $y^2 = \frac{x-4}{-2}$, so $a = -2$, $b = 1$, and $f = \frac{1^2}{-2 \cdot 4} = -0.125$. The vertex is $(4, 0)$. Subtract 0.125 from the $x$-coordinate of the vertex to get the focus, $(3.875, 0)$. Add 0.125 to the $x$-coordinate of the vertex to get the equation of the directrix, $x = 4.125$.

**e.** Focus: $(-1, 5)$; directrix: $y = 1$. Here $a = 4$ and $b = 2$, so $f = \frac{4^2}{2 \cdot 4} = 2$. The vertex is $(-1, 3)$. Add 2 to the $y$-coordinate of the vertex to get the focus, $(-1, 5)$. Subtract 2 from the $y$-coordinate of the vertex to get the equation of the directrix, $y = 1$.

**f.** Focus: $\left(\frac{61}{12}, 0\right)$; directrix: $x = \frac{11}{12}$. Here $a = 3$ and $b = 5$, so $f = \frac{5^2}{3 \cdot 4} = \frac{25}{12}$. The vertex is $(3, 0)$. Add $\frac{25}{12}$ to the $x$-coordinate of the vertex to get the focus, $\left(\frac{61}{12}, 0\right)$. Subtract $\frac{25}{12}$ from the $x$-coordinate of the vertex to get the equation of the directrix, $x = \frac{11}{12}$.

**4. a.** $(y - 2)^2 = x$. The vertex is at $(0, 2)$, and there are no stretches or reflections.

**b.** $\frac{y-4}{-1} = x^2$. The vertex is at $(0, 4)$; there is a reflection across the $x$-axis, so $b$ is negative.

**c.** $y + 1 = \left(\frac{x-3}{2}\right)^2$. The vertex is at $(3, -1)$ and the parabola is stretched horizontally by a factor of 2.

**d.** $\left(\frac{y-2}{3}\right)^2 = \frac{x+6}{-1}$. The vertex is at $(-6, 2)$ and the parabola is stretched vertically by a factor of 3 and reflected across the $y$-axis.

**5.** In 5a–d, use the parameter $t$ to represent the squared part of the equation.

**a.** $y - 2 = t$, so the equations are $x = t^2$, $y = t + 2$.

**b.** $\frac{y-4}{-1} = t^2$, so the equations are $x = t$, $y = -t^2 + 4$.

**c.** $t = \frac{x-3}{2}$ and $y + 1 = t^2$, so the equations are $x = 2t + 3$, $y = t^2 - 1$.

**d.** $t = \frac{y-2}{3}$ and $t^2 = \frac{x+6}{-1}$, so the equations are $x = -t^2 - 6$, $y = 3t + 2$.

**6.** $y^2 = -12x$. The directrix is 3 units to the right of the vertex, so $f = -3$. Thus the equation is $y^2 = (4)(-3x)$, or $y^2 = -12x$.

**7.** The path is parabolic. Answers may vary depending on how coordinates are chosen. One possibility is to put the rock at $(0, 2)$ and the shoreline at $y = 0$. Then $f = 1$ and the vertex is at $(0, 1)$, so the equation is $x^2 = 4(y - 1)$, or $y = \frac{1}{4}x^2 + 1$.

**8. a.** $y = \frac{1}{8}x^2 + 1$. Solve the original equation for $y$.

$x^2 + (y - 3)^2 = (y + 1)^2$    Original equation with both sides squared.

$x^2 + 8 = 8y$    Expand and combine terms.

$y = \frac{1}{8}x^2 + 1$    Divide both sides by 8.

**b.** The graph is a parabola with vertex at $(0, 1)$, focus at $(0, 3)$, and directrix $y = -1$.

**9.** $y = \frac{1}{8}(x - 1)^2 + 1$. The vertex of the parabola is halfway between the focus and the directrix, so it is at $(1, 1)$. The parabola is vertical and has the equation $y = \frac{1}{4f}(x - 1)^2 + 1$. The distance between the vertex and the focus is 2 units, so $f = 2$ and the equation is $y = \frac{1}{8}(x - 1)^2 + 1$.

**10.** The grill should be located 5 cm above the center of the dish.

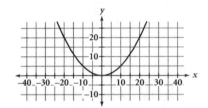

If you orient the dish on the coordinate axes so that it opens up and its vertex is at the origin, its equation in standard form is $\frac{y}{20} = \left(\frac{x}{20}\right)^2$. $f = \frac{20^2}{20 \cdot 4} = 5$, so its focus is at $(0, 5)$, 5 cm above the center of the dish.

**11. a., c.** The point of tangency is at $(0.5, 2)$ and the slope of the line is 2. To find the point of intersection, solve the system of equations

$$\begin{cases} y = 2x + 1 \\ y^2 = 8x \end{cases}$$

Solve the first equation for $x$: $x = \frac{1}{2}(y - 1)$. Substitute this expression for $x$ in the second equation to get $y^2 = 4y - 4$, and solve for $y$: $y^2 - 4y + 4 = 0$, so $(y - 2)^2 = 0$, and $y = 2$. Substitute 2 for $y$ in either of the original equations to find $x = 0.5$.

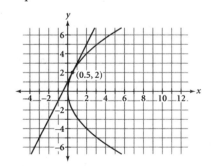

**b.** $f = \frac{8}{4} = 2$, so the focus is at $(2, 0)$.

**d.** *slope* $= 0$

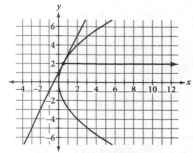

**e.** *slope* $= \dfrac{0 - 2}{2 - 0.5} = -\dfrac{4}{3}$

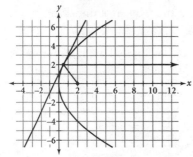

**f.** 63.4°; 63.4°; the angles are congruent. For the angle between the tangent line and the horizontal line, $\tan A = \dfrac{2 - 0}{1 + 2 \cdot 0} = 2$. For the other angle, $\tan B = \dfrac{-\frac{4}{3} - 2}{1 - \frac{4}{3} \cdot 2} = 2$.

The angles are both acute and have the same tangents, so they must be congruent, with measure $\tan^{-1} 2 \approx 63.4°$.

**12.** $y = -2.4x^2 + 21.12x - 44.164$. Start with the equation $y = ax^2 + bx + c$, and use the data points to get three linear equations in $a$, $b$, and $c$.

$$\begin{cases} 12.96a + 3.6b + c = 0.764 \\ 25a + 5b + c = 1.436 \\ 33.64a + 5.8b + c = -2.404 \end{cases}$$

Solve this system to find that $a = -2.4$, $b = 21.12$, and $c = -44.164$. The equation of the parabola is $y = -2.4x^2 + 21.12x - 44.164$.

**13.** Approximately 0.8660; approximately $(\pm 0.7071, 0.5)$. The coordinates of any point on the parabola are $(x, -x^2 + 1)$. The distance from the origin to a point on the parabola is then $d = \sqrt{(x - 0)^2 + ((-x^2 + 1) - 0)^2} =$

$\sqrt{x^2 + (-x^2 + 1)^2}$. Graph this function on your calculator and use the minimum function to find the smallest distance.

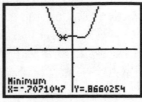

$[-4.7, 4.7, 1, -3.2, 3.2, 1]$

The smallest distance is about 0.8660, and it occurs at $x$-values of about $-0.7071$ and $0.7071$. Substitute these values in the equation for the parabola to find that $y \approx -(\pm 0.7071)^2 + 1 \approx 0.5$. The points closest to the origin are about $(\pm 0.7071, 0.5)$.

**14.** $\left(\dfrac{x - 2}{16}\right)^2 + \left(\dfrac{y - 1}{\sqrt{192}}\right)^2 = 1$, or $\left(\dfrac{x - 2}{16}\right)^2 + \left(\dfrac{y - 1}{8\sqrt{3}}\right)^2 = 1$. You are looking for an equation in the form $\left(\dfrac{x - h}{a}\right)^2 + \left(\dfrac{y - k}{b}\right)^2 = 1$. The center of the ellipse is halfway between the two foci, at $(2, 1)$, so $h = 2$ and $k = 1$. The major axis of the ellipse is horizontal, so the sum of the distances from the two foci to any point on the ellipse is $2a$. The distance from $(10, 13)$ to $(-6, 1)$ is 20 and the distance from $(10, 13)$ to $(10, 1)$ is 12, so $2a = 20 + 12$, or $a = 16$. The distance $c = 8$ from the center of the ellipse to one of the foci satisfies the equation $b^2 + c^2 = a^2$, so $b^2 + 8^2 = 16^2$ and $b = \pm\sqrt{192} = \pm 8\sqrt{3}$. Because $b$ is squared in the equation, it doesn't matter which sign it is, so use $b = 8\sqrt{3}$. The equation is $\left(\dfrac{x - 2}{16}\right)^2 + \left(\dfrac{y - 1}{8\sqrt{3}}\right)^2 = 1$.

**15. a.** $\pm 1, \pm 2, \pm 5, \pm 10, \pm\frac{1}{2}, \pm\frac{5}{2}$. By the Rational Root Theorem, the numerator must be a factor of 10 and the denominator must be a factor of 2.

**b.** Substitute each possible root into the function to find that $\frac{1}{2}$ is the only rational root.

**c.** $f(x) = (2x - 1)(x - 1 + 3i)(x - 1 - 3i)$. Because $\frac{1}{2}$ is a root, $(2x - 1)$ must be a factor. Use polynomial long division to factor.

$$\begin{array}{r} x^2 - 2x + 10 \\ 2x - 1 \overline{\smash{)}\ 2x^3 - 5x^2 + 22x - 10} \\ \underline{2x^3 - x^2} \phantom{+ 22x - 10} \\ -4x^2 + 22x \phantom{- 10} \\ \underline{-4x^2 + 2x} \phantom{- 10} \\ 20x - 10 \\ \underline{20x - 10} \\ 0 \end{array}$$

*Discovering Advanced Algebra Solutions Manual*
©2004 Key Curriculum Press

So $2x^3 - 5x^2 + 22x - 10 = (2x - 1)(x^2 - 2x + 10)$. Using the quadratic formula or completing the square, the two roots of $x^2 - 2x + 10 = 0$ are $1 \pm 3i$. Therefore the polynomial factors completely as $f(x) = (2x - 1)(x - 1 + 3i)(x - 1 - 3i)$.

**16.** $x = -1$, $y = 4$, $z = -6$. Represent the three linear equations in matrix form $[A][X] = [B]$.

$$\begin{bmatrix} 3 & 1 & 2 \\ -4 & 3 & 3 \\ 1 & -2 & -1 \end{bmatrix} \begin{bmatrix} x \\ y \\ z \end{bmatrix} = \begin{bmatrix} -11 \\ -2 \\ -3 \end{bmatrix}$$

Solve the equation by multiplying $[A]^{-1}[B]$.

$$[A]^{-1} = \begin{bmatrix} \frac{1}{6} & -\frac{1}{6} & -\frac{1}{6} \\ -\frac{1}{18} & -\frac{5}{18} & \frac{17}{18} \\ \frac{5}{18} & \frac{7}{18} & \frac{13}{18} \end{bmatrix}, \text{ so}$$

$$[A]^{-1}[B] = \begin{bmatrix} -1 \\ 4 \\ -6 \end{bmatrix}, \text{ and } x = -1, y = 4, \text{ and } z = -6.$$

### EXTENSIONS

**A.–C.** Answers will vary.

## LESSON 9.4

### EXERCISES

**1. a.** Vertices: $(-2, 0)$ and $(2, 0)$; asymptotes: $y = \pm 2x$. The center of the hyperbola is at $(0, 0)$. The upper corners of the box are $(2, 4)$ and $(-2, 4)$, so the slopes of the asymptotes are 2 and $-2$.

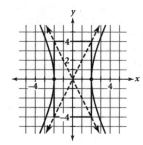

**b.** Vertices: $(2, -1)$ and $(2, -3)$; asymptotes: $y = \frac{1}{3}x - \frac{8}{3}$ and $y = -\frac{1}{3}x - \frac{4}{3}$. The center of the hyperbola is at $(2, -2)$. The upper corners of the box are $(5, -1)$ and $(-1, -1)$, so the slopes of the asymptotes are $\frac{1}{3}$ and $-\frac{1}{3}$.

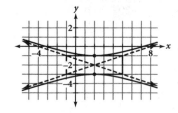

**c.** Vertices: $(1, 1)$ and $(7, 1)$; asymptotes: $y = x - 3$ and $y = -x + 5$. The center of the hyperbola is at $(4, 1)$. The upper corners of the box are $(1, 4)$ and $(7, 4)$, so the slopes of the asymptotes are 1 and $-1$.

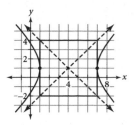

**d.** Vertices: $(-2, 1)$ and $(-2, -3)$; asymptotes: $y = \frac{2}{3}x + \frac{1}{3}$ and $y = -\frac{2}{3}x - \frac{7}{3}$. Rewrite the equation in standard form: $\left(\frac{y+1}{2}\right)^2 - \left(\frac{x+2}{3}\right)^2 = 1$. The center of the hyperbola is $(-2, -1)$. The right corners of the box are $(1, 1)$ and $(1, -3)$, so the slopes of the asymptotes are $\frac{2}{3}$ and $-\frac{2}{3}$.

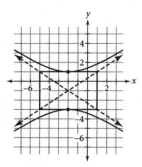

**e.** Vertices: $(-5, 3)$ and $(3, 3)$; asymptotes: $y = 0.5x + 3.5$ and $y = -0.5x + 2.5$. The center of the hyperbola is at $(-1, 3)$. The right corners of the box are $(3, 5)$ and $(3, 1)$, so the slopes of the asymptotes are 0.5 and $-0.5$.

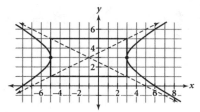

**f.** Vertices: $(3, 5)$ and $(3, -5)$; asymptotes: $y = \frac{5}{3}x - 5$ and $y = -\frac{5}{3}x + 5$. The center of the hyperbola is at $(3, 0)$. The upper corners of the box are $(0, 5)$ and $(6, 5)$, so the slopes of the asymptotes are $\pm\frac{5}{3}$.

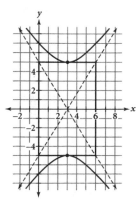

**2. a.** $2^2 + 4^2 = c^2$, so $c = \sqrt{20}$; the foci are at $\left(\sqrt{20}, 0\right)$ and $\left(-\sqrt{20}, 0\right)$, or $\left(2\sqrt{5}, 0\right)$ and $\left(-2\sqrt{5}, 0\right)$.

**b.** $1^2 + 3^2 = c^2$, so $c = \sqrt{10}$; the foci are at $\left(2, -2 + \sqrt{10}\right)$ and $\left(2, -2 - \sqrt{10}\right)$.

**c.** $3^2 + 3^2 = c^2$, so $c = \sqrt{18}$; the foci are at $\left(4 + \sqrt{18}, 1\right)$ and $\left(4 - \sqrt{18}, 1\right)$.

**d.** $2^2 + 3^2 = c^2$, so $c = \sqrt{13}$; the foci are at $\left(-2, -1 + \sqrt{13}\right)$ and $\left(-2, -1 - \sqrt{13}\right)$.

**e.** $4^2 + 2^2 = c^2$, so $c = \sqrt{20}$; the foci are at $\left(-1 + \sqrt{20}, 3\right)$ and $\left(-1 - \sqrt{20}, 3\right)$.

**f.** $3^2 + 5^2 = c^2$, so $c = \sqrt{34}$; the foci are at $\left(3, \sqrt{34}\right)$ and $\left(3, -\sqrt{34}\right)$.

**3. a.** $\left(\frac{x}{2}\right)^2 - \left(\frac{y}{1}\right)^2 = 1$. The center is at the origin, and by looking at the rectangle, $a = 2$ and $b = 1$. The hyperbola is horizontally oriented.

**b.** $\left(\frac{y + 3}{2}\right)^2 - \left(\frac{x - 3}{2}\right)^2 = 1$. The center is at $(3, -3)$, and by looking at the rectangle, $a = 2$ and $b = 2$. The hyperbola is vertically oriented.

**c.** $\left(\frac{x + 2}{3}\right)^2 - \left(\frac{y - 1}{4}\right)^2 = 1$. The center is at $(-2, 1)$, and by looking at the rectangle, $a = 3$ and $b = 4$. The hyperbola is horizontally oriented.

**d.** $\left(\frac{y - 1}{4}\right)^2 - \left(\frac{x + 2}{3}\right)^2 = 1$. The center is at $(-2, 1)$, and by looking at the rectangle, $a = 3$ and $b = 4$. The hyperbola is vertically oriented.

**4. a.** $x = \frac{2}{\cos t}$, $y = \tan t$

**b.** $x = 2 \tan t + 3$, $y = \frac{2}{\cos t} - 3$

**c.** $x = \frac{3}{\cos t} - 2$, $y = 4 \tan t + 1$

**d.** $x = 3 \tan t - 2$, $y = \frac{4}{\cos t} + 1$

**5. a.** $y = \pm 0.5x$

**b.** $y = x - 6$ and $y = -x$. The slopes of the lines are $\pm\frac{2}{2} = \pm 1$, and they both pass through $(3, -3)$, so the equations are $y = \pm(x - 3) - 3$, or $y = x - 6$ and $y = -x$.

**c.** $y = \frac{4}{3}x + \frac{11}{3}$ and $y = -\frac{4}{3}x - \frac{5}{3}$. The slopes of the lines are $\pm\frac{4}{3}$, and they both pass through $(-2, 1)$, so the equations are $y = \pm\frac{4}{3}(x + 2) + 1$, or $y = \frac{4}{3}x + \frac{11}{3}$ and $y = -\frac{4}{3}x - \frac{5}{3}$.

**d.** $y = \frac{4}{3}x + \frac{11}{3}$ and $y = -\frac{4}{3}x - \frac{5}{3}$. These are the same asymptotes as in 5c.

**6. a.** The lengths of the sides of the asymptote rectangle are $2a$ and $2b$. Using the Pythagorean Theorem, the length of the diagonal is $\sqrt{(2a)^2 + (2b)^2} = \sqrt{4a^2 + 4b^2} = \sqrt{4\left(a^2 + b^2\right)} = 2\sqrt{a^2 + b^2}$. Half this distance is $\sqrt{a^2 + b^2}$.

**b.** $\left(2, -2 + \sqrt{10}\right)$ and $\left(2, -2 - \sqrt{10}\right)$. The center of the hyperbola is $(2, -2)$; $a = 3$ and $b = 1$. Half the length of the diagonal is $\sqrt{1^2 + 3^2} = \sqrt{10}$. The hyperbola is vertically oriented, so the coordinates of the foci are $\left(2, -2 + \sqrt{10}\right)$ and $\left(2, -2 - \sqrt{10}\right)$, or about $(2, 1.16)$ and $(2, -5.16)$.

**7.** $\left(\frac{x - 1}{5}\right)^2 - \left(\frac{y - 1}{\sqrt{11}}\right)^2 = 1$. The center of the hyperbola is between the two foci, at $(1, 1)$. The distances from a point on the hyperbola to the foci always differ by $2a$ and in this case they differ by 10, so $a = 5$. The distance from each focus to the center is $c = 6$ units. Finally, use the equation $a^2 + b^2 = c^2$ to find $b$. $b = \sqrt{11}$, so the equation of the hyperbola is $\left(\frac{x - 1}{5}\right)^2 - \left(\frac{y - 1}{\sqrt{11}}\right)^2 = 1$.

**8.** $\left(\frac{y + 2.49}{3.95}\right)^2 - \left(\frac{x + 2.35}{2.63}\right)^2 = 1$

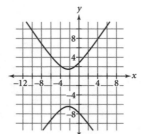

To find the $x$-coordinate of the upper right corner of the box, substitute the $y$-value of the vertex into the equation of the asymptote: $1.46 = 1.5x + 1.035$; $x = 0.2833$. The horizontal distance from the point $(0.2833, 1.46)$ to the vertex is $0.2833 - (-2.35) = 2.633$. Substituting the $x$-coordinate of the vertex into the equation for the asymptote provides the $y$-coordinate of the center of the hyperbola: $y = 1.5(-2.35) + 1.035 = -2.49$.

So the coordinates of the center are $(-2.35, -2.49)$. The vertical distance from the center to the vertex is $|-2.49 - 1.46| = 3.95$. Use this information to write the equation of the hyperbola: $\left(\frac{y + 2.49}{3.95}\right)^2 - \left(\frac{x + 2.35}{2.63}\right)^2 = 1$.

**9. a.** Possible answer: $\left(\frac{y}{3}\right)^2 - \left(\frac{x - 1}{2}\right)^2 = 1$. The center of the hyperbola is at $(1, 0)$ and the asymptote rectangle appears to be 4 units wide and 6 units high, so $a = 2$ and $b = 3$. The hyperbola is vertically oriented, so the equation is $\left(\frac{y}{3}\right)^2 - \left(\frac{x - 1}{2}\right)^2 = 1$.

*Discovering Advanced Algebra Solutions Manual*
©2004 Key Curriculum Press

**b.** Possible answer: $\left(\frac{x+4.5}{2.5}\right)^2 - \left(\frac{y+2}{3}\right)^2 = 1$.
The center of the hyperbola is at $(-4.5, -2)$ and the asymptote rectangle appears to be 5 units wide and 6 units high, so $a = 2.5$ and $b = 3$. The hyperbola is horizontally oriented, so the equation is $\left(\frac{x+4.5}{2.5}\right)^2 - \left(\frac{y+2}{3}\right)^2 = 1$.

**10. a.** Possible answer: $\left(\frac{y}{2.5}\right)^2 - \left(\frac{x-9.5}{2.5}\right)^2 = 1$. Plot the data points, using the distance the car has traveled as the $x$-coordinate and the strength of the signal as the $y$-coordinate.

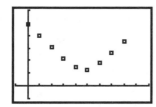

$[-2, 20, 2, -2, 12, 2]$

The vertex of the hyperbola appears to be near $(9.5, 2.5)$. Its asymptotes seem to have slope roughly $\pm 1$, making $a = b = 2.5$. The equation $\left(\frac{y}{2.5}\right)^2 - \left(\frac{x-9.5}{2.5}\right)^2 = 1$ fits the data quite well.

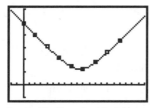

$[-2, 20, 2, -2, 12, 2]$

**b.** $(9.5, 0)$. When the car has traveled 9.5 mi, it is at its closest point, 2.5 mi from the transmitter.

**c.** 2.5 mi east or west of the road at mile 9.5

**11. a.**
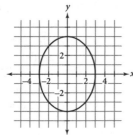

**b.**
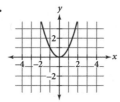

**c.**
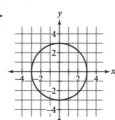

**d.**

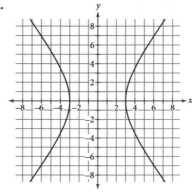

**e.** The resulting shapes are a paraboloid, a sphere, an ellipsoid, and a hyperboloid.

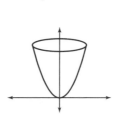

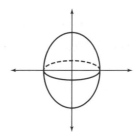

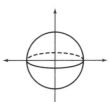

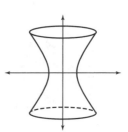

**12.**

| $x$-value | 5 | 10 | 20 | 40 |
|---|---|---|---|---|
| **Distance** | 0.83 | 0.36 | 0.17 | 0.08 |

The center of the hyperbola is $(2, -1)$ and the asymptotes are $y = \pm\frac{2}{3}(x - 2) - 1$. For each $x$-value, find the difference of the $y$-values of the point on the hyperbola and the point on the nearest asymptote. For example, for $x = 5$, the upper point on the hyperbola is $\left(5, 2\sqrt{2} - 1\right)$ and the nearest asymptote is $y = \frac{2}{3}x - \frac{7}{3}$, which contains the point $(5, 1)$. The lower point on the hyperbola is $\left(5, -2\sqrt{2} - 1\right)$ and the nearest asymptote is $y = -\frac{2}{3}x + \frac{1}{3}$, which contains the point $(5, -3)$. In both of these cases the vertical distance from the point on the hyperbola to the nearest asymptote is $2\sqrt{2} - 2 \approx 0.83$. Use the same procedure to find the other distances.

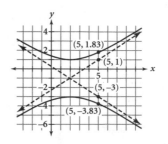

**13.** $x = 1$ or $x = 5$

$$0 = -x^2 + 6x - 5$$
$$0 = -(x^2 - 6x + 9 - 9) - 5$$
$$0 = -((x - 3)^2 - 9) - 5$$
$$0 = -(x - 3)^2 + 9 - 5$$
$$0 = 4 - (x - 3)^2$$
$$(x - 3)^2 = 4$$
$$x - 3 = \pm 2$$
$$x = 3 \pm 2$$
$$x = 1 \text{ or } x = 5$$

**14.** $\left(\frac{x - 16300000}{79000000}\right)^2 + \left(\frac{y}{77300000}\right)^2 = 1$. You are looking for an equation in the form $\left(\frac{x - h}{a}\right)^2 + \left(\frac{y - k}{b}\right)^2 = 1$. The major axis lies on the $x$-axis, so $k = 0$. The length of the major axis is $1.58 \times 10^8$ km, so $2a = 1.58 \times 10^8$ and $a = 7.9 \times 10^7$. You know that $h = c$, the distance from the center of the ellipse to a focus. The eccentricity of the ellipse is $\frac{c}{a} = 0.206$, so $c = 0.206a = 1.6274 \times 10^7$. Finally, use the equation $b^2 + c^2 = a^2$ to get $b = \sqrt{\left(7.9 \times 10^7\right)^2 - \left(1.6274 \times 10^7\right)^2} \approx 7.731 \times 10^7$. Thus the equation is $\left(\frac{x - 16300000}{79000000}\right)^2 + \left(\frac{y}{77300000}\right)^2 = 1$.

**15. a.** $y = -\frac{1}{8}(x - 10)^2 + 17.5$. The vertex of the parabola is at $(10, 17.5)$, so the equation is in the form $y = a(x - 10)^2 + 17.5$. Use the point $(0, 5)$ to find $a$.

$$5 = a(0 - 10)^2 + 17.5$$
$$-12.5 = 100a$$
$$a = -0.125 = -\frac{1}{8}$$

The equation is $y = -\frac{1}{8}(x - 10)^2 + 17.5$.

**b.** Approximately 18.5 ft or 1.5 ft. Solve the equation $8.5 = -\frac{1}{8}(x - 10)^2 + 17.5$ for $x$.

$$-9 = -\frac{1}{8}(x - 10)^2$$
$$72 = (x - 10)^2$$
$$x = 10 \pm 6\sqrt{2}$$
$$x \approx 1.5 \text{ or } x \approx 18.5$$

**16. a.** Vertex: $(-1, -2)$; focus: $(-1, -2.25)$; directrix: $y = -1.75$

$a = 1$ and $b = -1$, so $f = -0.25$. The focus is 0.25 unit below the vertex and the directrix is 0.25 unit above the vertex.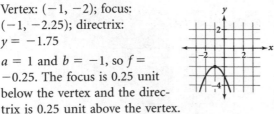

**b.** Vertex: $(3, 0.5)$; focus: $(3, 1)$; directrix: $y = 0$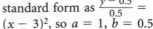

Rewrite the equation in standard form as $\frac{y - 0.5}{0.5} = (x - 3)^2$, so $a = 1$, $b = 0.5$, and $f = \frac{1^2}{0.5 \cdot 4} = 0.5$. The vertex is at $(3, 0.5)$, the focus is 0.5 unit above the vertex, and the directrix is 0.5 unit below the vertex.

**c.** Vertex: $(-6, 0)$; focus: $(-5.5, 0)$; directrix: $x = -6.5$

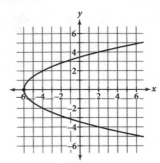

The vertex is at $(-6, 0)$, $a = \frac{1}{2}$, $b = 1$, and because the parabola is horizontally oriented, $f = \frac{b^2}{4a} = 0.5$. The focus is 0.5 unit to the right of the vertex, and the directrix is 0.5 unit to the left of the vertex.

**17. a.** $s = s_0\left(\frac{1}{2}\right)^{t/1620}$

**b.** Here $s_0 = 500$ and $t = 1000$, so $s = 500\left(\frac{1}{2}\right)^{1000/1620} \approx 326$ g.

**c.** About 13,331 yr. Solve the equation $10 = 3000\left(\frac{1}{2}\right)^{t/1620}$ for $t$.

$$\frac{1}{300} = \left(\frac{1}{2}\right)^{t/1620}$$
$$\log\frac{1}{300} = \frac{t}{1620}\log\frac{1}{2}$$
$$t = 1620 \cdot \frac{\log\frac{1}{300}}{\log\frac{1}{2}} \approx 13330.7$$

**18.** $n^2 + 3n - 24$. Use three terms of the sequence to write a system of equations and solve the system for $a$, $b$, and $c$.

**IMPROVING YOUR VISUAL THINKING SKILLS**

Circle: The slice is perpendicular to the cone's axis. Ellipse: The slice intersects only one branch of the cone and is not perpendicular to the axis or parallel to an edge. Parabola: The slice intersects only one branch of the cone and is parallel to an edge. Hyperbola: The slice intersects both branches of the cone but does not contain the cone's vertex. Point: The slice intersects only at the cone's vertex. One line: The slice is along an edge.

Two lines: The slice intersects both branches of the cone through the vertex, but not along an edge.

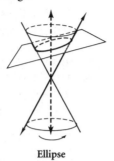

Circle          Parabola          Ellipse

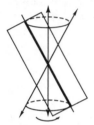
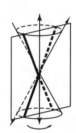

Hyperbola

## EXTENSIONS

**A.–C.** Answers will vary.

**D.** See the solution to Take Another Look activity 3 on page 237.

## EXPLORATION • CONSTRUCTING THE CONIC SECTIONS

### QUESTIONS

**1.** As the foci move farther apart, the minor axis of an ellipse becomes shorter and the major axis becomes longer. When the distance between the foci is greater than $AB$, an ellipse no longer exists because the two circles don't intersect. When the foci are both at the same point, you have a circle.

**2.** As $AB$ increases, both the major and minor axes become longer.

**3.** Construct a line (directrix) and focus ($F$). Construct $\overline{FB}$ to any point $B$ on the directrix. Construct the midpoint, $A$, of $\overline{FB}$ and then the perpendicular line through the midpoint. Construct the line perpendicular to the directrix through point $B$. Construct

the intersection, $P$, of the perpendicular bisector and the perpendicular. Construct $\overline{FP}$. Select points $P$ and $B$ to construct the locus. Because the construction produces congruent right triangles, $PF = PB$, so point $P$ is equidistant from the focus and the directrix, and the locus is a parabola.

**4.** Possible construction: Construct a line. On the line, construct $\overline{AB}$ and point $C$ outside $\overline{AB}$. Construct $\overline{AC}$ and $\overline{BC}$. Now follow Steps 4, 5, 6, and 9 of the ellipse instructions in the activity.

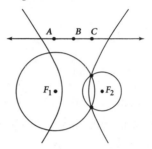

## LESSON 9.5

### EXERCISES

**1. a.** Expand to get $x^2 + 14x + 49 = 9y - 99$, then combine terms: $x^2 + 14x - 9y + 148 = 0$.

**b.** $x^2 + 9y^2 - 14x + 198y + 1129 = 0$

$$\frac{(x-7)^2}{9} + \frac{(y+11)^2}{1} = 1 \quad \text{Original equation.}$$

$$(x-7)^2 + 9(y+11)^2 = 9 \quad \text{Multiply both sides by 9.}$$

$$x^2 - 14x + 49 + 9y^2 + 198y + 1089 = 9 \quad \text{Expand and distribute.}$$

$$x^2 + 9y^2 - 14x + 198y + 1129 = 0 \quad \text{Combine terms.}$$

**c.** Expand to get $x^2 - 2x + 1 + y^2 + 6y + 9 = 5$, then combine terms: $x^2 + y^2 - 2x + 6y + 5 = 0$.

**d.** $9x^2 - 4y^2 - 36x - 24y - 36 = 0$

$$\frac{(x-2)^2}{4} - \frac{(y+3)^2}{9} = 1 \quad \text{Original equation.}$$

$$9(x-2)^2 - 4(y+3)^2 = 36 \quad \text{Multiply both sides by 36.}$$

$$9x^2 - 36x + 36 - 4y^2 - 24y - 36 = 36 \quad \text{Expand and distribute.}$$

$$9x^2 - 4y^2 - 36x - 24y - 36 = 0 \quad \text{Combine terms.}$$

**2.** $a = \frac{21}{15} = 1.4$; $b = \left(\frac{a}{2}\right)^2 = \left(\frac{1.4}{2}\right)^2 = 0.49$;

$c = 15b = 7.35$; $d = \frac{a}{2} = 0.7$

**3. a.** $\left(\dfrac{y-5}{\sqrt{11}}\right)^2 - \left(\dfrac{x+4}{\sqrt{11}}\right)^2 = 1$; hyperbola

$$x^2 + 8x - \left(y^2 - 10y\right) = -2$$

$$x^2 + 8x + 16 - \left(y^2 - 10y + 25\right) = -2 + 16 - 25$$

$$(x+4)^2 - (y-5)^2 = -11$$

$$\dfrac{(y-5)^2}{11} - \dfrac{(x+4)^2}{11} = 1$$

$$\left(\dfrac{y-5}{\sqrt{11}}\right)^2 - \left(\dfrac{x+4}{\sqrt{11}}\right)^2 = 1$$

**b.** $\left(\dfrac{x-3}{6}\right)^2 + \left(\dfrac{y-8}{\sqrt{72}}\right)^2 = 1$,

or $\left(\dfrac{x-3}{6}\right)^2 + \left(\dfrac{y-8}{6\sqrt{2}}\right)^2 = 1$; ellipse

$$2\left(x^2 - 6x\right) + y^2 - 16y = -10$$

$$2\left(x^2 - 6x + 9\right) + y^2 - 16y + 64 = -10 + 18 + 64$$

$$2(x-3)^2 + (y-8)^2 = 72$$

$$\dfrac{(x-3)^2}{36} + \dfrac{(y-8)^2}{72} = 1$$

$$\left(\dfrac{x-3}{6}\right)^2 + \left(\dfrac{y-8}{\sqrt{72}}\right)^2 = 1$$

**c.** $\left(\dfrac{x+5}{\sqrt{5}}\right)^2 = \dfrac{(y-15.8)}{-3}$; parabola

$$3\left(x^2 + 10x\right) = -5y + 4$$

$$3\left(x^2 + 10x + 25\right) = -5y + 4 + 75$$

$$3(x+5)^2 = -5(y-15.8)$$

$$\left(\dfrac{x+5}{\sqrt{5}}\right)^2 = \dfrac{(y-15.8)}{-3}$$

**d.** $(x+2)^2 + y^2 = 5.2$; circle

$$5\left(x^2 + 4x\right) + 5y^2 = 6$$

$$5\left(x^2 + 4x + 4\right) + 5y^2 = 6 + 20$$

$$5(x+2)^2 + 5y^2 = 26$$

$$(x+2)^2 + y^2 = 5.2$$

**4. a.** False; possible answer: $y^2 + 22y + 121 = (y+11)^2$

**b.** True

**c.** True

**d.** False; possible answers: $4x^2 + 48x + 144 = 4(x+6)^2$ or $4x^2 + 24x + 36 = 4(x+3)^2$

**5.** In 5a–d, rewrite the equation to identify the values of $a$, $b$, and $c$; then substitute them in the quadratic formula.

**a.** $y = \dfrac{\pm\sqrt{400x^2 + 1600}}{-8}$, or $y = \mp\dfrac{5}{2}\sqrt{x^2 + 4}$

$$-4y^2 + 0y + 25x^2 + 100 = 0;$$

$$a = -4;\ b = 0;\ c = 25x^2 + 100$$

$$y = \dfrac{0 \pm \sqrt{0^2 - 4(-4)\left(25x^2 + 100\right)}}{2(-4)}$$

$$y = \dfrac{\pm\sqrt{400x^2 + 1600}}{-8}$$

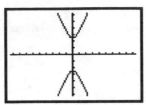

$$[-18.8, 18.8, 2, -12.4, 12.4, 2]$$

**b.** $y = \dfrac{-16 \pm \sqrt{160x - 320}}{8}$,

or $y = \dfrac{-4 \pm \sqrt{10x - 20}}{2}$

$$4y^2 + 16y - 10x + 36 = 0;$$

$$a = 4;\ b = 16;\ c = -10x + 36$$

$$y = \dfrac{-16 \pm \sqrt{16^2 - 4(4)(-10x + 36)}}{2(4)}$$

$$y = \dfrac{-16 \pm \sqrt{160x - 320}}{8}$$

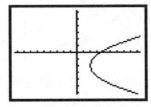

$$[-9.4, 9.4, 1, -6.2, 6.2, 1]$$

**c.** $y = \dfrac{8 \pm \sqrt{-64x^2 - 384x - 560}}{8}$,

or $y = 1 \pm \dfrac{\sqrt{-4x^2 - 24x - 35}}{2}$

$$4y^2 - 8y + 4x^2 + 24x + 39 = 0;$$

$$a = 4;\ b = -8;\ c = 4x^2 + 24x + 39$$

$$y = \dfrac{8 \pm \sqrt{8^2 - 4(4)\left(4x^2 + 24x + 39\right)}}{2(4)}$$

$$y = \dfrac{8 \pm \sqrt{-64x^2 - 384x - 560}}{8}$$

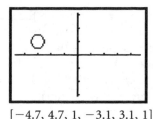

[−4.7, 4.7, 1, −3.1, 3.1, 1]

**d.** $y = \dfrac{-20 \pm \sqrt{-60x^2 + 240x + 240}}{10}$,

or $y = -2 \pm \dfrac{\sqrt{-15x^2 + 60x + 60}}{5}$

$5y^2 + 20y + 3x^2 - 12x + 8 = 0$;

$a = 5$; $b = 20$; $c = 3x^2 - 12x + 8$

$y = \dfrac{-20 \pm \sqrt{400 - 4(5)(3x^2 - 12x + 8)}}{10}$

$y = \dfrac{-20 \pm \sqrt{-60x^2 + 240x + 240}}{10}$

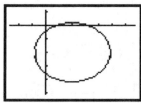

[2.7, 6.7, 1, −5.1, 1.1, 1]

**6. a.** $\left(\frac{3}{4}, \frac{73}{16}\right)$, or $(0.75, 4.5625)$. Substitution is simplest in this case.

$x^2 + 4 = (x - 2)^2 + 3$

$x^2 + 4 = x^2 - 4x + 4 + 3$

$0 = -4x + 3$

$x = \dfrac{3}{4}$

$y = \left(\dfrac{3}{4}\right)^2 + 4 = \dfrac{73}{16}$

The intersection point is $\left(\frac{3}{4}, \frac{73}{16}\right)$.

**b.** $(1.5, 0.5)$, $(1.5, -0.5)$, $(-1.5, 0.5)$, $(-1.5, -0.5)$. Elimination is simplest in this case. Subtract the second equation from the first to get $4y^2 = 1$, so $y = \pm\frac{1}{2}$. Substitute these values for $y$ in either of the original equations and solve for $x$.

$3x^2 + 9\left(\pm\dfrac{1}{2}\right)^2 = 9$

$3x^2 + \dfrac{9}{4} = 9$

$3x^2 = 6.75$

$x^2 = 2.25$

$x = \pm 1.5$

The intersection points are $(1.5, 0.5)$, $(1.5, -0.5)$, $(-1.5, 0.5)$, and $(-1.5, -0.5)$.

**c.** $(1.177, -1.240)$, $(-1.177, -1.240)$, $(2.767, -5.160)$, $(-2.767, -5.160)$. Elimination is simplest in this case. Subtract the first equation from the second and solve for $y$.

$\dfrac{y^2}{4} + (y + 4)^2 = 8$

$0.25y^2 + y^2 + 8y + 16 = 8$

$1.25y^2 + 8y + 8 = 0$

$y = \dfrac{-8 \pm \sqrt{64 - 40}}{2.5}$

$y \approx -1.240$ or $y \approx -5.160$

Solve the second equation for $x$:
$x = \pm\sqrt{9 - (y + 4)^2}$, and substitute the values for $y$. When $y \approx -1.240$, $x \approx \pm1.177$ and when $y \approx -5.160$, $x \approx \pm2.767$. The four intersection points are approximately $(1.177, -1.240)$, $(-1.177, -1.240)$, $(2.767, -5.160)$, and $(-2.767, -5.160)$.

**7.** Approximately 26.7 mi east and 13.7 mi north of the first station, or approximately 26.7 mi east and 13.7 mi south of the first station.

Orient the first station at the origin and the second station at the point $(50, 0)$. The epicenter is on the circles $x^2 + y^2 = 900$ and $(x - 50)^2 + y^2 = 729$. Use elimination to find the intersections of the two circles. Subtracting the second equation from the first, $x^2 - (x - 50)^2 = 171$, so $x^2 - x^2 + 100x - 2500 = 171$ and $x = 26.71$. Use the equation of either circle to find the $y$-coordinates, $y = \pm\sqrt{900 - 26.71^2} \approx \pm13.66$. The two intersection points are approximately $(26.7, \pm13.7)$. These are 26.7 mi east and 13.7 mi north or south of the first station.

**8. a.** D. Write the equation in standard form:

$9x^2 + 4y^2 = 36$

$\left(\dfrac{x}{2}\right)^2 + \left(\dfrac{y}{3}\right)^2 = 1$

This is an ellipse centered at the origin with horizontal stretch factor 2 and vertical stretch factor 3, so it is D.

**b.** B. Write the equation in standard form:

$x^2 - 8x + 16 - 4y^2 = 16$

$(x - 4)^2 - 4y^2 = 16$

$\left(\dfrac{x - 4}{4}\right)^2 - \left(\dfrac{y}{2}\right)^2 = 1$

This is a horizontally oriented hyperbola centered at $(4, 0)$, with horizontal stretch factor 4 and vertical stretch factor 2, so it is B.

**c.** C. Write the equation in vertex form:

$$3(x^2 - 10x + 25) - 75 + 55 = -5y$$

$$y = -\frac{3}{5}(x - 5)^2 + 4$$

This is a vertically oriented parabola that has its vertex at $(5, 4)$ and opens downward, so it is C.

**d.** A. Write the equation in standard form:

$$x^2 + 2x + 1 + y^2 - 6y + 9 = 15 + 1 + 9$$

$$(x + 1)^2 + (y - 3)^2 = 25$$

This is a circle centered at $(-1, 3)$ with radius 5, so it is A.

**9. a., b.** These constructions will result in a diagram similar to the one in the problem, which is on page 532 of your book.

**c.** $\triangle PAG$ is an isosceles triangle, so $PA = PG$. Thus $(FP + GP)$ remains constant because the distances sum to the radius.

**d.** An ellipse. The sum of the distances to two points remains constant.

**e.** Moving $G$ within the circle creates other ellipses. The closer $P$ is to $G$, the less eccentric the ellipse. Locations outside the circle produce hyperbolas.

**10. a.** 49 mi. The signal travels at a rate of 980 feet per microsecond and there is a difference of 264 microseconds in the time the two signals are received, so the difference in distances is $980 \cdot 264 = 258{,}720$ feet, or 49 miles.

**b.** 98 mi. The signal travels at a rate of 980 feet per microsecond and there is a difference of 528 microseconds in the time the two signals are received, so the difference in distances is $980 \cdot 528 = 517{,}440$ feet, or 98 miles.

**c.** $\frac{(x - 200)^2}{600.25} - \frac{y^2}{9399.75} = 1$. The center of the hyperbola is between stations $B$ and $C$, at $(200, 0)$. The difference of distances from a point on the hyperbola to the foci is $2a = 49$, so $a = 24.5$. Use the equation $a^2 + b^2 = c^2$ with $c = 100$ to find $b$: $b = \sqrt{100^2 - 24.5^2} = \sqrt{9399.75}$.

The equation is $\left(\frac{x - 200}{24.5}\right)^2 - \left(\frac{y}{\sqrt{9399.75}}\right)^2 = 1$, or $\frac{(x - 200)^2}{600.25} - \frac{y^2}{9399.75} = 1$.

**d.** $\frac{x^2}{2401} - \frac{y^2}{7599} = 1$. The center of the hyperbola is between stations $A$ and $B$, at $(0, 0)$. The difference of distances from a point on the hyperbola to the foci is $2a = 98$, so $a = 49$. Use the equation $a^2 + b^2 = c^2$ with $c = 100$ to find $b$: $b = \sqrt{100^2 - 49^2} = \sqrt{7599}$. The equation is $\left(\frac{x}{49}\right)^2 - \left(\frac{y}{\sqrt{7599}}\right)^2 = 1$, or $\frac{x^2}{2401} - \frac{y^2}{7599} = 1$.

**e.** Because the three transmitters are on the shoreline, the points below the $x$-axis are on land, so they are excluded. The point in the upper right is excluded because it is closer to transmitter $C$. The intersection point closest to $B$ is the location of the ship. The ship is at approximately $(137.3, 228.2)$.

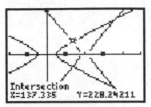

$$[-200, 500, 100, -800, 800, 800]$$

**11.** $x^2 + y^2 = 11.52$. The ellipses are centered at the origin, so the circle is also centered at the origin and has equation $x^2 + y^2 = r^2$. To find $r$, solve the first equation for $x^2$: $x^2 = 16\left(1 - \frac{y^2}{9}\right)$. Then substitute the expression for $x^2$ in the second equation and solve for $y$.

$$\frac{16}{9}\left(1 - \frac{y^2}{9}\right) + \frac{y^2}{16} = 1$$

$$\frac{16}{9} - \frac{16y^2}{81} + \frac{y^2}{16} = 1$$

$$\frac{7}{9} = \frac{16y^2}{81} - \frac{y^2}{16}$$

$$\frac{7}{9} = \frac{175y^2}{1296}$$

$$y^2 = \frac{9072}{1575} = \frac{144}{25}$$

$$y = \pm 2.4$$

Substitute the values for $y$ in either equation and solve for $x$ to get $x = \pm 2.4$. Substitute one of the points of intersection to get $r^2 = 2.4^2 + 2.4^2 = 5.76 + 5.76 = 11.52$. The equation is $x^2 + y^2 = 11.52$.

**12.** $y = -\frac{7}{24}x^2 - \frac{7}{12}x + 9$ and $x = 1.75y^2 - 25y + 83.25$

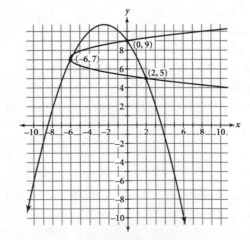

For the first equation, start with the equation $y = ax^2 + bx + c$ and use the given points to write a linear system.

$$\begin{cases} 4a + 2b + c = 5 \\ c = 9 \\ 36a - 6b + c = 7 \end{cases}$$

Use any method to solve the system and find that $a = -\frac{7}{24}$, $b = -\frac{17}{12}$, and $c = 9$. The equation is $y = -\frac{7}{24}x^2 - \frac{7}{12}x + 9$.

For the second equation, start with the equation $x = ay^2 + by + c$ and use the given points to write a linear system.

$$\begin{cases} 25a + 5b + c = 2 \\ 81a + 9b + c = 0 \\ 49a + 7b + c = -6 \end{cases}$$

Use any method to solve the system and find that $a = 1.75$, $b = -25$, and $c = 83.28$. The equation is $x = 1.75y^2 - 25y + 83.25$.

**13. a.** $\left(-2, 5 + 2\sqrt{5}\right)$ and $\left(-2, 5 - 2\sqrt{5}\right)$, or approximately $(-2, 0.53)$ and $(-2, 9.47)$. Here $a = 4$ and $b = 6$. Use the relation $a^2 + c^2 = b^2$ to find $c$, the distance from the center of the ellipse to its foci: $c = \sqrt{36 - 16} = 2\sqrt{5}$. The center of the ellipse is at $(-2, 5)$ and the major axis is vertical, so the foci lie $2\sqrt{5}$ units above and below the center, at $\left(-2, 5 + 2\sqrt{5}\right)$ and $\left(-2, 5 - 2\sqrt{5}\right)$.

**b.** $\left(1 + \frac{\sqrt{3}}{2}, -2\right)$ and $\left(1 - \frac{\sqrt{3}}{2}, -2\right)$, or approximately $(0.13, -2)$ and $(1.87, -2)$. Here $a = 1$ and $b = 0.5$. Use the relation $b^2 + c^2 = a^2$ to find $c$, the distance from the center of the ellipse to its foci: $c = \sqrt{1 - 0.25} = \frac{\sqrt{3}}{2}$. The center of the ellipse is at $(1, -2)$ and the major axis is horizontal, so the foci lie $\frac{\sqrt{3}}{2}$ units to the right and the left of the center, at $\left(1 + \frac{\sqrt{3}}{2}, -2\right)$ and $\left(1 - \frac{\sqrt{3}}{2}, -2\right)$.

**14.** $y = \frac{5}{12}x + \frac{47}{12}$ and $y = -\frac{5}{12}x + \frac{97}{12}$. The center of the hyperbola is between the two vertices, at $(5, 6)$. The distance from the center to a vertex is $b = 2.5$. The distance from the center to a focus is $c = 6.5$. Use the relation $a^2 + b^2 = c^2$ to find $a$: $a^2 = 6.5^2 - 2.5^2 = 36$, so $a = 6$. The slopes of the asymptotes are $\pm\frac{b}{a} = \pm\frac{5}{12}$, so the equations are $y = \pm\frac{5}{12}(x - 5) + 6$, or $y = \frac{5}{12}x + \frac{47}{12}$ and $y = -\frac{5}{12}x + \frac{97}{12}$.

**15.** 113°. Find the side lengths of the triangle.

$$AB = \sqrt{(10 - 4)^2 + (16 - 9)^2} = \sqrt{85}$$
$$AC = \sqrt{(10 - 8)^2 + (16 - 1)^2} = \sqrt{229}$$
$$BC = \sqrt{(4 - 8)^2 + (9 - 1)^2} = \sqrt{80}$$

Use the Law of Cosines to find the measure of the angle.

$$229 = 85 + 80 - 2\sqrt{85}\sqrt{80} \cos B$$
$$B = \cos^{-1}\left(\frac{64}{-2\sqrt{6800}}\right) \approx 113°$$

**16.** $(x - 1)(x - 2)\left(x - i\sqrt{2}\right)\left(x + i\sqrt{2}\right)$. First look for rational roots of the polynomial. Possibilities are $\pm 1$, $\pm 2$, and $\pm 4$. Substitute the possible values for $x$ to find that 1 and 2 are the only rational roots. Use synthetic division to factor the polynomial.

$$x^4 - 3x^3 + 4x^2 - 6x + 4 = (x - 1)(x - 2)\left(x^2 + 2\right)$$

The roots of $\left(x^2 + 2\right)$ are $\pm i\sqrt{2}$, so the polynomial factors completely as $(x - 1)(x - 2)\left(x - i\sqrt{2}\right)\left(x + i\sqrt{2}\right)$.

**17.** Square, trapezoid, kite, triangle, pentagon

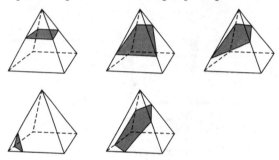

## EXTENSIONS

**A.** See the solution to Take Another Look activity 4 on page 237.

**B.** Construct $\overrightarrow{PQ}$ parallel to $\overline{AG}$. Then $\angle 1 \cong \angle 4$ (corresponding angles), $\angle 2 \cong \angle 3$ (alternate interior angles), and $\angle 3 \cong \angle 4$ ($\ell$ is the perpendicular bisector of $\overline{AG}$). Therefore $\angle 1 \cong \angle 2$; that is, the angle of incidence is congruent to the angle of reflection.

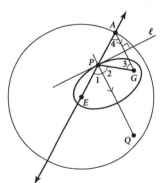

## QUESTIONS

**1.** (0.77, 5.33). Multiply the vector $\begin{bmatrix} 5 \\ 2 \end{bmatrix}$ by the rotation matrix

$$\begin{bmatrix} \cos 60° & -\sin 60° \\ \sin 60° & \cos 60° \end{bmatrix} = \begin{bmatrix} \dfrac{1}{2} & -\dfrac{\sqrt{3}}{2} \\ \dfrac{\sqrt{3}}{2} & \dfrac{1}{2} \end{bmatrix}$$

The new point is represented by the vector

$$\begin{bmatrix} \dfrac{5}{2} - \sqrt{3} \\ \dfrac{5\sqrt{3}}{2} + 1 \end{bmatrix} \approx \begin{bmatrix} 0.77 \\ 5.33 \end{bmatrix}$$

**2.** $x = -2.1t^2 - 3.5t - 2.1$, $y = 2.1t^2 - 3.5t + 2.1$.

Multiply the position vector $\begin{bmatrix} 3t^2 + 3 \\ 5t \end{bmatrix}$ by the rotation matrix

$$\begin{bmatrix} \cos 135° & -\sin 135° \\ \sin 135° & \cos 135° \end{bmatrix} = \dfrac{\sqrt{2}}{2}\begin{bmatrix} -1 & -1 \\ 1 & -1 \end{bmatrix}$$

The new position vector is

$$\dfrac{\sqrt{2}}{2}\begin{bmatrix} -3t^2 - 5t - 3 \\ 3t^2 - 5t + 3 \end{bmatrix} \approx \begin{bmatrix} -2.1t^2 - 3.5t - 2.1 \\ 2.1t^2 - 3.5t + 2.1 \end{bmatrix}$$

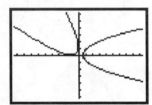

$[-47, 47, 5, -31, 31, 5]$
$-5 \le t \le 5$

**3.** $y = \frac{1}{2x}$. If a position vector $\begin{bmatrix} x \\ y \end{bmatrix}$ represents a point on the rotated hyperbola, then the position vector

$$\dfrac{\sqrt{2}}{2}\begin{bmatrix} 1 & 1 \\ -1 & 1 \end{bmatrix}\begin{bmatrix} x \\ y \end{bmatrix} = \dfrac{\sqrt{2}}{2}\begin{bmatrix} x + y \\ -x + y \end{bmatrix}$$

represents a point on the original hyperbola. Substitute the coordinates of this position vector into the equation of the original hyperbola.

$$\left(\dfrac{\sqrt{2}}{2}(x + y)\right)^2 - \left(\dfrac{\sqrt{2}}{2}(-x + y)\right)^2 = 1$$

$$\frac{1}{2}(x + y)^2 - \frac{1}{2}(-x + y)^2 = 1$$

$$(x + y)^2 - (-x + y)^2 = 2$$

$$x^2 + 2xy + y^2 - \left(x^2 - 2xy + y^2\right) = 2$$

$$4xy = 2$$

$$y = \frac{1}{2x}$$

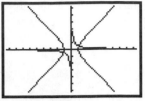

$[-9.4, 9.4, 1, -6.2, 6.2, 1]$

**4. a.** Sample answer: A vertically oriented hyperbola with vertices $(0, 1)$ and $(0, -1)$ and asymptotes $y = \pm x$; the standard form of the equation for this hyperbola is $y^2 - x^2 = 1$.

**b.** The graph of the hyperbola $y^2 - x^2 = 1$ rotated 50° counterclockwise about the origin

**c.**

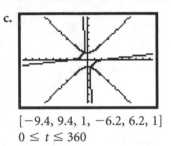

$[-9.4, 9.4, 1, -6.2, 6.2, 1]$
$0 \le t \le 360$

## EXTENSION

$x_1 = 2 \cos t$ and $y_1 = 2 \sin t$, with $t$-min $= 90°$, $t$-max $= 450°$, and $t$-step $= 120°$; $x_2 = 0.5x_1 \cos 60° - 0.5y_1 \sin 60°$ and $y_2 = 0.5x_1 \sin 60° + 0.5y_1 \cos 60°$

## LESSON 9.6

### EXERCISES

**1. a.** $f(x) = \dfrac{1}{x} + 2$

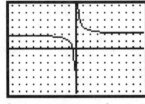

$[-9.4, 9.4, 1, -6.2, 6.2, 1]$

**b.** $f(x) = \dfrac{1}{x - 3}$

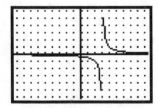

$[-9.4, 9.4, 1, -6.2, 6.2, 1]$

**c.** $f(x) = \dfrac{1}{x + 4} - 1$

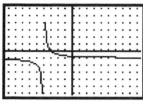

$[-9.4, 9.4, 1, -6.2, 6.2, 1]$

**d.** $f(x) = 2\left(\dfrac{1}{x}\right)$, or $f(x) = \dfrac{2}{x}$

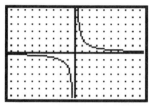

$[-9.4, 9.4, 1, -6.2, 6.2, 1]$

**e.** $f(x) = 3\left(\dfrac{1}{x}\right) + 1$, or $f(x) = \dfrac{3}{x} + 1$

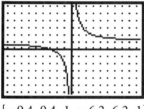

$[-9.4, 9.4, 1, -6.2, 6.2, 1]$

**2. a.** $y = 1,\ x = 0$

**b.** $y = 0,\ x = 4$

**c.** $y = -1,\ x = -2$

**d.** $y = -4,\ x = -3$

**3. a.** $x = -4$

$$12(x + 3) = x - 8$$
$$12x + 36 = x - 8$$
$$11x = -44$$
$$x = -4$$

**b.** $x = \dfrac{113}{18} = 6.2\overline{7}$

$$21(x - 5) = 3x + 8$$
$$21x - 105 = 3x + 8$$
$$18x = 113$$
$$x = \dfrac{113}{8} = 6.2\overline{7}$$

**c.** $x = 2.6$

$$3(4x - 7) = 2x + 5$$
$$12x - 21 = 2x + 5$$
$$10x = 26$$
$$x = 2.6$$

**d.** $x = -8.5$

$$-4(2x + 3) = -6x + 5$$
$$-8x - 12 = -6x + 5$$
$$-17 = 2x$$
$$x = -8.5$$

**4. a.** $y = \dfrac{1}{x} + 2$. The function $y = \dfrac{1}{x}$ is translated up 2 units.

**b.** $y = \dfrac{1}{x - 2} - 4$. The function $y = \dfrac{1}{x}$ is translated down 4 units and right 2 units.

**c.** $y = \dfrac{1}{x + 4} + 3$. The function $y = \dfrac{1}{x}$ is translated up 3 units and left 4 units.

**5.** 12 games. Let $x$ represent the number of consecutive games the team wins from now on. The team's winning percentage will then be $\dfrac{42 + x}{78 + x}$, so solve the equation $0.60 = \dfrac{42 + x}{78 + x}$.

$$0.6(78 + x) = 42 + x$$
$$4.8 = 0.4x$$
$$x = 12$$

**6. a.** $y = \dfrac{-1}{x + 5}$. The function $y = \dfrac{1}{x}$ is reflected across the $x$-axis and translated left 5 units.

**b.** $y = \dfrac{1}{x - 6} - 2$. The function $y = \dfrac{1}{x}$ is translated right 6 units and down 2 units.

**c.** $y = \dfrac{4}{x}$. The function $y = \dfrac{1}{x}$ is scaled (vertically or horizontally) by a factor of 4. Notice that it goes through the points $(1, 4)$ and $(4, 1)$.

**d.** $y = \dfrac{9}{x + 4}$. The function $y = \dfrac{1}{x}$ is scaled by a factor of 9 and then translated left 4 units. If you have trouble determining the scale factor, start with the equation $y = \dfrac{a}{x + 4}$ and then use a point on the graph to find $a$. For example, using the point $(-1, 3)$, $a = 3(-1 + 4) = 9$.

**7. a.** $0.38 \cdot 55 = 20.9$ mL

**b.** $f(x) = \dfrac{20.9 + x}{55 + x}$. After $x$ mL of pure acid are added to the solution, the amount of pure acid in the solution is $(20.9 + x)$ and the total amount of solution is $(55 + x)$. Thus the percentage of acid in the solution is $\dfrac{20.9 + x}{55 + x}$.

**c.** 39.72 mL

$$0.64 = \dfrac{20.9 + x}{55 + x}$$
$$0.64(55 + x) = 20.9 + x$$
$$14.3 = 0.36x$$
$$x \approx 39.72$$

**d.** The graph approaches $y = 1$. The more pure acid is added, the closer the solution comes to being 100% acid.

**8.** Approximately 0.013 gal. Let $x$ represent the number of gallons of milk emptied out and replaced with pure fat. Then the amount of pure fat in the milk is $0.02(1 - x) + x$ and the total amount of milk is 1 gal, so the fat percentage is $\frac{0.02(1 - x) + x}{1} =$ $0.98x + 0.02$. Solve the equation $0.0325 = 0.98x + 0.02$ to get $x \approx 0.013$.

**9. a.  i.** $y = 2 + \frac{-3}{x - 5}$

$y = \frac{2x - 13}{x - 5}$

$y = \frac{2(x - 5) - 3}{x - 5}$

$y = \frac{2(x - 5)}{x - 5} + \frac{-3}{x - 5}$

$y = 2 + \frac{-3}{x - 5}$

**ii.** $y = 3 + \frac{2}{x + 3}$

$y = \frac{3x + 11}{x + 3}$

$y = \frac{3(x + 3) + 2}{x + 3}$

$y = \frac{3(x + 3)}{x + 3} + \frac{2}{x + 3}$

$y = 3 + \frac{2}{x + 3}$

**b.  i.** For $y = 2 + \frac{-3}{x - 5}$, stretch vertically by a factor of $-3$, and translate right 5 units and up 2 units.

**ii.** For $y = 3 + \frac{2}{x + 3}$, stretch vertically by a factor of 2, and translate left 3 units and up 3 units.

**c.  i.**

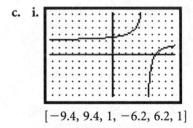

$[-9.4, 9.4, 1, -6.2, 6.2, 1]$

**ii.**

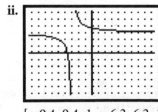

$[-9.4, 9.4, 1, -6.2, 6.2, 1]$

**10. a.**

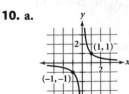

**b.**

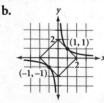

**c.** $a = b = \sqrt{2}$. The corners of the box are at $(2, 0)$, $(0, 2)$, $(-2, 0)$, and $(0, -2)$. The lengths of the sides are $2\sqrt{2}$ from the distance formula. So $a = b = \sqrt{2}$.

**d.** $c = 2$; foci: $\left(\sqrt{2}, \sqrt{2}\right)$ and $\left(-\sqrt{2}, -\sqrt{2}\right)$. Substitute $\sqrt{2}$ for $a$ and $b$ in the formula $a^2 + b^2 = c^2$.

$$\left(\sqrt{2}\right)^2 + \left(\sqrt{2}\right)^2 = c^2$$
$$2 + 2 = c^2$$
$$c^2 = 4$$
$$c = 2$$

The distance from the center, $(0, 0)$, to a focus is 2 and the focus is on the line $y = x$, so use the distance formula to find $x$.

$$\sqrt{(x - 0)^2 + (y - 0)^2} = 2$$
$$\sqrt{(x - 0)^2 + (x - 0)^2} = 2$$
$$\sqrt{x^2 + x^2} = 2$$
$$2x^2 = 4$$
$$x^2 = 2$$
$$x = \pm\sqrt{2}, y = \pm\sqrt{2}$$

The foci are at $\left(\sqrt{2}, \sqrt{2}\right)$ and $\left(-\sqrt{2}, -\sqrt{2}\right)$.

**11. a.** A rotated hyperbola

$[-5, 5, 1, -5, 5, 1]$

This is the equation $4xy - 1 = 0$, or $y = \frac{1}{4x}$.

**b.** The inverse variation function, $y = \frac{1}{x}$, can be converted to the form $xy = 1$, which is a conic section. Its graph is a rotated hyperbola.

**c.** $xy - 3x - 2y + 5 = 0$; $A = 0$, $B = 1$, $C = 0$, $D = -3$, $E = -2$, $F = 5$

$y = \frac{1}{x - 2} + 3$  Original equation.

$y(x - 2) = 1 + 3(x - 2)$  Multiply both sides by $(x - 2)$.

$xy - 2y = 1 + 3x - 6$  Distribute.

$xy - 3x - 2y + 5 = 0$  Combine terms and write in general quadratic form.

**12. a.** $8.33 = \frac{120}{R}$, so $R = \frac{120}{8.33} \approx 14.4$ ohms

**b.** $I = \frac{240}{14.4} \approx 16.7$ amps

**c.** $8.33 = \dfrac{240}{R}$, so $R = \dfrac{240}{8.33} \approx 28.8$ ohms

**13.**

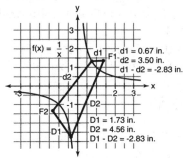

d1 = 0.67 in.
d2 = 3.50 in.
d1 - d2 = -2.83 in.

D1 = 1.73 in.
D2 = 4.56 in.
D1 - D2 = -2.83 in.

**14. a.** $(x - 5)(x - 2)$

**b.** $x^3 - 9x = x(x^2 - 9) = x(x - 3)(x + 3)$

**15.** $(x - 2)^2 + (y + 3)^2 = 16$

**16.** 9.8 m. Set up a coordinate system so that the base of the 2 m rod is at the origin and the base of the 5 m rod is at $(10, 0)$. Let $(x, 0)$ be the point where the wire should be fastened to the ground.

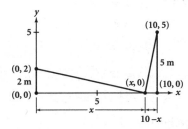

Using the distance formula and the fact that the wire is 15 m long, $\sqrt{(x - 0)^2 + (0 - 2)^2} + \sqrt{(10 - x)^2 + (5 - 0)^2} = 15$. Solve this equation for $x$.

$$\sqrt{(x - 0)^2 + (0 - 2)^2} + \sqrt{(10 - x)^2 + (5 - 0)^2} = 15$$

$$\left(\sqrt{x^2 + 4} + \sqrt{x^2 - 20x + 125}\right)^2 = 15^2$$

$$x^2 + 4 + 2\sqrt{(x^2 + 4)(x^2 - 20x + 125)} +$$
$$x^2 - 20x + 125 = 225$$

$$2x^2 - 20x - 96 = -2\sqrt{x^4 - 20x^3 + 129x^2 - 80x + 500}$$

$$x^2 - 10x - 48 = -\sqrt{x^4 - 20x^3 + 129x^2 - 80x + 500}$$

$$x^4 - 20x^3 + 4x^2 + 960x + 2304 = x^4 - 20x^3 + 129x^2 - 80x + 500$$

$$125x^2 - 1040x - 1804 = 0$$

$$x = \dfrac{1040 \pm \sqrt{1040^2 - 4(125)(-1804)}}{2(125)}$$

$$x \approx -1.47 \text{ or } x \approx 9.79$$

The wire is fastened to the ground between the two poles, so $x$ can't be $-1.47$. Therefore the wire is fastened to the ground approximately 9.8 m from the base of the 2 m pole.

**17.** Draw a diagram to represent the situation.

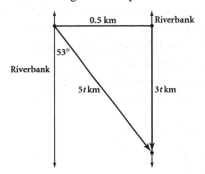

**a.** 53° to the riverbank. The angle between the direct route and the route Sarah should take is $\sin^{-1}\left(\frac{3}{5}\right) \approx 37°$, so the angle to the riverbank is approximately $90° - 37° = 53°$.

**b.** 375 m. By the Pythagorean Theorem, $0.5^2 + 9t^2 = 25t^2$, so $t = 0.125$. The distance along the opposite bank is $3t = 0.375$ km, or 375 m.

**c.** $x = 5t\cos 37°$, $y = 5t\sin 37° - 3t$

**18.** $x^2 + y^2 - 12x + 8y + 27 = 0$, $x^2 + y^2 - 12x + 8y - 12 = 0$

The equation for the first circle is $(x - 6)^2 + (y + 4)^2 = 5^2$. Expand to get $x^2 - 12x + 36 + y^2 + 8y + 16 = 25$, or $x^2 + y^2 - 12x + 8y + 27 = 0$.

The equation for the second circle is $(x - 6)^2 + (y + 4)^2 = 8^2$. Expand to get $x^2 - 12x + 36 + y^2 + 8y + 16 = 64$, or $x^2 + y^2 - 12x + 8y - 12 = 0$.

**19.** For 19a, c, and e, use the fact that $\sin 60° = \frac{\sqrt{3}}{2}$, $\cos 60° = \frac{1}{2}$, and $\tan 60° = \sqrt{3}$. For b, d, and e, use the fact that $\sin 45° = \cos 45° = \frac{\sqrt{2}}{2}$ and $\tan 45° = 1$.

**a.** $b = \sqrt{3}$, $c = 2$     **b.** $a = 1$, $c = \sqrt{2}$

**c.** $b = \frac{1}{2}$, $c = 1$     **d.** $a = \frac{\sqrt{2}}{2}$, $c = 1$

**e.** $\frac{\sqrt{2}}{2} : \frac{\sqrt{2}}{2} : 1$; $\frac{1}{2} : \frac{\sqrt{3}}{2} : 1$

## LESSON 9.7

### EXERCISES

**1. a.** $\dfrac{x^2 + 7x + 12}{x^2 - 4} = \dfrac{(x + 3)(x + 4)}{(x + 2)(x - 2)}$

**b.** $\dfrac{x^3 - 5x^2 - 14x}{x^2 + 2x + 1} = \dfrac{x(x - 7)(x + 2)}{(x + 1)(x + 1)}$

**2.** Use the factored forms from Exercise 1 to help identify the asymptotes. Find the values of $x$ that make the denominator (and not the numerator) equal to 0.

**a.** $x = 2$ and $x = -2$

**b.** $x = -1$

**3. a.** $3 + \dfrac{4x - 1}{x - 2} = \dfrac{3(x - 2)}{x - 2} + \dfrac{4x - 1}{x - 2} =$

$\dfrac{3x - 6 + 4x - 1}{x - 2} = \dfrac{7x - 7}{x - 2}$

**b.** $\dfrac{3x + 7}{2x - 1} - 5 = \dfrac{3x + 7}{2x - 1} - \dfrac{5(2x - 1)}{2x - 1} =$

$\dfrac{3x + 7 - 10x + 5}{2x - 1} = \dfrac{-7x + 12}{2x - 1}$

**4. a.** Hole at $x = 5$

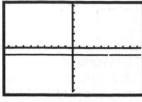

$[-9.4, 9.4, 1, -6.2, 6.2. 1]$

**b.** Hole at $x = -2$

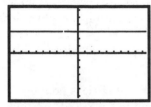

$[-9.4, 9.4, 1, -6.2, 6.2. 1]$

**c.** Hole at $x = 4$

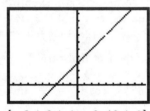

$[-9.4, 9.4, 1, -2, 10.4, 1]$

**d.** A hole occurs when both the numerator and the denominator are 0 for a value of $x$ and the zero appears the same number of times in the numerator as the denominator.

**5. a.** This is the line $y = 1$ with a hole at $x = -2$, so the equation is $y = 1 \cdot \dfrac{x + 2}{x + 2}$, or $y = \dfrac{x + 2}{x + 2}$.

**b.** This is the line $y = -2$ with a hole at $x = 3$, so the equation is $y = \dfrac{-2(x - 3)}{x - 3}$.

**c.** This is the line $y = x + 2$ with a hole at $x = -1$, so the equation is $y = \dfrac{(x + 2)(x + 1)}{x + 1}$.

**6.**

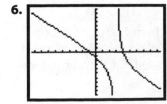

$[-9.4, 9.4, 1, -10, 10, 1]$

**a.** The graph has slant asymptote $y = -x$. As the absolute value of $x$ gets larger, the term $\dfrac{4}{x - 3}$ becomes smaller, so the graph of $y = -x + \dfrac{4}{x - 3}$ approaches the graph of $y = -x$.

**b.** The graph gets closer and closer to both sides of the vertical line $x = 3$.

**c.** $-x + \dfrac{4}{x - 3} = \dfrac{-x(x - 3)}{x - 3} + \dfrac{4}{x - 3} =$

$\dfrac{-x^2 + 3x + 4}{x - 3}$

**d.** $y = -\dfrac{(x - 4)(x + 1)}{x - 3}$. The $x$-intercepts are 4 and $-1$, and the vertical asymptote is $x = 3$.

**7. a.** Vertical asymptote $x = 0$, slant asymptote $y = x - 2$

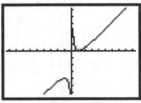

$[-9.4, 9.4, 1, -6.2, 6.2, 1]$

**b.** Vertical asymptote $x = 1$, slant asymptote $y = -2x + 3$

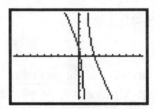

$[-9.4, 9.4, 1, -6.2, 6.2, 1]$

**c.** Hole at $x = 2$

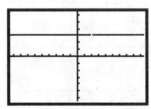

$[-9.4, 9.4, 1, -6.2, 6.2, 1]$

**d.** For 7a: $y = \dfrac{x^2 - 2x + 1}{x}$. The denominator is 0 and the numerator is nonzero when $x = 0$, so the vertical asymptote is $x = 0$.

$y = x - 2 + \dfrac{1}{x} = \dfrac{x^2}{x} - \dfrac{2x}{x} + \dfrac{1}{x} = \dfrac{x^2 - 2x + 1}{x}$

For 7b: $y = \dfrac{-2x^2 + 5x - 1}{x - 1}$. The denominator is 0 and the numerator is nonzero when $x = 1$, so the vertical asymptote is $x = 1$.

$y = \dfrac{(-2x + 3)(x - 1)}{x - 1} + \dfrac{2}{x - 1}$

$= \dfrac{-2x^2 + 5x - 1}{x - 1}$

*Discovering Advanced Algebra Solutions Manual*
©2004 Key Curriculum Press

For 7c: $y = \frac{3x - 6}{x - 2}$. A zero occurs once in both the numerator and the denominator when $x = 2$. This causes a hole in the graph.

$$y = \frac{7(x - 2)}{x - 2} + \frac{8 - 4x}{x - 2} = \frac{3x - 6}{x - 2}$$

**8. a.** The graph has slant asymptote $y = x$, vertical asymptote $x = -2$, and $x$-intercepts 1 and $-3$.

**b.** $y = x$

**c.** Possible answer: $y = \frac{1}{x + 2}$

**d.** Possible answer: $y = (x + 3)(x - 1)$

**e.** $y = \frac{(x + 3)(x - 1)}{x + 2}$, or $y = x + \frac{-3}{x + 2}$

**9.** $y = \frac{-(x + 2)(x - 6)}{3(x - 2)}$. By the first graph, the slant asymptote has slope $-\frac{1}{3}$. The second graph has $x$-intercepts $-2$ and 6, and vertical asymptote $x = 2$. Therefore the equation is $y = \frac{-(x + 2)(x - 6)}{3(x - 2)}$.

**10. a.** The graph has $x$-intercepts 1 and $-4$, vertical asymptotes $x = 2$ and $x = -3$, and $y$-intercept $\frac{2}{3}$.

**b.** The graph approaches horizontal asymptote $y = 1$.

**c.**

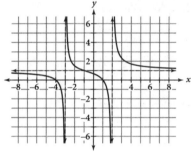

**11. a.** $x = 3 \pm \sqrt{2}$

$$\frac{2}{x - 1} + x = 5$$

$$\frac{2}{x - 1} + x \cdot \frac{x - 1}{x - 1} = 5 \cdot \frac{x - 1}{x - 1}$$

$$\frac{2 + x^2 - x}{x - 1} = \frac{5x - 5}{x - 1}$$

$$2 + x^2 - x = 5x - 5$$

$$x^2 - 6x = -7$$

$$x^2 - 6x + 9 = 2$$

$$(x - 3)^2 = 2$$

$$x = 3 \pm \sqrt{2}$$

**b.** No real solutions; $x = \frac{3 \pm i\sqrt{7}}{2}$

$$\frac{2}{x - 1} + x = 2$$

$$\frac{2}{x - 1} + x \cdot \frac{x - 1}{x - 1} = 2 \cdot \frac{x - 1}{x - 1}$$

$$\frac{2 + x^2 - x}{x - 1} = \frac{2x - 2}{x - 1}$$

$$2 + x^2 - x = 2x - 2$$

$$x^2 - 3x + 4 = 0$$

$$x = \frac{3 \pm \sqrt{3^2 - 4 \cdot 4}}{2} = \frac{3 \pm i\sqrt{7}}{2}$$

**12. a.** $x = 260$, so $y = \frac{60 \cdot 260}{1 + 0.625 \cdot 250} \approx 95$

**b.**

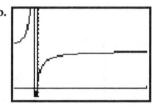

$[-10, 50, 50, -20, 200, 10]$

**c.** Vertical asymptote $x = -1.6$ and horizontal asymptote $y = 96$

**d.** The vertical asymptote is meaningless because there cannot be a negative number of moose. The horizontal asymptote means that as the density of the moose increases, more will be attacked, up to a maximum of 96 during 100 days.

**13. a.**

**b.** The height gets larger as the radius gets smaller. The radius must be greater than 2.

**c.** $V = \pi x^2 h - 4\pi h$

**d.** $h = \frac{V}{\pi(x^2 - 4)}$

**e.** Approximately 400 units$^3$. Substitute one of the data points in the equation for $V$: $V = \pi \cdot 2.5^2 \cdot 56.6 - 4\pi \cdot 56.6 \approx 400.08$. The constant volume is approximately 400 units$^3$.

**14.** $(-2, 4)$ and $(5, 5)$. Use substitution to solve the system of the two equations: $x = 7y - 30$ and $(x - 2)^2 + (y - 1)^2 = 25$.

$$(7y - 32)^2 + (y - 1)^2 = 25$$

$$49y^2 - 448y + 1024 + y^2 - 2y + 1 = 25$$

$$50y^2 - 450y + 1000 = 0$$

$$50(y - 4)(y - 5) = 0$$

$$y = 4 \text{ or } y = 5$$

If $y = 4$, then $x = 7 \cdot 4 - 30 = -2$, and if $y = 5$, then $x = 7 \cdot 5 - 30 = 5$. The two intersection points are $(-2, 4)$ and $(5, 5)$.

**15. a.** $83\frac{1}{3}$ g; approximately 17% almonds and 43% peanuts. Let $x$ be the number of grams of cashews you must to add to the mixture. In the original mixture, there are 0.30(500), or 150 g of cashews, 0.20(500), or 100 g of almonds, and 0.50(500), or 250 g of peanuts. The new mixture will have $(150 + x)$ g of cashews and will be a total of $(500 + x)$ g, so the new percentage of cashews will be $\frac{150 + x}{500 + x} = 0.40$. Solve this equation for $x$.

$$\frac{150 + x}{500 + x} = 0.40$$
$$150 + x = 200 + 0.40x$$
$$0.60x = 50$$
$$x = 83\frac{1}{3}$$

So you must add $83\frac{1}{3}$ g of cashews to the mixture to increase the percentage of cashews to 40%. Therefore the new percentage of almonds is $\frac{100}{583\frac{1}{3}} \approx 0.17$, or 17%, and the percentage of peanuts is $\frac{250}{583\frac{1}{3}} \approx 0.43$, or 43%.

**b.** 50 g; approximately 27.3% almonds, 27.3% cashews, and 45.5% peanuts. Let $x$ be the number of grams of almonds you must to add to the mixture. The original mixture contains 100 g of almonds and 150 g of cashews. The new mixture will have $(100 + x)$ g of almonds, 150 g of cashews, and will be a total of $(500 + x)$ g, so the new percentage of almonds will be $\frac{100 + x}{500 + x}$ and the new percentage of cashews will be $\frac{150}{500 + x}$. Set these expressions equal to each other and solve for $x$.

$$\frac{100 + x}{500 + x} = \frac{150}{500 + x}$$
$$100 + x = 150$$
$$x = 50$$

So you must add 50 g of almonds to make the percentage of almonds the same as the percentage of cashews. Now the percentage of almonds is $\frac{150}{550} \approx 27.3\%$, the percentage of cashews is $\frac{150}{550} \approx 27.3\%$, and the percentage of peanuts is $\frac{250}{550} \approx 45.5\%$.

**16. a.** $(2x + 1)(x - 3) = 0$, so $x = -\frac{1}{2}$ or $x = 3$

**b.** $x^2 + 4x + 4 = 4 + 4$, so $(x + 2)^2 = 8$, and $x = -2 \pm 2\sqrt{2}$

**c.** $x^2 + 4x + 4 = -1 + 4$, so $(x + 2)^2 = 3$, and $x = -2 \pm \sqrt{3}$

## EXTENSION

See the solution to Take Another Look activity 2 on page 237.

## LESSON 9.8

### EXERCISES

**1. a.** $\dfrac{x(x + 2)}{(x - 2)(x + 2)} = \dfrac{x}{x - 2}$

**b.** $\dfrac{(x - 1)(x - 4)}{(x + 1)(x - 1)} = \dfrac{x - 4}{x + 1}$

**c.** $\dfrac{3x(x - 2)}{(x - 4)(x - 2)} = \dfrac{3x}{x - 4}$

**d.** $\dfrac{(x + 5)(x - 2)}{(x + 5)(x - 5)} = \dfrac{x - 2}{x - 5}$

**2. a.** $(x + 3)(x - 3)(x - 2)$

**b.** $(2x + 1)(x - 4)(x + 1)(x - 2)$

**c.** $(x + 2)(x - 2)(x + 3)$. The first denominator factors as $(x + 2)(x - 2)$.

**d.** $(x - 3)(x + 2)(x + 3)$. The second denominator factors as $(x + 2)(x + 3)$.

**3. a.** $\dfrac{(2x - 3)(x + 1)}{(x + 3)(x - 2)(x - 3)}$

$\dfrac{x}{(x + 3)(x - 2)} + \dfrac{x - 1}{(x - 3)(x - 2)}$

$= \dfrac{x(x - 3) + (x - 1)(x + 3)}{(x + 3)(x - 2)(x - 3)}$

$= \dfrac{x^2 - 3x + x^2 + 2x - 3}{(x + 3)(x - 2)(x - 3)}$

$= \dfrac{2x^2 - x - 3}{(x + 3)(x - 2)(x - 3)}$

$= \dfrac{(2x - 3)(x + 1)}{(x + 3)(x - 2)(x - 3)}$

**b.** $\dfrac{-x^2 + 6}{(x + 2)(x + 3)(x - 2)}$

$\dfrac{2}{(x + 2)(x - 2)} - \dfrac{x}{(x + 3)(x - 2)}$

$= \dfrac{2(x + 3) - x(x + 2)}{(x + 2)(x + 3)(x - 2)}$

$= \dfrac{2x + 6 - x^2 - 2x}{(x + 2)(x + 3)(x - 2)}$

$= \dfrac{-x^2 + 6}{(x + 2)(x + 3)(x - 2)}$

**c.** $\dfrac{2x^2 - x + 9}{(x - 3)(x + 2)(x + 3)}$

$\dfrac{x + 1}{(x - 3)(x + 2)} + \dfrac{x - 2}{(x + 2)(x + 3)}$

$= \dfrac{(x + 1)(x + 3) + (x - 2)(x - 3)}{(x - 3)(x + 2)(x + 3)}$

$= \dfrac{x^2 + 4x + 3 + x^2 - 5x + 6}{(x - 3)(x + 2)(x + 3)}$

$= \dfrac{2x^2 - x + 9}{(x - 3)(x + 2)(x + 3)}$

**d.** $\dfrac{2x^2 - 5x + 6}{(x + 1)(x - 2)(x - 1)}$

$\dfrac{2x}{(x + 1)(x - 2)} - \dfrac{3}{(x + 1)(x - 1)}$

$= \dfrac{2x(x - 1) - 3(x - 2)}{(x + 1)(x - 2)(x - 1)}$

$= \dfrac{2x^2 - 2x - 3x + 6}{(x + 1)(x - 2)(x - 1)}$

$= \dfrac{2x^2 - 5x + 6}{(x + 1)(x - 2)(x - 1)}$

**4. a.** $\dfrac{x + 1}{(x + 2)(x - 3)} \cdot \dfrac{(x + 2)(x - 2)}{(x - 2)(x + 1)} =$

$\dfrac{(x + 1)(x + 2)(x - 2)}{(x + 2)(x - 3)(x - 2)(x + 1)} = \dfrac{1}{x - 3}$

**b.** $\dfrac{(x + 4)(x - 4)}{(x + 5)} \cdot \dfrac{(x + 5)(x - 2)}{(x + 4)(x + 4)} =$

$\dfrac{(x + 4)(x - 4)(x + 5)(x - 2)}{(x + 5)(x + 4)(x + 4)} = \dfrac{(x - 4)(x - 2)}{x + 4}$

**c.** $\dfrac{(x + 6)(x + 1)}{(x + 6)(x - 1)} \cdot \dfrac{2x(x - 1)}{x + 1} =$

$\dfrac{(x + 6)(x + 1) \cdot 2x(x - 1)}{(x + 6)(x - 1)(x + 1)} = 2x$

**d.** $\dfrac{x + 3}{x^2 - 8x + 15} \div \dfrac{x^2 - 9}{x^2 - 4x - 5} =$

$\dfrac{(x + 3)}{(x - 3)(x - 5)} \cdot \dfrac{(x - 5)(x + 1)}{(x + 3)(x - 3)} = \dfrac{x + 1}{(x - 3)^2}$

**5. a.** $\dfrac{\dfrac{x + 2}{x + 2} - \dfrac{x}{x + 2}}{\dfrac{x + 1}{x^2 - 4}} = \dfrac{\dfrac{2}{x + 2}}{\dfrac{x + 1}{(x + 2)(x - 2)}} =$

$\dfrac{2}{x + 2} \cdot \dfrac{(x + 2)(x - 2)}{x + 1} = \dfrac{2(x - 2)}{x + 1}$

**b.** $\dfrac{\dfrac{1}{x - 1} + \dfrac{1}{x + 1}}{\dfrac{x}{x - 1} - \dfrac{x}{x + 1}} = \dfrac{\dfrac{x + 1 + x - 1}{(x - 1)(x + 1)}}{\dfrac{x^2 + x - x^2 + x}{(x - 1)(x + 1)}} =$

$\dfrac{2x}{(x - 1)(x + 1)} \cdot \dfrac{(x - 1)(x + 1)}{2x} = 1$

**6.**

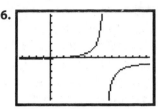

$[-4.4, 14.4, 1, -6.2, 6.2, 1]$

**a.** Vertical asymptote $x = 8$; horizontal asymptote $y = -0.5$; hole at $x = -1$; $y$-intercept: $-0.125$; $x$-intercept: 2

**b.** $\dfrac{x + 1}{(x + 1)(x - 8)} - \dfrac{x}{2(x - 8)} = \dfrac{2}{2(x - 8)} - \dfrac{x}{2(x - 8)} = \dfrac{2 - x}{2(x - 8)}$

**c.** The expression is undefined at $x = 8$ and the numerator is nonzero, causing the vertical asymptote. The factor $(x + 1)$ was canceled; this causes a hole. When $x = 0$, the expression has the value $-\frac{1}{8}$, or $-0.125$, the $y$-intercept. The numerator is 0 when $x = 2$; this is the $x$-intercept. For large values of $x$, the expression approaches the value $-0.5$, the horizontal asymptote.

**7. a.** $x = 3$ is a zero because that value causes the numerator to be 0. The vertical asymptotes are $x = 2$ and $x = -2$ because these values make the denominator 0 but do not make the numerator 0. The horizontal asymptote is $x = 0$ because this is the value that $y$ approaches when $|x|$ is large.

**b.**

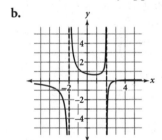

**8. a.** $y = x + 1$ is a slant asymptote; $x = 1$ is a vertical asymptote.

**b.** $y = \dfrac{(x + 1)(x - 1)}{x - 1} + \dfrac{1}{x - 1} = \dfrac{x^2 - 1 + 1}{x - 1}$

$= \dfrac{x^2}{x - 1}$

**c.**

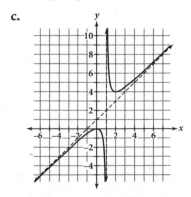

**d.**

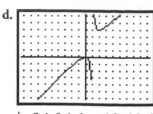

$[-9.4, 9.4, 1, -6.2, 6.2, 1]$

**9. a.** Answers will vary.

**b.** $-x^2 + xy - y = 0$; yes. Use the equation $y = \frac{x^2}{x-1}$ from 8b. $y(x - 1) = x^2$, so $-x^2 + xy - y = 0$. The equation can be written in general quadratic form, so its graph is a conic section. Therefore it is a hyperbola.

**c.** No

**d.** Not possible; no. If you try to put the equation in standard quadratic form, you get $x^2y - 4y - x - 3 = 0$. The term $x^2y$ does not belong in a general quadratic equation because its total degree is 3.

**e.** After reducing common factors, the degree of the numerator must be less than or equal to 2, and the degree of the denominator must be 1.

**10. a.** $y = 1 \cdot \frac{25v}{25v} + \frac{v}{25} \cdot \frac{v}{v} + \frac{50}{v} \cdot \frac{25}{25}$

$= \frac{v^2 + 25v + 1250}{25v}$

**b.** The equations are the same, so it was simplified correctly.

| X | Y₁ | Y₂ |
|---|---|---|
| 1 | 51.04 | 51.04 |
| 2 | 26.08 | 26.08 |
| 3 | 17.787 | 17.787 |
| 4 | 13.66 | 13.66 |
| 5 | 11.2 | 11.2 |
| 6 | 9.5733 | 9.5733 |
| 7 | 8.4229 | 8.4229 |

X=1

**c.** 4.4 s. First convert 45 mi/h to ft/s.

$\left(\frac{45 \text{ mi}}{1 \text{ h}}\right)\left(\frac{5280 \text{ ft}}{1 \text{ mi}}\right)\left(\frac{1 \text{ h}}{3600 \text{ s}}\right) = 66 \text{ ft/s}$

When $v = 66$, $y = 1 + \frac{66}{25} + \frac{50}{66} \approx 4.4$.

**d.** 3.8 s to 4.8 s. First convert 25 mi/h and 55 mi/h to ft/s.

$\left(\frac{25 \text{ mi}}{1 \text{ h}}\right)\left(\frac{5280 \text{ ft}}{1 \text{ mi}}\right)\left(\frac{1 \text{ h}}{3600 \text{ s}}\right) = 36\frac{2}{3} \text{ ft/s}$

$\left(\frac{55 \text{ mi}}{1 \text{ h}}\right)\left(\frac{5280 \text{ ft}}{1 \text{ mi}}\right)\left(\frac{1 \text{ h}}{3600 \text{ s}}\right) = 80\frac{2}{3} \text{ ft/s}$

When $x = 36\frac{2}{3}$, $y = 1 + \frac{36\frac{2}{3}}{25} + \frac{50}{36\frac{2}{3}} \approx 3.8$. When $x = 80\frac{2}{3}$, $y = 1 + \frac{80\frac{2}{3}}{25} + \frac{50}{80\frac{2}{3}} \approx 4.8$. Therefore the light should stay yellow for 3.8 s to 4.8 s.

**11. a.** $x = 3$, $y = 1$

**b.** Translation right 3 units and up 1 unit

**c.** $-2$. The equation must be in the form $y = 1 + \frac{a}{x-3}$. Use the point $(4, -1)$ to find $a$.

$-1 = 1 + \frac{a}{4-3}$, so $a = -2$

**d.** $y = 1 - \frac{2}{x-3}$ or $y = \frac{x-5}{x-3}$

**e.** $x$-intercept: 5; $y$-intercept: $\frac{5}{3}$

**12. a.**

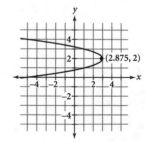

**b.** $v_i = 98 \sin 35° \approx 56$ N, $v_n = 98 \cos 35° \approx 80$ N

**13.** The new balance after 5 years, if the interest is compounded $n$ times per year, will be $1000\left(1 + \frac{0.065}{n}\right)^{5n}$, so the interest gained is $1000\left(1 + \frac{0.065}{n}\right)^{5n} - 1000$.

**a.** $370.09. $n = 1$, so the interest gained is $1000(1 + 0.065)^5 - 1000 = 370.09$.

**b.** $382.82. $n = 12$, so the interest gained is $1000\left(1 + \frac{0.065}{12}\right)^{60} - 1000 = 382.82$.

**c.** $383.75. $n = 52$, so the interest gained is $1000\left(1 + \frac{0.065}{52}\right)^{260} - 1000 = 383.75$.

**d.** $383.99. $n = 365$, so the interest gained is $1000\left(1 + \frac{0.065}{365}\right)^{18980} - 1000 = 383.99$.

## CHAPTER 9 REVIEW

### EXERCISES

**1. a.** The vertex of the parabola is at $(3, 2)$. $f = \frac{1}{4(-2)} = -0.125$ and the parabola is horizontally oriented, so the focus is at $(2.875, 2)$.

**b.**

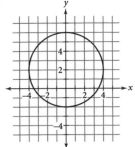

**c.**

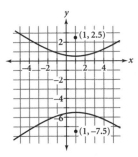

The center of the hyperbola is at $(1, -2.5)$. $a = 3$, $b = 4$, and $a^2 + b^2 = c^2$, so $c = 5$. The hyperbola is vertically oriented, so the foci are at $(1, 2.5)$ and $(1, -7.5)$.

**d.**

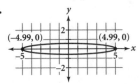

The center of the ellipse is at $(0, 0)$. $a = 5$, $b = \frac{1}{3}$, and $b^2 + c^2 = a^2$, so $c = \sqrt{25 - \frac{1}{9}} \approx 4.99$. The major axis of the ellipse is horizontal, so the foci are at $(\pm 4.99, 0)$.

**2. a.** $\left(\frac{x-5}{3}\right)^2 + \left(\frac{y+2}{4}\right)^2 = 1$. The center of the ellipse is at $(5, -2)$. Its horizontal axis is 6 units long, so $a = 3$. Its vertical axis is 8 units long, so $b = 4$.

**b.** $x = 3 \cos t + 5$ and $y = 4 \sin t - 2$

**c.** Center $(5, -2)$; foci $\left(5, -2 + \sqrt{7}\right)$ and $\left(5, -2 - \sqrt{7}\right)$. $a^2 + c^2 = b^2$, so $c = \sqrt{7}$. Therefore the foci are $\sqrt{7}$ units above and below the center.

**d.** $16x^2 + 9y^2 - 160x + 36y + 292 = 0$

$$\left(\frac{x-5}{3}\right)^2 + \left(\frac{y+2}{4}\right)^2 = 1$$

$$\frac{(x-5)^2}{9} + \frac{(y+2)^2}{16} = 1$$

$$16\left(x^2 - 10x + 25\right) + 9\left(y^2 + 4y + 4\right) = 144$$

$$16x^2 - 160x + 400 + 9y^2 + 36y + 36 = 144$$

$$16x^2 + 9y^2 - 160x + 36y + 292 = 0$$

**3. a.** $y = \pm 0.5x$

**b.** $x^2 - 4y^2 - 4 = 0$. This is the graph of $x^2 - y^2 = 1$, horizontally stretched by a factor of 2, so its equation is $\left(\frac{x}{2}\right)^2 - y^2 = 1$, or $x^2 - 4y^2 - 4 = 0$.

**c.** $d = 0.5x - \sqrt{\frac{x^2}{4} - 1}$. Solve the general quadratic equation from 3b for $y$.

$$-4y^2 = 4 - x^2$$

$$y^2 = \frac{x^2}{4} - 1$$

$$y = \pm\sqrt{\frac{x^2}{4} - 1}$$

The upper portion of the graph is represented by $y = \sqrt{\frac{x^2}{4} - 1}$. The vertical distance between the point on the asymptote and the point on the hyperbola is $d = 0.5x - \sqrt{\frac{x^2}{4} - 1}$.

**d.**

| $x$ | 2 | 10 | 20 | 100 |
|---|---|---|---|---|
| $d$ | 1 | 0.101 | 0.050 | 0.010 |

As $x$-values increase, the hyperbola gets closer to the asymptote.

**4.** $(x + 4)^2 + (y - 1)^2 = 25$. The graph is a circle with center $(-4, 1)$ and radius 5.

$$x^2 + y^2 + 8x - 2y = 8$$

$$x^2 + 8x + 16 + y^2 - 2y + 1 = 25$$

$$(x + 4)^2 + (y - 1)^2 = 25$$

**5.** $\left(\frac{y-4}{2}\right)^2 = x - 3$; vertex: $(3, 4)$, focus: $(4, 4)$, directrix: $x = 2$

$$y^2 - 8y - 4x + 28 = 0$$

$$y^2 - 8y + 16 = 4x - 12$$

$$(y - 4)^2 = 4(x - 3)$$

$$\left(\frac{y-4}{2}\right)^2 = x - 3$$

$f = \frac{2^2}{4 \cdot 1} = 1$ and the parabola is horizontally oriented, so the focus is at $(4, 4)$ and the directrix is $x = 2$.

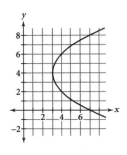

**6.** About 10 oz. Let $x$ be the amount of pure gold needed to mix with the 18-karat gold. In the current mixture, 75% of the 5 oz is pure gold, so there are 3.75 oz of pure gold. The new mixture will have $(3.75 + x)$ oz of pure gold and will be a total of $(5 + x)$ oz, so the new percentage of gold will be $\frac{3.75 + x}{5 + x}$.

$$\frac{3.75 + x}{5 + x} = 0.917$$
$$3.75 + x = 4.585 + 0.917x$$
$$0.083x = 0.835$$
$$x \approx 10.06$$

About 10 oz of pure gold must be mixed with the 5 oz of 18-karat gold.

**7. a.** $y = 1 + \frac{1}{x + 2}$, or $y = \frac{x + 3}{x + 2}$. The function $y = \frac{1}{x}$ is translated left 2 units and up 1 unit.

**b.** $y = -4 + \frac{1}{x}$, or $y = \frac{-4x + 1}{x}$. The function $y = \frac{1}{x}$ is translated down 4 units.

**8.**

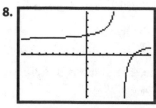

$[-9.4, 9.4, 1, -6.2, 6.2, 1]$

Horizontal asymptote $y = 2$, vertical asymptote $x = 5$. The denominator is 0 when $x$ is 5 and the numerator is nonzero, so the vertical asymptote is $x = 5$. The equation can be rewritten as $y = 2 - \frac{4}{x - 5}$, which shows that as $|x|$ gets larger, $y$ approaches 2. Therefore the horizontal asymptote is $y = 2$.

**9.** Multiply the numerator and the denominator by the factor $(x + 3)$.

$$y = \frac{(2x - 14)(x + 3)}{(x - 5)(x + 3)}$$

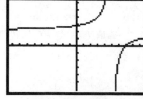

$[-9.4, 9.4, 1, -6.2, 6.2, 1]$

**10.** 23.3 mi/h and then 43.3 mi/h. Let $x$ represent Ellen's speed during the first portion of her trip, and let $y$ represent her speed during the second portion of her trip. Then $y = x + 20$ and $\frac{2}{x} + \frac{3.5}{y} = \frac{10}{60}$. Substitute $(x + 20)$ for $y$ in the second equation and solve for $x$.

$$\frac{2}{x} + \frac{3.5}{x + 20} = \frac{1}{6}$$
$$12(x + 20) + 21x = x(x + 20)$$
$$0 = x^2 - 13x - 240$$
$$x \approx -10.3 \text{ or } x \approx 23.3$$

It is impossible for $x$ to be negative in this context, so $x \approx 23.3$ and $y \approx 43.3$.

**11. a.** $\dfrac{3x^2 + 8x + 3}{(x - 2)(x + 1)(x + 2)}$

$$\frac{2x}{(x - 2)(x + 1)} + \frac{x + 3}{(x - 2)(x + 2)}$$
$$= \frac{2x(x + 2) + (x + 3)(x + 1)}{(x - 2)(x + 1)(x + 2)}$$
$$= \frac{2x^2 + 4x + x^2 + 4x + 3}{(x - 2)(x + 1)(x + 2)}$$
$$= \frac{3x^2 + 8x + 3}{(x - 2)(x + 1)(x + 2)}$$

**b.** $\dfrac{x^2}{x + 1} \cdot \dfrac{3x - 6}{x^2 - 2x} = \dfrac{x^2}{x + 1} \cdot \dfrac{3(x - 2)}{x(x - 2)} = \dfrac{3x}{x + 1}$

**c.** $\dfrac{x^2 - 5x - 6}{x} \div \dfrac{x^2 - 8x + 12}{x^2 - 1} =$

$$\frac{(x - 6)(x + 1)}{x} \cdot \frac{(x + 1)(x - 1)}{(x - 6)(x - 2)} =$$
$$\frac{(x + 1)^2(x - 1)}{x(x - 2)}$$

**12.** $(0.5, 1.936)$, $(0.5, -1.936)$, $(-2, 0)$. Solve the first equation for $y^2$: $y^2 = 4 - x^2$. Substitute this into the second equation and solve for $x$.

$$(x + 1)^2 - \frac{4 - x^2}{3} = 1$$
$$3(x + 1)^2 - 4 + x^2 = 3$$
$$3x^2 + 6x + 3 - 4 + x^2 = 3$$
$$4x^2 + 6x - 4 = 0$$
$$2(2x - 1)(x + 2) = 0$$
$$x = 0.5 \text{ or } x = -2$$

If $x = 0.5$, then $y^2 = 4 - 0.5^2 = 3.75$, so $y \approx \pm 1.936$. If $x = -2$, then $y^2 = 4 - (-2)^2$, so $y = 0$. The intersection points are $(0.5, \pm 1.936)$ and $(-2, 0)$. The graph confirms this.

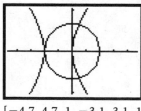

$[-4.7, 4.7, 1, -3.1, 3.1, 1]$

**13. a.** $y = 2|x|$

   **b.** $y = 2|x - 4|$

   **c.** $y = 2|x - 4| - 3$

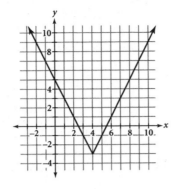

**14. a.** 91.45 million mi. Let $x$ be the distance from the perihelion to the Sun, and let $y$ be the distance from the Sun to the aphelion. Then $x + y = 186$ and $\frac{x}{y} = \frac{59}{61}$. Solve the second equation for $y$: $y = \frac{61}{59}x$. Substitute this into the first equation and solve for $x$: $x + \frac{61}{59}x = 186$, so $x = \frac{59}{120} \cdot 186 = 91.45$.

   **b.** 94.55 million mi. Using the equation from 14a, $y = 186 - x = 186 - 91.45 = 94.55$.

   **c.** $\frac{186}{2} = 93$ million mi

   **d.** $94.55 - 93 = 1.55$ million mi

   **e.** $1.55^2 + x^2 = 93^2$, so $x \approx 92.99$ million mi

   **f.** $\left(\dfrac{x}{93}\right)^2 + \left(\dfrac{y}{92.99}\right)^2 = 1$

**15. a.** Not possible. The number of columns in $[A]$ must match the number of rows in $[B]$.

   **b.** Not possible. To add matrices, they must have the same dimensions.

   **c.** $[A] - [C] = \begin{bmatrix} -2 - 1 & 0 - (-1) \\ 1 - 0 & -3 - 2 \end{bmatrix}$

      $= \begin{bmatrix} -3 & 1 \\ 1 & -5 \end{bmatrix}$

   **d.** $[B][A] = \begin{bmatrix} 0(-2) - 2(1) & 0(0) - 2(-3) \\ 5(-2) + 0(1) & 5(0) + 0(-3) \\ 3(-2) - 1(1) & 3(0) - 1(-3) \end{bmatrix}$

      $= \begin{bmatrix} -2 & 6 \\ -10 & 0 \\ -7 & 3 \end{bmatrix}$

   **e.** $3\begin{bmatrix} 1 & -1 \\ 0 & 2 \end{bmatrix} - \begin{bmatrix} -2 & 0 \\ 1 & -3 \end{bmatrix} = \begin{bmatrix} 5 & -3 \\ -1 & 9 \end{bmatrix}$

**16. a.** Arithmetic; 21, 24, 27; $u_1 = 9$ and $u_n = u_{n-1} + 3$ where $n \geq 2$

   **b.** Neither; 21, 34, 55; $u_1 = 1$, $u_2 = 1$, and $u_n = u_{n-1} + u_{n-2}$ where $n \geq 3$

   **c.** Geometric; $-48$, 96, $-192$; $u_1 = -3$ and $u_n = -2u_{n-1}$ where $n \geq 2$

**17. a.** 7.5 yd/s. The length of the diagonal is $\sqrt{100^2 + 52^2} \approx 112.7$ yd, so Spot's rate is $\frac{112.7 \text{ yd}}{15 \text{ s}} \approx 7.5$ yd/s.

   **b.** $\tan^{-1}\left(\frac{52}{100}\right) \approx 27.5°$

   **c.** $x = 7.5t\cos 27.5°$, $y = 7.5t\sin 27.5°$

   **d.** $x = 100 - 7.5t\cos 27.5°$, $y = 7.5t\sin 27.5°$

   **e.** Midfield (50, 26), at 7.5 s

**18. a.** $\bar{x} = 31.\overline{6}$; $median = 33$; $mode = 34$

   **b.** $Q_1 = 27$ and $Q_3 = 36$. The minimum is 18 and the maximum is 45.

      0   10   20   30   40   50

      **Number of students**

   **c.** $s = 7.57$. The data are fairly spread out from the mean. If the standard deviation were smaller, the data would be more closely grouped around 33 students per class.

**19. a.** $\left(\frac{y}{5}\right)^2 - \left(\frac{x}{2}\right)^2 = 1$; hyperbola. Divide both sides of the equation by 100 to get $\frac{x^2}{4} - \frac{y^2}{25} + 1 = 0$. Rewrite in standard form to get $\left(\frac{y}{5}\right)^2 - \left(\frac{x}{2}\right)^2 = 1$.

   **b.** $\dfrac{(y + 2)^2}{5} = \dfrac{x - 2}{2}$; parabola

$$4y^2 - 10x + 16y + 36 = 0$$
$$4(y^2 + 4y) = 10x - 36$$
$$4(y^2 + 4y + 4) = 10x - 20$$
$$4(y + 2)^2 = 10(x - 2)$$
$$\frac{(y + 2)^2}{5} = \frac{x - 2}{2}$$

   **c.** $(x + 3)^2 + (y - 1)^2 = \frac{1}{4}$; circle

$$4x^2 + 4y^2 + 24x - 8y + 39 = 0$$
$$4(x^2 + 6x) + 4(y^2 - 2y) = -39$$
$$4(x^2 + 6x + 9) + 4(y^2 - 2y + 1) = -39 + 36 + 4$$
$$4(x + 3)^2 + 4(y - 1)^2 = 1$$
$$(x + 3)^2 + (y - 1)^2 = \frac{1}{4}$$

   **d.** $\left(\dfrac{x - 2}{\sqrt{8}}\right)^2 + \left(\dfrac{y + 2}{\sqrt{4.8}}\right)^2 = 1$, or $\left(\dfrac{x - 2}{2\sqrt{2}}\right)^2 + \left(\dfrac{y + 2}{2\sqrt{1.2}}\right)^2 = 1$; ellipse

$$3x^2 + 5y^2 - 12x + 20y + 8 = 0$$
$$3(x^2 - 4x) + 5(y^2 + 4y) = -8$$
$$3(x^2 - 4x + 4) + 5(y^2 + 4y + 4) = -8 + 12 + 20$$
$$3(x - 2)^2 + 5(y + 2)^2 = 24$$
$$\frac{(x - 2)^2}{8} + \frac{(y + 2)^2}{4.8} = 1$$
$$\left(\frac{x - 2}{\sqrt{8}}\right)^2 + \left(\frac{y + 2}{\sqrt{4.8}}\right)^2 = 1$$

**20.** $y = 0.00115x^2 + 4$. The vertex of the parabola is at $(0, 4)$, so the equation is $y = ax^2 + 4$. Use the tip of one of the towers, at the points $(\pm200, 50)$, to find $a$. $50 = a(200^2) + 4$, so $a = \frac{46}{200^2} = 0.00115$. Therefore the equation is $y = 0.00115x^2 + 4$.

**21. a.** $5^x = 14$, so $x = \frac{\log 14}{\log 5} \approx 1.64$

   **b.** $0.5^{2x} = 2.5$, so $2x = \frac{\log 2.5}{\log 0.5} \approx -1.322$, and $x \approx -0.66$

   **c.** $x = 15$

   **d.** $x = \frac{\log 100}{\log 6} \approx 2.57$

   **e.** $\log x = 1.25$, so $x = 10^{1.25} \approx 17.78$

   **f.** $x = \log_5 5^3 = 3\log_5 5 = 3 \cdot 1 = 3$

   **g.** $\log x = \frac{1}{4}\log 16$, so $\log x = \log 16^{1/4} = \log 2$, and $x = 2$

   **h.** $x = 495$

   $$\log(5 + x) - \log 5 = 2$$
   $$\log\left(\frac{5 + x}{5}\right) = 2$$
   $$\frac{5 + x}{5} = 10^2$$
   $$5 + x = 500$$
   $$x = 495$$

   **i.** $x\log 5^x = 12$, so $x^2\log 5 = 12$, and $x = \pm\sqrt{\frac{12}{\log 5}} \approx \pm4.14$

**22. a.** $\hat{y} = 0.565x - 1100$. Use your calculator to calculate the median-median line.

   **b.** $s = \sqrt{\frac{48.61}{6}} \approx 2.8$

   **c.** In general, the median-median line model predicts results within 2.8 mi/gal of the actual results.

   **d.** Answers will vary. The model is likely a good model for the next few years at least. Eventually, however, alternative forms of fuel will make the model obsolete.

**23.** Set up a coordinate system with home plate at $(0, 0)$, first base at $(90, 0)$, second base at $(90, 90)$, and third base at $(0, 90)$. Write equations to simulate the motion.

Deanna: $x = 90$, $y = 28t + 12$

ball: $x = 125(t - 1.5)\cos 45°$, $y = 125(t - 1.5)\sin 45°$

Substitute $x = 90$ and $y = 90$ into each set of equations and solve for $t$ to find when Deanna and the ball reach second base. Deanna reaches second base at 2.79 s, and the ball reaches second at 2.52 s. Deanna is out.

**24. a.** $P + Q - R = 1 + 3i - 2 + i - 3 + 5i = -4 + 9i$

   **b.** $PQ = (1 + 3i)(-2 + i) = -2 - 5i + 3i^2 = -2 - 5i - 3 = -5 - 5i$

   **c.** $Q^2 = (-2 + i)(-2 + i) = 4 - 4i + i^2 = 4 - 4i - 1 = 3 - 4i$

   **d.** $P \div Q = \frac{1 + 3i}{-2 + i} \cdot \frac{-2 - i}{-2 - i} = \frac{-2 - 7i - 3i^2}{4 + 1} = \frac{1 - 7i}{5} = \frac{1}{5} - \frac{7}{5}i$

**TAKE ANOTHER LOOK**

**1.** To investigate the graph on your calculator, solve the equation $\left(\frac{x}{a}\right)^n + \left(\frac{y}{b}\right)^n = 1$ for $y$. Enter $Y_1 = b\left(1 - \left(\frac{x}{a}\right)^n\right)^{1/n}$ and, if $n$ is even, $Y_2 = -Y_1$. Then, on the Home screen, store values for $a$, $b$, and $n$.

For $n = 1$, the graph is a line. When $n$ is odd and greater than 1, the graphs are similar to the ones shown. As $n$ gets larger, the curve has "sharper" corners.

When $n$ equals 2, the graph of the equation is an ellipse with $x$-intercepts $a$ and $-a$, and $y$-intercepts $b$ and $-b$. As the even powers of $n$ get larger, the graph looks more like a rectangle.

$n = 4$          $n = 50$

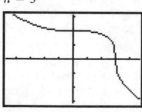 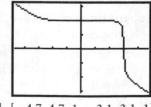

$[-4.7, 4.7, 1, -3.1, 3.1, 1]$   $[-4.7, 4.7, 1, -3.1, 3.1, 1]$

$n = 3$          $n = 7$

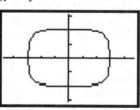 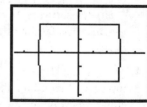

$[-4.7, 4.7, 1, -3.1, 3.1, 1]$   $[-4.7, 4.7, 1, -3.1, 3.1, 1]$

$n = 51$

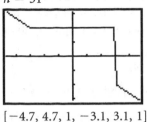

$[-4.7, 4.7, 1, -3.1, 3.1, 1]$

**2.** When the degree of the numerator is less than the degree of the denominator, the horizontal asymptote is the line $y = 0$. When the degree of the numerator is greater than the degree of the denominator, there is no horizontal asymptote. When the degree of the numerator equals the degree of the denominator, the horizontal asymptote is determined by the ratio of the leading coefficients.

**3.** A constant product gives a family of shapes called *Cassini ovals*. Depending on the product, the locus could form any of the shapes shown.

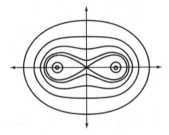

Using geometry software, graph a curve given by an equation in the form $y = \frac{a}{x}$, where $a$ is a constant, and measure the distances from a point on the curve to the $x$- and $y$-axes. These two measurements will have a constant product regardless of the location of the point on the curve. The rest of the construction is similar to the construction of the ellipse in the Exploration Constructing the Conic Sections.

When the ratio is constant, you get a circle around one of the foci. This can be demonstrated using geometry software, beginning with the function $y = ax$. This family of circles is called the *Apollonius circles*.

**4.** The highest degree on a variable determines the number of solutions for that variable. If a system of equations contains an $x^2$-term and a $y^2$-term, there are two solutions for $x$ and two corresponding solutions for $y$, making a total of four solutions. These solutions may be real or nonreal. If a system of equations contains an $x^2$-term and a $y$-term, there are two solutions for $x$, but only one corresponding solution for $y$, for a total of two solutions (real or nonreal). When the system contains a $y^2$-term and an $x$-term, the reverse is true, and there are still two solutions.

# CHAPTER 10

## LESSON 10.1

### EXERCISES

**1.** The $y$-value, or the frog's height, is $\sin 300° = -\frac{\sqrt{3}}{2} \approx -0.866$ m.

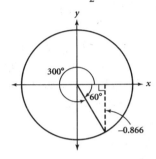

**2. a.** $-0.0872$; $\sin(-175°) = -\sin 5°$; reference angle $5°$

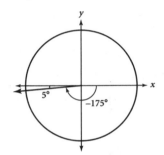

**b.** $-0.8387$; $\cos 147° = -\cos 33°$; reference angle $33°$

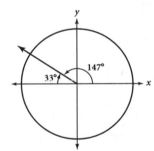

**c.** $-0.9848$; $\sin 280° = -\sin 80°$; reference angle $80°$

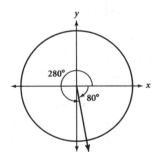

**d.** 0.6428; cos 310° = cos 50°; reference angle 50°

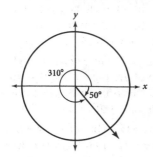

**e.** −0.7314; sin(−47°) = −sin 47°; reference angle 47°

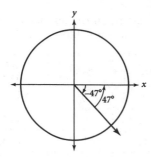

**3. a.** 2

  **b.** 4

**4. a.**

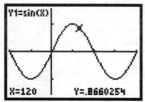

$[-180, 360, 90, -1.55, 1.55, 1]$

**b.**

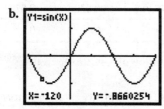

$[-180, 360, 90, -1.55, 1.55, 1]$

**c.**

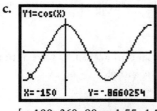

$[-180, 360, 90, -1.55, 1.55, 1]$

**d.**

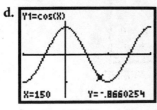

$[-180, 360, 90, -1.55, 1.55, 1]$

**5. a.** Periodic, 180°. The function repeats itself every 180°.

  **b.** Not periodic. The function does not repeat itself.

  **c.** Periodic, 90°. The function repeats itself every 90°.

  **d.** Periodic, 180°. The function repeats itself every 180°.

**6.** For 6a–d, add or subtract 360° from the angle until you reach an angle $\theta$ with $0° \leq \theta \leq 360°$.

  **a.** $\theta = -25° + 360° = 335°$

  **b.** $\theta = -430° + 2 \cdot 360° = 290°$

  **c.** $\theta = 435° - 360° = 75°$

  **d.** $\theta = 1195° - 3 \cdot 360° = 115°$

**7.** Quadrant I: $\cos \theta$ and $\sin \theta$ are both positive; Quadrant II: $\cos \theta$ is negative and $\sin \theta$ is positive; Quadrant III: $\cos \theta$ and $\sin \theta$ are both negative; Quadrant IV: $\cos \theta$ is positive and $\sin \theta$ is negative.

**8.** $x = \{-360°, -180°, 0°, 180°, 360°\}$

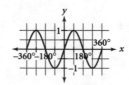

**9.** $x = \{-270°, -90°, 90°, 270°\}$

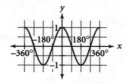

**10. a.**

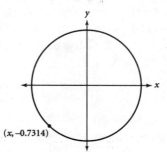

  **b.** $\theta \approx 227°$; $\cos \theta = -0.682$. $\sin^{-1}(-0.7314) \approx -47°$, so this is the reference angle for $\theta$. By looking at the graph, $\theta \approx 180° + 47° = 227°$.

  **c.** 133°. The other angle with the same cosine value is the angle in Quadrant II with reference angle 47°. This is $\alpha = 180° - 47° = 133°$.

*Discovering Advanced Algebra Solutions Manual*
©2004 Key Curriculum Press

**11.** The bearing on which a plane flies uses the positive *y*-axis (north) as its initial side, and the angle goes clockwise to its terminal side.

**a.** $\theta = -15°$

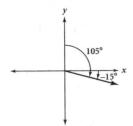

**b.** $\theta = 125°$

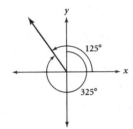

**c.** $\theta = -90°$

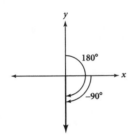

**d.** $\theta = 48°$

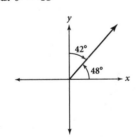

**12.** The distance from the origin to (2, 3) and from the origin to $(-2, 3)$ is $\sqrt{2^2 + 3^2} = \sqrt{13}$.

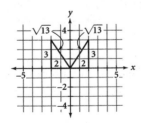

**a.** $\sin A = \dfrac{3}{\sqrt{13}}$, $\cos A = \dfrac{2}{\sqrt{13}}$

**b.** $\sin A = \dfrac{3}{\sqrt{13}}$, $\cos A = \dfrac{-2}{\sqrt{13}}$

**13. a.** $\theta = 150°$ and $\theta = 210°$. The reference angle is 30°. The cosine of an angle is negative in Quadrants II and III, so the two angles are $180° - 30° = 150°$ and $180° + 30° = 210°$.

**b.** $\theta = 135°$ and $\theta = 225°$. The reference angle is 45°. The cosine of an angle is negative in Quadrants II and III, so the two angles are $180° - 45° = 135°$ and $180° + 45° = 225°$.

**c.** $\theta \approx 217°$ and $\theta \approx 323°$. The reference angle is $\sin^{-1}\frac{3}{5} \approx 37°$. The sine of an angle is negative in Quadrants III and IV, so the two angles are approximately $180° + 37° = 217°$ and $360° - 37° = 323°$.

**d.** $\theta = 90°$. The only point on the unit circle with *y*-value 1 is (0, 1), where $\theta = 90°$.

**14.**

| $\theta$ | $\sin\theta$ | $\cos\theta$ | $\tan\theta$ | $\dfrac{\sin\theta}{\cos\theta}$ |
|---|---|---|---|---|
| 0° | 0 | 1 | 0 | 0 |
| 30° | 0.5 | 0.866 | 0.577 | 0.577 |
| 60° | 0.866 | 0.5 | 1.732 | 1.732 |
| 90° | 1 | 0 | undefined | undefined |
| 120° | 0.866 | $-0.5$ | $-1.732$ | $-1.732$ |
| 150° | 0.5 | $-0.866$ | $-0.577$ | $-0.577$ |
| 180° | 0 | $-1$ | 0 | 0 |
| 210° | $-0.5$ | $-0.866$ | 0.577 | 0.577 |
| 240° | $-0.866$ | $-0.5$ | 1.732 | 1.732 |
| 270° | $-1$ | 0 | undefined | undefined |
| 300° | $-0.866$ | 0.5 | $-1.732$ | $-1.732$ |
| 330° | $-0.5$ | 0.866 | $-0.577$ | $-0.577$ |
| 360° | 0 | 1 | 0 | 0 |

The values of $\tan\theta$ are equivalent to the ratio $\frac{\sin\theta}{\cos\theta}$.

$$\frac{\sin\theta}{\cos\theta} = \frac{\dfrac{\text{opposite}}{\text{hypotenuse}}}{\dfrac{\text{adjacent}}{\text{hypotenuse}}} = \frac{\text{opposite}}{\text{hypotenuse}} \cdot \frac{\text{hypotenuse}}{\text{adjacent}} =$$

$$\frac{\text{opposite}}{\text{adjacent}} = \tan\theta$$

**15. a.** The data are cyclical and appear to have a shape like a sine or cosine curve.

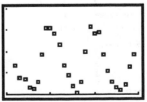

[1970, 2000, 10, 0, 200, 50]

**b.** 10–11 yr

**c.** 2001

**16. a.** $h = 1.5 + 20 \tan A$. Draw a diagram with Annie at the origin and the distance to the cliff on the positive *x*-axis.

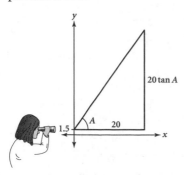

The vertical leg of the triangle, representing the height of the cliff, is $20 \tan A$. The triangle is 1.5 m above the *x*-axis, so the object she is looking at is $(1.5 + 20 \tan A)$ m above the ground.

**b.** $h = 1.5 + 20 \tan 58° \approx 33.5$ m

**c.** $h = 1.5 + 20 \tan 36° \approx 16.0$ m and $h = 1.5 + 20 \tan 40° \approx 18.3$ m

**d.** 23°. Substitute 10 for *h* and solve for *A*.
$10 = 1.5 + 20 \tan A$, so $A = \tan^{-1}\left(\frac{10 - 1.5}{20}\right) \approx 23°$.

**17. a.** $0.500 \text{ d} \cdot \dfrac{24 \text{ h}}{1 \text{ d}} \cdot \dfrac{60 \text{ min}}{1 \text{ h}} \cdot \dfrac{60 \text{ s}}{1 \text{ min}} = 43,200$ s

**b.** $\dfrac{3.0 \text{ mi}}{1 \text{ h}} \cdot \dfrac{5280 \text{ ft}}{1 \text{ mi}} \cdot \dfrac{1 \text{ h}}{60 \text{ min}} \cdot \dfrac{1 \text{ min}}{60 \text{ s}} = 4.4$ ft/s

**18.** $C \approx 29.7$ units, $A \approx 70.1$ units². Rewrite the equation in standard form by completing the square.

$$2x^2 + 2y^2 - 2x + 7y - 38 = 0$$

$$2(x^2 - x) + 2\left(y^2 + \frac{7}{2}y\right) = 38$$

$$x^2 - x + y^2 + \frac{7}{2}y = 19$$

$$x^2 - x + \frac{1}{4} + y^2 + \frac{7}{2}y + \frac{49}{16} = 19 + \frac{1}{4} + \frac{49}{16}$$

$$\left(x - \frac{1}{2}\right)^2 + \left(y + \frac{7}{4}\right)^2 = \frac{357}{16}$$

The radius is $r = \sqrt{\frac{357}{6}} \approx 4.72$ units, so the circumference of the circle is $2\pi r \approx 29.7$ units, and the area is $\pi r^2 \approx 70.1$ square units.

**19. a.** $\dfrac{3}{x - 4}$

$$\frac{x + 1}{x - 4} - \frac{x + 2}{x + 4} + \frac{4x}{-(x - 4)(x + 4)}$$

$$= \frac{(x + 1)(x + 4) - (x + 2)(x - 4) - 4x}{(x - 4)(x + 4)}$$

$$= \frac{x^2 + 5x + 4 - x^2 + 2x + 8 - 4x}{(x - 4)(x + 4)}$$

$$= \frac{3x + 12}{(x - 4)(x + 4)} = \frac{3(x + 4)}{(x - 4)(x + 4)} = \frac{3}{x - 4}$$

**b.** $\dfrac{2(x + 1)(x - 1)}{(x + 1)(x + 2)} \cdot \dfrac{(x + 2)(x - 3)}{(x - 1)(x - 3)} = 2$

**c.** $\dfrac{\frac{3 + a}{3}}{\frac{6 - a}{6}} = \dfrac{3 + a}{3} \cdot \dfrac{6}{6 - a} = \dfrac{2(3 + a)}{6 - a}$

**20.** $f(x) = \dfrac{2(x + 2)(x - 5)}{(x + 4)(x - 1)}$. The denominator should have roots $-4$ and 1, and the numerator should have roots $-2$ and 5. The ratio of leading coefficients should be 261.

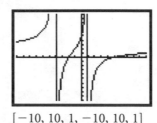

$[-10, 10, 1, -10, 10, 1]$

**EXTENSIONS**

**A.** See the solution to Take Another Look activity 1 on page 261.

**B.** See the Sketchpad demonstration Sine and Cosine.

## LESSON 10.2

**EXERCISES**

**1. a.** $80° \cdot \dfrac{\pi \text{ radians}}{180°} = \dfrac{4\pi}{9}$ radians

**b.** $570° \cdot \dfrac{\pi \text{ radians}}{180°} = \dfrac{19\pi}{6}$ radians

**c.** $-\dfrac{4\pi}{3}$ radians $\cdot \dfrac{180°}{\pi \text{ radians}} = -240°$

**d.** $\dfrac{11\pi}{9}$ radians $\cdot \dfrac{180°}{\pi \text{ radians}} = 220°$

**e.** $-\dfrac{3\pi}{4}$ radians $\cdot \dfrac{180°}{\pi \text{ radians}} = -135°$

**f.** $3\pi$ radians $\cdot \dfrac{180°}{\pi \text{ radians}} = 540°$

**g.** $-900° \cdot \dfrac{\pi \text{ radians}}{180°} = -5\pi$ radians

**h.** $\dfrac{5\pi}{6}$ radians $\cdot \dfrac{180°}{\pi \text{ radians}} = 150°$

**2.** In 2a–c, use the formula $s = r\theta$.

  **a.** $s = 3 \cdot \dfrac{2\pi}{3} = 2\pi$

  **b.** $s = 1 \cdot 1 = 1$

  **c.** $s = \dfrac{5}{2} \cdot \dfrac{\pi}{6} = \dfrac{5\pi}{12}$

**3. a, b.**

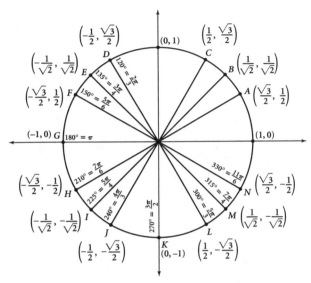

**4.** 1 radian $\cdot \dfrac{180°}{\pi \text{ radians}} \approx 57.3°$; $1° \cdot \dfrac{\pi \text{ radians}}{180°} \approx$ 0.017 radian

**5.** Less than; one rotation is $2\pi \approx 6.28$, which is more than 6.

**6. a.** 63.67 cm. The minute hand travels through 360° in 60 minutes, so in 40 minutes it goes through $\left(\dfrac{2}{3}\right)(360°) = 240° = \dfrac{4\pi}{3}$. The distance the tip of the minute hand travels is the arc length: $15.2 \cdot \dfrac{4\pi}{3} = 63.7$ cm.

  **b.** $\dfrac{63.8 \text{ cm}}{40 \text{ min}} \approx 1.6$ cm/min

  **c.** $\dfrac{\dfrac{4\pi}{3} \text{ radians}}{40 \text{ min}} \approx 0.105$ radian/min

**7. a, b.**

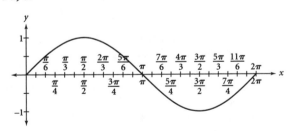

  **c.** Maximum: $\dfrac{\pi}{2}$; minimum: $\dfrac{3\pi}{2}$; $\sin x = 0$: 0, $\pi$, and $2\pi$

**8. a, b.**

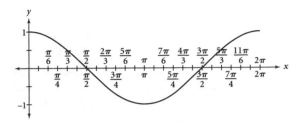

  **c.** Maximums: 0 and $2\pi$; minimum: $\pi$; $\cos x = 0$: $\dfrac{\pi}{2}$ and $\dfrac{3\pi}{2}$

**9. a.** $\dfrac{3}{2}$; $\dfrac{3}{2}$

  **b.** $-2$; $-2$

  **c.** They are equal. They are both the $y$-value divided by the $x$-value of any point on the terminal side of the angle.

  **d.** $\tan \dfrac{3\pi}{8} \approx 2.414$

**10.** Use the formula $s = r\theta$ to find that $12\pi = r \cdot \dfrac{\pi}{4}$, so $r = 48$.

**11. a.** $\theta = \pi + \dfrac{\pi}{3} = \dfrac{4\pi}{3}$. The reference angle is $\dfrac{\pi}{3}$ and the angle is in Quadrant III.

  **b.** $\theta = 2\pi - \dfrac{\pi}{4} = \dfrac{7\pi}{4}$. The reference angle is $\dfrac{\pi}{4}$ and the angle is in Quadrant IV.

  **c.** $\theta = \dfrac{\pi}{3}$. The reference angle is $\dfrac{\pi}{3}$ and the angle is in Quadrant I.

**12.** 31.3 radians/s. First convert your speed from mi/h to in./s.

$$\left(\dfrac{24 \text{ mi}}{1 \text{ h}}\right)\left(\dfrac{5280 \text{ ft}}{1 \text{ mi}}\right)\left(\dfrac{12 \text{ in.}}{1 \text{ ft}}\right)\left(\dfrac{1 \text{ h}}{60 \text{ min}}\right)\left(\dfrac{1 \text{ min}}{60 \text{ s}}\right) =$$
422.4 in./s

The circumference of the bike tire is $27\pi$ in., so the wheels are spinning at

$$\left(\dfrac{422.4 \text{ in.}}{1 \text{ s}}\right)\left(\dfrac{1 \text{ revolution}}{27\pi \text{ in.}}\right)\left(\dfrac{2\pi \text{ radians}}{1 \text{ revolution}}\right) \approx$$
31.3 radians/s

**13. a.** $A = \dfrac{1}{2}(8^2)\left(\dfrac{4\pi}{7}\right) = \dfrac{128\pi}{7} \approx 57.45 \text{ cm}^2$

  **b.** $\dfrac{A}{64\pi} = \dfrac{\dfrac{4\pi}{7}}{2\pi} = \dfrac{2}{7}$

  **c.** $A = 64\pi \cdot \dfrac{2}{7} = \dfrac{128\pi}{7} \approx 57.45 \text{ cm}^2$

**14. a.** $2\pi$ radians/day, or 0.26 radian/h

$$\left(\dfrac{2\pi \text{ radians}}{1 \text{ day}}\right)\left(\dfrac{1 \text{ day}}{24 \text{ h}}\right) = \dfrac{\pi}{12} \text{ radians/h} \approx$$
0.26 radian/h

  **b.** 1660 km/h. The radius of Earth is 6350 km, so its circumference is $12{,}700\pi$ km. Your speed is $\left(\dfrac{12700\pi \text{ km}}{2\pi \text{ radians}}\right)\left(\dfrac{\pi \text{ radians}}{12 \text{ h}}\right) \approx 1660$ km/h. Note that this is your speed if you are at the equator, traveling the full circumference of Earth. If you are not at the equator, you are not traveling as fast.

c. $(1660 \text{ km/h})(0.62 \text{ mi/km}) \approx 1030 \text{ mi/h}$

15. a. 1037 mi. The angular distance between the two cities is 15°, or $\frac{\pi}{12}$ radians. The distance between the two cities is the arc length, $s = 3960 \cdot \frac{\pi}{12} \approx 1037$ mi.

b. $10' \cdot \frac{1°}{60'} \approx 0.17°$, so $61°10' \approx 61.17°$

c. 2660 mi. Consider Anchorage city $A$ and Tucson city $B$. Convert the minutes into degrees using the process in 15b to get $\phi_A = 61.17°$, $\theta_A = 150.02°$, $\phi_B = 32.12°$, and $\theta_B = 110.93°$. Substitute these values and 3960 for $r$ in the formula.

$$D = \frac{3960\pi}{180} \cos^{-1}(\sin 61.17° \sin 32.12° + \cos 61.17° \cos 32.12° \cos(150.02° - 110.93°))$$

$$\approx 2660$$

16. a. Translated up 2 units and left 4 units

b. Stretched vertically by a factor of 3 and horizontally by a factor of 4, and translated right 5 units

c. Translated down 1 unit and right 3 units

d. Stretched vertically by a factor of 2, reflected across the $x$-axis, translated up 3 units and left 1 unit

17. a. $y = -2(x + 1)^2$. This is the graph of $y = x^2$ stretched vertically by a factor of 2, reflected across the $x$-axis, and translated left 1 unit.

b. $y + 4 = (x - 2)^2$, or $y = (x - 2)^2 - 4$. This is the graph of $y = x^2$ translated right 2 units and down 4 units.

c. $y + 2 = |x + 1|$, or $y = |x + 1| - 2$. This is the graph of $y = |x|$ translated left 1 unit and down 2 units.

d. $-\frac{y - 2}{2} = |x - 3|$, or $y = -2|x - 3| + 2$. This is the graph of $y = |x|$ stretched vertically by a factor of 2, reflected across the $x$-axis, and translated right 3 units and up 2 units.

18. a. 157°. The angle in Quadrant II with reference angle 23° is $180° - 23° = 157°$.

b. 324°. 216° is in Quadrant III and has reference angle 36°. The angle in Quadrant IV with reference angle 36° is $360° - 36° = 324°$.

c. 18°. 342° is in Quadrant IV and has reference angle 18°. The angle in Quadrant I with reference angle 18° is 18°.

d. 114°. 246° is in Quadrant III and has reference angle 66°. The angle in Quadrant II with reference angle 66° is $180° - 66° = 114°$.

19. a. 18 cm. When the slug is $\frac{1}{3}$ of the way around the wheel, it is at a 30° angle from the central horizontal axis of the wheel (the line parallel to the ground going through the center). This point is $12 \sin 30° = 6$ cm above the central horizontal axis, so it is $12 + 6 = 18$ cm above the ground.

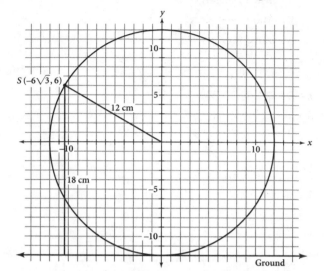

b. 166 cm. The car has moved forward $2\frac{1}{3}$ times the circumference of the wheel, or $2\frac{1}{3} \cdot 24\pi \approx 176$ cm. The slug is $6\sqrt{3} \approx 10$ cm behind the point where the wheel touches the ground, so it has traveled approximately 166 cm.

20.

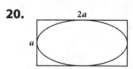

$\frac{\sqrt{3}}{2}$. The major axis is $a$ units long and the minor axis is $\frac{1}{2}a$ units long, so the foci are $\frac{\sqrt{3}}{2}a$ units from the center, along the major axis. Therefore the eccentricity is $\frac{\frac{\sqrt{3}}{2}a}{a} = \frac{\sqrt{3}}{2}$.

21. Possible answer: Construct $\overline{AP}$, $\overline{BP}$, and $\overline{CP}$. $\triangle APC$ is isosceles because $\overline{AP}$ and $\overline{CP}$ are radii of the same circle. $\angle A \cong \angle C$ because they are base angles of an isosceles triangle. $\angle ABP = 90°$ because the angle is inscribed in a semicircle. $\angle PBC = 90°$ because it is supplementary to $\angle APB$. $\triangle APB \cong \triangle CPB$ by SAA (two angles and a non-included side are congruent). Therefore $AB = BC$ because corresponding parts of congruent triangles are congruent.

**22. a.** $x = 1.5t$, $y = 80 - 4.9t^2$

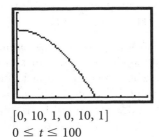

[0, 10, 1, 0, 10, 1]
$0 \le t \le 100$

**b.** About 4 s; about 6 m

**c.** Solve for $t$ when $y = 0$ and then substitute that value in the equation for $x$. $0 = 80 - 4.9t^2$, so $t \approx 4.04$ s, and $x \approx 6.06$ m.

## EXTENSION

See the solutions to Take Another Look activities 3 and 4 on page 261.

## LESSON 10.3

### EXERCISES

**1.** Possible answers:

**a.** $y = \sin x + 1$. This is the graph of $y = \sin x$ translated up 1 unit.

**b.** $y = \cos x - 2$. This is the graph of $y = \cos x$ translated down 2 units.

**c.** $y = \sin x - 0.5$. This is the graph of $y = \sin x$ translated down 0.5 unit.

**d.** $y = -3 \cos x$. This is the graph of $y = \cos x$ reflected across the $x$-axis and stretched vertically by a factor of 3 (amplitude is 3).

**e.** $y = -2 \sin x$. This is the graph of $y = \sin x$ reflected across the $x$-axis and stretched vertically by a factor of 2 (amplitude is 2).

**f.** $y = 2 \cos x + 1$. This is the graph of $y = \cos x$ stretched vertically by a factor of 2 (amplitude is 2) and translated up 1 unit.

**2.** Possible answers:

**a.** $y = \cos \frac{x}{0.5}$, or $y = \cos 2x$. This is the graph of $y = \cos x$ stretched horizontally by a factor of 0.5 (period is $\pi$).

**b.** $y = \sin\left(\frac{x}{2}\right) - 1$. This is the graph of $y = \sin x$ stretched horizontally by a factor of 2 (period is $4\pi$) and translated down 1 unit.

**c.** $y = -2 \sin 3x$. This is the graph of $y = \sin x$ reflected across the $x$-axis, stretched vertically by a factor of 2 (amplitude is 2), and stretched horizontally by a factor of $\frac{1}{3}$ (period is $\frac{2\pi}{3}$).

**d.** $y = \sin\left(x - \frac{\pi}{4}\right) + 1$. This is the graph of $y = \sin x$ translated right $\frac{\pi}{4}$ units (phase shift $\frac{\pi}{4}$) and up 1 unit.

**e.** $y = -\cos \frac{x}{0.5}$, or $y = -\cos 2x$. This is the graph of $y = \cos x$ reflected across the $x$-axis and stretched horizontally by a factor of 0.5 (period is $\pi$).

**f.** $y = \sin \frac{x + \frac{\pi}{2}}{2}$. This is the graph of $y = \sin x$ stretched horizontally by a factor of 2 (period $4\pi$) and translated left $\frac{\pi}{2}$ units (phase shift $-\frac{\pi}{2}$).

**3. a.** The $k$-value vertically translates the graph of the function.

**b.** The $b$-value vertically stretches or shrinks the graph of the function. The absolute value of $b$ represents the amplitude. When $b$ is negative, the curve is reflected across the $x$-axis.

**c.** The $a$-value horizontally stretches or shrinks the graph of the function. It also determines the period with the relationship $2\pi a = period$.

**d.** The $h$-value horizontally translates the graph of the function. It represents the phase shift.

**4.** The graph of $y = \sin x$ has been horizontally stretched by a factor of 3, vertically stretched by a factor of 2, and translated down 4 units.

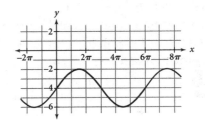

**5.** Horizontal translation left $\frac{\pi}{2}$ units (phase shift of $-\frac{\pi}{2}$ units); $y = \sin\left(x + \frac{\pi}{2}\right)$

**6.** Possible answer: $y = \sin\left(x - \frac{\pi}{2}\right)$, $y = -\sin\left(x + \frac{\pi}{2}\right)$, or $y = -\cos x$. You can think of this graph as a sine curve with a phase shift of $\frac{\pi}{2}$. This gives an equation of $y = \sin\left(x - \frac{\pi}{2}\right)$.

You can also think of this graph as a sine curve that has been reflected across the $x$-axis with a phase shift of $-\frac{\pi}{2}$. This gives an equation of $y = -\sin\left(x + \frac{\pi}{2}\right)$. This graph is also a cosine curve that has been reflected across the $x$-axis, $y = -\cos x$.

**7. a.** Let $x$ represent the number of days after a full moon (today), and let $y$ represent the percentage of lit surface that is visible. $y = 0.5 + 0.5 \cos\left(\frac{2\pi}{28}x\right)$. The period is 28 days, so the vertical stretch is $\frac{28}{2\pi}$. The range is from 0 to 1, so the amplitude is 0.5 and the vertical translation is up 0.5 unit. Use a cosine curve because it starts at 100%.

**b.** $y = 0.5 + 0.5 \cos\left(\frac{2\pi}{28} \cdot 23\right) \approx 0.7169$, so about 72% will be visible.

**c.** Day 5. Use the table function on your calculator to find the first day with $y$-value less than 0.75.

**8. a.** 3 cycles$\left(\dfrac{1\text{ s}}{60\text{ cycles}}\right) = 0.05$ s

**b.**

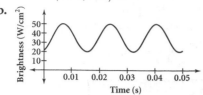

**c.** $y = 35 + 15\sin 120\pi(x - 0.003)$. The period is $\frac{1}{60}$, so the horizontal stretch factor is $120\pi$. The amplitude is $\frac{1}{2}(50 - 20) = 15$, the vertical translation is $\frac{1}{2}(50 + 20) = 35$, and the phase shift is 0.003.

**9.** *(See table at bottom of page.)*

**10.**

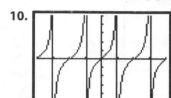

$[-2\pi, 2\pi, \pi/2, -5, 5, 1]$

**a.** A drag line appears. The value of $\tan\frac{\pi}{2}$ is undefined, so $x = \frac{\pi}{2}$ is a vertical asymptote. The vertical asymptotes are $x = \ldots -\frac{3\pi}{2}, -\frac{\pi}{2}, \frac{\pi}{2}, \frac{3\pi}{2} \ldots$, or $x = \frac{\pi}{2} + \pi n$, where $n$ is an integer.

**b.** $\pi$

**c.** On a unit circle, the point rotated $\frac{\pi}{5}$, the origin, and the point rotated $\frac{6\pi}{5}$ are collinear. So the segment from the origin to the point rotated $\frac{\pi}{5}$ has the same slope as the segment from the origin to the point rotated $\frac{6\pi}{5}$.

**d.**

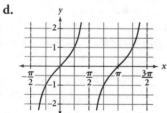

**11. a.** $y = 1.5\cos 2\left(x + \dfrac{\pi}{2}\right)$

**b.** $y = -3 + 2\sin 4\left(x - \frac{\pi}{4}\right)$. The period is $\frac{3\pi}{4} - \frac{\pi}{4} = \frac{\pi}{2}$, so the horizontal scale factor is $\frac{1}{4}$. The phase shift is $\frac{\pi}{4}$. The amplitude is $\frac{1}{2}(-1 - (-5)) = 2$, and the vertical translation is $\frac{1}{2}(-1 + (-5)) = -3$ units.

**c.** $y = 3 + 2\cos\dfrac{x - \pi}{3}$

**12. a.** $y = 2\sin\dfrac{2\pi(x - 80)}{365} + 12.15$

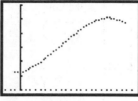

$[-30, 225, 10, 9, 15, 1]$

**b.** According to the equation, the least amount of daylight, 10.15 h, occurred on December 20. Use the minimum function on your calculator, or set the argument of the sine function equal to $-\frac{\pi}{2}$ and solve for $x$. $\frac{2\pi(x - 80)}{365} = -\frac{\pi}{2}$ when $x = -11.25$, and 11 days before December 31 is December 20.

**c.** The graph should be similar in shape but with a greater amplitude. It will have the same period of 365 days.

**13. a.** $\dfrac{2\pi}{8} \approx 0.79$ m

**b.** $\dfrac{2\pi}{8.5} \approx 0.74$ m

**c.** $\dfrac{2\pi}{7.75} \approx 0.81$ m

**14. a.** $A \approx 73.2°$ or $A \approx 106.8$. Use the Law of Sines: $\frac{\sin A}{7} = \frac{\sin 40°}{4.7}$, so $\sin A \approx 0.95734$. Therefore, $A \approx 73.2°$ or $A \approx 106.8°$.

**b.** $A \approx 59.6°$ or $A \approx 120.5°$. Use the Law of Sines: $\frac{\sin A}{7.5} = \frac{\sin 16.7°}{2.5}$, so $\sin A \approx 0.862$. Therefore, $A \approx 59.6°$ or $A \approx 120.5°$.

---

**Lesson 10.3, Exercise 9**

| Angle $A$ | 0 | $\dfrac{\pi}{6}$ | $\dfrac{\pi}{4}$ | $\dfrac{\pi}{2}$ | $\dfrac{3\pi}{4}$ | $\pi$ | $\dfrac{4\pi}{3}$ | $\dfrac{5\pi}{3}$ | $\dfrac{11\pi}{6}$ |
|---|---|---|---|---|---|---|---|---|---|
| $x$-coordinate | 1 | $\dfrac{\sqrt{3}}{2}$ | $\dfrac{\sqrt{2}}{2}$ | 0 | $-\dfrac{\sqrt{2}}{2}$ | $-1$ | $-\dfrac{1}{2}$ | $\dfrac{1}{2}$ | $\dfrac{\sqrt{3}}{2}$ |
| $y$-coordinate | 0 | $\dfrac{1}{2}$ | $\dfrac{\sqrt{2}}{2}$ | 1 | $\dfrac{\sqrt{2}}{2}$ | 0 | $-\dfrac{\sqrt{3}}{2}$ | $-\dfrac{\sqrt{3}}{2}$ | $-\dfrac{1}{2}$ |
| Slope or $\tan A$ | 0 | $\dfrac{1}{\sqrt{3}}$ | 1 | undefined | $-1$ | 0 | $\sqrt{3}$ | $-\sqrt{3}$ | $-\dfrac{1}{\sqrt{3}}$ |

*Discovering Advanced Algebra Solutions Manual*
©2004 Key Curriculum Press

**15.**

| Degrees | Radians |
|---------|---------|
| 0° | 0 |
| 15° | $\frac{\pi}{12}$ |
| 30° | $\frac{\pi}{6}$ |
| 45° | $\frac{\pi}{4}$ |
| 60° | $\frac{\pi}{3}$ |
| 75° | $\frac{5\pi}{12}$ |
| 90° | $\frac{\pi}{2}$ |
| 105° | $\frac{7\pi}{12}$ |
| 120° | $\frac{2\pi}{3}$ |
| 135° | $\frac{3\pi}{4}$ |
| 150° | $\frac{5\pi}{6}$ |
| 165° | $\frac{11\pi}{12}$ |
| 180° | $\pi$ |

| Degrees | Radians |
|---------|---------|
| 195° | $\frac{13\pi}{12}$ |
| 210° | $\frac{7\pi}{6}$ |
| 225° | $\frac{5\pi}{4}$ |
| 240° | $\frac{4\pi}{3}$ |
| 255° | $\frac{17\pi}{12}$ |
| 270° | $\frac{3\pi}{2}$ |
| 285° | $\frac{19\pi}{12}$ |
| 300° | $\frac{5\pi}{3}$ |
| 315° | $\frac{7\pi}{4}$ |
| 330° | $\frac{11\pi}{6}$ |
| 345° | $\frac{23\pi}{12}$ |
| 360° | $2\pi$ |

**16. a.** 1.884 m/h. The tip of the second hand travels $(2 \cdot 0.5\pi)$, or $\pi$ cm every minute.

$$\left(\frac{\pi \text{ cm}}{1 \text{ min}}\right)\left(\frac{60 \text{ min}}{1 \text{ h}}\right)\left(\frac{1 \text{ m}}{100 \text{ cm}}\right) \approx 1.884 \text{ m/h}$$

**b.** 30 cm. If the minute hand is $r$ cm long, then its speed in m/h is $\left(\frac{2\pi r \text{ cm}}{1 \text{ h}}\right)\left(\frac{1 \text{ m}}{100 \text{ cm}}\right) = \frac{\pi r}{50}$ m/h. Solve $\frac{\pi r}{50} = \frac{60\pi}{100}$ for $r$ to get $r = 30$ cm.

**c.** 360 cm. If the hour hand is $r$ cm long, then its speed in m/h is $\left(\frac{2\pi r \text{ cm}}{12 \text{ h}}\right)\left(\frac{1 \text{ m}}{100 \text{ cm}}\right) = \frac{\pi r}{600}$ m/h. Solve $\frac{\pi r}{600} = \frac{60\pi}{100}$ for $r$ to get $r = 360$ cm.

**d.** Second hand: 377 radians/h; minute hand: 6.28 radians/h; hour hand: 0.52 radian/h. Use the formula

$$\frac{\text{radians}}{\text{h}} = \left(\frac{\text{revolutions}}{\text{h}}\right)\left(\frac{2\pi \text{ radians}}{1 \text{ revolution}}\right)$$

where the second hand has 60 revolutions/h, the minute hand has 1 revolution/h, and the hour hand has $\frac{1}{60}$ revolution/h.

**e.** The speed of the tip of a clock hand varies directly with the length of the hand. Angular speed is independent of the length of the hand.

**17. a.** For each function, write $y = f(x)$, exchange $x$ and $y$, and then solve for $y$.

**i.** $f^{-1}(x) = -\frac{2}{3}x + 4$

$x = -\frac{3}{2}y + 6$, so $y = -\frac{2}{3}(x - 6) = -\frac{2}{3}x + 4$

**ii.** $f^{-1}(x) = \pm\sqrt{x + 4} - 2$

$x = (y + 2)^2 - 4$, so $y = \pm\sqrt{x + 4} - 2$

**iii.** $f^{-1}(x) = \frac{\log(x + 8)}{\log 1.3} - 6$

$x = 1.3^{y+6} - 8$, so $x + 8 = 1.3^{y+6}$, and

$y = \frac{\log(x + 8)}{\log 1.3} - 6$

**b. i.**

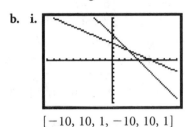

$[-10, 10, 1, -10, 10, 1]$

**ii.**

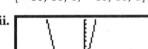

$[-10, 10, 1, -10, 10, 1]$

**iii.**

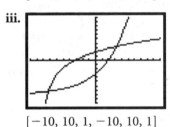

$[-10, 10, 1, -10, 10, 1]$

**c.** The inverses of i and iii are functions. The inverse of ii fails the vertical line test.

**18. a.** $\theta = 4°$ and $\theta = 356°$. Because 86° is 4° away from the vertical axis, and sine has a positive value at 86°, look for angles that have reference angle 4° and whose cosine is positive. These are 4° and $360° - 4° = 356°$.

**b.** $\theta = \frac{\pi}{12}$ and $\theta = \frac{11\pi}{12}$. The reference angle is $\frac{5\pi}{12}$, and cosine has a positive value at $\frac{19\pi}{12}$. Therefore look for angles that are $\frac{5\pi}{12}$ away from the vertical axis and whose sine is positive. These are $\frac{\pi}{2} - \frac{5\pi}{12} = \frac{\pi}{12}$ and $\frac{\pi}{2} + \frac{5\pi}{12} = \frac{11\pi}{12}$.

**c.** $\theta = 213°$ and $\theta = 327°$. The reference angle is 57°, and cosine has a negative value at 123°. Therefore look for angles that are 57° away from the vertical axis and whose sine is negative. These are $270° - 57° = 213°$ and $270° + 57° = 327°$.

**d.** $\theta = \frac{2\pi}{3}$ and $\theta = \frac{4\pi}{3}$. Because $\frac{7\pi}{6}$ is $\frac{\pi}{3}$ away from the vertical axis, and sine has a negative value at $\frac{7\pi}{6}$, look for angles that have reference angle $\frac{\pi}{3}$ and whose cosine is negative. These are $\pi - \frac{\pi}{3} = \frac{2\pi}{3}$ and $\pi + \frac{\pi}{3} = \frac{4\pi}{3}$.

**A.** Let $t$ be the time in minutes that the plane is in the air, starting with when it is 10 mi past the airport. Let $x$ be the east-west component of the distance from the plane to Detroit, and let $y$ be the north-south component of the distance from the plane to Detroit. Then the circular route of the plane has parametric equations $x = 300 + 10\cos\left(\frac{2\pi t}{15}\right)$ and $y = 10\sin\left(\frac{2\pi t}{15}\right)$. Use the distance formula to find the distance from the plane to the origin at a given time $t$,

$$d = \sqrt{\left(300 + 10\cos\left(\frac{2\pi t}{15}\right)\right)^2 + \left(10\sin\left(\frac{2\pi t}{15}\right)\right)^2}$$

The difference between this distance and the distance without the north-south component is

$$\left| 300 + 10\cos\left(\frac{2\pi t}{15}\right) - \sqrt{\left(300 + 10\cos\left(\frac{2\pi t}{15}\right)\right)^2 + \left(10\sin\left(\frac{2\pi t}{15}\right)\right)^2} \right|$$

Use the maximum function on your calculator to find that the maximum difference in distances is approximately 0.17 mi after 217 min. The difference is most likely insignificant because it is relatively small and doesn't reach its maximum until over 3 hours after the plane is put into its holding pattern.

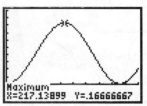

Maximum
X=217.13899  Y=.16666667

[0, 500, 50, −0.04, 0.2, 0.02]

**B.** Results will vary.

## LESSON 10.4

### EXERCISES

**1. a.** 27.8° and 0.49   **b.** −14.3° and −0.25

**c.** 144.2° and 2.52   **d.** 11.3° and 0.20

**2. a.** $\frac{\pi}{6}, \frac{5\pi}{6}, -\frac{11\pi}{6}, -\frac{7\pi}{6}$. All angles have reference angle $\frac{\pi}{6}$ and are in Quadrant I or II.

**b.** $\frac{3\pi}{8}, \frac{13\pi}{8}, -\frac{13\pi}{8}, -\frac{3\pi}{8}$. All angles have reference angle $\frac{3\pi}{8}$ and are in Quadrant I or IV.

**c.** 0.47, 5.81, −5.81, −0.47. All angles have reference angle 0.47 and are in Quadrant I or IV.

**d.** 1.47, 1.67, −4.81, −4.61. All angles have reference angle 1.47 and are in Quadrant I or III.

**3. a.** 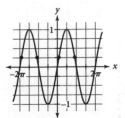   **b.**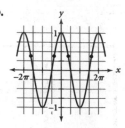

**c.** 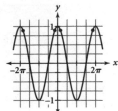   **d.**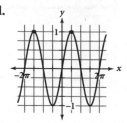

**4. a.**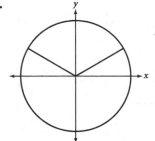

**b.**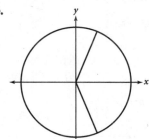

**c.**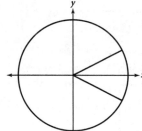

**d.**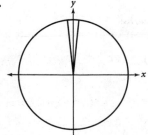

**5.** There is no angle whose sine is 1.28 because $-1 \le \sin x \le 1$.

**6.**

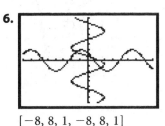

$[-8, 8, 1, -8, 8, 1]$

**7. a.** $x = \sin^{-1}(0.4665) \approx 0.485$ or $x \approx \pi - 0.485 \approx 2.656$

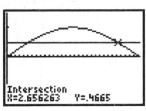

$[0, \pi, 0.1, -1.5, 1.5, 1]$

**b.** $x = -\cos^{-1}(-0.8113) \approx -2.517$ or $x = -2\pi + \cos^{-1}(-0.8113) \approx -3.766$

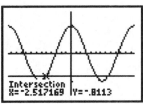

$[-2\pi, 2\pi, 0.5, -1.5, 1.5, 1]$

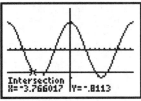

$[-2\pi, 2\pi, 0.5, -1.5, 1.5, 1]$

**8.** 6 solutions. There are six intersections of $y = -2.6$ and $y = 3 \sin x$ in the interval $0 \le x \le 6\pi$.

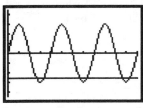

$[0, 6\pi, \pi/2, -4.5, 4.5, 1]$

**9.** $106.9°$. The largest angle is $A$, opposite the longest side. Use the Law of Cosines.

$$8.54^2 = 4.66^2 + 5.93^2 - 2(4.662)(5.932) \cos A$$

$$\cos A = \frac{8.54^2 - 4.66^2 - 5.93^2}{-2(4.66)(5.93)}$$

$$A \approx 106.9°$$

**10.** $55°$ or $125°$. Use the Law of Sines.

$$\frac{7}{\sin C} = \frac{3.9}{\sin 27°}, \text{ so } \sin C = \frac{7 \sin 27°}{3.9} \approx 0.8149$$

$\sin^{-1} 0.8149 \approx 55°$ is one possible angle. The other possible angle is $180° - 55° = 125°$.

**11. a.** Possible answer (using radians): $(10, 1.471)$, $(1, 0.785)$, $(0, 0)$, $(-1, -0.785)$, $(-10, -1.471)$

**b.** The domain is all real numbers. The range is $-\frac{\pi}{2} < y < \frac{\pi}{2}$ (or $-90° < y < 90°$). Sketches will vary.

**c.** The function $y = \tan^{-1} x$ is the portion of $x = \tan y$, such that $-\frac{\pi}{2} < y < \frac{\pi}{2}$ (or $-90° < y < 90°$).

**d.**

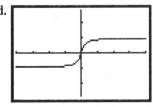

$[-20, 20, 5, -3\pi/2, 3\pi/2, \pi/2]$

**12.** $360° - 53.6° = 306.4°$; $360° + 53.6° = 413.6°$; $720° - 53.6° = 666.4°$

**13.** $650°$. The first point is $120°$ past the first maximum, so the next point is $120°$ before the second maximum, at $770° - 120° = 650°$.

**14. a.** $\frac{4}{5}$

**b.** $-\frac{2}{3}$

**c.** $\frac{\pi}{3}$. $\sin^{-1}\left(\sin \frac{2\pi}{3}\right)$ is the number between $-\frac{\pi}{2}$ and $\frac{\pi}{2}$ whose sine is the same as $\frac{2\pi}{3}$.

**d.** $45°$. $\cos^{-1}(\cos(-45°))$ is the angle between $0°$ and $180°$ whose cosine is the same as $\cos(-45°)$.

**15. a.** $8.0 \times 10^{-4}$ W/m$^2$; $6.9 \times 10^{-4}$ W/m$^2$

$$I_1 = 0.5\left(16 \times 10^{-4}\right) = 8.0 \times 10^{-4}$$

$$I_2 = \left(8 \times 10^{-4}\right) \cos^2 30° = \left(8 \times 10^{-4}\right)\frac{3}{4} \approx$$

$$6.0 \times 10^{-4}$$

**b.** $1.5 = 3 \cos^2 \theta$, so $\cos^2 \theta = 0.5$, and $\theta = \cos^{-1} \sqrt{0.5} = 45°$

**c.** $0 = 3 \cos^2 \theta$, so $\cos^2 \theta = 0$, and $\theta = \cos^{-1} 0 = 90°$

**16. a.** $\frac{7\pi}{10} \cdot \frac{180°}{\pi} = 126°$

**b.** $-205°\left(\frac{\pi}{180°}\right) = -\frac{41\pi}{36}$

**c.** $\left(\frac{5\pi \text{ radians}}{1 \text{ h}}\right)\left(\frac{180°}{\pi \text{ radians}}\right)\left(\frac{1 \text{ h}}{60 \text{ min}}\right) = 15°/\text{min}$

**17. a.** $y = \tan \frac{x + \frac{\pi}{2}}{2}$. The period is $2\pi$, so there is a horizontal stretch by a factor of 2. The phase shift is $-\frac{\pi}{2}$.

**b.** $y = 1 - 0.5 \tan\left(x - \frac{\pi}{2}\right)$. Phase shift may vary. The graph of $y = \tan x$ is shrunk vertically by a factor of 0.5 and reflected across the $x$-axis, then translated right $\frac{\pi}{2}$ units and up 1 unit. To understand the vertical shrink, note that the point $\left(\frac{\pi}{4}, 1.5\right)$ is on the graph, corresponding to the point $\left(\frac{\pi}{4}, 2\right)$ on the graph of $y = \tan x$.

**18. a.** Use the quadratic formula to get
$$x = \frac{6 \pm \sqrt{36 - 4(2)(3)}}{2(2)} = \frac{6 \pm \sqrt{12}}{4} = \frac{3 \pm \sqrt{3}}{2}.$$

**b.** $x = \frac{1}{2}$ or $x = 6$
$$2x^2 - 13x + 6 = 0$$
$$(2x - 1)(x - 6) = 0$$
$$x = \frac{1}{2} \text{ or } x = 6$$

**c.** Use the quadratic formula to get
$$x = \frac{-4 \pm \sqrt{16 - 4(3)(4)}}{2(3)} = \frac{-4 \pm \sqrt{-32}}{6} =$$
$$\frac{-4 \pm 4i\sqrt{2}}{6} = -\frac{2}{3} \pm \frac{2\sqrt{2}}{3}i.$$

**19. a.** Ellipse with center at origin, horizontal major axis of length 6 units, and vertical minor axis of length 4 units. The parametric equations are $x = 3 \cos t$ and $y = 2 \sin t$.

**b.** $\left(\frac{x + 1}{3}\right)^2 + \left(\frac{y - 2}{2}\right)^2 = 1$; $x = 3 \cos t - 1$ and $y = 2 \sin t + 2$

**c.** $(1.9, 1.5)$ and $(-2.9, 0.5)$

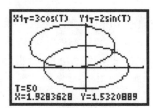

$[-5, 4, 1, -3, 5, 1]$
$0 \le t \le 360$

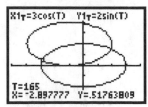

$[-5, 4, 1, -3, 5, 1]$
$0 \le t \le 360$

**d.** $(1.92, 1.54)$ and $(-2.92, 0.46)$. Write a system of equations.
$$\begin{cases} \left(\frac{x}{3}\right)^2 + \left(\frac{y}{2}\right)^2 = 1 \\ \left(\frac{x + 1}{3}\right)^2 + \left(\frac{y - 2}{2}\right)^2 = 1 \end{cases}$$

To solve the system, solve the first equation for $y$.
$$y = \pm 2\sqrt{1 - \left(\frac{x}{3}\right)^2}$$

Substitute this into the second equation, and solve for $x$.
$$\left(\frac{x + 1}{3}\right)^2 + \left(\frac{\pm 2\sqrt{1 - \left(\frac{x}{3}\right)^2} - 2}{2}\right)^2 = 1$$
Substitute.

$$\left(\frac{x + 1}{3}\right)^2 + \left(\pm\sqrt{1 - \left(\frac{x}{3}\right)^2} - 1\right)^2 = 1$$
Factor out 2 and divide.

$$\frac{x^2 + 2x + 1}{9} + 1 - \left(\frac{x}{3}\right)^2 - 2\sqrt{1 - \left(\frac{x}{3}\right)^2} + 1 = 1$$
Square.

$$\frac{2}{9}x + \frac{10}{9} = 2\sqrt{1 - \left(\frac{x}{3}\right)^2}$$
Combine terms.

$$\frac{1}{9}x + \frac{5}{9} = \sqrt{1 - \left(\frac{x}{3}\right)^2}$$
Divide both sides by 2.

$$\frac{1}{81}x^2 + \frac{10}{81}x + \frac{25}{81} = 1 - \left(\frac{x}{3}\right)^2$$
Square both sides.

$$\frac{10}{81}x^2 + \frac{10}{81}x - \frac{56}{81} = 0$$
Combine terms.

$$5x^2 + 5x - 28 = 0$$
Multiply both sides by $\frac{81}{2}$.

$$x = \frac{-5 \pm \sqrt{25 - 4(5)(-28)}}{2(5)}$$
Use the quadratic formula.

$$x \approx 1.92 \text{ or } x \approx -2.92$$
Evaluate

When $x \approx 1.92$, $y \approx 1.54$, and when $x \approx -2.92$, $y \approx 0.46$, so the two intersection points are $(1.92, 1.54)$ and $(-2.92, 0.46)$.

## LESSON 10.5

**EXERCISES**

**1. a.** $x = \left\{\frac{\pi}{3}, \frac{5\pi}{3}, \frac{7\pi}{3}, \frac{11\pi}{3}\right\}$. The reference angle is $\frac{\pi}{3}$, and it is in Quadrant I or IV because $\cos x$ is positive.

**b.** $x = \left\{\frac{7\pi}{6}, \frac{11\pi}{6}, \frac{19\pi}{6}, \frac{23\pi}{6}\right\}$. The reference angle is $\frac{\pi}{6}$, and it is in Quadrant III or IV because $\sin x$ is negative.

*Discovering Advanced Algebra Solutions Manual*
©2004 Key Curriculum Press

**2. a.** $x = \{1.831, 5.193\}$

$$2\sin(x + 1.2) - 4.22 = -4$$
$$2\sin(x + 1.2) = 0.22$$
$$\sin(x + 1.2) = 0.11$$

You need to find values between 1.2 and $(2\pi + 1.2)$ whose sine is 0.11. $\sin^{-1} 0.11 \approx 0.110$, so $x + 1.2 = \pi - 0.110 \approx 3.031$, and $x \approx 1.831$, or $x + 1.2 = 2\pi + 0.110 \approx 6.393$, and $x \approx 5.193$.

**b.** $x = \{1.784, 6.100\}$

$$7.4\cos(x - 0.8) + 12.3 = 16.4$$
$$7.4\cos(x - 0.8) = 4.1$$
$$\cos(x - 0.8) = 0.554$$

You need to find values between $-0.8$ and $(2\pi - 0.8)$ whose cosine is 0.554. $\cos^{-1} 0.554 \approx 0.984$, so $x - 0.8 \approx 0.984$, and $x \approx 1.784$, or $x - 0.8 = 2\pi - 0.984 \approx 5.300$, and $x \approx 6.100$.

**3. a.** Vertical translation: 5; average value: 5

**b.** Vertical stretch factor: 7; minimum: $5 - 7 = -2$; maximum: $5 + 7 = 12$; amplitude: $0.5(12 - (-2)) = 7$

**c.** Horizontal stretch factor: $\frac{11}{2\pi}$; period: 11

**d.** Horizontal translation: 9; phase shift: 9 (or 20 or 31 or 42 or 53 . . .)

**4. a.** Vertical translation: 18; average value: 18

**b.** Vertical stretch factor: $-17$; minimum: $18 - 17 = 1$; maximum: $18 + 17 = 35$; amplitude: $0.5(35 - 1) = 17$

**c.** Horizontal stretch factor: $\frac{15}{2\pi}$; period $= 15$

**d.** Horizontal translation: $-16$; phase shift: $-16$ (or $-1$ or 14 or 29 or 44 . . .)

**5.** $y = 1.2\sin\frac{2\pi t}{8} + 2$, or $y = 1.2\sin\frac{\pi t}{4} + 2$. The vertical stretch factor is 1.2, and the vertical translation is 2. The period is 8, so the horizontal stretch factor is $\frac{8}{2\pi}$. There is no horizontal translation because the curve starts at its average value. The equation is $y = 1.2\sin\left(\frac{2\pi x}{8}\right) + 2$.

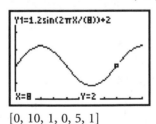

$[0, 10, 1, 0, 5, 1]$

**6.** 0.267 s, 0.533 s, 1.067 s, 1.333 s, 1.867 s. The amplitude of the vibration is 3 because the mass is pulled down 3 cm. There are 10 cycles in 8 s, so the period is 0.8 s. Because the spring begins at the bottom of its oscillation, use a reflection of a cosine curve. The equation is $y = -3\cos\left(\frac{2\pi x}{0.8}\right)$. Now find the times when the height, $y$, is 1.5 cm.

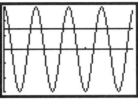

$[0, \pi, 1, -3, 3, 1]$

From the graph, you can see that there are five points of intersection in the interval $0 \le x \le 2$.

$$-3\cos\left(\frac{2\pi x}{0.8}\right) = 1.5$$
$$\cos\left(\frac{2\pi x}{0.8}\right) = -0.5$$
$$\frac{2\pi x}{0.8} = \frac{2\pi}{3}, \frac{4\pi}{3}, \frac{8\pi}{3}, \frac{10\pi}{3}, \frac{14\pi}{3}$$
$$\frac{x}{0.8} = \frac{1}{3}, \frac{2}{3}, \frac{4}{3}, \frac{5}{3}, \frac{7}{3}$$
$$x = 0.266667, 0.533333, 1.066667, 1.333333, 1.866667$$

The spring was 1.5 cm above its resting position at about 0.267 s, 0.533 s, 1.067 s, 1.333 s, and 1.867 s.

**7. a.** Possible answer: $v = 110\sqrt{2}\sin(120\pi t)$. The vertical stretch factor is $110\sqrt{2}$, and there is no vertical translation. The period is $\frac{1}{60}$ s, so the frequency is 60 cycles/s and the horizontal scale factor is $120\pi$. You can use either sine or cosine.

**b.**

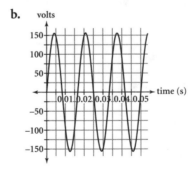

**8. a.** Possible answer: Let $t$ represent the number of hours after noon, and let $d$ represent the depth of the water in feet. $d = 11 + 5\cos\frac{\pi t}{7}$. The period is 14 h, so the horizontal stretch factor is $\frac{2\pi}{14}$, or $\frac{\pi}{7}$. The difference between the high-tide depth and the average depth, $16 - 11 = 5$, is the vertical scale factor. The average depth of 11 ft is the vertical shift. The curve starts at its maximum value, so use cosine.

**b.** Between 4:25 P.M. and 9:35 P.M., and between 6:25 A.M. and 11:35 A.M. the next day. Set $d$ equal to 9 and find the first four solutions.

$$11 + 5\cos\left(\frac{\pi t}{7}\right) = 9$$

$$5\cos\left(\frac{\pi t}{7}\right) = -2$$

$$\cos\left(\frac{\pi t}{7}\right) = -\frac{2}{5}$$

$$\frac{\pi t}{7} \approx 1.982,\ 4.301,\ 8.265,\ 10.584$$

$$t \approx 4.417,\ 9.583,\ 18.417,\ 23.583$$

The depth will be 9 ft at approximately 4 h 25 min, 9 h 35 min, 18 h 25 min, and 23 h 35 min after noon, so the boat will not be able to enter the harbor between 4:25 P.M. and 9:35 P.M., and between 6:25 A.M. and 11:35 A.M. the next day.

**9. a.** Possible answer: $y_1 = 3\sin 3\pi t$ and $y_2 = -4\cos 3\pi t$. The first mass has amplitude 3 cm, and the second mass has amplitude 4 cm. Both have period $\frac{8}{12} = \frac{2}{3}$, so the horizontal stretch factor is $\frac{2\pi}{\frac{2}{3}} = 3\pi$. At time $t = 0$, the first mass is at its resting position and rising, so use a sine curve for its equation; and the second mass is at a minimum height, so use a reflected cosine curve for its equation. Thus the equations are $y_1 = 3\sin 3\pi t$ and $y_2 = -4\cos 3\pi t$.

**b.** 0.2 s, 0.6 s, 0.9 s, 1.2 s, 1.6 s, 1.9 s. Use the intersect function on your calculator to find all intersections of the two graphs in the interval $0 \le t \le 2$.

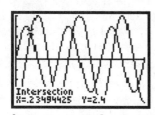

$[0, 2, 1, -4, 4, 1]$

**10. a.** $\frac{1}{1010000}$. The horizontal scale factor is $2000\pi \cdot 1010$, so the period is $\frac{2\pi}{2000\pi \cdot 1010} = \frac{1}{1010000}$.

**b.** 1,010,000 cycles/s

**c.** Answers will vary. Find the dial number of an AM radio station and substitute it for $n$. Period will be $\frac{1}{1000n}$. Frequency will be $1000n$.

**11. a.** $y = 12 + 2.4\sin\left(\frac{2\pi(354 - 80)}{365}\right) \approx 9.6$ h

**b.** Day 80, March 21, the spring equinox; and day 262.5, September 21 or 22, the autumn equinox. Graph the two functions $y_1 = 12 + 2.4\sin\left(\frac{2\pi(x - 80)}{365}\right)$ and $y_2 = 12$, and use the intersect function on your calculator to find the solutions for $0 \le x \le 365$.

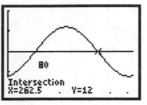

$[0, 365, 50, 8, 16, 2]$

$x = 80$ or $x = 262.5$. The 80th day of the year is March 21, and the 262nd day of the year is September 21.

**12. a.** Possible answer: $h = -10\cos\left(\frac{2\pi t}{20}\right)$. The period is 20 s, so the horizontal scale factor is $\frac{2\pi}{20}$. The diameter of the wheel is 20 ft, so the amplitude is 10. Sandra starts at the bottom of the wheel, so use a reflected cosine function. The equation is $h = -10\cos\left(\frac{2\pi t}{20}\right)$.

**b.** Possible answer: $h = 23 - 11\cos\left(\frac{2\pi t}{30}\right)$. The period is 30 s, so the horizontal scale factor is $\frac{2\pi}{30}$. The center of the two-wheel set is 23 ft above the ground, and the center of each wheel is 11 ft away from the center of the set. Therefore the vertical shift is 23 and the amplitude is 11. Sandra's wheel starts at the minimum height, so use a reflected cosine function. The equation is $h = 23 - 11\cos\left(\frac{2\pi t}{20}\right)$.

**c.** Possible answer: $h = 23 - 11\cos\left(\frac{2\pi t}{30}\right) - 10\cos\left(\frac{2\pi t}{20}\right)$

**d.** 6. Graph the functions $y = 23 - 11\cos\left(\frac{2\pi x}{30}\right) - 10\cos\left(\frac{2\pi x}{20}\right)$ and $y = 6$ on your calculator, and find the number of intervals the cosine curve is below $y = 6$ between 0 s and 5 min, or 360 s. There are 6 intervals.

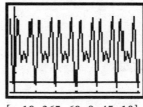

$[-10, 365, 60, 0, 45, 10]$

**13.** Construct a circle and its diameter for the main rotating arm. Construct a circle with a fixed radius at each end of the diameter. Make a point on each of these two circles. Animate these points and one endpoint of the diameter.

**14.** $\theta = \{-48°, 132°, 312°\}$. Graph the equations $y = \tan x$ and $y = -1.111$, and use the intersect function on your calculator.

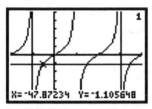

$[-180, 360, 90, -5, 5, 1]$

**15.** The sector has the larger area. The triangle's area is about 10.8 cm²; the sector's area is 12.5 cm². The area of the triangle is $\frac{1}{2}(5)(5)\sin 60° \approx 10.8$. To calculate the area of the sector, first find the angle. The radius and arc length are both 5 cm, so the angle is 1 radian. Therefore the area is $\frac{1}{2}(5)^2(1) = 12.5$.

**16.** $(x + 2)^2 + (y - 4)^2 = \frac{484}{13}$. To find the radius of the circle, calculate the distance from the tangent line to the center point, $(-2, 4)$. To do this, find the line perpendicular to the line $2x - 3y - 6 = 0$ that passes through the point $(-2, 4)$, and find its intersection with the line $2x - 3y - 6 = 0$.

The line perpendicular to the line $2x - 3y - 6 = 0$ that passes through the point $(-2, 4)$ is $3x + 2y - 2 = 0$.

Use any method to find the intersection of these two lines, which is the point $\left(\frac{18}{13}, -\frac{14}{13}\right)$.

The distance from $\left(\frac{18}{13}, -\frac{14}{13}\right)$ to $(-2, 4)$ is $\sqrt{\left(\frac{18}{13} + 2\right)^2 + \left(-\frac{14}{13} - 4\right)^2} = \sqrt{\frac{484}{13}}$.

Therefore the equation of the circle is $(x + 2)^2 + (y - 4)^2 = \frac{484}{13}$.

**17. a.** $\pm 1, \pm 5, \pm\frac{1}{2}, \pm\frac{5}{2}$. The numerator must be a factor of the constant term, 5, so it is $\pm 1$ or $\pm 5$. The denominator must be a factor of the leading coefficient, 2, so it is $\pm 1$ or $\pm 2$.

**b.** $x = \frac{1}{2}$. Substitute each possible root in the polynomial and evaluate.

**c.** $x = \pm\sqrt{5}$. Given the rational root $x = \frac{1}{2}$, use polynomial long division to divide $P(x)$ by $(2x - 1)$.

$$2x - 1 \overline{)\,2x^3 - x^2 - 10x + 5\,}$$

with work:

$$\begin{array}{r} x^2 - 5 \\ 2x^3 - x^2 \\ \hline 0 - 10x + 5 \\ -10x + 5 \\ \hline 0 \end{array}$$

So, $2x^3 - x^2 - 10x + 5 = (2x - 1)(x^2 - 5)$. The roots of $(x^2 - 5)$ are $\pm\sqrt{5}$.

**d.** $P(x) = 2\left(x - \frac{1}{2}\right)\left(x + \sqrt{5}\right)\left(x - \sqrt{5}\right)$, or $P(x) = (2x - 1)\left(x + \sqrt{5}\right)\left(x - \sqrt{5}\right)$

**18. a.** The radius of $C_2$ is 18. The radius of $C_3$ is 54. For each circle, draw a perpendicular line from the center of the circle to one of the legs of $\angle P$.

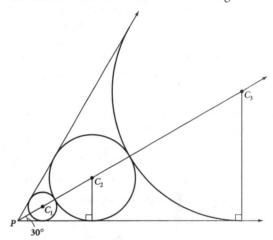

This gives a 30°-60°-90° triangle with the shortest side equal to the radius of the circle, so the hypotenuse is twice the radius. Therefore the distance from the angle's vertex to the closest point on the circle equals the radius of the circle. The distance from the vertex of the angle to the closest point of $C_1$ is 6, and the distance from the vertex of the angle to the farthest point of $C_1$ is $3(6) = 18$. Let $r_2$ be the radius of $C_2$. The distance from the vertex of the angle to the closest point of $C_2$ is $r_2$. This is also the farthest point of $C_1$, so $r_2 = 18$. Let $r_3$ be the radius of $C_3$. Using the same reasoning, $r_3 = 3(18) = 54$.

**b.** The radius of $C_n$ is $6\left(3^{n-1}\right)$. Let $r_n$ be the radius of $C_n$. Then $r_1 = 6$ and $r_n = 3r_{n-1}$ where $n \geq 2$. This can be written explicitly as $r_n = 6\left(3^{n-1}\right)$.

**EXTENSIONS**

**A.** Research results will vary.

**B.** Results will vary.

**EXERCISES**

**1.** Graph $y = \dfrac{1}{\tan x}$.

**2.** For 2a–d, graph the two equations on your calculator.

**a.** Yes

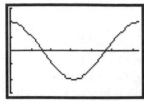

$[0, 2\pi, 1, -1.5, 1.5, 0.5]$

**b.** No

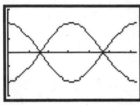

$[0, 2\pi, 1, -1.5, 1.5, 0.5]$

**c.** No

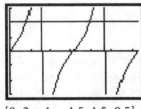

$[0, 2\pi, 1, -1.5, 1.5, 0.5]$

**d.** Yes

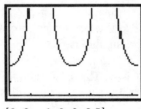

$[0, 2\pi, 1, 0, 3, 0.5]$

**3.** Proof: $\tan x(\cot x + \tan x) \overset{?}{=} \sec^2 x$   Original equation.

$\tan x \cot x + (\tan x)^2 \overset{?}{=} \sec^2 x$   Distribute.

$\tan x \cdot \dfrac{1}{\tan x} + \tan^2 x \overset{?}{=} \sec^2 x$   Reciprocal identity.

$1 + \tan^2 x \overset{?}{=} \sec^2 x$   Multiply.

$\sec^2 x = \sec^2 x$   Pythagorean identity.

**4. a.** $\sec \dfrac{\pi}{6} = \dfrac{1}{\cos \dfrac{\pi}{6}} = \dfrac{1}{\dfrac{\sqrt{3}}{2}} = \dfrac{2}{\sqrt{3}} = \dfrac{2\sqrt{3}}{3}$

**b.** $\csc \dfrac{5\pi}{6} = \dfrac{1}{\sin \dfrac{5\pi}{6}} = \dfrac{1}{\dfrac{1}{2}} = 2$

**c.** $\csc \dfrac{2\pi}{3} = \dfrac{1}{\sin \dfrac{2\pi}{3}} = \dfrac{1}{\dfrac{\sqrt{3}}{2}} = \dfrac{2}{\sqrt{3}} = \dfrac{2\sqrt{3}}{3}$

**d.** Undefined. $\sec x = \dfrac{1}{\cos x}$ and $\cos \dfrac{3\pi}{2} = 0$, so $\sec \dfrac{3\pi}{2}$ is undefined.

**e.** $\cot \dfrac{5\pi}{3} = \dfrac{1}{\tan \dfrac{5\pi}{3}} = -\dfrac{1}{\sqrt{3}} = -\dfrac{\sqrt{3}}{3}$

**f.** $\csc \dfrac{4\pi}{3} = \dfrac{1}{\sin \dfrac{4\pi}{3}} = \dfrac{1}{-\dfrac{\sqrt{3}}{2}} = -\dfrac{2}{\sqrt{3}} = -\dfrac{2\sqrt{3}}{3}$

**5.** A trigonometric equation may be true for some, all, or none of the defined values of the variable. A trigonometric identity is a trigonometric equation that is true for all defined values of the variable.

**6. a.** Odd. $\sin(-x) = -\sin x$

**b.** Even. $\cos(-x) = \cos x$

**c.** Odd. $\tan(-x) = \dfrac{\sin(-x)}{\cos(-x)} = \dfrac{-\sin x}{\cos x} = -\tan x$

**d.** Odd. $\cot(-x) = \dfrac{1}{\tan(-x)} = \dfrac{1}{-\tan x} = -\cot x$

**e.** Even. $\sec(-x) = \dfrac{1}{\cos(-x)} = \dfrac{1}{\cos x} = \sec x$

**f.** Odd. $\csc(-x) = \dfrac{1}{\sin(-x)} = \dfrac{1}{-\sin x} = -\csc x$

**7. a.** Proof:    $\cos 2A \overset{?}{=} 1 - 2\sin^2 A$   Original equation.

$\cos^2 A - \sin^2 A \overset{?}{=} 1 - 2\sin^2 A$   Given identity.

$1 - \sin^2 A - \sin^2 A \overset{?}{=} 1 - 2\sin^2 A$   Pythagorean identity.

$1 - 2\sin^2 A = 1 - 2\sin^2 A$   Combine terms.

**b.** Proof:    $\cos 2A \overset{?}{=} 2\cos^2 A - 1$   Original equation.

$\cos^2 A - \sin^2 A \overset{?}{=} 2\cos^2 A - 1$   Given identity.

$\cos^2 A - \left(1 - \cos^2 A\right) \overset{?}{=} 2\cos^2 A - 1$   Pythagorean identity.

$2\cos^2 A - 1 = 2\cos^2 A - 1$   Combine terms.

**8. a.**

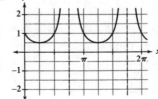

*Discovering Advanced Algebra Solutions Manual*

©2004 Key Curriculum Press

**b.**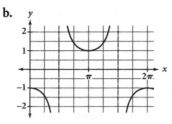

**9.** Possible answers:

   **a.** $y = \sin x$

   **b.** $y = \cos x$

   **c.** $y = \cot x$

   **d.** $y = \cos x$

   **e.** $y = -\sin x$

   **f.** $y = -\tan x$

   **g.** $y = \sin x$

   **h.** $y = -\sin x$

   **i.** $y = \tan x$

**10. a.** 1.98, 4.30, 8.27

$$\sec x = -2.5$$
$$\frac{1}{\cos x} = -2.5$$
$$\cos x = -0.4$$

The first three positive solutions are $\cos^{-1}(-0.4) \approx 1.98$, $2\pi - \cos^{-1}(-0.4) \approx 4.30$, and $2\pi + \cos^{-1}(-0.4) \approx 8.27$.

  **b.** No such values. If $\csc x = 0.4$, then $\sin x = \frac{1}{0.4} = 2.5$, which is impossible because $-1 \leq \sin x \leq 1$.

**11. a.**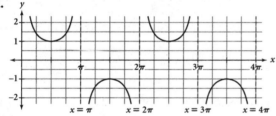

  **b.**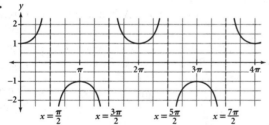

  **c.**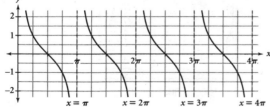

**12.** Possible answers:

  **a.** $y = \tan 2x - 1$. This is a transformation of the tangent graph. The period is $\frac{\pi}{2}$, so the horizontal stretch factor is 2. It is also translated down 1 unit.

  **b.** $y = \cot\left(x + \frac{\pi}{2}\right) + 1$. This is a transformation of the cotangent graph. The period is $\pi$, so there is no horizontal stretch factor. One possible phase shift is $-\frac{\pi}{2}$. It is also translated up 1 unit.

  **c.** $y = 0.5 \csc x + 1$. This is a transformation of the cosecant graph. The period is $2\pi$, so there is no horizontal stretch factor. The local minimums and maximums are 1 unit apart, at $y = 0.5$ and $y = 1.5$, so there is a vertical shrink factor of 0.5. It is also translated up 1 unit.

  **d.** $y = \tan\frac{1}{3}x$. This is a transformation of the tangent graph. The period is $3\pi$, so the horizontal stretch factor is $\frac{1}{3}$. There is no vertical stretch or translation.

**13. a.** 2; undefined at $\theta = 0$, $\theta = \pi$

| | |
|---|---|
| $2\cos^2\theta + \dfrac{\sin\theta}{\csc\theta} + \sin^2\theta$ | Original expression. |
| $2\cos^2\theta + \dfrac{\sin\theta}{\dfrac{1}{\sin\theta}} + \sin^2\theta$ | Reciprocal identity. |
| $2\cos^2\theta + \sin^2\theta + \sin^2\theta$ | Divide. |
| $2\left(\cos^2\theta + \sin^2\theta\right) = 2$ | Pythagorean identity. |

The original expression contains the cosecant function, so it is undefined at $\theta = 0$ and $\theta = \pi$.

  **b.** $3\cos\theta$; undefined at $\theta = 0$, $\theta = \frac{\pi}{2}$, $\theta = \pi$, $\theta = \frac{3\pi}{2}$

| | |
|---|---|
| $(\sec\theta)\left(2\cos^2\theta\right) + (\cot\theta)(\sin\theta)$ | Original expression. |
| $\left(\dfrac{1}{\cos\theta}\right)\left(2\cos^2\theta\right) + \left(\dfrac{\cos\theta}{\sin\theta}\right)(\sin\theta)$ | Reciprocal identities. |
| $2\cos\theta + \cos\theta = 3\cos\theta$ | Multiply. |

The original expression contains the cotangent function, so it is undefined at $\theta = 0$, $\theta = \frac{\pi}{2}$, $\theta = \pi$, and $\theta = \frac{3\pi}{2}$.

  **c.** $\tan^2\theta + \tan\theta$; undefined at $\theta = \frac{\pi}{2}$, $\theta = \frac{3\pi}{2}$

| | |
|---|---|
| $\sec^2\theta + \dfrac{1}{\cot\theta} + \dfrac{\sin^2\theta - 1}{\cos^2\theta}$ | Original expression. |
| $\dfrac{1}{\cos^2\theta} + \tan\theta + \dfrac{\sin^2\theta - 1}{\cos^2\theta}$ | Reciprocal identities. |
| $\dfrac{\sin^2\theta}{\cos^2\theta} + \tan\theta$ | Add first and last terms. |
| $\tan^2\theta + \tan\theta$ | Reciprocal identity. |

The original expression contains the cotangent function, so it is undefined at $\theta = \frac{\pi}{2}$ and $\theta = \frac{3\pi}{2}$.

**d.** $\sec\theta$; undefined at $\theta = 0$, $\theta = \frac{\pi}{2}$, $\theta = \pi$, $\theta = \frac{3\pi}{2}$

| | |
|---|---|
| $\sin\theta(\cot\theta + \tan\theta)$ | Original expression. |
| $\sin\theta\left(\dfrac{\cos\theta}{\sin\theta} + \dfrac{\sin\theta}{\cos\theta}\right)$ | Reciprocal identities. |
| $\cos\theta + \dfrac{\sin^2\theta}{\cos\theta}$ | Distribute. |
| $\dfrac{\cos^2\theta + \sin^2\theta}{\cos\theta}$ | Combine fractions. |
| $\dfrac{1}{\cos\theta} = \sec\theta$ | Pythagorean identity and reciprocal identity. |

The original expression contains the tangent and cotangent functions, so it is undefined at $\theta = 0$, $\theta = \frac{\pi}{2}$, $\theta = \pi$, and $\theta = \frac{3\pi}{2}$.

**14. a.** Sample answer: Select the second time value, 10:22, as time 0. The new time values are $-369$, 0, 378, 747, 1130, 1497, 1876, 2243.

**b.**

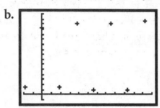

$[-400, 2400, 200, -1, 16, 1]$

**c.  i.** $\dfrac{1.6 + 1.42 + 1.01 + 0.94}{4} = 1.2425$ m

**ii.** $\dfrac{13.61 + 14.15 + 14.09 + 14.71}{4} = 14.14$ m

**iii.** $\dfrac{1.2425 + 14.14}{2} = 7.69125$ m

**iv.** 373 min. The times in minutes between tide changes are 369, 378, 369, 383, 367, 379, and 367. The average of these values is about 373.

**d.** Possible answer: $y = 6.45\cos\left(\frac{2\pi x}{746}\right) + 7.69$. The graph starts at a peak, so use a cosine curve. The average time between high tide and low tide is 373 min, so the period is $2(373) = 746$, and the horizontal stretch factor is $\frac{746}{2\pi}$. The amplitude is $0.5(14.14 - 1.24) = 6.45$, so this is the vertical stretch factor. The mean water level, 7.69, is the vertical translation. Therefore the equation is $y = 6.45\cos\left(\frac{2\pi x}{746}\right) + 7.69$.

**e.**

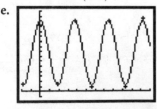

$[-400, 2400, 200, -1, 16, 1]$

**f.** 12.06 m. 12:00 on June 10 is 98 min after the starting time. Using the equation found in 14d, the tide is predicted to be at a height of $y = 6.45\cos\left(\frac{2\pi \cdot 98}{746}\right) + 7.69 \approx 12.06$ m.

**g.** Only one high tide at 12:06. Look for high tides in the interval $2258 \le x \le 3698$, which represents June 12. The peaks in the function come at multiples of 746 min. The only one of these in the given interval is $4 \cdot 746 = 2984$. The time 12:06 is 2984 min after the starting time (741 min after the last recorded time of 23:45 on June 11).

**15. a.** \$1505.12. The equation modeling the value of the savings bond is $P = 500\left(1 + \frac{0.065}{12}\right)^{12t}$, where $t$ represents the number of years since the bond was purchased. When Juan is 17, the value of the bond is $P = 500\left(1 + \frac{0.065}{12}\right)^{12 \cdot 17} = \$1505.12$.

**b.** Another 15 years, or until he's 32. Set $P$ equal to 4000 and solve for $t$.

$$4000 = 500\left(1 + \frac{0.065}{12}\right)^{12t}$$

$$8 = \left(1 + \frac{0.065}{12}\right)^{12t}$$

$$\frac{\log 8}{\log\left(1 + \frac{0.065}{12}\right)} = 12t$$

$$t = \frac{\log 8}{12\log\left(1 + \frac{0.065}{12}\right)} \approx 32$$

Juan would have to wait until he's 32, which is another 15 years.

**16. a.** $d(x) = \frac{60}{100 + x}$. The amount of pure medicine remains constant at 60 mL, while the total amount of medication becomes $(100 + x)$.

**b.** $\dfrac{60}{100 + 20} = 0.5$, or 50%

**c.** 100 mL. Solve the equation $0.30 = \frac{60}{100 + x}$ for $x$.

$$0.30(100 + x) = 60$$
$$100 + x = 200$$
$$x = 100$$

**d.** The asymptote is the $x$-axis, $y = 0$. The more water that is added, the closer the concentration will get to 0%. However, it will never actually become 0% because it will always have some medicine.

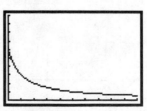

$[0, 1000, 100, 0, 1, 0.1]$

**17. a.** $c(x) = \frac{60 + x}{100 + x}$. The amount of pure medicine becomes $(60 + x)$, and the total amount of medication becomes $(100 + x)$.

**b.** $\frac{60 + 20}{100 + 20} = 0.\overline{6}$, or $66\frac{2}{3}\%$

**c.** 300 mL. Solve the equation $0.90 = \frac{60 + x}{100 + x}$ for $x$.

$$0.90(100 + x) = 60 + x$$
$$90 + 0.90x = 60 + x$$
$$30 = 0.10x$$
$$x = 300$$

**d.** The asymptote is the line $y = 1$. The more pure medicine that is added, the closer the concentration will get to 100%. However, it will never actually become 100% because it will always have some water.

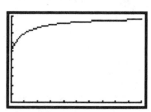

[0, 1000, 100, 0, 1, 0.1]

**e.** Use the diluting function to obtain concentrations less than 60%. Use the concentrating function to obtain concentrations greater than 60%.

**18. a.** $5^x = 14$, so $x = \frac{\log 14}{\log 5} \approx 1.64$

**b.** $\log_3 15 = \log_3 x$, so $x = 15$

**c.** $x = 1$

$$0.5^{2x} = 0.25$$
$$\left(2^{-1}\right)^{2x} = 2^{-2}$$
$$-2x = -2$$
$$x = 1$$

**d.** $x = \frac{\log 100}{\log 6} \approx 2.57$

**e.** $\log x = 1.25$, so $x = 10^{1.25} \approx 17.78$

**f.** $x = 3\log_5 5 = 3 \cdot 1 = 3$

**g.** $x = 2$

$$\log x = \frac{1}{4}\log 16$$
$$\log x = \log\left(16^{1/4}\right)$$
$$\log x = \log 2$$
$$x = 2$$

**h.** $x = 495$

$$\log\left(\frac{5 + x}{5}\right) = 2$$
$$\frac{5 + x}{5} = 10^2$$
$$5 + x = 500$$
$$x = 495$$

**IMPROVING YOUR VISUAL THINKING SKILLS**

Answers will vary. For the illustration in your book, a sample equation that models the water fountain is $y = -1.15x(x + 3.25)$.

**EXTENSIONS**

**A.** See the solutions to Take Another Look activities 1 and 2 on page 261.

**B.** The length of the secant line of an arc of length $x$ through the unit circle is sec $x$. Using similar triangles, the $y$-coordinate of the point $B$ is $\frac{\sin x}{\cos x} = \tan x$. Therefore, assuming $x$ is in Quadrant I, the secant line $\overrightarrow{OB}$ has length $\sqrt{1^2 + \tan^2 x} = \sec x$.

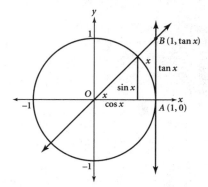

**LESSON 10.7**

**EXERCISES**

**1.** In 1a–d, look for substitutions of $A$ and $B$ demonstrating no identity. Suppose $A = 2$ and $B = 3$.

**a.** Not an identity

$$\cos(2 + 3) = \cos 5 \approx 0.2837$$
$$\cos 2 + \cos 3 \approx -0.4161 + -0.09900 \approx -1.4061$$

**b.** Not an identity

$$\sin 5 \approx -0.9589$$
$$\sin 2 + \sin 3 \approx 0.9093 + 0.1411 \approx 1.0504$$

**c.** Not an identity

$$\cos 4 \approx -0.6536$$
$$2\cos 2 \approx 2 \cdot -0.4161 \approx -0.8323$$

**d.** Not an identity

$\sin 4 \approx -0.7568$

$2 \sin 2 \approx 2 \cdot 0.9093 \approx 1.8186$

**2. a.** $\cos(2\pi - A) = \cos(2\pi) \cos A + \sin(2\pi) \sin A = 1 \cdot \cos A + 0 \cdot \sin A = \cos A$

  **b.** $\sin\left(\dfrac{3\pi}{2} - A\right) = \sin\dfrac{3\pi}{2} \cos A - \cos\dfrac{3\pi}{2} \sin A = -1 \cdot \cos A - 0 \cdot \sin A = -\cos A$

**3. a.** $\cos 1.5 \cos 0.4 + \sin 1.5 \sin 0.4 = \cos(1.5 - 0.4) = \cos 1.1$

  **b.** $\cos 2.6 \cos 0.2 - \sin 2.6 \sin 0.2 = \cos(2.6 + 0.2) = \cos 2.8$

  **c.** $\sin 3.1 \cos 1.4 - \cos 3.1 \sin 1.4 = \sin(3.1 - 1.4) = \sin 1.7$

  **d.** $\sin 0.2 \cos 0.5 + \cos 0.2 \sin 0.5 = \sin(0.2 + 0.5) = \sin 0.7$

**4. a.** $\sin -\dfrac{11\pi}{12} = \sin\left(\dfrac{\pi}{4} - \dfrac{7\pi}{6}\right)$

$= \sin\dfrac{\pi}{4} \cos\dfrac{7\pi}{6} - \cos\dfrac{\pi}{4} \sin\dfrac{7\pi}{6}$

$= \left(\dfrac{\sqrt{2}}{2}\right)\left(\dfrac{-\sqrt{3}}{2}\right) - \left(\dfrac{\sqrt{2}}{2}\right)\left(\dfrac{-1}{2}\right)$

$= \dfrac{-\sqrt{6} + \sqrt{2}}{4}$

  **b.** $\sin\dfrac{7\pi}{12} = \sin\left(\dfrac{\pi}{3} + \dfrac{\pi}{4}\right)$

$= \sin\dfrac{\pi}{3} \cos\dfrac{\pi}{4} + \cos\dfrac{\pi}{3} \sin\dfrac{\pi}{4}$

$= \left(\dfrac{\sqrt{3}}{2}\right)\left(\dfrac{\sqrt{2}}{2}\right) + \left(\dfrac{1}{2}\right)\left(\dfrac{\sqrt{2}}{2}\right)$

$= \dfrac{\sqrt{6} + \sqrt{2}}{4}$

  **c.** $\tan\dfrac{\pi}{12} = \tan\left(\dfrac{\pi}{3} - \dfrac{\pi}{4}\right)$

$= \dfrac{\tan\dfrac{\pi}{3} - \tan\dfrac{\pi}{4}}{1 + \tan\dfrac{\pi}{3} \tan\dfrac{\pi}{4}}$

$= \dfrac{\sqrt{3} - 1}{1 + \sqrt{3} \cdot 1}$

$= \left(\dfrac{\sqrt{3} - 1}{1 + \sqrt{3}}\right)\left(\dfrac{\sqrt{3} - 1}{\sqrt{3} - 1}\right)$

$= \dfrac{4 - 2\sqrt{3}}{3 - 1} = 2 - \sqrt{3}$

**d.** $\cos\dfrac{\pi}{8} = \cos\dfrac{\dfrac{\pi}{4}}{2} = \sqrt{\dfrac{1 + \cos\dfrac{\pi}{4}}{2}}$

$= \sqrt{\dfrac{1 + \dfrac{\sqrt{2}}{2}}{2}} = \sqrt{\dfrac{1}{2} + \dfrac{\sqrt{2}}{4}}$

(Note that $\dfrac{\pi}{8}$ is in Quadrant I, so $\cos\dfrac{\pi}{8}$ is positive.)

**5.** $\dfrac{4\sqrt{5}}{9}$. The angle is in Quadrant II, so $\cos x$ is negative. Therefore, $\cos x = -\sqrt{1 - \left(\dfrac{2}{3}\right)^2} = -\dfrac{\sqrt{5}}{3}$. Then $\sin 2x = 2 \sin x \cos x = 2\left(\dfrac{-2}{3}\right)\left(\dfrac{-\sqrt{5}}{3}\right) = \dfrac{4\sqrt{5}}{9}$.

**6.** Proof: $\sin(A + B) \overset{?}{=} \sin A \cos B + \cos A \sin B$

$\cos\left(\dfrac{\pi}{2} - (A + B)\right) \overset{?}{=} \sin A \cos B + \cos A \sin B$

$\cos\left(\left(\dfrac{\pi}{2} - A\right) - B\right) \overset{?}{=} \sin A \cos B + \cos A \sin B$

$\cos\left(\dfrac{\pi}{2} - A\right) \cos B + \sin\left(\dfrac{\pi}{2} - A\right) \sin B$

$\overset{?}{=} \sin A \cos B + \cos A \sin B$

$\sin A \cos B + \cos A \sin B = \sin A \cos B + \cos A \sin B$

**7.** Proof: $\sin(A - B) \overset{?}{=} \sin A \cos B - \cos A \sin B$

$\sin(A + (-B)) \overset{?}{=} \sin A \cos B - \cos A \sin B$

$\sin A \cos(-B) + \cos A \sin(-B)$

$\overset{?}{=} \sin A \cos B - \cos A \sin B$

$\sin A \cos B + \cos A(-\sin B)$

$\overset{?}{=} \sin A \cos B - \cos A \sin B$

$\sin A \cos B - \cos A \sin B = \sin A \cos B - \cos A \sin B$

**8.** Proof: $\sin 2A \overset{?}{=} 2 \sin A \cos A$

$\sin(A + A) \overset{?}{=} 2 \sin A \cos A$

$\sin A \cos A + \cos A \sin A \overset{?}{=} 2 \sin A \cos A$

$2 \sin A \cos A = 2 \sin A \cos A$

**9.** Proof: $\cos(2A) \overset{?}{=} \cos^2 A - \sin^2 A$

$\cos(A + A) \overset{?}{=} \cos^2 A - \sin^2 A$

$\cos A \cos A - \sin A \sin A \overset{?}{=} \cos^2 A - \sin^2 A$

$\cos^2 A - \sin^2 A = \cos^2 A - \sin^2 A$

**10.** Sample answer: $\cos(\tan x)$ is a composite function, and not a product. As an example of how this equation fails, substitute 0 for $x$. The left side of the equation is $\cos(\tan 0) = \cos 0 = 1$, and the right side of the equation is $\sin 0 = 0$.

**11.** Possible answer: Substitute 1 for *A* and 2 for *B*:
$\tan(1 + 2) \neq \tan 1 + \tan 2$; because $\tan 3 \approx -0.1425$, whereas $\tan 1 + \tan 2 \approx -0.6276$

$$\tan(A + B) = \frac{\sin(A + B)}{\cos(A + B)}$$

$$= \frac{\sin A \cos B + \cos A \sin B}{\cos A \cos B - \sin A \sin B}$$

$$= \frac{\dfrac{\sin A \cos B + \cos A \sin B}{\cos A \cos B}}{\dfrac{\cos A \cos B - \sin A \sin B}{\cos A \cos B}}$$

$$= \frac{\dfrac{\sin A}{\cos A} + \dfrac{\sin B}{\cos B}}{1 - \dfrac{\sin A}{\cos A} \cdot \dfrac{\sin B}{\cos B}}$$

$$= \frac{\tan A + \tan B}{1 - \tan A \tan B}$$

**12.** $\tan 2A = \tan(A + A) = \dfrac{\tan A + \tan A}{1 - \tan A \tan A} = \dfrac{2 \tan A}{1 - \tan^2 A}$

**13. a.** $\cos 2A = 1 - 2 \sin^2 A$

$2 \sin^2 A = 1 - \cos 2A$

$\sin^2 A = \dfrac{1 - \cos 2A}{2}$

**b.** $\cos 2A = 2 \cos^2 A - 1$

$2 \cos^2 A = \cos 2A + 1$

$\cos^2 A = \dfrac{\cos 2A + 1}{2}$

**14. a.**

| a | b | Period |
|---|---|--------|
| 1 | 2 | $2\pi$ |
| 2 | 3 | $2\pi$ |
| 2 | 4 | $\pi$ |
| 3 | 4 | $2\pi$ |
| 3 | 6 | $\dfrac{2\pi}{3}$ |
| 4 | 6 | $\pi$ |
| 4 | 8 | $\dfrac{\pi}{2}$ |
| 4 | 12 | $\dfrac{\pi}{2}$ |

Sample graph when $a = 3$ and $b = 4$:

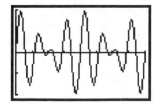

$[0, 4\pi, \pi/2, -2, 2, 1]$

**b.** The period is $2\pi$ divided by the greatest common factor of *a* and *b*.

**15. a.**

| a | b | Period |
|---|---|--------|
| 2 | 4 | $8\pi$ |
| 2 | 3 | $12\pi$ |
| 2 | 5 | $20\pi$ |
| 4 | 6 | $24\pi$ |
| 3 | 6 | $12\pi$ |

Sample graph when $a = 2$ and $b = 5$:

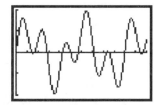

$[0, 24\pi, 2\pi, -2, 2, 1]$

**b.** The period is $2\pi$ multiplied by the least common multiple of *a* and *b*.

**c.** $48\pi$. Multiply $2\pi$ by the least common multiple of 3, 4, and 8, which is 24.

**16. a.** The period is $\dfrac{2\pi}{262 \cdot 2\pi} = \dfrac{1}{262} \approx 0.003817$ s.

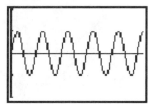

$[0, 0.02, 0, -2, 2, 1]$

**b.** The equation for the out-of-tune piano is $y = \sin(265 \cdot 2\pi x)$. The period of this function is $\dfrac{1}{265} \approx 0.003774$ s.

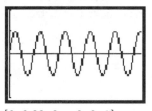

$[0, 0.02, 0, -2, 2, 1]$

**c.** $y = \sin(262 \cdot 2\pi x) + \sin(265 \cdot 2\pi x)$

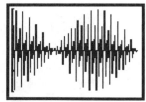

$[0, 0.5, 0, -2, 2, 1]$

**17. a.** $x = \dfrac{1}{\cos 144°} \approx -1.2361$

**b.** $x = \dfrac{1}{\sin \frac{24\pi}{9}} \approx 1.1547$

**c.** $x = \dfrac{1}{\tan 3.92} \approx 1.0141$

**d.** $x = \dfrac{\cos 630°}{\sin 630°} = \dfrac{0}{-1} = 0$

**18. a.** $\theta \approx 28°$ or $\theta \approx 208°$. The two values are $\tan^{-1} 0.5317 \approx 28°$ or about $180° + 28° = 208°$.

**b.** $\theta \approx 105°$ or $\theta \approx 255°$

$$\dfrac{1}{\cos \theta} = -3.8637$$

$$\cos \theta = \dfrac{1}{-3.8637} \approx -0.2588$$

The two values are $\cos^{-1} -0.2588 \approx 105°$ or about $360° - 105° = 255°$.

**c.** $\theta \approx 64°$ or $\theta \approx 116°$

$$\dfrac{1}{\sin \theta} = 1.1126$$

$$\sin \theta = \dfrac{1}{1.1126} \approx 0.8988$$

The two values are $\sin^{-1} 0.8988 \approx 64°$ or about $180° - 64° = 116°$.

**d.** $\theta \approx 167°$ or $\theta \approx 347°$

$$\dfrac{1}{\tan \theta} = -4.3315$$

$$\tan \theta = \dfrac{1}{-4.3315} \approx -0.2309$$

$$\tan^{-1}(-0.2309) \approx -13°$$

The two values are about $180° - 13° = 167°$ or about $360° - 13° = 347°$.

**19. a.** Let $x$ represent time in seconds, and let $y$ represent height in meters above the surface of the water if it were calm.

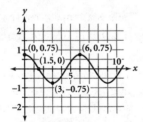

**b.** $y = 0.75 \cos \frac{\pi}{3}x$. The frequency is 10 cycles/min, or $\frac{1}{6}$ cycle/s, so the period is 6 s. Therefore the horizontal stretch factor is $\frac{2\pi}{6} = \frac{\pi}{3}$. The amplitude is $0.5(1.5) = 0.75$, so the function is $y = 0.75 \cos \frac{\pi}{3}x$.

**c.** $y = 0.75 \sin\left(\frac{\pi}{3}(x + 1.5)\right)$. Translate the sine curve $y = 0.75 \sin \frac{\pi}{3}x$ left 1.5 units $\left(\frac{1}{4}\right.$ of a cycle$\left.\right)$ to get the same curve as in 19b.

**A.** See the solution to Take Another Look activity 5 on page 261.

**B.** Results will vary. Here are graphs for some compositions.

$y = \cos(\tan x)$            $y = \tan(\cos x)$

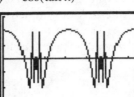 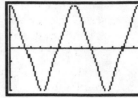

$[0, 2\pi, 1, -1.5, 1.5, 0.5]$    $[0, 4\pi, 1, -1.5, 1.5, 0.5]$

$y = \cos(\sin x)$            $y = \sin(\cos x)$

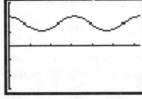 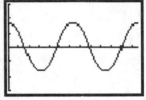

$[0, 2\pi, 1, -1.5, 1.5, 0.5]$    $[0, 4\pi, 1, -1.5, 1.5, 0.5]$

## EXPLORATION • POLAR COORDINATES

### QUESTIONS

**1.** The height ($y$-value) of a point on the graph of $y = a \cos nx$ corresponds to the value of $r$ when $x = \theta$. The number of local maximums and minimums of $y = a \cos nx$ in the domain $0° \leq x \leq 360°$ corresponds to the number of petals; if $n$ is even, the number of petals is the same as the number of local maximums and minimums in the domain $0° \leq x \leq 360°$; if $n$ is odd, the number of petals is half the number of local maximums and minimums.

**2. a.** The graphs are exactly the same. The difference is where the graph begins.

**b.** The graphs created with sine are rotated 90° counterclockwise in relation to the graphs created with cosine.

**c.** The coefficient $a$ is a dilation scale factor.

**3.** For 3a–d, use the general forms of equations you have already seen: $r = a \cos n\theta$ and $r = a \sin n\theta$ for rose curves, and $r = a(\cos \theta + 1)$ and $r = a(\sin \theta + 1)$ for cardioids. Possible answers:

**a.** $r = 3 \cos \theta$. This can be seen as a rose curve with one petal and maximum 3. The value for $\theta = 0$ is 3, so use a cosine curve.

**b.** $r = 3 \cos 2\theta$ and $r = 2 \sin 2\theta$. This is two rose curves, each with four petals, so $n = 2$. The larger curve has maximum value 3 and is at its maximum when $\theta = 0$, so it is a cosine curve. The smaller one has maximum value 2 and is 0 when $\theta = 0$, so it is a sine curve.

**c.** $r = -2(\cos \theta + 1)$. Start with the cardioid equation $r = a(\cos \theta + 1)$ because it is symmetric across the horizontal axis. The values of $|r|$ range from 0 to 4, so $|a| = 2$. Experiment to see that $a = -2$.

**d.** $r = 2(\cos \theta + 1)$ and $r = -2(\cos \theta + 1)$. See the solution to 3c.

**4. a.** General form: $r = a\theta$

**b.** The spiral continues to grow outward.

**c.** For negative values of $\theta$, the spiral reflects across the vertical axis.

**5.** Sample answer: In terms of rectangular coordinates, polar equations do not represent $y$ as a function of $x$; rose curves, cardioids, spirals, and so on, do not pass a vertical line test. In terms of polar coordinates, the polar equations in this exploration are functions, meaning $r$ is a function of $\theta$, as indicated by the notation $r = f(\theta)$; for any value of $\theta$, there is only one value of $r$.

**EXTENSION**
Results will vary.

## CHAPTER 10 REVIEW

### EXERCISES

**1. a.** Quadrant I; $60° + 360° = 420°$; $60° \cdot \dfrac{\pi}{180°} = \dfrac{\pi}{3}$

**b.** Quadrant III; $\dfrac{4\pi}{3} + 2\pi = \dfrac{10\pi}{3}$; $\dfrac{4\pi}{3} \cdot \dfrac{180°}{\pi} = 240°$

**c.** Quadrant IV; $330° - 360° = -30°$; $330° \cdot \dfrac{\pi}{180°} = \dfrac{11\pi}{6}$

**d.** Quadrant IV; $-\dfrac{\pi}{4} + 2\pi = \dfrac{7\pi}{4}$; $-\dfrac{\pi}{4} \cdot \dfrac{180°}{\pi} = -45°$

**2. a.** $\sin 60° = \dfrac{\sqrt{3}}{2}$; $\cos 60° = \dfrac{1}{2}$

**b.** $\sin \dfrac{4\pi}{3} = -\dfrac{\sqrt{3}}{2}$; $\cos \dfrac{4\pi}{3} = -\dfrac{1}{2}$. The reference angle is $\dfrac{\pi}{3}$; in Quadrant III, both sine and cosine are negative.

**c.** $\sin 330° = -\dfrac{1}{2}$; $\cos 330° = \dfrac{\sqrt{3}}{2}$. The reference angle is 30°; in Quadrant IV, sine is negative and cosine is positive.

**d.** $\sin\left(-\dfrac{\pi}{4}\right) = -\dfrac{\sqrt{2}}{2}$; $\cos\left(-\dfrac{\pi}{4}\right) = \dfrac{\sqrt{2}}{2}$. $\sin(-x) = -\sin x$ and $\cos(-x) = \cos x$.

**3.** In 3a–d, use the fact that the period of the function $y = b \cos a(x - h)$ is $\dfrac{2\pi}{a}$. Possible equations are given.

**a.** Period $= \dfrac{2\pi}{3}$; $y = -2 \cos\left(3\left(x - \dfrac{2\pi}{3}\right)\right)$

**b.** Period $= \dfrac{\pi}{2}$; $y = 3 \sin\left(4\left(x - \dfrac{\pi}{8}\right)\right)$

**c.** Period $= \pi$; $y = \csc\left(2\left(x + \dfrac{\pi}{4}\right)\right)$

**d.** Period $= \dfrac{\pi}{2}$; $y = \cot\left(2\left(x - \dfrac{\pi}{4}\right)\right) + 1$

**4. a.** Amplitude 2; phase shift $\dfrac{\pi}{6}$; translation 0; frequency $\dfrac{3}{2\pi}$

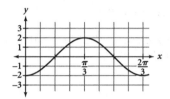

**b.** Amplitude 3; phase shift 0; translation 0; frequency $\dfrac{2}{\pi}$

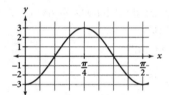

**5. a.** $y = -2 \sin 2x - 1$. This is a reflected sine curve with amplitude 2, so the vertical scale factor is $-2$. The period is $\pi$, so the horizontal scale factor is 2. The graph is translated down 1 unit.

**b.** $y = \sin 0.5x + 1.5$. This is a sine curve with amplitude 1. The period is $4\pi$, so the horizontal scale factor is 0.5. The graph is translated up 1.5 units.

**c.** $y = 0.5 \tan\left(x - \dfrac{\pi}{4}\right)$. This is a tangent curve shrunk vertically by a factor of 0.5 and translated right $\dfrac{\pi}{4}$ units.

**d.** $y = 0.5 \sec 2x$. This is a secant curve with local maximums and minimums at $\pm 0.5$, so the vertical scale factor is 0.5. The period is $\pi$, so the horizontal scale factor is 2. There is no translation.

**6.** Area: $\dfrac{1}{2}(3^2)\left(\dfrac{\pi}{4}\right) = \dfrac{9\pi}{8}$ cm$^2$; arc length: $3\left(\dfrac{\pi}{4}\right) = \dfrac{3\pi}{4}$ cm

**7.** For $\cos y = x$: domain: $-1 \le x \le 1$, range: all real numbers. For $y = \cos^{-1} x$: domain: $-1 \le x \le 1$, range: $0 \le y \le \pi$

**8.** For 8a and b, draw a right triangle with the appropriate side lengths.

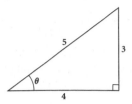

**a.** $\frac{3}{5}$

**b.** $\frac{4}{5}$

**c.** $\frac{8}{17}$ because $\sin\left(\sin^{-1} x\right) = x$.

**9.** $y = -3\sin\left(\frac{x - \frac{\pi}{2}}{4}\right)$. The curve is reflected across the $x$-axis and has amplitude 3, so the vertical scale factor is $-3$. The period is $8\pi$, so the horizontal scale factor is $\frac{2\pi}{8\pi} = \frac{1}{4}$. The phase shift is $\frac{\pi}{2}$, so there is a horizontal translation right $\frac{\pi}{2}$ units.

**10. a.** Proof: $\sec A - \sin A \tan A \stackrel{?}{=} \cos A$

$$\frac{1}{\cos A} - \sin A\left(\frac{\sin A}{\cos A}\right) \stackrel{?}{=} \cos A$$

$$\frac{1 - \sin^2 A}{\cos A} \stackrel{?}{=} \cos A$$

$$\frac{\cos^2 A}{\cos A} \stackrel{?}{=} \cos A$$

$$\cos A = \cos A$$

**b.** Proof: $\dfrac{1}{\sin^2 A} - \dfrac{1}{\tan^2 A} \stackrel{?}{=} 1$

$$\frac{1}{\sin^2 A} - \frac{\cos^2 A}{\sin^2 A} \stackrel{?}{=} 1$$

$$\frac{1 - \cos^2 A}{\sin^2 A} \stackrel{?}{=} 1$$

$$\frac{\sin^2 A}{\sin^2 A} \stackrel{?}{=} 1$$

$$1 = 1$$

**c.** Proof: $\dfrac{\sec A \cos B - \tan A \sin B}{\sec A} \stackrel{?}{=} \cos(A + B)$

$$\frac{\cos B}{\sec A} - \frac{\tan A \sin B}{\sec A} \stackrel{?}{=} \cos(A + B)$$

$$\cos B \cos A - \frac{\sin A}{\cos A} \sin B \cos A \stackrel{?}{=} \cos(A + B)$$

$$\cos B \cos A - \sin A \sin B \stackrel{?}{=} \cos(A + B)$$

$$\cos(A + B) = \cos(A + B)$$

**11.** 0.174 s, 0.659 s, 1.008 s, 1.492 s, 1.841 s, 2.325 s, 2.675 s. Let $x$ represent the time in seconds from when the mass is released, and let $y$ represent the height in cm of the mass relative to its resting position. The height of the mass can be represented by a reflected cosine curve with amplitude 2 and period $\frac{10}{12} = \frac{5}{6}$. Therefore the equation

is $y = -2\cos\left(\frac{12\pi}{5}x\right)$. Find all solutions to the equation $-0.5 = -2\cos\left(\frac{12\pi}{5}x\right)$ with $0 \leq x \leq 3$ by using the intersect function on your calculator. Graph the function to see that there are seven solutions.

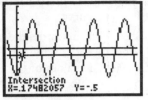

$[-0.25, 3.25, 1, -3, 3, 0.5]$

**12. a.** Let $x$ represent time in hours, and let $y$ represent tide height in meters.

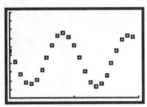

$[0, 24, 12, 0, 10, 1]$

**b.** Possible answer: $y = 2.985\cos\left(\frac{\pi}{6}(x - 10)\right) + 4.398$

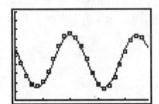

$[0, 24, 12, 0, 10, 1]$

The two occurrences of highest recorded tide are at 10:00 and 22:00, with heights 7.5 m and 7.33 m. Average these to get 7.415 m. The two occurrences of lowest recorded tide are at 4:00 and 16:00, with heights 1.56 m and 1.33 m. Average these to get 1.445 m. The average distance between high tide and low tide is then $7.415 - 1.445 = 5.97$ m, so the amplitude of the curve is $0.5 \cdot 5.97$, or 2.985 m. The high tides occur 12 h apart, as do the low tides, so the period is 12. Use an appropriate choice of sinusoidal curve and phase shift. For example, use a cosine curve with phase shift 10 (because the first high tide is at 10:00). Finally, the average tide height is 4.398, which is the vertical translation. Putting all of this information together, $y = 2.985\cos\left(\frac{\pi}{6}(x - 10)\right) + 4.398$.

**c.** Approximately 1.81 m. This time is represented by $x = 63$. Substitute this value in the equation from 12b to get $y = 2.985\cos\left(\frac{\pi}{6}(63 - 10)\right) + 4.398 \approx 1.81$ m.

**d.** Between 0:00 and 0:37, between 7:23 and 12:37, and between 19:23 and 23:59. Use the equation in 12b to find the values of $x$ for which $y \geq 5$, where $72 \leq x < 96$.

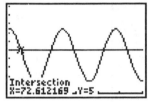

[70, 100, 5, 0, 10, 1]

The intersections occur at $x = 72.61$, $79.39$, $84.61$, and $91.39$, which translate in times on November 20, 2002, as 0:37, 7:23, 12:37, and 19:23. Use these intersections and look at where the graph is above the line $y = 5$. The ship can enter the harbor between 0:00 and 0:37, between 7:23 and 12:37, and between 19:23 and 23:59.

## TAKE ANOTHER LOOK

**1.** $AF = \sec\theta$; $GI = \cot\theta$; $AD = \sin\theta$; $AI = \csc\theta$; and $CF = \tan\theta$

$$\sec\theta = \frac{\text{hypotenuse}}{\text{adjacent}} = \frac{AF}{AC} = \frac{AF}{1}$$

$$\cot\theta = \frac{\text{adjacent}}{\text{opposite}} = \frac{AJ}{IJ} = \frac{GI}{AG} = \frac{GI}{1}$$

$$\sin\theta = \frac{\text{opposite}}{\text{hypotenuse}} = \frac{BE}{AE} = \frac{AD}{AE} = \frac{AD}{1}$$

$$\csc\theta = \frac{\text{hypotenuse}}{\text{opposite}} = \frac{AI}{IJ} = \frac{AI}{1}$$

$$\tan\theta = \frac{\text{opposite}}{\text{adjacent}} = \frac{CF}{AC} = \frac{CF}{1}$$

**2.** Possible answer:

$$\sin\frac{5\pi}{12} = \sin\left(\left(\frac{\pi}{3} + \frac{\pi}{4}\right) - \frac{\pi}{6}\right)$$

$$= \sin\left(\frac{\pi}{3} + \frac{\pi}{4}\right)\cos\frac{\pi}{6} - \cos\left(\frac{\pi}{3} + \frac{\pi}{4}\right)\sin\frac{\pi}{6}$$

$$= \left(\sin\frac{\pi}{3}\cos\frac{\pi}{4} + \cos\frac{\pi}{3}\sin\frac{\pi}{4}\right)\cos\frac{\pi}{6} -$$

$$\left(\cos\frac{\pi}{3}\cos\frac{\pi}{4} - \sin\frac{\pi}{3}\sin\frac{\pi}{4}\right)\sin\frac{\pi}{6}$$

$$= \left(\frac{\sqrt{3}}{2} \cdot \frac{\sqrt{2}}{2} + \frac{1}{2} \cdot \frac{\sqrt{2}}{2}\right)\frac{\sqrt{3}}{2} -$$

$$\left(\frac{1}{2} \cdot \frac{\sqrt{2}}{2} - \frac{\sqrt{3}}{3} \cdot \frac{\sqrt{2}}{2}\right)\frac{1}{2}$$

$$= \left(\frac{\sqrt{6}}{4} + \frac{\sqrt{2}}{4}\right)\frac{\sqrt{3}}{2} - \left(\frac{\sqrt{2}}{4} - \frac{\sqrt{6}}{4}\right)\frac{1}{2}$$

$$= \frac{\sqrt{2} + \sqrt{6}}{4}$$

You could also use the equations $\sin(\pi - x) = \sin x$ or $\sin x = \cos\left(\frac{\pi}{2}x\right)$.

$$\sin\frac{5\pi}{12} = \sin\left(\pi - \left(\frac{\pi}{3} + \frac{\pi}{4}\right)\right) = \sin\left(\frac{\pi}{3} + \frac{\pi}{4}\right)$$

$$\sin\frac{5\pi}{12} = \cos\left(\frac{\pi}{2} - \frac{5\pi}{12}\right) = \cos\frac{\pi}{12} = \cos\left(\frac{\pi}{3} - \frac{\pi}{4}\right)$$

The sine or cosine of any sum or difference of multiples of $\frac{\pi}{4}$ and $\frac{\pi}{3}$ can be evaluated by using the sum or difference identities repeatedly.

**3.** A circle can be divided into 400 gradians. Gradian measure has the convenient property that a right angle measures exactly 100 gradians. It is sometimes used in surveying and road grades. Gradians were proposed by the French shortly after the French Revolution.

A compass is divided into 32 points. For example, NE is between N and E, and NNE is between N and NE.

A mil is a military unit for measuring angles. It is based on the milliradian $\left(\frac{1}{1000}\text{ radian}\right)$, but instead of the approximately 6283.1583 milliradians in a circle, the U.S. military has standardized 6400 mils in a circle.

Just as a circle can be divided into degrees, radians, and gradians, a sphere can be divided into steradians. There are $4\pi$ steradians in a sphere.

**4.** The equations are $x = r(t - \sin t)$ and $y = r(1 - \cos t)$, where $r$ is the radius of the wheel. First, suppose you fix the wheel with point $A$ at the origin and that point $P$ travels around the circle in a clockwise direction. Then the position of $P$ relative to the angle $t$ (measured clockwise from the "down" position) is given by the parametric equations $x = -r\sin t$ and $y = -r\cos t$. Now consider the coordinates of point $P$ as the wheel travels. The $x$-coordinate is the same as the arc length from $C$ to $P$, which is $rt$. The $y$-coordinate is $r$. Therefore the path traveled by $P$ can be expressed parametrically as $x = rt - r\sin t$, $y = r - r\cos t$, or $x = r(t - \sin t)$, $y = r(1 - \cos t)$.

**5.** $\cos^2 A = \dfrac{1 + \cos 2A}{2}$

$$\cos A = \pm\sqrt{\frac{1 + \cos 2A}{2}}$$

$$\cos\frac{\theta}{2} = \pm\sqrt{\frac{1 + \cos\theta}{2}}$$

$$\sin^2 A = \frac{1 - \cos 2A}{2}$$

$$\sin A = \pm\sqrt{\frac{1 - \cos 2A}{2}}$$

$$\sin\frac{\theta}{2} = \pm\sqrt{\frac{1 - \cos\theta}{2}}$$

$$\tan\frac{\theta}{2} = \frac{\sin\frac{\theta}{2}}{\cos\frac{\theta}{2}} = \frac{\pm\sqrt{\dfrac{1 + \cos\theta}{2}}}{\pm\sqrt{\dfrac{1 - \cos\theta}{2}}} = \pm\sqrt{\frac{1 - \cos\theta}{1 + \cos\theta}}$$

## LESSON 11.1

### EXERCISES

**1.** $-3, -1.5, 0, 1.5, 3; u_1 = -3, d = 1.5$

**2.** $S_1 = 2, S_2 = 8, S_3 = 18, S_4 = 32, S_5 = 50$. The first term of the sequence, $u_1$, is 2 and the common difference, $d$, is 4, so the explicit formula for the partial sums of the series is $S_n = \left(\frac{4}{2}\right)n^2 + \left(2 - \frac{4}{2}\right)n = 2n^2$. Substitute values for $n$ to find the partial sums.

$S_1 = 2(1)^2 = 1$

$S_2 = 2(2)^2 = 8$

$S_3 = 2(3)^2 = 18$

$S_4 = 2(4)^2 = 32$

$S_5 = 2(5)^2 = 50$

**3. a.** $3 + 4 + 5 + 6; S_4 = 18$. Substitute the integers 1 through 4 for $n$ in the formula $u_n = n + 2$, and sum the resulting values to get $3 + 4 + 5 + 6 = 18$.

**b.** $-2 + 1 + 6; S_4 = 5$. Substitute the integers 1 through 3 for $n$ in the formula $u_n = n^2 - 3$, and sum the resulting values to get $-2 + 1 + 6 = 5$.

**4.** $S_{50} = 7650$. The first term of the sequence is 6 and the common difference is 6, so $S_n = \left(\frac{6}{2}\right)n^2 + \left(6 - \frac{6}{2}\right)n = 3n^2 + 3n$. To find the sum of the first 50 terms, substitute 50 for $n$: $S_{50} = 3(50)^2 + 3(50) = 7650$.

**5.** $S_{75} = 5700$. The first term of the sequence is 2 and the common difference is 2, so $S_n = \left(\frac{2}{2}\right)n^2 + \left(2 - \frac{2}{2}\right)n = n^2 + n$. To find the sum of the first 75 terms, substitute 75 for $n$: $S_{75} = (75)^2 + 75 = 5700$.

**6. a.** Substitute 75 for $n$: $u_{75} = 2(75) - 1 = 149$.

**b.** $S_{75} = 5625$. You can use either the explicit or alternative formula for the partial sum of an arithmetic series. $u_1 = 2(1) - 1 = 1$ and $u_2 = 2(2) - 1 = 3$, so $d = u_2 - u_1 = 3 - 1 = 2$. Using the explicit formula, $S_n = \left(\frac{2}{2}\right)n^2 + \left(1 - \frac{2}{2}\right)n = n^2$. Substitute 75 for $n$: $S_{75} = (75)^2 = 5625$.

Using the alternative formula, the first term, $u_1$, is 1 and the last term, $u_{75}$, is $2(75) - 1 = 149$, so $S_{75} = \frac{75(1 + 149)}{2} = 5625$.

**c.** $S_{75} - S_{19} = 5264$. The expression represents the sum of the first 75 terms minus the sum of the first 19 terms, or $S_{75} - S_{19}$. You know that $S_{75} = 5625$ from 6b. Using the explicit formula $S_n = n^2$ from 6b, substitute 19 for $n$: $S_{19} = (19)^2 = 631$. Therefore, $S_{75} - S_{19} = 5625 - 631 = 5264$.

**7. a.** $u_{46} = 229$. The first term is 4 and the common difference is $9 - 4$, or 5, so the formula is $u_n = 4 + (n - 1)5 = 5n - 1$. Substitute 46 for $n$: $u_{46} = 5(46) - 1 = 229$.

**b.** $u_n = 5n - 1$, or $u_1 = 4$ and $u_n = u_{n-1} + 5$ where $n \geq 2$

**c.** $S_{46} = 5359$. The first term is 4 and the common difference is 5, so $S_n = \left(\frac{5}{2}\right)n^2 + \left(4 - \frac{5}{2}\right)n = 2.5n^2 + 1.5n$. Substitute 46 for $n$: $S_{46} = 2.5(46)^2 + 1.5(46) = 5359$.

**8. a.** 1200 min, or 20 h. Each day represents a term in an arithmetic sequence, so the first term is 45 and the common difference is 5. The partial sums of the series are $S_n = \left(\frac{5}{2}\right)n^2 + \left(45 - \frac{5}{2}\right)n = 2.5n^2 + 42.5n$. Substitute 15 for $n$: $S_{15} = 2.5(15)^2 + 42.5(15) = 1200$. You will practice 1200 min, or 20 h.

**b.** 4550 min, or 75 h 50 min. Substitute 35 for $n$ in the formula from 8a: $S_{35} = 2.5(35)^2 + 42.5(35) = 4550$. You will practice 4550 minutes, or 75 hours 50 minutes.

**9. a.** 3, 6, 9, 12, 15, 18, 21, 24, 27, 30. There are 3 cans in the first row, 6 cans in the second row, and 9 cans in the third row as shown. The number of cans in each row forms an arithmetic sequence where the first term, $u_1$, is 3 and the common difference, $d$, is 3. Use Home screen recursion on your calculator to find the first ten terms of the sequence.

**b.** $u_1 = 3$ and $u_n = u_{n-1} + 3$ where $n \geq 2$

**c.** 3384 cans. $u_1 = 3$ and $d = 3$, so $S_n = \left(\frac{3}{2}\right)n^2 + \left(3 - \frac{3}{2}\right)n = 1.5n^2 + 1.5n$. Substitute 47 for $n$: $S_{47} = 1.5(47)^2 + 1.5(47) = 3384$. If the cans are stacked 47 rows high, it will take 3384 cans to build the display.

**d.** 13 rows with 15 cans left over. You know that $S_n = 288$, and you want to find $n$, the number of rows. Substitute 288 for $S_n$ in the explicit formula from 9c and solve for $n$.

$288 = 1.5n^2 + 1.5n$

$192 = n^2 + n$

$0 = n^2 + n - 192$

$n = \frac{-1 \pm \sqrt{1^2 - 4(1)(-192)}}{2(1)}$

$n \approx 13.365$ or $n \approx -14.365$

The number of rows must be a positive integer, so Jessica can make the display 13 rows high. $S_{13} = 1.5(13)^2 + 1.5(13) = 273$, so 273 cans are used to make the 13 rows with $288 - 273$, or 15 cans left over.

**10. a.** $S_{1000} = 500,500$. The first term, $u_1$, is 1 and the last term, $u_{1000}$, is 1000, so $S_{1000} = \frac{1000(1 + 1000)}{2} = 500,500$.

**b.** $S_{2000} - S_{1000} = 1,500,500$. Find the sum of the second 1000 positive integers by subtracting $S_{1000}$, the sum of the integers 1 through 1000, from $S_{2000}$, the sum of the integers 1 through 2000.

$$S_{2000} - S_{1000} = \frac{2000(1 + 2000)}{2} - 500500 =$$

$$2001000 - 500500 = 1500500$$

Alternatively, using $u_1 = 1001$ as the first term and $u_{1000} = 2000$ as the last term, the sum of the second 1000 positive integers is $\frac{1000(1001 + 2000)}{2} =$ 1,500,500.

**c.** Answers will vary. You may recognize that the sum is increased by exactly 1 million from 10a to 10b. The sum of the third 1000 positive integers may be the third term in an arithmetic sequence with a common difference of 1 million, so the value of the term would be $1,500,500 + 1,000,000 = 2,500,500$.

**d.** $S_{3000} - S_{2000} = 2,500,500$. Using the method in 10b, subtract $S_{2000}$, the sum of the integers 1 through 2000, from $S_{3000}$, the sum of the integers 1 through 3000.

$$S_{3000} - S_{2000} = \frac{3000(1 + 3000)}{2} + 2001000 =$$

$$4501500 - 2001000 = 2500500$$

Alternatively, using $u_1 = 2001$ as the first term and $u_{1000} = 3000$ as the last term, the sum of the third 1000 positive integers is $\frac{1000(2001 + 3000)}{2} =$ 2,500,500.

**e.** Each of these 1000 values is 2000 more than the corresponding value between 1 and 1000, so add $1000(2000)$ to the first sum.

**11.** $S_x = x^2 + 64x$. Write out the first few terms of the sequence: $u_1 = 65$, $u_2 = 67$, and $u_3 = 69$. The first term is 65 and the common difference is 2, so $S_x = \left(\frac{2}{2}\right)x^2 + \left(65 - \frac{2}{2}\right)x = x^2 + 64x$.

**12. a.** 21 trapezoids. The number of toothpicks needed to build each row can be expressed as an arithmetic sequence where the first term is 5, the second term is 9, and the third term is 13.

The common difference is 4 and $S_n = \left(\frac{4}{2}\right)n^2 + \left(5 - \frac{4}{2}\right)n = 2n^2 + 3n$. Substitute 1000 for $S_n$ to find $n$, the number of trapezoids in the last row.

$$1000 = 2n^2 + 3n$$

$$2n^2 + 3n - 1000 = 0$$

$$n = \frac{-3 \pm \sqrt{3^2 - 4(2)(-1000)}}{2(2)}$$

$$n \approx 21.62 \text{ or } n \approx -23.12$$

Only a positive integer answer makes sense, so there are 21 trapezoids in the last row.

**b.** 21 rows. The number of trapezoids in each row is the same as the row number, so the 21st row has 21 trapezoids.

**c.** 945 toothpicks. Using the formula for $S_n$, substitute 21 for $n$: $S_{21} = 2(21)^2 + 3(21) = 945$.

**d.** The numbers of toothpicks in each row form a sequence, whereas the total numbers of toothpicks used form a series.

**13. a.** $u_1 = 4.9$ and $u_n = u_{n-1} + 9.8$ where $n \geq 2$. The first term is 4.9, and in each subsequent second, 9.8 is added to the previous term.

**b.** $u_n = 4.9 + 9.8(n - 1) = 9.8n - 4.9$

**c.** 93.1 m. Substitute 10 for $n$ in the explicit formula to find that $u_{10} = 9.8(10) - 4.9 = 93.1$.

**d.** 490 m. You need to find the total distance the object has fallen during the first 10 seconds, so use the explicit formula for $S_n$. The first term is 4.9 and the common difference is 9.8, so $S_n = \left(\frac{9.8}{2}\right)n^2 + \left(4.9 - \frac{9.8}{2}\right)n = 4.9n^2$. Substitute 10 for $n$: $S_{10} = 4.9(10)^2 = 490$. The object falls 490 m during the first 10 seconds.

**e.** From 13d, the explicit formula is $S_n = 4.9n^2$.

**f.** Approximately 8.2 s. Substitute 331 for $S_n$ and solve for $n$: $331 = 4.9n^2$, so $67.55 = n^2$, and $n \approx 8.2$.

**14. a.** **i.** The values in the sequence increase by a factor of 2, so the long-run value of the sequence increases without bound.

  **ii.** The values in the sequence decrease by a factor of $\frac{1}{2}$, approaching a long-run value of 0.

**b.** **i.** 2

  **ii.** $\frac{1}{2}$

**c.** **i.** If you add all the terms of a sequence that increases without bound, the sum will be infinitely large.

  **ii.** Using Home screen recursion on your calculator, generate enough partial sums of the series to see that the sum approaches 4.

**15. a.** 576,443 people. After 1 hour, four 15-minute time periods have passed. If 42%, or 0.42 of the people who have not heard the warning become aware of the approaching tornado every 15 minutes, then $1 - 0.42$, or 0.58 of the people have not heard the warning each 15-minute time period. After the first 15 minutes, $650{,}000(0.58)$, or 377,000 people have not heard the news. After 30 minutes, $377{,}000(0.58)$, or 218,660 people have not heard the news. After 45 minutes, $218{,}660(0.58)$, or about 126,823 people have not heard the news. After 1 hour, $126{,}823(0.58)$, or about 73,557 people have not heard the news. Therefore, after 1 hour, $650{,}000 - 73{,}557$ or 576,433 people have heard the news.

**b.** 641,676 people. You may recognize from 15a that the number of people who have not heard the news after 1 hour is $650{,}000(0.58)^4$ where 4 is the number of 15-minute time periods. After 2 hours, eight 15-minute time periods have passed, so substitute 8 for 4: $650{,}000(0.58)^8 \approx 8324$. Therefore, after 2 hours, $650{,}000 - 8324$, or 641,676 people have heard the news.

**16. a.** $657.03. Write a recursive formula to represent the situation.

$$u_0 = 500 \text{ and } u_n = u_{n-1}\left(1 + \frac{0.055}{4}\right) \quad \text{where } n \geq 1$$

The interest is compounded $4 \cdot 5$, or 20 times in 5 years, so enter the recursive formula into your calculator to find that $u_{20} = 657.03$. After 5 years, you will have $657.03.

**b.** $4083.21. Change the recursive formula to add 150 to $u_n$.

$$u_0 = 500 \text{ and } u_n = u_{n-1}\left(1 + \frac{0.055}{4}\right) + 150$$
where $n \geq 1$

Use your calculator to find that $u_{20} = 4083.21$. After 5 years, you will have $4083.21.

**17. a.** $u_1 = 81$, $u_2 = 27$, $u_3 = 9$, $u_4 = 3$, $u_5 = 1$, $u_6 = \frac{1}{3}$

**b.** $u_1 = 81$ and $u_n = \frac{1}{3}u_{n-1}$ where $n \geq 2$. The common ratio is $\frac{1}{3}$.

**18. a.** 0.39, 0.0039, 0.000039, 0.00000039, 0.0000000039, 0.000000000039

**b.** $u_n = 39(0.01)^n$

**19. a.** $\cos 15° = \dfrac{\sqrt{6} + \sqrt{2}}{4}$

$\cos 15° = \cos(45° - 30°)$

$\quad = \cos 45° \cos 30° + \sin 45° \sin 30°$

$\quad = \dfrac{\sqrt{2}}{2} \cdot \dfrac{\sqrt{3}}{2} + \dfrac{\sqrt{2}}{2} \cdot \dfrac{1}{2}$

$\quad = \dfrac{\sqrt{6} + \sqrt{2}}{4}$

**b.** $\cos 75° = \dfrac{\sqrt{6} - \sqrt{2}}{4}$

$\cos 75° = \cos(45° + 30°)$

$\quad = \cos 45° \cos 30° - \sin 45° \sin 30°$

$\quad = \dfrac{\sqrt{2}}{2} \cdot \dfrac{\sqrt{3}}{2} - \dfrac{\sqrt{2}}{2} \cdot \dfrac{1}{2}$

$\quad = \dfrac{\sqrt{6} - \sqrt{2}}{4}$

**20. a.** $y = 2 + \dfrac{\frac{5}{2}}{x - \frac{1}{2}}$. Because the denominator is $(2x - 1)$, rather than $x$, try to get the expression $(2x - 1)$ in the numerator as well.

$$y = \frac{4x + 3}{2x - 1}$$

$$y = \frac{2(2x - 1) + 5}{2x - 1}$$

$$y = \frac{2(2x - 1)}{2x - 1} + \frac{5}{2x - 1}$$

$$y = 2 + \frac{5}{2x - 1} = 2 + \frac{\frac{5}{2}}{x - \frac{1}{2}}$$

The parent function has been vertically stretched by a factor of $\frac{5}{2}$, then translated right $\frac{1}{2}$ unit and up 2 units.

**b.** $x = \frac{1}{2}$, $y = 2$. $x = \frac{1}{2}$ is a vertical asymptote because this value makes the denominator, and not the nominator, equal to zero. Evaluating the function for large values shows that $y = 2$ is a horizontal asymptote.

**c.** $\left(\frac{3}{2}, \frac{9}{2}\right)$. The parent function has been translated right $\frac{1}{2}$ unit, so the $x$-coordinate of the image is $1 + \frac{1}{2}$, or $\frac{3}{2}$. It has been vertically stretched by a factor of $\frac{5}{2}$ and translated up 2 units, so the $y$-coordinate of the image is $\frac{5}{2}(1) + 2$, or $\frac{9}{2}$.

**EXTENSION**

To calculate the partial sums, imagine you have $n$ rows of boxes, where row $n$ contains $u_n$ boxes. The partial sum $S_n = \displaystyle\sum_{k=1}^{n} u_n$ gives the total number of boxes. For this example, $u_1 = 3$ and $d = 2$.

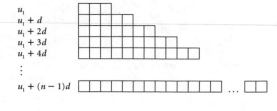

Now make a copy of this array of boxes, turn it upside down, and place it next to the original. You will get a rectangle with $n$ rows of boxes. Each row has $u_1 + (u_1 + (n-1)d) = 2u_1 + (n-1)d$ boxes in it.

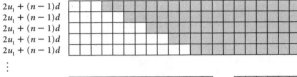

There are $n(2u_1 + (n-1)d)$ boxes in the full rectangle, and $\frac{n}{2}(2u_1 + (n-1)d)$ white boxes. Distribute the $\frac{n}{2}$ to get $S_n = u_1 n + \frac{d}{2}n^2 - \frac{d}{2}n$, and collect like terms to get $S_n = \frac{d}{2}n^2 + (u_1 - \frac{d}{2})n$.

To see the connection between this formula and the second formula for partial sums, $S_n = \frac{n(u_1 + u_n)}{2}$, recall that $u_n = u_1 + (n-1)d$. Substitute this into the second formula for partial sums, distribute, and collect like terms.

$$S_n = \frac{n(u_1 + u_1 + (n-1)d)}{2}$$

$$S_n = \frac{n}{2}(2u_1 + (n-1)d)$$

The expression $d(n-1)$ is the difference between the first and the last terms in the series.

## LESSON 11.2

### EXERCISES

**1. a.** $0.4 + 0.04 + 0.004 + \cdots$

   **b.** $u_1 = 0.4$, $r = 0.1$

   **c.** $S = \frac{0.4}{1 - 0.1} = \frac{0.4}{0.9} = \frac{4}{9}$

**2. a.** $0.47 + 0.0047 + 0.000047 + \cdots$

   **b.** $u_1 = 0.47$, $r = 0.01$

   **c.** $S = \frac{0.47}{1 - 0.01} = \frac{0.47}{0.99} = \frac{47}{99}$

**3. a.** $0.123 + 0.000123 + 0.000000123 + \cdots$

   **b.** $u_1 = 0.123$, $r = 0.001$

   **c.** $S = \frac{0.123}{1 - 0.001} = \frac{0.123}{0.999} = \frac{123}{999} = \frac{41}{333}$

**4.** 20, 19, 18.05, 17.1475, 16.290125. Substitute 20 for $u_1$ and 400 for $S$ in the formula for the sum of the series, and solve for $r$.

$$400 = \frac{20}{1 - r}$$

$$20 = \frac{1}{1 - r}$$

$$20(1 - r) = 1$$

$$1 - r = \frac{1}{20}$$

$$r = 1 - \frac{1}{20} = \frac{19}{20} = 0.95$$

The common ratio is 0.95, so find the first five terms of the sequence by multiplying each previous term by 0.95 or by using the explicit formula $u_n = 20(0.95)^{n-1}$.

**5.** $u_1 = 32768$. The common ratio is $\frac{32}{128}$, or 0.25. Substitute 0.25 for $r$ and $43{,}690.\overline{6}$ for $S$ in the formula for the sum, and solve for $u_1$.

$$43690.\overline{6} = \frac{u_1}{1 - 0.25}$$

$$u_1 = 43690.\overline{6}(0.75) = 32768$$

**6. a.** $S_{10} \approx 209.767$    **b.** $S_{20} \approx 232.291$

   **c.** $S_{30} \approx 234.709$    **d.** $S = \frac{47}{1 - 0.8} = 235$

**7. a.** $u_1 = 96$, $u_2 = 24$, $u_3 = 6$, $u_4 = 1.5$, $u_5 = 0.375$, $u_6 = 0.09375$, $u_7 = 0.0234375$, $u_8 = 0.005859375$, $u_9 = 0.00146484375$, $u_{10} = 0.0003662109375$. Substitute integers 1 through 10 for $n$ in the explicit formula, $u_n = 96(0.25)^{n-1}$, or use Home screen recursion on your calculator.

   **b.** $S_{10} \approx 128.000$. The recursive formula for the sequence of partial sums is $S_1 = 96$ and $S_n = S_{n-1} + 96(0.25)^{n-1}$ where $n \geq 1$. Enter the recursive formula into your calculator to find that $S_{10} \approx 128.000$.

   **c.**

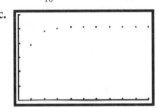

   $[0, 10, 1, 0, 150, 25]$

   **d.** $S = \frac{96}{1 - 0.25} = 128$

**8.** 900 cm. The total distance the ball travels both up and down is the sum of an infinite series. The ball is dropped from an initial height of 100 cm. After the first bounce, the ball rebounds to 80 cm, so let $u_1$ equal 80. After each additional bounce, the ball's rebound height is reduced by a common ratio. The second term divided by the first is $\frac{64}{80}$, the third term divided by the second is $\frac{51}{64}$, and the third term divided by the second is $\frac{41}{51}$, which are all approximately equal to 0.8, so the common ratio is 0.8. The sum of the series is $S = \frac{80}{1 - 0.8} = 400$. This represents only the sum of the rebound heights, or the upward distances. To find the total distance the ball travels, double $S$ and add 100 cm to account for the initial drop: $2S + 100 = 2(400) + 100 = 900$. Therefore the total distance traveled is 900 cm.

**9. a.** $50{,}000(\$500) = \$25{,}000{,}000$

**b.** $\$62{,}500{,}000$. The amount of income from visitors spent by the people of New Orleans each month forms a geometric sequence where the first term, $u_1$, is 25,000,000 and the common ratio, $r$, is 0.60. To find the long-run value, substitute these values in the formula for the sum: $S = \frac{25000000}{1 - 0.60} = 62500000$. In the long run the sporting event adds $\$62{,}500{,}000$ to the New Orleans economy.

**c.** 2.5. The ratio of the long-run value to the initial value is $\frac{62500000}{25000000}$, or 2.5.

**d.** 44.4%. The economic multiplier is 1.8, so $\frac{long\text{-}run\ amount}{10000000} = 1.8$, and $long\text{-}run\ amount = 18000000$. Substitute 18,000,000 for $S$ and 10,000,000 for $u_1$ in the formula for the sum and solve for $r$.

$$18000000 = \frac{10000000}{1 - r}$$

$$1 - r = \frac{10000000}{18000000}$$

$$1 - r = 0.\overline{5}$$

$$r = 0.\overline{4},\ or\ 44.\overline{4}\%$$

About 44.4% of the original amount is spent again and again in the local economy.

**10.** The point $\frac{1}{3}$ ft to the right of its starting point. The distance the flea jumps each time, alternating right and left, forms the geometric sequence $\frac{1}{2}, -\frac{1}{4}, \frac{1}{8}, \dots$. The first term, $u_1$, is $\frac{1}{2}$ and the common ratio, $r$, is $-\frac{1}{2}$, so using the formula for the sum,

$$S = \frac{\frac{1}{2}}{1 - \left(-\frac{1}{2}\right)} = \frac{\frac{1}{2}}{\frac{3}{2}} = \frac{1}{3}$$

The flea is zooming in to the point $\frac{1}{3}$ ft to the right of its starting point.

**11. a.** $\sqrt{2}$ in. The perimeters of the first three squares are 32 in., $16\sqrt{2}$ in., and 16 in., respectively, forming a geometric sequence with common ratio $\frac{\sqrt{2}}{2}$. Use the explicit formula $u_n = 32\left(\frac{\sqrt{2}}{2}\right)^{n-1}$ or use Home screen recursion on your calculator to find that $u_{10} = 32\left(\frac{\sqrt{2}}{2}\right)^9 = 32\left(\frac{16\sqrt{2}}{512}\right) = \frac{16\sqrt{2}}{16} = \sqrt{2}$.

**b.** 0.125 in.$^2$. The areas of the first three squares are 64 in.$^2$, 32 in.$^2$, and 16 in.$^2$, respectively, forming a geometric sequence with common ratio 0.5. Use the explicit formula $u_n = 64(0.5)^{n-1}$ or Home screen recursion on your calculator to find that $u_{10} = 64(0.5)^9 = 0.125$.

**c.** Approximately 109.25 in. From 11a, the first term, $u_1$, is 32 and the common ratio, $r$, is $\frac{\sqrt{2}}{2}$, so using the formula for the sum,

$$S = \frac{32}{1 - \frac{\sqrt{2}}{2}} = \frac{32}{\frac{2 - \sqrt{2}}{2}} = \frac{64}{2 - \sqrt{2}} \approx 109.25\ in.$$

**d.** 128 in.$^2$. From 11b, the first term, $u_1$, is 64 and the common ratio, $r$, is 0.5, so using the formula for the sum, $S = \frac{64}{1 - 0.5} = 128$.

**12. a.** Approaches 0. The perimeters of the equilateral triangles in the first three stages are 3 units, $\frac{3}{2}$ units, and $\frac{3}{4}$ units, respectively, forming a geometric sequence with common ratio $\frac{1}{2}$. In the long run the perimeter of each of the smaller triangles approaches 0.

**b.** Approaches 0. The areas of the equilateral triangles in the first three stages are $\frac{\sqrt{3}}{2}$ square units, $\frac{\sqrt{3}}{8}$ square units, and $\frac{\sqrt{3}}{32}$ square units, respectively, forming a geometric sequence with common ratio $\frac{1}{4}$. In the long run the area of each of the smaller triangles approaches 0.

**c.** Approaches infinity. The perimeter sum in Stage 0 is 3 units, in Stage 1 is $3\left(\frac{3}{2}\right)$, or $\frac{9}{2}$ units, and in Stage 2 is $9\left(\frac{3}{4}\right)$, or $\frac{27}{4}$ units, forming a geometric sequence with common ratio $\frac{3}{2}$. The common ratio is greater than 1, so the sum of the perimeters increases without bound and in the long run approaches infinity.

**d.** Approaches 0. The sums of the areas of the equilateral triangles in the first three stages are $\frac{\sqrt{3}}{4}$ square units, $3\left(\frac{\sqrt{3}}{8}\right)$ square units, and $9\left(\frac{\sqrt{3}}{32}\right)$ square units, respectively, forming a geometric sequence with common ratio $\frac{3}{4}$. In the long run the sum of the areas of the smaller triangles approaches 0.

**13.** $12.4 + 4.2(18) = 88$ gal

**14. i.** B. The $y$-intercept is at the origin on the graph. When you substitute 0 for $x$, only equation B gives $y = 0$.

**ii.** C. The $y$-intercept of the graph is at (0, 10). When you substitute 0 for $x$, only equations A and C give $y = 10$. However, when you substitute additional values for $x$, such as 10, $y = 10(0.8)^{10} \approx 1.07$ for equation A and $y = 3 + 7(0.7)^{10} \approx 3.2$ for equation C. The point (10, 3.2) is on the graph, so the graph matches equation C.

**iii.** D. The $y$-intercept of the graph is at (0, 3). When you substitute 0 for $x$, only equation D gives $y = 3$.

**iv. A.** The $y$-intercept of the graph is at $(0, 10)$. Using what you found in 14ii, when $x = 10$, $y = 10(0.8)^{10} \approx 1.07$ for equation A. The point $(10, 1.07)$ is on the graph, so the graph matches equation A.

**15. a.** $56,625. The expenses each week represent an arithmetic sequence where the first term is 955 and the common difference is 65. The explicit formula for the partial sum of the series is $S_n = \left(\frac{65}{2}\right)n^2 + \left(955 - \frac{65}{2}\right)n = 32.5n^2 + 922.5n$. To find how much of the development budget will be left after 25 weeks, first substitute 25 for $n$: $S_{25} = 32.5(25)^2 + 922.5(25) = 43375$. Then subtract this amount from 100,000 to get $100000 - 43375 = 56625$. After 25 weeks, $56,625 of the development budget will be left.

**b.** 43 weeks. Substitute 100,000 for $S_n$ in the explicit formula and solve for $n$, the number of weeks it will take to use the entire development budget.

$$100000 = 32.5n^2 + 922.5n$$

$$0 = 32.5n^2 + 922.5n - 100000$$

$$n = \frac{-922.5 \pm \sqrt{922.5^2 - 4(32.5)(-100000)}}{2(32.5)}$$

$$n \approx 43.06 \text{ or } n \approx -71.45$$

Only the positive answer makes sense, so it will take 43 weeks before the budget will not support another week of expenses.

**16.** $\displaystyle\sum_{n=1}^{5} 4^n = 1364$

The number of legs that Hans sees for each group of animals that follows the previous group forms a geometric sequence where the first term is 4 and the common ratio is 4. To find how many legs Hans sees, add the five terms generated by the explicit formula $u_n = 4(4)^{n-1}$, or $u_n = 4^n$, or in sigma notation

$$\sum_{n=1}^{5} 4^n = 4 + 16 + 64 + 256 + 1024 = 1364$$

Hans sees 1364 legs.

### IMPROVING YOUR VISUAL THINKING SKILLS

A good problem-solving technique when stuck is to ask what assumptions are being made. The assumption that the toothpicks can't overlap is a natural one, but it is not stated in the problem.

### EXTENSIONS

**A.** Any repeating decimal with $n$ repeating digits can be written as a fraction of those digits over $n$ 9's. For example, $0.\overline{1256} = \frac{1256}{9999}$.

**B.** Sample answer: Suppose there is a race between Achilles and the tortoise. Achilles runs 10 times as fast as the tortoise, so he decides to give the tortoise a 10 m head start. Zeno argued that Achilles would never be able to catch the tortoise.

By the time Achilles reaches the point where the tortoise began, the tortoise will have traveled 1 m. By the time Achilles covers that extra 1 m, the tortoise will have traveled another 0.1 m. Once Achilles covers that extra 0.1 m, the tortoise will have traveled another 0.01 m. Each time Achilles advances to where the tortoise once was, the tortoise has already left that spot and is still ahead of Achilles.

This scenario can be described using a geometric series. After Achilles has run the first 10 m, he has come 9 m closer to the tortoise. After he has gone another 1 m, Achilles has gained another 0.9 m on the tortoise. At the next step, when Achilles has gone another 0.1 m, he has gained 0.09 m on the tortoise. His total gain on the tortoise is the sum of these distances, $9 + 0.9 + 0.09 + \cdots$.

This forms the geometric series $\displaystyle\sum_{n=0}^{\infty} 9\left(\frac{1}{10}\right)^n$. The sum of the series is $\frac{9}{1 - \frac{1}{10}} = \frac{9}{\frac{9}{10}} = 10$.

So Achilles eventually covers the full 10 m gap between himself and the tortoise. However, this involves going through an infinite number of these steps, which makes it seem impossible. This can be remedied using another series.

Suppose Achilles runs 2.5 m/s, so he covers the first step (10 m) in 4 s. The next step (1 m) is covered in 0.4 s, the following step (0.1 m) is covered in 0.04 s, and so on. So the time that it takes for Achilles to catch up to the tortoise is represented by the sum $4 + 0.4 + 0.04 + \cdots$.

This forms the geometric series $\displaystyle\sum_{n=0}^{\infty} 4\left(\frac{1}{10}\right)^n$. The sum of this series is $\frac{4}{1 - \frac{1}{10}} = \frac{4}{\frac{9}{10}} = 4\frac{4}{9}$, so it only takes Achilles about 4.4 s to catch up to the tortoise.

**C.** See the Sketchpad demonstration Fractals.

**D.** See the solution to Take Another Look activity 1 on page 274.

**E.** Investigations will vary.

### EXERCISES

**1. a.** $u_1 = 12$, $r = 0.4$, $n = 8$

  **b.** $u_1 = 75$, $r = 1.2$, $n = 15$

  **c.** $u_1 = 40$, $r = 0.8$, $n = 20$. Rewrite in the form of an explicit formula for the partial sum of a geometric series.

$$\frac{40 - 0.46117}{1 - 0.8} = \frac{40(1 - 0.0115292)}{1 - 0.8} = \frac{40\left(1 - 0.8^{20}\right)}{1 - 0.8}$$

  **d.** $u_1 = 60$, $r = 2.5$, $n = 6$. Rewrite in the form of an explicit formula for the partial sum of a geometric series.

$$-40 + 40(2.5)^6 = \left(\frac{60}{1 - 2.5}\right) - \left(\frac{60}{1 - 2.5}\right)2.5^6$$

**2. a.** $u_8 = 34.171875$. Write an explicit formula for the terms of the geometric sequence: $u_n = 256(0.75)^{n-1}$. Substitute 8 for $n$ to find that $u_8 = 256(0.75)^7 = 34.171875$.

  **b.** $u_{10}$. The 8th term, $u_8$, is greater than 20, so continue by finding that $u_9 = 256(0.75)^8 \approx 25.63$ and $u_{10} = 256(0.75)^9 \approx 19.22$.

  **c.** $u_7 = 256(0.75)^6 = 45.5625$

  **d.** $S_7 = 887.3125$. The first term is 256, the common ratio is 0.75, and the number of terms is 7, so $S_7 = \frac{256\left(1 - 0.75^7\right)}{1 - 0.75} = 887.3125$.

**3. a.** $S_5 = 92.224$. The first term of the recursive sequence is 40, the common ratio is 0.6, and the number of terms is 5, so $S_5 = \frac{40\left(1 - 0.6^5\right)}{1 - 0.6} = 92.224$.

  **b.** $S_{15} = \frac{40\left(1 - 0.6^{15}\right)}{1 - 0.6} \approx 99.952$

  **c.** $S_{25} = \frac{40\left(1 - 0.6^{25}\right)}{1 - 0.6} \approx 99.9997$

**4. a.** $u_1 = 3.2$, $d = 1.05$, $S_5 = 26.5$. This is an arithmetic series with $u_1 = 3.2$, $d = 1.05$, and $n = 5$, so $S_5 = \frac{5(3.2 + 7.4)}{2} = 26.5$.

  **b.** $u_1 = 3.2$, $r = 1.5$, $S_7 = 102.95$. This is a geometric series with $u_1 = 3.2$ and $r = 1.5$. To find the partial sum, you need to first find the number of terms in the series. Use Home screen recursion, or use the explicit formula $u_n = 3.2(1.5)^{n-1}$, substitute 36.45 for $u_n$, and solve for $n$.

$$36.45 = 3.2(1.5)^{n-1}$$

$$11.390625 = (1.5)^{n-1}$$

$$\log 11.390625 = \log(1.5)^{n-1}$$

$$\log 11.390625 = (n - 1)\log 1.5$$

$$n - 1 = \frac{\log 11.390625}{\log 1.5} = 6$$

$$n = 7$$

Therefore the number of terms, $n$, is 7, so $S_7 = \frac{3.2\left(1 - 1.5^7\right)}{1 - 1.5} = 102.95$.

  **c.** $u_1 = 5.7$, $d = 2.5$, $S_{27} = 1031.4$. This is an arithmetic series with common difference 2.5. The first term is $3.2 + 2.5(1)$, or 5.7, and the last term, $u_{27}$, is $3.2 + 2.5(27)$, or 70.7. The number of terms in the series, $n$, is 27, so $S_{27} = \frac{27(5.7 + 70.7)}{2} = 1031.4$.

  **d.** $u_1 = 3.2$, $r = 4$, $S_{10} = 1118480$. This is a geometric series with common ratio 4. The first term is $3.2(4)^0$, or 3.2. The number of terms in the series, $n$, is 10, so $S_{10} = \frac{3.2\left(1 - 4^{10}\right)}{1 - 4} = 1118480$.

**5. a.** $S_{10} = \frac{3\left(1 - 2^{10}\right)}{1 - 2} = 3069$

  **b.** $n = 22$. To find $n$, substitute 9.999868378 for $S_n$, 4 for $u_1$, and 0.6 for $r$ in the explicit formula for the partial sum of a geometric series.

$$9.999868378 = \frac{4\left(1 - 0.6^n\right)}{1 - 0.6}$$

$$0.4(9.999868378) = 4\left(1 - 0.6^n\right)$$

$$\frac{3.999947351}{4} = 1 - 0.6^n$$

$$\frac{3.999947351}{4} - 1 = -0.6^n$$

$$-0.0000131622 = -0.6^n$$

$$0.0000131622 = 0.6^n$$

$$\log 0.0000131622 = n\log 0.6$$

$$n = \frac{\log 0.0000131622}{\log 0.6} = 22$$

  **c.** $u_1 = 2.8$. To find $u_1$, substitute 1081.976669 for $S_n$, 15 for $n$, and 1.4 for $r$ in the explicit formula for the partial sum of a geometric series.

$$1081.976669 = \frac{u_1\left(1 - 1.4^{15}\right)}{1 - 1.4}$$

$$-0.4(1081.976669) = u_1\left(1 - 1.4^{15}\right)$$

$$u_1 = \frac{-0.4(1081.976669)}{1 - 1.4^{15}} = 2.8$$

**d.** $r = 0.95$. To find $r$, substitute 66.30642497 for $S_n$, 5.5 for $u_1$, and 18 for $n$ in the explicit formula for the partial sum of a geometric series.

$$66.30642497 = \frac{5.5\left(1 - r^{18}\right)}{1 - r}$$

$$\frac{66.30642497}{5.5} = \frac{1 - r^{18}}{1 - r}$$

$$12.05571363 = \frac{1 - r^{18}}{1 - r}$$

You can't solve for $r$ explicitly, so graph the two functions $y = 12.05571363$ and $y = \frac{1 - r^{18}}{1 - r}$ and find their intersection.

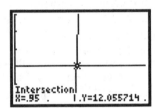

[0, 2, 0.5, 8, 18, 2]

The functions intersect at $r = 0.95$.

**6.** $n = 12$. Set the expression equal to 15 and solve for $n$.

$$15 = \frac{3.2\left(1 - 0.8^n\right)}{1 - 0.8}$$

$$0.2(15) = 3.2\left(1 - 0.8^n\right)$$

$$\frac{3}{3.2} = 1 - 0.8^n$$

$$0.9375 = 1 - 0.8^n$$

$$-0.0625 = -0.8^n$$

$$0.0625 = 0.8^n$$

$$\log 0.0625 = \log 0.8^n$$

$$\log 0.0625 = n \log 0.8$$

$$n = \frac{\log 0.0625}{\log 0.8} \approx 12.43$$

The nearest integer value for $n$ is 12.

**7. a.** $S_{10} = 15.984375$. Find the sum of the first ten terms of a geometric sequence with $u_1 = 8$ and $r = 0.5$.

$$S_{10} = \frac{8\left(1 - 0.5^{10}\right)}{1 - 0.5} = 15.984375$$

**b.** $S_{20} = \frac{8\left(1 - 0.5^{20}\right)}{1 - 0.5} \approx 15.99998474$

**c.** $S_{30} = \frac{8\left(1 - 0.5^{30}\right)}{1 - 0.5} \approx 15.99999999$

**d.** The partial sums continue to increase, but by a smaller amount each time, and they are approaching 16.

**8. a.** \$25,342.39. Let the starting salary of \$17,500 represent $u_1$ of a geometric sequence with $r = (1 + 0.042) = 1.042$. Each term in the sequence represents your increased salary each year. Write the explicit formula for the geometric sequence, $u_n = 17500(1.042)^{n-1}$, and substitute 10 for $n$ to find that $u_{10} = 17500(1.042)^9 \approx 25342.39$. Your salary in the tenth year after you start the job is \$25,342.39.

**b.** \$212,065.89. Use the explicit formula to find $S_{10}$, the sum of the first ten terms in the geometric series.

$$S_{10} = \frac{17500\left(1 - 1.042^{10}\right)}{1 - 1.042} \approx 212065.89$$

The total amount you earn in ten years is \$212,065.89.

**c.** About 30 yr. Substitute 1,000,000 for $S_n$ in the explicit formula and solve for $n$.

$$1000000 = \frac{17500\left(1 - 1.042^n\right)}{1 - 1.042}$$

$$-0.042(1000000) = 17500\left(1 - 1.042^n\right)$$

$$-42000 = 17500\left(1 - 1.042^n\right)$$

$$\frac{-42000}{17500} = 1 - 1.042^n$$

$$-2.4 = 1 - 1.042^n$$

$$-3.4 = -1.042^n$$

$$3.4 = 1.042^n$$

$$\log 3.4 = n \log 1.042$$

$$n = \frac{\log 3.4}{\log 1.042} \approx 29.75$$

You must work at this job about 30 years before your total earnings exceed \$1 million.

**9. a.  i.** 128 grains. The numbers of grains on each square of the chessboard form a geometric sequence with $u_1 = 1$ and $r = 2$. To find the number of grains on the 8th square, or the 8th term, $u_8$, write an explicit formula for the terms of the geometric sequence: $u_n = 1(2)^{n-1} = 2^{n-1}$. Substitute 8 for $n$ to find that $u_8 = 2^7 = 128$.

**ii.** More than $9 \times 10^{18}$ grains. Substitute 64 for $n$ to find that $u_{64} = 2^{63} \approx 9 \times 10^{18}$. More than $9 \times 10^{18}$ grains of wheat are needed for the 64th square.

**iii.** 255 grains. Add the number of grains in the first eight squares (the first row) using the explicit formula for the partial sum:
$$S_8 = \frac{1\left(1 - 2^8\right)}{1 - 2} = 255.$$

**iv.** More than $1.8 \times 10^{19}$ grains. There are 64 squares on a chessboard, so using the explicit formula for the partial sum, $S_{64} = \frac{1(1 - 2^{64})}{1 - 2} \approx 1.8 \times 10^{19}$.

**b.** $\sum_{n=1}^{64} 2^{n-1}$. The numbers of grains of wheat on each of the 64 squares represent the 64 terms in the geometric sequence with the explicit formula, $u_n = 2^{n-1}$, or, in sigma notation, $\sum_{n=1}^{64} 2^{n-1}$.

**10.** The second choice is more profitable by approximately $45 trillion. The first choice forms an arithmetic sequence with each additional monetary award per hour for the entire year representing a term in the series with $u_1 = 1000$ and $d = 1000$. The number of times you have been awarded, $n$, is $365(24)$, or 8760, which is the number of hours in a year. To find out how much you will receive by the end of the year using the explicit formula for $S_n$, you need to find the last term of the series, $u_{8760}$. Write the explicit formula for the terms of the arithmetic sequence: $u_n = 1000 + (n - 1)1000 = 1000n$. Then substitute 8760 for $n$ to find that $u_{8760} = 1000(8760) = 8760000$. Substitute these values into the explicit formula for $S_n$: $S_{8760} = \frac{8760(1000 + 8760000)}{2} = 38,373,180,000 \approx 3.8 \times 10^{10}$. At the end of one year, you will have been awarded approximately $38 billion if you make the first choice.

The second choice forms a geometric sequence with the amount received each week doubled. Each amount represents a term in the series with $u_1 = 0.01$ and $r = 2$. The number of times you have been awarded, $n$, is 52, the number of weeks in a year. To find out how much you will receive by the end of the year, use the explicit formula for $S_n$. Substitute 52 for $n$: $S_{52} = \frac{0.01(1 - 2^{52})}{1 - 2} = 45,035,996,270,000 \approx 4.5 \times 10^{13}$. At the end of one year, you will have been awarded approximately $45 trillion if you go with the second choice.

The difference between the two prizes is $45,035,996,270,000 - 38,373,180,000$, or $44,997,623,090,000$. Therefore the second choice is more profitable by almost $45 trillion.

**11. a.** 5, 15, 35, 75, 155, 315, 635. The first term of the series is 5 and the common ratio is 2, so the explicit formula for the partial sum of the series is $S_n = \frac{5(1 - 2^n)}{1 - 2} = -5(1 - 2^n)$. Use this formula to find the first seven partial sums.

$S_1 = -5(1 - 2^1) = 5$

$S_2 = -5(1 - 2^2) = 15$

$S_3 = -5(1 - 2^3) = 35$

$S_4 = -5(1 - 2^4) = 75$

$S_5 = -5(1 - 2^5) = 155$

$S_6 = -5(1 - 2^6) = 315$

$S_7 = -5(1 - 2^7) = 635$

**b.** No, they form a shifted geometric sequence. You need to multiply the previous term by 2 and then add 5 to get the next term in the sequence.

**c.** Not possible. The partial sums form a shifted geometric sequence and so there is no common ratio, $r$.

**12. a.** Neither. Subtracting the first term from the second term, $\frac{1}{2} - \frac{1}{1} = -\frac{1}{2}$, and the second term from the first term, $\frac{1}{3} - \frac{1}{2} = -\frac{1}{6}$, you can see that there is no common difference, so the series is not arithmetic. Divide the second term by the first term and the third term by the second term.

$$\frac{\frac{1}{2}}{\frac{1}{1}} = \frac{1}{2} \qquad \frac{\frac{1}{3}}{\frac{1}{2}} = \frac{2}{3}$$

There is no common ratio, so the series is not geometric.

**b.** $S_8 = \frac{1}{1} + \frac{1}{2} + \frac{1}{3} + \frac{1}{4} + \frac{1}{5} + \frac{1}{6} + \frac{1}{7} + \frac{1}{8} \approx 2.717857$

**13. a.** $1 + 4 + 9 + 16 + 25 + 36 + 49 = 140$. Substitute the integers 1 through 7 in the explicit formula, $u_n = n^2$, and then add the seven terms to find the sum of the series.

**b.** $9 + 16 + 25 + 36 + 49 = 135$. Substitute the integers 3 through 7 into the explicit formula, $u_n = n^2$, and then add the five terms to find the sum of the series.

**14. a.** 496 games. Every member of the chess team plays every other player, so $\frac{32 \cdot 31}{2}$, or 496 games need to be scheduled.

**b.** 31 games. For the first round, $\frac{32}{2}$, or 16 games need to be scheduled, 8 for the second round, 4 for the third round, and so forth. The number of games that need to be scheduled for the tournament is $16 + 8 + 4 + 2 + 1$, or 31 games.

**15.** \$637.95. Write the recursive formula for the situation, where $p$ represents the monthly payment.

$u_0 = 80000$ and $u_n = \left(1 + \dfrac{0.089}{12}\right)u_{n-1} - p$
where $n \geq 1$

Enter the recursive formula into your calculator. Use guess-and-check by substituting possible monthly payments for $p$ so that $u_{360} = 0$. Remember that there are 360 monthly payments in 30 years. When $p = 637.95$, $u_{360} \approx 0.43$, so by paying \$637.95 each month for 30 years, the balance owed is close to 0.

**16. a.** $x^2 - y^2 = 1$

**b.** Substitute $\frac{1}{\cos t}$ for $x$ and solve for $y$ in terms of $t$:
$\left(\frac{1}{\cos t}\right)^2 - y^2 = 1$, so $y^2 = \left(\frac{1}{\cos t}\right)^2 - 1$, and
$y = \pm\sqrt{\left(\frac{1}{\cos t}\right)^2 - 1}$.

**c.** The least common denominator for the terms under the radical is $(\cos t)^2$, so

$y = \pm\sqrt{\left(\dfrac{1}{\cos t}\right)^2 - 1}$

$= \pm\sqrt{\dfrac{1}{(\cos t)^2} - \dfrac{(\cos t)^2}{(\cos t)^2}}$

$= \pm\sqrt{\dfrac{1 - (\cos t)^2}{(\cos t)^2}}$

**d.** Substitute $(\sin t)^2 + (\cos t)^2$ for 1 and rewrite the numerator under the radical to get

$y = \pm\sqrt{\dfrac{(\sin t)^2 + (\cos t)^2 - (\cos t)^2}{(\cos t)^2}}$

$= \pm\sqrt{\dfrac{(\sin t)^2}{(\cos t)^2}}$

**e.** Because $\tan t = \frac{\sin t}{\cos t}$, $(\tan t)^2 = \left(\frac{\sin t}{\cos t}\right)^2 = \frac{(\sin t)^2}{(\cos t)^2}$. Substitute $(\tan t)^2$ for $\frac{(\sin t)^2}{(\cos t)^2}$ to get

$y = \pm\sqrt{\dfrac{(\sin t)^2}{(\cos t)^2}} = \pm\sqrt{(\tan t)^2} = \tan t$

**f.** $x = \frac{1}{\cos t}$ and $y = \tan t$

**g.** $x = \frac{a}{\cos t} + h$ and $y = b\tan t + k$

**17.** Yes. The long-run height is only 24 in. The weekly height increases form a geometric sequence where the first term, $u_1$, is 6, and the common ratio, $r$, is 0.75. Using Home screen recursion or the explicit formula $u_n = 6(0.75)^{n-1}$, the long-run height is $S = \frac{6}{1 - 0.75} = 24$ in.

**18.** $f(x) = 3x^3 + 16x^2 + 27x - 26$. If one of the zeros is $(-3 + 2i)$, another zero is its complex conjugate, $(-3 - 2i)$. Using the three zeros of the polynomial equation, $\frac{2}{3}$, $(-3 + 2i)$, and $(-3 - 2i)$, write the polynomial equation in factored form.

$f(x) = (3x - 2)(x - (-3 + 2i))(x - (-3 - 2i))$

Multiply the factors so that the polynomial has integer coefficients.

$f(x) = (3x - 2)\big(x^2 - (-3 - 2i)x - (-3 + 2i)x + (-3 + 2i)(-3 - 2i)\big)$

$= (3x - 2)\big(x^2 + 3x - 2ix + 3x + 2ix + 9 - 4i^2\big)$

$= (3x - 2)\big(x^2 + 6x + 13\big)$

$= 3x^3 + 18x^2 + 39x - 2x^2 - 12x - 26$

$f(x) = 3x^3 + 16x^2 + 27x - 26$

**IMPROVING YOUR REASONING SKILLS**

You might use Home screen recursion or a formula for the partial sum of a geometric series to find that at age 30 Pamela has \$35,120.59 (assuming she saves \$2,000 at age 20 and again each year until age 30). Candice has \$2,000 if she starts saving in her 30th year. Use a formula to find Candice's amount at age 65. To generate the geometric series, you might realize that the \$2,000 Candice deposited at age 64 will have grown to $2000(1 + 0.09)$, her deposit at age 63 will have increased to $2000(1 + 0.09)^2$, her previous deposit will have grown to $2000(1 + 0.09)^3$, and so on, down to her deposit at age 30, which will have grown to $2000(1 + 0.09)^{35}$. The sum of the 36 deposits, then, is $2000\frac{(1 - 1.09^{36})}{1 - 1.09}$, or \$472,249.45. Pamela's \$35,120.59 grows exponentially without further deposits, achieving an amount at age 65 of $(35120.59)(1.09)^{35}$, or approximately \$716,950.60.

**EXTENSIONS**

**A.** See the solutions to Take Another Look activities 1, 2, and 3 on page 274.

**B.** The harmonic series, $\displaystyle\sum_{n=1}^{\infty} \frac{1}{n}$, diverges. The alternating harmonic series, $\displaystyle\sum_{n=1}^{\infty} \frac{(-1)^{n+1}}{n}$, conditionally converges to $\ln 2$. These results can be proved using calculus.

**C.** One example is the function $y = \frac{1}{1 - x} = 1 + x + x^2 + x^3 + \cdots = \displaystyle\sum_{n=0}^{\infty} x^n$, which is a geometric series.

## EXPLORATION · SEEING THE SUM OF A SERIES

### QUESTIONS

**1.** $\sum\limits_{n=1}^{\infty} AB(0.6)^{n-1}$. For the example shown in your book,
$\sum\limits_{n=1}^{\infty} 3(0.6)^{n-1}$.

**2.** For the example shown in your book, by the 16th iteration the table values suggest that $S = 7.5$. This is confirmed by the explicit formula, $S = \frac{3}{1-0.6} = 7.5$.

**3.** Varying the length of $\overline{AB}$ reduces or enlarges the entire figure, but the sum is still finite. The series is always convergent for $r = 0.6$.

**4.** The figure continues to grow and does not converge.

**5.** Use $a$ as the initial length of $\overline{AB}$ and $\frac{-r}{1}$ as the dilation factor.

## CHAPTER 11 REVIEW

### EXERCISES

**1. a.** $u_{128} = 511$. The first term, $u_1$, is 3 and the common difference, $d$, is 4, so $u_n = 3 + (n-1)4 = 4n - 1$. Substitute 128 for $n$ to find that $u_{128} = 4(128) - 1 = 511$.

**b.** $u_{40} = 159$. Substitute 159 for $u_n$ and solve for $n$: $159 = 4n - 1$, so $4n = 160$, and $n = 40$.

**c.** Substitute 20 for $n$ to find that $u_{20} = 4(20) - 1 = 79$.

**d.** $S_{20} = 820$. The partial sums of the series are given by $S_n = \left(\frac{4}{2}\right)n^2 + \left(3 - \frac{4}{2}\right)n = 2n^2 + n$. Substitute 20 for $n$ to find that $S_{20} = 2(20)^2 + (20) = 820$.

**2. a.** $u_{11} \approx 17.490$. The first term, $u_1$, is 100 and the common ratio, $r$, is 0.84, so $u_n = 100(0.84)^{n-1}$. Substitute 20 for $u_{11}$ and solve for $n$.

$$20 = 100(0.84)^{n-1}$$

$$0.2 = 0.84^{n-1}$$

$$\log 0.2 = \log 0.84^{n-1}$$

$$n - 1 = \frac{\log 0.2}{\log 0.84}$$

$$n = \frac{\log 0.2}{\log 0.84} + 1 \approx 10.23$$

The terms are decreasing, so the first term smaller than 20 is $u_{11} = 100(0.84)^{10} \approx 17.490$.

**b.** $S_{10} \approx 515.687$. The 11th term is the first term in the sequence that is less than 20, so there are 10 terms that are greater than 20. The sum of these 10 terms is

$$S_{10} = \frac{100(1 - 0.84^{10})}{1 - 0.84} \approx 515.687$$

**c.** $S_{20} \approx 605.881$. $\sum\limits_{n=1}^{20} u_n = S_{20}$, so $\sum\limits_{n=1}^{20} u_n = \frac{100(1 - 0.84^{20})}{1 - 0.84} \approx 605.881$.

**d.** The partial sum approaches 625. The absolute value of $r$, 0.84, is less than 1, so the geometric series converges. The sum of the series is $S = \frac{100}{1 - 0.84} = 625$.

**3. a.** 144; 1728; 20,736; 429,981,696. Initially there are 12 bugs, half male and half female, or 6 pairs, so five days later when the female bugs are ready to reproduce, 6(24), or 144 bugs are born. On the 10th day $\frac{144}{2}$, or 72 females are ready to reproduce, so 72(24), or 1728 bugs are born. On the 15th day $\frac{1728}{2}$, or 864 females are ready to reproduce, so 864(24), or 20,736 bugs are born. The numbers of newborn bugs every five days form a geometric sequence with common ratio 12. Use Home screen recursion to find that on the 35th day 429,981,696 bugs are born.

**b.** $u_1 = 12$ and $u_n = 12u_{n-1}$ where $n \geq 2$ and where $n = \frac{d}{5} + 1$, where $d$ is the number of the day. The first term, $u_1$, is 12 and you must multiply the previous term by $r = 12$ to get the next term.

**c.** $u_n = 12^n$. The first term is 12 and the common ratio is 12, so $u_n = 12(12)^{n-1} = 12^n$.

**d.** Approximately $1.2 \times 10^{14}$. For the 60th day, $n = \frac{60}{5} + 1 = 13$. Using an explicit formula for the partial sum of a geometric series, substitute 13 for $n$ to find that $S_{13} = \frac{12(1 - 12^{13})}{1 - 12} \approx 1.2 \times 10^{14}$.

**4. a.** $-6639.7$. This is an arithmetic series with $u_1 = 125.3$ and $d = -6.8$, so $S_n = \left(-\frac{6.8}{2}\right)n^2 + \left(125.3 + \frac{6.8}{2}\right)n = -3.4n^2 + 128.7$. Substitute 67 for $n$ to find that $S_{67} = -3.4(67)^2 + 128.7(67) = -6639.7$.

**b.** $S_{67} = \sum\limits_{n=1}^{67} (125.3 - 6.8(n-1))$

**5. a.** Approximately 56.49 ft. The distances the golf ball travels after each putt from the initial position of 12 ft from the hole form a geometric sequence where the first term, representing the distance the ball travels after the first putt, is $12 + 12\left(\frac{2}{3}\right)$, or 20, the second term is $8 + 8\left(\frac{2}{3}\right)$, or $13\frac{1}{3}$, and the third term is $5\frac{1}{3} + 5\frac{1}{3}\left(\frac{2}{3}\right)$, or $8\frac{8}{9}$. The common ratio is $\frac{2}{3}$. An explicit formula for the partial sum is

$$S_n = \frac{20\left(1 - \left(\frac{2}{3}\right)^n\right)}{1 - \frac{2}{3}}$$

To find how far the golf ball travels in seven putts, substitute 7 for $n$.

$$S_7 = \frac{20\left(1 - \left(\frac{2}{3}\right)^7\right)}{1 - \frac{2}{3}} \approx 56.49$$

The ball travels approximately 56.49 ft in seven putts.

**b.** 60 ft. Use the formula for the sum of a geometric series.

$$S = \frac{20}{1 - \frac{2}{3}} = 60$$

The ball travels 60 ft in the long run.

**6. a.** Geometric; $r = \frac{1}{2}$. The distance the flea jumps each time is $\frac{1}{2}$ the previous distance, so the distances form a geometric sequence with common ratio $\frac{1}{2}$.

**b.** 0.0039 ft; 0.996 ft to the right. You need to find the 8th term of the sequence. Using Home screen recursion, begin with $\frac{1}{2}$ and multiply each previous term by $\frac{1}{2}$ to get the first eight terms of the sequence: $\frac{1}{2}, \frac{1}{4}, \frac{1}{8}, \frac{1}{16}, \frac{1}{32}, \frac{1}{64}, \frac{1}{128}$, and $\frac{1}{256}$. The 8th term is $\frac{1}{256}$, or approximately 0.0039. To find the flea's total distance from its starting point, add the first eight terms of the sequence to get $\frac{1}{2} + \frac{1}{4} + \frac{1}{8} + \frac{1}{16} + \frac{1}{32} + \frac{1}{64} + \frac{1}{128} + \frac{1}{256} = \frac{255}{256} \approx 0.996$.

**c.** Approximately $9.5 \times 10^{-7}$ ft; approximately 1 ft to the right of its starting point. Using Home screen recursion, continue the sequence from 6b to find that the 20th term of the sequence is approximately $9.5 \times 10^{-7}$. The total distance the flea has jumped is

$$S_{20} = \frac{\frac{1}{2}\left(1 - \left(\frac{1}{2}\right)^{20}\right)}{1 - \frac{1}{2}} \approx 1$$

**d.** $u_n = 0.5^n$; $S_n = \frac{0.5(1 - 0.5^n)}{1 - 0.5}$. The first term of the geometric sequence is $\frac{1}{2}$, so the explicit formula for the jump length is $u_n = 0.5(0.5)^{n-1} = 0.5^n$. Using the same values, an explicit formula for the flea's location after any jump, or for the partial sum of the geometric series, is $S_n = \frac{0.5(1 - 0.5^n)}{1 - 0.5}$.

**e.** The point 1 ft to the right of its starting point. Using the formula for the sum of a geometric series: $S = \frac{0.5}{1 - 0.5} = 1.0$. The flea is zooming in to the point 1 ft to the right of its starting point.

**7. a.** $S_{10} = \frac{4\left(1 - 0.7^{10}\right)}{1 - 0.7} \approx 12.957$;

$$S_{40} = \frac{4\left(1 - 0.7^{40}\right)}{1 - 0.7} \approx 13.333$$

**b.** $S_{10} \approx \frac{4\left(1 - 1.3^{10}\right)}{1 - 1.3} = 170.478$;

$$S_{40} = \frac{4\left(1 - 1.3^{40}\right)}{1 - 1.3} \approx 481571.531$$

**c.** $S_{10} = 40$; $S_{40} = 160$. You cannot use an explicit formula for the partial sum of the geometric sequence because when $r = 1$, you will have 0 in the denominator, so the expression is undefined. The geometric sequence is 4, 4, 4, . . . , so the sum of the first 10 terms, $S_{10}$, is 4(10), or 40. Similarly, the sum of the first 40 terms, $S_{40}$, is 4(40), or 160.

**d.** For $r = 0.7$      For $r = 1.3$

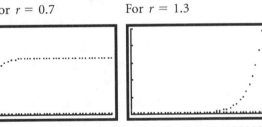

[0, 40, 1, 0, 20, 1]     [0, 40, 1, 0, 500000, 100000]

For $r = 1$

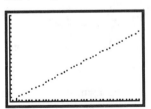

[0, 40, 1, 0, 200, 10]

**e.** 0.7. When $|r| < 1$, as in the case for $r = 0.7$, the geometric series converges.

**8. a.** $S_{10} = 0.8888888888$. This is a geometric series where the first term is 0.8 and the common ratio is 0.1, so the partial sums are $S_n = \frac{0.8\left(1 - 0.1^n\right)}{1 - 0.1}$. Substitute 10 for $n$ to find that $S_{10} = \frac{0.8\left(1 - 0.1^{10}\right)}{1 - 0.1} = 0.8888888888$.

**b.** Substitute 15 for $n$ to find that $S_{15} = \frac{0.8(1 - 0.1^{15})}{1 - 0.1}$
$= 0.888888888888888$.

**c.** $\frac{8}{9}$. Use the formula for the sum of a series and reduce to a ratio of integers.

$$S = \frac{0.8}{1 - 0.1} = \frac{0.8}{0.9} = \frac{\frac{8}{10}}{\frac{9}{10}} = \frac{8}{9}$$

You might also recognize this series as the repeating decimal $0.\overline{8}$, which is equal to $\frac{8}{9}$.

**TAKE ANOTHER LOOK**

**1.** The total distance the ball has fallen is modeled by the function $y = \frac{200(1 - 0.8^x)}{1 - 0.8}$. A graph of this equation gives a smooth curve that fits the data points representing the partial sums. Evaluating the equation for any integer value of $x$ gives a partial sum; evaluating the equation for a large positive value of $x$ (or tracing the curve toward its long-run value) approximates the sum of infinitely many terms. In general, a geometric series is modeled by the function $y = \frac{u_1(1 - r^x)}{1 - r}$, and an arithmetic series is modeled by the function $y = \left(\frac{d}{2}\right)x^2 + \left(u_1 - \frac{d}{2}\right)x$.

**2.** If $|r| < 1$, then as $n$ approaches infinity, $r^n$ approaches 0 and $\frac{u_1(1 - r^n)}{1 - r}$ approaches $\frac{u_1(1 - 0)}{1 - r}$, or $\frac{u_1}{1 - r}$, which is the explicit formula for the sum of infinitely many terms of a convergent geometric series. If $r > 1$, then $r^n$ gets larger without bound, and $(1 - r)$ will be a fixed negative number; therefore $\frac{u_1(1 - r^n)}{1 - r}$ also gets larger without bound. If $r < -1$, the expression $r^n$ alternates sign, getting farther from 0, so $\frac{u_1(1 - r^n)}{1 - r}$ also gets farther from 0.

**3.** The equation for the last unpaid balance is
$A_n = A_0(1 + r)^n - P(1 + r)^{n-1} - P(1 + r)^{n-2} - P(1 + r)^{n-3} - \cdots - P(1 + r)^1 - P$.

The part of the equation with the $P$'s is a geometric series of $n$ terms in reverse order with $u_1 = -P$ and constant ratio $(1 + r)$. By the formula, the partial sum equals $\frac{-P(1 - (1 + r)^n)}{1 - (1 + r)}$, or $\frac{P(1 - (1 + r)^n)}{r}$. The equation for $A_n$ then becomes $A_n = A_0(1 + r)^n + \frac{P(1 - (1 + r)^n)}{r}$. Substituting 0 for $A_n$ and solving for $P$ yields the equation $P = -\frac{A_0 r(1 + r)^n}{1 - (1 + r)^n}$, or $P = \frac{A_0 r(1 + r)^n}{(1 + r)^n - 1}$.

**a.** Substitute 11,000 for $A_0$, 60 for $n$, and $\frac{0.049}{12}$ for $r$ in the formula for $P$.

$$P = \frac{11000 \cdot \frac{0.049}{12}\left(1 + \frac{0.049}{12}\right)^{60}}{\left(1 + \frac{0.049}{12}\right)^{60} - 1} \approx 207.08$$

A monthly payment of \$207.08 is required.

**b.** Substitute 620 for $P$, 30(12), or 360 for $n$, and $\frac{0.075}{12}$ for $r$ in the formula for $P$ and solve for $A_0$.

$$620 = \frac{A_0 \cdot \frac{0.075}{12}\left(1 + \frac{0.075}{12}\right)^{360}}{\left(1 + \frac{0.075}{12}\right)^{360} - 1}$$

$$620\left(1 + \frac{0.075}{12}\right)^{360} - 620 = A_0 \cdot \frac{0.075}{12}\left(1 + \frac{0.075}{12}\right)^{360}$$

$$A_0 = \frac{620\left(1 + \frac{0.075}{12}\right)^{360} - 620}{\frac{0.075}{12}\left(1 + \frac{0.075}{12}\right)^{360}} \approx 88670.93$$

The maximum home mortgage for which Tina Fetzer can qualify is \$88,670.93.

## CHAPTER 12

**LESSON 12.1**

**EXERCISES**

**1. a.** $\frac{6}{15} = .4$. In the 15 days of observation, Nina's coach wore black socks 6 times, so the probability that he will wear black socks on any given day is $\frac{6}{15}$.

**b.** $\frac{7}{15} \approx .467$. In the 15 days of observation, Nina's coach wore white socks 7 times, so the probability that he will wear black socks on any given day is $\frac{7}{15}$.

**c.** $\frac{2}{15} \approx .133$. In the 15 days of observation, Nina's coach wore red socks 2 times, so the probability that he will wear black socks on any given day is $\frac{2}{15}$.

**2. a.** $\frac{698}{1424} \approx .490$. There are 1424 students in total, and 698 of them are female.

**b.** $\frac{477}{1424} \approx .335$. There are 1424 students in total, and 477 of them are 11th graders.

**c.** $\frac{228}{435} \approx .524$. There are 435 12th graders in total, and 228 of them are male.

**d.** $\frac{263}{726} \approx .362$. There are 726 males in total, and 263 of them are 10th graders.

*Discovering Advanced Algebra Solutions Manual*
©2004 Key Curriculum Press

**3.** The total area of the shaded region is 14 square units. In 3a–e, find the area of the region specified.

**a.** $\frac{4}{14} \approx .286$. The area of the shaded region where $x$ is between 0 and 2 is 4 square units, so the probability that $x$ is between 0 and 2 is $\frac{4}{14}$.

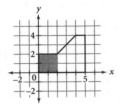

**b.** $\frac{10}{14} \approx .714$. The area of the shaded region where $y$ is between 0 and 2 is 10 square units, so the probability that $y$ is between 0 and 2 is $\frac{10}{14}$.

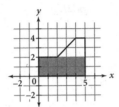

**c.** $\frac{7.5}{14} \approx .536$. The area of the shaded region where $x$ is greater than 3 is 7.5 square units, so the probability that $x$ is greater than 3 is $\frac{7.5}{14}$.

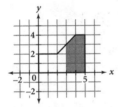

**d.** $\frac{1.5}{14} \approx .107$. The area of the shaded region where $y$ is greater than 3 is 1.5 square units, so the probability that $y$ is greater than 3 is $\frac{1.5}{14}$.

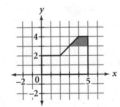

**e.** $\frac{2}{14} \approx .143$. The area of the portion of the shaded region where $x + y$ is less than 2 is 2 square units, so the probability that $x + y$ is less than 2 is $\frac{2}{14}$.

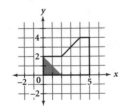

**4. a.** $\frac{5}{30} \approx .167$

**b.** $\frac{100 - 2.5}{100} = \frac{97.5}{100} = .975$

**c.** $\frac{36 - 5}{36} = \frac{31}{36} \approx .861$

**5. a.** Experimental

**b.** Theoretical

**c.** Experimental

**6. a.** Answers will vary.

**b.** Possible answer: Use the random integer command on the calculator to simulate rolling a die.

**c.** Answers will vary.

**d.** Answers will vary. Sum your answers from 6c and divide the answer by 10.

**e.** Answers will vary. Long-run averages should tend toward 6 turns in order to roll a 6.

**7.** Answers will vary. Each of these procedures has shortcomings.

**i.** Middle numbers (3–7) are more common than getting only 1 or 2 or 8 or 9 heads in one trial of dropping pennies.

**ii.** Very few pencils will be at 0 or 1 in.; students throw away their pencils long before that.

**iii.** This is the best method, although books tend to open to pages that are used more than others.

**8. a.** Answers will vary.

**b.** The long-run experimental probability should show that $\frac{1}{6}$ of all rolls will be a 3.

**c.** Answers will vary. The points should level out to a straight line at $y = 0.1\overline{6}$. If you considered 5's instead of 3's, the data should level out to the same value.

**d.** Answers will vary but should be close to $\frac{1}{6}$.

**e.** $P(3) = \frac{1}{6} \approx .167$. There are six equally likely outcomes, and 3 is one of them, so the theoretical probability is $\frac{1}{6}$.

**9. a.** 36. There are 6 possibilities for the green die and 6 possibilities for the white die, so there are $6 \cdot 6 = 36$ possible outcomes for the two-die roll.

**b.** $6; \frac{1}{6} \approx .167$

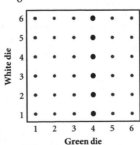

**c.** $12; \frac{12}{36} \approx .333$. There are 6 possibilities for the green die and 2 possibilities for the white die, so there are $6 \cdot 2 = 12$ possible outcomes for the two-die roll. Therefore the probability of rolling a 2 or 3 on the white die is $\frac{12}{36}$.

**d.** $3; \frac{3}{36} \approx .083$. There are 3 possibilities for the green die and 1 possibility for the white die, so there are $3 \cdot 1 = 3$ possible outcomes for the two-die roll. Therefore the probability of rolling an even number on the green die and a 2 on the white die is $\frac{3}{36}$.

**10. a.** $4; \frac{4}{36} \approx .111$. The possible outcomes are $(3, 6)$, $(4, 5)$, $(5, 4)$, $(6, 3)$.

**b.** $5; \frac{5}{36} \approx .139$. The possible outcomes are $(1, 5)$, $(2, 4)$, $(3, 3)$, $(4, 2)$, $(5, 1)$.

**c.** $10; \frac{10}{36} \approx .278$. The possible outcomes are $(1, 2)$, $(2, 3)$, $(3, 4)$, $(4, 5)$, $(5, 6)$, $(6, 5)$, $(5, 4)$, $(4, 3)$, $(3, 2)$, $(2, 1)$.

**d.** $2; \frac{2}{36} \approx .056$. The possible outcomes are $(2, 4)$, $(4, 2)$.

**e.** $10; \frac{10}{36} \approx .278$. The possible outcomes are $(1, 1)$, $(1, 2)$, $(1, 3)$, $(1, 4)$, $(2, 1)$, $(2, 2)$, $(2, 3)$, $(3, 1)$, $(3, 2)$, $(4, 1)$.

**11. a.** $12 \cdot 12 = 144$ square units

**b.** $\frac{1}{2}(11)(8) = 44$ square units

**c.** $\frac{44}{144}$

**d.** $\frac{44}{144} \approx .306$

**e.** $\frac{100}{144} \approx .694$

**f.** $0; 0$. The area of a point or of a line is 0, so the probability of a randomly selected point landing on a specific point or line is $\frac{0}{144} = 0$.

**12. a.** $x + y \leq 6$

**b.**

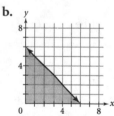

**c.** $\frac{18}{64} \approx .281$. The area of the shaded triangle is $\frac{1}{2}(6)(6) = 18$ square units and the area of the entire feasible region, the 8-by-8 square, is 64 square units, so the probability that a point in the square lands in the shaded triangle is $\frac{18}{64}$.

**13. a.** 270

**b.** 1380. The approximate sum of frequencies is $180 + 240 + 210 + 300 + 270 + 180 = 1380$.

**c.** $\frac{270}{1380} \approx .196$

**d.** $\frac{1380 - 270}{1380} = \frac{1110}{1380} \approx .804$

**14.** To cut up the cube into 27 smaller cubes, divide each edge into three equal parts.

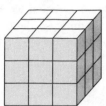

**a.** $\frac{6}{27} \approx .222$. There are 6 cubes with exactly one painted face, one in the middle of each face of the large cube.

**b.** $\frac{12}{27} \approx .444$. There are 12 cubes with exactly two painted faces, one in the middle of each edge of the large cube.

**c.** $\frac{8}{27} \approx .296$. There are 8 cubes with exactly three painted faces, one at each corner of the large cube.

**d.** $\frac{1}{27} \approx .037$. There is 1 cube with no painted faces, in the center of the large cube.

Three painted faces is the most that any of the small cubes has, so the probabilities in 14a–d should sum to 1.

$$\frac{6}{27} + \frac{12}{27} + \frac{8}{27} + \frac{1}{27} = \frac{27}{27} = 1$$

**15. a.** 53 pm, at point $C$

**b.** 0 pm, at point $A$, the nucleus

**c.** The probability starts at zero at the nucleus, increases and peaks at a distance of 53 pm, and then decreases quickly, then more slowly, but never reaches zero.

**16.** $x^4 - 4x^3y + 6x^2y^2 - 4xy^3 + y^4$

$(x - y)^4 = (x - y)^2(x - y)^2$

$\qquad = \left(x^2 - 2xy + y^2\right)\left(x^2 - 2xy + y^2\right)$

$\qquad = x^4 - 2x^3y + x^2y^2 - 2x^3y + 4x^2y^2 - 2xy^3 + x^2y^2 - 2xy^3 + y^4$

$\qquad = x^4 - 4x^3y + 6x^2y^2 - 4xy^3 + y^4$

**17.** $\log\left(\frac{ac^2}{b}\right)$

$\log a - \log b + 2 \log c = \log\left(\frac{a}{b}\right) + \log\left(c^2\right)$

$\qquad\qquad = \log\left(\frac{a}{b}\right)\left(c^2\right) = \log\left(\frac{ac^2}{b}\right)$

**18.** $x = 5000$

| | |
|---|---|
| $\log 2 + \log x = 4$ | Original equation. |
| $\log 2x = 4$ | Product property of logarithms. |
| $10^4 = 2x$ | Definition of logarithm. |
| $x = 5000$ | Evaluate $10^4$ and divide both sides by 2. |

**19. a.**

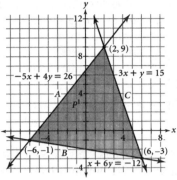

**b.** $(2, 9), (-6, -1), (6, -3)$. Find the intersections of each of the lines that border the triangle by using substitution, elimination, or matrix inverses.

Intersection of $3x + y = 15$ and $-5x + 4y = 26$: $(2, 9)$

Intersection of $x + 6y = -12$ and $-5x + 4y = 26$: $(-6, -1)$

Intersection of $3x + y = 15$ and $x + 6y = -12$: $(6, -3)$

**c.** 68 square units. Inscribe the triangle in a square with side length 12 units. The area of the triangle is equal to the area of the square minus the areas of the surrounding triangles.

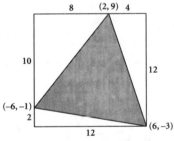

The area of the triangle is $(12)(12) - \frac{1}{2}(8)(10) - \frac{1}{2}(12)(2) - \frac{1}{2}(4)(12) = 68$ square units.

**20.** A vertical parabola with focus $(3, 0)$ and directrix $y = 6$; $y = -\frac{1}{12}x^2 + \frac{1}{2}x + \frac{9}{4}$

**21. a.** Set i should have a larger standard deviation because the values are more spread out.

**b. i.** $\bar{x} = 35, s \approx 22.3$

**ii.** $\bar{x} = 117, s \approx 3.5$

**c.** The original values of $\bar{x}$ and $s$ are multiplied by 10.

**i.** $\bar{x} = 350, s \approx 223.5$

**ii.** $\bar{x} = 1170, s \approx 35.4$

**d.** The original values of $\bar{x}$ are increased by 10, and the original values of $s$ are unchanged.

**i.** $\bar{x} = 45, s \approx 22.3$

**ii.** $\bar{x} = 127, s \approx 3.5$

## EXTENSION

Results will vary.

## EXPLORATION · GEOMETRIC PROBABILITY

### QUESTIONS

**1.** Sample answer: A quarter (diameter 24 mm) is tossed onto a grid of squares with side length 27 mm and line thickness 3 mm.

**2.** $P(\text{success}) = \frac{(a - d)^2}{(a + t)^2}$. When looking at a single square of the grid (and half of its borders with neighboring squares), its total area is $(a + t)^2$. The coin must land so that its center is at least $\frac{d}{2}$ units away from any border of the square, so it must land inside a square of area $\left(a - 2\left(\frac{d}{2}\right)\right)^2 = (a - d)^2$. Therefore the probability that the coin does not touch the border when it is tossed is $\frac{(a - d)^2}{(a + t)^2}$.

**3.** Approximately .321. Consider a single triangle. Its total area is $400\sqrt{3}$ mm². The coin must land so that its center is at least 5 mm from any edge of the triangle, so it must land in an equilateral triangle of side length $\left(40 - 10\sqrt{3}\right)$ mm. The area of this triangle is $\frac{1}{2}\left(40 - 10\sqrt{3}\right)^2\left(\frac{\sqrt{3}}{2}\right) = \left(475\sqrt{3} - 600\right)$ mm². Therefore the probability that the coin will land entirely inside a triangle is $\frac{475\sqrt{3} - 600}{400\sqrt{3}} \approx .321$.

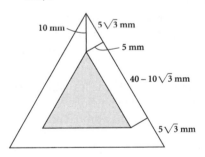

### IMPROVING YOUR REASONING SKILLS

Trish should put 49 of the red marbles into the box with the blue marbles, leaving only 1 red marble in the other box. If the box with 99 marbles is chosen, the probability of choosing a red marble is $\frac{49}{99}$. If the box with 1 marble is chosen, the probability of choosing a red marble is 1. It is equally likely that either box will be chosen, so the overall probability of Trish winning is the average of $\frac{49}{99}$ and 1, or $.\overline{74}$.

**EXERCISES**

**1.**

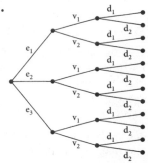

**2.** $P(a) = (.75)(.9) = .675$; $P(b) = (.75)(.1) = .075$; $P(c) = (.25)(.2) = .05$; $P(d) = (.25)(.8) = .2$; the values sum to 1.

**3.** $P(a) = .7$; $P(b) = .3$; $P(c) = .18$; $P(d) = .4$; $P(e) = .8$; $P(f) = .2$; $P(g) = .08$

$.6P(a) = .42$, so $P(a) = \frac{.42}{.6} = .7$

$P(b) = 1 - P(a) = 1 - .7 = .3$

$P(c) = .6P(b) = (.6)(.3) = .18$

$P(d) = 1 - .6 = .4$

$P(d) \cdot P(e) = .32$, so $P(e) = \frac{.32}{.4} = .8$

$P(f) = 1 - P(e) = 1 - .8 = .2$

$P(g) = P(d) \cdot P(f) = (.4)(.2) = .08$

**4.** Because each branching has two choices, each branch in the tree has probability $\frac{1}{2}$.

**a.** $\frac{1}{8} = .125$. There is only one path with all S's, so it has probability $\left(\frac{1}{2}\right)\left(\frac{1}{2}\right)\left(\frac{1}{2}\right) = \frac{1}{8}$.

**b.** $\frac{3}{8} = .375$. There are three paths with two S's and one F. Each of these paths has probability $\frac{1}{8}$, so the probability of ending up on one of those paths is $\frac{1}{8} + \frac{1}{8} + \frac{1}{8} = \frac{3}{8}$.

**c.** $\frac{2}{3} \approx .667$. There are two paths for which Celina is one of exactly two students who are successful. Each of these two paths has probability $\frac{1}{8}$, so the probability of this event is $\frac{1}{8} + \frac{1}{8} = \frac{1}{4}$. Divide this by the probability found in 4b to get $\frac{1}{4} \div \frac{3}{8} = \frac{2}{3}$.

**5.** For the first choice, the probability of choosing a sophomore is $\frac{14}{21}$, and the probability of choosing a junior is $\frac{7}{21}$. Once the first student is chosen, the class total is reduced by 1 and either the junior or sophomore portion is reduced by 1.

**6. a.** From the top: $\frac{182}{420} = \frac{13}{30} \approx .433$; $\frac{98}{420} = \frac{7}{30} \approx .233$; $\frac{98}{420} = \frac{7}{30} \approx .233$; $\frac{42}{420} = \frac{1}{10} = .1$

**b.** No, because the probabilities of the four paths are not all the same.

**c.** $\frac{420}{420} = 1$

**7. a.** 24. There are 4 choices for what to put in first, and then 3 choices for what to put in second, then 2 choices for what to put in third, and only 1 choice for the last item. Therefore there are $4 \cdot 3 \cdot 2 \cdot 1 = 24$ possible orders in which Chris can add the ingredients.

**b.** .25. There are 4 possibilities for what should be first, so the probability that milk should be first is $\frac{1}{4} = .25$.

**c.** $\frac{2}{24} \approx .083$. There are two paths having flour first and shortening second (FSBM, FSMB), and each path has probability $\frac{1}{24}$, so the probability is $\frac{2}{24}$.

**d.** $\frac{1}{24} \approx .042$. Each path has probability $\frac{1}{24}$.

**e.** $\frac{24 - 1}{24} = \frac{23}{24} \approx .958$

**f.** $\frac{12}{24} = .5$. There are 12 paths that have flour and milk next to each other:

FMBS, FMSB, BFMS, SFMB, BSFM, SBFM, MFBS, MFSB, BMFS, SMFB, BSMF, SBMF

**8. a.**

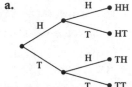

**b.**

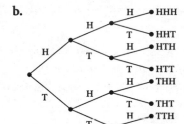

**c.**

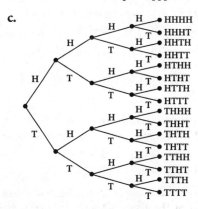

**9. a.** 4       **b.** 8       **c.** 16

**d.** 32       **e.** 1024       **f.** $2^n$

**10.** For 10a–c, use a tree diagram similar to the one in 8c.

**a.** $\frac{1}{16} = .0625$. There is 1 possible path.

**b.** $\frac{4}{16} = .25$. There are 4 possible paths.

**c.** $\frac{6}{16} = .375$. There are 6 possible paths.

**d.** $\frac{4}{16} = .25$. There are 4 possible paths.

**e.** $\frac{1}{16} = .0625$. There is 1 possible path.

**f.** 1

**g.** Add the probabilities from 10d and e:
$.25 + .0625 = .3125$.

**11. a.**
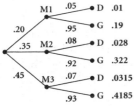

To fill in the diagram, remember that the probabilities of all branches coming out of any node must sum to 1, and the probability of any path is the product of probabilities of all the branches in that path.

**b.** .08. $P$(a phone from site M2 is defective) $=$
$P(\text{D} \mid \text{M2}) = 1 - P(\text{G} \mid \text{M2}) = 1 - .92 = .08$

**c.** .0695. $P$(a randomly chosen phone is defective) $=$
$P(\text{D}) = P(\text{M1 and D}) + P(\text{M2 and D}) +$
$P(\text{M3 and D}) = .01 + .028 + .0315 = .0695$

**d.** .4029. $P$(a phone was manufactured at site M2 if you already know it is defective) $= P(\text{M2} \mid \text{D}) =$
$\frac{P(\text{M2 and D})}{P(\text{D})} = \frac{.028}{.0695} \approx .4029$

**12.** The shots are independent events, so multiply the probabilities of each event to answer 12a–d.

**a.** .0289. $P$(he misses both shots) $= P$(he misses a shot) $\cdot$ $P$(he misses a shot) $= (.17)(.17) = .0289$

**b.** .9711. $P$(he makes at least one shot) $=$
$P$(he makes the first shot and misses the second shot) $+$ $P$(he misses the first shot and makes the second shot) $+$ $P$(he makes both shots) $= (.83)(.17) + (.17)(.83) + (.83)(.83) = .9711$

**c.** .6889. $P$(he makes both shots) $= (.83)(.83) = .6889$

**d.** .9711. The Pistons free thrower needs to make only one of his shots in order to win the game, so by 12b, $P$(the Pistons win the game) $=$ $P$(he makes at least one shot) $= .9711$.

**13.** $\frac{6}{16} = .375$. There is a total of $2^4 = 16$ possibilities for the genders of the four children. Of these, there are 6 with exactly two girls: GGBB, GBGB, GBBG, BGGB, BGBG, BBGG. Therefore, $P$(exactly 2 girls in a family with 4 children) $= \frac{6}{16} = .375$.

**14.** Dependent; $P$(10th grade $\mid$ female) $= \frac{249}{698} \approx .357$, but $P$(female) $= \frac{698}{1424} \approx .490$. So the probability of choosing a female from the 10th grade is less than the probability of choosing a female.

**15. a.** $10^5 = 100,000$

**b.** $10^9 = 1,000,000,000$

**c.** 17,576,000. There are 10 digits and 26 letters, so in choosing 3 digits and 3 letters there are $10^3 \cdot 26^3 = 17,576,000$ possible mailing codes.

**d.** 7,200,000. There are still 10 digits to choose from in each occurrence. There are 18 choices for the first letter and 20 choices for each of the other two letters. Hence there are $10^3 \cdot 18 \cdot 20^2 = 7,200,000$ possible mailing codes.

**16.** 64. There are six positions, each with two possible states, so there are $2^6 = 64$ possible Braille characters.

**17. a.** $(2 + 4i) - (5 + 2i) = (2 - 5) + (4 - 2)i = -3 + 2i$

**b.** $(2 + 4i)(5 + 2i) = 10 + 4i + 20i + 8i^2 = 10 + 24i - 8 = 2 + 24i$

**c.** $\dfrac{2 + 4i}{5 + 2i} = \dfrac{2 + 4i}{5 + 2i} \cdot \dfrac{5 - 2i}{5 - 2i} =$
$\dfrac{10 - 4i + 20i - 8i^2}{25 - 4i^2} = \dfrac{10 + 16i + 8}{25 + 4} =$
$\dfrac{18 + 16i}{29} = \dfrac{18}{29} + \dfrac{16}{29}i$

**18.** $P$(orange) $= .152$; $P$(blue) $\approx .457$. The full rectangle has area $20 \cdot 15 = 300$ square units. The area of the orange region is $\frac{1}{2}(7)(13) = 45.5$ square units, so $P$(orange) $= \frac{45.5}{300} = .152$.

To find the area of the blue triangle, subtract the areas of the three outer triangles from the area of the whole rectangle. The blue triangle's area is $(20)(15) - \frac{1}{2}(7)(13) - \frac{1}{2}(13)(15) - \frac{1}{2}(20)(2) = 137$ square units. Therefore $P$(blue) $= \frac{137}{300} \approx .457$.

**19. a.** $P$(a junior is female) $= \dfrac{\textit{number of female juniors}}{\textit{total number of juniors}} = \dfrac{50}{110} \approx .455$

**b.** $P$(a student is a senior) $= \dfrac{\textit{total number of seniors}}{\textit{total number of students}} = \dfrac{120}{230} \approx .522$

**20.** $8\sqrt{2}$. The length of the first diagonal is $4\sqrt{2}$. The second square has side length 2, so its diagonal has length $2\sqrt{2}$. The third square has side length 1, so its diagonal has length $\sqrt{2}$. The lengths of the individual diagonals form a geometric sequence with initial value $4\sqrt{2}$ and common ratio 0.5. Therefore the long-run length of the spiral made by the diagonals is the sum of the geometric series
$$\sum_{n=1}^{\infty} 4\sqrt{2}(0.5)^{n-1} = \frac{4\sqrt{2}}{1 - 0.5} = 8\sqrt{2}$$

## QUESTIONS

**1.** For more cases, the shape of the histogram is closer to what it theoretically should be.

**2.** For more cases, the relative range of the data becomes smaller.

**3.** Rerandomize many times and look for a pattern. For 1000 cases it should be very easy to determine how the die was loaded, but for only 10 cases it can be more difficult.

**4.** The Law of Large Numbers is demonstrated by this exploration. The more cases you look at, the closer the histogram gets to the theoretical probability, for both fair and loaded dice.

### IMPROVING YOUR REASONING SKILLS

Angelina can put one-third of the coins into each pan. If they don't balance, the lighter coin is in the lighter third. If they do balance, the omitted third contains the lighter coin. She then repeats the process with the lighter third and isolates the lighter coin in four balancings.

## LESSON 12.3

### EXERCISES

**1.** 10% of the students are sophomores and not in advanced algebra. 15% are sophomores in advanced algebra. 12% are in advanced algebra but are not sophomores. 63% are neither sophomores nor in advanced algebra.

**2. a.** $P(S) = .10 + .15 = .25$

**b.** $P(A \text{ and not } S) = .12$

**c.** $P(S \mid A) = \dfrac{P(S \text{ and } A)}{P(A)} = \dfrac{.15}{.15 + .12} \approx .56$

**d.** $P(S \text{ or } A) = .10 + .15 + .12 = .37$

**3.**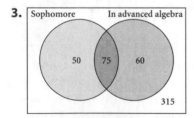

To find the frequency of any event, multiply its probability by 500. For example, the frequency of (S and A) is $.15 \cdot 500 = 75$.

**4.** No. $P(S) \cdot P(A) = .25 \cdot .27 = .0675$, while $P(S \text{ and } A) = .15$. These must be equal if the events are independent.

**5. a.** Yes, because they do not overlap.

**b.** No. $P(A \text{ and } B) = 0$, but $P(A) \cdot P(B) \neq 0$. These two probabilities would be the same if the events were independent.

**6. a.**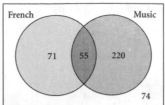

Use the fact that 20% of the 275 music students take French to find that 55 students are in both music and French. This puts $126 - 55 = 71$ students in French but not music, $275 - 55 = 220$ students in music but not French, and $420 - (71 + 55 + 220) = 74$ students in neither music nor French.

**b.** $\dfrac{55}{420} \approx 0.13$, or 13%    **c.** 74

**7. a.**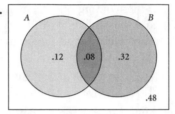

$P(A \mid B) = \dfrac{P(A \text{ and } B)}{P(B)}$, so $P(A \text{ and } B) = P(B) \cdot P(A \mid B) = (.4)(.2) = .08$.

$P(A \text{ and not } B) = P(A) - P(A \text{ and } B) = .2 - .08 = .12$

$P(B \text{ and not } A) = P(B) - P(A \text{ and } B) = .4 - .08 = .32$

$P(\text{not } (A \text{ or } B)) = 1 - .12 - .08 - .32 = .48$

**b. i.** .08    **ii.** .60    **iii.** .48

**8.** $0 \le P(A \text{ and } B) \le .4$, $.5 \le P(A \text{ or } B) \le .9$. The first diagram shows $P(A \text{ and } B) = 0$ and $P(A \text{ or } B) = .9$. The second diagram shows $P(A \text{ and } B) = .4$ and $P(A \text{ or } B) = .5$.

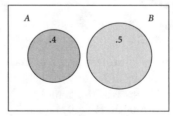 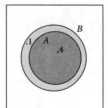

**9.** If there are 800 students in the school, this is the original frequency diagram.

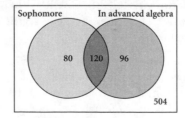

If 20 sophomores move from geometry to advanced algebra, take 20 students out of (S and not A) and add 20 students to (S and A) to get the new frequency diagram.

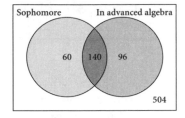

Divide each of the frequencies by 800 to obtain the new Venn diagram of probabilities.

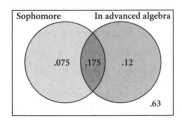

**10. a.** Yellow     **b.** Cyan     **c.** White

   **d.** Blue     **e.** Green     **f.** Black

**11. a.**

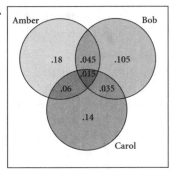

Use the independence of the events to find the probabilities.

$P(A \text{ and } B) = P(A) \cdot P(B) = (.3)(.2) = .06$

$P(A \text{ and } C) = P(A) \cdot P(C) = (.3)(.25) = .075$

$P(B \text{ and } C) = P(B) \cdot P(C) = (.2)(.25) = .05$

$P(A \text{ and } B \text{ and } C) = P(A) \cdot P(B) \cdot P(C) = (.3)(.2)(.25) = .015$

Now subtract appropriate probabilities to fill in the Venn diagram.

$P(A \text{ and } B, \text{ but not } C) = P(A \text{ and } B) - P(A \text{ and } B \text{ and } C) = .06 - .015 = .045$

$P(A \text{ and } C, \text{ but not } B) = P(A \text{ and } C) - P(A \text{ and } B \text{ and } C) = .075 - .015 = .06$

$P(B \text{ and } C, \text{ but not } A) = P(B \text{ and } C) - P(A \text{ and } B \text{ and } C) = .05 - .015 = .035$

$P(A, \text{ but not } B \text{ or } C) = P(A) - P(A \text{ and } B) - P(A \text{ and } C, \text{ but not } B) = .3 - .06 - .06 = .18$

$P(B, \text{ but not } A \text{ or } C) = P(B) - P(A \text{ and } B) - P(B \text{ and } C, \text{ but not } A) = .2 - .06 - .035 = .105$

$P(C, \text{ but not } A \text{ or } B) = P(C) - P(A \text{ and } C) - P(B \text{ and } C, \text{ but not } A) = .25 - .075 - .035 = .14$

  **b.** $P(A \text{ and } B \text{ and } C) = .015$

  **c.** .42. The probability that at least one of Kendra's three friends will be on the phone is the sum of all the probabilities in the circles, which is .58. Therefore, $P$(none of her friends will be on the phone) $= 1 - .58 = .42$.

**12. a.** $\frac{280}{1500} \approx .187$. There are 280 liberals over 45 years old, out of a total 1500 interviewed voters.

  **b.** $\frac{775}{1500} \approx .517$. There are 775 conservatives, out of a total 1500 interviewed voters.

  **c.** $\frac{145}{355} \approx .408$. Among the 355 interviewed voters under 30 years old, there are 145 conservatives.

  **d.** $\frac{145}{775} \approx .187$. Among the 775 conservative voters interviewed, there are 145 under 30 years old.

**13.** $\bar{x} = \dfrac{74 + 71 + 87 + 89 + 73 + 82 + 55 + 78 + 80 + 83 + 72}{11}$

$= 76.\overline{72}$, or approximately 77

**14.** $\frac{324}{15625} \approx .02$. The flips are independent events, so multiply the probabilities of the individual flips.

$$\left(\frac{2}{5}\right)\left(\frac{3}{5}\right)\left(\frac{3}{5}\right)\left(\frac{3}{5}\right)\left(\frac{2}{5}\right)\left(\frac{3}{5}\right) = \frac{324}{15625} \approx .02$$

**15. a.** $\sqrt{18} = \sqrt{3^2 \cdot 2} = 3\sqrt{2}$

  **b.** $\sqrt{54} = \sqrt{3^2 \cdot 6} = 3\sqrt{6}$

  **c.** $\sqrt{60x^3y^5} = \sqrt{2^2x^2y^4 \cdot 15xy} = 2xy^2\sqrt{15xy}$

**16.** They meet 6.68 h after Patrick and Ben leave, or at 12:56 P.M., 534 km from Port Charles. Let $t$ represent the time in hours from when Patrick and Ben start driving until they meet Carl and Louis. Carl and Louis start driving 3.25 h later, so their driving time is $t - 3.25$. Between the two vehicles, there were 860 km covered. Therefore, solve the equation $860 = 80t + 95(t - 3.25)$.

$860 = 80t + 95(t - 3.25)$

$860 = 175t - 308.75$

$1168.75 = 175t$

$6.68 = t$

They meet 6.68 h after Patrick and Ben leave. At that time Patrick and Ben have traveled $(80 \text{ km/h})(6.68 \text{ h}) \approx 534$ km.

**EXERCISES**

**1. a.** Yes; the number of children will be an integer, and it is based on a random process.

   **b.** No; the length may be a non-integer.

   **c.** Yes; there will be an integer number of pieces of mail, and it is based on random processes of who sends mail when.

**2. a.** Yes; the result of each call is independent of other calls, and she stops calling when she is successful.

   **b.** No; the number of cats is a discrete random variable, but because you don't stop counting when you get the first cat, it is not geometric.

   **c.** No; you are counting minutes until you hear a song, but because all songs are not the same length and minutes are not equivalent to songs, you are working with two different types of variables.

**3. a.** Approximately .068. You must first find two right-handed people, and then a left-handed person, so the probability is $(.92)(.92)(.08) = .067712$.

   **b.** Approximately .203. There are three ways to find exactly one left-handed person in three tries, depending on whether the left-handed person is the first, second, or third person you meet. Each of these events has probability $(.92)(.92)(.08) = .067712$. Therefore the probability of finding exactly one left-handed person in three tries is $3(.067712) = .203136$.

**4. a.** 0. The probability that you answer a question correctly is $\frac{1}{6}$, the probability that you answer a question incorrectly is $\frac{4}{6} = \frac{2}{3}$, and the probability that you leave a question blank is $\frac{1}{6}$. Therefore the expected value of a question is $\frac{1}{6}(1) + \frac{2}{3}\left(-\frac{1}{4}\right) + \frac{1}{6}(0) = 0$.

   **b.** 0. The expected value for each question is 0 points, so the expected value for a 30-question test is $30(0) = 0$.

**5. a.** Theoretically, after 10 games Sly should get about 23 points and Andy should get about 21.

   **b.** Theoretically, it should be close to .41.

   **c.**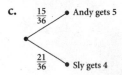

   There are 15 ways to roll a sum greater than 7 and 21 ways to roll a sum less than 8.

**d.** $-0.25$. The expected outcome is $\frac{15}{36}(5) + \frac{21}{36}(-4) = -0.25$.

**e.** Possible answer: 5 points for Sly if the sum is less than 8 and 7 points for Andy if the sum of the dice is greater than 7. Then the expected value from Andy's point of view is $\frac{15}{36}(7) + \frac{21}{36}(5) = 0$, which means that neither player is favored.

**6. a.** Answers will vary.

   **b.** Sample answer: Assign each of the letters in the word CHAMPION a different number from 1 to 8. Randomly generate numbers between 1 and 8. Count how many digits you must generate until you have at least one of each number.

   **c.** Answers will vary.

   **d.** Theoretically, the average number of boxes should be about 22 boxes.

   **e.** Average numbers of boxes should be about 22 boxes.

**7. a.** $.16(35) + .24(30) + .32(25) + .28(15) = \$25$

   **b.** $P(C \mid (A \text{ or } C)) = \dfrac{P(C)}{P(A \text{ or } C)} = \dfrac{.32}{.16 + .32} = \dfrac{2}{3} = .67$

   **c.** \$28.33. The expected value of the ticket is $P(A \mid (A \text{ or } C))(35) + P(C \mid (A \text{ or } C))(25) = \frac{1}{3}(35) + \frac{2}{3}(25) = \$28.33$.

**8. a.** Approximately 7 points. The expected number of points for player 1 is $6(.25)(.6) + 10(.75)(.4)$, and the expected number of points for player 2 is $8(.25)(.4) + x(.75)(.6)$. To find the value of $x$ for which these expected numbers are equal, write and solve an equation.

$$6(.25)(.6) + 10(.75)(.4) = 8(.25)(.4) + x(.75)(.6)$$
$$.9 + 3 = .8 + .45x$$
$$3.1 = .45x$$
$$x \approx 6.9$$

Therefore, for $x = 7$ the two players have approximately the same expected number of points, 3.9 for player 1 and 3.95 for player 2.

   **b.** Answers will vary.

**9. a.** .2. This is the case where Bonny makes her shot and Sally misses the return, so the probability is $(.80)(.25) = .2$.

   **b.** .12. This is the case where Bonny makes both of her shots and Sally makes the first return shot but misses the second return. The probability is $(.80)(.75)(.80)(.25) = .12$.

**c.**

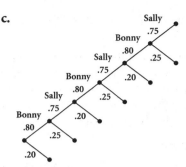

$(.80)(.75) \cdot (.80)(.75) \cdot (.80)(.25) = .072$

**d.** This is the sum of the probabilities in 9a–c: $.2 + .12 + .072 = .392$.

**e.** Geometric; $u_1 = .20$, $r = .6$

$u_1 = (.80)(.25) = .20$

$u_2 = (.80)(.75)(.80)(.25) = (.6)(.2)$

$u_3 = ((.80)(.75))^2(.80)(.25) = (.6)^2(.2)$

$u_n = ((.80)(.75))^n(.80)(.25) = (.6)^n(.2)$

**f.** $.476672$. The probability is the sum of the first six terms in the sequence from 9e: $.2 + (.6)(.2) + (.6)^2(.2) + (.6)^3(.2) + (.6)^4(.2) + (.6)^5(.2) = .476672$.

**g.** $.5$. The long-run probability is the sum of a geometric series.

$$\sum_{n=1}^{\infty} (.6)^{n-1}(.2) = \frac{.2}{1 - .6} = .5$$

**10. a.** Sample answer: Use your calculator to randomly generate two integers. Assign one of the integers to be the red candy, and count how many times it takes for the integer to come up. In the long run, you need to pick 2 candies before you get a red one.

**b.** The long-run average number of blue candies should be 1. Calculate the probabilities of a person pulling out various numbers of blue candies before pulling out a red. Assume an infinite supply of candies.

$P(0) = .5$

$P(1) = .5^2$

$P(2) = .5^3$

$P(3) = .5^4$

This forms a geometric sequence with $u_0 = .5$ and $r = .5$. The expected number of blue candies pulled out in the long run is

$$.5(0) + .5^2(1) + .5^3(2) + .5^4(3) + \cdots = \sum_{n=1}^{\infty} .5^n(n - 1)$$

Use your calculator to estimate the sum of the series to be 1.

**11. a.** $1 - P(0) = 1 - .420 = .580$

**b.**

| Number of defective radios $x$ | Probability $P(x)$ | $x \cdot P(x)$ |
|---|---|---|
| 0 | .420 | 0 |
| 1 | .312 | 0.312 |
| 2 | .173 | 0.346 |
| 3 | .064 | 0.192 |
| 4 | .031 | 0.124 |
| 5 | .000 | 0 |

**c.** $0.974$

**d.** On average, the engineer should expect to find 0.974 defective radio in a sample of 5.

**12.** Approximately $.0465$. You must roll something other than a 6 for the first 7 rolls and then roll a 6 on the eighth roll. The probability is $\left(\frac{5}{6}\right)^7\left(\frac{1}{6}\right) \approx .0465$.

**13.** Because $E_1$ and $E_2$ are complementary, $P(E_1 \text{ or } E_2) = 1$.

**14.** $.4$. The possible numbers of the varieties for a person to get are 0, 1, or 2, and these are mutually exclusive events. You are given $P(2) = .18$ and $P(0) = .42$, therefore $P(1) = 1 - (.18 + .42) = .4$.

**15. a.**

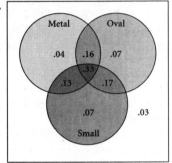

There are 144 paperclips in total. The Venn diagram has eight regions, and the table in your book gives the frequencies for each of those regions. So the probability of each region is the frequency for that region divided by 144.

$P(\text{M and O and S}) = \frac{47}{144} \approx .33$

$P(\text{M and O, but not S}) = \frac{23}{144} \approx .16$

$P(\text{O and S, but not M}) = \frac{25}{144} \approx .17$

$P(\text{O, but not M or S}) = \frac{10}{144} \approx .07$

Continue in this manner until you have filled in the entire Venn diagram.

**b.**

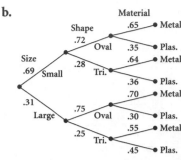

Use the table to fill in the tree diagram. The probabilities in a tree diagram are conditional probabilities.

There are $47 + 25 + 18 + 10 = 100$ small paperclips, so $P(S) = \frac{100}{144} \approx .69$. There are 44 large paperclips, so $P(L) = \frac{44}{144} \approx .31$. Of the 100 small paperclips, $47 + 25 = 72$ are oval, so $P(O|S) = \frac{72}{100} \approx .72$. Similarly $P(T|S) = \frac{18 + 10}{100} \approx .28$. Of the 72 small oval paperclips, 47 are metal, so $P(M|L \text{ and } O) = \frac{47}{72} \approx .65$. Continue in this manner to finish filling in the tree diagram.

**16.** $n \geq \dfrac{-5}{\log\left(\frac{1}{2}\right)}$, or $n \geq 16.61$

$$\left(\frac{1}{2}\right)^n \leq 10^{-5}$$

$$n\log\left(\frac{1}{2}\right) \leq -5\log 10$$

$$n \geq \frac{-5\log 10}{\log\left(\frac{1}{2}\right)} = \frac{-5}{\log\left(\frac{1}{2}\right)} \approx 16.61$$

**17.** 44. Calculate $(.9)^n$ for increasing values of $n$ until the result is less than .01.

**EXTENSION**

Results will vary.

## LESSON 12.5

**EXERCISES**

**1. a.** Yes. Different arrangements of scoops are different.

**b.** No. Different arrangements are not counted separately.

**c.** No. Repetition is not allowed in permutations.

**d.** No. Repetition is not allowed in permutations.

**2. a.** $\dfrac{12!}{11!} = \dfrac{12 \cdot 11!}{11!} = 12$

**b.** $\dfrac{7!}{6!} = \dfrac{7 \cdot 6!}{6!} = 7$

**c.** $\dfrac{(n + 1)!}{n!} = \dfrac{(n + 1)n!}{n!} = n + 1$

**d.** $\dfrac{n!}{(n - 1)!} = \dfrac{n(n - 1)!}{(n - 1)!} = n$

**e.** $\dfrac{120!}{118!} = \dfrac{120 \cdot 119 \cdot 118!}{118!} = 120 \cdot 119 = 14{,}280$

**f.** $\dfrac{n!}{(n - 2)!} = \dfrac{n(n - 1)(n - 2)!}{(n - 2)!} = n(n - 1)$

**g.** Using the solution to 2c, $\dfrac{(n + 1)!}{n!} = n + 1 = 15$, so $n = 14$.

**3. a.** $_7P_3 = \dfrac{7!}{(7 - 3)!} = 7 \cdot 6 \cdot 5 = 210$

**b.** $_7P_6 = \dfrac{7!}{(7 - 6)!} = 7! = 5040$

**c.** $_{n+2}P_n = \dfrac{(n + 2)!}{((n + 2) - n)!} = \dfrac{(n + 2)!}{2!} = \dfrac{(n + 2)!}{2}$

**d.** $_nP_{n-2} = \dfrac{n!}{(n - (n - 2))!} = \dfrac{n!}{2!} = \dfrac{n!}{2}$

**4. a.** $4! = 24$

**b.** 18. Subtract the number of permutations with 0 first from the answer in 4a. The number of permutations with 0 first is the number of permutations of the numbers 3, 5, and 8, or 3!. Thus, $4! - 3! = 18$ numbers can be formed.

**c.** $4^4 = 256$

**d.** 192. There are 3 choices for the first digit and 4 choices for each of the other three digits, so the number of possible I.D. numbers is $3 \cdot 4^3 = 192$.

**5. a.** 10,000; $27.\overline{7}$ h. There are $10^4 = 10{,}000$ possible combinations. It would take $10(10{,}000) = 100{,}000$ s, or $(100{,}000 \text{ s})\left(\frac{1 \text{ m}}{60 \text{ s}}\right)\left(\frac{1 \text{ h}}{60 \text{ m}}\right) = 27.\overline{7}$ h to try all possible combinations.

**b.** 100,000; approximately 11.57 days. There are $10^5 = 100{,}000$ possible combinations. It would take $10(100{,}000) = 1{,}000{,}000$ s, or $(1{,}000{,}000 \text{ s})\left(\frac{1 \text{ m}}{60 \text{ s}}\right)\left(\frac{1 \text{ h}}{60 \text{ m}}\right)\left(\frac{1 \text{ d}}{24 \text{ h}}\right) \approx 11.57$ days to try all possible combinations.

**c.** 10. There are 10 times as many combinations in a 5-dial lock, so it is 10 times more secure.

**6.** $n = r = 6$, or $n = 6$ and $r = 5$, or $n = 10$ and $r = 3$, or $n = 720$ and $r = 1$

**7.** $r$ factors. Rewrite the factors as

$$(n - 0)(n - 1)(n - 2)(n - 3) \cdots (n - (r - 1))$$

Counting the number of factors is the same as counting the number of integers from 0 to $r - 1$, which is $r$.

**8.** $_5P_3 = 5 \cdot 4 \cdot 3 = 60$

**9. a.** $8! = 40{,}320$ **b.** $7! = 5040$ **c.** $\dfrac{7!}{8!} = \dfrac{1}{8} = .125$

**d.** Sample answer: There are 8 possible positions for Volume 5, all equally likely. So $P(5 \text{ in rightmost slot}) = \frac{1}{8} = .125$.

**e.** .5. Sample answer: There are 4 even-numbered books that can be in the rightmost position out of the eight books. So the probability of an even-numbered book being on the right is $\frac{4}{8} = .5$.

*Discovering Advanced Algebra Solutions Manual*
©2004 Key Curriculum Press

**f.** 1  **g.** $40320 - 1 = 40{,}319$

**h.** $\frac{1}{40320} \approx .000025$

**10.** Using the first two entries, you can see that it takes the computer $\left(N! \cdot 10^{-6}\right)$ s to list all permutations of $N$ items. Use this to complete the table.

| $N$ | Number of permutations of $N$ items | Time |
|---|---|---|
| 12 | 479,001,600 | $\approx$ 8 min |
| 13 | 6,227,020,800 | $\approx$ 1.7 h |
| 15 | $\approx 1.31 \times 10^{12}$ | $\approx$ 15 d |
| 20 | $\approx 2.43 \times 10^{18}$ | $\approx$ 77,100 yr |

**11. a.** $\frac{4 \cdot 46 \cdot 45}{50 \cdot 49 \cdot 48} \approx .070$. There is 1 first-prize ticket, and 4 ways you could get it: as your first, second, third, or fourth ticket. So there are $1 \cdot 4$ ways to get first prize. For your 3 remaining tickets, there are 47 non-prize tickets which could be the first remaining ticket, then 46 which could be the second, and then 45 which could be the third. Thus the number of ways to get only first prize is $1 \cdot 4 \cdot {}_{47}P_3 = 1 \cdot 4 \cdot 47 \cdot 46 \cdot 45$. The number of ways to get *any* 4 tickets is ${}_{50}P_4 = 50 \cdot 49 \cdot 48 \cdot 47$. Thus the probability of getting only first prize is $\frac{1 \cdot 4 \cdot 47 \cdot 46 \cdot 45}{50 \cdot 49 \cdot 48 \cdot 47} = \frac{4 \cdot 46 \cdot 45}{50 \cdot 49 \cdot 48} \approx .070$.

**b.** $\frac{4 \cdot 3 \cdot 46}{50 \cdot 49 \cdot 48} \approx .005$. As in 11a, there are $1 \cdot 4$ ways to get first prize. Then there are $1 \cdot 3$ ways to get second prize as one of your 3 remaining tickets. Finally, there are ${}_{47}P_2 = 47 \cdot 46$ ways for your two remaining tickets to not be prize tickets. Thus there are $1 \cdot 4 \cdot 1 \cdot 3 \cdot {}_{47}P_2 = 1 \cdot 4 \cdot 1 \cdot 3 \cdot 47 \cdot 46$ ways to get first and second prize only, so the probability is $\frac{1 \cdot 4 \cdot 1 \cdot 3 \cdot 47 \cdot 46}{50 \cdot 49 \cdot 48 \cdot 47} = \frac{4 \cdot 3 \cdot 46}{50 \cdot 49 \cdot 48} \approx .005$.

**c.** $1 - \frac{46 \cdot 45}{50 \cdot 49} \approx .155$. $P$(second or third) $= 1 - P$(not second and not third). There are 48 tickets which are neither second prize nor third prize, and ${}_{47}P_4 = 48 \cdot 47 \cdot 46 \cdot 45$ ways to get four of them. So the probability of *not* getting second or third prize is $\frac{48 \cdot 47 \cdot 46 \cdot 45}{50 \cdot 49 \cdot 48 \cdot 47} = \frac{46 \cdot 45}{50 \cdot 49}$. Thus the probability of *getting* second or third prize is $1 - \frac{46 \cdot 45}{50 \cdot 49} \approx .155$.

**d.** $3.20

$$P(\text{exactly one prize}) = \frac{4 \cdot 46 \cdot 45}{50 \cdot 49 \cdot 48} = \frac{69}{980}$$

$$P(\text{exactly two prizes}) = \frac{4 \cdot 3 \cdot 46}{50 \cdot 49 \cdot 48} = \frac{23}{4900}$$

$$P(\text{all three prizes}) = \frac{4 \cdot 3 \cdot 2}{50 \cdot 49 \cdot 48} = \frac{1}{4900}$$

The expected value of your winnings is $P$(first prize only)(25) $+ P$(second prize only)(10) $+ P$(third prize only)(5) $+ P$(first and second prizes only)(35) $+ P$(first and third prizes only)(30) $+ P$(second and third prizes only)(15) $+ P$(all three prizes)(40) $= \frac{69}{980}(25) + \frac{69}{980}(10) + \frac{69}{980}(5) + \frac{23}{4900}(35) + \frac{23}{4900}(30) + \frac{23}{4900}(15) + \frac{1}{4900}(40) \approx \$3.20$.

**12. a.** 0. There is no possible way to get a bb gene combination.

**b.** $\frac{1}{4} = .25$. There is 1 bb out of 4 possible gene combinations.

**c.** $\frac{2}{4} = .5$. There are 2 bb's out of 4 possible gene combinations.

**d.** It is not possible because there are no brown-eyed (B) genes in the mixture.

**e.** $\frac{4}{16} = .25$. There are 4 possible combinations creating blue eyes and brown hair (bbEe) out of 16 possible gene combinations. You may notice that one parent's hair-color gene combination is EE, so the child is guaranteed to have brown hair. Therefore you can calculate this probability by ignoring the hair color, as in 12b.

**13. a.** $\frac{30}{50} = .6$

**b.** $\frac{16}{30} \approx .533$

**14. a.** $E(x) = P(1)(1) + P(2)(-2) + P(3)(3) + P(4)(-4) + P(5)(5) + P(6)(-6) = \frac{1}{6}(1 - 2 + 3 - 4 + 5 - 6) = -0.5$

**b.** You would expect to lose 0.50 point on each of the ten tosses, for a total loss of 5 points.

**15. a.** $\left(\frac{1}{2}\right)^3 = \frac{1}{8} = .125$

**b.** $\frac{3}{8} = .375$. Any particular ordering of three children has probability $\frac{1}{8}$ of occurring. There are three different ways to have two girls and a boy, so the probability is $3\left(\frac{1}{8}\right) = \frac{3}{8}$.

**c.** $\frac{1}{2} = .5$. The genders of the three children are independent.

**16. a.** $y = -0.25x^2 + 2.5x - 3.25$. Start with the equation $y = ax^2 + bx + c$, and use the points $(0, -3.25)$, $(3, 2)$, and $(8, 0.75)$ to find $a$, $b$, and $c$.

$$\begin{cases} c = -3.25 \\ 9a + 3b + c = 2 \\ 64a + 8b + c = 0.75 \end{cases}$$

Use any method to solve this system of equations. The solution is $a = -0.25$, $b = 2.5$, $c = -3.25$, so the equation of the parabola is $y = -0.25x^2 + 2.5x - 3.25$.

**b.** $y = -0.25(x - 5)^2 + 3$. Complete the square on the equation $y = -0.25x^2 + 2.5x - 3.25$, found in 16a.

$$y = -0.25x^2 + 2.5x - 3.25$$
$$y = -0.25(x^2 - 10x) - 3.25$$
$$y = -0.25(x^2 - 10x + 25 - 25) - 3.25$$
$$y = -0.25((x - 5)^2 - 25) - 3.25$$
$$y = -0.25(x - 5)^2 + 6.25 - 3.25$$
$$y = -0.25(x - 5)^2 + 3$$

**c.** $y = -0.25(x - 5 + 2\sqrt{3})(x - 5 - 2\sqrt{3})$. Use either of the forms found in 16a and b to find the $x$-intercepts. Using the quadratic formula, they are $x = \dfrac{-2.5 \pm \sqrt{2.5^2 - 4(-0.25)(-3.25)}}{2(-0.25)} = 5 \pm 2\sqrt{3}$. Therefore the factored form is $y = -0.25(x - 5 + 2\sqrt{3})(x - 5 - 2\sqrt{3})$.

**17. a.** 41. The side lengths of the boxes form a geometric sequence with $u_1 = 4$ and $r = 0.95$. Use your calculator to find the first term in the sequence that is less than 0.5. $u_{41} \approx 0.514$ and $u_{42} \approx 0.488$, so Jesse can make 41 boxes in one set.

**b.** About 808.3 in.² The area of paper needed for a box of side length $u_n$ is $5u_n^2$. Use your calculator to add the first 41 terms in the sequence.

$$\sum_{n=1}^{41} 5u_n^2 = \sum_{n=1}^{41} 5(4 \cdot 0.95^{n-1})^2 \approx 808.3$$

**IMPROVING YOUR VISUAL THINKING SKILLS**

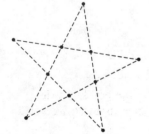

**EXTENSION**

Results will vary.

## LESSON 12.6

**EXERCISES**

**1. a.** $\dfrac{10!}{3!\,7!} = \dfrac{10 \cdot 9 \cdot 8}{3 \cdot 2 \cdot 1} = 10 \cdot 3 \cdot 4 = 120$

**b.** $\dfrac{7!}{4!\,3!} = \dfrac{7 \cdot 6 \cdot 5}{3 \cdot 2 \cdot 1} = 7 \cdot 5 = 35$

**c.** $\dfrac{15!}{13!\,2!} = \dfrac{15 \cdot 14}{2 \cdot 1} = 15 \cdot 7 = 105$

**d.** $0! = 1$, so $\dfrac{7!}{7!\,0!} = \dfrac{7!}{7!} = 1$

**2.** Use the results from 1a–d.

  **a.** 120    **b.** 35    **c.** 105    **d.** 1

**3. a.** $\dfrac{_7P_2}{2!} = {_7}C_2$    **b.** $\dfrac{_7P_3}{3!} = {_7}C_3$

  **c.** $\dfrac{_7P_4}{4!} = {_7}C_4$    **d.** $\dfrac{_7P_7}{7!} = {_7}C_7$

  **e.** $\dfrac{_nP_r}{r!} = {_n}C_r$

**4.** Neither; they are the same. Because you divide $n!$ by both $r!$ and $(n - r)!$, it will always be true that ${_n}C_r = {_n}C_{n-r}$. The number of $n$ things taken $r$ at a time is equal to the number of $n$ things omitted $(n - r)$ at a time.

**5.** $n = 7$ and $r = 3$, or $n = 7$ and $r = 4$, or $n = 35$ and $r = 1$, or $n = 35$ and $r = 34$

**6.** $r = 6$; $\dfrac{10!}{4!\,6!} = \dfrac{10!}{6!\,4!}$. The number of 10 things taken 4 at a time is equal to the number of 10 things omitted 6 at a time.

**7. a.** ${_7}C_4 = 35$

  **b.** $\dfrac{20}{35} \approx .571$. The number of question combinations including Essay Question 5 is ${_6}C_3 = 20$, so the probability is $\dfrac{20}{35} \approx .571$.

**8.** Sample answer: In a combination lock, the order of the numbers matters, so it does not really use combinations. It does not use permutations either, because repetitions are not permitted in permutations. To open a true combination lock, you could enter the correct numbers in any order.

**9. a.** $\dfrac{2!}{0!\,2!} + \dfrac{2!}{1!\,1!} + \dfrac{2!}{2!\,0!} = 1 + 2 + 1 = 4$

  **b.** $\dfrac{3!}{0!\,3!} + \dfrac{3!}{1!\,2!} + \dfrac{3!}{2!\,1!} + \dfrac{3!}{3!\,0!} = 1 + 3 + 3 + 1 = 8$

  **c.** $\dfrac{4!}{0!\,4!} + \dfrac{4!}{1!\,3!} + \dfrac{4!}{2!\,2!} + \dfrac{4!}{3!\,1!} + \dfrac{4!}{4!\,0!} = 1 + 4 + 6 + 4 + 1 = 16$

  **d.** The sum of all possible combinations of $n$ things is $2^n$. Test this conjecture for five things: $2^5 = 32$, and this is the same as ${_5}C_0 + {_5}C_1 + {_5}C_2 + {_5}C_3 + {_5}C_4 + {_5}C_5$.

**10. a.** Approximately 3.4 yr. There are ${_{47}}C_6 = 10{,}737{,}573$ possible tickets. At 10 s per ticket, it would take 107,375,730 s, or

$$(107375730 \text{ s})\left(\dfrac{1 \text{ m}}{60 \text{ s}}\right)\left(\dfrac{1 \text{ h}}{60 \text{ m}}\right)\left(\dfrac{1 \text{ d}}{24 \text{ h}}\right)\left(\dfrac{1 \text{ yr}}{365 \text{ d}}\right) \approx 3.4 \text{ yr}$$

to fill out all possible tickets.

  **b.** $\dfrac{1000}{_{47}C_6} \approx .000093$

**11. a.** 6    **b.** 10    **c.** 36

  **d.** ${_n}C_2 = \dfrac{n!}{2(n - 2)!}$. Given $n$ points, you need two of them to draw a chord. The order of the two points doesn't matter, therefore the total number of possible chords is ${_n}C_2$.

**12. a.** 26,466,926,850. There are $_{30}C_{12} = 86,493,225$ ways to choose the 12 jurors, leaving 18 people in the pool. Order matters with the alternates, so there are $_{18}P_2 = 18 \cdot 17 = 306$ ways to choose the alternates. Therefore there are $(86,493,225)(306) = 26,466,926,850$ ways to choose 12 jurors and 2 alternates from 30 people.

**b.** Approximately $2.134 \times 10^{19}$. Use the strategy from 12a to see that there are $\left(_{64}C_{12}\right)\left(_{52}P_4\right) \approx 2.134 \times 10^{19}$ possible ways to choose 12 jurors and 4 alternates from a pool of 64 prospective jurors.

**13. a.** $(x + y)^2 = (x + y)(x + y) = x^2 + xy + xy + y^2 = x^2 + 2xy + y^2$

**b.** $x^3 + 3x^2y + 3xy^2 + y^3$

$(x + y)^3 = (x + y)(x + y)^2$

$\quad = (x + y)\left(x^2 + 2xy + y^2\right)$

$\quad = x^3 + 2x^2y + xy^2 + x^2y + 2xy^2 + y^3$

$\quad = x^3 + 3x^2y + 3xy^2 + y^3$

**c.** $x^4 + 4x^3y + 6x^2y^2 + 4xy^3 + y^4$

$(x + y)^4 = (x + y)(x + y)^3$

$\quad = (x + y)\left(x^3 + 3x^2y + 3xy^2 + y^3\right)$

$\quad = x^4 + 3x^3y + 3x^2y^2 + xy^3 + x^3y + 3x^2y^2 + 3xy^3 + y^4$

$\quad = x^4 + 4x^3y + 6x^2y^2 + 4xy^3 + y^4$

**14.** $3 \cdot 5 = 15$ speeds

**15. a.** $(.97)(.02) = .0194$ is the probability that someone is healthy but tests positive.

**b.** .02 is the probability that a healthy person tests positive.

**c.** .0491 is the probability that a person tests positive.

$P(P) = P(D) \cdot P(P\,|\,D) + P(H) \cdot P(P\,|\,H) = (.03)(.99) + (.97)(.02) = .0491$

**d.** .395 is the probability that a person who tests positive is healthy. Use your results from 15a and c to calculate $P(H\,|\,P)$.

$P(H\,|\,P) = \dfrac{P(H \text{ and } P)}{P(P)} = \dfrac{.0194}{.0491} \approx .395$

**16.** $C < \frac{157}{4}$, or $C < 39.25$. Complete the square to put the equation in standard form.

$$x^2 + y^2 + 6x - 11y + C = 0$$

$$x^2 + 6x + 9 + y^2 - 11y + \frac{121}{4} + C = 9 + \frac{121}{4}$$

$$x^2 + 6x + 9 + y^2 - 11y + \frac{121}{4} = -C + 9 + \frac{121}{4}$$

$$(x + 3)^2 + \left(y - \frac{11}{2}\right)^2 = -C + \frac{157}{4}$$

For this to be the equation of a circle, the right side of the final equation must be positive. That is, $-C + \frac{157}{4} > 0$, so $C < \frac{157}{4}$.

**17.** Approximately 19.5 m from the tree; approximately 26.2 m from the owl. Let $x$ represent the distance Angelo got from the tree, let $y$ represent the height of the owl in the tree, and let $z$ represent the distance Angelo got from the owl. Draw a diagram and then use the tangent function two equations in $x$ and $y$, and solve for $x$.

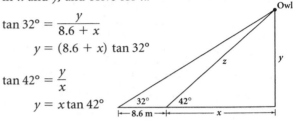

$\tan 32° = \dfrac{y}{8.6 + x}$

$y = (8.6 + x)\tan 32°$

$\tan 42° = \dfrac{y}{x}$

$y = x \tan 42°$

$x \tan 42° = 8.6 \tan 32° + x \tan 32°$

$x(\tan 42° - \tan 32°) = 8.6 \tan 32°$

$x = \dfrac{8.6 \tan 32°}{\tan 42° - \tan 32°} \approx 19.5$

Therefore, Angelo got about 19.5 m from the tree. To find out how close he was to the owl, use the cosine function. $\cos 42° = \frac{x}{z}$, so $z = \frac{x}{\cos 42°} = \frac{19.5}{\cos 42°} \approx 26.2$. Therefore, Angelo got about 26.2 m from the owl.

**18. a.** $36500(1 - 0.06)^{5.25} = \$26,376.31$

**b.** 20 yr 11 mo. Solve the equation $36500(1 - 0.06)^n = 10000$.

$$0.94^n = \frac{10000}{36500}$$

$$n \log 0.94 = \log \frac{10000}{36500}$$

$$n = \frac{\log \frac{10000}{36500}}{\log 0.94} \approx 20.925$$

Convert the decimal part of $n$ into months: $(0.925)(12) = 11.1$. Therefore the building will be worth less than \$10,000 after about 20 years 11 months.

### IMPROVING YOUR REASONING SKILLS

If Angelo had waited for his mother, his trip from the time he arrived at the station until the time he arrived home would have been an hour longer than usual. Because he walked, he cut off 20 minutes— 10 minutes off his mother's driving time each way. He was with her for 10 of those minutes; the other 10 came off the hour he was early, so he must have walked for 50 minutes.

You might also sketch a picture with variables representing the times in minutes.

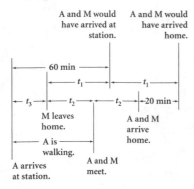

A and M would have arrived at station.
A and M would have arrived home.
60 min
$t_1$
$t_1$
$t_3$
$t_2$
$t_2$
20 min
M leaves home.
A and M arrive home.
A is walking.
A and M meet.
A arrives at station.

From this diagram, $2t_1 - 2t_2 = 20$ min, so $t_1 - t_2 = 10$ min, and $t_3 + t_2 = (60 - t_1) + t_2 = 60 - (t_1 - t_2) = 60 - 10 = 50$ min.

## LESSON 12.7

### EXERCISES

1. In 1a–d, the $(r + 1)$st term is $_{47}C_{47-r}x^{47-r}y^r$.

   a. $_{47}C_{47-0}x^{47-0}y^0 = x^{47}$

   b. $_{47}C_{47-10}x^{47-10}y^{10} = 5{,}178{,}066{,}751x^{37}y^{10}$

   c. $_{47}C_{47-40}x^{47-40}y^{40} = 62{,}891{,}499x^7y^{40}$

   d. $_{47}C_{47-46}x^{47-46}y^{46} = 47xy^{46}$

2. a. $1 - .25 = .75$

   b. $(.25)(.25) = .0625$

   c. $(.25)^n$

   d. Approximately .264. The probability of any one particular ordering of two successes and three failures in five trials is $(.25)^2(.75)^3$. There are $_5C_2 = 10$ such orderings, so the probability of having some combination of two successes and three failures in five trials is $10(.25)^2(.75)^3 \approx .264$.

3. Answers to 3b and c may vary slightly, depending on your method of calculation.

   a. .299

   b. .795, .496

   $P$(at most 4 birds survive)
   $= P(0) + P(1) + P(2) + P(3) + P(4)$
   $= .005 + .045 + .157 + .289 + .299$
   $= .795$

   $P$(at most 3 birds survive)
   $= P(0) + P(1) + P(2) + P(3)$
   $= .005 + .045 + .157 + .289$
   $= .496$

   c. .203, .502, .791

   $P$(at least 5 birds survive) $= P(5) + P(6)$
   $= .165 + .038 = .203$

   $P$(at least 4 birds survive) $= P(4) + P(5) + P(6)$
   $= .299 + .165 + .038$
   $= .502$

   $P$(at least 3 birds survive)
   $= P(3) + P(4) + P(5) + P(6)$
   $= .289 + .299 + .165 + .038 = .791$

   d. Both the "at most" and the "at least" numbers include the case of "exactly," so if you add the two together, any "exactly" cases will be counted twice. Probabilities sum to 1 for mutually exclusive, complementary events, but the events in the "at most" and "at least" rows are not mutually exclusive, so you cannot just add probabilities.

4. $_{50}C_{35}(.62)^{35}(.38)^{15} \approx .0606$

5. $p < \dfrac{25}{33}$

   | | |
   |---|---|
   | $_{32}C_{24}p^{24}q^8 > {}_{32}C_{25}p^{25}q^7$ | Original inequality. |
   | $_{32}C_{24}q > {}_{32}C_{25}p$ | Divide both sides by $p^{24}q^7$. |
   | $\dfrac{32!}{24!\,8!}q > \dfrac{32!}{25!\,7!}p$ | Substitute numbers of combinations for $_{32}C_{24}$ and $_{32}C_{25}$. |
   | $\dfrac{q}{24!\,8!} > \dfrac{p}{25!\,7!}$ | Divide both sides by 32!. |
   | $25q > 8p$ | Multiply both sides by 25! 8!. |
   | $25(1 - p) > 8p$ | Replace $q$ with $1 - p$. |
   | $25 > 33p$ | Add $25p$ to both sides. |
   | $p < \dfrac{25}{33}$ | Divide both sides by 33. |

6. a. HH, HT, TH, TT     b. HH, HT, TH, TT

   c. Both diagrams would look the same.

   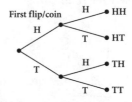

   Second flip/coin
   First flip/coin
   H — HH
   H
   T — HT
   T
   H — TH
   T — TT

   d. $_2C_0 = 1$ is the number of ways of getting 0 tails, $_2C_1 = 2$ is the number of ways of getting 1 tail, and $_2C_2 = 1$ is the number of ways of getting 2 tails.

   e. There is 1 way of getting 2 heads, 2 ways of getting 1 head and 1 tail, and 1 way of getting 2 tails.

**7.** In 7a–d, use the binomial coefficients from Pascal's triangle or the Binomial Theorem to expand the expressions.

a. $x^4 + 4x^3y + 6x^2y^2 + 4xy^3 + y^4$

b. $p^5 + 5p^4q + 10p^3q^2 + 10p^2q^3 + 5pq^4 + q^5$

c. $(2x + 3)^3 = (2x)^3 + 3(2x)^2(3) + 3(2x)(3)^2 + 3^3 = 8x^3 + 36x^2 + 54x + 27$

d. $(3x - 4)^4 = (3x)^4 + 4(3x)^3(-4) + 6(3x)^2(-4)^2 + 4(3x)(-4)^3 + (-4)^4 = 81x^4 - 432x^3 + 864x^2 - 768x + 256$

**8. a.** $_{50}C_{10}p^{10}q^{40}$ or $_{50}C_{40}p^{10}q^{40}$. Assuming that $p$ is the probability that a randomly chosen person supports a new traffic circle and $q = 1 - p$, the probability that 10 people chosen from a pool of 50 would support a new traffic circle is $_{50}C_{10}p^{10}q^{40}$.

b. $_{50}C_{10}p^{10}q^{40} > {_{50}C_{11}}p^{11}q^{39}$

c. $_{50}C_{10}p^{10}q^{40} > {_{50}C_9}p^9q^{41}$

d. $\frac{10}{51} < p < \frac{11}{51}$, or $.1961 < p < .2157$. Solve each inequality individually.

| | |
|---|---|
| $_{50}C_{10}p^{10}q^{40} > {_{50}C_{11}}p^{11}q^{39}$ | Original inequality from 8b. |
| $_{50}C_{10}q > {_{50}C_{11}}p$ | Divide both sides by $p^{10}q^{39}$. |
| $\frac{50!}{10!\,40!}q > \frac{50!}{11!\,39!}p$ | Substitute numbers of combinations for $_{50}C_{10}$ and $_{50}C_{11}$. |
| $\frac{q}{10!\,40!} > \frac{p}{11!\,39!}$ | Divide both sides by 50!. |
| $11q > 40p$ | Multiply both sides by 11! 40!. |
| $11(1 - p) > 40p$ | Replace $q$ with $1 - p$. |
| $11 > 51p$ | Add $11p$ to both sides and simplify. |
| $p < \frac{11}{51}$ | Divide both sides by 51. |
| $_{50}C_{10}p^{10}q^{40} > {_{50}C_9}p^9q^{41}$ | Original inequality from 8c. |
| $_{50}C_{10}p > {_{50}C_9}q$ | Divide both sides by $p^9q^{40}$. |
| $\frac{50!}{10!\,40!}p > \frac{50!}{9!\,41!}q$ | Substitute numbers of combinations for $_{50}C_{10}$ and $_{50}C_9$. |
| $\frac{p}{10!\,40!} > \frac{q}{9!\,41!}$ | Divide both sides by 50!. |
| $41p > 10q$ | Multiply both sides by 10! 41!. |
| $41p > 10(1 - p)$ | Replace $q$ with $1 - p$. |
| $51p > 10$ | Add $10p$ to both sides and simplify. |
| $p > \frac{10}{51}$ | Divide both sides by 51. |

Therefore, to satisfy both of the inequalities in 8b and c, $\frac{10}{51} < p < \frac{11}{51}$.

**9. a.** $(.97)^{30} \approx .401$

b. .940. Add the last three terms of the expanded expression $(.97 + .03)^{30}$, corresponding to the probabilities of having 2, 1, or 0 failures in 30 days.

$_{30}C_2(.97)^{28}(.03)^2 + {_{30}C_1}(.97)^{29}(.03)^1 + {_{30}C_0}(.97)^{30}(.03)^0$

$= 435(.97)^{28}(.03)^2 + 30(.97)^{29}(.03) + (.97)^{30}$

$\approx .940$

c. $Y_1(x) = {_{30}C_x}(.97)^{30-x}(.03)^x$

d. .940. See the solution to 9b. Add $Y_1(2) + Y_1(1) + Y_1(0)$ to find the probability of fewer than 3 failures in 30 treatments.

**10.** .007. Add the last 21 terms of the expanded expression $(.88 + .12)^{100}$, corresponding to the probabilities of having 20 or fewer incorrect readings in 100 applications of the test. This gives the probability of having at most 20 incorrect readings, so subtract it from 1 to find the probability of having over 20 incorrect readings.

$P(20 \text{ or fewer incorrect readings}) =$

$\sum_{n=0}^{20} {_{100}C_n}(.88)^{100-n}(.12)^n \approx .993$

$P(\text{more than 20 incorrect readings}) \approx 1 - .993 = .007$

**11. a.** .000257. $P(\text{fewer than 25 such coins}) =$

$\sum_{n=0}^{24} {_{100}C_n}(.12)^n(.88)^{100-n} \approx .999743$, so $P(\text{at least 25 such coins}) \approx 1 - .999743 = .000257$.

b. .446. $P(\text{fewer than 25 such coins}) =$

$\sum_{n=0}^{24} {_{200}C_n}(.12)^n(.88)^{200-n} \approx .554$, so $P(\text{at least 25 such coins}) \approx 1 - .554 = .446$.

c. .983. $P(\text{fewer than 25 such coins}) =$

$\sum_{n=0}^{24} {_{300}C_n}(.12)^n(.88)^{300-n} \approx .017$, so $P(\text{at least 25 such coins}) \approx 1 - .017 = .983$.

**12. a.** $.47^4 \approx .049$

b. $.53^4 \approx .079$

**c.** 1.88 birds, or approximately 2 birds. The expected number of surviving birds is

$$0P(0) + 1P(1) + 2P(2) + 3P(3) + 4P(4)$$
$$= 0(.53)^4 + 1(4)(.53)^3(.47) + 2(6)(.53)^2(.47)^2$$
$$\quad + 3(4)(.53)(.47)^3 + 4(.47)^4$$
$$= 1.88$$

**13.** Answers will vary. This event will happen in approximately 15.6% of trials. The probability of this event happening is $_5C_4(.5)^4(.5) = 5(.5)^5 = .15625$.

**14. a.** $_7C_5(.30)^5(.70)^2 \approx .02500$

 **b.** $_7C_6(.30)^6(.70) \approx .00357$

 **c.** $_7C_7(.30)^7 \approx .00022$

 **d.** .02880. Add the probabilities found in 14a–c (without rounding them).

**15. a.**

| $x$ | 1 | 2 | 3 | 4 |
|---|---|---|---|---|
| $y$ | 2 | 2.25 | $\approx 2.370$ | $\approx 2.441$ |

 **b.** $f(10) \approx 2.5937$, $f(100) \approx 2.7048$, $f(1000) \approx 2.7169$, $f(10000) \approx 2.7181$

 **c.** There is a long-run value of about 2.718.

**16.** 65,780. Sample answer: Either the group of 5 students includes the new student or it doesn't. If the new student is included, then the other 4 are selected from the remaining 25 class members and this can be done $_{25}C_4 = 12{,}650$ ways. If the new student is not selected, then all 5 are selected from the 25 original members and this can be done $_{25}C_5 = 53{,}130$ ways. This means there are 12,650 ways that the new student is part of the group and 53,130 ways that he or she is not. This makes $12{,}650 + 53{,}130 = 65{,}780$ ways to select 5 students.

**17.** 37.44 cm². The experimental probability that a randomly chosen point lands inside the curve is $\frac{156}{350} \approx .4457$. The area of the rectangle is 84 cm², so the area within the curve is estimated to be $\frac{156}{350}(84) = 37.44$ cm².

**18. a.** The experimental probabilities are likely to be different from .5 and .5. In this sample simulation, $P(H) = .6$ and $P(T) = .4$.

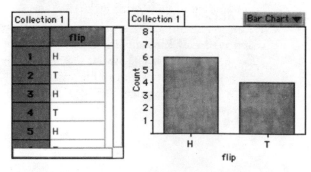

**b.** The experimental probabilities should be closer to .5 and .5, but are likely to not yet be exact. In this sample simulation, $P(H) = .49$ and $P(T) = .51$.

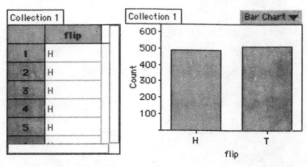

**c.** Using Fathom, you can create an unfair coin by defining **randomPick** with more heads to choose from. For example, **randomPick("H","H","H","T")** would make the experimental probability of heads approximately .75.

**19. a.** Graph the four combinations of *distance*, *period*, and their logarithms.

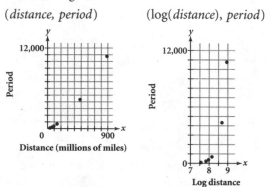

*(distance, period)*     *(log(distance), period)*

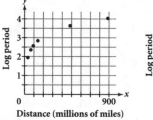 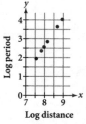

*(distance, log(period))*     *(log(distance), log(period))*

*(log(distance), log(period))* is the most linear of the four graphs, so use the median-median line to find an equation to fit these points. Let $x$ represent log(*distance*), let $y$ represent log(*period*), let $d$ represent *distance*, and let $p$ represent *period*.

| | |
|---|---|
| $y = 1.50x - 9.38$ | Median-median line. |
| $\log p = 1.50 \log d - 9.38$ | Substitute log $d$ for $x$ and log $p$ for $y$. |
| $10^{\log p} = 10^{1.50 \log d - 9.38}$ | Raise 10 to both sides. |
| $\hat{p} = 10^{-9.38} d^{1.50}$ | Evaluate. |

**b.** 31,385; 61,566; 92,535; errors may be due to rounding. For more accurate results, the $a$- and $b$-values found from regression can be stored in variables in the calculator.

**c.** $p^2 = 10^{-18.76}d^3$. Start with the equation $p = 10^{-9.38}d^{1.5}$ from 19a and square both sides.

$$p^2 = \left(10^{-9.38}d^{1.5}\right)^2$$

$$p^2 = 10^{-18.76}d^3$$

## EXTENSIONS

**A.** See the solutions to Take Another Look activities 1 and 2 on page 293.

**B.** .03283; .06; .000071. Use the formula for trinomial expansion from Take Another Look activity 2,

$$(x + y + z)^n = \sum_{i=0}^{n}\sum_{j=0}^{n-i} \frac{n!}{i!\,j!\,(n-i-j)!}\,x^i y^j z^{(n-i-j)}$$

The probability that, of 81 seats sold, 4 are sold in first class, 6 in business class, and 71 in coach is $\frac{81!}{4!\,6!\,71!}(.05)^4(.08)^6(.87)^{71} \approx .03283$. (On many calculators, 81! and 71! will cause an overflow error—the numbers are too big for the calculator to handle. But notice that $\frac{81!}{4!6!71!} = \frac{81!}{71!10!} \cdot \frac{10!}{4!6!} = \left(_{81}C_{71}\right)\left(_{10}C_4\right)$. The calculator calculates combinations by a method that does not involve first calculating the large factorials, so using combinations avoids the overflow error.)

Use your calculator to find the probability that each section is oversold. Pay careful attention to the limits of summation in the expressions below. The index $i$ represents the number of first-class tickets sold, the index $j$ represents the number of business-class tickets sold, and $(81 - i - j)$ represents the number of coach tickets sold.

$P(\text{first class is oversold}) =$

$$\sum_{i=11}^{90}\sum_{j=0}^{81-i} \frac{81!}{i!\,j!\,(81-i-j)!}(.05)^i(.08)^j(.87)^{81-i-j} \approx$$
$.00232$

$P(\text{business class is oversold but first class is } not$ oversold$) =$

$$\sum_{i=0}^{10}\sum_{j=11}^{81-i} \frac{81!}{i!\,j!\,(81-i-j)!}(.05)^i(.08)^j(.87)^{81-i-j} \approx$$
$.05765$

$P(\text{only coach is oversold}) = (.87)^{81} \approx .00001$

These probabilities are of mutually exclusive events, so add them to find the probability that one section is oversold: $.00232 + .05765 + .00001 = .05998$. The probability that one section is oversold is approximately .06.

The probability that both first class and business class are oversold (there are at least 11 tickets sold for each section) is

$$\sum_{i=11}^{81}\sum_{j=11}^{81-i} \frac{81!}{i!\,j!\,(81-i-j)!}(.05)^i(.08)^j(.87)^{81-i-j} \approx$$
$.00071$

## CHAPTER 12 REVIEW

### EXERCISES

**1.** Answers will vary depending on whether you interpret the problem to imply random decimal numbers (between 0 and 10, non-inclusive) or random integers (0 to 10, inclusive). To generate random decimal numbers, you might look at a random-number table and place the decimal point after the first digit in each group of numbers. Alternatively, you could use a calculator command, such as **10*rand** on the TI-83 Plus. To generate random integers, you might number 11 chips or slips of paper and select one. Alternatively, you could use a calculator command, such as **randInt(0,10)** on the TI-83 Plus.

**2. a, b.**

**c.** $\frac{10}{64} \approx .156$. There are 10 outcomes in which the sum is less than 6, out of 64 possible outcomes, so the probability that the sum is less than 6 is $\frac{10}{64}$.

**d.** $\frac{49}{64} \approx .766$. There are 10 outcomes in which the sum is less than 6 and 5 outcomes in which the sum is exactly 6. That leaves 49 outcomes in which the sum is more than 6, out of a total 64 possible outcomes. The probability that the sum is more than 6 is $\frac{49}{64}$.

**3. a.** .5. The area of the rectangle is $6 \cdot 9 = 54$. The area of the shaded region is $6\left(\frac{6+3}{2}\right) = 27$. Therefore the probability of a randomly plotted point landing in the shaded region is $\frac{27}{54} = .5$.

**b.** 17.765 square units. The experimental probability that a randomly chosen point lands inside the curve is $\frac{374}{1000} = .374$. The area of the rectangle is $5 \cdot 9.5 = 47.5$ square units, so the area within the curve is approximately $(0.374)(47.5) = 17.8$ square units.

**4. a.**

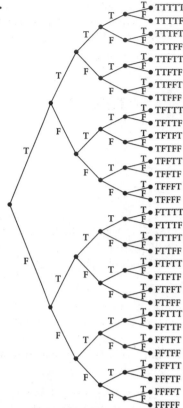

**b.** 10. Count the number of such results from your diagram in 4a.

**c.** Because the order in which the true and false answers occur doesn't matter, use combinations: $_5C_3 = 10$.

**d.** $\frac{3}{8} = .375$. There are $2^3 = 8$ possible answer combinations on the last three problems, of which $_3C_2 = 3$ contain two false answers. Therefore the probability of such an event is $\frac{3}{8}$.

**5. a.**

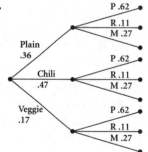

**b.** $(.47)(.11) = .0517$

**c.** .8946. $P(\text{veggie dog on plain bun}) = (.17)(.62) = .1054$, therefore $P(not \text{ veggie dog on plain bun}) = 1 - .1054 = .8946$.

**d.** $(.36)(.62) + (.47)(.27) = .3501$

**6. a.**

|  | 9th grade | 10th grade | 11th grade | 12th grade | Total |
|---|---|---|---|---|---|
| Ice cream | 18 | 37 | 85 | 114 | 254 |
| Whipped cream | 5 | 18 | 37 | 58 | 118 |
| Total | 23 | 55 | 122 | 172 | 372 |

**b.** $\frac{37}{55} \approx .673$. Of the 55 10th graders, 37 prefer ice cream.

**c.** $\frac{37}{122} \approx .303$. Of the 122 11th graders, 37 prefer whipped cream.

**d.** $\frac{18}{254} \approx .071$. Of the 254 students who prefer ice cream, 18 are in 9th grade.

**e.** $\frac{118}{372} \approx .317$. Of the 372 students surveyed, 118 prefer whipped cream.

**7.** 110.5. Rita's expected score on a single throw is $.30(20) + .40(10) + .20(5) + .05(1) = 11.05$. Her expected score on 10 throws is $10(11.05) = 110.5$.

**8.**

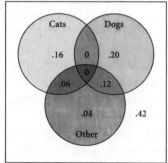

Using the fact that the ownership of cats and dogs is mutually exclusive, $P(\text{cats and dogs}) = 0$ and $P(\text{cats or dogs}) = P(\text{cats}) + P(\text{dogs})$. Therefore, $.54 = P(\text{cats}) + .32$, so $P(\text{cats}) = .22$. 16% of homes have only a cat, leaving 6% to have a cat and another pet, which must be in the "other" category. Therefore, $P(\text{cats and other, but no dogs}) = .06$. Given the final bit of information, $P(\text{other, but no cats}) = .16$. Now use all of this information to find $P(\text{dogs and other, but no cats})$. The probabilities of all the mutually exclusive events must sum to 1.

$P(\text{only cats}) + P(\text{other}) + P(\text{only dogs}) + P(\text{no animals}) = 1$

$P(\text{only cats}) + P(\text{other}) + (P(\text{dogs}) - P(\text{dogs and other})) + P(\text{no animals}) = 1$

$.16 + .22 + (.32 - P(\text{dogs and other})) + .42 = 1$

$.32 - P(\text{dogs and other}) = .36$

$P(\text{dogs and other}) = .12$

This leaves $P(\text{only other}) = .04$ and $P(\text{only dogs}) = .20$.

*Discovering Advanced Algebra Solutions Manual*
©2004 Key Curriculum Press

**9.** .044. Sum the first four terms of the expanded expression $(.65 + .35)^{20}$, which corresponds to the probabilities of Elliott receiving more than 16 orders for pepperoni pizza.

$$.65^{20} + {}_{20}C_{19}(.65)^{19}(.35) + {}_{20}C_{18}(.65)^{18}(.35)^2 + {}_{20}C_{17}(.65)^{17}(.35)^3 \approx .044$$

**10. a.** 1      **b.** $\dfrac{x^{99}}{12^{99}}$

    **c.** ${}_{21}C_9 a^{20-9}b^9 = 293{,}930a^{12}b^9$

**TAKE ANOTHER LOOK**

**1.** Sample patterns: The first and last digits in every row are 1; the second and second-to-last digits are equal to the row number (if the row with only one 1 is called row 0); the next numbers in row $n$ are ${}_nC_2$; numbers in each row are symmetric. Adding two numbers next to each other in a row gives the number between them in the next row down. If you shade even numbers one color and odd numbers another color, you get a pattern that resembles a Sierpiński triangle. (Similar patterns appear when you color multiples of other factors as well.) Adding the numbers in rows gives powers of 2. Adding numbers next to each other in the diagonal starting with 1, 3 gives square numbers. Looking at the numbers in a row as digits in a number gives powers of 11 (with a procedure to deal with numbers of more than two digits). Fibonacci numbers can be found in diagonals; these diagonals are parallel to the one starting in row 3, which contains 1, 6, 5, 1.

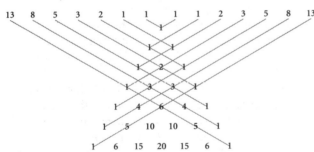

**2.** $(x + y + z)^2 = x^2 + y^2 + z^2 + 2xy + 2xz + 2yz$

$(x + y + z)^3 = x^3 + y^3 + z^3 + 3x^2y + 3x^2z + 3xy^2 + 3xz^2 + 3y^2z + 3yz^2 + 6xyz$

$(x + y + z)^4 = x^4 + y^4 + z^4 + 4x^3y + 4x^3z + 4xy^3 + 4xz^3 + 4y^3z + 4yz^3 + 6x^2y^2 + 6x^2z^2 + 6y^2z^2 + 12x^2yz + 12xy^2z + 12xyz^2$

$(x + y + z)^n = \displaystyle\sum_{i=0}^{n} \sum_{j=0}^{n-i} \frac{n!}{i!\,j!\,(n-i-j)!} x^i y^j z^{(n-i-j)}$

Another way to write this is

$(x + y + z)^n = \displaystyle\sum_{(i,j,k)} \frac{n!}{i!\,j!\,k!} x^i y^j z^k$

where the sum runs over all ordered triples $(i, j, k)$ where $i + j + k = n$. The factors $\frac{n!}{i!\,j!\,k!}$ are called multinomial coefficients, which are a generalization of the binomial coefficients ${}_nC_r$.

# CHAPTER 13

## LESSON 13.1

### EXERCISES

**1.** A: $\dfrac{1}{8}$; B: $\dfrac{1}{12}$; C: $\dfrac{1}{10}$; D: $\dfrac{1}{10}$

For Distribution A, the shaded region is a triangle with base 4 and area 1. To find the height of the triangle, solve the equation $\frac{1}{2} \cdot 4 \cdot h = 1$ to find that $h = \frac{1}{2}$. Therefore the height of one grid box is $\frac{1}{2} \div 4 = \frac{1}{8}$.

For Distribution B, the shaded region is a triangle with base 6 and area 1. To find the height of the triangle, solve the equation $\frac{1}{2} \cdot 6 \cdot h = 1$ to find that $h = \frac{1}{3}$. Therefore the height of one grid box is $\frac{1}{3} \div 4 = \frac{1}{12}$.

For Distribution C, the shaded region is a rectangle with base 5 and area 1. To find the height of the rectangle, solve the equation $5 \cdot h = 1$ to find that $h = \frac{1}{5}$. Therefore the height of one grid box is $\frac{1}{5} \div 2 = \frac{1}{10}$.

For Distribution D, the region between 0 and 5 is made up of 10 shaded grid boxes with area 1, so the area of one grid box is $\frac{1}{10}$. The width of one grid box is 1, so $1 \cdot h = \frac{1}{10}$ and the height of one grid box is $\frac{1}{10}$.

**2.** A: $\dfrac{9}{16}$; B: $\dfrac{3}{8}$; C: $\dfrac{3}{5}$; D: $\dfrac{2}{5}$

For Distribution A, the region between 0 and 3 is a triangle with width 3 and height $\frac{3}{8}$. Its area is $\frac{1}{2} \cdot 3 \cdot \frac{3}{8} = \frac{9}{16}$, so the probability that a randomly chosen value is between 0 and 3 is $\frac{9}{16}$.

For Distribution B, the region between 0 and 3 is a triangle with width 3 and height $\frac{3}{12}$. Its area is $\frac{1}{2} \cdot 3 \cdot \frac{3}{12} = \frac{3}{8}$, so the probability that a randomly chosen value is between 0 and 3 is $\frac{3}{8}$.

For Distribution C, the region between 0 and 3 is a rectangle with width 3 and height $\frac{2}{10}$, or $\frac{1}{5}$. Its area is $3 \cdot \frac{1}{5} = \frac{3}{5}$, so the probability that a randomly chosen value is between 0 and 3 is $\frac{3}{5}$.

For Distribution D, the region between 0 and 3 is a trapezoid with bases 3 and 1 and height $\frac{2}{10}$, or $\frac{1}{5}$. Its area is $\frac{1}{2}(3 + 1)\left(\frac{1}{5}\right) = \frac{2}{5}$, so the probability that a randomly chosen value is between 0 and 3 is $\frac{2}{5}$.

**3.** Sample estimates: A: 2.8; B: 3.5; C: 2.5; D: 3.3. (Exact answers: A: $\sqrt{8} = 2\sqrt{2}$; B: $\sqrt{12} = 2\sqrt{3}$; C: 2.5; D: $3\frac{1}{3}$.) For Distributions A–D, estimate the vertical line that divides the figure into two regions, each having area 0.5.

For Distribution A, trial and error shows that the median is about 2.8. Then the triangle formed to the left of the median has base 2.8 and height approximately 0.36.

$A \approx 0.5 \cdot 2.8 \cdot 0.36 \approx 0.5$

For Distribution B, trial and error shows that the median is about 3.5. The triangle formed to the left of the median has base 3.5 and height approximately 0.3.

$A \approx 0.5 \cdot 3.5 \cdot 0.3 \approx 0.5$

For Distribution C, the median is exactly 2.5. The rectangle formed to either side of the median has base 2.5 and height 0.2.

$A = 2.5 \cdot 0.2 = 0.5$

For Distribution D, trial and error shows that the median is about 3.3. Then the rectangle formed to the right of the median has base 1.7 and height 0.3.

$A \approx 1.7 \cdot 0.3 \approx 0.5$

**4.** Sample estimates: A: 2.7; B: 3.3; C: 2.5; D: 3.2

For Distributions A and B, recall from geometry that the coordinates of the centroid are the means of the coordinates of the vertices. The $x$-coordinate of the centroid, then, is the mean of the $x$-coordinates of the vertices.

A: $\dfrac{0 + 4 + 4}{3} = \dfrac{8}{3} = 2\dfrac{2}{3} \approx 2.7$

B: $\dfrac{0 + 4 + 6}{3} = \dfrac{10}{3} = 3\dfrac{1}{3} \approx 3.3$

For Distribution C, the mean of the distribution is the $x$-coordinate of the center of the rectangle. The center is $(2.5, 0.1)$, so the mean is approximately 2.5.

For Distribution D, trace the figure, then cut it out and balance it on the eraser end of a pencil. The $x$-coordinate of the balancing point, approximately 3.2, is the mean of the distribution.

**5. a.** 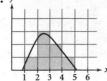  **b.**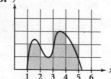

**6. a.** Answers will vary, but the values range from 1 to 8, and mean values 1 and 8 are very rare. Sample histogram:

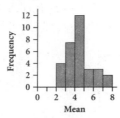

**b.** Sample estimates: $mode = 4.5$, $median \approx 4$

**7. a.** False. Possible counterexample:

**b.** True. A probability distribution shows only what fraction of values fall within each bin. It does not show the number of values.

**c.** False. If the distribution is symmetric, then they can all be the same.

**8.** Solutions will vary. General shapes are shown below.

**a.**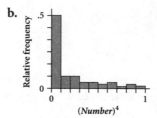

The range is still 0 to 1. If you square a number less than 1, the result is smaller than the original number.

**b.**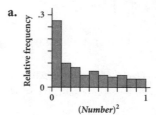

Raising numbers between 0 and 1 to the power of 4 gives even smaller results than squaring them, but they still remain between 0 and 1.

**c.**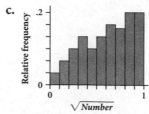

If you take the square root of a number between 0 and 1, the result is larger than the original number, but still never larger than 1.

*Discovering Advanced Algebra Solutions Manual*
©2004 Key Curriculum Press

**9.** To do this with a calculator, create a list of 100 random decimals between 0 and 1 (see Calculator Note 1L) and store them in list L1. For 9a, define list L2 as $(L_1)^2$. For b, define list L3 as $(L_1)^4$. For 9c, define list L4 as $\sqrt{(L_1)}$. Sample histograms for 100 trials:

**a.**

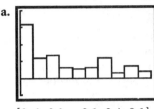

[0, 1, 0.1, −0.1, 0.4, 0.1]

**b.**

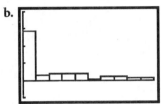

[0, 1, 0.1, −0.1, 0.4, 0.1]

**c.**

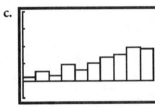

[0, 1, 0.1, −0.1, 0.4, 0.1]

**10. a.** For the mean and median to be the same value, the distribution must be symmetric. Possible answer:

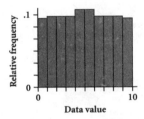

**b.** For the mean to be larger than the median, the distribution must be skewed right. Possible answer:

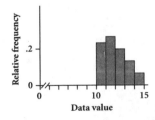

**11. a.** Sample answer: The histogram is perfectly symmetric. The data set that might produce this distribution is the percentile rankings of high school students' standardized test scores where the distribution is predetermined and the ranking

is based on the comparison of all students' performances or scores. The range on the x-axis is 0% to 100%.

**b.** Sample answer: The histogram is slightly skewed left. The data set that might produce this distribution is the first walking times of babies in months. The range on the x-axis would be 9 to 18 months, where the mean walking age is approximately 14 months.

**c.** Sample answer: The histogram is approximately symmetric. The data set that might produce this distribution is the average amount of sleep a sample group of college students receives each night. The range on the x-axis would be 1 to 10 hours per night.

**12. a.** President: $\bar{x} = 54.8$, $s = 6.3$, *median* = 54.5, *IQR* = 7
Vice president: $\bar{x} = 54.0$, $s = 8.5$, *median* = 53, *IQR* = 11

The mean and median ages are close, but there is more spread in the vice presidents' ages.

**b.** President

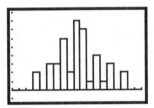

[36, 74, 2, −1, 9, 1]

Vice President

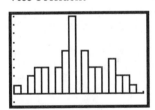

[36, 74, 2, −1, 9, 1]

The histogram for presidents' ages has less spread, so more presidents' ages are clustered around the mean and median. The histogram for vice presidents' ages is more spread out, resulting in a larger *IQR* and standard deviation.

**c.** Create these lists on your calculator. If list L1 contains presidents' ages, define list L3 as $(L_1 - 54.8)/6.3$. If list L2 contains vice presidents' ages, define list L4 as $(L_2 - 54)/8.5$.

**d.** Range for standardized age of president: −2.0 to 2.3; range for standardized age of VP: −2.1 to 2.0. These numbers represent how many standard deviations above or below the mean the presidents' ages or vice presidents' ages are.

**e.** President

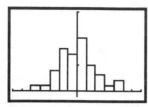

$[-3.5, 3.5, 0.5, -1, 15, 5]$

Vice President

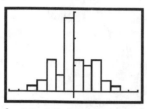

$[-3.5, 3.5, 0.5, -1, 15, 5]$

**f.** Sample answer: The graphs are reasonably symmetric with most values near the *y*-axis. All values are within the $-3.5 \leq x \leq 3.5$ domain, and most are within $-2.0 \leq x \leq 2.0$.

**13. a.**

| x | P(x) |
|------|------|
| 0–3 | .015 |
| 3–6 | .046 |
| 6–9 | .062 |
| 9–12 | .092 |
| 12–15 | .2 |
| 15–18 | .138 |
| 18–21 | .123 |
| 21–24 | .154 |
| 24–27 | .092 |
| 27–30 | .062 |
| 30–33 | .015 |

**b, d.**

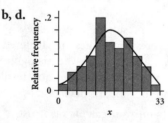

**c.** 15–18 min. There are 65 customers who called in for help the entire evening and 36 customers, over half, have hung up by a call duration of 15–18 minutes. Therefore the median length of time a customer waited before hanging up is 15–18 min.

**14. a.** *(See table at bottom of page.)*

Let *x* represent the probability of heads and let *y* represent the probability of tails in the expression $(x + y)^{15}$. Use the binomial expansion of $(.5 + .5)^{15}$ to find the probability distribution for $P(x)$. Note that each probability becomes $_{15}C_x(.5)^{15}$.

$(.5 + .5)^{15} = {}_{15}C_0(.5)^{15} + {}_{15}C_1(.5)^{14}(.5)^1 +$
${}_{15}C_2(.5)^{13}(.5)^2 + {}_{15}C_3(.5)^{12}(.5)^3 + {}_{15}C_4(.5)^{11}(.5)^4 +$
${}_{15}C_5(.5)^{10}(.5^5)^5 + {}_{15}C_6(.5)^9(.5)^6 + {}_{15}C_7(.5)^8(.5)^7 +$
${}_{15}C_8(.5)^7(.5)^8 + {}_{15}C_9(.5)^6(.5)^9 + {}_{15}C_{10}(.5)^5(.5)^{10} +$
${}_{15}C_{11}(.5)^4(.5)^{11} + {}_{15}C_{12}(.5)^3(.5)^{12} + {}_{15}C_{13}(.5)^2(.5)^{13}$
$+ {}_{15}C_{14}(.5)(.5)^{14} + {}_{15}C_{15}(.5)^{15}$

$= 1(.5)^{15} + 15(.5)^{15} + 105(.5)^{15} + 455(.5)^{15} +$
$1365(.5)^{15} + 3003(.5)^{15} + 5005(.5)^{15} +$
$6435(.5)^{15} + 6435(.5)^{15} + 5005(.5)^{15} +$
$3003(.5)^{15} + 1365(.5)^{15} + 455(.5)^{15} +$
$105(.5)^{15} + 15(.5)^{15} + 1(.5)^{15}$

$= .00003 + .0005 + .003 + .014 + .042 + .092 +$
$.153 + .196 + .196 + .153 + .092 + .042 +$
$.014 + .003 + .0005 + .00003$

Now find the frequencies by multiplying each probability by 500.

**b.**

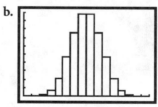

$[0, 16, 1, 0, 100, 10]$

**c.** $\bar{x} = 7.5, s = 1.94$

---

**Lesson 13.1, Exercise 14a**

| Heads (x) | 0 | 1 | 2 | 3 | 4 | 5 | 6 | 7 |
|-----------|------|------|------|------|------|------|------|------|
| P(x) | .00003 | .0005 | .003 | .014 | .042 | .092 | .153 | .196 |
| Frequency | 0 | 0 | 2 | 7 | 21 | 46 | 76 | 98 |
| Heads (x) | 8 | 9 | 10 | 11 | 12 | 13 | 14 | 15 |
| P(x) | .196 | .153 | .092 | .042 | .014 | .003 | .0005 | .00003 |
| Frequency | 98 | 76 | 46 | 21 | 7 | 2 | 0 | 0 |

*Discovering Advanced Algebra Solutions Manual*
©2004 Key Curriculum Press

**d.** 348 trials. $7.5 - 1.94 = 5.56$ and $7.5 + 1.94 = 9.44$, so the number of trials resulting between 6 and 9 heads is within one standard deviation of the mean. Therefore the number of trials is $76 + 98 + 98 + 76 = 348$.

**e.** $\dfrac{348}{500} = 0.696$, or 69.6%

**f.** 96.4%. $7.5 - 2(1.94) = 3.62$ and $7.5 + 2(1.94) = 11.38$, so the number of trials resulting between 4 and 11 heads is within two standard deviations of the mean. The number of trials is $21 + 46 + 76 + 98 + 98 + 76 + 46 + 21 = 482$, so $\dfrac{482}{500} = 0.964$, or 96.4% of the data is within two standard deviations of the mean.

**g.** 100%. $7.5 - 3(1.94) = 1.68$ and $7.5 + 3(1.94) = 13.32$, so the number of trials resulting between 2 and 13 heads is within two standard deviations of the mean. The number of trials is $2 + 7 + 21 + 46 + 76 + 98 + 98 + 76 + 46 + 21 + 7 + 2 = 500$, so $\dfrac{500}{500} = 1$, or 100% of the data is within three standard deviations of the mean.

**15.** .022. The probability of rolling a sum of 8 one time is $\dfrac{5}{36} \approx .14$, so the probability of rolling a sum of 8 at least three times is $P(x \geq 3) = P(3) + P(4) + P(5) = {}_5C_3(.14)^3(.86)^2 + {}_5C_4(.14)^4(.86)^1 + {}_5C_5(.14)^5 \approx .022$.

**16. a.** $d = \left| \tan\left(\frac{\pi}{10}t\right) \right|$, $0 \leq t \leq 60$ where $t$ represents time in seconds and $d$ represents distance in units.

**b.** Note that distance is always positive.

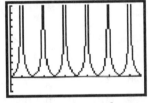

$[0, 60, 5, -2, 10, 1]$

**17.** $QR$ is 0 when $P$ overlaps $R$, then grows larger and larger without bound until $P$ reaches the $y$-axis, at which time $Q$ is undefined because $\overrightarrow{PQ}$ and $\overrightarrow{RT}$ are parallel and do not intersect. As $P$ moves through Quadrant II, $QR$ decreases to 0. Then, as $P$ moves through Quadrant III, $QR$ again increases without bound. When $P$ reaches the $y$-axis, point $Q$ is again undefined. As $P$ moves through Quadrant IV, $QR$ again decreases to 0. These patterns correspond to the zeros and vertical asymptotes of the graph in Exercise 16.

**18.** The expected value of points per spin is $+0.5$, so the game should last 100 spins. The expected value is $.1(-1) + .1(2) + .1(-3) + .1(4) + .1(-5) + .1(6) + .1(-7) + .1(8) + .1(-9) + .1(10)$, or 0.5. Multiply 0.5 by 100 games to get a score of $+50$.

**19.** In all cases, the area remains the same. The relationship holds for all two-dimensional figures.

Rectangle: $A = bh$

$(2b)\left(\dfrac{h}{2}\right) = bh$

$(3b)\left(\dfrac{h}{3}\right) = bh$

Triangle: $A = \dfrac{1}{2}bh$

$\dfrac{1}{2}(2b)\left(\dfrac{h}{2}\right) = \dfrac{1}{2}bh$

$\dfrac{1}{2}(3b)\left(\dfrac{h}{3}\right) = \dfrac{1}{2}bh$

## LESSON 13.2

### EXERCISES

**1. a.** The tables and graphs of both functions agree.

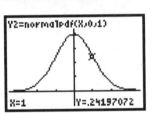

$[-3.5, 3.5, 1, -0.1, 0.5, 0.1]$

**b.** $y \approx .242$. Trace either graph to show that $y \approx .242$ when $x = 1$. (See the graph above.) Or evaluate $n(1, 0, 1)$ to get approximately .242.

**2.** In 2a and b, the equations are in the form $y = \dfrac{1}{\sigma\sqrt{2\pi}}(\sqrt{e})^{-((x-\mu)/\sigma)^2}$, so you can determine the exact value of the mean, $\mu$, and the standard deviation, $\sigma$.

**a.** $\mu = 47$, $\sigma = 5$

**b.** $\mu = 250$, $\sigma = 23$

In 2c and d, the coefficient $c$ in $y = cb^d$ must equal $\dfrac{1}{\sigma\sqrt{2\pi}}$. You still identify the mean, $\mu$, from the expression $(x - \mu)$ in the exponent.

**c.** $\mu = 5.5$, $1.29 = \dfrac{1}{\sigma\sqrt{2\pi}}$, so $\sigma = \dfrac{1}{1.29\sqrt{2\pi}} \approx 0.31$

**d.** $\mu = 83$, $0.054 = \dfrac{1}{\sigma\sqrt{2\pi}}$, so $\sigma = \dfrac{1}{0.054\sqrt{2\pi}} \approx 7.4$

**3.** Because each normal curve is symmetric, you estimate the mean by locating the maximum of the curve. You can estimate the standard deviation of any normal distribution by locating the inflection points of its graph, which are the points where it changes between curving downward and curving upward.

**a.** $\mu = 18$, $\sigma \approx 2.5$. The inflection points are located at about 15.5 and 20.5, approximately 2.5 units from the mean.

**b.** $\mu = 10$, $\sigma \approx 0.8$. The inflection points are located at about 9.2 and 10.8, approximately 0.8 unit from the mean.

**c.** $\mu \approx 68$, $\sigma \approx 6$. The inflection points are located at about 62 and 74, approximately 6 units from the mean.

**d.** $\mu \approx 0.47$, $\sigma \approx 0.12$. The inflection points are located at about 0.35 and 0.59, approximately 0.12 unit from the mean.

**4.** In 4a–d, substitute into the equation $y = \frac{1}{\sigma\sqrt{2\pi}}\left(\sqrt{e}\right)^{-((x-\mu)/\sigma)^2}$ the mean and standard deviation that you found in 3a–d.

**a.** $y = \dfrac{1}{2.5\sqrt{2\pi}}\left(\sqrt{e}\right)^{-((x-18)/2.5)^2}$

**b.** $y = \dfrac{1}{0.8\sqrt{2\pi}}\left(\sqrt{e}\right)^{-((x-10)/0.8)^2}$

**c.** $y = \dfrac{1}{6\sqrt{2\pi}}\left(\sqrt{e}\right)^{-((x-68)/6)^2}$

**d.** $y = \dfrac{1}{0.12\sqrt{2\pi}}\left(\sqrt{e}\right)^{-((x-0.47)/0.12)^2}$

**5.** Sketch a normal curve. The maximum represents the mean, $x = 1.8$, and the inflection points represent one standard deviation below and above the mean, at $x = 1.8 - 0.8 = 1$ and $x = 1.8 + 0.8 = 2.6$. Label the mean and the standard deviation, then shade the area beneath the curve between $x = 1$ and $x = 1.8$.

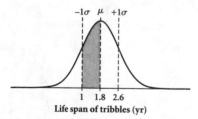

−1σ  μ  +1σ

1  1.8  2.6
**Life span of tribbles (yr)**

On your calculator use the command to shade a normal curve (see Calculator Note 13C) to find that this area represents approximately 34% of tribbles.

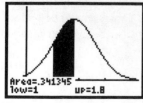

Area=.341345
low=1        up=1.8

$[-0.6, 4.2, 1, -0.1, 0.6, 0]$

**6. a.** Sketch a normal curve. The maximum represents the mean in inches, $x = 68$, and the inflection points represent one standard deviation below and above the mean, $x = 68 - 7.2 = 60.8$ and $x = 68 + 7.2 = 75.2$.

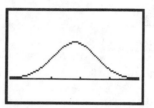

−1σ  μ  +1σ

60.8  68  75.2
**Height of male gorilla (in.)**

On your calculator, graph the normal distribution $n(x, 68, 7.2)$.

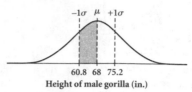

$[46.4, 89.6, 10, -0.03, 0.1, 0]$

**b.** Because the standard deviation has decreased, the normal curve will not have as much spread. However, because the area under the curve must remain 1, the area will be redistributed making the curve taller. Sketch a normal curve that is narrower yet taller than the one you sketched for 6a. Use the maximum and inflection points to label the mean and one standard deviation below and above the mean.

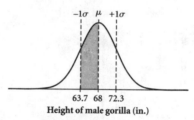

−1σ  μ  +1σ

63.7  68  72.3
**Height of male gorilla (in.)**

On your calculator, graph the normal distribution $n(x, 68, 4.3)$. Notice how the graph has a horizontal shrink and a vertical stretch compared with the graph in 6a.

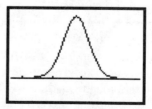

$[46.4, 89.6, 10, -0.03, 0.1, 0]$

**c.** The second graph has less spread and more area under the central portion of the curve. Hence, there will be less area under the tail where $x > 72$. Using your calculator's shade command shows that the areas representing heights greater than 72 inches (6 feet) are about 0.29 for the first graph and 0.18 for the second graph.

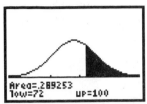

$[46.4, 89.6, 10, -0.03, 0.1, 0]$

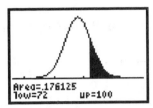

$[46.4, 89.6, 10, -0.03, 0.1, 0]$

**7. a.** Graph the normal distribution $n(x, 16.8, 0.7)$ and shade the area where $x < 16$.

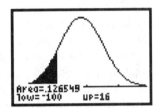

$[14.7, 18.9, 1, -0.1, 0.6, 0]$

**b.** 12.7%. Sample answer: No, more than 10% of boxes do not meet minimum weight requirements. The area of the shaded portion of the graph is about 0.127, so about 12.7% of the boxes are below advertised weight.

**8. a.** Use guess-and-check to find that the mean should be set at about 12.96 oz so that the region where $x > 12$ provides an area of 0.90.

$[10, 16, 20, -0.2, 0.6, 1]$

**b.** Using your calculator, $N(13.5, 20, 12.96, 0.75)$ is approximately 0.24, so 24% of the bottles will overflow at the setting suggested in 8a.

**9.**

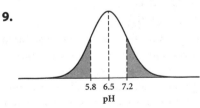

The maximum of the graph represents the mean, $x = 6.5$, and the inflection points, 7.2 and 5.8, represent one standard deviation above and below the mean. Shade the area greater than or less than one standard deviation away from the mean.

**10. a.** Use the median of each range as a representative value for that range. For example, assume that 149 represents the two women with heights between 148 and 150. $\mu \approx 165; \sigma \approx 5.90$

$[148, 180, 2, -5, 70, 5]$

**b.** $y = 66(0.99)^{(x-165)^2}$. Any curve in this form is bell-shaped, is symmetric about the $y$-axis, and has a maximum at $(0, a)$. To make the curve symmetric about the line $x - 165$ with maximum $(165, 66)$, substitute $(x - 165)$ for $x$, and substitute 66 for $a$. Then use guess-and-check to find that the value of $b$ should be 0.99.

**c.** $y = \frac{1}{5.90\sqrt{2\pi}}\left(\sqrt{e}\right)^{-((x-165)/5.90)^2}$. Substitute 165 for $\mu$ and 5.90 for $\sigma$ into the equation for a normal distribution.

**11. a.** $\mu = 79.1, \sigma \approx 7.49$

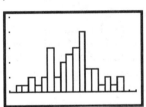

$[60, 100, 2, -1, 10, 2]$

**b.** Sample answer:

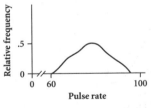

**c.** $y = \frac{1}{7.49\sqrt{2\pi}}\left(\sqrt{e}\right)^{-((x-79.1)/7.49)^2}$. Substitute 79.1 for $\mu$ and 7.49 for $\sigma$ into the equation for a normal distribution.

**d.** Sample answer: The data do not appear to be normally distributed. They seem to be approximately symmetrically distributed with several peaks.

**12. a.** Approximately .68. The probability that a randomly chosen individual has a ridge count between 100 and 200 is equal to the area under the normal curve between 100 and 200. You can find this area on your calculator using $N(100, 200, 150, 50)$. The area is about 0.68, so there is a 68% chance that a randomly chosen individual has a ridge count between 100 and 200.

**b.** Approximately .16. Find the area under the normal curve between 200 and 1000 on your calculator using $N(200, 1000, 150, 50)$. The area is about 0.16, so there is a 16% chance that a randomly chosen individual has a ridge count of more than 200.

**c.** Approximately .16. Find the area under the normal curve between 0 and 100 on your calculator using $N(0, 100, 150, 50)$. The area is about 0.16, so there is a 16% chance that a randomly chosen individual has a ridge count of less than 100. Alternatively, notice that the answers to 12a and b combined, .84, represent the probability of a ridge count of greater than 100. Subtract this from 1 to find the probability of a ridge count of less than 100: $1 - .84 = .16$.

**13. a.** Possible answers: The means for both the French and Spanish tests are lower than that for the Mandarin test, which may indicate more difficult tests. Also, the larger standard deviation on the French exam indicates that there is a larger variation in scores, meaning that more students did worse. However, it is difficult to compare three completely different exams.

**b.** The French exam, because it has the greatest standard deviation

**c.** Determine how many standard deviations each student's score is from the mean.

Paul: $\dfrac{88 - 72}{8.5}$, or about $1.88\sigma$ above

Kenyatta: $\dfrac{84 - 72}{5.8}$, or about $2.07\sigma$ above

Rosanna: $\dfrac{91 - 85}{6.1}$, or about $0.98\sigma$ above

Kenyatta's score is better than Paul's and Rosanna's because her score is 2.07 standard deviations above the mean.

**14.** $_6C_3 \cdot _4C_2 = 20 \cdot 6 = 120$

**15.** The term in the expansion containing $y^7$ is $_{12}C_7(2x)^5y^7$, so the coefficient is $_{12}C_72^5 = 792 \cdot 32 = 25344$.

**16. a.** Possible answers: $y = \frac{37}{56}x^2 + \frac{95}{56}x - \frac{197}{28}$ or $x = \frac{37}{30}y^2 - \frac{7}{2}y - \frac{41}{15}$. Substitute the point's coordinates

into the quadratic equation $y = ax^2 + bx + c$ (for a vertically oriented parabola) or $x = ay^2 + by + c$ (for a horizontally oriented parabola). Write a system of equations and then solve for $a$, $b$, and $c$ using any method.

vertical:

$$\begin{cases} 25a - 5b + c = 1 \\ 4a + 2b + c = -1; \ a = \frac{37}{56}, \ b = \frac{95}{56}, \ c = -\frac{197}{28} \\ 9a + 3b + c = 4 \end{cases}$$

horizontal:

$$\begin{cases} a + b + c = -5 \\ a - b - c = 2 \quad ; \ a = \frac{37}{30}, \ b = -\frac{7}{2}, \ c = -\frac{41}{15} \\ 16a + 4b + c = 3 \end{cases}$$

Substituting the values for $a$, $b$, and $c$, the possible equations for a parabola are $y = \frac{37}{56}x^2 + \frac{95}{56}x - \frac{197}{28}$ or $x = \frac{37}{30}y^2 - \frac{7}{2}y - \frac{41}{15}$.

**b.** Possible answer: $\left(x + \frac{65}{74}\right)^2 + \left(y - \frac{161}{74}\right)^2 = \frac{50297}{2738}$, or $(x + 0.878)^2 + (y - 2.176)^2 = 18.370$. Substitute the points' coordinates into the standard equation for a circle, $(x - h)^2 + (y - k)^2 = r^2$. Write a system of equations and then solve for $h$, $k$, and $r^2$ using any method.

$$\begin{cases} (-5 - h)^2 + (1 - k)^2 = r^2 \\ (2 - h)^2 + (-1 - k)^2 = r^2 \\ (3 - h)^2 + (4 - k)^2 = r^2 \end{cases}$$

$$h = -\frac{65}{74} \approx -0.878, \ k = \frac{161}{74} \approx 2.176,$$

$$r^2 = \frac{50297}{2738} \approx 18.370$$

Substituting the values for $h$, $k$, and $r^2$ into the standard equation for a circle, the equation is $\left(x + \frac{65}{74}\right)^2 + \left(y - \frac{161}{74}\right)^2 = \frac{50297}{2738}$, or $(x + 0.878)^2 + (y - 2.176)^2 = 18.370$.

**EXTENSION**

See the solutions to Take Another Look activities 3 and 4 on page 319.

**EXPLORATION · NORMALLY DISTRIBUTED DATA**

**QUESTIONS**

**1.** Sample answer: Rural areas tend to have more young people. This could be either because people in rural areas have more children than people in urban areas or because more adults leave rural areas and move to urban areas. Income is not normally distributed because many young and old people have no income, and some adult women also have no income. If you look at men only, it is more normally distributed, but there is still a relatively large number of men with no income. Educational code was normally distributed with a peak at 8–12 years. This implies that most people attend high school, with fewer people having lower or higher levels of schooling.

2. Data sets that are not normally distributed are usually skewed right and occasionally skewed left.

## LESSON 13.3

### EXERCISES

1.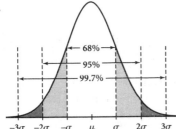

2. For this data set, $\mu = 63$ and $\sigma = 1.4$. In 2a–d, use the formula $z = \frac{x - \mu}{\sigma}$ to standardize each data value.

   a. $z = \frac{64.4 - 63}{1.4} = \frac{1.4}{1.4} = 1$

   b. $z = \frac{58.8 - 63}{1.4} = \frac{-4.2}{1.4} = -3$

   c. $z = \frac{65.2 - 63}{1.4} = \frac{2.2}{1.4} \approx 1.57$

   d. $z = \frac{62 - 63}{1.4} = \frac{-1}{1.4} \approx -0.71$

3. For this data set, $\mu = 125$ and $\sigma = 2.4$. First solve the formula $z = \frac{x - \mu}{\sigma}$ for $x$: $x - \mu = \sigma z$, so $x = \mu + \sigma z$. Now use $x = 125 + 24z$ to convert each $z$-value in 3a–d back to an $x$-value.

   a. $x = 125 + 2.4(-1) = 122.6$

   b. $x = 125 + 2.4(2) = 129.8$

   c. $x = 125 + 2.4(2.9) = 131.96$

   d. $x = 125 + 2.4(-0.5) = 123.8$

4. a. 2. Use the 68-95-99.7 rule.

   b. 1.645. Use the table on page 748 of your book.

   c. 2.576. Use the table on page 748 of your book.

5. a. $z = 1.8$. Using $\mu = 58$ and $\sigma = 4.5$, the $z$-value of $x = 66.1$ is $\frac{66.1 - 58}{4.5}$, or 1.8.

   b. $z = -0.\overline{6}$. Using $\mu = 58$ and $\sigma = 4.5$, the $z$-value of $x = 55$ is $\frac{55 - 58}{4.5}$, or $-0.\overline{6}$.

   c. Approximately .71. Find the area under the normal curve and between 55 and 61.1. Use your calculator to find that $N(55, 61.1, 58, 4.5)$ is approximately .71.

6. a. Approximately 50%. Use your calculator to find that $N(45, 47, 47, 0.6)$ is approximately .50.

b. Approximately 1.2%. The endpoints are $47 \pm 1.5$, or 45.5 and 48.5. Use your calculator to find the area between these endpoints: $N(45.5, 48.5, 47, 0.6) \approx 0.98$. So the percentage of data greater than 48.5 and less than 45.5 is $1 - 0.98 = 0.012$, or approximately 1.2%.

7. a. (3.058, 3.142). Using the table on page 748 of your book, the $z$-value for 90% is 1.645. The confidence interval is $\left(3.1 - \frac{1.645(0.14)}{\sqrt{30}}, 3.1 + \frac{1.645(0.14)}{\sqrt{30}}\right)$, or about (3.058, 3.142).

   b. (3.049, 3.151). Using the 68-95-99.7 rule, the $z$-value for 95% is about two standard deviations. The confidence interval is $\left(3.1 - \frac{2(0.14)}{\sqrt{30}}, 3.1 + \frac{2(0.14)}{\sqrt{30}}\right)$, or about (3.049, 3.151).

   c. (3.034, 3.166). Using the table on page 748 of your book, the $z$-value for 99% is 2.576. The confidence interval is $\left(3.1 - \frac{2.576(0.14)}{\sqrt{30}}, 3.1 + \frac{2.576(0.14)}{\sqrt{30}}\right)$, or about (3.034, 3.166).

8. a. $\left(3.1 - \frac{1.645(0.14)}{\sqrt{100}}, 3.1 + \frac{1.645(0.14)}{\sqrt{100}}\right)$, or about (3.077, 3.123)

   b. $\left(3.1 - \frac{2(0.14)}{\sqrt{100}}, 3.1 + \frac{2(0.14)}{\sqrt{100}}\right)$, or about (3.072, 3.128)

   c. $\left(3.1 - \frac{2.576(0.14)}{\sqrt{100}}, 3.1 + \frac{2.576(0.14)}{\sqrt{100}}\right)$, or about (3.064, 3.136)

9. a. Decrease. The denominator, $\sqrt{n}$, will increase as $n$ increases. As the denominator increases, the fractions, and the confidence intervals, decrease. Verify this by the answers to Exercises 7 and 8.

   b. Increase. The 99% confidence interval is larger than the 90% confidence interval, so increasing your confidence increases the interval.

   c. Stay the same size. Using the calculations from 7a, substitute a larger value, such as 5, for the mean. The confidence interval becomes $\left(5 - \frac{1.645(0.14)}{\sqrt{30}}, 5 + \frac{1.645(0.14)}{\sqrt{30}}\right)$, or about (4.958, 5.042). The original interval is $3.142 - 3.058 = 0.084$ and the new interval is $5.042 - 4.958 = 0.084$, so the interval stays the same size. Essentially, you horizontally translate both endpoints by the same amount.

   d. Increase. As the standard deviation increases, the distribution has more spread. So it will require a larger interval to capture the same percentage of confidence.

10. Between 30.3 and 31.7 mi/gal. By the 68-95-99.7 rule, the $z$-value for 95% is about two standard deviations. The endpoints of the confidence interval,

then, are $31 \pm \frac{2(2.6)}{\sqrt{50}}$, or about $31 \pm 0.7$. You can be 95% confident that an actual automobile's mileage is between approximately 30.3 and 31.7 mi/gal.

**11. a.** Between 204.4 and 210.6 passengers. By the 68-95-99.7 rule, the *z*-value for 95% is about two standard deviations. The endpoints of the confidence interval are $207.5 \pm \frac{2(12)}{\sqrt{60}}$, or about $207.5 \pm 3.1$. You can be 95% confident that the actual number of passengers showing up for the 7:24 A.M. flight is between approximately 204.4 and 210.6 passengers.

**b.** .07. Find the area beneath the curve and to the right of 225. The probability is $N(225, 250, 207.5, 12)$, or about .07, that the plane will be overbooked.

**12. a.** 68%. The data values 44.95 and 45.05 are one standard deviation below and above the mean, so by the 68-95-99.7 rule, 68% of the output is acceptable.

**b.** $1 - .68 = .32$, so 32% of the output is unacceptable.

**c.** 5%. If the standard deviation is cut in half to 0.025, then the data values 44.95 and 45.05 are two standard deviations below and above the mean. So by the 68-95-99.7 rule, 95% of the output is acceptable and therefore $1 - .95 = .05$, or 5% is unacceptable.

**d.** $\frac{.05}{3}$, or $0.1\overline{6}$. By cutting the standard deviation by one-third, the data values 44.95 and 45.05 become three standard deviations below and above the mean, so by the 68-95-99.7 rule, 99.7% of the output would be acceptable.

**13. a.** The area of the entire distribution is $80a$, so $80a = 1$, and $a = \frac{1}{80}$, or .0125.

**b.** The area of the distribution between 0 and 30 is $55a = 55(.0125) = .6875$, so the probability that a number is less than 30 is 68.75%.

**c.** The area of the distribution between 20 and 40 is $15a = 15(.0125) = .1875$, so the probability that a number is between 20 and 40 is 18.75%.

**d.** The area of the distribution at 30, or at any single value, is 0.

**e.** The area of the distribution at 15, or at any single value, is 0.

**f.** $18\frac{1}{3}$. The area of the distribution between 0 and the median is $\frac{80a}{2}$, or $40a$. The area between 0 and 10 is $15a$. The area between 10 and 20 is $30a$, but you only need $25a$ to reach the median area of $40a$. The median occurs $\frac{25}{30}$ of the distance between 10 and 20, or $10 + 10\left(\frac{25}{30}\right) = 18\frac{1}{3}$.

**14. a.** $P(-3) = \frac{32}{500} = .064$

**b.** $P(\text{less than } 0) = P(-1) + P(-2) + P(-3) = \frac{153 + 60 + 32}{500} = \frac{245}{500} = .49$

**c.** $P(\text{not } 2) = 1 - P(2) = 1 - \frac{90}{500} = 1 - .18 = .82$

**d.** $-1.2$. The expected value of the random integers is $-3(.064) + -2(.12) + -1(.306) + 0(.184) + 1(.09) + 2(.18) + 3(.056) = -0.12$. So the expected sum of the next ten selected values is $-0.12(10) = -1.2$.

**15. a.** Let *n* represent the number of months, and let $S_n$ represent the accumulated total in dollars. Plan 1: $S_n = 398n + 2n^2$; Plan 2: $S_n = \frac{75(1 - 1.025^n)}{1 - 1.025}$.
Plan 1: The first term of the sequence is $u_1 = 400$ and the common difference is $d = 4$, so the explicit formula for the arithmetic series is $S_n = \left(\frac{4}{2}\right)n^2 + \left(400 - \frac{4}{2}\right)n = 2n^2 + 398n$.

Plan 2: The first term is $u_1 = 75$ and the common ratio is $r = 1.025$, so the explicit formula for the geometric series is $S_n = \frac{75(1 - 1.025^n)}{1 - 1.025}$.

**b.**
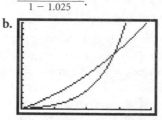
[0, 200, 50, 0, 150000, 10000]

**c.** The graphs intersect at (141.91, 96756.89), so at 141.91 months, or 11 years 9 months, you would have paid the same total amount for rent. Before this time, the total rent you would have paid for Plan 2 is less, so choose Plan 2. If you stay longer, the total rent you will pay for Plan 1 is less, so choose Plan 1.

## LESSON 13.4

### EXERCISES

**1. a.** The probability that a value is 195 or less is $N(0, 195, 200, 12) \approx .3385$, or 33.85%.

**b.** The standard deviation of the distribution of means is $\frac{12}{\sqrt{4}}$, or 6, so the probability of a mean of 195 or less is $N(0, 195, 200, 6) \approx .2023$, or 20.23%.

**c.** The standard deviation of the distribution of means is $\frac{12}{\sqrt{9}}$, or 4, so the probability of a mean of 195 or less is $N(0, 195, 200, 4) \approx .1057$, or 10.57%.

**d.** The standard deviation of the distribution of means is $\frac{12}{\sqrt{36}}$, or 2, so the probability of a mean of 195 or less is $N(0, 195, 200, 2) \approx .006210$, or 0.6210%.

**2. a.** $\bar{x} \le 76$ or $\bar{x} \ge 84$. To find the values that are two standard deviations from the sample mean, calculate $80 \pm \frac{2(10)}{\sqrt{25}}$, or 76 or 84. Therefore, all the values on the interval $\bar{x} \le 76$ or $\bar{x} \ge 84$ would indicate a significant event.

**b.** $\bar{x} \le 128$ or $\bar{x} \ge 132$. Calculate $130 \pm \frac{2(6)}{\sqrt{36}}$, or 128 or 132. Therefore, all the values on the interval $\bar{x} \le 128$ or $\bar{x} \ge 132$ would indicate a significant event.

**c.** $\bar{x} \le 17.5$ or $\bar{x} \ge 18.5$. Calculate $18 \pm \frac{2(2)}{\sqrt{64}}$, or 17.5 or 18.5. Therefore, all the values on the interval $\bar{x} \le 17.5$ or $\bar{x} \ge 18.5$ would indicate a significant event.

**d.** $\bar{x} \le 0.50$ or $\bar{x} \ge 0.54$. Calculate $0.52 \pm \frac{2(0.1)}{100}$, or 0.50 or 0.54. Therefore, all the values on the interval $\bar{x} \le 0.50$ or $\bar{x} \ge 0.54$ would indicate a significant event.

**3.** 31.28%. The probability it will take more than 25 min is $N(25, 40, 23, 4.1) \approx .3128$.

**4. a.** 80% of the time the candy bars will weigh at least 71.3 g, so advertise this as the weight. One standard deviation below the mean is $71.3 - 4.7$, or 70.6, so $N(70.6, 90, 75.3, 4.7)$, or about 84%, of the candy bars weigh at least this much. Use guess-and-check on your calculator to obtain a larger value than 70.6 that has 80% of the data to the right of it. This value is 71.3 g, so 80% of the time the candy bars will weigh at least 71.3 g.

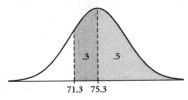

**b.** 90% of the time the candy bars will weigh at least 69.2 g, so advertise this as the weight. Use guess-and-check on your calculator to obtain a smaller value than 70.6 that has 90% of the data to the right of it. This value is 69.2, so 90% of the time the candy bars will weigh at least 69.2 g.

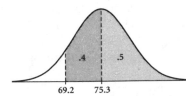

**c.** 95% of the time the candy bars will weigh at least 67.5 g, so advertise this as the weight.

Two standard deviations below the mean is $71.3 - 2(4.7)$, or 65.9, so $N(65.9, 90, 75.3, 4.7)$, or about 97.6%, of the candy bars weigh at least this much. Use guess-and-check on your calculator to obtain a smaller value than 65.9 that has 95% of the data to the right of it. This value is 67.5 g, so 95% of the time the candy bars will weigh at least 67.5 g.

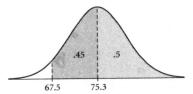

**5. a.** $224 < \mu < 236$. 95% of the sample means lie within two standard deviations of the population mean, or within $\frac{2(12)}{\sqrt{16}} = 6$ mg. So you can be 95% confident that the actual population mean lies between $230 \pm 6$, or in the interval $224 < \mu < 236$.

**b.** $227.6 < \mu < 232.4$. 95% of the sample means lie within two standard deviations of the population mean, or within $\frac{2(12)}{\sqrt{100}} = 2.4$ mg. So you can be 95% confident that the actual population mean lies between $230 \pm 2.4$, or in the interval $227.6 < \mu < 232.4$.

**c.** $228 < \mu < 232$. 95% of the sample means lie within two standard deviations of the population mean, or within $\frac{2(12)}{\sqrt{144}} = 2$ mg. So you can be 95% confident that the actual population mean lies between $230 \pm 2$, or in the interval $228 < \mu < 232$.

**6. a.** Null hypothesis: The mean number of chips is equal to 20.

**b.** $\bar{x} = 17.33$, $s = 3.80$

**c.** 0.006%. The standard deviation of the distribution of means is $\frac{3.80}{\sqrt{30}}$, or about 0.694. The probability of a mean of 17.33 chips or less is $N(0, 17.33, 20, 0.694)$, or about .00006. This means that there is only a 0.006% chance that a sample's mean would be 17.33 chips or less.

**d.** There is significant evidence to reject the claim of 20 chips per cookie. Collecting a sample with a mean of 17.33 chips is an extremely rare event, and the cookie company's claim of 20 chips per chocolate chip cookie is open to question.

**7.** $s = 0.43$. First, assume that the 300 samples are normally distributed. 225 out of 300 samples, or 75%, have pH between 5.5 and 6.5. Use your calculator and guess-and-check to find the sample standard deviation, $s$, that makes $N(5.5, 6.5, 6, s)$ approximately equal to .75 is 0.43.

Use the Central Limit Theorem to make a graph of the pH distribution for the entire lake (a population). Treat each individual sample as a sample of size $n = 1$. The Central Limit Theorem states that the population mean is approximately the mean of the sample means. By treating each sample individually, the mean of the sample means simply is the mean of the samples, or 6. So the population mean is $\mu = 6$. The Central Limit Theorem also states that the standard deviation of the sample means is approximately the population standard deviation divided by the square root of the sample size, so $0.43 = \frac{\sigma}{\sqrt{1}}$, or $\sigma = 0.43$. A graph of the pH distribution in the lake, therefore, will be identical to a graph of the distribution of the samples.

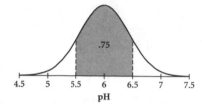

**8. a.** $\bar{x} = 2.5$, $s \approx 2.53$. No, the distribution of the accident data is skewed right. You can use a calculator histogram to verify this.

[0, 11, 1, 0, 8, 1]

**b.** $\bar{x} = median = mode = 2.5$

**c.** The means are the same. The median of the original data ($median = 2$) is less than the median in 8b. The mode of the original data ($mode = 2$) is less than the mode in 8b. The median will always be less than the mean for a skewed-right distribution.

**9. a.** 5 samples. The samples with a concentration of cadmium of 0.89, 0.89, 0.88, 0.98, and 0.95 mg/kg are contaminated.

**b.** $\bar{x} = 0.56$, $s = 0.20$

**c.** Approximately 0. The standard deviation of the distribution of means is $\frac{0.20}{\sqrt{50}}$, or about 0.028. The probability of a mean concentration of cadmium of 0.56 mg/kg or less is $N(0, 0.56, 0.8, 0.028)$, or 0. This means that there is a 0% chance that a sample's mean would be 0.56 mg/kg or less.

**d.** Probably, because these results are highly unlikely if the site is contaminated.

**10.** The graph appears to sit on a horizontal line and has a line of symmetry at $x = 10$.

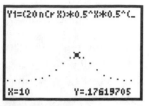

[0, 18.8, 5, −0.1, 0.5, 0.1]

**11.** The graph appears to sit on a horizontal line. The graph is skewed right, so it doesn't have a line of symmetry.

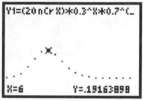

[0, 18.8, 5, −0.1, 0.5, 0.1]

**12. a.** $f(-19.5) = 16.8(-19.5) + 405 = 77.4$

**b.** $501.096 = 16.8x + 405$, so $16.8x = 96.096$, and $x = 5.72$

**c.** $y = 16.8x + 407.4$, $y = 16.8x + 402.6$. The slope remains the same, and the y-intercepts of the two parallel lines above and below the line $y = f(x)$ are $405 \pm 2.4 = 407.4$ or $402.6$.

**13.** $\hat{y} = 4.53x + 12.98$; 6.2. The three summary points are $M_1(2, 23)$, $M_2(5.5, 36)$, and $M_3(9.5, 57)$. The slope of the line through $M_1$ and $M_3$ is $\frac{57 - 23}{9.5 - 2} \approx$ 4.53. The equation of this line is $y = 23 + 4.53(x - 2)$, or $y = 4.53x + 13.94$. Using the same slope, the equation of the line through $M_2$ is $y = 36 + 4.53(x - 5.5)$, or $y = 4.53x + 11.085$. The y-intercept of the median-median line is the mean of the y-intercepts, $\frac{13.94 + 13.94 + 11.085}{3} \approx$ 12.98. Therefore the final equation of the median-median line is $\hat{y} = 4.53x + 12.98$.

The root mean square error for the data is 6.2.

**14. a.** $z = \frac{12 - 12.45}{0.36} = -1.25$

**b.** 32%. The probability is $N(12.30, 12.60, 12.45, 0.36)$, or about .32. This means there is a 32% chance that a randomly chosen measurement is between 12.30 and 12.60 m.

**c.** 79%. The standard deviation of the distribution of means is $\frac{0.36}{\sqrt{9}}$, or about 0.12. The probability that the mean of their measurements is between 12.30 and 12.60 m is $N(12.30, 12.60, 12.45, 0.12)$, or about .79. This means that there is a 79% chance that the sample's mean would be between 12.30 and 12.60 m.

**d.** (11.73, 13.17). 95% of the measurements of the sample means lie within two standard deviations of the population mean, or within 2(0.36) = 0.72 m. So you can be 95% confident that the actual population mean lies between 12.45 ± 0.72, or in the interval (11.73, 13.17).

**e.** (12.21, 12.69). 95% of the sample means lie within two standard deviations of the population mean, or within 2(0.12) = 0.24 m. So you can be 95% confident that the actual population mean lies between 12.45 ± 0.24, or in the interval (12.21, 12.69).

### IMPROVING YOUR VISUAL THINKING SKILLS

Imagine a horizontal number line through the base of the tree, where negative numbers represent "behind" the tree and positive numbers represent "in front of" the tree. For any one line, the mean is 0—at the trunk. Along all horizontal lines through the base, the acorns fall normally, so use $\mu = 0$ and $\sigma = 20$.

**1.** .6171. The probability that an acorn falls less than 10 ft is $N(-10, 10, 0, 20)$, or approximately .3829. The probability of more than 10 ft is $1 - .3829 = .6171$.

**2.** .3173. The probability that 4 acorns fall less than 10 ft is $N\left(-10, 10, 0, \frac{20}{\sqrt{4}}\right)$, or approximately .6827. The probability of more than 10 ft is $1 - .6827 = .3173$.

**3.** .0455. The probability that 16 acorns fall less than 10 ft is $N\left(-10, 10, 0, \frac{20}{\sqrt{16}}\right)$, or approximately .9545. The probability of more than 10 ft is $1 - .9545 = .0455$.

### EXPLORATION · CONFIDENCE INTERVALS FOR BINARY DATA

#### QUESTIONS

**1.** The percentiles vary because each time you use **Collect More Measures** you are dealing with new samples, and every sample or set of samples from a population varies slightly. To more precisely determine the percentiles, you could collect the measures multiple times and average the results for the 2.5 and 97.5 percentiles, or you could increase the number of sample polls that are simulated.

**2.** The formula gives values between .39 and .67 for a poll result of 53%, and between .67 and .89 for a poll result of 78%. These answers are close to experimental results found in Step 5 of the activity.

#### EXTENSIONS

**A.** The number of voters polled is not specified, so answers will vary. However, with a sample size of

only 10, the 95% confidence interval for a poll result of 65% is .499 to .801. This means that you can be 95% confident that the actual percentage of support is between 50% and 80%. For a sample size of 10 with a poll result of 45%, you can be 95% confident that the actual percentage of support is between 29% and 61%. If the sample size increased to 100, the confidence interval would be 40% to 50%. For a sample size of 1000, the interval is 43% to 47%.

**B.** Results will vary.

### LESSON 13.5

#### EXERCISES

**1. a.** .95. The graph increases, so it has a positive correlation coefficient. The relationship is very strong, so the correlation coefficient should be close to 1.

**b.** −.95. The graph decreases, so it has a negative correlation coefficient. The relationship is very strong, so the correlation coefficient should be close to −1.

**c.** −.6. The graph decreases, so it has a negative correlation coefficient. The relationship is weaker than in 1b, so the correlation coefficient should be midrange between 0 and 1.

**d.** .9. The graph increases, so it has a positive correlation coefficient. The relationship is strong (but not quite as strong as in 1a), so the correlation coefficient should be close to 1.

**2.** Possible answers:

**a.**

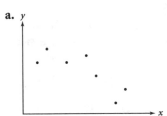

The graph should decrease and have a moderately strong correlation.

**b.**

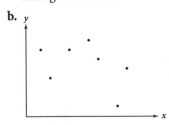

The graph should decrease and have a weak correlation.

**c.**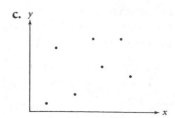

The graph should increase and have a weak correlation.

**d.**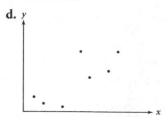

The graph should increase and have a moderately strong correlation.

**3.** $\bar{x} = 17$; $\bar{y} = 6$

| $x$ | $y$ | $x - \bar{x}$ | $y - \bar{y}$ | $(x - \bar{x})(y - \bar{y})$ |
|---|---|---|---|---|
| 12 | 8 | −5 | 2 | −10 |
| 14 | 8 | −3 | 2 | −6 |
| 18 | 6 | 1 | 0 | 0 |
| 19 | 5 | 2 | −1 | −2 |
| 22 | 3 | 5 | −3 | −15 |

**a.** The sum of the last column in the table is
$-10 + (-6) + 0 + (-2) + (-15) = -33$.

**b.** $\bar{x} = 17$ and $s_x = 4$

**c.** $\bar{y} = 6$ and $s_y = 2.1213$

**d.** −.9723. Substitute the values from 1a, 1b, and 1c into the formula for the correlation coefficient.

$$\frac{\sum (x - \bar{x})(y - \bar{y})}{(4)(2.1213)(5 - 1)} = \frac{-33}{33.9408} \approx -.9723$$

**e.** There is a strong negative correlation in the data.

**f.**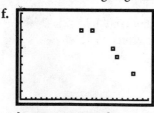

[0, 25, 1, 0, 10, 1]

**4. a.** Explanatory variable: amount of sleep; response variable: ability to learn the finger-tapping pattern

**b.** Explanatory variable: weight of mammal; response variable: weight of brain

**c.** Explanatory variable: university enrollment; response variable: algebra class enrollment

**5. a.** Correlation. Weight gain probably has more to do with amount of physical activity (the lurking variable) than with television ownership.

**b.** Correlation. The age of the children may be the lurking variable controlling both size of feet and reading ability.

**c.** Correlation. The size of the fire may be the lurking variable controlling both the number of firefighters and the length of time.

**6. a.**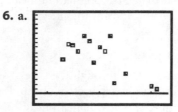

[2.8, 5.4, 1, −2, 17, 1]

**b.** Possible answer: The variables appear to have a negative correlation. As the soil pH increases, the percent of dieback decreases.

**c.** $r \approx -.740$. This value confirms a fairly strong negative correlation. Enter the data into lists and use your calculator to find the correlation coefficient.

**d.** There is a correlation, but you cannot assume it is causation. Other lurking variables, such as temperature, location, and amount of sunlight, would also have to be considered.

**7.** $r \approx .915$. There is a strong positive correlation between the number of students and the number of faculty. Use your calculator to find the correlation coefficient.

**8. a.** .862; .419. Use your calculator to find the correlation coefficients.

**b.** Number of volumes is more strongly correlated with operating cost. A correlation coefficient of .862 is closer to 1 than .419 and means there is a stronger correlation between the number of bound volumes and the operating cost than there is between the number of books that are checked out and the operating cost.

**9. a.**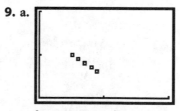

[0, 2, 1, 0, 2, 1]

$r = -1$. This value of $r$ implies perfect negative correlation, which is consistent with the plot. Use your calculator to find the correlation coefficient.

**b.**

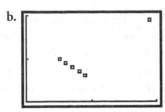

$[0, 2, 1, 0, 2, 1]$

$r \approx .833$. This value of $r$ implies strong positive correlation, but the plot suggests negative correlation with one outlier. Use your calculator to find the correlation coefficient.

**c.**

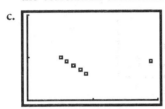

$[0, 2, 1, 0, 2, 1]$

$r = 0$. This value of $r$ implies no correlation, but the plot suggests negative correlation with one outlier. Use your calculator to find the correlation coefficient.

**d.** Yes, one outlier can drastically affect the value of $r$.

**10. a.**

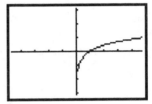

$[0, 2, 1, 0, 2, 1]$

$r = 0$. This value of $r$ implies no correlation; however, the plot suggests a circular relationship. Use your calculator to find the correlation coefficient.

**b.**

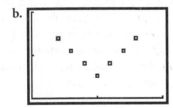

$[0, 2, 1, 0, 2, 1]$

$r = 0$. This value of $r$ implies no correlation; however, the plot suggests an absolute-value function. Use your calculator to find the correlation coefficient.

**c.** In 10a the data are circular, and in 10b the data appear to fit an absolute-value function. However, the values of $r$ are 0, implying that there is no correlation. This is because there is no *linear* correlation, although there is in fact a strong relationship in the data.

**11. 12.** Parallel lines have the same slope and the line $y = 12(x - 5) + 21$ has slope 12, so the slope of the line that passes through $(4, 7)$ is also 12.

**12.** $\hat{y} = 0.045x - 3.497$; 0.48. Use your calculator to find the equation for the median-median line and the root mean square error.

**13.** $y = 0 - 1.5(x - 4)$, or $y = -3 - 1.5(x - 6)$, or $y = -1.5x + 6$. The slope of the line is $\frac{-3 - 0}{6 - 4} = -\frac{3}{2}$, or $-1.5$, so using point-slope form, $y = 0 - 1.5(x - 4)$ or $y = -3 - 1.5(x - 6)$. In intercept form, $y = -1.5x + 6$.

**14.** Graph $y = \dfrac{\log x}{\log 5}$.

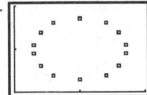

$[-4.7, 4.7, 1, -3.1, 3.1, 1]$

**15.** 60 km/h. Average speed is $\frac{total\ distance}{total\ time}$. The distance $d$ is the same in each direction, so $2d$ is the *total distance*, the time $t$ is $\frac{distance}{rate}$, or $\frac{d}{r}$, so $\frac{d}{50} + \frac{d}{75}$ is the *total time*, and the average speed is

$$\frac{2d}{\frac{d}{50} + \frac{d}{75}} = \frac{2d}{\frac{75d + 50d}{3750}} = \frac{2d}{\frac{125d}{3750}}$$

$$= \frac{2d \cdot 3750}{125d} = \frac{7500}{125} = 60$$

Your average speed for the entire trip is 60 km/h.

**16.** David got a thin box 4 feet long and 3 feet wide. By the Pythagorean Theorem, $3^2 + 4^2 = 5^2$, so he fit the fishing rod into the box along the 5-foot diagonal.

## LESSON 13.6

### EXERCISES

**1.** Enter the data from the table into lists in your calculator to find the values in 1a–d.

   **a.** $\bar{x} = 1975$

   **b.** $\bar{y} = 40.15$

   **c.** $s_x = 18.71$

   **d.** $s_y = 8.17$

   **e.** Use the formula for the correlation coefficient to find $r \approx .9954$.

**2. a.** $\hat{y} = 54 + 2(x - 18)$, or $\hat{y} = 18 + 2x$. The slope of the least squares line is $b = r\left(\frac{s_y}{s_x}\right) = .8\left(\frac{5}{2}\right) = 2$. Substitute the values of $b$, $\bar{x}$, and $\bar{y}$ into the equation of the least squares line: $\hat{y} = 54 + 2(x - 18)$.

**b.** $\hat{y} = 5 - 22.5(x - 0.31)$, or $\hat{y} = 11.975 - 22.5x$. The slope of the least squares line is $b = -.75\left(\frac{1.2}{0.04}\right) = -22.5$. Substitute the values of $b$, $\bar{x}$, and $\bar{y}$ into the equation of the least squares line: $\hat{y} = 5 - 22.5(x - 0.31)$.

**c.** $\hat{y} = 6 - 0.36(x - 88)$, or $\hat{y} = 37.68 - 0.36x$. The slope of the least squares line is $b = -.9\left(\frac{2}{5}\right) = -0.36$. Substitute the values of $b$, $\bar{x}$, and $\bar{y}$ into the equation of the least squares line: $\hat{y} = 6 - 0.36(x - 88)$.

**d.** $\hat{y} = 40 + 0.4203(x - 1975)$, or $\hat{y} = -790.1 + 0.4203x$. The slope of the least squares line is $b = .9975\left(\frac{7.88}{18.7}\right) \approx 0.4203$. Substitute the values of $b$, $\bar{x}$, and $\bar{y}$ into the equation of the least squares line: $\hat{y} = 40 + 0.4203(x - 1975)$.

**3.** On your calculator, enter the data into lists $L_1$ and $L_2$, and enter the equation into $Y_1$.

**a.** 0.3166, −0.2292, 0.1251, 0.1794, −1.3663, 0.9880. Use list algebra.

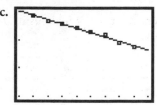

**b.** 0.01365. Either sum the values in 3a or calculate one-variable statistics for list $L_3$, the residuals. The sum of the residuals is $\sum x = 0.01365$.

**c.** 0.1002, 0.0525, 0.0157, 0.0322, 1.8667, 0.9761. Use list algebra.

**d.** 3.0435. Either sum the values in 3c or use the one-variable statistics in 3b. The sum of the squares of the residuals is $\sum x^2 \approx 3.0435$.

**e.** The root mean square error is $\sqrt{\frac{\sum x^2}{n-2}} \approx \sqrt{\frac{3.0435}{4}} \approx 0.8723$.

**4.** Substitute each $x$-value in 4a–d into the equation $y = -818.13 + 0.434571x$ to predict a $y$-value.

**a.** $y = -818.13 + 0.434571(1954) \approx 31.02$, or 31.02%

**b.** $y = -818.13 + 0.434571(1978) \approx 41.45$, or 41.45%

**c.** $y = -818.13 + 0.434571(1989) \approx 46.23$, or 46.23%

**d.** $y = -818.13 + 0.434571(2004) \approx 52.75$, or 52.75%

**5. a.**

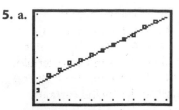

[1978, 1991, 1, 85, 105, 5]

$\hat{y} = 1.3115x - 2505.3782$. Enter the data into lists on your calculator, and calculate and graph the equation for the least squares line.

**b.** $y = 1.3115(2005) - 2505.3782 \approx 124.2$ ppt

**c.**

[1989, 1998, 1, 90, 105, 5]

$\hat{y} = -0.7714x + 1639.4179$. Enter the data into lists on your calculator, and calculate and graph the equation for the least squares line.

**d.** $y = -0.7714(2005) + 1639.4179 \approx 92.8$ ppt. This is $92.8 - 124.2$, or 31.4 ppt lower than the amount predicted in 5b.

**6. a.** $\hat{y} = -2660.8 + 1.5875x$. Enter the data into lists on your calculator, and calculate the equation for the least squares line.

**b.** The correlation coefficient, $r \approx .985$, is close to 1, so a linear model is a good fit for the data.

**c.** $\bar{x} = 1995.\overline{6}$; $\bar{y} = 507.\overline{3}$. The point is on the line. Use your calculator to find that $\bar{x} = 1995.\overline{6}$ and $\bar{y} = 507.\overline{3}$. Substitute $\bar{x}$ into the equation of the least squares line: $\hat{y} = -2660.8 + 1.5875(1995.\overline{6}) = 507.\overline{3}$. The predicted value of $y$ is equivalent to $\bar{y}$, so the point $(\bar{x}, \bar{y})$ is on the line.

**d.** $\hat{y} = -2660.8 + 1.5875(1994) = 504.675$. This is within one point of the actual mean score of 504.

**e.** $\hat{y} = -2660.8 + 1.5875(2010) = 530.075$. This is possible, but because it is ten years beyond the current data, it is difficult to know if the trend will continue.

**7. a.** $\hat{y} = -1.212x + 110.2$. Enter the data into lists on your calculator, and calculate the equation for the least squares line.

**b.** Possible answer: 10°N to 60°N. The minimum latitude is 16.85°N and the maximum latitude is 58.3°N, so an appropriate domain would be 10°N to 60°N.

**c.** Denver, Mexico City, Phoenix, Quebec, Vancouver. Sample reasons: Denver is a high mountainous city; Mexico City is also a high mountainous city; Phoenix is in desert terrain; Quebec is subject to the Atlantic currents; and Vancouver is subject to the Pacific currents.

**d.** Sample answer: The latitude of Dublin, Ireland, is $53°22'$, or $53.3\overline{6}°$. The model in 7a predicts $\hat{y} = -1.212(53.3\overline{6}) + 110.2 = 45.5196$, or approximately $46°F$. According to the *New York Times 2002 Almanac,* the average high temperature for Dublin in April is $54°F$.

**8. a.** $\hat{y} = 7.56 + 0.4346x$. Rewrite the table using 1900 as the reference year.

| Year | 50 | 60 | 60 | 80 | 90 | 100 |
|---|---|---|---|---|---|---|
| Percentage | 29.6 | 33.4 | 38.1 | 42.5 | 45.3 | 52.0 |

Enter the data into lists on your calculator to find the equation for the least squares line.

**b.** The slope, 0.4346, means that each year, 0.435% more of the U.S. labor force was female. The $y$-intercept, 7.56, means that in 1900, 7.56% of the labor force was female.

**c.** Sample answer: For 2003, $x = 103$, so $\hat{y} = 7.56 + 0.4346(103) = 52.3$. Therefore the model predicts about 52.3% of the labor force is female.

**9.** Sample answer: The least squares equation for the line uses all of the data, whereas the median-median equation for the line uses only three summary points. The least squares line minimizes the residuals, whereas the median-median line ignores outliers. The least squares equation gives you other values useful for fitting a line; the median-median equation can be found easily even without a calculator.

**10.** The root mean square error is the square root of the average of the squares of the residuals, and the average is proportional to the sum. If one is minimized, the other is as well.

**11. a.** Rewrite the equation in exponential form: $10^3 = y$, so $y = 1000$.

**b.** $y = \frac{100}{\sqrt{x}}$. Use the power property, the product property, and the definition of logarithm.

$$\log x + 2\log y = 4$$
$$\log x + \log y^2 = 4$$
$$\log xy^2 = 4$$
$$xy^2 = 10^4$$
$$y^2 = \frac{10^4}{x}$$
$$y = \sqrt{\frac{10^4}{x}} = \frac{100}{\sqrt{x}}$$

**12. a.** $r \approx -.95$. As the population increased, the number of daily papers decreased. Enter the data into lists on your calculator, and calculate the least squares line to find $r \approx -.95$. This is a high negative correlation, which indicates that as the population increased, the number of daily papers decreased.

**b.** $r \approx .91$. Enter the data into lists on your calculator, and calculate the least squares line to find $r \approx -.91$. The high, positive correlation indicates that as the population increased, the circulation increased.

**c.** $\frac{15.1}{76.2} \approx 0.20 = 20\%$, $\frac{27.8}{106.0} \approx 0.26 = 26\%$, $\frac{41.1}{132.1} \approx 0.31 = 31\%$, $\frac{58.9}{179.3} \approx 0.33 = 33\%$, $\frac{62.2}{226.5} \approx 0.27 = 27\%$, $\frac{55.8}{248.7} \approx 0.22 = 22\%$. Sample answer: Midway through the century almost a third of the population read a daily paper. Perhaps in recent years the decline in the percentage reading is due to TV or Internet news coverage. The average circulation per paper is increasing, whereas the number of papers is decreasing. Maybe this is due to people moving to cities and small rural papers going out of business.

**13.** $y = 1.2(x - 1)^2(x + 2)(x + 5)^2$. Based on the graph, $(-5, 0)$ and $(1, 0)$ are double roots. An equation with $x$-intercepts $(-5, 0)$ [double root], $(-2, 0)$, and $(1, 0)$ [double root] is in the form $y = a(x - 1)^2(x + 2)(x + 5)^2$. To solve for $a$, substitute the coordinates of the $y$-intercept $(0, 60)$: $60 = a(0 - 1)^2(0 + 2)(0 + 5)^2$, $60 = 50a$, and $a = 1.2$. Therefore the equation that will produce the given graph is $y = 1.2(x - 1)^2(x + 2)(x + 5)^2$.

**14.** 45. Your expected score for one spin is $-5\left(\frac{145}{360}\right) + 10\left(\frac{80}{360}\right) + 100\left(\frac{15}{360}\right) + -10\left(\frac{70}{360}\right) + 15\left(\frac{50}{360}\right) \approx 4.5$. Therefore, for ten spins your expected score is $10(4.5)$, or 45 points.

**15.** The length will increase without bound. If the original segment is 18 cm, the length is modeled by the geometric sequence $18, 18\left(\frac{4}{3}\right), 18\left(\frac{16}{9}\right), \ldots, 18\left(\frac{4}{3}\right)^n$. Because the common ratio, $r = \frac{4}{3}$, is greater than 1, the sequence will increase without bound.

**IMPROVING YOUR REASONING SKILLS**

Your reasoning might go something like this: You need a 1 oz bag to measure a 1 oz block. You could use a second 1 oz bag to measure a 2 oz block, but you could also measure the 2 oz block if you put it on the same side as the 1 oz bag and had a 3 oz bag on the other side. With the 1 oz and 3 oz bags, you can measure every size block up through 4 oz; if you put the 1 oz bag and the 3 oz bag on the side with a 5 oz block, you can balance them against a 9 oz bag. With 1, 3, and 9 oz bags, you can measure every size block up through 13 oz. By similar reasoning, you can make a 27 oz bag and measure blocks up to 27 + 9 + 3 + 1, or 40 oz. For example, if a block together with the 3 oz bag balances with the 27 oz bag, you know the block weighs 24 oz.

## LESSON 13.7

### EXERCISES

1. For 1a–d, enter the data into lists on your calculator, transform the data using additional lists, and then graph each data set.

   a.
   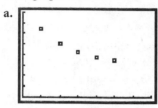
   [0, 7, 1, 0, 80, 10]

   b.
   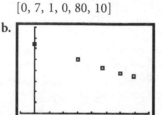
   [−0.1, 0.8, 0.1, 0, 80, 10]

   c.
   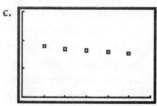
   [0, 6, 1, 0, 3, 1]

   d.
   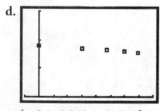
   [−0.1, 0.8, 0.1, 0, 3, 1]

   e. It is difficult to tell visually, but (log x, log y) has the strongest correlation coefficient, $r \approx -.99994$.

2. Rewrite the table, subtracting 20 from each y-value. Enter the new y-values into a list on your calculator, and create scatter plots of the transformed data for 2a–d. (Unless you used dynamic definitions for the transformed lists, you'll need to recalculate the transformations.)

   | Time (h) x | 1 | 2 | 3 | 4 | 5 |
   |---|---|---|---|---|---|
   | Percentage y | 45.0 | 30.0 | 22.5 | 18.0 | 15.0 |

   a.
   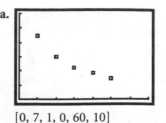
   [0, 7, 1, 0, 60, 10]

   b.
   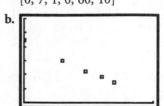
   [0, 1, 1, 0, 60, 10]

   c.
   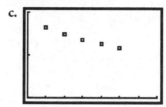
   [0, 7, 1, 0, 2, 1]

   d.
   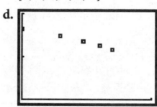
   [0, 1, 1, 0, 2, 1]

   e. It is difficult to tell visually, but (log x, log y) has the strongest correlation coefficient, $r \approx -.9974$.

3. a. $\hat{y} = 67.7 - 7.2x$. Add 20 to each side. The equation is in the form $\hat{y} = a + bx$.

   b. $\hat{y} = 64 - 43.25 \log x$. Add 20 to each side. The equation is in the form $\hat{y} = a + b \log x$.

   c. $\hat{y} = 54.4 \cdot 0.592^x + 20$. Solve for $\hat{y}$ by rewriting the equation in exponential form.

   $$\log(\hat{y} - 20) = 1.7356 - 0.227690x$$

   $$\hat{y} - 20 = 10^{1.7356 - 0.227690x}$$

   $$\hat{y} = 10^{1.7356 - 0.227690x} + 20$$

   $$= 10^{1.7356} \cdot 10^{-0.227690x} + 20$$

   $$= 54.4 \cdot 0.592^x + 20$$

   The equation $\hat{y} = 54.4 \cdot 0.592^x + 20$ is in the form $\hat{y} = ab^x + c$.

*Discovering Advanced Algebra Solutions Manual*
©2004 Key Curriculum Press

**d.** $\hat{y} = 46.33x^{-0.68076} + 20$. Solve for $\hat{y}$ by rewriting the equation in exponential form.

$$\log(\hat{y} - 20) = 1.66586 - 0.68076 \log x$$
$$\hat{y} - 20 = 10^{1.66586 - 0.68076\log x}$$
$$\hat{y} = 10^{(1.66586 - 0.68076\log x)} + 20$$
$$= 10^{1.66586} \cdot 10^{-0.68076\log x} + 20$$
$$= 10^{1.66586} \cdot 10^{\log x - 0.68076} + 20$$
$$= 46.33x^{-0.68076} + 20$$

The equation $\hat{y} = 46.33x^{-0.68076} + 20$ is in the form $\hat{y} = ax^b + c$.

**4. a.** $\hat{y} = 1.93x^2 - 18.77x + 81.2$. Use your calculator's quadratic regression command to find a second-degree polynomial that is a good fit.

**b.** $\hat{y} = -0.5x^3 + 6.43x^2 - 30.57x + 89.6$. Use your calculator's cubic regression command to find a third-degree polynomial that is a good fit.

**c.** $\hat{y} = 0.125x^4 - 2x^3 + 12.625x^2 - 40.75x + 95$. Use your calculator's quartic regression command to find a fourth-degree polynomial that is a good fit.

**d.** 1.115; 0.207; 0. Paste each regression equation into the Y= menu, and use list algebra and one-variable statistics to calculate the residuals and the root mean square error. For the quadratic regression, the root mean square error is approximately 1.115.

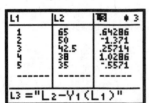 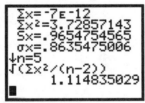

For the cubic regression, the root mean square error is approximately 0.207.

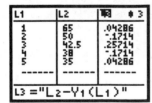 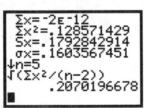

For the quartic regression, the root mean square error is 0.

 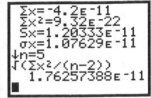

If you manually enter the equations using rounded values, your answers may vary slightly.

**5. a.** $\hat{y} = -3.77x^3 + 14.13x^2 + 8.23x - 0.01$. Use your calculator's cubic regression command.

**b.** 0.079. Paste the cubic equation into the Y= menu, and use list algebra and one-variable statistics to calculate the residuals and root mean square error.

**c.** 12.52 m³. $y = -3.77(0.75)^3 + 14.13(0.75)^2 + 8.23(0.75) - 0.01 \approx 12.52$.

**d.** Because the root mean square is 0.079, you can expect the predicted volume to be within approximately 0.079 cubic meter of the true value.

**6. a.** $\hat{y} = -0.00303125x^2 + 0.223875x + 2.1125$; $\hat{y} = 0.0000947917x^3 - 0.01725x^2 + 0.85708x - 5.85$. Use your calculator's quadratic and cubic regression commands.

**b.** Quadratic: approximately 37%; cubic: approximately 35%. Graph the quadratic equation and calculate that the maximum weight occurs at $x \approx 37$.

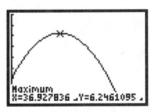

[0, 100, 10, 0, 8, 1]

Graph the cubic equation and calculate that the maximum weight occurs at $x \approx 35$.

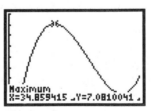

[0, 100, 10, 0, 8, 1]

**c.** The difference is only about 2%.

**7. a.** $\bar{y} = 4.2125$

**b.** $\sum (y_i - \bar{y})^2 = 43.16875$

**c.** $\sum (y_i - \hat{y})^2 = 6.28525$

**d.** Substitute the appropriate values from 7b and c to find

$$R^2 = \frac{\sum (y_i - \bar{y})^2 - \sum (y_i - \hat{y})^2}{\sum (y_i - \bar{y})^2}$$

$$= \frac{43.16875 - 6.28525}{43.16875} \approx .8544$$

**e.** .90236. The cubic model is a better fit. For the cubic model, the mean $y$-value and the sum of the squares of the deviations for the $y$-values remain the same as for the quadratic model: $\bar{y} = 4.2125$ and $\sum (y_i - \bar{y})^2 = 43.16875$. The sum of the squares of the residuals predicted by the cubic model is $\sum (y_i - \hat{y})^2 = 4.215$. Substitute these values to find

$$R^2 = \frac{\sum (y_i - \bar{y})^2 - \sum (y_i - \hat{y})^2}{\sum (y_i - \bar{y})^2}$$

$$= \frac{43.16875 - 4.215}{43.16875} \approx .90236$$

The value of $R^2$ for the cubic model is closer to 1 than it is for the quadratic model, which indicates that the cubic model is a better fit.

**f.** $\hat{y} = -0.07925x + 8.175$; $R^2 \approx .582$. The values of $R^2$ and $r^2$ are equal for the linear model. Use your calculator's linear regression command. Notice that the value of $r^2$ is approximately .582.

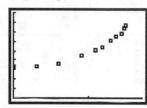

```
LinReg
 y=ax+b
 a=-.07925
 b=8.175
 r²=.5819545389
 r=-.762859449
```

For the linear model, $\bar{y} = 4.2125$ and $\sum (y_i - \bar{y})^2 = 43.16875$, the same as for the quadratic and cubic models. The sum of the squares of the residuals predicted by the linear model is $\sum (y_i - \hat{y})^2 = 18.0465$. Substitute these values to find

$$R^2 = \frac{\sum (y_i - \bar{y})^2 - \sum (y_i - \hat{y})^2}{\sum (y_i - \bar{y})^2}$$

$$= \frac{43.16875 - 18.0465}{43.16875} \approx .582$$

Therefore the values of $R^2$ and $r^2$ are equal for the linear model.

**8. a.**

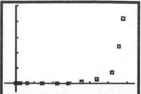

$[-3, 32, 5, -7000000, 50000000, 10000000]$

The data are not linear.

**b.** $(x, \log y)$ is most linear.

$(\log x, y)$

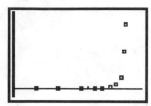

$[0, 1.7, 1, -5000000, 50000000, 1]$

$(x, \log y)$

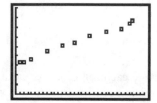

$[0, 33, 1, 0, 9, 1]$

$(\log x, \log y)$

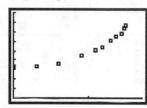

$[0, 1.7, 1, 0, 9, 1]$

**c.** $\hat{y} = 0.144x + 3.217$. Use your calculator's linear regression command.

**d.** $\hat{y} = 10^{0.144x + 3.217}$, or $\hat{y} = 1648.162(1.393)^x$. Replace $y$ in the equations for the least squares line with $(\log y)$, and then solve for $y$.

$$\log y = 0.144x + 3.217$$

$$y = 10^{0.144x + 3.217}$$

$$y = 10^{0.144x} \cdot 10^{3.217}$$

$$y = 1.393^x \cdot 1648.162$$

$$\hat{y} = 1648.162(1.393)^x$$

The equation that models the data is $\hat{y} = 10^{0.144x + 3.217}$, or $\hat{y} = 1648.162(1.393)^x$.

**e.** Approximately 1,320,000,000. Find $y$ when $x = 41$: $y = 10^{0.144(41) + 3.217} = 1,321,295,634$. There will be approximately 1,320,000,000 transistors on a microchip in 2011.

**9. a.** $83 + 3.2 = 86.2$

**b.** $83 - 3.2 = 79.8$

**c.** $83 + 2(3.2) = 89.4$

**10.** Approximately .137. Use your calculator's binomial probability distribution command. (See Calculator Note 12F.)

**11. a.** Approximately 1910. Find the least squares line for the data. Let $x$ represent the year, and let $y$ represent the number of country stations. Use your calculator's linear regression command to find the linear model for the data: $y = -68.418x + 13088.443$. Paste the exact equation into the $Y=$ menu, and evaluate the function at $x = 2005$ to find $y \approx 1910$. Therefore, there will be approximately 1910 country stations in 2005.

**b.** Approximately 847. Find the least squares line for the data. Let $x$ represent the year, and let $y$ represent the number of oldies stations. Use your calculator's linear regression command to find the linear model for the data: $y = 12.008x - 23229.656$. Paste the exact equation into the $Y=$ menu, and evaluate the function at $x = 2005$ to find $y \approx 847$. Therefore, there will be approximately 847 oldies stations in 2005.

**c.** Approximately 919. Scroll through a table of function values until $y \approx 1500$ for the least squares line from 11a. The number of country radio stations reaches approximately 1500 in 2011. Look at the corresponding $y$-value for the least squares line from 11b. The $y$-value is 918.83. In 2011 there will be approximately 919 oldies stations.

| X | Y1 | Y2 |
|------|--------|--------|
| 2009 | 1636.6 | 894.81 |
| 2010 | 1568.2 | 906.82 |
| 2011 | 1499.8 | 918.83 |
| 2012 | 1431.4 | 930.84 |
| 2013 | 1362.9 | 942.84 |
| 2014 | 1294.5 | 954.85 |
| 2015 | 1226.1 | 966.86 |

Y2=918.827868852

**12. a.** Approximately .003. $P(\text{all three born on Wednesday}) = \left(\frac{1}{7}\right)^3 = \frac{1}{343} \approx .003$. The probability is about 0.3% that the three students picked at random were all born on a Wednesday.

**b.** Approximately .370. $P(\text{at least one born on Wednesday}) = P(\text{one born on Wednesday}) + P(\text{two born on Wednesday}) + P(\text{all three born on Wednesday}) = {}_3C_1\left(\frac{6}{7}\right)^2\left(\frac{1}{7}\right) + {}_3C_2\left(\frac{6}{7}\right)\left(\frac{1}{7}\right)^2 + {}_3C_3\left(\frac{1}{7}\right)^3 = \frac{108}{343} + \frac{18}{343} + \frac{1}{343} = \frac{127}{343} \approx .370$. The probability is about 37% that at least one student picked at random was born on a Wednesday.

**c.** Approximately .612. $P(\text{all three born on a different day}) = 1\left(\frac{6}{7}\right)\left(\frac{5}{7}\right) = \frac{30}{49} \approx .612$. The probability is about 61% that three students picked at random were each born on a different day of the week.

**EXTENSIONS**

**A.** Results will vary.

**B.** Sample answer: Assume a set of data for the Investigation A Leaky Bottle Experiment was collected from a cylindrical bottle with radius 60 mm. *(See table at bottom of page.)*

A graph of the data curves similar to the original time-height data, so an exponential, quadratic, or cubic model may be appropriate.

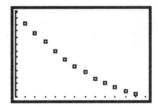

[0, 130, 10, 400000, 1700000, 100000]

In fact, each volume data value is $\pi(60)^2$ times greater than the original data. So the time-volume data are a vertical stretch of the original time-height data. Hence, to find the exponential, quadratic, and cubic models, multiply the models that you found in Step 3 of the investigation by $\pi(60)^2$:

$y = \pi(60)^2(151.234)(0.989)^x$

$y = \pi(60)^2(0.005x^2 - 1.500x + 149.110)$

$y = \pi(60)^2(-0.000005x^3 + 0.006x^2 - 1.544x + 149.456)$

You can verify these equations using your calculator's regression commands.

---

**Lesson 13.7, Extension B**

| Time (s) | 0 | 10 | 20 | 30 | 40 | 50 | 60 |
|---|---|---|---|---|---|---|---|
| Volume (mm³) | 1,696,460 | 1,515,504 | 1,357,168 | 1,232,761 | 1,097,044 | 972,637 | 870,849 |

| Time (s) | 70 | 80 | 90 | 100 | 110 | 120 |
|---|---|---|---|---|---|---|
| Volume (mm³) | 769,062 | 678,584 | 610,726 | 542,867 | 486,319 | 441,080 |

**EXERCISES**

**1. a.** $0.5(20)(.1) = 1$. The area of the shaded region is the area of a triangle, which is $0.5bh$.

**b.** 7.75. Find the vertical line that divides the triangle into two regions, each having area 0.5. To calculate the median, use the equations of the lines that form the boundaries of the region. The equation of the line through $(5, .1)$ and $(20, 0)$ is $y = -\frac{1}{150}(x - 20)$. Use this equation to find the value of the median, $d$, so that the area of the triangle to the right of the median is 0.5.

$$A = 0.5bh$$
$$0.5 = 0.5(20 - d)\left(-\frac{1}{150}(d - 20)\right)$$
$$1 = -\frac{1}{150}(-d^2 + 40d - 400)$$
$$-150 = -d^2 + 40d - 400$$
$$d^2 - 40d + 250 = 0$$
$$d \approx 32.25 \text{ or } d \approx 7.75$$

Only 7.75 makes sense and is inside the domain, so the median of the distribution is about 7.75.

**c.** .09. Find the area of the region between 0 and 3, which is a triangle with base 3. The equation of the line through $(0, 0)$ and $(5, .1)$ is $y = 0.02x$, so the height at $x = 3$ is $y = 0.02(3) = 0.06$. $A = 0.5(3)(0.06) = .09$.

**d.** $\frac{77}{300} = .25\overline{6}$. The region between 3 and 6 is a pentagon. The area is difficult to find, so instead subtract from 1 the area of the triangles on either side. The area of the triangle on the left—the region between 0 and 3—is .09 from 1c. Next, find the area of the triangle on the right—the region between 6 and 20—with base 14 and height $-\frac{1}{150}(6 - 20) = \frac{7}{75} = .09\overline{3}$. The area of that region is $0.5(14)(.09\overline{3}) \approx .65\overline{3}$. Now subtract the sum of these regions from 1: $1 - (.09 + .65\overline{3}) = 0.25\overline{6}$. If you work with fractions, the sum is $\frac{77}{300}$. Therefore the probability that the data value is between 3 and 6 is .25$\overline{6}$.

**2.** $\sqrt{\frac{2}{\pi}}$. The area of a semicircle with radius $r$ is $A = \frac{1}{2}\pi r^2$. The region under a probability distribution must have area 1, so $\frac{1}{2}\pi r^2 = 1$, $r^2 = \frac{2}{\pi}$, and $r = \sqrt{\frac{2}{\pi}}$. So the radius of the semicircle is $\sqrt{\frac{2}{\pi}}$.

**3. a.** $\bar{x} = 10.55$ lb; $s = 2.15$ lb. The mean is the midpoint of the confidence interval, so $\bar{x} = \frac{8.4 + 12.7}{2} = 10.55$ lb. The endpoints of a 68% confidence interval are one standard deviation above and below the mean, so $12.7 - 10.55 = 2.15$ and $10.55 - 8.4 = 2.15$, so $s = 2.15$ lb.

**b.** Between 6.25 and 14.85 lb. The endpoints of a 95% confidence interval are two standard deviations above and below the mean: $10.55 + 2(2.15) = 14.85$ and $10.55 - 2(2.15) = 6.25$.

**4. a.** $\bar{x} \approx 67.8$; $s \approx 3.6$. Sample answer: Approximately 68% of the 5-year-old trees are between 64.2 and 71.4 in. tall.

**b.**

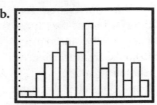

[60, 76, 1, 0, 15, 1]

The distribution is approximately normal, although slightly skewed to the right.

**5. a.**

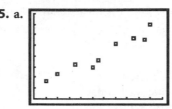

[0, 11, 1, 0, 80, 10]

**b.** Yes, there does seem to be a linear relationship; $r \approx .965$. Enter the data into lists, and use your calculator to evaluate the two-variable statistics.

$$\bar{x} = 5.\overline{7}, \ s_x \approx 3.2318$$
$$\bar{y} = 41.\overline{3}, \ s_y \approx 17.8185$$

Then use the two-variable statistics in the formula for the correlation coefficient.

$$r = \frac{\sum (x - 5.\overline{7})(y - 41.\overline{3})}{(3.2318)(17.8185)(9 - 1)} \approx \frac{444.6666}{460.9452} \approx .965$$

**c.** $\hat{y} = 5.322x + 10.585$, or $\hat{y} = 41.\overline{3} + 5.321(x - 5.\overline{7})$. The slope of the least squares line is $b = r\left(\frac{s_y}{s_x}\right) = \frac{.965 \cdot 17.8185}{3.2318} \approx 5.321$. Substitute the values for $b$, $\bar{x}$, and $\bar{y}$ into the equation of the least squares line: $\hat{y} = 41.\overline{3} + 5.321(x - 5.\overline{7})$, or $\hat{y} = 5.321x + 10.590$. You can also use your calculator to find a more accurate equation for the least squares line without rounding errors: $\hat{y} = 5.322x + 10.585$.

**d.** The rolling distance increases 5.322 in. for every additional inch of wheel diameter. The skateboard will skid approximately 10.585 in. even if it doesn't have any wheels.

**e.** 7.5 in. Substitute 50.5 for $y$ into the equation from 5c: $50.5 = 5.322x + 10.585$, so $5.322x = 39.915$, and $x = 7.5$. The diameter of the wheel needs to be 7.5 in. for the skateboard to roll 50.5 in.

**6. a.** Approximately 32.3%. Find the area under the normal curve between 180 and 200 lb. The mean is 175 and the standard deviation is 14 lb, so the area is $N(180, 200, 175, 14)$, or approximately .323.

**b.** Approximately 14.2%. Find the area under the normal curve between 0 and 160 lb, or $N(0, 160, 175, 14) \approx .142$.

**c.** Between 152 and 198 lb. The $z$-value for 90% is 1.645, so the endpoints of the confidence interval are $175 \pm 14(1.645)$, or 152 and 198.

**d.** $y = \frac{1}{14\sqrt{2\pi}} \left(\sqrt{e}\right)^{-((x-175)/14)^2}$. Using the standard deviation for a normal distribution, substitute 175 for the mean, $\mu$, and 14 for the standard deviation, $\sigma$.

**7.** Approximately .062. The standard deviation of the distribution of means is $\frac{1.3}{\sqrt{4}}$, or 0.65, so the probability of a mean of 283 or less is $N(0, 283, 284, 0.65)$, or about .062.

**8. a.** $\hat{y} = 19.373x - 6.676$. Use your calculator's linear regression command.

**b.**

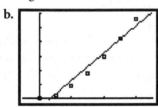

$[-0.5, 3.5, 1, -1, 60, 10]$

It looks like a fairly close fit, but there is a distinct pattern of residuals.

**c.** $r \approx .978$, $r^2 \approx .956$. The value of $r$ is close to 1, so a linear model is a good fit.

**d.** $\hat{y} = 4.712x^2 + 5.236x - 0.785$; $\hat{y} = -1.047x^3 + 9.424x^2 + 0.0004x$. Use the quadratic and cubic regression commands on your calculator.

Graph the curves with the data.

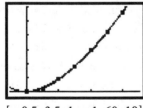

$[-0.5, 3.5, 1, -1, 60, 10]$

**e.** The cubic model fits best.

**f.** Quadratic: $R^2 \approx .999$, cubic: $R^2 \approx 1.000$. The value of $R^2$ for the cubic model is closer to 1 than the value of $R^2$ for the quadratic model or $r^2$ for the linear model, so the cubic model is a best fit.

**9. a.**

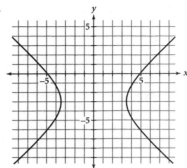

Hyperbola. This is a standard equation of a hyperbola with center $(0, -3)$ and vertices at $\left(0 \pm \sqrt{12}, -3\right)$, or about $(\pm 3.46, -3)$. The equations of the asymptotes are $y = \pm \frac{3}{\sqrt{12}}x$ or $y = \pm \frac{\sqrt{3}}{2}x$.

**b.**

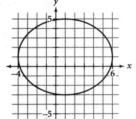

Ellipse. This is a standard equation of an ellipse with center $(1, 1)$, vertices at $(6, 1)$, $(-4, 1)$, $(1, 5)$, and $(1, -3)$, and major axis on the $x$-axis.

**c.**

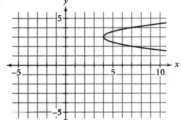

Parabola. This is a standard equation of a parabola with vertex $(4, -3)$ and axis of symmetry $y = -3$. The parabola opens right and is stretched horizontally by a factor of 3.

**d.**

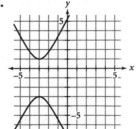

Hyperbola. Rewrite the equation of the conic section so that it is an equation for a hyperbola in standard form.

$$-4x^2 - 24x + y^2 + 2y = 39$$

$$-4(x^2 + 6x) + y^2 + 2y = 39$$

$$-4(x^2 + 6x + 9) + (y^2 + 2y + 1) = 39 + (-36 + 1)$$

$$-4(x + 3)^2 + (y + 1)^2 = 4$$

$$\frac{(y + 1)^2}{4} - (x + 3)^2 = 1$$

$$\left(\frac{y + 1}{4}\right)^2 - (x + 3)^2 = 1$$

This is an equation of a hyperbola with center $(-3, -1)$ and vertices at $(-3, 1)$ and $(-3, -3)$. The equations of the asymptotes are $y = \pm 2x$.

**10.** .751. The probability of a snowstorm in July or an A in algebra is $.004 + .75 - (.004 \cdot .75) = .754 - .003 = .751$.

**11.** The sequence of odd positive integers—1, 3, 5, 7, 9, . . .—is an arithmetic sequence with $u_1 = 1$ and $d = 2$. In 11a–c, use the formula for the partial sum of an arithmetic series, $S_n = \left(\frac{d}{2}\right)n^2 + \left(u_1 - \frac{d}{2}\right)n$.

**a.** $S_{12} = \left(\frac{2}{2}\right)(12)^2 + \left(1 - \frac{2}{2}\right)(12) = 144 + 0 = 144$

**b.** $S_{20} = \left(\frac{2}{2}\right)(20)^2 + \left(1 - \frac{2}{2}\right)(20) = 400 + 0 = 400$

**c.** $S_n = \left(\frac{2}{2}\right)n^2 + \left(1 - \frac{2}{2}\right)(n) = n^2 + 0 = n^2$

**12. a.** $\begin{bmatrix} \frac{7}{8} & \frac{1}{8} \\ \frac{1}{12} & \frac{11}{12} \end{bmatrix}$

**b.** Approximately 439 cars in Detroit and 561 in Chicago; approximately 400 cars in Detroit and 600 in Chicago. Multiply the initial condition, [500  500], by the transition matrix from 12a four times or multiply by the transition matrix raised to the power of 4.

The product is [439.28  560.72], so after four months, approximately 439 cars are in Detroit and 561 cars are in Chicago. By raising the transition matrix to a higher power, such as 30 or 40, you will see that the long-run values are [400.01  599.99].

Therefore, in the long run, approximately 400 cars are in Detroit and 600 are in Chicago.

**13. a.** $y = -20x^2 + 332x$. Create a table of values. Use finite differences to determine the degree of a polynomial model.

| Price ($) | 6.60 | 7.10 | 7.60 | 8.10 | 8.60 |
|---|---|---|---|---|---|
| Number sold | 200 | 190 | 180 | 170 | 160 |
| Revenue ($) | 1320 | 1349 | 1368 | 1377 | 1376 |

$D_1$        29    19    9    −1

$D_2$          10    10    10

The second differences are constant, so you can model the price-revenue data with a quadratic equation. Find the quadratic equation by selecting three data points, substituting them into $y = ax^2 + bx + c$, and solving the system of equations. Using (6.60, 1320), (7.10, 1349), and (7.60, 1368), you get

$$\begin{cases} 43.56a + 6.6b + c = 1320 \\ 50.41a + 7.1b + c = 1349 \\ 57.76a + 7.6b + c = 1368 \end{cases}$$

Solve this system on your calculator with row reduction to find $a = -20$, $b = 322$, and $c = 0$. So the quadratic equation is $y = -20x^2 + 332x$.

**b.** $8.30; $1377.80. Graph the quadratic equation $y = -20x^2 + 332x$, and calculate that the maximum point of the graph is at (8.30, 1377.80).

Charging $8.30 for a flashlight provides the maximum weekly revenue of $1377.80.

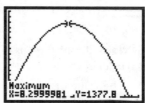

Maximum
X=8.2999981  Y=1377.8

[0, 18, 1, 0, 1600, 100]

**14. a.** $y = -\frac{1}{2}\cos\left(\frac{1}{2}x\right) + 6$. Write the equation of the image after each transformation.

| | |
|---|---|
| $y = \cos x$ | Parent function. |
| $y = -\cos x$ | Reflect across the $x$-axis. |
| $y = -\frac{1}{2}\cos x$ | Shrink by a vertical scale factor of $\frac{1}{2}$. |
| $y = -\frac{1}{2}\cos\left(\frac{1}{2}x\right)$ | Stretch by a horizontal scale factor of 2. |
| $y = -\frac{1}{2}\cos\left(\frac{1}{2}x\right) + 6$ | Translate up 6 units. |

**b.** Period: $4\pi$; amplitude: $\frac{1}{2}$; phase shift: none. The period of the function $y = b\cos(a(x - h))$ is $\frac{2\pi}{a}$, the amplitude is $|b|$, and the phase shift is $h$. So the period of the image is $\frac{2\pi}{\frac{1}{2}} = 4\pi$, the amplitude is $\frac{1}{2}$, and there is no phase shift.

**c.**

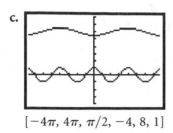

$[-4\pi, 4\pi, \pi/2, -4, 8, 1]$

**15.**

|  |  | Test results | |
|---|---|---|---|
|  |  | Accurate | Inaccurate |
| Patient's condition | Doesn't have the disease | .72 | .08 |
|  | Has the disease | .18 | .02 |

The probability that the 20% who have the disease are given an accurate test is $.90(.20) = .18$, and the probability they are given an inaccurate test is $.10(.20) = .02$. The probability that the 80% who do not have the disease are given an accurate test is $.90(.80) = .72$, and the probability that they are given an inaccurate test is $.10(.80) = .08$. This means that out of 100 people with the symptoms, 20 will have the disease and 80 will not have the disease. The test will accurately confirm that 72 do not have the disease and mistakenly suggest that 8 do have the disease. The test will accurately indicate that 18 do have the disease and mistakenly suggest that 2 do not have the disease.

**16. a.** Possible answer: 3.5% per year. Set up an exponential relationship where $5.8 = 2.9b^{20}$, so $b^{20} = 2$, and $b = 2^{1/20} \approx 1.035$. This means that a good estimate of the growth rate is 0.035, or 3.5% per year.

**b.** Possible answer: In 1970 the population of Bombay was 5.8 million and the growth rate was 3.5% per year, so an exponential function in point-ratio form is $\hat{y} = 5.8(1 + 0.035)^{x-1970}$.

**c.** Possible answer: 27.3 million. Substitute 2015 for $x$ to find that $y = 5.8(1 + 0.035)^{2015-1970} \approx 27.3$.

**d.** The population predicted by the equation is somewhat higher. The difference is $27.3 - 26.1 = 1.3$ million.

**17. a.** Seats versus cost: $r \approx .9493$

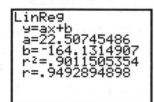

**Speed versus cost:** $r \approx .8501$

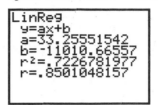

**b.** The number of seats is more strongly correlated to cost. Sample answer: The increase in number of seats will cause an increase in weight (both passengers and luggage) and thus cause an increase in the amount of fuel needed.

**18. a.** Geometric; $u_1 = 3$ and $u_n = 3u_{n-1}$ where $n \geq 2$; $u_n = 3(3)^{n-1}$, or $u_n = 3^n$

**b.** Arithmetic; $u_1 = -1$ and $u_n = u_{n-1} - 2$ where $n \geq 2$; $u_n = -2n + 1$

**c.** The pattern is neither arithmetic nor geometric. You are not expected to write a recursive formula. However, the sequence is quadratic (by finite differences), so an explicit formula is $u_n = n^2 + 1$.

**d.** Geometric; $u_1 = 1$ and $u_n = -\frac{1}{2}u_{n-1}$ where $n \geq 2$; $u_n = \left(-\frac{1}{2}\right)^{n-1}$

**19. a.** $m\angle ACB = 55° \cdot \frac{\pi \text{ radians}}{180°} = \frac{11\pi}{36}$ radians

**b.** Approximately 3.84 cm. The length of an intercepted arc, $s$, is given by $s = r\theta$, where $r$ is the radius of the circle and $\theta$ is the central angle in radians.

$$s = (4)\left(\frac{11\pi}{36}\right) = \frac{11\pi}{9} \approx 3.84 \text{ cm}$$

**c.** Approximately 7.68 cm². The area of an intercepted sector is given by $A = \frac{1}{2}r^2\theta$.

$$A = \frac{1}{2}(4)^2\left(\frac{11\pi}{36}\right) = \frac{176\pi}{72} = \frac{22\pi}{9} \approx 7.68 \text{ cm}^2$$

**20. a.** Mean: approximately 1818.4 ft; median: 1572.5 ft; mode: 1600 ft

**b.** The data are skewed right.

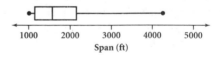

**c.** Approximately 878.6 ft

**21. a.** (1, 4). Use elimination to solve for $x$.

$$\begin{array}{r} 3x - y = -1 \\ \underline{2x + y = \phantom{-}6} \\ 5x \phantom{+ y} = \phantom{-}5 \end{array}$$

$$x = 1$$

Substitute 1 for $x$ and solve for $y$: $2(1) + y = 6$, so $y = 4$. The solution of the system is (1, 4).

**b.** $(-5.5, 0.5)$. Rewrite the second equation in terms of $x$: $x = y - 6$. Then substitute $y - 6$ for $x$ in the first equation and solve for $y$:

$$2(y - 6) + 4y = -9$$
$$2y - 12 + 4y = -9$$
$$6y = 3$$
$$y = 0.5$$

Substitute 0.5 for $y$ into either of the original equations, and solve for $x$: $x - 0.5 = -6$, so $x = -5.5$. The solution of the system is $(-5.5, 0.5)$.

**22. a.** $S_5 = \frac{121}{810} \approx 0.149$. The series is geometric with $u_1 = \frac{1}{10}$ and $r = \frac{1}{3}$, so

$$S_5 = \frac{\frac{1}{10}\left(1 - \left(\frac{1}{3}\right)^5\right)}{1 - \frac{1}{3}} = \frac{\frac{1}{10}\left(\frac{242}{243}\right)}{\frac{2}{3}} = \frac{\frac{242}{2430}}{\frac{2}{3}}$$

$$= \frac{121}{810} \approx 0.149$$

**b.** $S_{10} = \frac{\frac{1}{10}\left(1 - \left(\frac{1}{3}\right)^{10}\right)}{1 - \frac{1}{3}} = \frac{\frac{1}{10}\left(\frac{59048}{59049}\right)}{\frac{2}{3}}$

$$= \frac{\frac{59048}{590490}}{\frac{2}{3}} = \frac{29524}{196830} \approx 0.150$$

**c.** $S = \frac{\frac{1}{10}}{1 - \frac{1}{3}} = \frac{\frac{1}{10}}{\frac{2}{3}} = \frac{3}{20} = 0.15$

**23. a.** Domain: $x \geq \frac{3}{2}$; range: $y \geq 0$. To find the domain, you know that $2x - 3 \geq 0$, so $x \geq \frac{3}{2}$. To find the range, note that $f\left(\frac{3}{2}\right) = 0$, so $y \geq 0$.

**b.** Domain: any real number; range: $y \geq 0$. There are no restrictions on the domain, so $x$ can be any real number. The output values of the quadratic function $g(x)$ are always positive, so $y \geq 0$.

**c.** $f(2) = \sqrt{2(2) - 3} = \sqrt{1} = 1$

**d.** $2 = 6x^2$, so $x^2 = \frac{1}{3}$, and $x = \pm\sqrt{\frac{1}{3}} \approx \pm 0.577$

**e.** $f(3) = \sqrt{2(3) - 3} = \sqrt{3}$, so $g(f(3)) = g(\sqrt{3}) = 6(\sqrt{3})^2 = 6 \cdot 3 = 18$

**f.** $f(g(x)) = f(6x^2) = \sqrt{2(6x^2) - 3} = \sqrt{12x^2 - 3}$

**24. a.** Possible answer: $x = 2.4t$, $y = 1$ and $x = 400 - 1.8t$, $y = 2$; $0 \leq t \leq 95.24$. To find the maximum $t$-value for the range—the time when the people meet—set the two $x$-equations equal and solve for $t$: $2.4t = 400 - 1.8t$, and $4.2t = 400$, so $t \approx 95.24$.

**b.** The faster person runs approximately 229 m; the slower person runs approximately 171 m.

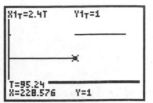

$[0, 500, 1, -0.5, 3, 1]$
$0 \leq t \leq 95.24$

The faster person runs 229 m, whereas the slower person runs $400 - 229 = 171$ m.

**c.** 95.24 s. When $t = 95.24$, the runners are at the same point, so it takes them 95.24 s to meet.

**25. a, b.**

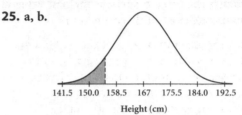

Height (cm)

Using your calculator, graph this normal curve using $n(x, 167, 8.5)$. Sketching the graph, remember to put the maximum at the mean at $x = 167$ and inflection points one standard deviation above and below the mean at $x = 158.5$ and $x = 175.5$. Then shade the area beneath the curve between 0 and 155.

**c.** Approximately 7.91%. Find the area under the normal curve between 0 and 155 on your calculator, or $N(0, 155, 167, 8.5) \approx .079$. Approximately 7.91% of the people are shorter than 155 cm.

**TAKE ANOTHER LOOK**

**1.** Sample answer: Squaring the residuals makes them all positive, so the minimum sum is an indicator of a better fit. If one line has two residuals 1 and 5 and another line has residuals 3 and 3, the sum of the residuals would be the same (6) in both cases, but the sum of the squares of the residuals would be 26 and 18, respectively.

**2. Equations**

linear: $y = 13.727 - 0.15727x$

quadratic: $y = 0.00110x^2 - 0.25614x + 15.045$

cubic: $y = 0.0000036908x^3 + 0.00060023x^2 - 0.23912x + 14.952$

quartic: $y = 0.000000029138x^4 - 0.0000015540x^3 + 0.00089452x^2 - 0.24437x + 14.965$

*Discovering Advanced Algebra Solutions Manual*
©2004 Key Curriculum Press

**Coefficient of Determination**

linear: $R^2 = .96930$

quadratic: $R^2 = .99956$

cubic: $R^2 = .99976$

quartic: $R^2 = .99977$

**Adjusted Coefficient of Determination**

linear: $R_A^2 = .96546$

quadratic: $R_A^2 = .99943$

cubic: $R_A^2 = .99964$

quartic: $R_A^2 = .99959$

It appears that the cubic model has the best value of the adjusted coefficient of determination.

3. Summaries should emphasize that the width and height of the normal curve vary inversely, so the area under the curve always remains 1. That is, as $\sigma$ increases, the curve widens and gets shorter; as $\sigma$ decreases, the curve narrows and gets taller.

If you are using a graphing calculator, graph in the same window several equations of the form

$$y = \frac{1}{\sigma\sqrt{2\pi}}\left(\sqrt{e}\right)^{-(x/\sigma)^2}$$

and change the value of $\sigma$ slightly in each (such as $\sigma = \{0.5, 1.0, 1.5, 2.0\}$). If you are using geometry software, create a slider whose length represents the value of $\sigma$ and then define and graph the function $f(x) = \frac{1}{\sigma\sqrt{2\pi}}\left(\sqrt{e}\right)^{-(x/\sigma)^2}$. Changing the length of the segment will dynamically change the curve. If you are using geometry software, use a rectangular coordinate grid in which the scale of the $x$-axis can be adjusted independent of the $y$-axis.

4. You may find that the equation

$$y = \frac{1}{\sigma\sqrt{2\pi}}\left(1 - \frac{1}{2\sigma^2}\right)^{x^2}$$

is a particularly good approximation when $\sigma$ is greater than 2. For the interval $\sqrt{0.5} < \sigma \le 2$, the curve is narrower than the actual normal curve. For $\sigma$ less than or equal to $\sqrt{0.5}$ $\left(\text{or } \frac{\sqrt{2}}{2}, \text{ or approximately } 0.7\right)$, the function is undefined.

If you are using a graphing calculator, graph the equations

$$y = \frac{1}{\sigma\sqrt{2\pi}}\left(\sqrt{e}\right)^{-(x/\sigma)^2}$$

$$y = \frac{1}{\sigma\sqrt{2\pi}}\left(1 - \frac{1}{2\sigma^2}\right)^{x^2}$$

in the same window, and change the value of $\sigma$ in both equations to see how they compare (such as $\sigma = \{0.4, 0.5, 0.6, 0.7, 0.8, 0.9, 1.0, 1.1, \ldots\}$). If you are using geometry software, create a slider whose length represents the value of $\sigma$ and then define and graph the functions $f(x) = \frac{1}{\sigma\sqrt{2\pi}}\left(\sqrt{e}\right)^{-(x/\sigma)^2}$ and $g(x) = \frac{1}{\sigma\sqrt{2\pi}}\left(1 - \frac{1}{2\sigma^2}\right)^{x^2}$. Changing the length of the segment will dynamically change the curves. If you are using geometry software, use a rectangular coordinate grid in which the scale of the $x$-axis can be adjusted independent of the $y$-axis.